GLOBAL STRATEGIC MANAGEMENT
The Essentials

GLOBAL
STRATEGIC
MANAGEMENT
The Essentials

Second Edition

HEIDI VERNON-WORTZEL
Northeastern University

LAWRENCE H. WORTZEL
Boston University and
The M.A.C. Group

WILEY

JOHN WILEY & SONS

New York   Chichester   Brisbane   Toronto   Singapore

ACQUISITIONS EDITOR   Cheryl Mehalik
DESIGNER   Ann Marie Renzi
PRODUCTION SUPERVISOR   Gay Nichols
MANUFACTURING MANAGER   Lorraine Fumoso
COPY EDITING SUPERVISOR   Gilda Stahl

Recognizing the importance of preserving what has been written, it is a policy of John Wiley & Sons, Inc. to have books of enduring value published in the United States printed on acid-free paper, and we exert our best efforts to that end.

Library of Congress Cataloging in Publication Data:

Vernon-Wortzel, Heidi, 1938-
    Global strategic management: the essentials/Heidi Vernon-Wortzel, Lawrence H. Wortzel.—2nd ed.
    p.   cm.
    Includes bibliographical references and index.
    ISBN 0-471-61788-1 (paper)

    1. International business enterprises—Management.   2. International business enterprises—Planning.   3. Strategic planning.   4. International economic relations.   I. Wortzel, Lawrence H.   II. Title.

HD62.4.V483   1990
658.4′012—dc20   90-44777
                                                                          CIP

Printed in the United States of America

10 9 8 7 6 5 4 3 2 1

*To Joshua and Jennifer who
continue to provide the incentive*

PREFACE

More and more, U.S. managers are discovering that the business world does not begin and end in New York, Washington, D.C., or San Francisco. Increasingly, U.S. firms are facing foreign competition inside their home markets. Foreign investment in American companies, either through joint ventures or outright purchases, increased tremendously in the 1980s. By 1990, foreign firms controlled more than 12 percent of manufacturing assets in the United States and employed nearly 10 percent of all workers in manufacturing. Robert B. Reich observed that "in 20 years, or even sooner perhaps, a majority of Americans will be working directly or indirectly for global entities, which have no particular nationality.

To compete successfully in such a world, American firms must look for opportunities abroad as well as in the United States American managers must know how to search for, identify, and capitalize on overseas ventures. Many U.S.-based multinational companies have been operating huge networks of international subsidiaries for years. These firms recognized global opportunities and responded to competitive pressures. But other U.S. firms are frightened by foreign competition on their own turf and are reluctant to venture abroad. Instead, they pressure the U.S. government to restrict foreign investment and protect domestic industry.

There seems no question that restrictive national legislation at home and abroad will have little impact on the trend toward globalization. More and more, U.S. companies will need to adopt a global outlook to remain competitive. Corporations of all nationalities will make investments wherever the opportunities lie. National borders and protectionist legislation will be annoyances but will not seriously hinder investments, mergers, acquisitions, and takeovers.

Several major factors are contributing to globalization. The establishment of a single European market in 1992, *perestroika* in the Soviet Union and Eastern

Europe, the U.S.-Canadian Free Trade Pact, and Third World development all foster worldwide demand for consumer and industrial goods. In the European Community, hundreds of U.S. firms are trying to beat the 1992 deadline.

Companies like Coca-Cola, Heinz, IBM, Ford, and Honeywell are deeply entrenched and have the European expertise they will need. They are already in an excellent competitive position. New American entrants are positioning themselves to take advantage of the unified market. Some firms are setting up manufacturing operations or rationalizing existing operations while others are buying European companies outright. For example, in the first quarter of 1989, U.S. purchases of European firms doubled over the previous year.

The Soviet Union and Eastern bloc countries have huge pent-up demand. Although there are major impediments to foreign investment in the Soviet Union, some U.S. companies have already formed alliances with Soviet counterparts. Eastman Kodak initially proposed nine joint venture projects but negotiated only two successfully. Nevertheless, Kodak remains optimistic and has a long-term goal of generating distribution ventures for a full range of standard Kodak products.

RJR Nabisco plans to make and sell crackers, cereal, and cigarettes in the Soviet Union. In Hungary, Western European firms have launched more than 300 deals with local partners. U.S. firms are more cautious than Europeans about Hungary's political situation, but they too are forming joint ventures.

The U.S.-Canadian trade pact which abolishes all tariffs between the two countries by 1998, promises enormous opportunity for U.S. and Canadian firms. Canadian Prime Minister Mulroney predicted that the pact would give Canada access to a market 10 times Canada's size. The trade pact sparked an ongoing wave of mergers and acquisitions among Canadian and U.S. firms.

Developing countries, particularly in Asia and Southeast Asia, are generating markets for Japanese, American, and European goods. The region is the fastest growing on earth. Thailand, South Korea, Singapore, and Taiwan have growth rates in the double digits. Hong Kong, Indonesia, Malaysia, and the Philippines have huge potential. But Japanese companies are extremely aggressive in the Pacific Rim. They account for much of the 30 percent annual growth in trade in the region. Whether American companies will rise to the Japanese challenge in Asia remains to be seen.

Across the globe, Japanese multinationals provide intense competition. In the United States, Japanese make everything from automobiles to hamburger. Japanese cowboys ride American cattle ranges, transport American-made goods on Japanese ships, and supply their American factories with parts made in Mexican *maquiladoras*. In Europe, Japanese companies are anticipating 1992. Nissan expects to make nearly a quarter of a million cars in England and Spain by the deadline. Eight big Japanese banks have branches in Milan, and Fujitsu announced plans to build a $675 million chip-fabrication plant in northeast England.

Clearly, the challenges for American corporations and their managers in the 1990s are enormous. When we wrote the preface for the first edition of this book in 1984, we observed that worldwide competition was increasing and that

U.S. managers would have to meet competition from foreign investors on their home turf. Neither we nor other observers of the competitive environment foresaw the full effects of cooperative regional agreements, the fragmentation of the Soviet bloc, or the events in the People's Republic of China. Nor could we have fully appreciated the results of waves of mergers and acquisitions that fostered giant global conglomerates.

Global corporate restructuring and a ferociously competitive international environment make even more imperative that managers develop new skills. Strategic planning must encompass foreign as well as domestic opportunities. Managers must make their plans in risky, volatile political environments and disparate cultures. Managing in the 1990s will require new and more sophisticated planning tools. The business functions—marketing, production, finance and control, and research and development—will be more complex to manage and more difficult to control. Although the world of business seems terribly uncertain and even uncontrollable, it offers exciting opportunities and tremendous potential gains for internationally educated managers.

In the current edition of this book, we have kept some of the classic readings in international business and have added many new articles. We have responded to the comments of faculty and students who told us what they thought was valuable and what we could have done better. As in the previous edition, we have tried to keep the "essentials," the ideas, concepts, techniques, and knowledge that provide the best possible base for strategic management in a global environment. In selected readings, we have tried to pay close attention to the 3Rs: readability, recency, and relevance.

We designed the book to give upper-level undergraduates and M.B.A. students a firm grasp of issues central to the management of multinational and global corporations. Instructors will find they can use these readings, in combination with internationally focused cases, in lieu of a textbook. Or the volume can be integrated with a text if the instructor wants to focus more closely on the environment. We are grateful to those who reviewed the introductory essays and suggested additions and deletions of article: Latheef N. Ahmed, University of Missouri-Kansas City, Charlie Cole, University of Oregon, Farok Contractor, Rutgers University-Newark, Bruce Kogut, University of Pennsylvania, Briance Mascarenhas, New York University, John Stanbury, Ohio State University, George Yip, Georgetown University.

Heidi Vernon-Wortzel
Northeastern University

Lawrence H. Wortzel
Boston University and the MAC Group

CONTENTS

SECTION 6
PRODUCTION MANAGEMENT

SECTION 7
R&D AND INNOVATION MANAGEMENT

SECTION 8
CORPORATE CULTURE AND HUMAN RESOURCE MANAGEMENT

SECTION 1

THE STRATEGIC PLANNING ENVIRONMENT

Strategic planning is a key activity in both multinational and domestic firms. Critical to successful strategic planning is identifying and then correctly interpreting those elements of the environment most critical to the success of the firm. Strategic planners in domestic as well as multinational firms must understand the global environment as well as their own domestic environment.

Increasingly, we must operate in a world in which foreign or global competitors affect the prospects of local firms and industries. Fewer and fewer domestic firms can isolate themselves from the effects of events or from competitors outside their own domestic markets. Events and competitors in the Italian pasta industry, the Korean steel industry, and the Hong Kong electronics industry can have a significant impact on their counterpart domestic industries in other countries.

The "basics" of analysis are the same for both the domestic and the global environment. Planners in both cases must identify strategic opportunities and threats. They must analyze the economic and consumer environments and their own and competitors' strengths and weaknesses. In a multinational environment, the analysis is considerably more subtle and complex. Similarities and differences exist side by side.

Countries have become more similar in industrial structure and consumption patterns. Interdependencies among countries have increased. But political environments are more diverse. International trade is becoming both more and less restrictive, depending on where one looks. A country at a given stage of economic development may differ from other countries at the same stage, or may in some ways resemble countries at more or less advanced stages. To identify strategic threats and opportunities, we must be able to identify both the relevant similarities and the relevant differences.

READING SELECTIONS

In pointing out how much the world economy has changed, Peter Drucker also identifies the salient characteristics of the new world economy. In Drucker's view, demand for primary products no longer follows demand for manufactured goods; primary products demand has slackened, while demand for manufactured goods continues to increase. Because of the capital and knowledge intensiveness of new industries, increases in manufacturing output no longer mean automatic increases in employment. And flows of capital, rather than trade flows, drive the world economy.

Drucker then argues that these changes in the world economy will profoundly affect national economies. Based on the effects of world economic changes on national economies, it is not difficult to visualize the pressures firms face operating in this new world economy. The pressures come both from increasing competition and from the policies that national governments may introduce to maintain employment and growth.

Doz, in looking at some of the determinants of industry structure, identifies these pressures more specifically. He first presents and discusses enabling conditions that have driven industries toward globalization. Then he identifies and discusses forces that are driving industries in the opposite direction, toward fragmentation. The article points up the interplay among factors such as technological advancement, industry economics, managerial abilities, and government policies in determining industry structure.

Welch and Luostarinen take us down to firm level, offering an historical perspective to help understand how global firms evolved. They first present a framework that links foreign operation methods and organizational capacity. The framework identifies the major decisions firms must make as they go through the internationalization process. They then analyze studies showing paths firms have taken as they internationalized. The authors conclude that, in a reasonably wide series of cases, internationalization has followed a typical path.

The abilities to predict the future behavior of present competitors and to identify potential new competitors are important to a firm's success. It is worthwhile to ask, in light of the two previous readings, whether the process described in this reading will predict firms' behavior in the future. If we think not, it would be useful to explore what might be different and why.

Schwartz and Saville present some alternative scenarios for the 1990s. They base their scenarios on identifying the driving forces for change, the uncertainties about the future, and the capabilities that exist to respond. Their conception can serve as a useful device for integrating the readings in this section of the book.

If we add to the discussion of these issues appearing in Schwartz and Saville the topics and viewpoints expressed in the Drucker and Doz readings, for example, we can gain a richer perspective on change, uncertainty, and response. If we then add in the perspective on the firm's internationalization process as presented by Welch and Luostarinen, we can further enrich our perspective on response capabilities.

1

<hr>

THE CHANGED WORLD ECONOMY
PETER F. DRUCKER

A collapsing raw materials economy, the decoupling of labor from production, and the growing importance of global capital movements versus international trade have caused a decisive and—the author maintains—irreversible shift in economic dynamics from the national economy to the world economy. From now on, he argues, any country—and company—if it is to prosper will have to subordinate domestic considerations to securing its international competitive position and base its plans and policies on exploiting the opportunities opened up by changes in the world economy.

The talk today is of the "changing world economy." I wish to argue that the world economy is not "changing"; it has *already changed*—in its foundations and in its structure—and in all probability the change is irreversible.

Within the last decade or so, three fundamental changes have occurred in the very fabric of the world economy:

- The primary-products economy has come "uncoupled" from the industrial economy.

- In the industrial economy itself, production has come "uncoupled" from employment.

- Capital movements rather than trade (in both goods and services) have become the driving force of the world economy. The two have not quite come uncoupled, but the link has become loose and, worse, unpredictable.

These changes are permanent rather than cyclical. We may never understand what caused them—the causes of economic changes are rarely simple. It may be a long time before economic theorists accept that there have been fundamental changes, and longer still before they adapt their theories to account for them. Above all, they will surely be most reluctant to

Source: *The McKinsey Quarterly* (Autumn 1986), pp. 2–26. This article first appeared in the Spring 1986 issue of *Foreign Affairs*. Copyright © 1986 by the Council on Foreign Relations, Inc.

accept that it is the world economy in control, rather than the macroeconomics of the nation-state on which most economic theory still exclusively focuses. Yet this is the clear lesson of the success stories of the last 20 years—of Japan and South Korea; of West Germany (actually a more impressive though far less flamboyant example than Japan); and of the one great success within the United States, the turnaround and rapid rise of an industrial New England, which only 20 years ago was widely considered moribund.

Practitioners, whether in government or in business, cannot afford to wait until there is a new theory. They have to act. And their actions will be more likely to succeed the more they are based on the new realities of a changed world economy.

UNCOUPLED PRIMARY PRODUCTS

First, consider the primary-products economy. The collapse of non-oil commodity prices began in 1977 and has continued interrupted only once (right after the 1979 petroleum panic), by a speculative burst that lasted less than six months; it was followed by the fastest drop in commodity prices ever registered. By early 1986 raw material prices were at their lowest levels in recorded history in relation to the prices of manufactured goods and services—in general as low as the depths of the Great Depression, and in some cases (e.g., lead and copper) lower than their 1932 levels.[1]

This collapse of prices and the slowdown of demand stand in startling contrast to what had been confidently predicted. Ten years ago the Club of Rome declared that desperate shortages of *all* raw materials were an absolute certainty by the year 1985. In 1980 the Carter Administration's *Global 2000 Report to the President: Entering the Twenty-first Century* concluded that world demand for food would increase steadily for at least 20 years; that worldwide food production would fall except in developed countries; and that real food prices would double. This forecast helps to explain why American farmers bought up all available farmland, thus loading on themselves the debt burden that now so threatens them.

Contrary to all these expectations, global agricultural output actually rose almost one-third between 1972 and 1985 to reach an all-time high. It rose the fastest in less-developed countries. Similarly, production of practically all forest products, metals, and minerals has gone up between 20 and 35 percent in the last 10 years—again with the greatest increases in less-developed countries. There is not the slightest reason to believe that the growth rates will slacken, despite the collapse of commodity prices. Indeed, as far as farm products are concerned, the biggest increase—at an almost exponential rate of growth—may still be ahead.[2]

Perhaps even more amazing than the contrast between such predictions and what has happened is that the collapse in the raw materials economy seems to have had almost no impact on the world industrial economy. If there was one thing considered "proven" beyond doubt in business cycle theory, it is that a sharp and prolonged drop in raw material prices inevitably, and within 18 to 30 months, brings on a worldwide depression in the industrial economy.[3] While the industrial economy of the world today is not "normal" by any definition of the term, it is surely not in a depression. Indeed, industrial production in the developed non-communist countries has continued to grow steadily, albeit at a somewhat slower rate in Western Europe.

PERPLEXING PROSPERITY

Of course, a depression in the industrial economy may only have been postponed and may still be triggered by a banking crisis caused by massive defaults on the part of commodity producing debtors, whether in the Third World or in Iowa. But for almost 10 years the industrial world has run along as though there were no raw materials crisis at all. The only explanation is that for the developed countries—excepting only the Soviet Union—the primary-products sector has become marginal where before it had always been central.

In the late 1920s, before the Great Depression, farmers still constituted nearly one-third of the US population and farm income accounted for almost a quarter of the gross national product. Today they account for less than 5 percent of population and even less of GNP. Even adding the contribution that foreign raw material and farm producers make to the American economy through their purchases of American industrial goods, the total contribution of the raw material and food producing economies of the world to the American GNP is, at most, one-eighth. In most other developed countries, the share of the raw materials sector is even lower. Only in the Soviet Union is the farm still a major employer, with almost a quarter of the labor force working on the land.

The raw materials economy has thus come uncoupled from the industrial economy. This is a major structural change in the world economy, with tremendous implications for economic and social policy, as well as economic theory, in developed and developing countries alike.

---

[1]References appear at the end of this reading.

For example, if the ratio between the prices of manufactured goods and the prices of non-oil primary products (that is, foods, forest products, metals and minerals) had been the same in 1985 as it had been in 1973, the 1985 US trade deficit might have been a full one-third less—$100 billion as against an actual $150 billion. Even the US trade deficit with Japan might have been almost one-third lower, some $35 billion as against $50 billion. American farm exports would have bought almost twice as much. And industrial exports to a major US customer, Latin America, would have held; their near-collapse alone accounts for a full one-sixth of the deterioration in US foreign trade over the past five years. If primary-product prices had not collapsed, America's balance of payments might even have shown a substantial surplus.

Conversely, Japan's trade surplus with the world might have been a full 20 percent lower. And Brazil in the last few years would have had an export surplus almost 50 percent higher than its current level. Brazil would then have had little difficulty meeting the interest on its foreign debt and would not have had to endanger its economic growth by drastically curtailing imports as it did. Altogether, if raw material prices in relationship to manufactured goods prices had remained at the 1973 or even the 1979 level, there would be no crisis for most debtor countries, especially in Latin America.[4]

FACTS ABOUT FOOD

What accounts for this change? Demand for food has actually grown almost as fast as the Club of Rome and the *Global 2000 Report* anticipated. But the supply has grown much faster; it has not only kept pace with population growth, it has steadily outrun it. One cause of this, paradoxically, is surely the fear of world-wide food shortages, if not world famine, which resulted in tremendous efforts to increase food output. The United States led the parade with a farm policy of subsidizing increased food production. The European Economic Community followed suit, and even more successfully. The greatest increases, both in absolute and in relative terms, however, have been in developing countries: in India, in post-Mao China and in the rice-growing countries of Southeast Asia.

And there is also the tremendous cut in waste. In the 1950s, up to 80 percent of the grain harvest of India fed rats and insects rather than human beings. Today in most parts of India the wastage is down to 20 percent. This is largely the result of unspectacular but effective "infrastructure innovations" such as small concrete storage bins, insecticides and three-wheeled motorized carts that take the harvest straight to a processing plant instead of letting it sit in the open for weeks.

It is not fanciful to expect that the true "revolution" on the farm is still ahead. Vast tracts of land that hitherto were practically barren are being made fertile, either through new methods of cultivation or through adding trace minerals to the soil. The sour clays of the Brazilian highlands or the aluminum-contaminated soils of neighboring Peru, for example, which never produced anything before, now produce substantial quantities of high-quality rice. Even greater advances have been registered in biotechnology, both in preventing diseases of plants and animals and in increasing yields.

In other words, just as the population growth of the world is slowing down quite dramatically in many regions, food production is likely to increase sharply.

Import markets for food have all but disappeared. As a result of its agricultural drive, Western Europe has become a substantial food exporter plagued increasingly by unsalable surpluses of all kinds of foods, from dairy products to wine, from wheat to beef. China, some observers predict, will have become a food exporter by the year 2000. India is about at that stage, especially with wheat and coarse grains. Of all major non-communist countries, only Japan is a substantial food importer, buying abroad about one-third of its food needs. Today most of this comes from the United States. Within five or ten years, however, South Korea, Thailand and Indonesia—low-cost producers that are fast increasing food output—are likely to try to become Japan's major suppliers.

The only remaining major food buyer on the world market may then be the Soviet Union—and its food needs are likely to grow.[5] However, the food surpluses in the world are so large—maybe five to eight times what the Soviet Union would ever need to buy—that its food needs are not by themselves enough to put upward pressure on world prices. On the contrary, the competition for access to the Soviet market among the surplus producers—the United States, Europe, Argentina, Australia, New Zealand (and probably India within a few years)—is already so intense as to depress world food prices.

MAKING MORE WITH LESS

For practically all non-farm commodities, whether forest products, minerals or metals, world demand is shrinking—in sharp contrast to what the Club of Rome so confidently predicted. Indeed, the amount of raw material needed for a given unit of economic output has been dropping for the entire century, except in wartime. A recent study by the International Monetary Fund calculates the decline as 1.25 percent a year (compounded) since 1900.[6] This would mean that the amount of industrial raw materials needed for one unit of industrial production is now no more than two-fifths of what it was in 1900. And the decline is accelerating. The Japanese experience is particularly striking. In 1984, for every unit of industrial production, Japan consumed only 60 percent of the raw materials required for the same volume of industrial production in 1973, 11 years earlier.

Why this decline in demand? It is not that industrial production is fading in importance as the service sector grows—a common myth for which there is not the slightest evidence. What

is happening is much more significant. Industrial production is steadily switching away from heavily material-intensive products and processes. One of the reasons for this is the new high-technology industries. In a semiconductor microchip the raw materials account for 1 to 3 percent of total production cost; in an automobile their share is 40 percent, and in pots and pans 60 percent. But also in older industries the same scaling down of raw material needs goes on, and with respect to old products as well as new ones. Fifty to 100 pounds of fiberglass cable transmit as many telephone messages as does one ton of copper wire.

This steady drop in the raw material intensity of manufacturing processes and manufacturing products extends to energy as well, and especially to petroleum. To produce 100 pounds of fiberglass cable requires no more than 5 percent of the energy needed to produce one ton of copper wire. Similarly, plastics, which are increasingly replacing steel in automobile bodies, represent a raw material cost, including energy, less than half that of steel.

Thus it is quite unlikely that raw material prices will ever rise substantially as compared to the prices of manufactured goods (or knowledge-intensive services such as information, education, or health care) except in the event of a major prolonged war.

AN END TO FREE TRADE?

One implication of this sharp shift in the terms of trade of primary products concerns the developed countries, both major raw material exporters like the United States and major raw material importing countries such as Japan. For two centuries the United States has made maintenance of open markets for its farm products and raw materials a central element of its international trade policy. This is what it has always meant by an "open world economy" and by "free trade."

Does this still make sense, or does the United States instead have to accept that foreign markets for its foodstuffs and raw materials are in a long-term and irreversible decline? Conversely, does it still make sense for Japan to base its international economic policy on the need to earn enough foreign exchange to pay for imports of raw materials and foodstuffs? Since Japan opened to the outside world 120 years ago, preoccupation—amounting almost to a national obsession—with its dependence on raw material and food imports has been the driving force of Japan's policy, and not in economics alone. Now Japan might well start out with the assumption—a far more realistic one in today's world—that foodstuffs and raw materials are in permanent oversupply.

Taken to their logical conclusion, these developments might mean that some variant of the traditional Japanese policy—highly mercantilist with a strong de-emphasis of domestic consumption in favor of an equally strong emphasis on capital formation and protection of infant industries—might suit the United States better than its own tradition. The Japanese might be better served by some variant of America's traditional policies, especially a shift from favoring savings and capital formation to favoring consumption. Is such a radical break with more than a century of political convictions and commitments likely? From now on the fundamentals of economic policy are certain to come under increasing criticism in these two countries—and in all other developed countries as well.

These fundamentals will, moreover, come under the increasingly intense scrutiny of major Third World nations. For if primary products are becoming of marginal importance to the economies of the developed world, traditional development theories and policies are losing their foundations.[7] They are based on the assumption—historically a perfectly valid one—that developing countries pay for imports of capital goods by exporting primary materials—farm and forest products, minerals, metals. All development theories, however much they differ otherwise, further assume that raw material purchases by the industrially developed countries must rise at least as fast as in-

dustrial production in these countries. This in turn implies that, over any extended period of time, any raw material producer becomes a better credit risk and shows a more favorable balance of trade. These premises have become highly doubtful. On what foundation, then, can economic development be based, especially in countries that do not have a large enough population to develop an industrial economy based on the home market? As we shall presently see, these countries can no longer base their economic development on low labor costs.

PRODUCTION AND LABOR

The second major change in the world economy is the uncoupling of manufacturing production from manufacturing employment. Increased manufacturing production in developed countries has actually come to mean *decreasing* blue-collar employment. As a consequence, labor costs are becoming less and less important as a "comparative cost" and as a factor in competition.

There is a great deal of talk these days about the "deindustrialization" of America. In fact, manufacturing production has risen steadily in absolute volume and has remained unchanged as a percentage of the total economy. Since the end of the Korean War, that is, for more than 30 years, it has held steady at 23 to 24 percent of America's total GNP. It has similarly remained at its traditional level in all of the other major industrial countries.

It is not even true that American industry is doing poorly as an exporter. To be sure, the United States is importing from both Japan and Germany many more manufactured goods than ever before. But it is also exporting more, despite the heavy disadvantages of an expensive dollar, increasing labor costs and the near-collapse of a major industrial market, Latin America. In 1984—the year the dollar soared—exports of American manufactured goods rose by 8.3 percent; and they went up again in 1985. The share of US-manufactured exports in world exports was 17 percent in

1978. By 1985 it had risen to 20 percent—while West Germany accounted for 18 percent and Japan 16. The three countries together thus account for more than half of the total.

Thus it is not the American economy that is being "deindustrialized." It is the American labor force. Between 1973 and 1985, manufacturing production (measured in constant dollars) in the United States rose by almost 40 percent. Yet manufacturing employment during that period went down steadily. There are now 5 million fewer people employed in blue-collar work in American manufacturing industry than there were in 1975.

Yet in the last 12 years total employment in the United States grew faster than at any time in the peacetime history of any country—from 82 to 110 million between 1973 and 1985—that is, by a full one-third. The entire growth, however, was in non-manufacturing, and especially in non–blue-collar, jobs.

The trend itself is not new. In the 1920s one out of every three Americans in the labor force was a blue-collar worker in manufacturing. In the 1950s the figure was one in four. It is now down to one in every six—and dropping. While the trend has been running for a long time, it has lately accelerated to the point where—in peacetime at least—no increase in manufacturing production, no matter how large, is likely to reverse the long-term decline in the number of blue-collar jobs in manufacturing or in their proportion of the labor force.

This trend is the same in all developed countries, and is, indeed, even more pronounced in Japan. It is therefore highly probable that in 25 years developed countries such as the United States and Japan will employ no larger a proportion of the labor force in manufacturing than developed countries now employ in farming—at most, 10 percent. Today the United States employs around 18 million people in blue-collar jobs in manufacturing industries. By 2010, the number is likely to be no more than 12 million. In some major industries the drop will be even sharper. It is quite unrealistic, for instance, to expect that the American auto-

mobile industry will employ more than one-third of its present blue-collar work force 25 years hence, even though production might be 50 percent higher.

DEVELOPMENTS IN EMPLOYMENT

If a company, an industry or a country does not in the next quarter century sharply increase manufacturing production and at the same time sharply reduce the blue-collar work force, it cannot hope to remain competitive—or even to remain "developed." It would decline fairly fast. Britain has been in industrial decline for the last 25 years, largely because the number of blue-collar workers per unit of manufacturing production went down far more slowly than in all other non-communist developed countries. Even so, Britain has the highest unemployment rate among non-communist developed countries—more than 13 percent.

The British example indicates a new and critical economic equation: a country, an industry or a company that puts the preservation of blue-collar manufacturing jobs ahead of international competitiveness (which implies a steady shrinkage of such jobs) will soon have neither production nor jobs. The attempt to preserve such blue-collar jobs is actually a prescription for unemployment.

So far, this concept has achieved broad national acceptance only in Japan.[8] Indeed Japanese planners, whether in government or private business, start out with the assumption of a doubling of production within 15 or 20 years based on a cut in blue-collar employment of 25 to 40 percent. A good many large American companies such as IBM, General Electric and the big automobile companies have similar forecasts. Implicit in this is the conclusion that a country will have less overall unemployment the faster it shrinks blue-collar employment in manufacturing.

This is not a conclusion that American politicians, labor leaders or indeed the general public can easily understand or accept. What confuses the issue even more is that the United States is experiencing several separate and different shifts in the manufacturing economy. One is the acceleration of the substitution of knowledge and capital for manual labor. Where we spoke of mechanization a few decades ago, we now speak of "robotization" or "automation." This is actually more a change in terminology than a change in reality. When Henry Ford introduced the assembly line in 1909, he cut the number of man-hours required to produce a motor car by some 80 percent in two or three years—far more than anyone expects to result from even the most complete robotization. But there is no doubt that we are facing a new, sharp acceleration in the replacement of manual workers by machines—that is, by the products of knowledge.

A second development—and in the long run this may be even more important—is the shift from industries that were primarily labor-intensive to industries that, from the beginning, are knowledge-intensive. The manufacturing costs of the semiconductor microchip are about 70 percent knowledge—that is, research, development and testing—and no more than 12 percent labor. Similarly with prescription drugs, labor represents no more than 15 percent, with knowledge representing almost 50 percent. By contrast, in the most fully robotized automobile plant, labor would still account for 20 or 25 percent of the costs.

QUESTIONS OF SCALE

Another perplexing development in manufacturing is the reversal of the dynamics of size. Since the early years of this century, the trend in all developed countries has been toward ever larger manufacturing plants. The economies of scale greatly favored them. Perhaps equally important, what one might call the "economies of management" favored them. Until recently, modern management techniques seemed applicable only to fairly large units.

This has been reversed with a vengeance over the last 15 to 20 years. The entire shrinkage in manufacturing jobs in the United States has occurred in large companies, beginning with the giants in steel and automobiles. Small and especially medium-sized manufacturers have either held their own or actually added employees. In respect to market standing, exports and profitability too, smaller and middle-sized businesses have done remarkably better than big ones.

The reversal of the dynamics of size is occurring in the other developed countries as well, even in Japan where bigger was always better and biggest meant best. The trend has reversed itself even in old industries. The most profitable automobile company these last years has not been one of the giants, but a medium-sized manufacturer in Germany—BMW. The only profitable steel companies, whether in the United States, Sweden or Japan, have been medium-sized makers of specialty products such as oil drilling pipe.

In part, especially in the United States, this is a result of a resurgence of entrepreneurship.[9] But perhaps equally important, we have learned in the last 30 years how to manage the small and medium-sized enterprise to the point where the advantages of smaller size, for example, ease of communications and nearness to market and customer, increasingly outweigh what had been forbidding management limitations. Thus, in the United States, but increasingly in the other leading manufacturing nations such as Japan and West Germany as well, the dynamism in the economy has shifted from the very big companies that dominated the world's economy for 30 years after World War II to companies that, while much smaller, are professionally managed and largely publicly financed.

THE NEW "MANUFACTURERS"

Two distinct kinds of "manufacturing industry" are emerging. One is material-based, represented by the industries that provided economic growth in the first three-quarters of this century. The other is information- and knowledge-based: pharmaceuticals, telecommunications, analytical instruments and information processing such as computers. It is largely the information-based manufacturing industries that are growing.

These two groups differ not only in their economic characteristics but especially in their position in the international economy. The products of material-based industries have to be exported or imported as "products." They appear in the balance of trade. The products of information-based industries can be exported or imported both as "products" and as "services," which may not appear accurately in the overall trade balance.

An old example is the printed book. For one major scientific publishing company, "foreign earnings" account for two-thirds of total revenues. Yet the company exports few, if any, actual books—books are heavy. It sells "rights," and the "product" is produced abroad. Similarly, the most profitable computer "export sales" may actually show up in trade statistics as an "import." This is the fee some of the world's leading banks, multinationals and Japanese trading companies get for processing in their home office data arriving electronically from their branches and customers around the world.

In all developed countries, "knowledge" workers have already become the center of gravity of the labor force. Even in manufacturing they will outnumber blue-collar workers within 10 years. Exporting knowledge so that it produces license income, service fees and royalties may actually create substantially more jobs than exporting goods.

This in turn requires—as official Washington seems to have realized—far greater emphasis in trade policy on "invisible trade" and on abolishing the barriers to the trade in services. Traditionally, economists have treated invisible trade as a stepchild, if they noted it at all. In-

creasingly, it will become central. Within 20 years major developed countries may find that their income from invisible trade is larger than their income from exports.

INDUSTRIAL POLICIES

Another implication of the "uncoupling" of manufacturing production from manufacturing employment is, however, that the choice between an industrial policy that favors industrial *production* and one that favors industrial *employment* is going to be a singularly contentious political issue for the rest of this century. Historically these have always been considered two sides of the same coin. From now on the two will increasingly pull in different directions; they are indeed already becoming alternatives, if not incompatible.

Benign neglect—the policy of the Reagan Administration these last few years—may be the best policy one can hope for, and the only one with a chance of success. It is probably not an accident that the United States has, after Japan, by far the lowest unemployment rate of any industrially developed country. Still, there is surely need also for systematic efforts to retrain and to place redundant blue-collar workers—something no one as yet knows how to do successfully.

Finally, low labor costs are likely to become less of an advantage in international trade simply because in the developed countries they are going to account for less of total costs. Moreover, the total costs of automated processes are lower than even those of traditional plants with low labor costs; this is mainly because automation eliminates the hidden but high costs of "not working," such as the expense of poor quality and rejects, and the costs of shutting down the machinery to change from one model of a product to another. Consider two automated American producers of televisions, Motorola and RCA. Both were almost driven out of the market by imports from countries with much lower labor costs. Both subsequently automated, with the result that these American-made products now successfully compete with foreign imports. Similarly, some highly automated textile mills in the Carolinas can underbid imports from countries with very low labor costs such as Thailand. On the other hand, although some American semiconductor companies have lower labor costs because they do the labor-intensive work offshore, for example, in West Africa, they are still the high-cost producers and easily underbid by the heavily automated Japanese.

The cost of capital will thus become increasingly important in international competition. And this is where, in the last 10 years, the United States has become the highest-cost country—and Japan the lowest. A reversal of the US policy of high interest rates and costly equity capital should thus be a priority for American decision makers. This demands that reduction of the government deficit, rather than high interest rates, becomes the first defense against inflation.

For developed countries, especially the United States, the steady downgrading of labor costs as a major competitive factor could be a positive development. For the Third World, especially rapidly industrializing countries such as Brazil, South Korea or Mexico, it is, however, bad news.

In the rapid industrialization of the nineteenth century, one country, Japan, developed by exporting raw materials, mainly silk and tea, at steadily rising prices. Another, Germany, developed by leap-frogging into the "high-tech" industries of its time, mainly electricity, chemicals and optics. A third, the United States, did both. Both routes are blocked for today's rapidly industrializing countries—the first because of the deteriorioration of the terms of trade for primary products, the second because it requires an infrastructure of knowledge and education far beyond the reach of a poor country (although South Korea is reaching for it). Com-

petition based on lower labor costs seemed to be the only alternative; is this also going to be blocked?

CAPITAL FLOWS

The third major change that has occurred in the world economy is the emergence of the "symbol" economy—capital movements, exchange rates and credit flows—as the flywheel of the world economy, in place of the "real" economy—the flow of goods and services. The two economies seem to be operating increasingly independently. This is both the most visible and the least understood of the changes.

World trade in goods is larger, much larger, than it has ever been before. And so is the "invisible trade," the trade in services. Together, the two amount to around $2.5 to $3 trillion a year. But the London Eurodollar market, in which the world's financial institutions borrow from and lend to each other, turns over $300 billion each working day, or $75 trillion a year, a volume at least 25 times that of world trade.[10] In addition, there are the foreign exchange transactions in the world's money centers, in which one currency is traded against another. These run around $150 billion a day, or about $35 trillion a year—12 times the worldwide trade in goods and services.

Of course, many of these Eurodollars, yen, and Swiss francs are just being moved from one pocket to another and may be counted more than once. A massive discrepancy still exists, and there is only one conclusion: capital movements unconnected to trade—and indeed largely independent of it—greatly exceed trade finance.

There is no one explanation for this explosion of international—or, more accurately, transnational—money flows. The shift from fixed to floating exchange rates in 1971 may have given an initial impetus (though it was meant to do the opposite) by inviting currency speculation. The surge in liquid funds flowing to oil producers after the 1973 and 1979 oil shocks was surely a major factor.

But there can be little doubt that the US government deficit also plays a big role. The American budget has become a financial "black hole," sucking in liquid funds from all over the world making the United States the world's major debtor country.[11] Indeed it can be argued that it is the budget deficit that underlies the American trade and payments deficit. A trade and payments deficit is, in effect, a loan from the seller of goods and services to the buyer, that is, to the United States. Without it Washington could not finance its budget deficit, at least not without the risk of explosive inflation.

The way major countries have learned to use the international economy to avoid tackling disagreeable domestic problems is unprecedented: the United States has used high interest rates to attract foreign capital and avoid confronting its domestic deficit; the Japanese have pushed exports to maintain employment despite a sluggish domestic economy. This politicization of the international economy is surely also a factor in the extreme volatility and instability of capital flows and exchange rates.

REALITY AND SYMBOL

Whichever of these causes is judged the most important, together they have produced a basic change: in the world economy of today, the "real" economy of goods and services and the "symbol" economy of money, credit and capital are no longer bound tightly to each other; they are, indeed, moving further and further apart.

Traditional international economic theory is still neoclassical, holding that trade in goods and services determines international capital flows and foreign exchange rates. Capital flows and foreign exchange rates since the first half of the 1970s have, however, moved quite independently of foreign trade, and indeed (for example, in the rise of the dollar in 1984–85) have run counter to it.

But the world economy also does not fit the Keynesian model in which the "symbol" economy determines the "real" economy. The relationship between the turbulences in the world economy and the various domestic economies has become quite obscure. Despite its unprecedented trade deficit, the United States has had no deflation and has barely been able to keep inflation in check; it also has the lowest unemployment rate of any major industrial country except Japan, lower than that of West Germany, whose exports of manufactured goods and trade surpluses have been growing as fast as those of Japan. Conversely, despite the exponential growth of Japanese exports and an unprecedented Japanese trade surplus, the Japanese domestic economy is not booming but has remained remarkably sluggish and is not generating any new jobs.

Economists assume that the "real" economy and the "symbol" economy will come together again. They do disagree, however—and quite sharply—as to whether they will do so in a "soft landing" or in a head-on collision.

The "soft-landing" scenario—the Reagan Administration is committed to it, as are the governments of most of the other developed countries—expects the US government deficit and the US trade deficit to go down together until both attain surplus, or at least balance, some time in the early 1990s. Presumably both capital flows and exchange rates will then stabilize, with production and employment high and inflation low in major developed countries.

HARD LANDINGS

In sharp contrast to this are the "hard-landing" scenarios.[12] With every deficit year the indebtedness of the US government goes up, and with it the interest charges on the US budget, which in turn raises the deficit even further. Sooner or later, the argument goes, foreign confidence in America and the American dollar will be undermined—some observers consider this practically imminent. Foreigners would stop lending money to the United States and, indeed, try to convert their dollars into other currencies. The resulting "flight from the dollar" would bring the dollar's exchange rates crashing down, and also create an extreme credit crunch, if not a "liquidity crisis" in the United States. The only question is whether the result for the United States would be a deflationary depression, a renewed outbreak of severe inflation or, the most dreaded affliction, "stagflation"—a deflationary, stagnant economy combined with an inflationary currency.

There is, however, a totally different "hard-landing" scenario, one in which Japan, not the United States, faces an economic crisis. For the first time in peacetime history the major debtor, the United States, owes its foreign debt in its own currency. To get out of this debt it does not need to repudiate it, declare a moratorium, or negotiate a "roll-over." All it has to do is devalue its currency and the foreign creditor has effectively been expropriated.

For "foreign creditor," read Japan. The Japanese by now hold about half of the dollars the United States owes to foreigners. In addition, practically all of their other claims on the outside world are in dollars, largely because the Japanese have resisted all attempts to make the yen an international trading currency lest the government lose control over it. Altogether, Japanese banks now hold more international assets than do the banks of any other country, including the United States. And practically all these assets are in US dollars—$640 billion of them. A devaluation of the US dollar would thus fall most heavily on the Japanese.

The repercussions for Japan extend deep into its trade and domestic economy. By far the largest part of Japan's exports goes to the United States. If there is a "hard landing," the United States might well turn protectionist almost overnight; it is unlikely that Americans would let in large volumes of imported goods were the unemployment rate to soar. But this would immediately cause severe unemployment in Tokyo and Nagoya and Hiroshima, and might indeed set off a true depression in Japan.

There is still another "hard-landing" scenario. In this version neither the United States, nor Japan, nor the industrial economies altogether, experience the "hard landing"; it would hit the already depressed producers of primary products.

Practically all primary materials are traded in dollars, and their prices might not go up at all should the dollar be devalued (they actually went down when the dollar plunged by 30 percent between summer 1985 and February 1986). Thus Japan may be practically unaffected by a dollar devaluation; Japan needs dollar balances only to pay for primary-product imports, as it buys little else on the outside and has no foreign debt. The United States, too, may not suffer, and may even benefit as its industrial exports become more competitive.

But while the primary producers sell mainly in dollars, they have to pay in other developed nations' currencies for a large part of their industrial imports. The United States, after all, although the world's leading exporter of industrial goods, still accounts for only one-fifth of the total. And the dollar prices of the industrial goods furnished by others—the Germans, the Japanese, the French, the British, and so on—are likely to go up. This might bring about a further drop in the terms of trade for the already depressed primary producers. Some estimates of the possible deterioration go as high as 10 percent, which would entail considerable hardship not only for metal mines in South America and Zimbabwe, but also for farmers in Canada, Kansas and Brazil.

A STATUS QUO

One more possible scenario involves no "landings," either "soft" or "hard." What if the economists were wrong and both the American budget deficit and American trade deficit continue, albeit at lower levels than in recent years? This would happen if the outside world's willingness to put its money into the United States were based on other than purely economic considerations—on their own internal domestic politics, for example, or simply on the desire to escape risks at home that appear to be far worse than a US devaluation.

This is the only scenario that is so far supported by hard facts rather than by theory. Indeed, it is already playing. The US government talked the dollar down by almost one-third (from a rate of 250 yen to 180 yen to the dollar) between summer 1985 and February 1986—one of the most massive devaluations ever of a major currency, though called a "readjustment." America's creditors unanimously supported this devaluation and indeed demanded it. More amazing still, they responded by increasing their loans to the United States, and substantially so. International bankers seem to agree that the United States is more creditworthy the more the lender stands to lose by lending to it!

A major reason for this Alice-in-Wonderland attitude is that the biggest US creditors, the Japanese, clearly prefer even very heavy losses on their dollar holdings to domestic unemployment. And without exports to the United States, Japan might have unemployment close to that of Western Europe, 9 to 11 percent, and concentrated in the most politically sensitive smokestack industries in which Japan is becoming increasingly vulnerable to competition from newcomers such as South Korea.

Similarly, economic conditions alone will not induce Hong Kong Chinese to withdraw the money they have transferred to American banks in anticipation of Hong Kong's reversion to Chinese sovereignty in 1997. These deposits amount to billions. The even larger amounts—at least several hundred billion—of "flight capital" from Latin America that have found refuge in the US dollar will also not be lured away by purely economic incentives such as higher interest rates.

The sum needed from the outside to maintain both a huge US budget deficit and a huge US trade deficit would be far too big to make this the most probable scenario. But if political factors are in control, the "symbol" economy is indeed truly "uncoupled" from the "real" economy, at least in the international sphere. Whichever scenario proves right, none promises a return to any kind of "normalcy."

COMPARATIVE ADVANTAGES

From now on exchange rates between major currencies will have to be treated in economic theory and business policy alike as a "comparative-advantage" factor, and a major one.

Economic theory teaches that the comparative-advantage factors of the "real" economy—comparative labor costs and labor productivity, raw material costs, energy costs, transportation costs and the like—determine exchange rates. Practically all businesses base their policies on this notion. Increasingly, however, it is exchange rates that decide how labor costs in country A compare to labor costs in country B. Exchange rates are thus a major "comparative cost" and one totally beyond business control. Any firm exposed to the international economy has to realize that it is in two businesses at the same time. It is both a maker of goods (or a supplier of services) and a "financial" business. It cannot disregard either.

Specifically, the business that sells abroad—whether as an exporter or through a subsidiary—will have to protect itself against three foreign exchange exposures: proceeds from sales, working capital devoted to manufacturing for overseas markets, and investments abroad. This will have to be done whether the business expects the value of its own currency to go up or down. Businesses that buy abroad will have to do likewise. Indeed, even purely domestic businesses that face foreign competition in their home market will have to learn to hedge against the currency in which their main competitors produce. If American businesses had been run this way during the years of the overvalued dollars, from 1982 through 1985, most of the losses in market standing abroad and in foreign earnings might have been prevented. They were management failures, not acts of God. Surely stockholders, but also the public in general, have every right to expect management to do better the next time around.

In respect to government policy there is one conclusion: don't be "clever." It is tempting to exploit the ambiguity, instability and uncertainty of the world economy to gain short-term advantages and to duck unpopular political decisions. But it does not work. Indeed, disaster is a more likely outcome than success, as all three of the attempts made so far amply indicate.

COURTING DISASTER

In the first attempt, the Carter Administration pushed down the US dollar to artificial lows to stimulate the American economy through the promotion of exports. American exports did indeed go up—spectacularly so. But far from stimulating the domestic economy, this depressed it, resulting in simultaneous record unemployment and accelerated inflation—the worst of all possible outcomes.

President Reagan a few years later pushed up interest rates to stop inflation, and also pushed up the dollar. This did indeed stop inflation. It also triggered massive inflows of capital. But it so overvalued the dollar as to create a surge of foreign imports. As a result, the Reagan policy exposed the most vulnerable of the smokestack industries, such as steel and automobiles, to competition they could not possibly meet. It deprived them of the earnings they needed to modernize themselves. Also, the policy seriously damaged, perhaps irreversibly, the competitive position of American farm products in the world markets, and at the worst possible time. Worse still, his "cleverness" defeated Mr. Reagan's major purpose: the reduction of the US government deficit. Because of the losses to foreign competition, domestic industry did not grow enough to produce higher tax revenues. Yet the easy and almost unlimited availability

of foreign money enabled Congress (and the Administration) to postpone again and again action to cut the deficit.

In the third case the Japanese, too, may have been too clever in their attempt to exploit the disjunction between the international "symbol" and "real" economies. Exploiting an undervalued yen, the Japanese have been pushing exports—a policy quite reminiscent of America under the Carter Administration. But the Japanese policy similarly has failed to stimulate the domestic economy; it has been barely growing these last few years despite the export boom. As a result, the Japanese have become dangerously overdependent on one customer, the United States. This has forced them to invest huge sums in American dollars, even though every thoughtful Japanese (including, of course, individuals in the Japanese government and the Japanese central bank) has known all along that these investments would end up being severely devalued.

Surely these three lessons should have taught us that government economic policies will succeed to the extent to which they try to harmonize the needs of the two economies, rather than to the extent to which they try to exploit the disharmony between them. Or to repeat very old wisdom, "in finance don't be clever; be simple and conscientious." I am afraid this is advice that governments are not likely to heed soon.

FUTURE ACTIONS

It is much too early to guess what the world economy of tomorrow will look like. Will major countries, for instance, succumb to traditional fears and retreat into protectionism? Or will they see a changed world economy as an opportunity?

Some parts of the main agenda, however, are fairly clear by now. Rapidly industrializing countries like Mexico or Brazil will need to formulate new development concepts and policies. They can no longer hope to finance their development by raw material exports, for example, Mexican oil. It is also becoming unrealistic for them to believe that their low labor costs will enable them to export large quantities of finished goods to developed countries—something the Brazilians, for instance, still expect. They would do much better to go into "production sharing," that is, to use their labor advantage to become subcontractors to developed-country manufacturers for highly labor-intensive work that cannot be automated—some assembly operations, for instance, or parts and components needed only in relatively small quantities. Developed countries no longer have the labor to do such work, which even with the most thorough automation will still account for 15 to 20 percent of manufacturing work.

Such production sharing is, of course, how Singapore, Hong Kong and Taiwan bootstrapped their development. Yet in Latin America production sharing is still politically unacceptable and, indeed, anathema. Mexico, for instance, has been deeply committed since its beginnings as a modern nation in the early years of this century to making its economy less dependent on, and less integrated with, that of its big neighbor to the north. That this policy has been a total failure for 80 years has only strengthened its emotional and political appeal.

Even if production sharing is implemented to the fullest, it would not by itself provide enough income to fuel development, especially of countries so much larger than the Chinese "city-states." We thus need a new model and new policies.

LESSONS FROM INDIA

Can we learn something from India? Everyone knows of India's problems—and they are legion. Few people seem to realize, however, that since independence India has done a better development job than almost any other Third World country: it has enjoyed the fastest increase in farm production and farm yields; a growth rate in manufacturing production equal to that of Brazil, and perhaps even of South Korea (India now has a bigger industrial economy than any but a handful of developed countries); the emergence of a large and highly entrepreneurial middle class; and arguably, the greatest achievement in providing schooling and health care in the villages.

Yet the Indians followed none of the established models. They did not, like Stalin, Mao and so many leaders of newly independent African nations, despoil the peasants to produce capital for industrial development. They did not export raw materials. And they did not export the products of cheap labor. Instead, since Nehru's death in 1964, India has followed a policy of strengthening agriculture and encouraging consumer goods production. India and its achievement are bound to get far more attention in the future.

The developed countries, too, need to think through their policies in respect to the Third World—and especially in respect to the "stars" of the Third World, the rapidly industrializing countries. There are some beginnings: the debt proposals recently put forward by Treasury Secretary James A. Baker, or the new lending criteria recently announced by the World Bank for loans to Third World countries, which will be made conditional on a country's overall development policies rather than on the soundness of individual projects. But these proposals are aimed more at correcting past mistakes than at developing new policies.

The other major agenda item is—inevitably—the international monetary system. Since the Bretton Woods Conference in 1944, the world monetary system has been based on the US dollar as the reserve currency. This clearly does not work any more. The reserve-currency country must be willing to subordinate its domestic policies to the needs of the international economy, for example, risk domestic unemployment to keep currency rates stable. And when it came to the crunch, the United States refused to do so—as Keynes, by the way, predicted 40 years ago.

The stability supposedly supplied by the reserve currency could be established today only if the major trading countries—at a minimum the United States, West Germany and Japan— agreed to coordinate their economic, fiscal and monetary policies, if not to subordinate them to joint (and this would mean supranational) decision making. Is such a development even conceivable, except perhaps in the event of worldwide financial collapse? The European experience with the far more modest European Currency Unit is not encouraging; so far, no European government has been willing to yield an inch for the sake of the ECU. But what else can be done? Have we come to the end of the 300-year-old attempt to regulate and stabilize money on which, after all, both the modern nation-state and the international system are largely based?

THE GLOBAL FRAMEWORK

We are left with one conclusion: economic dynamics have decisively shifted from the national economy to the world economy.

Prevailing economic theory—whether Keynesian, monetarist, or supply-side—considers the national economy, especially that of the large developed countries, to be autonomous and the unit of both economic analysis and economic policy. The international economy may be a restraint and a limitation, but it is not central, let alone determining. This "macroeconomic axiom" of the modern economist has become increasingly shaky. The two major subscribers to this axiom, Britain and the United States, have done least well economically in the last 30 years, and have also had the most economic instability.

West Germany and Japan never accepted the "macroeconomic axiom." Their universities teach it, of course, but their policymakers, both in government and in business, reject it. Instead, both countries all along have based their economic policies on the world economy, have systematically tried to anticipate its trends and exploit its changes as opportunities. Above all, both make the country's competitive position in the world economy the first priority in their policies—economic, fiscal, monetary, even social—to which domestic considerations are normally subordinated. And these two countries have done far better—economically and socially—than Britain and the United States these last 30 years. In fact, their focus on the world economy and the priority they give it may be the real "secret" of their success.

Similarly the "secret" of successful businesses in the developed world—the Japanese, the German carmakers like Mercedes and BMW, Asea and Ericsson in Sweden, IBM and Citibank in the United States, but equally of a host of medium-sized specialists in manufacturing and in all kinds of services—has been that they base their plans and their policies on exploiting the world economy's changes as opportunities.

From now on any country—but also any business, especially a large one—that wants to prosper will have to accept that it is the world economy that leads and that domestic economic policies will succeed only if they strengthen, or at least do not impair, the country's international competitive position. This may be the most important—it surely is the most striking—feature of the changed world economy.

NOTES

1. When the price of petroleum dropped to $15 a barrel in February 1986, it was actually below its 1933 price (adjusted for the change in the purchasing power of the dollar). It was still, however, substantially higher than its all-time low in 1972–73, which in 1986 dollars amounted to $7–$8 a barrel.

2. On this see two quite different discussions by Dennis Avery, "U.S. Farm Dilemma: The Global Bad News Is

Wrong," *Science,* October 25, 1985; and Barbara Insel, "A World Awash in Grain," *Foreign Affairs,* Spring 1985.

3. The business cycle theory was developed just before World War I by the Russian mathematical economist, Nikolai Kondratieff, who made comprehensive studies of raw material price cycles and their impacts all the way back to 1797.

4. These conclusions are based on static analysis, which presumes that which products are bought and sold is not affected by changes in price. This is of course unrealistic, but the flaw should not materially affect the conclusions.

5. Although the African famine looms large in our consciousness, the total population of the affected areas is far too small to make any dent in world food surpluses.

6. David Sapsford, "Real Primary Commodity Prices: An Analysis of Long-Run Movements," International Monetary Fund memorandum, May 17, 1985 (unpublished).

7. This was asserted as early as 1950 by the South American economist Raúl Prebisch in *The Economic Development of Latin America and Its Principal Problems* (E/CN.

12/89/REV. 1), United Nations Economic Commission for Latin America. But then no one, including myself, believed him.

8. The Japanese government, for example, sponsors a finance company that makes long-term, low-interest loans to small manufacturers to enable them to automate rapidly.

9. On this see my book, *Innovation and Entrepreneurship: Practice and Principle* (New York: Harper & Row, 1985).

10. A Eurodollar is a U.S. dollar held outside the United States.

11. This is cogently argued by Stephen Marris, for almost 30 years economic advisor to the Organization for Economic Cooperation and Development (OECD), in his *Deficits and the Dollar: The World Economy at Risk* (Washington, D.C.: Institute of International Economics, December 1985).

12. In ibid., the author gives the clearest and most persuasive presentation of the hard-landing scenarios.

2

INTERNATIONAL INDUSTRIES: FRAGMENTATION VERSUS GLOBALIZATION
YVES DOZ

Since World War II, growth in international trade has exceeded world economic growth by a substantial margin, and national economies have become increasingly dependent on world trade. Up to 50 percent of the gross national product (GNP) of small European countries is traded internationally, whereas only about 25 percent of GNP in larger European countries and 10 to 15 percent of GNP in the comparatively isolated large economies of the United States and Japan is traded internationally. Markets for many industrial goods have become increasingly homogeneous. Simultane-

ously, foreign investment has grown rapidly, both in developed and in developing countries.[1] Not only has the total stock of capital grown rapidly, but, more significantly, there has been growth in the number of subsidiaries of multinational companies (MNCs); growth in the number of countries in which specific firms were active; and increasing diversity in the products manufactured and sold abroad through subsidiaries of MNCs (Vernon and Davidson, 1979).

As both international trade and investment grew rapidly, international competition became more intense, and many national industries became global industries. Similarity of markets in different countries and intense global competition drove international competi-

Source: Bruce K. Guile and Harvey Brooks, eds. *Technology and Global Industry* (Washington, D.C.: National Academy Press, 1987), pp. 96–118.

tors to coordinate their market and competitive strategies between countries more actively. The relevant scope of strategy thus shifted from discrete national markets to global markets, and coordinated worldwide competitive actions between the various subsidiaries of MNCs became more important.

As national competition shifted to global competition, foreign investment also shifted. Protectionism in the 1930s, the trauma of World War II, and national reconstruction policies led the early multinational investors to fragment their operations into discrete market-servicing, self-sufficient investments with little interdependence between operations in separate countries. The developing countries' import substitution policies had similar effects. With freer trade and more intense competition, both the possibility of, and the need for, sourcing investments in manufacturing arose: International corporations started to specialize and rationalize their plants to exploit national comparative advantages. Even where economic and technical conditions prohibited such specialization—for example, for cement, glass, or industrial gases—competitive actions became coordinated across subsidiaries as the companies realized they were competing in a very concentrated global oligopoly. As a result, portfolio foreign investments, where only intangible assets are leveraged, gave way to strategically coordinated integrated operations worldwide, exploiting comparative advantages of different countries for various types of activities. Labor-intensive activities were sited in locations where labor costs were low and from which the world markets were served. Such advantages were most often exploited by owned subsidiaries—through "internalization" —rather than through subcontracting or licensing.[2] This, in turn, led to the development of intrafirm international trade. Such trade may be intraindustry (e.g., the processing of semiconductors overseas for reimport into the United States) or intrafirm but interindustry (e.g., General Electric "off-setting" the

sale of jet engines to the Canadian Armed Forces with exports of consumer goods from Canada).

With some significant exceptions—usually government imposed—the trend toward industry globalization and toward MNC integration has affected most countries and most internationally traded goods. The proportion of internationally traded goods in the GNP of countries also increased substantially, so that by 1980 internationally traded goods with substantial trade levels comprised more than 80 percent of the industrial sectors in Western Europe (Orléan, 1986). This trend was particularly strong between 1968 and 1978.

Since the late 1970s, however, three sets of factors have come to limit such globalization. First, the technology no longer always drives toward globalization: New manufacturing techniques may reverse the trend toward "world-scale" plants and allow differentiation and segmentation with smaller cost penalties. Second, protectionism is on the rise and limits the strategic freedom of global competitors. Protectionism applies not only to trade in goods, but also increasingly to trade in knowledge, technology in particular. Third, the organizational and strategic capabilities of global competitors often lag the competitive opportunities available to them, and many firms are less than fully successful in exploiting their opportunities.

The impact of the three sets of limiting factors mentioned above deserves more attention. This chapter reflects this interest, beginning with a selective review of the abundant, if still fragmentary, evidence on the trends toward market homogenization, industry globalization and firm integration, and the underlying forces that drive them. These issues are discussed at three complementary levels of aggregation: the international economic relations framework; individual industries and their competitive dynamics; and the logistics, organizational structures, and management processes of individual firms. Finally, the recent evolution of the three sets of moderating factors—technologies, government policies leading to growing protectionism, and the limited organizational capabilities of firms—and what their effect may be on the fragmentation or globalization of international industries are analyzed.

GLOBALIZATION OF INDUSTRIES

Enabling Conditions

Globalization is rooted in several key enabling conditions: the homogenization of markets, the decreasing costs of transport and communication, decreasing trade barriers, and the competitive pressures from new competitors. First, national markets have become increasingly similar in taste as income distributions in industrialized nations have equalized. The result has been the development of relatively homogeneous market segments that cross borders (Levitt, 1983). Though national markets may have been more similar in the past than was generally recognized (Helleiner, 1981), the media (mainly television), international travel, and the action of active multinational marketers have contributed to the homogenization of markets across national boundaries. Furthermore, global market segments appear in industries as different as automobiles (to the advantage of BMW or AMC's "Jeep") and beer (to the advantage of Heineken and a few others). Higher disposable incomes also encouraged the development of a market for fashionable "world products" in a number of countries, be these products British raincoats, Italian sweaters, Swiss watches (Rolex or Swatch), French wines, or Japanese consumer electronics.

Lower communication and transportation costs—the second enabling condition—also made serving these homogeneous markets from centralized locations economical, even for relatively bulky products such as cars. Real-time low-cost communication also made the coordination of a complex worldwide logistics system

feasible. The globalization of manufacturing in certain industries where products are complex and differentiated might not have happened without the drastic reductions in transportation and telecommunication costs between 1950 and 1980.

That trade barriers were removed between the 1950s and the 1980s is well known and needs no detailed analysis here. The removal of these barriers provided a third enabling condition for the globalization of industries. Only in some industries where government-controlled customers predominate, and where national defense considerations are relevant, did trade barriers stay in place (Doz, 1986). Specific trade agreements (e.g., the Lomé convention), as well as the extension of credit to developing countries, allowed these countries to participate in this move toward free trade, initiated by traditional industrialized countries. The recognition that across-the-board import substitution measures usually fail, and the successful example of the newly industrialized countries (NICs), also provided an incentive for developing countries to participate actively in the world economy.

A fourth enabling condition, usually at the level of individual firms, was the existence of the organizational infrastructure for globalization. In the mid-1960s, when trade liberalization was initiated and national markets started to converge visibly, many MNCs were already in place, with their infrastructure of sales subsidiaries and foreign plants. This gave them the capability both to gather data worldwide and to respond quickly—at least in theory—to globalization trends. Global information networks and means of global market reach were already in place, decreasing the cost of transition from national to global competition for the major competitors. Experience in handling foreign manufacture, new product introduction, and technology transfer facilitated a prompt response to industry globalization by MNCs (Vernon, 1979). Where such networks and means did not exist, helping hands could be found. Initially, for example, Japanese exporters relied on Japanese trading companies, importing countries' mass merchandisers (e.g., Sears in the United States), mass buyers (e.g., TV rental companies in the United Kingdom), and original equipment manufacturer (OEM) customers (e.g., for computer peripherals). This allowed the new competitors to skip both the market intelligence tasks (Sears, for instance, specified the TV sets it wanted) and the initial market access cost and delay. More complex, more fragmented, less transparent, and less willing distribution structures would have been a formidable barrier to globalization and, where present, remain a source of asymmetry in globalization (witness the painful efforts of many European and American firms to establish a significant market presence in Japan).

Driving Forces for Sourcing and Marketing Globalization

The enabling conditions summarized above were necessary, though not sufficient, for industry globalization to take place. They had to be exploited by firms trying to gain a permanent competitive advantage. The intense competition created by these firms was in most cases the main driving force for integration and globalization to actually take place. Intense competition itself depended on the opportunity for substantial gains through globalization, the existence or the creation of destabilizing conditions, and the presence of competitors with the strategic intent and capabilities to exploit destabilizing conditions to their advantage.

Growing economies of scale in R&D and in production provided the most frequent opportunity for increased profits through globalization. Changes in product and process technology have increased the minimum efficient size of production in a variety of industries, such as cars, chemicals, consumer electronics, semiconductors, and machinery. Combined with

the emergence of smaller differentiated global segments, this is a powerful incentive to pool demand from a variety of national markets and serve such demand from large, optimally sited specialized plants. New product development costs have also risen considerably in a range of industries, the best-known of which are aircraft, telephone switching, cars, and semiconductors. These higher costs have created a strong incentive for industries to serve the world market to spread R&D costs over a larger production. There is a further incentive to serve the world market quickly to minimize the financing cost of the initial investment and the competitive risk of technological obsolescence (Hamel and Prahalad, 1985).

In some capital goods industries, such as papermaking machinery, electrical equipment, and railroad equipment, the cyclicality of domestic demand and the uncertainty of future domestic orders have led to chronic overcapacity and to the need for national firms to diversify their customer base by selling abroad. Intense competition, though, is the key driving force. In Europe, following the European Economic Community's (EEC) lowering of trade barriers, little change toward a more efficient industry structure took place unless triggered and stimulated by intense competition (Owen, 1983).

The emergence of a period of intense competition was facilitated by technological or market discontinuities that destabilized the existing market and industry structures. Increases in energy costs, for example, destabilized the structure of such industries as automobiles and papermaking machinery, making it possible for new global competitors to emerge. Shifts from electromechanical to electronic technologies in industries ranging from watches to digital switching systems and avionics have similarly allowed new competitors to establish themselves and occasionally to render a whole industry obsolete (e.g., the mechanical Swiss watch industry). Wide fluctuations in exchange rates have occasionally had significant effects, helping new competitors to penetrate mature industries, even in the absence of new technology or changing economies of scale. In 1983 and 1984, for example, the overvaluation of the U.S. dollar helped Komatsu gain overseas customers at the expense of Caterpillar (Bartlett, 1985).

Ambitious competitors, with a vision of how to turn situations to their advantage, were also needed to make competition more intense. These competitors, such as Komatsu, have the long-term strategic intent to dominate their industry, and they are able to exploit opportunities as they arise. While the new competitors have usually been Japanese, they are also occasionally European (e.g., Leroy Somer in small electric motors) or American (e.g., Otis in the small-elevator industry). Confronted with intense competition from new competitors intent on exploiting economies of scale, new product and process technology, and other destabilizing factors such as exchange rate fluctuations, established competitors have typically reacted in two complementary ways: (1) reducing costs through the exploitation of economies of scale or through economies of location; and (2) gaining worldwide market access through their own efforts or through networks of partnerships and coalitions.[3] First, many companies attempted to reduce costs by exploiting potential economies of large scale, typically by integrating and rationalizing production in a region (e.g., Philips rationalizing its television tube and receiver plants in Europe and Ford doing the same with cars). Companies also searched for lower factor costs and other locational advantages (e.g., the moves offshore in the U.S. electronics industry in the late 1960s and 1970s, or the relocation of the aluminum smelting industry). Demands for cost competitiveness led to sourcing globalization. This practice was sometimes encouraged by governments, either through factor subsidization (small open countries such as Ireland or Singapore) or by the imposition of export performance requirements in exchange for access to local markets, typi-

cally in large "promising" countries such as Spain, Brazil, and recently India (Guysinger et al., 1984).

Managing costs is not enough, however, as companies have also come to recognize the value of worldwide market access (Hamel and Prahalad, 1985). Such access is becoming critical not only as a response to rising R&D costs but also as a way of providing potential for competitive retaliation. Goodyear responded to Michelin's inroads into the U.S. tire market by competing more actively in Europe, where Michelin was dominant, thus depriving Michelin of the cash flow it needed to continue its investments to gain market share in the United States. A fight confined to the U.S. market would have been more costly for Goodyear than for Michelin. Similarly, IBM fights Japanese computer manufacturers not so much in the United States, where it would hurt itself, as in Japan, where IBM hurts its Japanese competitors most at the least cost to itself (*New Scientist,* 1985). U.S. makers of consumer electronics had no such option and fell almost defenseless to the Japanese and to Philips.[4]

Where firms were not yet global enough and could not establish market presence quickly (either because of government restrictions, or because distribution channels are hard to penetrate, or both), strategic partnerships and coalitions developed in industries that were becoming global. The primary motive of most partnerships and coalitions is to shore up market presence and technological competence to establish quickly a defensible position in a global industry. While these do provide a viable option, the sharing of strategic control over competitive actions by several partners usually results in tensions as soon as the external technological and market conditions evolve or the relative strategic importance of the joint activities to the various partners changes. This is probably the single largest cause of mortality in collaborative agreements. Even when the collaboration endures, conflicting priorities may result in delays that blunt its competitiveness (for example, the 2-year delay in the launch of the A-320 airplane by Airbus Industries and the continuing tensions between the main partners on future product policy and on acceptable financial performance).

Empirical Evidence

Although anecdotal evidence of industry globalization and MNC integration abounds, systematic measurable data on their extent remain scarce and fragmentary. Some industries are well documented (e.g., automobiles, textiles, electronic components, aerospace) through numerous industry studies, but most others are much less well analyzed.[5] Aggregate statistics using proxies such as intrafirm trade also suggest that integration of operations within MNCs is important, with 20 to 30 percent of the international trade of countries such as the United States, the United Kingdom, and Sweden being intrafirm trade. Intrafirm trade seems to be more prevalent in R&D-intensive industries, with high wages and large plants, which is consistent with the driving forces hypothesized above (Dunning and Pearce, 1985; Lall, 1978; United Nations Center on Transnational Corporations, 1983). Yet, even the most detailed studies are fraught with problems in the availability and interpretation of data (Hood and Young, 1980). There is a convergence between findings from studies that start with trade statistics (e.g., based on the U.S. Department of Commerce Annual Survey of U.S. corporations), those that start with a survey of large samples of firms (e.g., Dunning and Pearce, 1985), and those that start with an analysis of the strategic behavior of firms (e.g., Hood and Young, 1980). The more anecdotal evidence from individual "case" studies and from industry-specific studies also points in the same direction.

Industry studies also provide evidence that even in industries that are traditionally nationally fragmented, pressures for integration and globalization are being felt. In the furniture in-dustry, for instance, companies such as IKEA or Habitat-Mothercare are exploiting economies of scale in purchasing, subcontracting, advertising, and brand image, shifting the bottom end of the furniture market away from a fragmented national structure to an integrated multinational one. Similar moves are made at the top end of this market with international designers' brands and with global distributors, such as Roche-Bobois. Even where national prestige, national defense, and strategic independence have traditionally weighed more heavily than competitiveness in industrial choices, original patterns of globalization and integration develop. By and large, European integration in aerospace is making progress under tight supervision from governments. The failure to agree on a single design for a future fighter plane may ultimately be beneficial in offering two complementary products and maintaining spirited competition for export orders: Britain, Italy, Germany, and Spain joined forces and will compete against France and smaller countries. Similarly, the European microelectronics industry is evolving out of a stalemate. We see cooperation between large firms that traditionally were competitors as in the joint development of "megachips" by Philips and Siemens, and we see new ventures occasionally being funded by old firms, as when European Silicon Structures is financed by a group of large European electronic industry firms to make semi-custom chips economically in Europe. Although these collaborative ventures may not operate under the best possible conditions, and their cost of coordination is high, they at least overcome the worst aspects of fragmentation.[6]

Besides the turnaround in many governments in favor of government-sponsored transnational cooperation, it is also important to note that pressure groups that might have tried to block globalization and integration by and large have failed. Although in the early 1970s it seemed plausible that unions would gain a strong say in MNC management, they have now been ruled out as a severe barrier to globalization and integration. This is the result of a combination of factors, namely, the change of attitude in Europe (both the effect of the unemployment crisis and also of an ideological shift away from statism and socialism), the failure of unions to lock MNCs into transnational bargaining, the lack of support provided by governments (e.g., the inability to get the Vredeling proposal off the ground), and the divisive aspects of MNC integration itself on international labor cooperation. Where unions succeeded in gaining a say, as they did with the German codetermination laws, their representatives quickly aligned their positions on those of management.

Economically weak but politically strong national industrial companies could also be barriers to globalization, but by and large they fell to competitive pressures in Europe. Only in a few partly competitive but largely government-controlled sectors, such as electrical equipment for railroads, do the old industry structures survive largely unchanged. Even in some of these industries, there are encouraging signs of possible rationalization, such as the investments by Compagnie Générale d' Electricité into Ateliers de Constructions Electriques de Charleroi. Computer manufacturers are victims of probably the worst stalemate along these lines in Europe. Britain, Germany, and France each have their "national champion," hopelessly small for global competitiveness, and unable to renew its product line without much outside help—usually Japanese. Yet each of these national champions is well enough ensconced in its national political and economic environment to survive, to prevent its merger into a transnational alliance, and to block the development of new, more entrepreneurial national or international competitors. First-class customers desert European suppliers—mainly to IBM—despite the switching costs involved, and the technical capability of European computer companies is withered by their Japanese partners, who provide them with components, critical subsystems, and peripherals. The continuation of this stalemate threatens the European computer industry with extinction. In Europe, though, this is more the exception than the rule, and most industries—aerospace, chemicals and plastics, pharmaceuticals, and even now automobiles—are taking on the challenge of global competition with a fair measure of success.

Research and Development

Unlike marketing and manufacturing, research and development have not been significantly affected by globalization and have remained principally home-country activities. In a world of sequential market development, where new products and new processes were first developed and put to use on the domestic market or in the home plants, home-country R&D made good sense. As foreign markets developed to resemble the domestic markets, or as foreign plants were built, new products and technologies were transferred abroad once they had been proved domestically. Foreign R&D was mainly devoted to the adaptation of transferred products and processes to local conditions such as taste, product features, norms and standards, and climate (Fischer and Behrman, 1979; Hirschey and Caves, 1981). The role of foreign subsidiaries was not to innovate on their own but to absorb and apply technology developed in the parent company's laboratories. Technology was in fact global from the start, but research was centrally performed and leveraged internationally through product life cycle phenomena or through transfers to foreign subsidiaries. Even a group such as Brown Boveri, which epitomized the nationally responsive—and fragmented—MNC, leveraged its Swiss-developed technology in its foreign operations (Doz, 1978).

In a more complex world, where the United States no longer clearly leads in product innovation, nor Europe in process innovation, centralized R&D is less effective. First, the leading users—those who can contribute their experience to the success of an innovation—are no longer necessarily available in the domestic market. Although this is truest for MNCs in small countries (e.g., Holland, Sweden, Switzerland, Korea), it is also applicable to U.S. or Japanese companies. Leading markets for medical electronics, for example, may be in the United States and in Japan and Sweden for factory automation, in France for nuclear engineering, and in Britain for consumer electronics. Second, key scientists, like the leading users, are potentially more dispersed geographically than they have ever been. Some European pharmaceuticals or electronics firms find it easier to locate laboratories for new technologies such as genetic engineering or microchips in the United States than in Europe. Conversely, India may offer the potential for a large number of inexpensive software specialists and Italy for creative ones. Several U.S. electronics companies, such as Control Data, Motorola, and Texas Instruments, are setting up software R&D centers in India and Italy. Exploiting a larger pool of talent and avoiding the cost of expatriation are strong motives to locate R&D in various countries. Third, locating R&D in host countries may also help placate their governments' desires for more higher skilled jobs (see Branscomb in this volume [i.e., *Technology and Global Industry*—eds.]).[7] It may also make the firm eligible for national R&D subsidies or access to national collaborative projects. Finally, the mobility and transfer of knowledge within MNCs is neither easy nor costless (Teece, 1977).

Despite these trends, the forces favoring centralization of R&D remain strong. First, as markets become increasingly homogeneous, the need for specific local product adaptation or for autonomous product development is lessened. Second, the benefits of close proximity of researchers are strong. Although esti-

mates of the distance beyond which easy informal communication between scientists breaks down range from a few yards to a 1-day plane commute, observers agree that the scattering of related research activities is detrimental to their effectiveness (Allen, 1977). Third, there are often economies of scope in R&D, particularly where technologies are interdependent, which make the scattering of R&D laboratories costly since they cannot be made self-contained. Fourth, considerations of political risk seem to have limited the willingness of major firms to be dependent in their home markets on technologies developed abroad.

It is thus no great surprise to observe that, with a few notable exceptions, the performance of the R&D function in firms has neither been globalized nor integrated to any extent comparable to that of manufacturing and marketing. The results of R&D are global, not the performance of the R&D tasks. With a few significant exceptions, R&D remained centralized, at least in the technology-intensive sectors. Foreign R&D labs do mostly product development and adaptation to local conditions, or sometimes basic research, but seldom have broad research mandates, except in some of the most mature MNCs (e.g., IBM, Dow Chemical Company, and Ciba-Geigy). Further, few firms seem to have developed systematic processes for the coordination of R&D activities across regions of the world, again with a few notable exceptions, such as IBM.

Yet, as the home market can no longer be equated with the lead market, centrally performed R&D needs to be responsive to the needs of distant potential users. This may be easy to achieve for engineered commodities, such as consumer durables, photocopiers, and typewriters, but it is more difficult where needs can be defined only in close conjunction with users rather than through market research (von Hippel, 1982). Whereas Japanese successes have been confined mainly to engineered commodities, European exporters and MNCs cover a wider spectrum of products. Large European companies have particularly difficult problems with their U.S. subsidiaries. Their products are often developed with too much of a "technology-push" by central labs whose scientists and managers may have gained a sense for European needs but are insensitive to U.S. needs. In some cases, they seem to be following what they think is the "right" path from a technological rather than market standpoint without considering the lead users' needs. As a result, it is not uncommon for U.S. subsidiaries of European groups to avoid marketing products developed in Europe, thus ensuring that their volumes will be too low to break even. Instead, they develop new products at great cost, take a license from a competitor, or buy the products directly on an OEM basis.

The issue is not who is right or wrong between the U.S. subsidiary and headquarters, but the fact that a European group facing such a situation gains little competitive advantage from being in the United States at all. The converse example, of insensitivity by U.S.-based companies to non-U.S. market needs in their product development, is better known and more easily explicable, given the historical dominance—in the operation of most U.S. MNCs—of the U.S. market over smaller fragmented national markets. Faced with the dilemma between economies of centralization and the market access advantages of R&D dispersion, MNCs have occasionally done both; some U.S. MNCs have maintained central laboratories but located the primary labs for a set of products in the lead market away from headquarters.

In summary, R&D activities have not changed as dramatically over time as manufacturing and marketing: Their activities have remained largely centralized—most often in the home country—and their output leveraged through transfer to foreign subsidiaries or through embodiment in exported products (Hirschey and Caves, 1981). For most MNCs, the arguments for centralization seem to have outweighed those favoring geographical fragmentation.

Summary Observations

Although it has to remain impressionistic, since detailed data are lacking, the analysis of the balance between forces of global homogenization and integration and forces of fragmentation clearly shows the balance tilting toward globalization. The removal of trade barriers, and the growing similarity of national markets created the potential for globalization of markets and competition. The development of MNCs, or of global networks allying independent firms, and the technology of cheap effective transportation and communication provided the practical means necessary for the integration of supply. These conditions were necessary, though not sufficient. Intense competition in most industries was the driving force necessary for integration and globalization. During the same period, actors who might have stalled globalization either did not act or acted ineffectively.

Thus, homogenization of markets has increased, industries have globalized, and firms have responded by geographic integration of their activities. Such integration took place (1) for sourcing—usually driven by manufacturing cost-reduction opportunities stemming from growing economies of scale and from economies of location; (2) for marketing—usually driven by a mix of economies of scale in distribution and manufacturing; and (3) by the competitive leverage brought by market scope. Coalitions and partnerships of all kinds provide an attractive low-cost alternative to single-firm manufacturing and market access investments. They do not, however, provide the strategic freedom and control available through a company's own investments.

Research and development activities have typically remained in the home country. However, as more and more products are developed for world markets, usually for simultaneous rather than sequential introduction, the need for a better integration of foreign subsidiaries and domestic labs has arisen. Evidence from specific product innovation studies in the United States and in Europe tends to suggest that this need for integration is not well met. Conversely, there is little to suggest that MNCs successfully apply innovations that originate in one subsidiary outside of that subsidiary.

The next section discusses three sets of factors that suggest the trends toward homogenization, globalization, and integration may slow down or even reverse themselves in the coming decade. Some of the underlying conditions or driving forces will have run their course, and new limits may appear.

LIMITS TO GLOBALIZATION

Manufacturing Technology

The evolution of manufacturing technology—in particular the increase in economies of scale in manufacture—has been one of the key conditions in favor of market globalization and MNC integration in a number of industries. Several factors may now slow down this trend. First, new technology has been so successful at reducing manufacturing unit costs that these costs now account for only a small proportion of total delivered costs. Further reduction of manufacturing cost will be of lesser impact than in the past, as other elements of cost play a much greater role, namely overheads, R&D recovery, and distribution.

Second, economies of scale may no longer increase in the same way as in the past. Some new technologies may abruptly decrease economies of scale. New multipurpose smaller processors in the chemical industry are an example of this type of technology. Even in the absence of genuinely new technology that would reduce economies of scale, the advantage of manufacturing systems—from the well-known materials and resource planning systems to the embryonic

"factory-of-the-future" concepts—are based on cost reduction from better managing the manufacturing system rather than from increasing the plant size or the length of the production run. Better manufacturing processes allow more flexibility in production. For instance, multiple car models can be produced in varying proportions on the same assembly line with relatively little cost penalty. This could allow car manufacturers to move back from large single-model factories serving multicountry markets to multimodel factories serving single-country markets. Although there may still be some cost penalty to setting up a flexible factory rather than a narrowly focused one, at least the trade-off between increasing flexibility and decreasing costs can be explicitly considered.

The impact of flexible manufacturing on the trade-off between integration and fragmentation of manufacturing is still unclear, however. Greater flexibility allows producers to cater to shifts in consumer preference—as their discretionary income increases—from cheap standardized goods toward customized products. Flexible manufacturing systems may allow both product customization—at least so long as such customization can be achieved through featurization around a common core—and low cost. These systems may shift the basis for cost advantage from scale to scope and thus make it possible for an integrated manufacturer to serve differentiated worldwide needs.

Third, the "just-in-time" manufacturing concept works best with the collocation of various facilities into an integrated system. This polarizes globalization and integration to the extremes: either a series of small "local-for-local" plants, each by and large self-sufficient, or, at the opposite extreme, a single integrated source for everything (e.g., Toyota City, or to a lesser extent, Boeing around Seattle, or Caterpillar around Peoria). A widely dispersed integrated manufacturing network (such as Ford of Europe), where plants are distant and supply each other with components and subassemblies, is least amenable to just-in-time manufacturing management. Buffer inventories must be kept to allow for transportation delays, localized strikes and disruptions, and slowdowns in custom clearance. This would suggest that the initial patterns of integration within MNCs, particularly in Europe, may not endure. Either the advantages of collocation and flexibility will be such that we will witness a return to largely local plants, or the advantages of focus and specialization will continue to exceed those of flexibility, and the advantages of collocation will lead to even further centralization of manufacturing.

Fourth, the trends toward vertical deintegration may allow more creative combinations between independent firms at different stages in a value-added structure. This would allow producers to continue to draw benefits from economies of scale for components and to gain flexibility for end products. Large-scale component manufacturing can be delegated to independent suppliers serving multiple smaller-scale assemblers, for instance. This may lead to different balances between integration and fragmentation at various stages of the value-added chain in the same industry.

Most industries and firms are not yet affected by all of these trends, but economies of scale in production are unlikely to be the opportunity they were in the 1960s and 1970s. As a result, economies of scale will no longer be a driving force toward globalization and integration. Choices for MNC managers will be more complex than just building up the largest plants with the aim of regaining competitiveness. Most companies are likely to end up with a mix of plants of various sizes and locations, and with various degrees of focus or flexibility.

Economies of location are also likely to become less important. With a few exceptions—such as aluminum—economies of location derive mainly from labor cost advantages. Several observations can be made. Not only has manufacturing cost decreased in relation to delivered cost for a whole range of industrial products, but also labor costs will decrease in relation to manufacturing costs with any shift toward more capital-intensive technologies. Stable or increasing real wages in Europe, despite the recent recessions, have accelerated the substitution of capital for labor. Even with relatively low wages, the product quality provided by automation in consumer electronics, for instance, may lead to rapidly decreasing labor content and to the repatriation and automation of plants previously dispersed from developed countries.

Locations with low labor costs also tend to catch up with locations with higher costs if only because skilled labor is scarce and the general wage structure moves up. Location advantages based on cheap labor are thus often temporary. Although labor may remain cheap in countries where political risks, government policies, or financial problems deter foreign investors—and thus limit the competition for labor—countries such as Singapore, Korea, and Taiwan, which have been hosts to massive foreign investments, have often seen their real-term wage rates increase significantly. In some industries—such as garment production—firms may shift their manufacturing locations in a search for cheaper labor. Where developed countries' firms subcontract to local producers—a prevalent practice for garments—shopping around for cheaper subcontractors is easy; when the foreign MNC sets up its own sourcing plants, however, closing down and relocating elsewhere is a much more costly and difficult process.

Differences in the cost of capital between countries also tend to decrease as the world's capital market becomes more integrated and as MNCs cross-finance themselves on multiple markets and arbitrage between them. Although domestic firms may still benefit from favorable institutional arrangements, for example, the institutional structure of Japanese capitalism, or from specific government assistance, for example, European exporters, these advantages are limited, not always accessible to MNC subsidiaries, and not often sufficient to justify location.[8]

Finally, exploiting economies of location also entails certain risks, for instance, exchange risks. If the mix of manufacturing locations differs significantly from that of selling locations, the firm is exposed to currency risks. Whereas this can play in their favor occasionally (e.g., the hefty margins made by European companies exporting to the United States in 1984–1985), it can also play the other way around as in the plight of U.S. exporters. Various hedging approaches can be adopted, but they usually either run counter to the search for economies of location, or they result in the creation of abundant "buffer" excess capacity. Instability of the exchange rate only increases the difficulties and costs of these approaches.

Protectionism

Since 1975 protectionist pressures on the U.S. Congress have increased largely as a result of the globalization process. Outright protectionist bills have been avoided only by successive administrations' careful negotiation of selected "voluntary" protection. Examples include the "Orderly Marketing Agreements" for TV sets and the "trigger prices" for steel or other commodities. Proposals such as the Burke-Hartke Act, which would have considerably limited the opportunity for U.S. firms to import goods made by their overseas subsidiaries, have been turned down, but at an increasing political price. The overvaluation of the dollar in 1983–1985, and the huge U.S. trade deficit only made matters worse. In the fall of 1985, only the shift in the U.S. position toward an active intervention policy to devalue the dollar staved off strong protectionist measures.

Europe, while making only slow progress toward a true free internal market, has resorted to protectionism toward a variety of industries, particularly those threatened by Japanese imports. Government purchasing policies that favor national suppliers also endure and close whole industries to foreign suppliers. Whether the Japanese market is closed or just hard to enter is an old debate, but it is clear that market access to Japan in critical industries is extremely difficult.

What is impotant here is not so much the exact extent of protectionism, but that recent evolutions do not allow managers to make a safe assumption about freer trade. The risk of a widespread return to protectionism puts a damper on globalization strategies that imply high levels of trade and adds fuel to strategies that return to traditional foreign investment as a way of overcoming trade barriers. Indeed, the purpose of many of the Japanese investments in Western Europe and in the United States is to overcome trade barriers, or at least to serve as "insurance" against new trade barriers, should they be implemented.

Among the less-obvious aspects of protectionism that may hamper MNC integration strategies are the issues of data flow across borders. Several countries have argued that data should be likened to raw material and processed locally rather than internationally. The issues are manifold and vary from country to country. Among the most prominent are (1) the importance of local data processing for stimulating the national demand for electronic data processing hardware and services and for telecommunication services; (2) the disadvantage of local firms and governments in relation to MNCs and their access to global market information; and (3) the threat of more centralization of decision making in MNCs, a process directly related to integration strategies. Canada has clearly articulated concerns about transborder data flows. Brazil and France have followed suit, with somewhat different concerns and priorities. Although policies on data flow are often lent moral legitimacy by being amalgamated with a series of regulations to protect the privacy of individuals, economic and political considerations drive the development of such policies. Countries do compete for the location of data processing centers by MNCs, and they also compete for international data transmission and value-added services. A few countries, including the United States and Britain, have taken an aggressive commercial position by lowering packet-switching charges, for example, and others try to regulate data flows. Although the current impact of data flow regulations is limited, it is a concern for at least some firms.[9] In addition, regulation of data flows may also be a way to ensure that critical knowledge exists within the country. One widespread concern, for instance, is that some U.S. suppliers of computers keep debugging software at home, where it can only be accessed by telephone lines from Europe. Should denial measures be taken by the U.S. government, whatever the reasons (as was done in 1982 in the Dresser case), such critical software might no longer be available.[10]

More broadly, protectionism in technology has become a major issue. In the 1980s the U.S. government, as well as several U.S. firms, became worried about the transfer of technology to Japan and to the USSR. This concern arose as the extent and success of efforts by Japanese firms and the Soviet government to appropriate Western technologies became clear. With regard to Japan, the issue is competition, particularly in industries such as semiconductors. In this industry, in particular, manufacturing equipment is critical to success, and the U.S. industry became concerned that process technology was transferred too easily to Japan. The concern was heightened as Japan came to be seen in the United States as an "unfair" competitor. Similar concerns have been voiced in other industries, such as aerospace and computers, as evidenced by IBM's actions against Mitsubishi and Hitachi.

With regard to the USSR, the issue is twofold: first, to deny the USSR access to the core technologies of military systems, a priority widely shared in the West; and second, to limit the USSR's access to technologies that may allow faster economic growth and thus make large military expenditures more affordable to the Soviets. The second point is a matter of debate between U.S. government hard-liners and more liberal circles in the United States and among European governments. The issue gained prominence with the discovery, probably by French counterespionage in early 1982, of the magnitude of the Soviet effort to spy on the West, and of the success of that effort.[11] Later updates, based on captured Soviet documents, kept the issue salient. Also giving prominence to the issue were several instances of discreet reexport of classified U.S. equipment via Sweden and Austria and several cases of industrial espionage in major West European and American companies, including MBB, Dassault, and Hughes. Although studies suggest that the Soviets are not able to absorb and finance the use of the new technology they obtain from the West, legally or otherwise, the Reagan administration took it to heart to stem the flow of technology to the Soviet bloc (Bornstein, 1985).

The Export Administration Amendment Act of July 1985 extends the list of goods subject to U.S. export licenses to "dual-use" equipment, civilian in principle, but using technologies or components with potential military use. The U.S. policy of reexport control also considerably limits the mobility of components to be incorporated into systems assembled in another country, and sold in yet another. European integrated MNCs, such as Philips, suffer great logistic complications from this new set of laws (Dekker, 1985). This leads them to substitute, where possible, non-U.S. for U.S. components and subsystems. Although such substitution is a boost to some European industries, it leads to an inefficient duplication of effort between the United States and Europe.

Protectionism in technology—be it through limiting the transfer of data or through restrictions on exports of goods possibly related to the manufacture of defense-related equipment— makes it difficult for technology-intensive MNCs to adopt integration strategies, since the various parts of the company need to be technologically autonomous. It also makes it difficult for U.S. firms to cooperate with foreign partners on joint R&D and casts doubt on the ability of European firms to use technology they would have acquired through collaborative efforts with the United States or with U.S. government support. Although Japanese firms are more strongly encouraged than their European counterparts to participate in U.S. defense projects, the same issues arise between the United States and Japan as between the United States and Europe. Conversely, IBM's or Texas Instruments' access to the results of joint Japanese research projects is a difficult issue.

These concerns have prompted Europe into action, first with the European Strategic Program for Research and Development in Information Technology (ESPRIT) and with specialized projects, such as Research in Advanced Communications in Europe (RACE) and more recently with a program called EUREKA. ESPRIT's relative success was a surprise, but by the end of 1985 about 195 projects shared 1.4 billion European Currency Units, and many of them looked promising. EUREKA, launched as a civilian equivalent to the U.S. Strategic Defense Initiative, is still embryonic and funding is uncertain. Despite widespread skepticism, it may take hold and lead to interesting projects. This direct subsidy approach addresses only one facet of European competitiveness, however, and maybe not the most important: European firms show inferiority not in the development of new technology but in its exploitation. Technology may not be the critical issue. Market structure and management are. Although much attention in Europe is focused on making Europe a true "common" market, remarkably little attention is devoted to manage-

to the successful exploitation of global technological and competitive opportunities.

Organizational Capabilities

The various elements discussed above suggest that large international competitors will face a world of neither fragmentation nor global integration, but a mixture of both, with many shades of gray and complex patterns of international operations that are unlikely to fall neatly into any category. Thus, there will be many trade-offs between industry fragmentation and globalization and strategies of integration and subsidiary autonomy, and they will vary by function, country, and business. Differences between industries, between segments within the same industry, and even between stages in the value-added chain are going to be important. This will introduce considerable variety in the situations faced by MNCs. Further, strategies will vary from free and competitive to negotiated and collaborative through complex networks of collaborative agreements, coalitions and joint ventures among firms, and occasionally between them and governments (Doz, 1986).

Not all global competitors are able, organizationally, to cope with such diversity. Most started as national companies (e.g., most Japanese competitors) or with fragmented organizational structures loosely "federated" by headquarters. Such fragmented structures, leaving a lot of autonomy to individual subsidiaries in various countries, fit well with the fragmented environment faced by MNCs prior to the 1970s.

The initial transition from autonomous subsidiaries to coordinated international strategies and integrated manufacturing and marketing networks has been a traumatic experience for many companies. The process has been slow (typically 3 to 7 years), painful, and not always successful (Doz and Prahalad, 1981; Prahalad and Doz, 1981). For a while in the mid-1970s, matrix organizations were seen as the answer to complex trade-offs between integration and fragmentation. Though a matrix organization may achieve such trade-offs, it achieves them well only if a number of conditions are met.

First, a matrix organization is not merely a different form of organization. Rather, it is a different mode of making decisions and ensuring that relevant data and perspectives are brought to bear on the choices, that trade-offs are made explicit, and that well-considered decisions are reached. This requires both a well-developed management system infrastructure, the involvement of top management, and much attention to the quality of the executive process. Observations of many companies suggest that not all are able to meet these conditions. Hence the widespread disillusionment with matrix organizations (Prahalad and Doz, 1987).

Although the "ideal" MNC organization is easy to spell out in principle, it is difficult to put in place and make work. Yet, as discussed in the earlier sections, the conflicting demands for flexibility and responsiveness, on the one hand, and for global competitiveness and integration, on the other, call for complex trade-offs. Such conflicting demands thus further limit the capabilities of firms to succeed in global industries.

Moreover, in many industries, speed and interdependence in action become increasingly critical. Product cycles are shorter, and the maintenance of competitive advantage requires coordinated policies across product lines and business units, both for technology development and for market access (Hamel and Prahalad, 1985). The growing number and variety of collaborative arrangements also make it more difficult for companies to maintain conventional configurations of strategic control, as can be more easily done with fully owned operations (Doz, 1986). As a result, a gap develops between the demands put on companies by global competition and the capability of their organizations and management to meet them.

CONCLUSION

The three sets of factors outlined above—manufacturing technology, protectionism, and organizational capabilities—may limit the growth of integrated multinational companies and tilt the balance again toward fragmentation. Collaborative agreements and strategic partnerships may increasingly represent an alternative to direct investment for gaining market access, achieving volume production, or leveraging technology. These may deeply modify the nature of global competition and international industries by creating a series of intermediate positions between national and global competitors.

NOTES

1. For summary data, see Dunning and Pearce (1985); Stopford (1983); Vernon (1977); Franko (1976). See also, for U.S. multinationals, U.S. Bureau of Economic Analysis (1986).

2. For a summary of the internalization argument, see Casson (1979); Rugman (1981); Dunning (1979). Many authors draw on Hymer (1976).

3. For a general argument on the dynamics of global competition, illustrated with the example of color television sets, see Hamel and Prahalad (1985).

4. See Hamal and Prahalad (1985), for a summary argument. For a more detailed analysis, see Millstein (1983).

5. For a series of industrial studies, see Zysman and Tyson (1983); Hochmuth and Davidson (1985).

6. For an early analysis of these problems in collaborative ventures, see Hochmuth (1974).

7. The argument cuts both ways, though, as it may be argued that local scientists or technicians employed by MNCs develop knowledge, the economic benefits from which may well accrue to another country where the MNC operates, whereas local firms would have a greater propensity to export innovative goods and processes, thus creating more value for the country.

8. For a more detailed discussion of the limits to the competitive advantage that can be obtained from multinational resource deployment, see Doz and Prahalad (1986).

9. For a summary analysis, see Kane (1985), and United Nations Center on Transnational Corporations (1982).

10. For a detailed discussion of the Dresser case, see Bettis (1984).

11. Although not publicly available, the various CIA reports to the U.S. Congress did much to increase the politi-

cal salience of the transfer of technology to the Soviet Union.

REFERENCES

Allen, T. A. 1977. *The Flow of Technology.* Cambridge, Mass.: MIT Press.

Bartlett, C. 1985. Komatsu Limited. Harvard Business School Case Study. HBSCS0-385-277.

Bettis, R. A. 1984. Dresser Industries and the pipeline. Southern Methodist University Case Study.

Bornstein, M. 1985. *East-West Technology Transfer: The Transfer of Western Technology to the USSR.* Paris: Organization for Economic Cooperation and Development.

Casson, M. 1979. *Alternatives to the Multinational Enterprise.* London: Macmillan.

Dekker, W. 1985. The technology gap: Western countries growing apart. Speech presented at the Atlantic Institute for International Affairs, Paris, December 5, 1985.

Doz, Y. 1978. Brown Boveri & Cie. Harvard Business School Case Study, HBSCS 4-378-115.

Doz, Y. 1986. Government policies and global competition. In M. E. Porter, ed., *Competition in Global Industries.* Boston: Harvard Business School Press.

Doz, Y., and C. K. Prahalad. 1981. Headquarter influence and strategic control in multinational companies. *Sloan Management Review* 23(1).

Doz, Y., and C. K. Prahalad. 1986. Quality of management: An emerging source of global competitive advantage? In N. Hood and J. E. Vahlne, eds., *Strategies in Global Competition.* London: John Wiley & Sons.

Dunning, J. 1979. Explaining changing patterns of international production: In defense of the eclectic theory. *Oxford Bulletin of Economics and Statistics* 41 (November):269–296.

Dunning, J. H., and R. D. Pearce. 1985. *The World's Largest Industrial Enterprises, 1962–1983.* New York: St. Martin's Press.

Fischer, W. A., and J. N. Behrman. 1979. The coordination of foreign R&D activities by transnational corporations. *Journal of International Business Studies* 10 (3) (winter):28–35.

Franko, L. G. 1976. *The European Multinationals.* Stamford, Conn.: Greylock.

Guysinger, S., et al. 1984. *Investment Incentives and Performance Requirements.* Washington, D.C.: The World Bank Mimeographed Report.

Hamel, G., and C. K. Prahalad. 1985. Do you really have a global strategy? *Harvard Business Review* (July–August):139–148.

Helleiner, G. K. 1981. *Intra Firm Trade and the Developing Countries.* New York: St. Martin's Press.

Hirschey, R. C., and R. E. Caves. 1981. Research and the transfer of technology by multinational enterprises. *Oxford Bulletin of Economics and Statistics* 43(2): 115–130.

Hochmuth, M. S. 1974. *Organizing the Transnational: The Experience with Transnational Enterprise in Advanced Technology.* Cambridge, Mass.: Harvard University Press.

Hochmuth, M. S., and W. Davidson. 1985. *Revitalizing American Industry.* Cambridge, Mass.: Ballinger.

Hood, N., and S. Young. 1980. *European Development Strategies of U.S.-Owned Manufacturing Companies Located in Scotland.* Edinburgh: Her Majesty's Stationery Office.

Hymer, S. 1976. *The International Operations of National Firms: A Study of Foreign Investment.* Cambridge, Mass.: MIT Press.

Kane, M. J. 1985. A study of the impact of transborder data flow: Regulation on large U.S.-based corporations using an extended information systems interface model. Ph.D. dissertation. College of Business Administration, University of South Carolina.

Lall, S. 1978. The pattern of intra firm exports by U.S. multinationals. *Oxford Bulletin of Economics and Statistics* 40(3):209–223.

Levitt, T. 1983. The globalization of markets. *Harvard Business Review* (May–June):92–102.

Millstein, J. E. 1983. Decline in an expanding industry: Japanese competition in color television. In J. Zysman and L. Tyson, eds., *American Industry in International Competition.* Ithaca, N.Y.: Cornell University Press.

New Scientist. 1985. IBM begins its Japanese assault. (17 October):22–23.

Orléan, A. 1986. "L'insertion dans les échanges internationaux: comparison de cinq grands pays développés. *Economie et Statistiques* 184(Janvier):25–39.

Owen, N. 1983. *Economies of Scale, Competitiveness and Trade Patterns Within the European Community.* Oxford: Clarendon Press.

Prahalad, C. K., and Y. Doz. 1981. An approach to strategic control in multinational companies. *Sloan Management Review* 22(4):5–13.

Prahalad, C. K., and Y. Doz. 1987 (forthcoming). *The Multinationals' Mission.* New York: The Free Press.

Rugman, A. M. 1981. *Inside the Multinatonals: The Economies of Internal Markets.* London: Croom Helm.

Stopford, J. M. 1983. *The World Directory of Multinational Enterprises, 1982–83.* London: Macmillan.

Teece, D. J. 1977. Technology transfer by multinational firms: The resource cost of transferring technological know-how. *The Economic Journal* 87(June):242–261.

United Nations Center on Transnational Corporations. 1982. *Transnational Corporations and Transborder Data Flows: A Technical Paper.* New York: United Nations.

United Nations Center on Transnational Corporations. 1983. *Transnational Corporations in World Development: Third Survey.* New York: United Nations.

U.S. Bureau of Economic Analysis. 1986. *U.S. Direct Investment Abroad: 1982 Benchmark & Survey Data.* Washington, D.C.: U.S. Government Printing Office.

Vernon, R. 1977. *Storm over the Multinationals.* Cambridge, Mass.: Harvard University Press.

Vernon, R. 1979. The product cycle hypothesis in a new international environment. *Oxford Bulletin of Economics and Statistics* 41(4).

Vernon, R., and W. H. Davidson. 1979. Foreign production

of technology-intensive products by U.S.-based multinational enterprises. Harvard Business School Working Paper, HBS 79-5.

von Hippel, E. 1982. Appropriability of innovation benefit as a predictor of the functional locus of innovation. *Research Policy* 11(2):95–115.

Zysman, J., and L. Tyson, eds. 1983. *American Industry in International Competition.* Ithaca, N.Y.: Cornell University Press.

3

INTERNATIONALIZATION: EVOLUTION OF A CONCEPT

LAWRENCE S. WELCH AND REIJO LUOSTARINEN

Over the last two decades there has been growing interest in the international operations of business companies. Academic activity in the area has both stimulated and been stimulated by the many strands of concern—for example, the business firms themselves, with a concern to make such operations more effective and efficient in a more competitive global environment; governments, with a concern to ensure that the overall process has a positive effect on the national interest; and trade unions, with a concern about the impact on working conditions, wages and their own power.

At the outset much academic interest and analysis focused on the multinational corporation. Studies such as Servan Schreiber's[1] American Challenge alerted governments and others to the already extensive international operations of these companies. Much of the academic research in the early stages was involved with documenting and explaining the spread of multinational corporations, and assessing their impact, with an emphasis on their foreign investment activities. This was reflected in a spate of studies of foreign investment in various recipient countries.[2–4]

However, much of the early research took the multinational, or at least foreign investment, as a starting point in the analysis, leaving many questions unanswered regarding the development process which preceded this stage, and undoubtedly affected the later steps. Horst,[5] for example, after finding that firm size was a significant factor in the firm's decision to invest abroad concluded that: "The principal deficiency in this line of analysis, I believe, is the absence of dynamic considerations. Nowhere is there a description of how a firm came to acquire its current attributes. . . . But if we are even to unravel the complexity of the foreign investment decision process, a systematic study of the dynamic behaviour of firms must be undertaken."[1] In essence a more longitudinal view, a process perspective, was called for.

Already, though, a shift in this direction had begun with Aharoni's[6] study of the various steps involved in the foreign investment decision process. As well, Wilkins[7,8] had begun to delineate some of the dynamic factors contributing to the historical evolution of American multinational corporations.

This developing longitudinal approach was taken a stage further with a number of studies of the international operations of Nordic-based companies, studies which considered the ex-

Source: *Journal of General Management,* Vol. 14, no. 2 (Winter 1988), pp. 34–55.

pansion activity as an internationalization process.[9-11] Specifically, their research was important in advancing our knowledge of the process not only because of its identification of patterns of internationalization, and a method for examining them, but also because of the attempt to outline the key dynamic factors which formed the basis of forward progress. In the Nordic case the overall pattern was one of gradual, sequential development of international operations.

At the same time as this overall longitudinal research was developing in the 1970s, an interest was growing in the analysis of specific steps which contribute to the ongoing process. Inevitably, the shift to a more longitudinal approach led to an interest in the earlier steps which formed a foundation for later moves. For example, considerable analysis of early exporting activity has been undertaken in a number of countries.[12-16] While each new step of the development of international operations can be considered unique, each nevertheless provides insight into the broader longitudinal forces at work.

In general therefore research into the process of internationalization has tended to be carried on at the level of specific decisions to increase involvement as well as overall patterns and dynamic causative factors. Nevertheless, although considerable progress has and is being made in unravelling the nature and cause of internationalization—much remains to be accomplished. The various contributions represent an incomplete patchwork. As Buckley has noted, "This development from naive entrant to established multinational has been inadequately modelled ... and its implications for theory are as yet unassimilated."[17]

THE MEANING OF "INTERNATIONALIZATION"?

At the very outset it is difficult to discuss a "theory of internationalization" because even the term itself has not been clearly defined. Al-

though widely used, the term "internationalization" needs clarification. It tends to be used roughly to describe the outward movement in an individual firm's or larger grouping's international operations.[18-20] As a starting point this common usage could be broadened further to give the following definition: "the process of increasing involvement in international operations." An important reason for adopting a broader concept of internationalization is that both sides of the process, that is, both inward and outward, have become more closely linked in the dynamics of international trade.

The growth of countertrade in its many forms, from pure barter to buy-back arrangements and offset policies, is indicative of the way in which outward growth has become tied in with inward growth.[21,22] In effect, countertrade has meant that, for many companies, success in outward activities is partly dependent on inward performance. This, in combination with supportive government action in some cases, has led to a number of large companies setting up trading arms to facilitate the process.[23,24] The inward-outward interlink is further illustrated in the growth of international subcontracting which has played an important role in the international viability of many companies through the ability to tie in cheap component/raw materials imports from international suppliers—from clothing manufacture through to sophisticated systems selling.[25-27] From a general perspective therefore, it seems to be inappropriate to restrict the concept of increasing international involvement merely to the outward side, given the growing inward-outward interconnection.

Having put forward a working definition of "internationalization" it should be stressed that once a company has embarked on the process, there is no inevitability about its continuance. In fact the evidence indicates that reverse or "de-internationalization" can occur at any stage, as the example of Chrysler and other disinvestments in the late-1970s illustrate, but is particularly likely in the early stages of export development.[28,29]

So far the concept of "internationalization" has been couched in relatively broad terms deliberately, to cover a multitude of possibilities. However, to apply the concept, considerable elaboration is required. For example, on what basis can we assess the degree of internationalization of one firm versus another? What does the concept mean as an outcome? Perhaps the simplest objective basis for assessing the degree of internationalization is some measure of foreign sales relative to total sales. The proportion of total sales exported has often been used as an indication of export performance despite its drawbacks.[30] Such a measure can also be extended out to the national economy as exports/gross domestic product. Although this measure is attractive because of its simplicity and measurability it provides very little information about the nature of and capacity to conduct international operations. Given the diversity of international operations, types of markets, degree of organizational commitment and types of international offering, there is obviously a need for a broader framework for assessing the extent of "increased international involvement"—that is, on a number of different dimensions. An example of such a framework is presented in Figure 1. In general internationalization can be expected to be associated with, and perhaps dependent upon, developments along each of the dimensions shown:

Operation Method (How)

Evidence indicates that as companies increase their level of international involvement there is a tendency for them to change the method/s by which they serve foreign markets.[31-33] The Nordic studies indicate that this change occurs in the direction of increasing commitment, a typical pattern being from no exporting, to exporting via an agent, to a sales subsidiary and finally to a production subsidiary. One of the reasons for the considerable attention on the operational method as a means of assessing a pattern of internationalization is that it does represent a clearly overt manifestation of the overall process.

As well as increasing commitment though, the pattern appears to be one of greater operational diversity as internationalization proceeds.[34] This appears to be related not only to the greater experience, skills, and knowledge of foreign markets and marketing which develops within the firm, but also to the exposure of a wider range of opportunities and threats. Sometimes the sheer success of one method of operation, for example, exporting, causes the erection of import barriers by a foreign government thereby necessitating a shift to some other form such as licensing or foreign investment if a market presence is to be maintained. An Australian study found that outward foreign licensing was mainly adopted because of various constraints on the use of other, more preferred methods of operation in foreign markets.[34] The recent strong move by Japanese firms into foreign investment has been partly stimulated by the various forms of protection imposed in key markets.[35,36] In a similar manner, the exploitation of market opportunities in the socialist countries, because of the emphasis of their governments on countertrade, is likely to force some shift toward operational diversity. Clearly, the degree of market diversity has an impact on the degree of operational diversity.

Thus, on the method of operation dimension we would expect internationalization to be reflected in both increasing depth and diversity of operational methods. At a global level, this is evident not just in the growth of foreign investment but also in the rise of countertrade in its various guises, of the technology trade, of franchising, of management contracts and so on. It is difficult, if not impossible, to go far in the internationalization process simply by using one preferred operational method. One can perhaps argue that the future international success

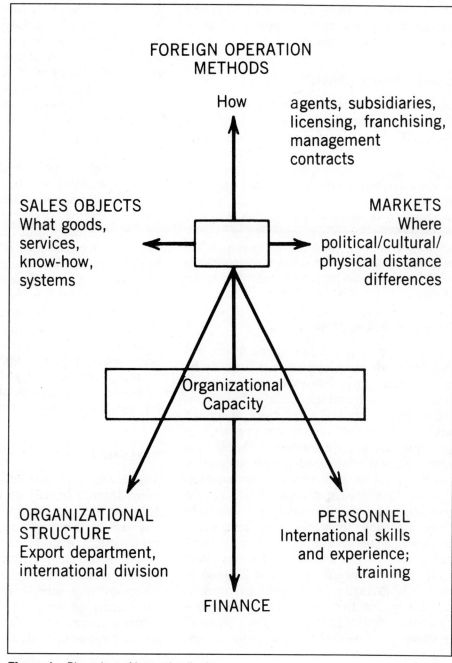

Figure 1. Dimensions of Internationalization

of companies will partly depend on their ability to master and successfully apply a range of methods of foreign operation.

Sales Objects (What)

As a company increases its involvement in international operations there is also a tendency for its offering to foreign markets to deepen and diversify.[37] This may occur at two levels:

• Expansion within an existing, or into a new, product line.[38]

• Change in the whole product concept to include "software" components such as services, technology, know-how, or some combination. Over time the blending of hardware and software components is often developed into more packaged forms, representing project or systems solutions.[39]

Target Markets (Where)

As with sales objects and operation forms, it is difficult to develop internationally merely by concentrating on a limited number of countries. Expanded operations and offerings increasingly link with a wider range of foreign markets—typically more distant over time in political, cultural, economic and physical terms. There is a basic tendency for companies, particularly in the early stages of internationalization, to approach markets which appear simpler, more familiar and less costly to penetrate—and these are most commonly those which are closest in physical and cultural terms.[40,41] It is not uncommon for Australian firms to view operations in New Zealand as merely an extension of domestic activities, as also for Finnish firms moving into Sweden. A company's shift of activities to more "distant" locations can therefore be seen as one indication of greater maturation in its internationalization process.

Organisational Capacity

The internationalization process of a company is perhaps most overtly demonstrated by the preceding three dimensions: the further advanced a firm is along them the more "internationalized" it may be regarded as being. For example, a Finnish company with a high export/total sales ratio of say 80 per cent but which is selling only one product, via an agent, to one country, Sweden, would be regarded, according to the above framework, as still being only in the earliest stages of international development.

Nevertheless, although providing a broader-based assessment of internationalization, the first three dimensions concentrate on the components of actual foreign market activity. Such an approach leaves aside the variety of internal company changes which are consequent upon, and therefore reflect, the degree of internationalization but also form the foundation for additional steps forward in the overall process.[42] In the resources area finance and personnel are obviously important, but so also is the organisation structure developed for handling foreign activities. In Figure 1, three of these areas—finance, personnel and organisation structure—are noted because of their importance, but they are by no means exclusively so.

Personnel

The success of internationalization in any company depends heavily on the type of people both initiating and carrying through the various steps in the process, and on overall personnel policies. Lorange[43] has recently argued that "the human resource function is particularly critical to successful implementation of (such) co-operative ventures (joint ventures, licensing agreements, project co-operation, . . .)." In the initial exporting phase the background of the decision-maker, in such areas as work and foreign experience, education and language training, has been shown to be potentially important in the preparedness to commit a firm to the exporting activity.[44,45] At a general level though, internationalization both feeds upon and contributes to the development of international knowledge, skills and experience of the people involved.[46] While learning-by-doing appears to be a key part of the whole process, it is also possible to obtain some assistance through effective training and recruitment policies. Tung,[47] for example, concluded from a study of a number of US, European and Japanese companies that "the more rigorous the selection and training procedures used, the less the incidences of poor performance or failure to work effectively in a foreign country." Clearly, unless the people involved, through whatever means, become more international in their capacities and outlook, the ability to carry through any international strategy is bound to be severely constrained. International personnel development therefore remains as a prime indication of the internal extent to which a company has effectively become internationalized, although it is perhaps more difficult to measure than the preceding three dimensions.

Organisational Structure

As the administrative and organisational demands generally of carrying out international operations grow and diversify, the organisational structure for handling such demands ultimately needs to respond. A variety of formal and informal organisational arrangements have been used by companies in different countries to cope with the increasing amount and complexity of continuing internationalisation.[48–50] The changes, and their sophistication, as the company seeks to improve the organisational mechanism and focus of international operations, provide a further signpost of the state of internationalisation. Organisational changes are often a clear statement of commitment to the objectives of international involvement. In an Australian study the shift from experimental to committed exporting was often marked by the establishment of an export section or division in some form.[51]

Finance

The growth of international operations inevitably also places increasing demands on the avail-

ability of funds to support the various activities. The nature and extent of the company's financing activities for international operations provide a further indicator of the degree of internationalization. We might expect that the range of finance sources (both local and international) and the sophistication of financing techniques would develop with international growth. However, the relationship is by no means clear-cut—depending on such aspects as the type of product/service, operation methods and payment method, as well as the extent of government support.[52]

Framework Overview

By examining the above six dimensions it is possible to derive a substantial overview of the state of internationalization of a given company, which could then form the basis of comparison to others. It is not the intention at this stage to consider scales of measurement along the different dimensions, although work has already taken place in this area—as for example in Luostarinen's [53] composite of business distance (including cultural, economic and physical distance). At a general level, though, it is possible to foresee the development of more precise composite measures along the various dimensions, providing a better basis for relative assessment of the internationalization progress of different companies. For example, the hypothetical patterns for two companies are presented in Figure 2. Comparing the two patterns it is clear that company 1 has gone further than company 2 in its foreign market activities, yet its internal development to support these is less developed than company 2. Perhaps this is a sign of potential problems for company 1.

PATTERNS OF INTERNATIONALIZATION

From the discussion so far it is clear that there is a wide range of potential paths any firm might take in internationalization. Neverthe-

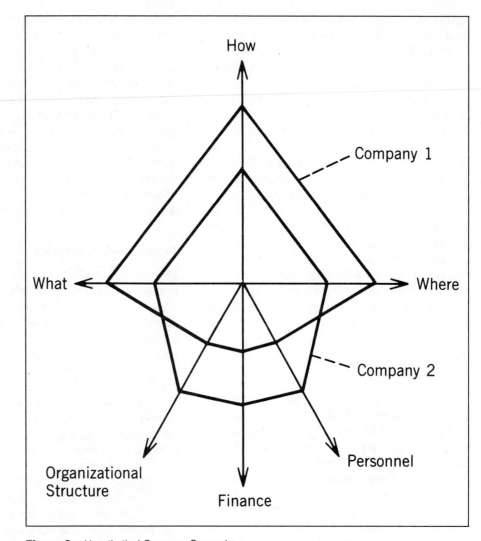

Figure 2. Hypothetical Company Comparison

less, are there any consistent patterns observable from the research? In answering this question a major contribution has been made by Nordic researchers.[54-56] Their work points generally to a process of evolutionary, sequential build-up of foreign commitments over time. Johanson and Wiedersheim-Paul studied the establishment chains of four large Swedish multinationals from the beginning of their operations. Typically the growth of foreign establishments was distinguished by a series of small, cumulative steps over time: the setting-up of a sales subsidiary was preceded by an agency operation in about three-quarters of cases.

This general pattern of evolutionary development was perhaps most strongly confirmed in Finnish research. In a study of around three-quarters of the population of Finnish industrial companies with foreign operations of any type

Luostarinen found that, in 1976, 65 per cent of the companies had only non-investment marketing operations abroad, 33 per cent had production operations abroad which had been preceded by non-investment marketing operations, whereas in only 2 per cent of the total had production operations abroad begun without preceding operations. This result has apparently continued, although being less pronounced, according to a more recent examination of the shift to foreign direct manufacturing investment during the period 1980–82 by Finnish companies.[57] In only 13 per cent of cases did the shift occur without preceding alternative operations in the country concerned.

Luostarinen's research revealed a process of evolutionary development not only in terms of the depth of operational mode, but also in terms of the diversity of modes used, as well as in product offerings and the range of markets penetrated. For example, product offerings were divided into four categories: goods, services, systems and know-how. The offering to foreign markets consistently began in the simplest form—that is, goods (for 99 per cent of companies)—while sales of services, systems and know-how came later, and approximately in that order.[58] The gradual development towards systems or package selling has also been noted in the growth of Swedish multinational corporations where skills and knowledge (software) were added to the hardware sale until a more complete problem-solving package was on offer.[59] This trend has broader implications as a growing software/service component clearly places greater stress on effective communication skills and understanding of user needs and the user's environment, which is a more demanding exercise once cultural and other distance barriers have to be surmounted, thereby reinforcing the impact of such distance variables on internationalization.

Research in other countries, although differing in sample size, period of study and subject of analysis, nevertheless has revealed a degree of consistency with the results of Nordic research. In examining Japanese foreign investment in South-East Asia, Yoshihara[60] found that "the pattern of investment seems to substantiate the evolutionary theory of foreign investment." This echoes a similar conclusion drawn from a longitudinal study of American direct investment abroad.[61] Small sample studies of first time UK smaller firm direct investors and of Continental European direct investors in the UK have confirmed the pattern of intermediate steps being used as a build-up to foreign investment.[62,63] While 15.4 per cent of cases involved a direct move to foreign investment, "over half of these firms were prevented from exporting by the nature of their product—transport cost barriers or a high 'service' element effectively ruled out exporting as a means of servicing the foreign markets."[64]

The pattern is not completely consistent though an Australian study of 228 outward direct investment cases revealed that in 39 per cent of these cases there was no pre-existing host country presence.[65] To some extent this can be explained by the high proportion (43.8 per cent) of service companies involved in the investment activity, given that it is often more difficult to operate with intermediate steps to the foreign investment stage in the services sector. However, service companies were only slightly under-represented (40.7 per cent) amongst those affiliates with a pre-existing presence.[66] Of particular note though is the fact that 65.5 per cent of the investments were undertaken during the period 1970–79. This is perhaps suggestive of a change in the rate at which firms have been accomplishing internationalization in more recent times, through leapfrogging of intermediate steps to the foreign investment stage in some countries. Further support for this development has been forthcoming in the more direct move to foreign investment by Swedish companies into the Japanese market from the early 1970s.[67] Perhaps a more general indication of the desire by companies to short-circuit the process of gradually building-up activities in foreign markets over time has been the switch in foreign investment towards acquisition and away from greenfield ventures.[68-70] Acquisition is not only a path to more rapid establishment in a given foreign market, which has become a more important consideration in the light of stronger global competition, but it is also potentially a means of obtaining faster access to a developed international network. For example, when the Australian company Wormald International purchased Mather and Platt in the UK it obtained as well a network of subsidiaries in Europe, Japan, Brazil, South Africa and New Zealand. The managing director commented that to have built such a network from scratch would have taken 20–30 years.[71,72]

Of course, it should be expected that observed patterns of internationalization will vary from country to country, and over time, because of environmental differences at the outset, as well as the inevitable changes in the environment. A combination of the more competitive international environment of the 1980s and the general demonstration effects of other companies' increased international efforts from different national environments has probably contributed to a less cautious approach to internationalization, at least in the latter stages.

It should also be stressed that the concept of a sequential, cumulative process of internationalization does not necessarily mean some smooth, immutable path of development. The actual paths taken are often irregular. Commitments are frequently lumpy over time, with plateaux while previous moves are absorbed and consolidated. Particular steps are affected by the emergence of opportunities and/or threats which do not usually arrive in a continuous or controlled manner. The outcome tends to be derived from a mixture of deliberate and emergent strategies.[73]

In fact, some of the argument which appears to be developing about the evolutionary or stages model of internationalization[74] seems to have occurred because of a lack of specification of what this process actually means for an individual company: does it mean evolution or a stepwise process for each individual foreign market or rather development of involvement in an overall sense? So far concentration has been on the former situation where the number and type of steps up to, for example, foreign investment are considered. A reduction in, or absence of, intervening steps in a foreign market is taken as some indication that the evolutionary or stages model is not functioning.[75] Such a result is of course more likely in particular markets where unique circumstances might apply, perhaps in the form of government policy. More importantly though it is probably more appropriate to analyse the process of international involvement at the company level, looking across total foreign market activities. As skills, experience and knowledge in the use of a more advanced form of operations are developed in some foreign markets we might expect that this will eventually allow a company to leapfrog some intermediate steps in others.[76] This proposition is illustrated in Figure 3. Taken on its own, company X's move directly to foreign investment in Foreign Market No. 6 might be regarded as a shift away from the sequentialist pattern revealed in other markets. However, when taken in the overall context of the steps taken in other markets it is certainly far removed from a leap into the unknown. Thus, leapfrogging moves in given markets should be examined as part of the overall operational pattern of the company before any definitive conclusions can be drawn about a "shift" from the evolutionary pattern.

Likewise the concept of what is evolutionary could be related back to the type of preceding experience of international operations that key individuals in the company might have had. For example an Australian company with four years of operating and marketing experience in a small Australian city (Toowoomba) considered its first "export" move as an attempt to penetrate a large Australian city 130 kilometres away (Brisbane). By contrast a Sydney com-

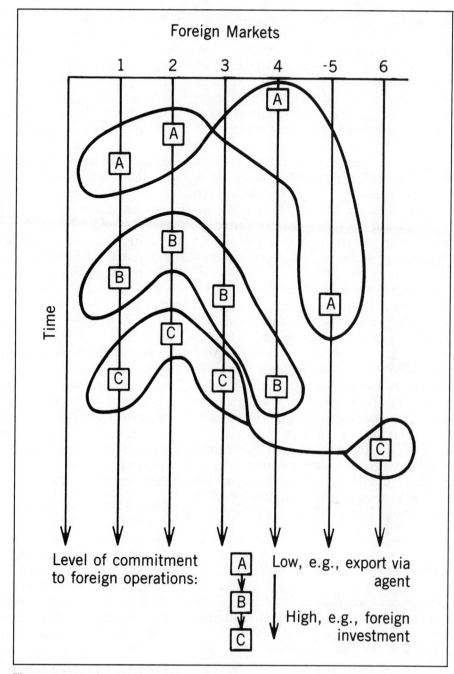

Figure 3.   Company X—Foreign Operations

pany was exporting within three months of beginning operations and to 52 countries in three years. The differences in behaviour were strongly related to the owner-managers of each company. In the Toowoomba example the individual had very limited personal or company experience beyond the local area, whereas in the second case the manager was a migrant with over 20 years of international experience in the industry concerned which had exposed an unexploited market niche. His perception of the market place was international in character from the outset. In this context, the international moves of the Sydney company were less startling than at first sight. One person's (or company's) evolution often appears as a revolution to others.[77,78]

Overall then, the research has revealed a reasonable degree of consistency, at least up to the mid-1970s, that the pattern of internationalization for most firms has been marked by a sequential, stepwise process of development. More recently, limited evidence has been emerging of a departure from the gradualist path as some firms seek to by-pass the steps to deeper commitment, resulting in a speeding up of the whole process. Just how widespread the change is can only be determined from further research, but pattern variation should be expected in response to the many environmental changes, both nationally and globally, which have occurred in the 1970s and 1980s.

WHY INTERNATIONALIZATION?

While we can expect continued debate on the nature of the shifting pattern of internationalization, an important question remains to be settled: why internationalization? What is it that drives the process, leading a firm from little or no involvement to, in some cases, widespread multinational investments? Obviously, if we are to understand the process then we have to explain why a company undertakes each particular step in an overt pattern. As Starbuck[79] has noted, growth is not spontaneous, it is the result of decisions. As such, the separate analysis of these distinct steps contributes to our understanding of why and how the internationalization process is initiated and maintained. For example, the recent research on the export involvement decision has considerably elucidated how and why a company's internationalization begins, and what sort of base is established for subsequent forward moves, if any.[80-82] However, each of the decision points inevitably has a variety of unique causative elements as well as bearing the impact of any general ongoing influential factors, as noted in Figure 4. In developing any overall explanation of internationalization it is important to examine those continuing influences which play such a key role in maintaining forward momentum—in building the company to the point where it is more receptive to the possibilities of increased involvement, and better prepared to respond to them. These dynamic factors also help to explain why there is some degree of consistency of internationalization patterns across countries because of their general effect. At the same time they represent reasons why so many companies feel constrained to a more gradual, sequential path of development, as revealed in the research noted earlier.

Overall Pattern Explanatory Factors Resources Availability The ability to undertake any form of international operations is clearly limited by the means accessible to the firm to carry it out. For smaller firms, given their limitations in many areas, this is an obvious reason why less demanding directions of international development can be undertaken first, with major commitments only occurring well into the longer run. By the same token, this means that we should expect larger firms, based in large domestic markets, to reveal more advanced involvement far earlier, and generally to move through the overall process at a faster rate. While there is some argument about the re-

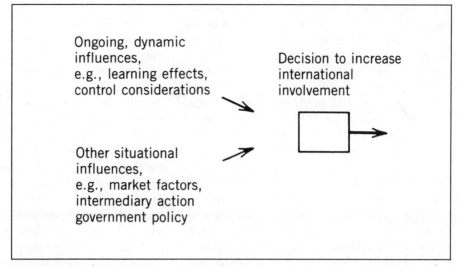

Figure 4. Determinants of Forward Momentum

search results which consider the impact of size, there does not appear to be any clear relationship between size of firm and export performance.[83,84] Instead of size, Czinkota and Johnston[85] concluded that "what really does seem to make for export success is the attitude of management." Some of the constraints which face companies of whatever size, when considering international expansion, particularly financial ones, are sometimes more apparent than real. Outside financial sources and creative funding of takeovers, have been used by some companies to permit faster expansion than directly accessible means would imply.[86] While resource availability may limit expansion at any given point in time, the constraint is not static, so that any action or developments which widen availability provide the basis for increased foreign operations over time.

Knowledge Development Clearly, there is something more to the resources question than just physical or financial capacity. A critical factor in the ability to carry out chosen international activities is the possession of appropriate knowledge: this includes knowledge about foreign markets, about techniques of foreign operation, about ways of doing business, about key people in buyer organisations, and so on. Such information and understanding is not easily, cheaply or rapidly acquired. Much of it is not readily acquired "off-the-shelf" as it is developed through the actual experience of foreign operations.[87] The learning-by-doing process explains much in the evolutionary patterns of internationalization revealed in research.[88]

Communication Networks Personal contact and social interaction play an important part in the development of international markets—especially where more complex industrial products are concerned.[89] Networks between buyers and sellers which form the basis of effective communication must be established. Network establishment can be a demanding and time consuming process where the gap between buyer and seller is large due to an initial lack of knowledge of each other and is accentuated by physical and cultural distance barriers. There is considerable inertia amongst buyers who feel more secure with suppliers from familiar sources and locations. While this constrains the development of operations at the outset, the initial gaps are not necessarily static: they are susceptible to reduction over time. With wider experience, greater contact at all levels and more diverse cultural exposure on both sides, there is a potential for deeper and more long-standing relationships to evolve, forming the basis for deeper commitments.[90]

Risk and Uncertainty As foreign buyers are loath to establish networks with unknown foreign suppliers at the outset so too the foreign suppliers, because of initial lack of knowledge and experience, tend to feel uncertainy about taking on additional or new foreign operations, especially in unfamiliar locations. Inevitably there is a response of seeking ways to reduce the uncertainty exposure. It is not surprising therefore to find the pattern noted earlier that companies are attracted to foreign operations first in more familiar (culturally) and closer locations and that only small steps in operational commitments are undertaken initially thereby limiting exposure. This also allows experimentation without high risk and the time required to gather relevant knowledge and experience, before any deeper commitment is contemplated.

In general therefore the need to develop relevant knowledge and skills and communication networks, as well as to reduce risk and uncertainty exposure, interact and play a key role at given points in constraining international moves. Over time, however, the inevitable changes in these areas consequent upon foreign activities also change the capacity of the company to contemplate and carry through more involving commitments.[91]

Control Given the limited foreign market knowledge and experience of many companies during the early stages of internationalization it is not surprising that they will often look to outside foreign intermediaries to assist in market penetration. With more experience, however, if a company's knowledge about a given market increases through active involvement, there is a tendency for it to scrutinise the activities of its foreign intermediary more closely, especially when sales potential has been proven by preceding operations. The concern about control is reflected in a variety of efforts to more closely direct the operations of the intermediary on its behalf. Sometimes this will result in "positive" steps such as training or the provision of promotional materials. In other cases a more "negative" approach will be adopted, leading to more stringent checks and guidelines. Under these changing circumstances, with the power positions being subtly reversed and the principal feeling less dependent on its foreign intermediary, it is not uncommon for dissatisfaction about perceived under-performance to grow. Ultimately, perhaps sparked by other developments, the principal may feel that the effective way of dealing with the "problem" is for it to take over the running of the foreign operation itself, in some altered form. Inevitably this will mean increasing its commitment in the given foreign market. Thus, the control factor, interacting with knowledge development and risk perception, tends to be a growing influence over time which pushes a company towards increasing involvement in foreign operations. In general, increasing market control means inceasing involvement and thereby greater cost and risk.[92]

Commitment As international operations are developed there is necessarily a commitment of resources, and by people, to the process. This commitment is particularly strong when key management staff are involved in developing the international strategy.[93] It creates a need for fulfilment and provides strong forward momentum whereby justification is sought in further operations and deeper involvement along the same line.[94] The commitment factor therefore represents a further dynamic driving force in the overall internationalization process.

The above factors taken together help to explain the continued forward momentum of the internationalization process of individual companies and also why the evolutionary pattern has been found in so many studies in different countries.[95] In essence, these factors, apart from any general market size and potential considerations, help us to understand why for example a given environmental change—such as protectionist action by a foreign government or a change in foreign investment rules—is unlikely to cause a shift to foreign investment by a company with limited foreign experience but is more likely to do so at a later stage after the development of market knowledge, contacts, a sales organization, and so on, as illustrated in Figure 5.

CONCLUSION

Taken overall the concept of internationalization has yet to be clearly developed as a research object. Nevertheless, considerable progress has been made in establishing its conceptual and empirical foundations, while the emerging debate about the "stages thesis" or "gradual internationalization" can be considered a healthy step in clarifying the subject.

Given the focus of the concept, a development process through time, much research remains to be conducted that is responsive to its longitudinal character. Inevitably this is a difficult activity:[96] take for example the attempt to trace the impact of individuals and the evolution of communication patterns in the past. It can be expected however that research will continue along the dual lines of analysis of par-

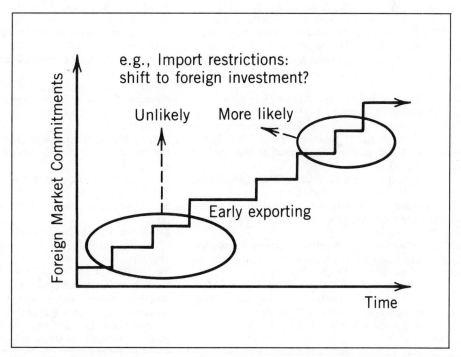

Figure 5. Response to Environmental Change

ticular decisions or steps in the overall process and those elements which tie together total progress.

NOTES

1. J. J. Servan-Schreiber, *Le Defi American* (Paris: Editions de Noel, 1967).

2. D. T. Brash, *American Investment in Australian Industry* (Cambridge, Mass.: Harvard University Press, 1966).

3. A. E. Safarian, *Foreign Ownership of Canadian Industry* (Toronto: McGraw-Hill, 1966).

4. J. H. Dunning, *American Investment in British Manufacturing* (London: Allen and Unwin, 1958).

5. T. Horst, "Firm and Industry Determinants of the Decision to Invest Abroad," *Review of Economics and Statistics,* Vol. 54 (1972), pp. 264–265.

6. Y. Aharoni, *The Foreign Investment Decision Process* (Cambridge, Mass.: Harvard University Press, 1966).

7. M. Wilkins, *The Emergence of Multinational Enterprise* (Cambridge, Mass.: Harvard University Press, 1970).

8. M. Wilkins, *The Maturing of Multinational Enterprise* (Cambridge, Mass.: Harvard University Press, 1974).

9. J. Johanson and F. Wiedersheim-Paul, "The Internationalization of the Firm—Four Swedish Cases," *Journal of Management Studies,* Vol. 12, no. 3 (October 1975).

10. J. Johanson and J.-E. Vahlne, "The Internationalization Process of the Firm," *Journal of International Business Studies,* Vol. 8 (Spring–Summer 1977).

11. R. Luostarinen, *The Internationalization of the Firm* (Helsinki: Acta Academic Oeconomica Helsingiensis, 1979).

12. W. J. Bilkey and G. Tesar, "The Export Behavior of Smaller Wisconsin Manufacturing Firms," *Journal of International Business Studies,* Vol. 8 (Spring–Summer 1977).

13. L. S. Welch and F. Wiedersheim-Paul, "Initial Exports—A Marketing Failure?" *Journal of Management Studies,* Vol. 17 (October 1980).

14. P. Joynt, "An Empirical Study of Norwegian Export Behavior," *Skriftserie,* no. 1 (1981).

15. N. Piercy, "Company Internationalisation: Active and Reactive Exporting," *European Journal of Marketing,* Vol. 15, no. 3 (1981).

16. J.-E. Denis and D. Depelteau, "Market Knowledge, Diversification and Export Expansion," *Journal of International Business Studies,* Vol. 16 (Fall 1985).

17. P. J. Buckley, "New Theories of International Business," in M. Casson (ed.), *The Growth of International Business* (London: Allen and Unwin, 1983), p. 48.

18. Johanson and Wiedersheim-Paul, "The Internationalization of the Firm."

19. Piercy, "Company Internationalisation."

20. P. Turnbull, "Internationalisation of the Firm—A Stages Process or Not?", paper presented at the conference on Export Expansion and Market Entry Modes, Dalhousie University, Halifax, October 15/16, 1985.

21. S. J. Koury, "Countertrade: Forms, Motives, Pitfalls, and Negotiaton Requisites," *Journal of Business Research,* Vol. 12, no. 2 (June 1984).

22. S. M. Huszagh and F. W. Huszagh, "International Barter and Countertrade," *International Marketing Review,* Vol. 3, no. 2 (Summer 1986).

23. J. W. Dizard, "The Explosion of International Barter," *Fortune,* Vol. 107, no. 3 (February 7, 1983).

24. S. S. Cohen and J. Zysman, "Countertrade, Offsets, Barter, and Buybacks," *California Management Review,* Vol. 28, no. 2 (Winter 1986).

25. R. Carstairs and L. S. Welch, "Australian Offshore Investment in Asia," *Management International Review,* Vol. 20, no. 4 (1980).

26. E. Hornell and J.-E. Vahlne, "The Changing Structure of Swedish Multinational Companies," working pap?er 1982/12, Centre for International Business Studies, University of Uppsala.

27. *Business Week,* "The Hollow Corporation," March 3, 1986.

28. J. J. Boddewynn, "Foreign Divestment: Magnitude and Factors," *Journal of International Business Studies,* Vol. 10 (Spring–Summer 1979).

29. Welch and Wiedersheim-Paul, "Initial Exports."

30. S. T. Cavusgil and Y. M. Godiwalla, "Decision-Making for International Marketing: A Comparative Review," *Management Decision,* Vol. 20, no. 4 (1982).

31. Johanson and Wiedersheim-Paul, "The Internationalization of the Firm."

32. Luostarinen, *The Internationalization of the Firm.*

33. Ibid., pp. 105–124.

34. R. T. Carstairs and L. S. Welch, "Licensing and the Internationalization of Smaller Companies: Some Australian Evidence," *Management International Review,* Vol. 22, no. 3 (1982), p. 35.

35. B. Roscoe, "Getting Round Protectionism by the Direct Route," *Far Eastern Economic Review* (June 13, 1985), pp. 82–83.

36. B. Emmott, "Japan: A Survey," *Economist* (December 7, 1985), pp. 26–30.

37. Luostarinen, *The Internationalization of the Firm,* pp. 95–105.

38. Price Waterhouse Associates, *Successful Exporting* (Canberra: Australian Government Publishing Service, 1982), pp. 30–34.

39. E. Hornell and Vahlne, "The Changing Structure of Swedish Multinational Companies," p. 8.

40. J.-E. Vahlne and F. Wiedersheim-Paul, "Psychic Distance—An Inhibiting Factor in International Trade," working paper, 1977/2, Centre for International Business Studies, University of Uppsala, Sweden.

41. Luostarinen, *The Internationalization of the Firm,* pp. 124–172.

42. Cavusgil and Godiwalla, "Decision-Making for International Marketing."

43. P. Lorange, "Human Resource Management in Multinational Cooperative Ventures," *Human Resource Management,* Vol. 25, no. 1 (Spring 1986), p. 133.

44. S. D. Reid, "The Decision-Maker and Export Entry and Expansion," *Journal of International Business Studies,* Vol. 12 (Fall 1981).

45. L. S. Welch, "Managerial Decision-Making: The Case of Export Involvement," *Scandinavian Journal of Materials Administration,* Vol. 9, no. 2 (1983).

46. Johanson and Vahlne, "The Internationalization Process of the Firm."

47. R. L. Tung, "Selection and Training of U.S., European, and Japanese Multinationals," *California Management Review,* Vol. 25, no. 1 (Fall 1982). p. 70.

48. J. M. Stopford and L. T. Wells, *Managing the Multinational Enterprise* (New York: Basic Books, 1972).

49. C. A. Bartlett, "Multinational Structural Change: Evolution Versus Reorganization," in L. Otterbeck (ed.), *The Management of Headquarters—Subsidiary Relationships in Multinational Corporations* (Aldershot: Gower, 1981).

50. G. Hedlund, "Organization In-Between," *Journal of International Business Studies,* Vol. 15 (Fall 1984).

51. Welch and Wiedersheim-Paul, "Initial Exports."

52. Price Waterhouse Associates, *Successful Exporting,* pp. 56–62.

53. Luostarinen, *The Internationalization of the Firm,* p. 151.

54. Johanson and Wiedersheim-Paul, "The Internationalization of the Firm."

55. Luostarinen, *The Internationalization of the Firm.*

56. Juul and Walters.

57. J. Larimo, "The Foreign Direct Manufacturing Investment Behaviour of Finnish Companies," paper presented at the 11th European International Business Association Conference, Glasgow, December 15–17, 1985.

58. Luostarinen, *The Internationalization of the Firm,* pp. 95–105.

59. Hornell and Vahlne, "The Changing Structure of Swedish Multinational Companies", p. 8.

60. K. Yoshihara, "Determinants of Japanese Investment in South-East Asia," *International Social Science Journal,* Vol. 30, no. 2 (1978), p. 372.

61. Wilkins, *The Maturing Multinational Enterprise,* p. 414.

62. P. J. Buckley, G. D. Newbould, and J. Thurwell, "Going International—The Foreign Direct Investment Behaviour of Smaller U.K. Firms," in L. G. Mattsson and F. Wiedersheim-Paul (eds.), *Recent Research on the Internationalization of Business,* (Uppsala: Acta Universitatis Upsaliensis, 1979).

63. P. J. Buckley, G. D. Newbould, and Z. Berkova, "Direct Investment in the U.K. by Smaller Continental European Firms," working paper, University of Bradford, 1981.

64. P. J. Buckley, "The Role of Exporting in the Market Servicing Policies of Multinational Manufacturing Enterprises," in M. Czinkota and G. Tesar (eds.), *Export Management* (New York: Praeger, 1982), pp. 178–79.

65. Bureau of Industry Economics, *Australian Direct Investment Abroad* (Canberra: Australian Government Publishing Service, 1984), p.115.

66. Bureau of Industry Economics, *Australian Direct Investment Abroad,* p. 128.

67. G. Hedlund and A. Kverneland, "Are Establishments and Growth Strategies for Foreign Markets Changing?" paper presented at the 9th European International Business Association Conference, Oslo, December 18–20, 1983.

68. Hornell and Vahlne, "The Changing Structure of Swedish Multinational Companies."

69. Larimo, "The Foreign Direct Manufacturing Investment Behaviour of Finnish Companies."

70. OECD, "International Direct Investment: A Change in Pattern," *OECD Observer,* No. 112 (September 1981).

71. G. Korporaal, *Yankee Dollars: Australian Investment in America* (London: Allen and Unwin, 1986), Ch. 12.

72. Department of Trade, "Fire Protection Firm Sparks New Sales in China, U.S.S.R.," *Overseas Trading,* Vol. 31, no. 10 (May 25, 1979), p. 345.

73. H. Mintzberg and A. McHugh, "Strategy Formation in an Adhocracy," *Administrative Science Quarterly,* Vol. 30 (June 1985).

74. Turnbull, "Internationalisation of the Firm."

75. Hedlund and Kverneland, "Are Establishments and Growth Strategies for Foreign Markets Changing?"

76. Buckley, "The Role of Exporting . . . "

77. L. S. Welch and F. Wiedersheim-Paul, "Domestic Expansion: Internationalization at Home," *Essays in International Business,* No. 2 (December 1980).

78. R. Layton (ed.), "Magna Alloys and Research Pty. Ltd.," *Australian Marketing Projects* (Sydney: Halstead Press, 1969).

79. W. H. Starbuck, "Organizational Growth and Development," in W. H. Starbuck (ed.), *Organizational Growth and Development* (Harmondsworth: Penguin, 1971).

80. Welch and Wiedersheim-Paul, "Initial Exports."

81. S. T. Cavusgil, "Organizational Characteristics Associated with Export Activity," *Journal of Management Studies,* Vol. 21, no. 1 (January 1984).

82. A. Yaprak, "An Empirical Study of the Differences Between Small Exporting and Non-Exporting U.S. Firms," *International Marketing Review,* Vol. 2, no. 2 (Summer 1985).

83. M. R. Czinkota and W. J. Johnston, "Exporting: Does Sales Volume Make a Difference," *Journal of International Business Studies,* Vol. 14 (Spring–Summer 1983).

84. Cavusgil, "Organizational Characteristics Associated with Export Activity."

85. Czinkota and Johnston, "Exporting," p. 153.

86. *Euromoney,* "Elders IXL," Supplement, August 1985.

87. Johanson and Vahlne, "The Internationalization Process of the Firm."

88. S. Carlson, *How Foreign Is Foreign Trade* (Uppsala: Acta Universitatis Upsaliensis, 1975).

89. H. Hakansson (ed.), *International Marketing and Purchasing of Industrial Goods* (Winchester: John Wiley, 1982).

90. D. Ford, "The Development of Buyer-Seller Relationships in Industrial Markets," *European Journal of Marketing,* Vol. 14, 5/6 (1980).

91. Johanson and Vahlne, "The Internationalization Process of the Firm."

92. Luostarinen, *The Internationalization of the Firm,* p. 117.

93. Aharoni, *The Foreign Investment Decision Process.*

94. Johanson and Vahlne, "The Internationalization Process of the Firm."

95. Cavusgil and Godiwalla, "Decision-Making for International Marketing."

96. Mintzberg and McHugh, "Strategy Formation in an Adhocracy."

4

MULTINATIONAL BUSINESS IN THE 1990S—A SCENARIO
PETER SCHWARTZ AND JERRY SAVILLE

A multinational business cannot expect to develop one single scenario which represents the development of world society in the coming decade. There is scope for substantial economic growth of an order which has not been seen since the 1960s, but fear of failure and the caution which are inevitable after the crisis-ridden and disturbed business environment of the 1970s and early 1980s could mean that the opportunities are missed. Multinationals will have to develop flexible strategies for a wide variety of possible environments and management styles to operate in a highly competitive environment.

As the next decade draws near, multinational businesses must ask themselves what new challenges they may face and what responses they should make in a highly uncertain environment. The rapid economic developments of this century have been characterized by periods of growth followed by periods of transition before further growth could be realized. Since World War II there has been one period of prolonged and predictable growth until the late 1960s followed by nearly 20 years of highly unpredictable economic behaviour which was often unexplicable by traditional concepts of economic theory.

The developed economies have generally gone through a period of "stagflation" since the first oil shock of 1973 and many LDCs have experienced financial turmoil as import bills have risen and could not be offset by exports because of limited growth in the world economy. There have been exceptions. Inevitably wealth has shifted to oil-exporting countries which have consequently undergone major transformations in their economies. Some developed economies have fared well—the Japanese being the obvious example. Some less-developed countries such as South Korea have grown to a point where they represent a major threat to the competitiveness of traditional players in some markets.

Many multinationals have gone through difficult times in the last decade. They must now ask themselves whether low growth and poor returns on capital invested are primarily a result of the inevitable ups and downs of a busi-

Source: *Long Range Planning,* Vol. 19, no. 6 (December 1986), pp. 31–37. Printed in Great Britain.

ness cycle or the result of more fundamental changes in the environment. The case is set out below for the view that major changes are occurring and will make the task of planning for the future even more difficult.

The multinational corporation (MNC) has a particular need to understand the driving forces behind the transformations which affect the performance of global economies in absolute and relative terms. The domestic firm which exports finished goods to a number of markets is concerned with such issues as the growth of foreign markets and the likely development of exchange rates. The MNC, with capital invested overseas and with commitments to indigenous work forces, is exposed to more risks and conflicts. Political risks arise from concerns about the stability of particular political institutions and their attitude towards foreign investment. Conflicts of interest frequently arise between sovereign states and the business goals of multinational corporations. MNCs have significant impact on the development of nations because they transfer technology around the world and seek trained labour to create and market their products. Cognizance must be given to the wide range of regulatory, advisory and political bodies which operate at national, regional and international level. Operations in multiple environments require new concepts, analytical methods and information.

The ability to wrestle with the political risks of foreign investment is a skill which most multinationals have developed since the postwar expansion in world trade. The skill was often centred on a narrow and relatively static view of the business environment. Capital investment was derived from a small number of developed and politically stable nations in Europe and North America. The political world order and elements of neo-colonialism enabled ethnocentric thinking to persist until it was realized that apparently insignificant players could create major international turbulence which fundamentally shifted attitudes and fu-

ture behaviour. On the political front Vietnam, Iran and Libya have rocked the faith of the U.S.A. in its ability to influence the destiny of events outside its own shores.

The core of economic growth is now more dispersed. The dominance of Europe and the U.S.A. has been diluted by the emergence of Japan, Canada and Australia. Other nations, such as South Korea and Brazil, are waiting in the wings getting ready to move towards centre stage.

Any MNC which is to prosper in the 1990s and beyond is faced with the need to undergo a constant adaptation and development of its conceptual thinking, modes of analysis, systems of control and management style. Whatever the rate of growth in world economies it is certain that global competition will increase. Inability to adapt will therefore generate casualties who may only survive with the help of government intervention. The principal issues to which the MNC must address itself are:

- What are the fundamental driving forces which will dictate the type of future which unfolds?
- What are the major uncertainties about the future which have a relevance to the performance and strategies of MNCs?
- What capabilities exist to respond to the future environment, that is, what are the appropriate strategies, management styles, organizational structure and control systems?
- What will be the consequences of the transition to the post-war generation of corporate leaders?

THE DRIVING FORCES

It has been suggested above that the world economy is in a period of transition. Any analysis of the driving forces which will mould the future must look at the dynamics of transition and the transformation into expansion.

Transitions are marked by a mismatch of skills, capital stock and institutions to the circumstances of the times. They occur when production and consumption potential are nearly fully exploited or the underlying conditions which support the established order change substantially. Potential for new expansion derives from technological innovation and improved human capabilities brought about by social development. The evolution of a system through alternating phases of transition and expansion is regulated by institutions at national, regional, and international level.

At national level the realization of new potential can be exemplified by the emergence of co-operative efforts of governments, business and financial institutions in the development of both the German and Japanese economies. At the other extreme, economic nationalism and protectionism tend to stifle expansionary forces. It may be impossible to bring innovations profitably to world markets because protectionist measures prevent global economies of scale being achieved. Individual societies may have no faith that benefits will accrue directly to them or that there will be any alleviation in high levels of unemployment.

A prerequisite of expansion is that the "old order" is in some measure swept aside and support is given to new institutional frameworks. Emergence from the current transition may require significant turbulence in order to release economic potential. The recent dramatic fall in oil prices could be a spark which ignites a transformation. Alternatively, the wave of economic nationalism brought about by the major recessions of the early 1980s may have induced considerable institutional inertia which will continue well into the 1990s. If systemic resistance is high then it is important to understand the strength of human and technological potential which is an underlying driving force for change (see Figure 1).

The world population is growing but at a slower rate than in the past and the growth is almost exclusively in developing countries. As population growth slows in the developing world there is an opportunity for *human potential* to increase. Resources can be devoted in principle to the improvement of the quality, rather than quantity, of human and physical resources. Improvements in social development have taken place, providing healthier and better educated populations. The size and diver-

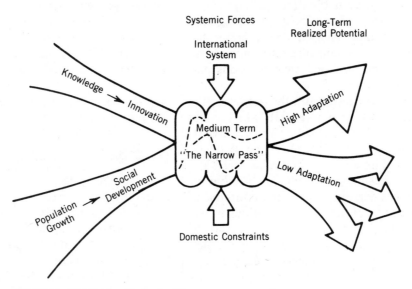

Figure 1. The Driving Forces for Change

sity of markets can increase, which leads to opportunities for economies of scale, higher productivity and higher incomes. MNCs recognize that steps forward are highly susceptible to political and economic shocks and LDCs are often considered as high-risk investments.

Improvements are not, of course, true of all countries. Africa continues to experience an increasing population growth rate with attendant political, social and economic consequences. It must also be remembered that some nations trade off the benefits of economic development against cherished social or political values. India and China are countries which, for different reasons, have chosen a different set of trade-offs for various social and political values, having sacrificed some income in their pursuit. Many LDCs do not have a choice. They are caught in a vicious circle which inhibits development. Population growth requires capital for expanded social systems but the infrastructure is not well enough developed to generate sufficient export earnings or be competitive with goods produced elsewhere (except in the case of oil exporters). Foreign aid becomes a vital lifeline.

Improving the human potential of a society involves such forces as health care and housing, but among the most important is education. It is no accident that the Japanese have gained enormous economic benefit from the high quality of its labour force, which was the product of a great emphasis given to education (of the "right" sort). MNCs have an increasing influence on this process. Among the indirect influences are the requirements it establishes for hiring. More directly it engages in extensive training and development programmes of its own. The choices it makes in these will have an increasing influence as technology advances and competition becomes more global.

The demographics of developed countries is leading to ageing populations as life expectancy increases and birth rates decline. Apart from the effects this will have on the structure of de-

mand, there could be important consequences for institutional change. An older population is likely to be more rigid and resistant to change. This would affect a country's ability to adapt in a world of rapid technological change and shifting international competitiveness. The situation is exacerbated when money has to be diverted to large sectors of the community which have ceased to be economically active.

In the developed world *technological potential* is a dominant factor for change. R&D investment in OECD countries has grown since 1975 in real terms despite recent severe recessions and the decline of major industries. In addition the type of technical innovation is leading to some optimism that new technologies may generate "a second Industrial Revolution." In the areas of electronics, communications, biotechnology, chemicals and materials there is large potential for growth which could revitalize declining or mature industries at the same time as new industries are formed. MNCs are in a unique position to take advantage of such developments. They have global infrastructures which can potentially utilize resources and technology in the most efficient way to bring new products to market. What they must realize, however, is that a combination of increasing globalization of markets and high rewards for technological innovation will attract intense competition. MNCs whose employees and managers are drawn from developed countries, where the quality of life has been high for some time, may have difficulty maintaining the drive for competitiveness. Emerging MNCs, from countries where there is an under-developed middle class, will have a strong appetite for improving living standards. The efficiencies of traditional MNCs are further threatened by continuing rigidities in some institutional structures, notably in Europe.

However strongly the forces of human and technological potential strive to emerge they can be thwarted by systemic barriers. They will eventually find an outlet if old barriers are not removed but the interim may be marked by stagnation and protectionism in developed economies as vibrant economies in such regions as the Pacific Basin forge ahead.

In one sense economic growth and consumer demand have enabled MNCs to develop at a faster pace than international institutions:

the emergence of the multinational corporation reflects a differential pace in the evolution of political institutions relative to business organisations. While business institutions have become more and more internationalised, the development of international governmental organisations has not accompanied business and economic trends.[1]

It is doubtful that MNCs would welcome an increase in *regulation* at international level but the release of significant potential will be dependant on favourable institutional environments. In such a case the accelerated evolution of integrated international bodies may be an advantage to world growth and the prosperity of MNCs. The absence of such bodies undoubtedly contributes to fears that MNCs are "uncontrolled" and accusations that they are sometimes more powerful than the sovereign states in which they operate. However, as Behrman suggests,[2] integration initiated by nations needs the willingness of one, or a few, key countries to bear the costs of adjustment and assistance to less fortunate members and few seem prepared to take this initiative except at regional level (e.g., EEC).

A further driving force which is of particular significance to the MNC and which demonstrates the way in which radical shifts in institutional controls can occur, is international financial trade. Since the abandonment of the Bretton Woods agreement there has been a gradual increase in deregulation, greater fluctuation in exchange rates, higher levels of competition and a massive growth in the volume of financial trade between countries. The freedom of movement for capital and the creation of a multitude of new financial instruments creates opportunities for the MNC but dictates that a positive and clear approach to financing strategy exists. The inability to respond effectively to signals in the capital markets creates risks. These range from the risk of severe exchange losses, as unhedged revenues or payments cross national boundaries, to the risk of takeover in which the "small fish," aided by new forms of financing, swallow the "big fish" bringing a new meaning to "megamerger." There is some concern that deregulation has proceeded too far but many of the changes in the nature of international finance are now irreversible.

The MNC business planner can thus expect that economic developments will be characterized by formidable constraints in the 1990s despite the presence of considerable human and technological potential. What are the major uncertainties with which MNC managements will have to grapple?

UNCERTAINTIES

The underlying driving forces of human potential, technological potential and financial deregulation are, to some extent, predetermined elements in the future which will unfold in the 1990s. It is not known how the forces will develop or interact or how fast change will occur but failure to take account of these forces would be a serious error in environmental assessment for the strategist who seeks to chart a way through the 1990s and beyond.

Even if the effects of the driving forces are understood there remain other uncertainties which complicate strategy formulation.

• What are the long-term economic prospects of countries whose manufacturing base is eroding? For example, will the U.K. become a test case for the notion that "a nation cannot survive by selling hamburgers to itself"?

• Can any accommodation be made between the "rich North" and the "poor South" or will the fortunes of developed countries and NICs continue to diverge from those of the poor LDCs?

• Will political objectives tend towards social concerns or wealth creation? In a world in which both exist, what are the long-term prospects for nations which choose to forego economic development in order to retain a cherished social tradition?

• How far will the nexus of economic power slip away from Europe and North America towards the Pacific Basin? Does China threaten to destabilize traditional international competition in the foreseeable future?

The analysis so far permits the construction of two archetypes for the 1990s which take account of diverse developments in uncertainties and the driving forces.

In the first, structural rigidities persist. The potential benefits of such shocks as the collapse in oil prices are lost. This could be because institutions (including MNCs) decide to "save" the income transferred to them so that they reduce deficit and debt problems rather than "spend" it. There would be a feeling that improvements in economic performance were fragile and transient. In the longer term regional trading patterns would predominate over global trade as economic nationalism and protectionism were seen as the only viable ways of creating some stability and minimizing the effects of future shocks. Growth rates would vary considerably by region with the Pacific Basin showing particularly high rates. The problem of "Eurosclerosis" could remain and result in little innovation, increasing unemployment and limited improvement in standards of living. European nations could rationalize their position as a trade-off between the benefits and high risks of economic growth and the maintenance of traditions within a less stressful environment.

A second archetype would not allow many institutions the luxury of a choice between "save" and "spend" because many would be radically altered or abandoned as the forces for change placed pressure on systemic processes. In the

longer term technological potential could be taken up as Europe and the U.S.A. participate in efficient innovation which can compete with NICs in Latin America and the Far East. Interdependence between developed countries, NICs and LDCs for the factors of production and the need for market outlet begins to produce institutions in which economic cooperation is effective but at the expense of some national sovereignty.

STRATEGIES AND CAPABILITIES

MNCs will have to develop strategies now which are resilient to both archetypes. Neither world is necessarily good or bad for the MNC. A world in which *new institutions* emerge may be dominated by economic values but regulation of MNCs, affairs might become more effective at international level. MNCs should welcome international institutions which support wealth creation even if they give the appearance of increasing the general level of regulatory power. A situation in which wealth creation is aggressively pursued by the majority of nations without adequate control of international private corporations is potentially unstable and not in the long-term interests of MNCs.

A return to levels of growth last seen in the 1960s would attract high levels of competition. In the 1960s the lack of suitable technology and trained labour often dictated that growth proceeded at the rate chosen by the *producer*. This is unlikely to be the case again. The *consumer* will determine the pace of innovation.

Manufacturing technology has made major advances so that the mass production of a wide variety of products, or varieties of a particular product, can be produced with great efficiency. Manufacturers will be expected to produce differentiated products into an ever increasing number of markets. A world in which capital, labour and products can be freely moved around the world would offer the MNC profitable opportunities. Flexibility of response would be at a premium as producers sought to meet consumer demand ahead of rivals. Liberated world trade would make comparative advantages for the factor costs of production less relevant than at present. The emphasis would be on entrepreneurialism. In such an environment there would be winners and losers but the latter would receive less and less protection from social legislation. In periods of stable high growth societies would recognize that, with sufficient labour mobility and retraining, there would be little risk of raising unemployment levels permanently when corporations failed.

If Europe cannot abolish some of its institutional barriers then it is unlikely to gain very much from the early stages of a new expansionary period. MNCs would operate elsewhere, using Europe as a source of trained labour and venture capital. Europe would be a non-participant in growth centred on the Pacific Basin and successful NICs elsewhere.

Sustained growth and changing political and social institutions has risks. Potential losers will seek to protect their interests. Shocks to a highly interdependent economic system can have a multiplier effect which creates severe booms and busts while maintaining a high average rate of growth. For such an archetype to succeed it has to be believed that global macro-economic management would generally be effective in preventing periods of prolonged and damaging recession. Successful MNCs would exercise centralized control to manage resources so as to take full advantage of variations in regional performance.

The alternative archetype, which is characterized by wide and persistent variations in economic performance and development among nations and regions, would require MNCs to consider other strategies. Intense intra-regional competition will require good knowledge of local conditions and an ability to co-exist successfully with political and social institutions which are suspicious of strong dependency on foreign capital. MNCs are likely to be faced with social costs, difficulties in re-

patriation of funds and protectionist measures. In general they would be faced with a world of reliable, but limited, rewards for low-risk exposure. Above average rewards are likely for those which can exploit comparative advantages and co-exist successfully with a wide range of differing political, economic and social environments. A narrow ethnocentric view of the world will limit potential. The MNC which is seen to make a significant contribution to the social, in addition to the economic, development of nations will be more sought after than the MNC which is seen to pursue primarily economic goals.

LDC economies would grow on average more quickly than those of developed countries, whose growth would be limited by self-imposed strictures. In LDCs high rewards at high risk could be available for MNCs. It would have to be recognized that the "North-South" divide is likely to grow as the developed world looks increasingly to its own interests at the expense of aid to the poorer nations. MNCs will have to operate across a divide which at best operates as an uneasy co-existence of contrasting political, social and economic objectives.

MANAGEMENT STYLE AND CONTROL SYSTEMS

The evolution of MNCs has created a number of different ways in which international corporations can be effectively managed. Are there particular modes which are more suited than others to the vicissitudes of the 1990s and beyond?

A first observation is that organizations must be sensitive to environmental changes. The balance of power is shifting from supply push to demand pull, the reaction of markets and external institutions has to be taken into account as economies oscillate between good and poor performance. Managers at corporate and subsidiary level must be in a position to analyse and act upon such changes in the environment.

There must be an open-mindedness to developments which, however costly, may cause the MNC to reassess its strategies and tactics. The corporation whose managers carry a static mental model of the interaction of the organization with its environment will be at a disadvantage. A constant process of questioning assumptions is vital but must be based on sound and perceptive observations.

It follows that the best forms of bureaucratic control may be inadequate if they serve to reinforce existing "conventional wisdoms." They will serve MNCs least well in a world where regional issues predominate over global integration. They will be more appropriate where competitive advantage is to be gained from exploiting the interdependency between economies on a global scale.

The social, or cultural, dimension of control also has to be considered. MNCs must study their *modus operandi* and the environment in which they will operate in order to determine the level they wish to internationalize their management system. A number of choices exist. A company "way" can be a powerful source of efficiency but may prove resistant to change and inappropriate to a world in which there are marked differences in the most effective modes of conducting business around the world. It will also be resisted in a world where nationalism is a major feature and pride is taken in national differences in culture and behaviour.

EXPECTATIONS AND VALUES

Archetypes of the environments in which MNCs may have to operate and the possible types of response have been described. On the assumption that an MNC has resolved these issues in order to develop a sound and resilient strategy for the 1990s, will it have the appropriate managers to implement the strategy?

The next generation of managers who will have sufficient experience to control MNCs differs in several respects from the preceding generation. In the developed world there is substantial suspicion of corporate power and values. The most able individuals, brought up in the absence of a World War or major depression, have a high degree of personal independence and do not need the security of a large organization:

This post-war generation, born in the joy of victory and a surge of unprecedented affluence, represents a sharp change in the social fabric of American life. In stark contrast to the overly ambitious hopes of their parents, the baby boomers are less motivated towards success, less optimistic and certainly less committed to the large institutions that make up this society than any previous generation of Americans.

The study which prompted these comments[3] was carried out in AT&T and assessed the appetite for leadership and management among two groups of AT&T staff—one recruited in the 1950s and one in the 1970s. There was a significantly lower drive for advancement in the later group.

The decline of the "Protestant work ethic" has been noted frequently in North America. Many dreams have been realized, a high quality of life can be derived from sources other than advancement in corporate life. The challenges for today's corporation which operates on a global basis will come from MNCs in emerging nations where individual ambitions have not been realized and can best be served by aiding in the creation of wealth. The MNC has two possible responses. It can pursue aggressively those individuals who show the values it cherishes. They still exist, even if their predominance has waned. Alternatively it can reassess its reward and career development systems and method of organization to seek accommodation with the values it finds in abundance in the labour market. The diversity of opportunities which now exists outside corporate life suggests that the second route will provide the better long-term investment in human resources.

It is not surprising that the concept of adaptation keeps arising in this discussion. The fundamental issue that is at the heart of the problem, is evolutionary adaptation. The emergent global corporation has defined a new competitive niche, that is the entire planet. Their principal evolutionary strength is intelligence, embodied in a knowledge elite. The role of that elite is the shaping and guiding of the structure, culture and strategy of the MNC based on a systematic interaction with its environment.

The central task is fostering the process of constant and timely adaptation. This is not to say that the process can be designed *a priori.* The operational problems in the adaptive process are not the engineering problems. They are more like hermeneutics as applied to biblical studies rather than the precision and predictability of scientific method. As such they involve issues such as:

- decentralization vs centralization,
- co-operation vs independence,
- role of culture,
- investment in human assets and
- the management of conflict.

CONCLUSIONS

The multinational cannot expect to develop one scenario which represents the development of the world's institutions and societies in the 1990s. There is scope for a return to substantial and sustained economic growth which was last seen in the 1960s but it will be easy to "miss the boat" because fear of failure has become deeply

entrenched after the shocks and recessions of the 1970s and 1980s.

MNCs will have to develop strategies which take account of a wide variety of possible environments. They will also have to pay attention to appropriate management styles and control systems which can generate acceptable profits in a highly competitive environment while remaining flexible to shifts in the environment which are of significance to its operations.

The MNC is an impressive invention for accomplishing things and this will be a highly valued asset in a world poised for sustained growth. In a world of conflict and confusion, the adaptive MNC is a remarkable system for corporate survival. Perhaps, an analogy can be drawn with history of migrating families as they moved outward from Europe. There are often conflicts inside families, but the ties of blood are often strong enough to overcome such conflicts. Families have a long lineage. Families give people a sense of belonging and role in the world: they are the social fabric. It is not far fetched to see the MNC of the future like an enduring family. The great centuries-old companies of Japan provide an historical precedent. Perhaps the emerging MNC may be more like Sumitomo and Mitsui than IBM and Citicorp.

NOTES

1. S. F. Robock and K. Simmonds, *International Business and Multinational Enterprise* (Homewood, Ill.: Richard D. Irwin, 1983).
2. J. N. Behrman, *Industrial Policies: International Restructuring and Transnationals* (Lexington, Mass.: Lexington Books, 1984).
3. A. Howard and J. A. Wilson, "Leadership in a Declining Work Ethic," *California Management Review* (Summer 1982).

Section 2

CONCEPTS AND TOOLS FOR COMPETITIVE ANALYSIS AND STRATEGIC PLANNING

Any business, whether domestic or global, will not prosper unless it can identify opportunities to develop a competitive advantage and then capitalize on those opportunities. The tasks of competitive analysis and strategic planning are central to building a competitive advantage. Competitive analysis and strategic planning are complex enough exercises for a business that is purely domestic; where the scope of the business is international or global, the complexities multiply.

As the geographic scope of a business broadens, the business strategist must contend with a considerably wider variety of competitors, consumers, and business environments. The multinational or global firm must compete not just against domestic firms in each country in which it markets, but also worldwide against other multinational and global firms. Domestic firms as well must take into account foreign competitors as they plan. In many countries, domestic firms' toughest competitors are not other domestics, but multinational and global firms headquartered elsewhere.

The core problem of strategic planning, specifying the products with which the business will compete and the markets in which it will compete with those products, is common to both the smallest domestic and the largest global business. But this problem is considerably more difficult for the multinational or global firm to handle.

To market automobiles in any one country, for example, General Motors must identify consumer segments and then design and position specific cars for each segment in which it wants to compete. It must go through a similar segmentation and positioning exercise for each country in which it wants to market. Then it must come up with a product line that—taking into account manufacturing and shipping economics, as well as consumer desires—gives it the maximal competitive advantage in each country.

A product line consideration specific to multinational and global firms is whether they should standardize their products worldwide or customize them for individual countries or regions. The advantages of one tack versus the other have been the subject of much debate. From the firm's standpoint, the advantages of standardization are clear: the result is a much simpler, more easily managed business that may be able to offer lower prices than competitors offering customized products. Consumers, on the other hand, may be willing to pay somewhat more for a customized product they believe will fit their needs more precisely.

In many industries, choosing the right production location(s) is also critical to maintaining a competitive advantage. This is true for domestic firms and even more so for multinational and global firms. With so many potential sites around the world, the choices are not easy because the many issues involved are complex and the advantages of one site over another can rapidly shift.

In this section, we explore these and related strategic planning questions from a corporate and SBU perspective, looking across the business functions. We will focus on some of the important concepts and techniques useful in competitive analysis. In later sections of the book, we shall explore in more depth and from the perspective of the individual business functions many of the issues raised here.

READING SELECTIONS

Kenichi Ohmae addresses the question of market selection, which he then relates to decisions about manufacturing location and corporate form. He argues that firms desiring to compete globally must build strong internal positions in the "Triad" markets: Japan, Europe, and the United States. He points out that the Triad countries account for the bulk of world demand in many products, have similar markets, and face similar problems.

Ohmae's view is that, despite the similarities among the Triad markets, a growing trend toward protectionism will push firms to manufacture within the markets in which they sell. Capital-intensive, flexible manufacturing processes, he suggests, will make it possible for global firms to produce efficiently within local markets; the advantages of producing in low-labor-cost countries and then exporting to the Triad are eroding. Traveling the road to Triad power may require forming joint ventures and consortia as well as wholly owned subsidiaries.

Balaji Chakravarthy and Howard Perlmutter pick up and expand on themes introduced by Doz and Ohmae. They point out that a firm's strategic planning must reconcile economic and political imperatives while at the same time fitting the firm's strategic predisposition. They then review four alternative systems for strategic planning and discuss the appropriateness of each in light of different economic and political imperatives and strategic predispositions. Chakravarthy and Perlmutter recommend value chain analysis as a tool for determining the economic component of the firm's strategy. Succeeding articles show how to use the value chain as an analytic tool.

Bruce Kogut, in his two articles, shows how to use value chain analysis. In the first article, he discusses the competitive importance of both production location and activity decisions. A key concept in this article is the interplay between comparative advantage (where to perform an activity) and competitive advantage (what activities to perform) in developing an effective global strategy. He presents a framework for analyzing the economic effects of selecting alternative manufacturing sites, of splitting a manufacturing operation among two or more countries, and of vertical integration.

In his second article, Kogut points out the uncertainties involved in manufacturing location decisions due to exchange rate movements. He shows us that exchange rate differences and labor-cost differentials across countries often do not correspond. Therefore, he argues, the firm that wants to be a low-cost producer must remain flexible enough to shift its production from country to country in response to exchange rate movements. His analysis applies to goods a firm purchases as well as to goods it manufactures.

Michael Porter introduces configuration and coordination as concepts for organizing the firm's value chain activities. A firm's *configuration* is the deployment of its various activities around the globe; *coordination* is the extent to which similar activities are coordinated indifferent countries. Porter then discusses the advantages of concentrated versus dispersed configurations and of tight versus loose coordination. He argues that successful global strategies require an increasing degree of both dispersion and coordination.

Lawrence Wortzel focuses on the standardization versus customization debate. He identifies the assumptions each side makes in putting forth its point of view and concludes that both standardization and customization can be viable strategies, depending on the product. He suggests that, in setting a global strategy, we must consider two key product characteristics: the extent to which consumers will accept a standardized product and the speed at which the product changes. He then recommends an appropriate global strategy for each set of characteristics.

Deepak Datta picks up a theme that has run through several of the articles in this section, the use of joint ventures. He notes that they are growing in number among multinational and global firms. His article covers two important, but neglected, aspects of joint venture decisions and management. He presents a framework for assessing the desirability of using a joint venture and strategies for making them work. Techniques such as value chain analysis and concepts such as configuration/coordination presented in earlier articles in this section may be useful additions to Datta's framework.

5

BECOMING A TRIAD POWER: THE NEW GLOBAL CORPORATION
Kenichi Ohmae

Three major markets—"Triad" of Japan, Europe and the United States—are emerging as the most important strategic battlefield for any company operating on a global scale. The author pinpoints four trends—increasing capital intensity, soaring R&D costs, converging worldwide consumer tastes and intensifying protectionism—which together make it imperative for a company to have an inside presence in all three Triad regions. He looks at the steps some companies have already taken toward becoming a Triad power.

Three great market regions—Japan, Europe and the United States—dominate the world of multinational business today. The combined gross national products of Japan and the United States now account for 30 per cent of the free world's total. Add in the GNP of the four biggest Western European nations—the United Kingdom, West Germany, France and Italy—and the figure reaches 45 per cent. Customers in the Japan-Europe-US Triad buy over 85 per cent of all computers and consumer electronics products. Japan, the United States and West Germany alone comprise 70 per cent of the global market for numerically controlled machine tools.

The Triad countries all have similar problems: mature economies, escalating social costs, aging propulations, a growing scarcity of skilled jobs, dynamic technologies and escalating R&D costs. Triad markets, too, are increasingly similar. Capital equipment until recently reflected its country of origin. Now the best-selling factory machines have become almost identical not only in appearance but in the skills required to operate them. There are 600 million consumers in the Triad with converging needs and preferences. Gucci bags, Sony Walkmans and McDonald's golden arches are seen on the streets of Tokyo, London, Paris and New York. Companies like Seiko, Sony, Canon, Matsushita, Casio and Honda are now routinely developing products for a world market, with minor modifications depending on local tastes.

All this has far-reaching consequences for multinational business. Quite simply, global enterprises organized for doing business in the 1960s are out of date.

Following World War II, American multinationals enjoyed a virtually insurmountable technological and competitive edge and could straddle Latin America, Asia and Europe. From 1945 to 1965 some 2,800 US businesses had stakes in 10,000 direct investments abroad, aimed in most cases at exploiting a technological advantage (IBM, Texas Instruments, Xerox), a unique product (Gillette, Kellogg), or a leading position in US industry (General Motors, International Telephone & Telegraph). Most of these subsidiaries were clones, so to speak, of the parent organisation, each with its miniature version of corporate headquarters.

Many of today's leading world enterprises are still structured along traditional lines. Yet the world around them has changed dramatically. Consider:

- Siting production facilities in low-labour-cost locations—the "global enterprise" model—is still

Source: This article is taken with special permission from *McKinsey Quarterly* (Spring 1985), pp. 7–20.

the fashion. Yet the economic advantages of doing so are likely to be short-lived. Most competitive Japanese companies, for instance, are today pulling out of Southeast Asia and investing in capital-intensive robots and machines.

• A strategy favoured by American MNCs has been to develop a proprietary technology and exploit it first domestically and then abroad. Today, they don't have time leisurely to market new and probably much more expensive technological developments; many competitors possess comparable technological skills, making it almost impossible to sustain a technological monopoly; and the global diffusion of new technology has become a matter of months, not years.

• In the Triad markets, a new breed of consumers is emerging, similar in education, income, life style and aspirations. These 600 million customers exhibit the same basic demand patterns and can be treated for marketing purposes as a single species. They all want the best products at the best price, regardless of origin.

• At the same time, protectionist pressures in each of the OECD countries are mounting, and economic nationalism is fueling a global trend toward bloc economies.

These interrelated forces have momentous implications.

CAPITAL-INTENSIVE OPERATIONS

Automation, robots, machining centres and numerical controls have vastly increased productivity in the past decade. They have halved the labour content of traditional assembly operations, facilitated quick changeovers in manufacturing processes and made possible greater flexibility in plant siting. Microprocessors have swiftly driven down the cost of computer power. Computer-aided design and manufacturing (CAD/CAM) are begetting a manufacturing revolution.

The competitive repercussions of this shift from labour to capital in production are already evident in the automobile industry. To produce over 13 million vehicles a year, the entire Japanese automobile industry (automakers, component suppliers and automobile contractors) employs only 670,000 people— slightly fewer than the global workforce of the single largest US automaker.

During the past decade, Toyota, while increasing its output 3½ times—to 3.3 million units a year—has, by reducing production man-hours, managed to maintain its workforce at about 45,000. The productivity of Toyota's rival Nissan is likewise about twice that of its global competitors. These companies have changed the traditionally labour-intensive auto industry into a capital-intensive business.

The story is the same in electronics. During the past five years, the workforce required to assemble a given consumer electronics product has been halved, and direct labour costs have been driven down to an average five per cent of total costs. Likewise, the semiconductor industry has become a fixed-cost, capital-intensive game, as opposed to the variable-cost, "learning"-intensive business of only five years ago.

The trend is even more prevalent in continuous processing industries like chemicals, textiles and steel, where automated control systems enhance productivity and competitiveness. In two of Japan's leading steel mills, Nippon Steel and Nippon Kokan KK, the labour tab hovers around ten per cent of total costs.

This shift from labour to capital intensity shatters the mirage of low-cost labour in developing countries. Companies used to locate their operations in low-labour-cost countries so as to bring down variable costs. Third World labour costs still average only a third of those in developed nations—but when direct labour content accounts for less than ten per cent of total manufacturing costs, the costs of transport and insurance can more than offset the advantages of cheap labour. For example, the typical cost of transporting a colour television set from Southeast Asia to California, including duties and insurance, is 13 per cent of free on board (FOB), totally out-weighing the ten per cent savings in labour cost.

CHANGED ECONOMICS

Typically, therefore, the economic tradeoff will favour siting a production facility either where the product will be sold or where important component parts are available. The same logic applies in industries where product life cycles are short: constant changes in moulds, jigs, tools and components make production locations remote from the core engineering group very inconvenient.

Together with the lack of qualified workers and local managers, these factors have reduced the attractiveness of siting production facilities in developing countries. The Japanese chipmakers have been the latest to learn first hand what the colour television (CTV) and textile industries discovered earlier: cheap, inexperienced labour must be trained and, once trained and experienced, does not stay cheap very long.

Managers in automated industries who fail to recognize the implications of this shift from labour to capital will find their profit margins severely squeezed. Automated operations are better equipped to fight inflation, since the ratio of labour cost to total manufacturing is bound to increase when sales are declining or wages rising. Automated operations also resist recession. Highly automated Japanese facilities such as Yamazaki (machine tools) and Fujitsu Fanuc (numerical controls) are said to break even at ten per cent of capacity. Other manufacturers like Toyota claim that they can operate at 70 per cent and still not lose money.

But this shift from labour- to capital-intensive production has a further consequence. To achieve the economies of scale needed to defray the heavy initial investment and the outlays for continuing production process innovation, deep and immediate market penetration becomes necessary. In the semiconductor and machine tool industries, even domestic markets as large as Japan or the United States have proved too small to support global-class automated plants.

At the same time, to keep product lines attuned to the demands of the market and to be responsive to competitive challenges, it is more vital than ever to be close to the customer. Constant product innovation and strongly entrenched distribution channels to reach prime markets may be key success factors. Once a product becomes, in effect, a commodity that can be made by numerous competitors, and cost-reduction opportunities are roughly the same for all participants, a superior distribution capability that enables a company to sell large volumes of non-differentiated products at the lowest cost to the end user becomes the key to survival.

COSTS OF DEVELOPMENT

The interaction between scientific disciplines, between industries, and between industries and services is blurring existing economic power patterns. So rapid has the pace of technological innovation and its commercialization become in the high-tech industries that a technological advantage can be eroded virtually overnight.

Five vanguard high-technology industries (electronics, data processing, telecommunications, fine chemicals and pharmaceuticals), accounting today for just over six per cent of GNP in the OECD nations, contributed no less than 16 per cent of their economic growth between 1975 and 1980. The same high-technology group averaged 1.49 times the sales growth, 2.8 times the labour productivity growth, and 2.75 times the profit growth of six medium-technology industries—iron and steel, automobiles, organic chemicals, textiles, non-ferrous metals, and pulp and paper. As can be seen from Exhibit 1, which compares the two groups in terms of the net profit on sales, it has become very difficult to make money in old-line industries that have become "engineered commodities."

The industries critical to wealth generation in the 1980s are all concentrated in Japan, Europe and the United States. More than 80 per

Exhibit 1   High Profits from High Technology

Net profit/sales ratio*

High technology industry	Old-line industry
Fine chemicals	Steel
Electronics	Light electric industry
Communications equipment	Automobiles
Office equipment	Petroleum refining
Computers	Textiles
Pharmaceuticals	Nonferrous metals
	Paper and paper products
	Fabricated metal products
	Ceramic, earths and stone

*World leading companies: weighted average of 1980 and 1981.

Source: *Economic Analysis of World Enterprise—International Comparison*, MITI, 1982.

cent of global production and consumption, and 85 per cent of patent registrations, are also taking place in the Triad.

As the costs of developing and commercialising new technologies keep rising, companies are moving in three directions to gain the benefits of integration and cross-fertilisation: (1) downstream, to control the interface with the customer, (2) upstream, to acquire new technologies or protect sources of expensive raw materials, and (3) horizontally, to share complementary technologies with the object of creating or exploiting new market opportunities.

The first two moves are obvious. As global competition intensifies, the management of fixed costs, particularly in R&D and distribution, becomes critical for creating wealth. The fixed cost of R&D, especially the cost of developing breakthrough technologies, is becoming so high that their global potential must be quickly exploited to the fullest. But this demands the ability to penetrate deeply into all critical markets.

Few corporations—apart, possibly, from the IBMs, Xeroxes and Kodaks of this world—command a distribution network capable of establishing a share of foreign markets comparable to their established domestic positions. For example, Toyota and Nissan, with domestic market shares of 38 per cent and 28 per cent respectively, have a combined share of only five per cent of the European Community (EC) and 12 per cent of the US markets. Even Sony has only an eight per cent market share in the US consumer television market, as against a 19 per cent share at home.

A natural strategic move, therefore, is to concentrate on strengthening R&D and domestic distribution. Once a corporation develops a unique technology, it can cross-license it to foreign counterparts in the other two regions of the Triad. Beside achieving high penetration and reducing marketing risks in difficult foreign markets, it can thereby gain attractive new technologies in return to be exploited in its own home markets. Such cross-licensing typically doubles or triples the potential of a technology, and maximises the contribution to the fixed costs of domestic distribution through the handling of products and technologies of foreign origin.

CO-OPERATIVE INITIATIVES

The third type of crossover is horizontal. In today's high-technology industries, no single company can control all the critical technological elements, ranging from memory microchips, image sensors and laser emitters to modems, optical transmission devices and the time division multiplex technique for the simultaneous transmission of voice and data over the same phone line.

As a result, any company that wants to compete in office automation, robotics, or consumer electronics markets must concentrate on a few critical internal R&D projects and develop a supersensitive control-tower function to constantly scan and monitor externally available technologies. In order to avoid the risk of losing out totally in a new game, a corporation may very well cross-fertilise with a complementary company, domestic or foreign, across a wide spectrum of the business system, from procurement, design and manufacturing to sales and servicing.

The signposts of structural shifts on a cross-national basis are all there. Companies vying for a piece of the potentially lucrative computer and communications pie are coming from all directions.

One example is the technological patent exchange between the two leviathans in telecommunications and computers, respectively—Japan's Nippon Telegraph and Telephone (NTT) and America's IBM. In Europe, American Telephone and Telegraph (AT&T) is invading IBM's turf with a computer, with help from Philips and Olivetti. American contenders in the Japanese office automation equipment market today include all the traditional and plug-compatible computer competitors, entrants from traditional "office equipment" makers (such as Xerox and Hewlett-Packard), a host of word-processor entrants led by Wang, and even a personal computer manufacturer or two.

Several of Japan's office automation leaders are arming themselves for the coming global battle for dominance through international alliances with competitors. Burroughs, which is trying to latch on to Hitachi's technological edge, is already packaging Fujitsu's high-speed facsimiles and is manufacturing Nippon Electric Company's (NEC's) optical character reading techniques under a royalty license. Toshiba's high-speed facsimiles are being distributed in the United States by Pitney Bowes and Telautograph, a subsidiary of the Arden Group, and by International Telephone & Telegraph (ITT) in Europe.

Even now, as the divergent, Japanese contenders and giant European computer and communications firms, each with different core strengths and economic bases, mingle with the more precisely defined American entrants in the office automation fray, the entire structure of the industry is undergoing a major transition. Meanwhile, to build the volume needed to survive in what promises to be a hotly contested share war, most major global players are tapping markets outside the Triad. Japan is pushing its office automation products in Asia, while US and European manufacturers are vying for a beachhead in Latin America. And everyone is hastening to establish procurement agents in East Asia to buy crucial components and subassemblies such as keyboards, disk drives, cathode ray tubes and printers.

ACCELERATING TIME FRAMES

The rapid rate of technological dispersal is a distinct and important phenomenon of its own. The basic research on the transistor, developed at Bell Laboratories in 1947, took over a decade. It was commercially introduced four years later, and another six years passed before it was incorporated into the computer. The integrated circuit, developed by Texas Instruments in 1958, took three years to become a viable product.

Now consider the accelerated time frame for major developments in the semiconductor during the past decade. It took two years in the United States for the chip to move from 4K- to 16K-bit random access memory (RAM). Less than eight months later the Japanese caught up with the United States. It took two years for the United States to move from 16K to 32K chips, less than three months for Japan to catch up. Then, in 1978, Japan's Fujitsu leap-frogged US suppliers and introduced the 64K microchip with a 3-month lead. In 1983, the Japanese started sample shipment of the 256K N-MOS dynamic RAM, and early in 1984 they started its commercial production. American firms are lagging behind by about a year on average.

The story is much the same in computers. In 1952, when IBM introduced its 701 model, it had four years' lead before competitors caught up. By 1980, when IBM introduced its powerful 308X model, it met competition head on. The rate of diffusion has become so fast that no one can hold a technological monopoly for long.

The strategic implications are threefold. First, technologically advanced companies cannot rest on their laurels. Second, challengers with me-too products may nevertheless have the clout to erode the leader's market share. Third, it costs so much to develop a technologically advanced and differentiated product that the producer must be able to sell to the entire world simultaneously in order to amortize the heavy front-end investment. Companies that choose to develop domestic markets first before going overseas may find themselves totally blocked out by well entrenched competitors set to invade their own home markets.

UNIVERSAL USERS

Whether it produces capital equipment or consumer goods, a company that ignores the universal market potential of the Triad does so at its peril. Not too long ago, capital equipment exhibited clear cultural distinctions: West German machines reflected that nation's penchant for craftsmanship, American equipment was often extravagant in its use of raw materials, and so on. Today, the best-selling factory machines have lost these distinguishing "art" elements. They have become alike in appearance and in the level of skills they require.

Even more conspicuously, consumers in the Triad have become increasingly alike. In his dark blue suit, Regal shoes and Céline necktie, carrying a Casio pocket calculator in his Mark Cross wallet, frequenting a nearby *sushi* bar for lunch, and commuting in a Celica, the typical New York businessman would not draw a second glance on the streets of Düsseldorf or Tokyo. Youngsters in Denmark, Germany, Japan and California are all growing up with ketchup, jeans and guitars and worshipping the universal "now" gods—ABBA, Levi's and Arpège. Within the Triad countries, in fact, age-group differences—the so-called generation gap—are more pronounced than differences of taste across national boundaries.

The Triad consumption pattern, which is both a cause and an effect of cultural patterns, is rooted largely in the educational system. As more people learn to use technology, their differences tend to disappear; thus, educating people to higher levels of technological achievement tends to eradicate differences in life styles. The nearly universal penetration of television has accelerated the trend.

A prime force behind the similarities and commonalities in the demand and life patterns of Triad consumers is purchasing power. In terms of per capita discretionary income, the purchasing power of Triad residents is more than ten times that of dwellers in the less-developed countries (LDCs) and newly-industralized countries (NICs). More than 94 per cent of households in Triad countries have television sets, as compared to about 60 per cent for the NICs and less than 20 percent for the LDCs. One-third of both Japanese and American consumers have a high-school education or better, as compared with 15 per cent of the population in NICs, and even fewer in the LDCs. Their purchasing power, their educational level, and what they read and see unite the Triadians and distinguish them from the rest of the world.

Another factor making for uniform Triadian demand patterns is similarity of technological infrastructure. For example, over 50 per cent of Triadian households have telephones, creating a hospitable environment for products like facsimile, telex and digital data transmission/processing equipment. High ratios of physicians to population stimulate the demand for pharmaceuticals and medical electronics. Well developed highway systems foster the rapid penetration of radial tires and sports cars—higher value-added products based on a higher level of technology.

Once these commonalities are recognized, universal products can be designed. The increasing commonality of life styles in Triad countries means that the company that comes up first with a universal product has the best chance of winning the global race for consumer acceptance. Companies like Seiko, Sony, Canon, Matsushita, Casio and Honda now routinely develop products against a global perspective. Their product designers spend as much as half their time abroad talking directly with their customers and dealers. When they return, they design and synthesise their global product based directly on their personal impressions.

This concentration of consumer and capital goods users within Japan, Europe and the United States is probably the primary trigger of global high-technology competition. The Triad is where the main action is.

NEO-PROTECTIONISM

Most Free World economies were in a severe slump in the early 1980s. High unemployment reduced purchasing power, leading to slowdowns in the automobile, consumer goods and construction industries, and in dependent businesses such as steel and component parts. These economic dislocations made it very difficult for national governments to resist political pressures for short-term remedies in the form of trade barriers. Some countries put up quotas and duties against all imports, others against imports of specific products coming from particular countries.

In consequence, if a company is not a recognized "insider" in a country important to its share growth, it may find the doors to that market tightly closed. The outsider's trade base is always fragile, whereas the insider's position is secure. For instance, Sony, which has a sizable plant in San Diego, escaped the quota and surcharge litigations and much of the ill-will directed against other Japanese colour television producers during the uproar over Japanese colour televisions in the United States.

Of course, governmental regulations and media headlines don't necessarily reflect the attitude of the public at large. The Japanese government may take a tough negotiating stance with the United States on beef and orange quotas, but that doesn't mean that Japanese consumers are any less keen to buy American oranges or beef. And, despite quotas, the American people clearly like Japanese colour televisions and automobiles.

Quite simply, customers everywhere want the best product for the price from anywhere in the world. That is the reason behind the increase in transnational trade, and hence in trade friction and artificial obstacles to the transnational flow of goods. That is why it is so important for a global corporation-to-be to establish a *de facto* insider position.

Paradoxically, this fragmentation of developed markets is taking place (and seemingly even intensifying) at a time when the residents of the Triad are emerging as a nearly homogeneous buying group. To respond to these two contrary phenomena, pragmatic business strategists must simultaneously develop a Triad perspective and accelerate their companies' "insiderization" in key markets.

TRIADIC STRATEGIES

As we have seen, the Japan-Europe-US Triad is where the major markets are. It is where the competitive threat comes from. It is where new technologies will originate. And, as competition becomes keener, it is where preventive action against protectionism will be needed most. Thus, in order to take advantage of the Triad's markets and emerging technologies and to prepare for new competitors, every multinational corporation must seek to become a true insider in all three regions.

An early presence in a new market provides clear advantages. When Tokyo Electric Company first introduced its electronic cash register and began to eat away at National Cash Register's (NCR's) market share in Japan, NCR's subsidiary operation in Japan was able to switch from electromechanical to electronic technology to stem the erosion before its domestic position was severely threatened. Xerox's pre-eminence in Japan helped it anticipate and respond to low-end technology being introduced by the Japanese plain paper copier manufacturers. Texas Instruments was able to produce 64K memory chips in Japan quickly, while other US companies were fighting off the intrusion of Japanese semiconductor houses in the United States. Each of these companies was able to adapt quickly to an emerging competitive situation by virtue of its insider position.

A company that can ensure it has equal penetration and exploitation capabilities in each of the Triad regions—and no blind spots—stands a good chance of becoming an effective Triad power. The first condition will ensure that it recovers its investment in unique and diversified products; the second, that it avoids surprises from foreign competitors, or from domestic competitors forming alliances with foreign companies. Failure to satisfy these two conditions allows a company to slip into a vicious cycle of decline: giving up its main market segments, concentrating on relatively peaceful niches, confining its activities to the domestic market, repeating the "cost reduction and removal of overhead" cycle, and ultimately losing its position as a major contender in the global marketplace.

The most significant advantage of becoming a Triad power, however, is not simply to stop this vicious cycle, but to pursue a positive and more offensive strategy. Knowing the basic desires of Triad consumers, the company can come up with a universal product. Or, having come up with a highly competitive basic product at home, it can tailor features and looks to local tastes. And it can market simultaneously to 600 million people.

With mighty salesforces in each of the three Triad regions, either their own or a partner's, companies can strike into the market in a rela-

tively short time, preempting both local and other global competitors and realizing high returns on their initial investment. With this profit, they can reinvest in more sophisticated and complex facilities and/or R&D, redoubling their competitive muscle. Should any local company come up with a high-potential new product, the Triad power can swiftly copy it and preempt the local competitors' opportunities in the other two Triad markets. With the profit thus generated, it can then comfortably engage in a head-to-head battle with the originating company on its own turf. That company must generate funds to fight back, although its profits from domestic sales may be hardly enough to recover its developments and launching costs.

The advantages of knowing the Triad customers and competitors as a true insider are so clear that the issue is not whether a company should become a Triad power, but how.

THE ROAD TO TRIAD POWER

Three vehicles can be used, alone or in combination, to become an effective Triad insider: wholly-owned subsidiaries, joint ventures, and consortia.

The Wholly Owned Subsidiary

This, the traditional MNC vehicle, needs no detailed discussion, but for successful implementation in the Triad context three points should be borne in mind: first, a "regional" rather than country-level structure should be established to share common resources; second, headquarters should play the role of strategic lubricator across key regions of the Triad rather than acting primarily as a controller; and finally, equal "citizenship" should be given to each of the Triad regions—and to any region outside the Triad where the company operates on a major scale (we could call this a "tetrahedral" model).

For example, the German chemical giant BASF, which reorganized in 1981, preserves the regional grouping of its nonstrategic areas, but treats the key strategic countries completely separately. The heads of BASF's US, Japanese and Brazilian subsidiaries (Brazil is an important "hinterland" for the company) each report directly to a member of the executive board. Tailor-made policies are worked out for each of the three areas. This kind of organisation is one realistic model for a multinational enterprise.

Despite Japan's critical strategic difference from other Asian countries, too many multinationals consign it to the Far East Department or the Pacific Basin Division of the International Business Sector, with the head of Japanese operations five levels below the CEO— literally, in some cases, below the level of a sales manager in Denver. Japanese companies make the same mistake when they send a deputy general manager from Production Planning to head up their US operations. This is the quickest way for a multinational corporation to undermine its prospects of succeeding as a Triad power.

The Joint Venture

Joint ventures are normally designed to take advantage of the strong functions of the partners and supplement their weak functions, be they management, research, or marketing. The recent announcement of a joint-venture plan in small business computers between Matsushita and IBM is a good example of resource sharing, with each company supplementing the other's functional strengths. This joint venture also testifies that even the biggest companies in two regions of the Triad cannot fight and win the electronics war single-handed.

Yamatake-Honeywell, in which Honeywell owns 50 per cent, the Yasuda group about 16.5 per cent, with the rest traded on the Tokyo Stock Exchange, has grown to be No. 2 in the Japanese process control and instrumentation field. Honeywell has been able to inject needed technologies, and the Japanese partner has supplied a stable management team.

American-Japanese joint ventures such as Yamatake-Honeywell, Carterpillar-Mitsubishi, Sumitomo-Minnesota Mining and Manufacturing (3M), and Fuji-Xerox are all ranked among the top three in their respective industries. Ebara-Infilco, owned until recently by Westinghouse's Infilco Division, is the biggest firm in the Japanese water treatment industry. This is doubly astonishing because more than 90 per cent of this company's work was in the public sector, which is notoriously intolerant of outsiders.

Philips has a long and successful history of joint ventures with Matsushita in electronic components. Similarly, Caterpillar's joint venture with Mitsubishi Heavy Industries has given it real staying power in the rather conservative earth-moving equipment market of Japan. High Voltage Industries (HVI), a 50:50 joint venture between GE and Hitachi in gas switch gear in Philadelphia, uses GE's mighty pooled sales force for utility customers and Hitachi's advanced gas diffusion technology.

Too often, however, joint ventures fail because of differences between the partners. Since a joint venture is a legal entity with equity sharing, the partners must decide formally how to share profit (or loss) and where and how to reinvest for the future. Unless their management philosophies are compatible, disputes over investments or resource allocation can frustrate common goals. All concerned need to understand at the outset that making a success of a joint venture involves at least as much pain and effort as building a new greenfield plant. Like a marriage, it will demand a lot of effort by both parties over a long period that may bring changes in the environment, in the aspirations of the partners, and in their relative strengths.

Unlike a marriage, though, a joint venture is constrained by numerous legal contracts and forms of capital participation. Instead of talking out their frustrations and differences, the partners are frequently all too quick to point out each other's violations of these legal contracts. Often, critical matters tend to be decided by vote, based on the partners' respective proportions of equity holding.

In my observation, majority voting seldom represents good business judgment and rarely favours entrepreneurial decisions. Indeed, if a voting process is needed to decide on critical matters, the chances are the joint venture has already failed. To put it another way, if your company needs the world's best lawyers to spell out all the possible details and countermeasures in potential disputes, you lack a sound basis for the joint venture. Two companies with "natural" fit are a rarity. Extremely careful planning, and a lot of giving, will be needed before the partners can begin thinking about jointly harvesting the fruits.

In short, the joint-venture route can be difficult because it involves matching two different corporate cultures by the artificial means of legal contracts. Ownership and control issues, which are fundamentally at odds with the spirit of pragmatic, entrepreneurial business, come into the picture. Unless the corporation is fully prepared to maintain the spirit of the joint venture without having recourse to contract, the long-term viability of the enterprise is questionable.

Companies that choose the joint-venture route to becoming a Triad power will be wise to follow a few simple guidelines:

• Make sure there is at least one key top management sponsor on each side of the venture, each firmly convinced that the undertaking is meaningful and will be good for his company.

• Keep these sponsors responsible for the joint venture for a decade at least.

• Ensure active cross-fertilization and frequent mutual face-to-face communications at the top management, operations management and workforce levels.

• Above all, communicate rather than control.

On the organisational side, a joint venture must be clearly positioned relative to existing divisions. Many joint ventures are formed by a handful of top executives and staff members, and their position in relation to the existing corporate functions and operating divisions is often unclear. Without full co-operation or resource reallocation, the joint venture becomes a stepchild.

The Consortium

Traditional multinationals tried to do everything on their own as they entered each market. Today, the skills and resources required to compete worldwide have increased so enormously that they can no longer "go it alone." All but a very few must rely for success on their ability to develop and enhance company-to-company relationships, particularly across national and cultural boundaries.

Given the difficulties a company faces in penetrating the major Triad markets on its own, or in adapting its established corporate culture to establish an insider position in the other regions of the Triad, the strategic benefits of forming a consortium of true insiders in the respective key regions are obvious. Such a consortium can enable each member company to enjoy almost instant access to a vast number of potential customers, and gain vital insight into the purchasing, manufacturing, marketing, distribution, personnel and financing aspects of operating everywhere in the tough but lucrative Triad markets.

The trend of recent consortia is toward sharing resources and swapping products to avert development risk. Instead of geographically close competitors joining forces, distant competitors are merging and sharing functions such as R&D and production: British Leyland produces a medium-sized Honda in the United Kingdom, while Nissan produces Volkswagen's Santana Model in Japan.

Many examples of emerging loose consortia can be seen today in such key industries as automobiles, semiconductors and steel. The rationale is to seek partners in other Triad regions to supplement functional shortcomings in order to survive and even expand in home regions. Typically, these consortia are formed to share or trade certain upstream functions such as R&D, production and technology, and to stay abreast of the leading-edge competitors. Sometimes they involve swapping certain product categories in order to take advantage of synergies made possible by sharing critical functions. Rarely does a partner give up an entire function.

This form of co-operation is becoming increasingly popular in industries once proverbial for tough competition. An executive vice president of a large US chemical company recently visited several Japanese chemical firms to explore areas of potential synergy. To his surprise, more than half of them expressed strong interest in sharing various resources. Many global enterprises today are willing to cooperate with their Triad-region competitors rather than fight them off in destructive trade wars.

Consortium alliances between competitors in the same Triad region should be avoided, however. Distant foes can be real friends, while close cousins can be enemies. Most of the European transnational mergers of the 1960s, involving links between similar companies, failed. Because they were too close, they could not work as partners and ended up at loggerheads.

The most useful ground rule in forming a consortium is to maximize the contribution to critical fixed costs. If R&D becomes expensive, make sure the resulting products are sold all over the world by licensing them to consortium allies, even though you may have some selling capabilities of your own in certain regions. If you have a costly, state-of-the-art production facility that could operate at low cost if fully utilised, then you should think about selling your products through any company with strong distribution capabilities, to original equipment manufacturers or under your own brand name. If you have a well-developed salesforce and/or distribution channel, but your laboratories cannot pump out enough new products, then think about importing attractive products made by other companies. Most product lines acquire a larger value-added increment during distribution than in production.

All these measures aim at maximizing the product's contribution to fixed costs by drawing on a global range of options. The message is: Enlarge your search for sources and potential contributors beyond your traditional neighborhood "shopping areas." Go global for the hunt. If your traditional rival is going global, then your only option is to do the same—but do it better.

The organizational implications of international consortia are complex. Collaborative arrangements with traditional competitors are seldom welcomed by middle managers, whose interest is to show top management that they are as capable as anyone else.

One essential step, therefore, is to conduct a good internal communications campaign to explain the intent of the consortium. Building executive relationships on several levels between the partners, and positioning a strong liaison officer at the top, are also vitally important. Too many consortia have been launched on a great wave of enthusiasm, only to fail subsequently for lack of any built-in means of sustaining it.

Most companies, while generously forgiving themselves their own mistakes, have a terrible habit of recriminating over their trading partner's errors. Maturity and diplomacy are required in a consortium to sustain constructive intercompany relationships.

Any corporation entering into consortium arrangements will need to keep two points in mind:

• Instead of cautious, suspicious and distant alliances of convenience, it will need to allow positive, proactive and strategic interlinkages—ultimately, if not at the outset—among all the participating partners.

• It must be prepared to gradually adjust its business system and terminology in order to minimize friction among the consortium members in communicating and agreeing on critical matters. Smooth communication among the partners at all times and at all levels of management is vital to the long-term success of a Triad consortium.

MARKS OF A TRIAD POWER

Whether it has achieved "insider" status through wholly-owned subsidiaries, joint-venture entities or loose consortium alliances, a true Triad power can be identified by a few distinctive characteristics:

1. Well established management systems in each of the Triad regions.
2. A full set of functions (possibly supplemented by headquarters or other regions where that makes strategic sense), fully responsive to local conditions.
3. Managers who are wholly familiar with local and regional customers and competitors.
4. Continuity of management, mostly with home-grown, overseas-trained personnel.
5. Swift, autonomous decision making, fully synchronized with the rest of the corporation. (Corporate headquarters, though fully informed, seldom interferes with regional management.)
6. Strong "staying power" in the key markets during periods of difficulty, and the capacity to come up with creative solutions to problems of market change.
7. Constant active communications—by telephone, personal visits and long-term exchange of people—within the corporation, at the interfaces with affiliated companies, and with headquarters.
8. Intolerance of the customary "it's out of my control" excuses for shortcomings and mistakes.
9. Significant presence and weight in the communities where its operations are located.
10. A corporate headquarters that functions simultaneously in three roles: as resource mobil-

iser, as interface lubricator and as strategic sensitiser.

The "resource mobiliser" role is self-evident in the case of wholly-owned subsidiaries. But even if a company takes the joint-venture or consortium route to Triad "insider" status, it must be prepared to allocate substantial funds and human resources to the venture with its partners. These alternatives to the on-your-own approach reduce the necessary commitment of management resources, but they must not be used to choke off the allocation of resources. Even a technical tie-up will not bear fruit unless both parties are willing to exchange people and experiment together, and prepared for plenty of "nice tries."

By the same token, corporate headquarters should take every opportunity to act to facilitate and lubricate the implementation strategies of consortia and/or joint ventures, rather than sit and wait for results to come in from the four corners of the world.

The final critical headquarters role is that of strategic sensitiser. If you are in the office automation industry, you had better be in California or Japan so that you can feel the "breathing" of the business. If you are a semiconductor manufacturer you need to visit Hamilton-Avnet, a large microchip distributor in the United States, or Kyushu, Japan's "silicon island," to feel the vibrations of the industry. These are the sensitive zones where trends can be detected first and where insiders can pick up market signals far ahead of competitors based elsewhere. Triad insiders in Japan were the first to pick up such subtle signals as the entry of Japanese sewing machine companies into the electronic typewriter business, or that of Sumitomo and Furukawa Copper Wire Works into fiber optics.

A true Triad insider can extract the strategic essence from these "sensitive zones" on behalf of its Triad partners. In its role as strategic sensitiser, headquarters will act to maximise corporate wealth by finding opportunities and eliminating blind spots over the entire Triad and its submarkets. It will pick up critical information in one region and preempt the opportunities of competitors in other regions. It will be alert to signals of structural change in consumers' desires, so that the company can come up with new product and/or service concepts. It will be able to identify and link up with dynamic new partners, catching its domestic and global competitors off guard.

CHALLENGE AND OPPORTUNITY

To sum up: Old strategies and organizational frameworks designed to reach 200 million customers at most have become obsolete in the Triad's new and dynamic markets of 600 million people, where consumers and industrial customers alike are becoming more and more homogeneous in their basic needs.

This growing universality of user characteristics and requirements gives global enterprises a powerful incentive to find ways of doing business in all parts of the Triad. But neither consumers nor industrial customers can be captured at a single sweep, using a monolithic approach and a single business system around the world.

Regional differences in business practice and in the local infrastructures of distribution, personnel, production and engineering, coupled with the political pressures of protectionism, make it necessary for the global enterprise to establish a true insider position in each of the key Triad regions. To succeed, it must be prepared to change its strategy, its structure and its traditional culture and value system, transforming itself into a new global entity with a significantly different chemistry and blood type—a Triad power.

STRATEGIC PLANNING FOR A GLOBAL BUSINESS

Balaji S. Chakravarthy
Howard V. Perlmutter

Strategic planning in a multinational corporation (MNC) has become progressively more complex over the years due to the globalization of its businesses and the increasing activism of its stakeholders. This paper reviews four generic planning systems that are available to an MNC for meeting this challenge and discusses the context in which each should be used.

Two recent trends have made strategic planning more complex in a multinational corporation

Professors Franklin Root, Peter Lorange, and Bruce Kogut offered valuable comments on an earlier version of this paper.

Source: Columbia Journal of World Business (Summer 1985), pp. 3–10.

(MNC): globalization of several industries and increased activism of its stakeholders. Until a decade ago, most multinational corporations did not seriously deal with either global integration or stakeholder activism.

A globally focused firm uses its worldwide system of resources to compete in national markets (Hout, Porter, and Rudden, 1982). Various country subsidiaries consequently become highly interdependent in their operational strategies, since the minimum volume necessary to exploit scale economies and experience effects is unavailable within a single national market. In order to be a viable competitor in a global business, an MNC must ensure tight integration of its worldwide operations.

Concurrent with the above trend has been the increasing pressure on MNCs from host governments. These stakeholders are forcing MNCs to concern themselves more with issues of legitimacy, that is, whether the actions of MNCs are consonant with the interests of the host country.

The fundamental planning challenge for an MNC is one of balancing the economic imperative of global integration with the political imperative of prudent stakeholder management (Doz, 1980). In an extreme case, the two can pull in opposite directions. Giving the subsidiary autonomy to pursue a strategy responsive to host government needs can nurture legitimacy, but it must be balanced with suitable controls to ensure proper integration of the subsidiary's strategy with that of other subsidiaries. This paper focuses on the role of strategic planning systems in bringing about such a balance.

The paper is divided into two main sections. The first section elaborates the planning challenge. The second section describes briefly the choice of strategic planning systems currently available to an MNC and assesses their relevance for a global business.

THE CHALLENGES FOR STRATEGIC PLANNING

Three important contextual factors define the business planning challenge faced by an MNC:

- The *economic imperative* that determines where the MNC should locate various elements of the value chain for a given business;
- The *political imperative* as shaped by the demands of the host countries in which the MNC operates; and
- The MNC's own *strategic predisposition*.

The Economic Imperative

Based on the economic forces operating in an industry, Porter (1984) offers two distinct strategic options for an MNC: a global strategy (cost leadership, differentiation, and segmentation) and a country-centered strategy (national responsiveness, or protected markets). Each of these strategies is distinguished by two criteria: (1) extent of global centralization/coordination, and (2) breadth of target segments within the industry (see Chart 1).

A primary determinant of whether a firm should pursue a global or country-centered strategy is the proportion of value added in the upstream activities of the industry's value chain. In industries such as automobiles, motorcycles, chemicals, steel, and heavy electrical systems, where significant value is added in upstream activities (i.e., R&D and manufac-

Chart 1   Strategic Alternatives in a Global Industry

		Extent of Global Centralization/Coordination		
Breadth of Broad		Global Cost Leadership	Global Differentiation	Protected Markets
Target Segments Within the Industry Narrow		Global Segmentation		National Responsiveness
		Global Strategy		Country-Centered Strategy

Source: Porter (1984).

turing), MNCs have found it advantageous to pursue a global strategy. On the other hand, in industries such as insurance and consumer packaged goods, where a substantial proportion of value is added in downstream activities (i.e., marketing, sales and service), a country-centered strategy has been more viable.

However, even within an industry, the choice of strategy depends on the segments of the value chain that a firm competes in. For example, if a firm in the aircraft industry merely sells and services aircrafts worldwide, a country-centered strategy may be appropriate to it. Similarly, if there are global customers for an insurance company's product (e.g., marine insurance), the company may have to pick a global strategy. As a corollary, a vertically integrated firm can choose to pursue different strategies for different segments of the industry's value chain.

Globalization of industries is on the rise because of the increasing potential for centralization and coordination of business activities (Porter, 1984). The move towards centralization is helped by the continuing homogenization of product needs among countries and the marketing systems and business infrastructure through which these needs are served. Cheaper and more reliable transportation has also contributed to centralization. (The lack of such transportation was a major deterrent to intercountry shipments in the past.) Greater coordination is being facilitated primarily by the international communications revolution. Integrated transmission of voice, data, and video signals worldwide is projected to become a reality in the near future. The emergence of global buyers and suppliers also calls for greater coordination between the various subsidiaries of an MNC.

The above analysis of the economic imperatives confronting an MNC would suggest that global strategies (both cost leadership and differentiation) will displace country-centered strategies in several industries. However, the new political imperatives faced by an MNC

represent a countertrend towards national responsiveness. These will be examined next.

The Political Imperative

Doz and Prahalad (1980) offer a useful framework for understanding the political imperatives that drive the business strategies of an MNC. They define two important determinants of business context: (1) the bargaining power of the MNC, and (2) the bargaining power of the host government. The bargaining power of the MNC is based on three sources: proprietary technology, worldwide market share (economies of scale), and product differentiation. The bargaining power of the host government is derived from its desire and ability to control market access, and the size and attractiveness of the national market that it controls.

In situations where the MNC is a technology or market leader and where the bargaining power of the host government is weak, a global integration strategy is appropriate. For example, Boeing could choose a global integration strategy in Europe because of its relative power over host governments (Doz and Prahalad, 1980). Boeing is a technology leader with a dominant share of the world market. Consequently, the host governments could not force it to adopt a more country-centered strategy.

On the other hand, in situations where the power balance is skewed in favor of the host government, a country-centered strategy is more appropriate. Examples of such an approach are provided by Honeywell in France and Chrysler in the UK (Doz and Prahalad, 1980).

The push towards country-centered strategies comes from the growing number of powerful external stake-holders. Management must not only worry about an MNC's viability (i.e., meeting its profit objectives), but also about its legitimacy (i.e., stakeholder perceptions as to whether the firm's activities are consonant with the values of the host country), (Heenan and Perlmutter, 1979).

Home and host governments are key external stakeholders, and both have begun to regulate MNC activities with increasing sophistication. In addition to its role as a regulator, the host government can engage in other relationships with an MNC: as a co-negotiator (along with unions in labor relations), as a supplier (where public utilities and raw material industries may be state owned), as a competitor (through its public sector corporations), or even as a distributor (where channels are state owned). In coping with powerful external stakeholders such as the host government, the MNC requires strategies that are tailored to each national context.

Strategic Predisposition

The strategic predisposition of a firm is shaped by a number of factors: the circumstances of its birth, the leadership style of its CEOs, its past administrative practices, the myths and folklore that have endured in the organization, etc. Heenan and Perlmutter (1979) describe four distinct predispositions in an MNC:

- *Ethnocentrism* is a predisposition where all strategic decisions are guided by the values and interests of the parent. Such a firm is predominantly concerned with its viability worldwide and legitimacy only in its home country.
- *Polycentrism* is a predisposition where strategic decisions are tailored to suit the cultures of the various countries in which the MNC competes. A polycentric multinational is primarily concerned with legitimacy in every country that it operates in, even if that means some loss of profits.
- *Regiocentrism* is a predisposition that tries to blend the interests of the parent with that of the subsidiaries at least on a limited regional basis. A regiocentric multinational tries to balance viability and legitimacy at the regional level.
- *Geocentrism* is a predisposition that seeks to integrate diverse subsidiaries through a global systems approach to decision making. A geocentric firm tries to balance viability and legitimacy through a global networking of its businesses. On occasion, these networks may even include the firm's stakeholders and

competitors. Geocentrism can be further classified as enclave or integrative geocentrism. The former deals with high priority problems of host countries in a marginal fashion; the latter recognizes that the MNC's key decisions must be separately assessed for their impact on each country.

The above predispositions are seldom found in their pure form. An MNC's predominant predisposition is called its EPRG profile. An ethnocentric or polycentric EPRG profile is very common (Perlmutter, 1969), while a regiocentric or geocentric EPRG profile is relatively new among MNCs. Each EPRG profile is associated with a distinct social architecture (Perlmutter, 1984). The mission, governance structure, strategy, organization structure, and culture associated with the four EPRG profiles are described in Table 1.

The administrative systems associated with each EPRG profile reinforce one another and over a period of time define the distinct mode in which an MNC adapts to its environment. In a sense, the profile gets institutionalized and dictates the firm's behavior in a variety of functions (Table 2). In an ethnocentric multinational, for example, marketing, manufacturing, finance, and personnel decisions are typically made at headquarters with very little input from country managers.

The predisposition of an MNC can be at odds with the strategy appropriate to its economic or political imperatives. For example, an ethnocentric firm may find it difficult to adopt a nationally responsive strategy, or a polycentric firm may not be successful in implementing a global integration strategy.

STRATEGIC PLANNING SYSTEMS: CHOICES AND LIMITATIONS

The three forces described in the previous section can and often do pull in different directions. In fact, the planning challenge is to reconcile their differences. For ease of exposition, we will represent the various business con-

Table 1 Orientation of the Firm under Different EPRG Profiles

Orientation of the Firm	EPRG PROFILE:			
	Ethnocentric	Polycentric	Regiocentric	Geocentric
1. MISSION	Profitability (viability)	Public acceptance (legitimacy)	Both profitability and public acceptance (viability and legitimacy)	
2. GOVERNANCE • Direction of goal setting	Top down	Bottom up (each subsidiary decides upon local objectives)	Mutually negotiated between region and its subsidiaries	Mutually negotiated at all levels of the corporation
• Communication	Hierarchical, with headquarters giving high volume of orders, commands and advice	Little communication to and from headquarters and between subsidiaries	Both vertical and lateral communication within region	Both vertical and lateral communication within the company
• Allocation of resources	Investment opportunities decided at headquarters	Self-supporting subsidiaries, no cross-subsidies	Regions allocate resources, under guidelines from headquarters	Worldwide projects, allocation influenced by local and headquarters' managers
3. STRATEGY	Global integrative	National responsiveness	Regional integrative and national responsiveness	Global integrative and national responsiveness
4. STRUCTURE	Hierarchical product divisions	Hierarchical area divisions, with autonomous national units	Product and regional organizations tied through a matrix	A network of organizations, (including some stakeholders and competitor organizations)
5. CULTURE	Home country	Host country	Regional	Global

Source: Perlmutter (1984); Heenan and Perlmutter (1979).

texts that an MNC can experience in a two dimensional framework (Chart 2).

The strategic planning systems that have been used in the past by large diversified corporations fall under four distinct categories: Model I, or top-down planning; Model II, or bottom-up planning; Model III, or portfolio planning; and Model IV, or dual structure planning (Chakravarthy and Lorange, 1984). The ability of each of these systems to balance viability and legitimacy in the distinct business contexts defined by Chart 2 are discussed below.

Model I: Planning for Cell 4

Model I, a top-down approach to planning, seeks to provide the MNC with a global competitive advantage through tight integration of its worldwide activities.

A Model I company is typically organized into several product groups worldwide. It is the responsibility of each product group manager to ensure the needed global integration through an elaborate formal plan that is monitored for progress each month at all levels of management. This planning system is associated with a

Table 2 EPRG Profile in Different Functional Areas

Functional Area	EPRG PROFILE:			
	Ethnocentric	Polycentric	Regiocentric	Geocentric
TECHNOLOGY				
Production technology	Mass production	Batch production	Flexible manufacturing	Flexible manufacturing
MARKETING				
Product planning	Product development determined primarily by the needs of home country customers	Local product development based on local needs	Standardize within region, but not across	Global product, with local variations
Marketing mix decisions	Made at headquarters	Made in each country	Made regionally	Made jointly with mutual consultation
FINANCE				
Objective	Repatriation of profits to home country	Retention of profits in host country	Redistribution within region	Redistribution globally
Financing relations	Home country institutions	Host country institutions	Regional institutions	Other global institutions
PERSONNEL PRACTICES				
Perpetuation	People of home country developed for key positions everywhere in the world	People of local nationality developed for key positions in their own country	Regional people developed for key positions anywhere in the region	Best people everywhere in the world developed for key positions everywhere in the world
Evaluation and control	Home standards applied for persons and performance	Determined locally	Determined regionally	Standards which are universal, weighted to suit local conditions

Source: Heenan and Perlmutter (1979); Perlmutter (1984).

large and powerful planning staff at the headquarters, who carefully scrutinize and independently double check all strategic plans proposed by the national unit managers.

The legitimacy issue is dealt with in such a system through additional "citizenship costs" incurred by each subsidiary (Doz and Prahalad, 1980).

In other words, the MNC using a Model I planning system chooses to pay the penalty for nonconformance with the host government's demands in the forms of higher import duties and taxes. For a period under Harold Geneen, ITT was a company that followed such a system of planning (Kotter, Schlesinger and Sathe, 1979).

Chart 2 A Framework for Choosing Strategic Planning Systems

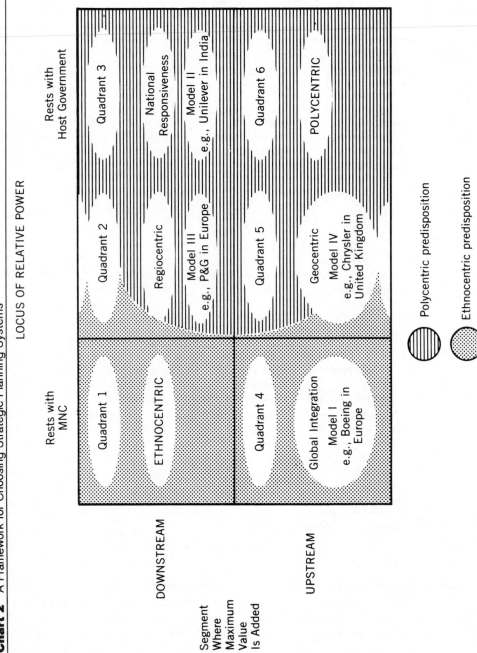

The business context to which this system is best suited is cell 4. Cell 4 represents a business context where global integration is desirable and possible. The relatively high value that is added upstream suggests that the pooling of R&D and manufacturing activities among the MNC's various subsidiaries can result in important cost savings. A centrally coordinated strategic plan can facilitate the proper scheduling of these activities. Moreover, given that the locus of relative power rests with the MNC, it will face few obstacles from the host government for such an integration. Boeing's aircraft business in Europe falls in this cell. Other examples are IBM or AT&T (eventually) in world markets. This is not to suggest that these companies are restricted only to a Model I planning system, but to point out that given their contexts, they can use such a system.

It must be noted, however, that the locus of relative power can shift back to the host government if there are other eager competitors who are willing to collaborate with it. In fact, like in the case of Honeywell in France, the host government can provide suitable incentives to attract a "weak" MNC. This can mean loss of market for a Model I MNC. A Model I planning approach must be tempered, therefore, with some sensitivity to the needs of the host country.

Model II: Planning for Cell 3

A firm using a Model II planning system is typically organized by geographic areas (as opposed to product groups as in Model I). The smallest geographic unit is a national unit. Each national unit is delegated the responsibility for balancing its legitimacy and viability goals within broad guidelines issued by headquarters. The subsidiaries behave as if they are national companies. There are very few functional interdependencies across national units, and headquarters seldom resort to cross-subsidies. Typically, monitoring and control

are financially oriented in a Model II planning system. The headquarters has a very thin corporate planning staff who act primarily as consolidators of national unit business plans.

Theoretically, a Model II planning system can be very responsive to the needs of the host government, but at costs in the duplication of resources and limits to the economic advantages of multinationality. A Model II firm has competitive advantages over a national firm only in a few domains: pooling of financial risks, sharing of R&D costs, coordination of export marketing, and some skill transfers among subsidiaries. If Model I was overly focused on the economic imperative, Model II is especially partial to the political imperative.

Model II is best suited to a cell 3 business. Cell 3 represents a business where the economic imperative (high value added downstream) and the political imperative both point to a national responsiveness strategy. Unilever's operations in India are a case in point. The subsidiary sells consumer products, toiletries and animal feed, none of which lies in the core of essential industrial sectors as defined by the Indian government. Consequently, Unilever can operate in India only on the government's terms. In such a setting, a Model II planning process is quite appropriate. The parent exercises largely financial control and provides the subsidiary with technical and managerial assistance and with help in its export efforts when sought.

Model III: Portfolio Planning

Models I and II are suitable only for select business segments of a MNC and cannot be used consistently throughout the firm. Model I presumes that national stakeholders can be appeased by paying suitable citizenship costs. As the recent woes of Union Carbide in Bhopal, India, would point out, citizenship costs currently are being measured by more exacting world standards. Consequently, a planning orientation like Model I that completely ignores legitimacy issues can eventually hurt even the firm's viability.

On the other hand, a planning orientation that is predominantly responsive to national interests ignores the many advantages of multinationality. Given the trend towards globalization in many industries, a Model II planning orientation can hurt the competitive position of an MNC in world markets.

Instead of selecting one of the two pure archetypes discussed above, a diversified MNC can use both planning systems to suit its different business contexts. This approach is also called portfolio planning. An MNC using a Model III planning system is typically organized in global product divisions like a Model I firm. However, unlike a Model I firm, it uses a top-down or bottom-up planning process, depending on the context of each of its businesses. This is a popular approach among MNCs. According to a recent survey, over fifty percent of all US-based diversified MNCs use this system of planning (Haspeslagh, 1982).

The attractiveness of an industry environment and the competitive strengths of the firm in that industry are normally the two determinants of whether the business will be subjected to a Model I or Model II planning system. A business in a growing national market where the company is trying to build market share will typically employ Model II planning, while a business in a maturing or mature national market where the company has a strong competitive position will generally use a Model I planning process. This is consistent with the emphasis on marketing (country-centered strategy) in the first business as the MNC tries to build market share, and on manufacturing and distribution (global integration strategy) in the second business as it seeks to improve operational efficiency.

Portfolio planning is best suited to a cell 1 or cell 2 business context. In either case, given the MNC's relative power over its host countries, it is free to attempt at least limited coordination among groups of countries in a region. Each such region is treated as a planning unit in a Model III system.

The Model III planning approach is most effective only when the planning challenge can be neatly compartmentalized as either integrative (regional integration) or adaptive (national responsiveness), (Lorange, 1980). This is indeed possible in several business contexts. The economic forces faced by a firm need not always be in conflict with the political forces. As Porter (1984) points out:

Some economic forces favor standardization (e.g., scale economies) but others favor country-centered strategies (e.g., product heterogeneity and transport costs). Similarly, there are political forces working towards a country-centered strategy (e.g., local content rules and local ownership laws) and political forces favoring global strategies (export subsidies, R&D support for targeted industries). (p. 30)

Designing a planning system that simultaneously encourages adaptation and integration within a region is, however, difficult. For example, in industries like telecommunications, a global integration strategy can optimally exploit special upstream resources like R&D and manufacturing; however, given the salience of this industry to national economies, host governments are likely to insist on a country-centered strategy.

Moreover, the assumption of Model III that a country unit can be initially subjected to a country-centered strategy (Model II) and then switched to a regional integration strategy (Model I), may be untenable in countries where such integration implies retrenchment in investment. This is especially true in countries where the MNC has several business interests. The host country can use its leverage in one business to extract concessions in another, where the MNC supposedly has more power over the host country. A sequential attention to the legitimacy and viability needs of a business, as proposed in Model III, needs to be replaced therefore with a system that can ensure simultaneous attention to these needs. Model IV on Dual Structure Planning is such a system.

Model IV: Dual Structure Planning

A cell 5 or cell 6 business context is the most difficult since it simultaneously requires a global integration and national responsiveness orientation. For example, Chrysler's operations in the UK should be responsive to the host government, while at the same time derive global integrative advantages to compete successfully with other international auto manufacturers.

In order to use a dual structure planning system, the MNC must be organized in a matrix structure, with product and area as its two dimensions. A planning system can then be designed to stress adaptation along one dimension and integration along the other (Lorange, 1976). If, for example, the corporation wants the subsidiary to be country-centered, it should use an adaptive orientation for strategies formulated by the business side of the matrix, and use the area dimension of the matrix for integration. In other words, while national unit managers have leeway in adapting the company's business to their local environments, they would still be answerable for profit performance set through the budgeting process. Conversely, to implement a global business strategy, the MNC should allow adaptation on the area dimension at the national unit level while ensuring integration through the product dimension of the matrix. Thus, the integrative side of the matrix becomes in effect the operating structure, while the adaptive dimension becomes the strategic structure (Lorange, 1984).

The relative emphasis on adaptation or integration within a national market can be altered by moving key managers to the appropriate side of the matrix, and by altering the planning, control, and reward systems used in that country (Prahalad, 1976). The planning system acts

like a lens to focus the matrix structure toward a national responsive or global integrative orientation as required from country to country. It also leads to a more balanced orientation within each country than that provided by a Model III, especially if the MNC's culture encourages healthy confrontation between the two sides of the matrix. An example of a company that uses a dual structure planning is IBM. It is most useful to firms that are not widely diversified and that derive their competitive advantage from a common product-market, technology, or operation base.

A Model IV planning system can theoretically provide the simultaneous balance required between legitimacy and viability. The relative power difference between the two dimensions of the global matrix can be set at different equilibrium levels to suit each business context. However, fine tuning a global matrix structure through a Model IV planning system requires the simultaneous support of several other administrative systems including staffing, control, and reward systems. (Doz and Prahalad, 1981). The orchestration of all of these systems can easily become an administrative nightmare (Davis and Lawrence, 1977). A recent survey showed that less than 5 percent of all MNCs attempted such a planning system (Haspeslagh, 1982).

CONCLUSIONS

The discussion in the previous sections showed how currently available planning systems are not quite suited to the needs of a global business. One way of dealing with this problem would be for the MNC to position itself in quadrants where the economic and political pressures are not conflicting. It can also attempt to rectify power imbalances with the host government by manipulating the resource dependencies of the subsidiary. However, as was pointed out earlier, current trends suggest that increasing numbers of global businesses will face the simultaneous challenge of global integration and national responsiveness. A hybrid of Model III and Model IV will be the best initial option for meeting this twin challenge.

A Hybrid Planning System

The Model IV planning system proposed in the previous section can theoretically help balance the visibility and legitimacy goals of an MNC. However, as mentioned earlier, dual structure planning is relatively new. Instead of attempting a company wide Model IV planning approach, it is perhaps more prudent to first attempt Model IV planning only within select regions where there are strong pressures for both legitimacy and viability (Chakravarthy, 1984). Other regions can be managed using a Model III planning system.

In such a system, the headquarters must help balance the region's orientation towards integration and national responsiveness by maintaining a counterbalancing functional and administrative view. In other words, if the region seems to be veering off to a nationally responsive orientation, staff advisors at the headquarters must be managers who are biased towards global integration. Finally, the monitoring, control, and reward systems must acknowledge performance towards the goals of all major stakeholders of the firm, and not merely those of the stockholders of the parent company. The proposed hybrid system is discussed at length in a follow-up paper.

Strategic Predisposition

The major bottleneck we anticipate in implementing the hybrid planning system discussed above is the predominant ethnocentric predisposition exhibited by most MNCs. An ethnocentric firm essentially focuses on bottom line profits, and treats all political imperatives as unnecessary constraints. Even a polycentric firm pursues a country-centered strategy vigorously only when it is dictated by an economic

imperative (cell 3 in Chart 2), and not as enthusiastically when imposed by a political imperative (cells 1 and 2 in Chart 2). The governing management paradigm in most MNCs seem to be overly biased towards viability (Perlmutter, 1984).

On the other hand, most host governments expect the MNC to treat political imperatives as goals and economic imperatives (reasonable profits) as constraints. The mindsets of the MNC managers and their international stakeholders would seem to be irreconcilably different. Unless an MNC begins to change its predisposition, it is headed on a collision course with its stakeholders, regardless of the planning system that it uses.

The real challenge for an MNC is then to alter its predisposition to a more regiocentric or geocentric orientation (Perlmutter, 1984). On occasion, the MNC may have to seek the cooperation of select competitors and important stakeholders in order to proactively simplify the environment in which it competes. Cooperation and competition are both accepted strategies under a geocentric predisposition.

The most important instrument available for changing the predisposition of an MNC is human resource management. Very few managers have personally internalized and resolved the tension between maximizing the firm's profit goals and emphasizing the needs of the host government. It is important, therefore, that the personnel policies of an MNC ensure: (1) that the proper mix of attitudes is nurtured through job rotation, promotion, and placement; and (2) that job assignments are carefully made in keeping with the manager's attitudes. The critical determinant of an MNC's successful adaptation to its environment is its ability to nurture relevant attitudes in its managerial work force.

REFERENCES

Chakravarthy, B. S., "Strategic Adaptation to Deregulation: Toward a Conceptual Framework," working paper

WP 84-07, Reginald Jones Center, The Wharton School, 1985.

Chakravarthy, B. S., "Strategic Self-renewal: A Planning Framework for Today," *The Academy of Management Review,* 1984, 9(3), 536–547.

Chakravarthy, B. S., and P. Lorange, "Managing Strategic Adaptation: Options in Administrative Systems Design," *Interfaces,* 1984, 14(1), 34–46.

Davis, S., and P. Lorange, *Matrix.* Reading, Mass.: Addison-Wesley, 1977.

Doz, Y. L., "Strategic Management in Multinational Companies," *Sloan Management Review,* 1980, 21(2), 27–46.

Doz, Y. L., and C. K. Prahalad, "Headquarters Influence and Strategic Control in MNCs," *Sloan Management Review,* Fall 1981, 15–29.

Haspeslagh, P., "Portfolio Planning: Uses and Limits," *Harvard Business Review,* 1982, 60(1), 58–73.

Heenan, D. A., and H. V. Perlmutter, *Multinational Organizational Development: A Social Architecture Perspective.* Reading, Mass.: Addison-Wesley, 1979.

Hout, T., M. E. Porter, and E. Rudden, "How Global Companies Win Out," *Harvard Business Review,* 1982, 60(5), 98–108.

Kotter, J. P., L. A. Schlesinger, and V. Sathe, *Organization:* *Text, Cases and Readings.* Homewood, Ill.: Richard D. Irwin, 1979, 271–310.

Lorange, P., "A Framework for Strategic Planning in Multinational Corporations," *Journal of Long Range Planning,* June 1976, 276–288.

Lorange, P., *Corporate Planning: An Excessive View Point.* Englewood-Cliffs, N.J.: Prentice-Hall, 1980.

Lorange, P., "Organizational Structure and Management Processes: Implications for Effective Strategic Management," in W. Guth (ed.), *Handbook of Strategic Management.* New York: Warren, Gorham, and Lamont, 1984.

Perlmutter, H. V., "The Tortuous Evolution of the Multinational Corporation," *Columbia Journal of World Business,* January–February 1969, 9–18.

Perlmutter, H. V., "Building the Symbiotic Societal Enterprise: A Social Architecture for the Future," *World Futures,* 1984, 19(3/4), 271–284.

Porter, M. E., "Competition in Global Industries: A Conceptual Framework," paper presented at the Prince Bertil Symposium on Strategies for Global Competition, Stockholm School of Economics, November 7–9, 1984.

Prahalad, C. K., "Strategic Choices in Diversified MNCs," *Harvard Business Review,* 1976, 54(4), 67–78.

7

DESIGNING GLOBAL STRATEGIES: COMPARATIVE AND COMPETITIVE VALUE-ADDED CHAINS
Bruce Kogut

The design of international strategies is based upon the interplay between the comparative advantages of countries and the competitive advantages of firms. These two advantages

Research for this article was funded by the Reginald H. Jones Center of The Wharton School. The author thanks Ned Bowman, Paul Browne, Jean Francois Hennart, Laurent Jacque, Franklin Root, Harbir Singh, and Louis Wells for their help.

Source: Sloan Management Review (Summer 1985), pp. 15–28.

determine the answer to the two principal questions in international strategy:

1. Where should the value-added chain be broken across borders?
2. In what functional activities should a firm concentrate its resources?

Answers to both of these questions are affected by comparative and competitive advantage. Comparative advantage, sometimes referred to as location-specific advantage, influences the decision of *where* to source and market. It is based on the lower cost of a factor (labor, for example) in one country relative to another, favoring industries that use this factor intensively. Competitive advantage, sometimes referred to as firm-specific advantage, influences the decision of *what* activities and technologies along the value-added chain a firm should concentrate its investment and managerial resources in, relative to other firms in its industry. It stems from some proprietary characteristic of the firm, such as a brand name, which cannot be imitated by rivals without substantial cost and uncertainty.[1] The value-added chain is the process by which technology is combined with material and labor inputs, and then processed inputs are assembled, marketed, and distributed. A single firm may consist of only one link in this process, or it may be extensively vertically integrated, such as steel firms that carry out operations that range from mining ore to fabricating final goods.

Competitive and comparative advantages are not completely independent of each other. Firms differ in location of sourcing of their production and can, therefore, acquire a competitive edge with superior exploitation of the comparative advantages among countries. Thus, differences between firms regarding the location of their sourcing can give rise to strategic advantages. It is therefore important to distinguish between strategies based on competitive advantage and those based on comparative advantage.

It is the interaction between comparative and competitive advantage in the international strategy of firms that is examined in this article. The concept of the value-added chain is developed in order to analyze the competitive position of the firm in a global industry. The first section develops the use of the value-added chain for structuring the strategic allocation decision. The second section turns to developing the concept of comparative advantage; an international production chain for countries is derived from differences in factor costs. The third and fourth sections illustrate the use of the value-added chain as a tool in delineating the interplay of comparative and competitive advantages by analyzing changes in the world economy. From this analysis, three generic modes of international competition emerge.

COMPETITIVE ADVANTAGE AND THE VALUE-ADDED CHAIN

Strategy formulation can be seen as the selection of product/market allocation decisions that promise to generate what economists call economic rents. In layman's terms, this means profitability in excess of the competitive norm. To capture economic rents, a firm must devise a strategy that is superior to the competition. Techniques of strategy formulation are heuristic guides that aid firms in analyzing their competition and allocating resources to the most profitable courses of action. One such technique is industry competitive analysis. A second, and complementary, technique is the analysis of market segments in search of insights that will guide the allocation of resources to different productive units of the corporation. These productive units can be depicted, as will be shown later, by a value-added chain.

Consider first the technique of industry competitive analysis.[2] This technique implicitly begins with a static model of profit determination which is then expanded to incorporate how firms "game" against one another. The logic of the model commonly specifies two kinds of generic strategies. The first is characteristic of firms in a highly competitive industry in which products are qualitatively similar. In such industries, strategies tend to be *low-cost* oriented in order to either increase margins or lower prices. The danger of the latter strategy, of course, is that firms will simultaneously cut prices in anticipation of scale or experience economies, resulting in cutthroat competition. In less competitive industries, firms follow revenue-oriented strategies by *differentiating* their products. Rivalry by physically or psychologically differentiating products also spills back into price competition, as products invariably face competition from approximate substitutes.

The generic strategies of low-cost and differentiation are useful for categorizing competitive strategies but in themselves do not suggest where costs should be cut or how products should be differentiated. For these purposes, the value-added chain is a surprisingly easy yet powerful concept.[3] The measurement of the links of the value-added chain should be defined differently depending upon whether the firm is pursuing a low-cost or a differentiated strategy.

THE VALUE-ADDED CHAIN

For designing strategies in highly competitive markets, the value-added chain is best defined in terms of each link's contribution to total cost. (In the case of multiproduct firms, there may be horizontal links as well.) For many of these links, there exist price data on the value of intermediate products when these products are traded in markets. In some cases, firms have, or can acquire, fairly accurate estimates of the production costs of competitors. By comparing the costs incurred by each link and against competitors, a firm can locate the "critical success factors" that must be addressed. Such a comparison can lead to radical changes in strategy, such as the decision to divest or to acquire new technologies in certain links.[4]

The example of the American steel industry can be used to illustrate an application of value-added chain analysis in this vein. The American steel industry has consisted traditionally of large, vertically integrated carbon steel makers, some of whom are integrated from ore mining to finished products. Recently, their profitability has been abysmal, the result of in-roads made by mini-mills in long products (e.g., rails and bars) and import competition. Because of the increased competition, the carbon steel manufacturers have little power in influencing the price they charge on long products. (Flat products, e.g., sheet, tend to be more differentiated.) Faced with increased price competition and large investments in fixed assets, carbon steel producers must choose either a dramatic curtailment of crude steel production and a focus on flat and specialty steel products, or a cut in costs. In this context, the value-added chain has been particularly useful in suggesting those links that are not cost competitive.[5]

For designing strategies in industries where competition is driven by product differentiation, the value-added chain is best defined in terms of the contribution of each link to market value. The estimation of contribution to market value is not straight-forward, but such a calculation underlies any strategic plan that seeks to generate economic rents. The determination of market value contribution leads to a mapping of the product attributes most strongly desired by consumers back upon the links of the value-added chain that generate this attribute.[6] For example, if consumers desire a home computer that is supported by strong after-sales service, and the firm is able to provide this service better than its competition, the implication for resource allocations is to shift investment from other links of the value-added chain in order to invest in the downstream link of servicing channels. The key question becomes what links of the value-added chain generate those attributes most strongly desired by consumers and which of those attributes correspond to the present and potential competitive advantage of a firm.

It is important to emphasize the last phrase of the above sentence. If the only issue were to determine demand for product attributes, strategy would simply be a market research question. But assets that underlie the production of these attributes are not easily redeployed along the value-added chain, nor is product or process imitation between competitors without uncertainty and risk. Because of the costs and risks of redeploying assets, firms can be found competing in an industry while pursuing different strategies, even though some strategies are recognized as dominant in terms of profitability.[7] Strategy is thus not just the selection of profitable product markets; it is also the attempt to create a competitive advantage by investing in the link that generates the product attribute most strongly desired by consumers and which corresponds to the firm's distinctive competence relative to its competitors.

An example of the contribution of value-added chain analysis for strategies of product differentiation is the selection of acquisition targets. Ebeling and Doorley compare, for ex-

ample, the structural characteristics of value-added chains for three competitors by estimating the contribution of each link to market value and the extent to which each link is done in-house or sourced outside.[8] (Two of these chains are depicted in Figure 1.) There is no reason that the links should reflect the same value across firms, and they can, in fact, be expected to differ as each firm pursues a different product-market strategy. (Some links, such as R&D and after-sales service, are not shown.) Observations on activities sourced or contract-

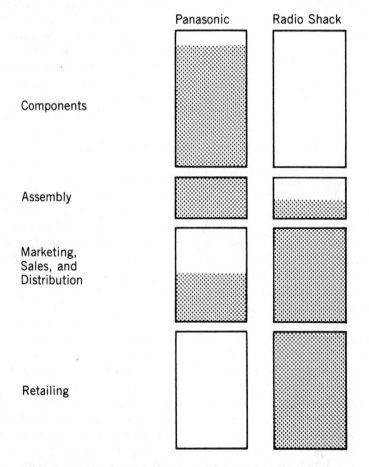

*Shaded portion represents proportion kept in-house.

Source: Ebeling and Doorley (1983).

Figure 1 Value-Added Analysis for Consumer Electronic Products*

ed out externally permit insight into the question of which firm is best situated for entry into the home computer market. An application of the value-added chain in this context rests on the identification of the characteristics of consumer demand and the strategic positioning of firms in terms of their control over the critical links that supply these characteristics. If component manufacture is critical, then Panasonic is best placed because of its ownership of production activities. If the consumer desires easy access to distribution centers and after-sales service, then Radio Shack has the better position. Once the attributes desired by the customer and the relative strengths of the competition have been determined, a firm can determine its present strength in a business and decide either to redeploy its assets or pursue its traditional competence, withdraw from the business, or acquire the critical assets.

In conclusion, the value-added chain is a useful tool in isolating the critical success factors of a strategy. For strategies in competitive industries, the chain isolates those links that are not currently viable relative to competition. For strategies of product differentiation, the chain indicates those links that generate downstream economic rents. Before turning to its extension in the international context, the chain of comparative advantage for countries must first be explored.

THE CHAIN OF COMPARATIVE ADVANTAGE

The international environment differs from a purely domestic setting for two reasons. The first is that institutional and cultural factors establish powerful barriers to the easy transfer of competitive advantages among countries. These barriers may be particularly effective in blocking the transfer of the final links of the value-added chain. Marketing programs must often be redesigned, distribution networks established, and after-sales service—which is becoming an increasingly critical variable in many industries—backed by a trained team. Where these barriers are reported to be unusually strong, which is commonly the case with firms' experiences in Japan, there is a tendency to move toward cooperative ventures with domestic firms that possess the knowledge and infrastructure to market, distribute, and service the goods.

The second reason is that the factor costs (e.g., wages, materials, capital charges) differ remarkably from one country to the next. These differences in macroeconomic variables greatly increase the risk associated with a firm's product/market and resource allocation decisions. The sheer number of variables reflects the most potent fact of international competition. That is, global competition brings together in multiple markets firms that differ widely in where they source and in their access to national markets.

Differences in factor costs have powerful implications for where a firm should locate the links of its value-added chain internationally. The general rule, as developed below, is that a firm should locate its activities in those countries that possess a comparative advantage in terms of the relevant intensive factor. Because countries differ in factor costs and the intensity of factor use varies along the value-added chain, the distribution of value-added activities between countries will tend to differ. Research and development is, of course, intensive in human capital, that is, in highly trained workers. Basic manufacturing is more variable, but it is certainly less intensive in human capital than research and development and can be relatively labor intensive, especially in assembly. Manufacturing of new products tends to rely on sophisticated process technologies that cannot be separated from the use of a trained and educated work force or engineering crew.[9] Because countries differ in factor costs, labor-intensive activities can be expected to be located where unskilled labor is inexpensive, and capital (including human)-intensive activities located where capital is inexpensive.

For simplicity, some implications for international strategies can be captured by considering a stylized model of comparative advantage and the location of economic activity first introduced by Deardorff.[10] A few assumptions are necessary, although they will be relaxed later. One assumption is that markets are competitive, and thus the same price exists in all national markets for a good. Another assumption is that all firms have the same production technology, which is not characterized by economies of scale. There are only two factors of production: labor and capital.

ISOCOST LINES AND ISOQUANTS

Based on these assumptions, countries can be ordered by a chain of comparative advantage along isocost lines. An isocost line shows the proportions of factor inputs that equal one dollar. (It can also be called a one-dollar cost line.) For Country I, where labor is relatively inexpensive, isocost line 1 is drawn in Figure 2. For Country II, where capital is relatively inexpensive, isocost line 2 is drawn. The lines for the countries differ because the factor costs of labor and capital are different between countries. Tangent to the isocost lines are unit-value isoquants whereby an isoquant represents the proportions of capital and labor that produce the same value of output. This value is set equal in Figure 2 to one dollar. (These isoquants can also be called one-dollar production curves.)

The tangency of the unit-value isoquants implies that firms are earning market returns. An isoquant inside an isocost line represents a state of excess profits as the unit cost of factors used in production is less than the dollar unit value of production.[11] Excess profits (also called economic rents) lead to an increase in competition and lower prices: as prices fall, production must increase to earn the same dollar of revenue, increasing the required amount of factor inputs. Thus, the isoquants move outward. If the isoquants were outside the isocost lines, then

the value of production is less than cost and unprofitable. The result of all this is that, for production under competition, the isoquants must be tangent to the isocost line farthest from the origin.

Isoquants are drawn in Figure 2 for a few economic activities and goods.[12] Some of these goods are raw materials; some are intermediate products, such as labor-intensive assembly or human-capital-intensive research and development. This description of goods and economic activities implies that they have been unbundled in terms of their contribution to the value-added chain. By examining the value-added chain, it can be determined which activities will be placed in countries where the comparative advantage is most favorable.[13] Only the goods for isoquants below point A will be produced by the labor-intensive country; the goods for isoquants above point A will be produced by the country with an advantage in capital-intensive production.

The ordering of isoquants along an isocost line corresponds to what can be termed a chain of comparative advantage for countries. This chain reflects the differences in factor costs between countries and the differences in factor intensities in the production of intermediate and final goods. The chain derived from Figure 2 shows that each country specializes in producing those goods for which it has a comparative advantage.

FACTORS AFFECTING COMPARATIVE ADVANTAGE

The derivation of the chain of comparative advantage is based on strong assumptions. When the assumptions of perfect competition and the same price for a good across countries are relaxed, the argument must be modified strongly. Two factors prevent, in particular, the clean and tidy ordering of industries along the chain of comparative advantage.

The first factor is the cost of transportation

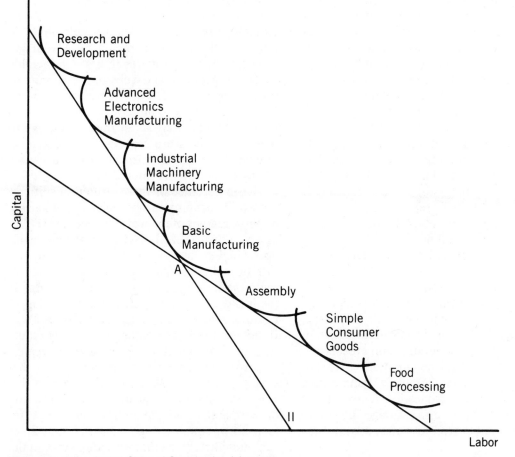

Figure 2 Value-Added Chain of Comparative Advantage

and tariffs, which can create strong barriers between nations and permit domestically located firms to survive despite a disadvantage in f.o.b. prices. These costs are especially effective for goods characterized by low value to weight. Tariffs and transportation costs may prevent a clean ordering of trade between countries, but the general tendency of trade to reflect the comparative advantages of nations is certain to influence the allocation of world resources. The chain of comparative advantage will not hold for industries where factor cost differences between countries are small. It can be expected to

hold for industries where these differences are large, although governments can, of course, strongly affect the allocation of production.

The second factor is the difference in competitive advantages among firms. Firms can, in particular, exploit certain economies along and between value-added chains which create competitive advantages that can sometimes be transferred globally. Three economies are particularly relevant: scale, scope, and learning. If the economies captured by large-scale production outweigh the disadvantage in factor costs, then a firm can remain competitive despite a poor location. Similarly, the production of one good might lower the costs for the production of another. Thus, if a firm has a competitive advantage in one good, the production of a second may be profitable despite a location disadvantage. Finally, a firm may possess an advantage in knowledge or skill gained over time. Japanese trading companies have no apparent competitive or location advantage in acting as agents for non-Japanese firms selling outside of Japan, yet they have knowledge of trading on world markets. Learning might also take the form of superior technology in the manufacturing or marketing of goods. Because learning is not easily transferred or replicated, some firms maintain a competitive advantage through product or process technologies.

The second factor is particularly pertinent to analysis of the interplay between the comparative advantages of countries and the competitive advantages of firms. When firms achieve a competitive advantage in terms of scale, scope, or learning, firms can be disadvantaged in terms of their location but still compete successfully. In other words, the competitive advantage of a firm can overcome the comparative disadvantage of country location. However, the stronger the location disadvantage, the more potent the competitive advantage of the firm must be.

There is a common tendency to suggest that a firm change its strategy in response to international competition rather than recognize that its industry may be in decline because of a change in comparative advantage. In industries characterized by differentiated goods, firms can respond to international competition by investing in new competitive advantages. But in industries characterized by commodities or close substitutes, shifts in comparative advantage dictate only four responses, namely, divestiture, switching of technologies to use factors favored by a firm's country location, investment in overseas plants as source sites, or lobbying for government intervention.

SHIFTS IN THE CHAIN OF COMPARATIVE ADVANTAGE

Not all industries are equally vulnerable to long-term shifts in the comparative advantages among nations. Industries that are vulnerable consist of goods or activities in the vicinity of point A of Figure 2. They represent the *weak links* of the chain of comparative advantage. Industries that embody goods that correspond to these weak links are especially vulnerable to fluctuations in factor costs and exchange rates when competition is international.

The importance of these structural shifts in the world economy can be isolated by focusing on three regions of the world: developed (DCs), newly industrialized (NICs), and less-developed (LDCs) countries. Figure 2 can be altered to reflect this perspective. If Country I represents the developed countries and Country II the less-developed countries, the allocation of world production that existed after World War II and until recently can be seen in rough illustration. Through the 1970s, a third region consisting of NICs has been interpolated between LDCs and DCs. Figure 3 depicts this emergence and its implications on the ordering of comparative advantage for these three regions. If we compare Figure 3 with Figure 2, we can immediately see that a major change in the allocation of global production has been emerging from newly industrializing countries.

This emergence has placed tremendous pressure on the weak links of the post-war chain of comparative advantage. The rise of Japan, which was already fairly industrialized by the start of this period, affected most strongly the industries for which comparative and competitive advantage were weakest, such as steel, and, over time, auto production, which had been labor-intensive in the United States relative to current factor use. The more recent industrialization of countries such as Brazil, Korea, and Taiwan is similarly displacing some traditional industries, although the extent of this shift has

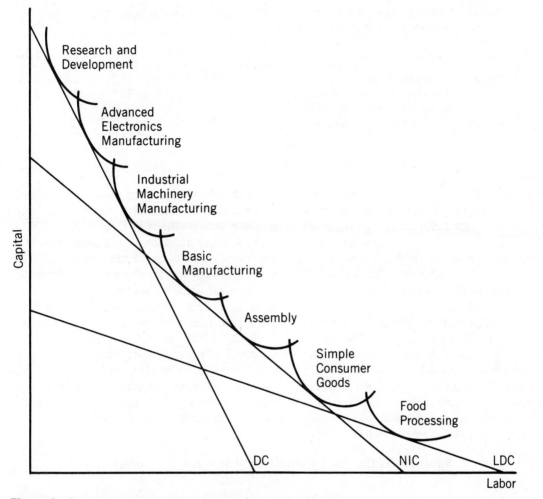

Figure 3 Changes in the Value-Added Chain of Comparative Advantage

been restrained by the tariff intervention of developed countries.

Table 1 documents the extent of this shift. Between 1963 and 1980, the share of value-added in world manufacturing fell in developed countries (not including the socialist bloc) from 77.3 percent to 65.2 percent. For the newly industrializing countries, it rose from 5.5 to 7.7 percent. The percentile change may not seem dramatic, but the absolute value in dollar terms is staggering. The change for the socialist countries is more dramatic, though its impact on world markets is not as critical given the substantial barriers to trade between the East and West. (The share of world manufacturing trade for the East, in fact, fell from 11 percent in 1966 to 8 percent in 1980.)

The brunt of this change is not, however, felt equally by every industry, but rather is borne primarily by the weak links in the chain of comparative advantage. Semiconductor and robotic production are less vulnerable to shifts in comparative advantage than crude steel production, the lower line of automobiles, or basic

Table 1 Estimated Shares in World Manufacturing Value Added by Country Groupings and Subgroups, Selected Years*

	1963	1970	1975	1978	1980
Developed Countries	77.3	73.4	67.5	66.8	65.2
Developed Socialist Countries	14.6	17.8	22.5	22.9	23.8
Newly Industrializing Countries	5.5	6.0	7.0	7.2	7.7
Less Developed Countries	2.6	2.8	3.0	3.1	3.3

*At constant 1975 prices.

Source: Ballance and Sinclair (1983, p. 14).

manufacturing. Table 2 provides some evidence on changes in output for steel and autos. Clearly, the most dramatic change has occurred in LDCs, with much of the increase stemming from economic growth in the NICs. For certain consumer electronic industries, the change has been equally dramatic; for example, the share of world production by LDCs of radio receivers grew from 33.3 percent in 1966 to 83.1 percent in 1979. Even during the difficult period of 1974 to 1980, the LDC share of world manufacturing value-added grew by 32 percent.[14]

Of course, not all changes in the distribution of value-added in manufacturing is reflected in changes in trade patterns. Part of the shift goes to satisfy the increased demand in LDCs. Also, as the developed countries move away from infrastructural investments, demand for such intermediate products as steel falls relative to that for other products. Yet a considerable effect does reverberate in the pattern of trade between countries, an effect that is dampened by the imposition of quotas and tariffs. Thus, whereas trade in manufactured goods for developed countries grew at 5.6 percent between 1966 and 1980, for LDCs, it expanded at 9.8 percent for the same time period. Again, certain industries were affected more than others. Machinery and transport vehicles contributed to only 7 percent of LDCs' manufacturing exports in 1966; by 1980, they contributed to 25 percent.

Table 2 The Changing Pattern of World Production in Automobiles and Steel, 1950–80

	Year	Advanced Market Economies	Advanced Socialist Economies	LDCs and NICs
Automobiles	1950	10147	394	36
(in 1000s)	1960	15325	730	322
	1965	23058	936	548
	1970	27245	1530	912
	1975	28810	2851	1604
	1980	24972	3110	2275
Steel	1950	148.9	35.9	5.2
(in millions	1960	228.5	86.5	20.0
of tons)	1965	301.6	119.6	32.8
	1970	388.5	155.6	49.9
	1975	381.0	192.6	86.1
	1980	394.9	209.1	113.4

Source: Ballance and Sinclair (1983, p. 74).

Underneath this macroeconomic picture, though, lies the efforts of firms trying to benefit from the differences in comparative advantages. These efforts have partly resulted in a tendency to enforce firm-specific advantages through the creation of cost economies and the application of new technologies that substitute capital for labor. They have also resulted in a greater dispersion of production within the firm over geographical boundaries. Thus, recent studies estimate that almost 50 percent of U.S. manufactured imports reflect the exports of foreign affiliates and related firms to the parent corporations.[15]

The international dispersion of American transnational corporations has, moreover, been echoed in recent years by similar trends among the major European and, to a lesser extent, Japanese firms. The German and Japanese share of world foreign direct investment rose from 1.2 to 7.3 percent and 0.5 to 6.8 percent, respectively, between 1960 and 1978. During the same time period, the U.S. share fell from 49.2 percent to 41.4 percent.[16]

Because of the vast dispersion of the production activities of American, European, and Japanese firms, competition in international markets is a combination of both competitive and comparative advantage. In a global industry, firms differ in the configuration of bets they place on different sourcing locations and on links along the value-added chain. Moreover, because of the relative unfamiliarity between the major firms in these industries, there is frequently an absence of historical rules upon which to base the nature of the competition. Competitive signals, even if sent, are harder to detect when firms have yet to perceive historical patterns in the multiple markets in which they confront each other.

ANALYSIS OF THE INTERNATIONAL VALUE-ADDED CHAIN

A value-added chain analysis of competition for a global industry is useful for outlining the nature and stakes of the different wagers placed on sourcing locations and on different links along the value-added chain. The value-added chain can be applied under two different assumptions. The first is that competitors have the same technology, but costs vary because of differences in location sites. Under this assumption, costs can be readily estimated by incorporating foreign wage and material rates into the estimates of production costs. The second assumption allows for differences in technologies, and estimates production costs when competitors may be at an advantage or a disadvantage in terms of firm-specific assets. This second calculation is far more difficult, but even without precise data, a sensitivity analysis around the benchmark measure calculated under the first assumption can be estimated. Moreover, only the second calculation provides a reasonable answer to whether investment in new technologies overcomes the advantage of firms sourcing in cheaper sites. By focusing on competitors' locations and technological advantages, the above analysis, in an international context, is fundamental in determining where the value-added chain should be broken across borders and where new investments should be located.

In addition to analyzing global competitiveness in terms of costs, the value-added chain is useful for designing integrated strategies that address particular national characteristics while exploiting upstream competitive advantages in the value-added chain. The key challenge of a global strategy is to determine which links are to be centralized and which links decentralized. Clearly, centralization is critical in order to maintain control over, or exploit, economies of scale in the use of strategic assets. An example of a decentralized link is marketing to the extent that products must be redesigned or packaged to correspond to differences in the attributes demanded by the various national markets. Decentralized marketing programs that exploit upstream competitive advantages in terms of low-cost production are the cutting edge of a global strategy.

On the other hand, if the advantage stemming from a strategic link cannot be internationally transferred, then an industry is consequently national in terms of competition. The primary example of a nontransferable advantage is distribution, though some firms have been able to build their competitive advantages precisely by developing franchising networks that overcome distributional barriers. A pivotal factor in the gaming behavior of firms in international markets is the attempt of national firms to close distribution, service, or customer ties to foreign competitors who, in turn, seek to overcome their disadvantage by innovative marketing programs and investments in channel access.

Developments in the world television industry illustrate the usefulness of a value-added chain defined in terms of market value. The initial entry of Japanese firms into the American market relied upon exports from home plants that operated at full economies of scale and that, initially, benefited from inexpensive labor. Although the share of the market captured by Japanese television manufacturers rose dramatically in both black-and-white and color sets, most of the sales were made under private labels through large department stores. The weakness of the Japanese firms in marketing (brand labels), distribution, and after-sales service poses, then, the question of who was capturing the downstream profits: the manufacturer or the distributor.

To overcome their downstream weakness, Japanese firms invested heavily in product quality, reducing the need for servicing relative to American producers. Yet, as American manufacturers began to compete on new product and process technologies, margins became increasingly squeezed and brand labeling and distribution grew in importance. By the late 1970s, competition had shifted to the later stages of the value-added chain in terms of market value. Japanese firms responded by investing in distribution channels and brand labeling. Thus, the industry had evolved into cost competition in the lower line of television sets and marketing and distribution competition in the top line. The initial global advantage in terms of location and economies of scale for a world market largely evaporated by 1980.

MODES OF INTERNATIONAL COMPETITION

The above discussion suggests that a distinction can be drawn between three modes of competition. One mode rests upon the dispersion of the links in the chain of comparative advantage among countries. Comparative advantage implies that international competition will be between commodity exports from countries with similar factor endowments, resulting in distinct patterns of trade. Trading between countries with dissimilar comparative advantages will be interindustry; that is, there will be no cross flows of similar commodities. Thus, it is primarily comparative advantage that explains the pattern of competition between exports from the various offshore plants which supply the American black-and-white television market. This sourcing can be from unaffiliated firms or, if there are reasons to coordinate and guarantee delivery and pricing, from overseas plants that are elements in the international vertical integration of the multinational corporation.

A second mode of competition rests upon differences in the chain of competitive advantage among firms. If relative factor costs among nations are similar, then competition is driven entirely by differences in the competitive advantages between firms. Competition is characterized by cross flows in the trade of similar goods and foreign direct investment for market penetration.[17] Such patterns of trading and investment are called, respectively, intraindustry and horizontal. The automobile industry is one such example. There is considerable intraindustry trade of vehicles which are differentiated on the basis of styling, quality, or advertising. And, as an alternative to trading, auto firms can invest in each other's country of origin and in other parts of the world. Such overseas investments are elements in the international horizontal integration of the multinational corporation.

The third mode of competition consists of the interplay between competitive and comparative advantage along a value-added chain. Whereas differences in competitive advantage promote intraindustry trade or horizontal investments in other countries, the combination of comparative and competitive advantages generates a complex pattern of the international dispersion of the firm's activities. These activities are conducted in-house, for the competitive strength of the firm rests on its ownership of specialized production processes, technologies, or quality control measures that cannot be easily bought in the marketplace.[18] Under the third mode of competition, firms compete on the basis of the relative superiority of their *configuration* of overseas sourcing locations, competitive advantages, and product/market decisions.

These three modes of competition generate the pattern shown in Figure 4. Box I reflects the first mode outlined above, where competition is driven by comparative advantage in the form of exports and imports of intermediate and final goods. Box II reflects the second mode, whereby firms have no factor cost incentive to locate in a particular country but compete internationally in terms of their distinctive competencies and the competitive structure of the market, much as they do in the purely domestic case. The third mode is represented by Box III. Here, differences in both comparative and competitive advantages generate the international dispersion of the firm's sourcing and market penetration activities. The upper left-hand corner represents the endpoint case in which the similarity of factor costs between countries and competitive advantages between firms segments markets along national boundaries. Therefore, because of transportation and other costs, there is no international competition in the absence of comparative and competitive advantages.

Although useful in structuring the complex interrelations of competitive and comparative advantage, Figure 4 omits the extent to which the firm's global position augments its strategic position in its national markets. There are generally three sources for a sustainable global advantage: increase in economies of scale as a

	Comparative Advantages of Countries	
	No Advantage	**Advantaged**
No Advantage	• Nationally Segmented Markets	• Interindustry Trade • International Vertical Integration of Firms I
Advantaged	• Intraindustry Trade • International Horizontal Integration of Firms II	• Internationally Vertically and Horizontally Integrated Firms with Different Configurations of Market Penetrations and Sourcing Sites III

Competitive Advantages of Firms labels the vertical axis.

Figure 4 Modes of International Competition

result of the increase in market size; increase in economies of scope as a result of the increase in product lines supporting the fixed costs of logistics, control, or downstream links of the value-added chain; and experience as a result of the knowledge gained regarding market opportunities or new technologies.[19] When these economies exist, industries are global in the sense that firms must compete in world markets in order to survive.

CONCLUSION

There is thus a difference between competing on the initial *transfer* of an advantage, through exporting a good from a plant favored by its location or a firm advantage by investing overseas, and competing on the basis of the *subsequent* advantages gained by being global. The Japanese entry into the United States frequently assumes a historical pattern of competition based upon an initial transfer of a comparative advantage in exports stemming from low wages, and a later transfer of a competitive advantage in the form of exporting by or investing overseas in capital-intensive production at minimum efficient scale. As comparative and competitive advantages between American and Japanese firms grow more similar, competition in the large North American market (which can often by itself support minimum efficient scale in production) takes on an increasingly domestic character, though the names of some of the players are foreign. Thus, the initial *global* advantage of Japanese firms is frequently not sustainable. New competitive advantages, such as brand labeling, must therefore be developed, but these advantages are not global as they are not uniquely acquired by virtue of participating in world markets.

What is often overlooked is that the creation of a global network provides the benefit of profiting from the uncertainty of the world market. A critical element of formulating an international strategy is creating the organizational flexibility and incentives that respond to changes in economic parameters between countries. To this extent, the international firm can be viewed as representing investments in flexibility that permit the exploitation of profit opportunities generated by environmental turbulence. Thus, the key operating dimensions in a global strategy are one, to recognize the potential profit opportunities, and two, to create the organizational flexibility that responds to changes in the environment. A number of the elements that compose this flexibility will be explored with regard to the multinational corporation in Part 2 of this article.

NOTES

1. For a discussion of location- and firm-specific advantages in terms of foreign direct investment, see the seminal article by John Dunning, "Trade, Location of Economic Activity and the MNE: A Search for an Eclectic Theory," in *The International Allocation of Economic Activity,* edited by B. Ohlin et al. (London: Holmes and Meier, 1979).

2. For a complete statement, see Michael Porter, *Competitive Strategy* (New York: Basic Books, 1981).

3. Although the concept of the value-added chain has been circulated among consultants and academics for several years, it has only recently been discussed in academic publications. See, for example, Bruce Kogut, "Normative Observations on the International Value-Added Chain and Strategic Groups," *Journal of International Business Studies* (Fall 1984): 151–167, and Michael Porter, *Competitive Advantage* (New York: The Free Press, 1985).

4. Although we cannot pursue this point further, it is important to note that the decision to divest because of a relative cost disadvantage may be deterred because of supply or price uncertainty arising from a scarcity of suppliers. For the impact of small numbers of suppliers on the decision to source externally, see Oliver Williamson, "Transaction-Cost Economics: The Governance of Contractual-Relations," *Journal of Law and Economics* (October 1979): 233–261.

5. I thank Stephen Schaubert for his description of how Bain & Company have applied the value-added chain to an analysis of the steel industry.

6. The microeconomic underpinnings of our approach is the treatment of goods as bundles of attributes that differ in terms of consumer demand. For this line of inquiry, see the seminal article by Kevin Lancaster, "A New Approach to Consumer Demand," *Journal of Political Economy* 74 (1966): 132–157, and the interesting extension to product rivalry by Richard Schmalensee, "The Ready-to-Eat Breakfast Cereal Industry," *Bell Journal of Economics* 9 (1978): 305–327.

7. The costs of redeploying assets result in the existence, to use a term from the strategy literature, of different "strategic groups." These different product-market strategies can be mapped back upon the value-added chain.

8. See H. Ebeling and L. Doorley, "A Strategic Approach to Acquisitions," *Journal of Business Strategy* 3 (1983): 44–55.

9. Our discussion is consistent with a theory of foreign direct investment called the international product life cycle, which predicts that as products become more standardized, their production shifts to sourcing from overseas plants. See the collection of articles edited by Louis Wells, *The Product Life Cycle* (Boston: Harvard Business School Press, 1972).

10. See Alan Deardorff, "Weak Links in the Chain of Comparative Advantage," *Journal of International Economics* 9 (1979): 97–209.

11. The term "profits" may cause some confusion. Profits are earned as a competitive payment to capital. Earnings in excess of the competitive return to capital are considered excess profits or economic rents.

12. Our ordering is drawn from data given by Chad Leechor, Harinder Kohli, and Sujin Hur in *Structural Changes in World Industry: A Quantitative Analysis of Recent Developments* (Washington, D.C.: World Bank, 1983).

13. Assuming competitive markets, the production of intermediate goods is defined as the value of the output minus the intermediate good inputs. Because labor and capital are paid their marginal products, and there are no excess profits, we can also order intermediate products along an isocost line.

14. This and the following data are drawn from Robert Ballance and Stuart Sinclair, *Collapse and Survival: Industry Strategies in a Changing World* (London: George Allen & Unwin, 1983), and Leechor et al. (1983).

15. See Gerald Helleiner, "Transnational Corporation and Trade Structure: The Role of Intra-firm Trade," in *On the Economics of Intra-industry Trade,* edited by H. Giersch (Tubingen: J. C. B. Mohr, 1979).

16. See John Dunning, "Changes in the Level and Structure of International Production: The Last One Hundred Years," in *The Growth of International Business,* edited by M. Casson (London: George Allen & Unwin, 1983).

17. The inadequacy of the Heckscher-Ohlin model, which rests upon comparative advantage, to explain intra-industry foreign direct investment and trade has led to a number of new theories which incorporate product differentiation and economies of scale as critical variables. For a representative work, see Paul Krugman, "Increasing Returns, Monopolistic Competition, and International Trade," *Journal of Political Economy* 9 (1979): 469–479.

18. For a variety of reasons, firms may choose to enter into joint ventures, license, or franchise. Most studies show, however, that a firm tends to maintain full ownership over its strategic assets unless it can arrange enforceable claims on their use and derived profits.

19. See Kogut, "Normative Observations."

8

DESIGNING GLOBAL STRATEGIES: PROFITING FROM OPERATIONAL FLEXIBILITY

Bruce Kogut

In a companion article, global strategies were analyzed in terms of their interplay of competitive and comparative advantages. Comparative advantage is driven by differences in the costs of inputs (e.g., unskilled and skilled workers or

Research for this paper has been funded by the Reginald H. Jones Center of The Wharton School. The author thanks Laurent Jacque and Louis Wells for their comments.

Source: Sloan Management Review (Fall 1985), pp. 27–38.

capital equipment) among countries.[1] Competitive advantage is driven by differences among firms in their abilities to transform these inputs into goods and services at maximum profit. The outstanding feature of global competition is the uncertainty over these advantages. This uncertainty stems from three factors:

1. The world economy is undergoing a fundamental shift in terms of the comparative advantages of countries. This shift is manifested in changes in

the *intersectoral* allocation of world industry and trends toward protectionism.

2. Global competition consists of firms which differ radically in the constellation of bets they have placed along the value-added chain and on different sourcing and marketing sites.

3. Global competition is often characterized by a lack of historical rules for industry competition. As a result, there is uncertainty over the initial moves and competitive reactions in terms of pricing and market penetration.

From this perspective, the thesis is developed that the unique content of a *global* versus a purely domestic strategy lies less in the methods to design long-term strategic plans than in the construction of flexibility which permits a firm to exploit the uncertainty over future changes in exchange rates, competitive moves, or government policy. This flexibility can be attained, for example, by building excess capacity into dispersed sourcing platforms or by arbitraging between different tax regimes. In short, flexibility is gained by decreasing the firm's dependence on assets already in place.

A largely neglected question is whether firms have indeed developed the organizational structures and incentives to profit from changes in the environment and coordinate an international response. The question is more than a matter of whether subsidiaries are integrated into headquarters' strategic plans or whether they report data which reflects their contribution to these plans. Rather, the question is whether there exists either a centralized organizational unit which is responsible, for example, for the shifting of production schedules and the transshipment of goods or a decentralized system which provides the proper incentives to subsidiaries to respond to changes in exchange rates and relative price movements. The exercise of strategic flexibility is a moot question unless the organizational wherewithal exists to coordinate activities internationally.

This article explores the creation of the operational flexibility of the multinational corpo-

ration in order to benefit from being global. There are many sources of environmental volatility, such as new product entries, new government policies, or new international competitors, to which firms can respond and exploit to their advantage. Section one examines only one of these sources, namely, fluctuations in exchange rates and the impact on the real cost of labor. The second section continues to examine exchange rate fluctuations, but this time in terms of the impact upon the decision of where to source and how much risk should be borne. The third section of the article widens the analysis to look more broadly at the kinds of strategic flexibility that the multinational corporation can exercise. Two kinds of flexibility are described, one is the arbitrage of market imperfections, the second is leverage, by which a firm's position in one national market is enhanced by its position in a second. A key question is whether firms recognize and have created organizational structures to respond proactively to these opportunities. This question is expanded further in the fourth section to a consideration of integrative systems that promote flexibility by managerial incentives.

VOLATILITY IN INTERNATIONAL MARKETS

Volatility in world markets affects both the firm's cost structure and its choice of technology along the value-added chains. When applied to the study of international strategies, the concept of the value-added chain pinpoints two methods with which to analyze the implications of this uncertainty. The first involves tracing out the current and future cost advantages of competitors under different assumptions regarding factor payments and technologies. The second involves determining the demand characteristics of different national markets and designing tailored marketing programs that exploit economies of scale and scope in upstream links.

The value-added chain exercise outlined above does not appear to be greatly different if conducted in an international or national setting with regional differences in wage rates and market prices. Yet, there is a critical difference that cannot be underestimated, and that is the tremendous variability of macroeconomic parameters between countries. Though southern parts of the United States tend toward lower wage rates than the North, this differential will not be strongly affected by fluctuating exchange rates or by changes in other macroeconomic parameters, such as interest rates.[2] On the other hand, the international economy is rocked to a much greater extent by the variability of exchange rates and movements in the relative factor costs between countries.

The extent of this variability can be suggested by considering, first, movements in wage rates between sourcing platforms over time and, second, movements in real (i.e., inflation) adjusted exchange rates over time. The impact on profitability because of unexpected movements in exchange rates can be naively illustrated by considering the decision of an American firm to source in Singapore in the mid-1970s. The success of such a venture is dependent upon what happens to the Singapore wage rates over time relative to the location decisions of competitors. Data on wage rates in dollar terms is given in Table 1 for Singapore and Sri Lanka. Clearly, the firm's competitive position would have deteriorated had it invested in Singapore and relied on the expectation that the wage rate differential vis-à-vis Sri Lanka (where its competitors sourced) would remain the same over time.

The quintessential element of volatility in international markets, however, is the fluctuation in exchange rates. One theory which explains the determination of exchange rates is that of purchasing power parity (PPP). Stated with unabashed simplicity, PPP claims that the price of foreign goods sold in their home markets should be equal to the price of these goods at home, adjusted for exchange rates and transportation costs. Based on this supposi-

Table 1 Hourly Wage Rates in Manufacturing (in U.S. dollars)

	Sri Lanka	Singapore
1973	.13	.36
1974	.16	.45
1975	.16	.50
1976	.14	.54
1977	.11	.56
1978	.15	.61
1979	.12	.88
1980	.11	.80
1981	.11	1.05
1982	.14	1.17

Source: Compiled from *Yearbook of Labour Statistics.* 1983, ILO; *International Financial Statistics,* IMF.

tion, and holding transportation costs constant, it proposes that changes in observed or nominal exchange rates must, therefore, be linked to changes in the prices of goods in one country relative to prices in another country. Exchange rate movements should reflect, then, differences in inflation between countries. The relevance of PPP for our purposes is that deviations from the predicted value of an exchange rate under this theory imply that there has been a change in *real* economic variables between countries, such as wage rates adjusted for inflation.

Because exchange rates are no longer pegged, a major source of uncertainty is the impact of exchange rate fluctuations precisely on these real economic variables. Figure 1 graphs nominal exchange rates for Germany, Japan, and the United States against a basket of currencies weighted by the significance of the trade with the country of issuance. Clearly, the German mark and Japanese yen appreciated in nominal terms against the currencies of their trading partners throughout the 1970s, whereas the dollar's value is fairly stable until its rapid rise beginning in 1982. Curiously, the Japanese yen appears to evidence the greatest volatility, fluctuating dramatically between 1978 and 1983.

The impact of these changes on competitive

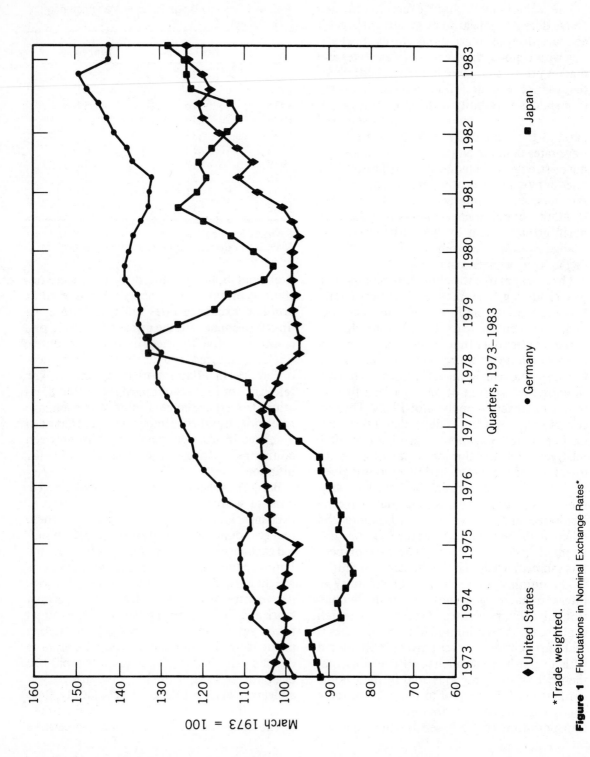

Figure 1 Fluctuations in Nominal Exchange Rates*

*Trade weighted.

◆ United States   ● Germany   ■ Japan

Quarters, 1973–1983

March 1973 = 100

positions becomes more transparent when the effect of movements in real exchange rates on nominal wages is isolated. In Table 2, manufacturing wages for Germany, Japan, and the United States are listed. All wages are calculated in dollars. The wages have been calculated in two ways, the first showing nominal wages calculated using the prevailing exchange rate for each year, the second showing wages if purchasing power parity had held. (Under PPP, changes in exchange rates would only reflect differences in inflation rates between the United States and its trading partners, Germany and Japan.) As seen in the PPP-adjusted rates, if PPP had held, the wage bill paid by German and Japanese firms in the 1970s would have tracked more closely that of their American competitors. In nominal terms, the wage increases for Japan and Germany are even more impressive, but when compared to the PPP-adjusted wage estimates, a substantial portion of this increase can be attributed to the *real* appreciation of the yen and deutsche mark against the dollar throughout the 1970s. Because of the real appreciation of the dollar between 1980 and 1982, this pattern was reversed. American wages rose 17 percent, whereas German and Japanese nominal wages

calculated in dollars rose only 6.1 percent and 10.2 percent respectively.

Changes in real economic variables are difficult to forecast for the very reason that they are affected by both nominal fluctuations in foreign exchange rates and by structural shifts in the economy. Because these variables cannot be perfectly forecasted, firms bear the risk of their fluctuations whenever a contract is signed or an investment is made. There are no financial markets where the risk of real foreign exchange rate fluctuations can be shifted.

RISK PROFILES AND INVESTMENT DECISIONS

The absence of financial markets to lay off this risk does not mean, though, that firms cannot affect their risk profiles in reference to these variables. On the contrary, sourcing policy can radically influence the risk borne. Three types of risk profile policies, namely, the speculative, the hedged, and the flexible.

The speculative consists of betting on one sourcing site. Such a strategy is warranted when advantages stemming from economies of scale override the costs attached to the risk that rela-

Table 2 Changes in Nominal and PPP-adjusted Wage Rates* (in U.S. dollars)

	U.S.	Germany		Japan	
	Nominal	Nominal	PPP-adjusted	Nominal	PPP-adjusted
1973	100	100	100	100	100
1974	108	123	116	115	114
1975	118	128	129	133	124
1976	128	153	140	157	134
1977	139	177	153	200	143
1978	151	199	168	246	158
1979	164	218	189	209	180
1980	178	214	218	274	204
1981	195	216	240	295	228
1982	208	227	254	302	244

Source: Complied from Yearbook of Labour Statistics, 1983, ILO; International Financial Statistics, various years, IMF.

*Calculated at purchasing power parity exchange rates by consumer price index.

tive factor costs may change drastically. Without economies of scale, an investment in a single site is a bet, albeit perhaps an informed one, that the relative factor cost advantage will persist in the future.

Like all risky bets, however, the potential return is highly variable. In part, this captures the phenomenal success of Japanese firms, who bet consistently through the 1970s and early 1980s that the increasing costs of home wages could be offset by new home investments and an ensuant rise in labor productivity.[3] For Germany, the United States, and the United Kingdom, less than 30 percent of their foreign direct investment stock is in services, the remainder consists of extractive and manufacturing operations. For Japan, approximately 45 percent is in services, commonly in the form of sales offices of trading companies. Moreover, Japanese overseas operations are generally not sourcing platforms for intermediate components. On the contrary, the overseas operations are dependent on components manufactured by the Japanese firms. Whereas only 6 percent of production of Japanese overseas affiliates is exported back to Japan, some 47 percent of the procurements by these same affiliates originated in Japan.[4]

This trend appears to contravene strongly the tendency of American firms to source overseas component manufacture or assembly of goods that are later sold in the United States. The Japanese strategy suggests, therefore, the gamble that exchange rates might move back to long-term parity or that new investments in technology might overcome the higher labor costs. The first gamble represents a bet on the comparative advantage of Japan; the second, a bet on the competitive advantage of the firm.

In the absence of large economies of scale or technological advantages, a firm can reduce its risk exposure by sourcing from multiple locations. An example of this strategy is illustrated by Volkswagen, which suffered large losses in the early 1970s as the real cost of German wages rose relative to its competitors in its principal export markets. This experience led to invest-

ments in plants in Mexico and Brazil for its low end of the line cars, in the United States for its middle line, and a concentration of mid and upper lines in Germany. The logic of the policy was that by keeping the top of the line production in Germany, Volkswagen was able to "pass through" the impact of exchange rate movements to foreign and domestic consumers who are less sensitive to price increases of the higher quality cars. On the other hand, placing plants in Mexico, Brazil, and the United States for primarily local sales reflected the greater restraint on a complete pass through in the case of the lower line of cars. Thus, by matching the exchange exposure on the cost side to that on the revenue side, Volkswagen hedged a considerable portion of its operating margin against exchange rate fluctuations. That this hedged strategy did not meet expectations in the United States can be attributed partly to the fact that the Japanese speculative bet paid off in the American market.

A hedged position can lead, though, to a flexible strategy which permits the firm to exploit valuable options. One option is to invest in excess capacity in plants in multiple countries. In response to a movement in real exchange rates, a firm can shift production between sites to the extent that labor can work overtime or be placed on shortened schedules. Another option is to invest in flexible technologies that increase capital leverage but permit firms to tailor products to other markets in response to competitive in-roads caused by shifts in real economic variables between countries.[5] Though such options incur costs in terms of loss of scale economies, their distinctive feature is that they become more valuable the greater the unpredictability of the environment. Under this strategy, variance implies greater profit opportunities.

IDENTIFYING AND MANAGING GLOBAL OPPORTUNITIES

The value of these opportunities depends on the answer to three questions: the first is a strategic issue, the second, cognitive, and the third, organizational.

• Are the benefits sufficient to justify the costs attached to the loss of scale economies in production or to the organizational support systems?

• Do managers perceive and identify potential options generated by being multinational?

• Are there organizational mechanisms that permit the coordination of the international activities essential to the exploitation of flexibility?

Based on a series of interviews with managers from American and European multinational corporations, I found that firms vary widely in the recognition of, and their organizational capabilities to capitalize on, these opportunities. Some firms have failed to exercise these options as a result of cognitive factors, namely, the tendency to extend the historical organization to overseas operations or to treat each subsidiary as an individual business.[6] In part, these styles reflect the salient features of the relevant environment. It is not surprising that American firms, given the size of the home market, should resist having the international tail of their operations wag the dog. Nor is it surprising that European firms, many of whom developed multinational operations during a period of extensive tariff barriers, tended toward loose headquarters/subsidiary relations in order to establish an identity as a collection of national companies. Running a truly global company is costly, and a policy of home organization extension or local market adaptation may be the most cost effective choice in many environments.

Whatever these cost tradeoffs may have been, though, several elements have increased the benefits of developing organizational structures along global lines. These elements are, principally, the continual reduction of tariffs since 1950; a greater similarity in incomes in developed countries; a reputed convergence in cultures and consumer tastes; and a growth in the economies of scale of production in some industries such as steel, auto components, and television tubes. Evidence from numerous case and cross-sectional studies over the past decade and more have shown a remarkable trend toward organizational structures better suited to a global orientation.[7] These structures include the creation of world product lines, divisions along regions—with the United States being one or part of North America—and matrix structures.

This transformation notwithstanding, multinational corporations appear to vary substantially in the coordination of their international activities and response to the market place. In part, the coordination of a global strategy is constrained by the imposition of governments demanding local content or performance requirements. Yet, even here, concessions and bargaining positions can be coordinated in terms of the larger strategic considerations of maintaining global cost economies in the relevant links of the value-added chain.

From the perspective of managing the strategic flexibility embedded in the multinational corporation, there are six tasks that need to be centralized in order to benefit from being global. Four of these tasks concern the exercise of *arbitrage* opportunities. The other two concern the identification of points of *leverage* to enhance the strategic gaming position of the international firm vis-à-vis competitors and governments.

ARBITRAGE OPPORTUNITIES

Production Shifting

As discussed above, production shifting permits the firm to respond to movements in exchange rates. The exercise of such an option is characterized minimally by two features. First, the loss in economies of scale must be less than the value of the option to shift production and the added cost of holding excess capacity.[8] Thus, in industries where economies of scale are significant, the cost of building two plants with excess capacity may be unjustified, especially if real exchange rates do not fluctuate greatly. Second, the value of shifting of production rests on the ability of firms to capitalize on differences in variable costs between plants located in separate countries because of fluctuations in exchange rates. The most relevant of these variable costs are locally sourced inputs that are not priced on world markets, the best example being labor. Yet, the degree to which labor is a fixed or variable cost will differ greatly between countries in terms of layoff and overtime constraints. As a result, the successful exercise of this option requires that, one, industrial relations be included in the investment decision and, two, that overtime provisions be made a central feature of labor contracts.[9]

As a result of the interaction between investments and strategic flexibility, the decision of where to locate a plant is frequently centralized. The extent to which corporations have adopted a policy of *internal flexible sourcing* by establishing a central committee to monitor exchange rates and costs and shift production in response to exchange rate movements is less clear. For many corporations, this decision cannot be left to divisions, for plants can often be shared between different product lines or areas. A major problem, as reported by a few interviewed firms, is the lack of incentives for divisions to cooperate in production shifting. This problem is treated in the next section.

Tax Minimization

One of the more touted features of the multinational corporation is its ability to minimize its tax bill through thoughtful adjustments of transfer prices and choice of remittance channels. The issue of transfer prices is sufficiently well known to warrant only a short discussion. When operating in two countries with different rates of taxation on corporate income, a multinational corporation can, unlike the entirely domestic firm, adjust its mark-up on intra-company sales of goods in order to realize profits in the low tax jurisdiction. Given the tremendous contribution transfer pricing can make to after-tax income, the administration of intra-firm prices for the purpose of income reporting is invariably centralized.

A more subtle form of tax minimization involves establishing multiple channels for income remittance.[10] In many countries, dividends, royalties, fees, and interest payments are taxed at differential rates. To a significant extent, a multinational corporation has the flexibility of choosing to transfer intangibles, such as technology or brand labels, to its subsidiaries in the form of a capitalized equity investment, a sale financed by corporate debt, or as a license. By under- or overevaluating the transferred intangibles, a firm can shift reported profits to subsidiaries in low tax countries. Similarly, interest payments and royalties can be adjusted to minimize taxes on remitted income. Finally, a firm has some discretion over the timing of remittances, and can, thus, choose to remit according to its tax situation. All of these potential tax benefits stem from the attributes of being a multinational corporation.

Financial Markets

The above two cases represent factor market and institutional arbitrage. Arbitrage in financial markets represents a combination of the two, for it is often the imposition of government barriers or subsidies which creates riskless profit opportunities. For example, domestic credit rationing and cross-border capital flows are commonly imposed by governments seeking to equilibrate the balance of payments. A multinational corporation, often in cooperation with an international bank, can circumvent many of these restrictions by its transfer price and remittance policy and also by innovative financial products, such as parallel loans and back-to-back loans. By similar mechanisms, a multinational corporation can often benefit from subsidized loans intended for local investment, but, in fact, transfer the loans outside a country by its remittance, transfer pricing, and financing flexibility.

Often, however, governments cooperate to provide financial incentives for multinational corporations. To this extent, governments by policy intention create arbitrage incentives. For example, export credits have been a heated point of competition between western governments in recent years. Among some developed, and a considerable number of developing countries, competition has centered around investment incentives such as tax holidays, duty relief on imported components, and guaranteed loans. As a result, some corporations centralize the decision of where to locate export activity in order to benefit from the best package of export credit and investment incentive programs.

Information Arbitrage

The final arbitrage opportunity for the multinational corporation concerns information. This information may concern scanning world markets to match sellers and buyers. An increasing characteristic of world trade is the growth of countertrade demands by governments. Estimates of countertrade vary substantially, with some corporations reporting that as much as 25 percent of their world business is in this form. The export firm is dramatically hindered in its ability to absorb the countertraded goods and use them externally or trade them on world markets. On the contrary, a number of large American firms, following a Japanese and, to a lesser extent, European tradition, have created world trade divisions that exploit profitably their multinational subsidiary network for the location of potential buyers for the traded goods. These trading services also reflect arbitrage benefits in terms of avoiding capital constraints on trade as well as tariffs imposed on the monetary value of the traded goods.

In addition to arbitraging informational imperfections in product markets, the multinational corporation can also benefit by transferring new product and process developments from one location to the next. For example, innovations are often stochastic in nature. With differences in expenditures on research and development between nations growing smaller, it is often necessary to monitor multiple national markets in order to exploit potential innovations. In some industries, the impetus to being global consists largely of scanning innovations in foreign markets. For this reason, it has been a common practice for firms in technologically advanced industries to set up research and development offices in the United States, and similar trends are apparent for American firms regarding monitoring the Japanese market.

LEVERAGE OPPORTUNITIES

Global Coordination

Unlike arbitrage, leverage reflects not the exploitation of differences in the price of an asset, product, or factor of production between markets, but rather, the creation of market or bargaining power because of the global position of the firm. One of the more important sources of this power for the international firm is the ability to differentiate prices according to its world competitive posture. For example, in response to Michelin's entry into North America, Goodyear dropped its prices on tires in Europe, forcing the family-held French company to slow its investment program and, eventually, to issue outside equity. Much like the reputed benefits embedded in portfolio models that encourage firms to diversify in order to cross-subsidize between product lines, a benefit of global activity is the possibility of carrying out an aggressive price cutting strategy in one region by relying on profits gained in other regions of the world. Of course, laws, as well as political pressures in the form of government retaliatory policies, limit the extent to which prices can be cut.

Global coordination can take forms other than price differentiation. A multinational firm can build overseas coalitions between suppliers or between a group of competitors in order to exercise leverage on the behavior of a rival firm.

Boeing's sub-contracting and recent Japanese joint ventures are examples of moves to preempt Airbus. Thus, Boeing's advances toward multinationality are almost entirely promoted by the benefits of acquiring competitive leverage.

Centralization policy varies according to the context and type of strategic decision. Pricing coordination is easily centralized when the firm is organized along global product or area lines. It becomes more difficult under a structure that includes a weak international division, for external pricing then often becomes entangled in the complex issue of establishing the transfer price between divisions. Centralization of joint venture and long-term supply decisions appears to vary substantially between firms. A few of the firms interviewed for this study delegated these decisions without specifying its place in the long-term plan. Another firm had a central office to oversee the joint venture policy, but its posture was more reactive to local government policy than proactive in the sense of coalition building.

The benefits of coalition building need to be balanced by a clear understanding of the costs. It is unlikely a firm will have the resources to compete in every regional market without adjusting its entry strategy. Because some assets are not transferable between countries, such as distribution or, to a lesser extent, marketing research, a trend in several industries, such as telecommunications, has been to form joint ventures with local firms that provide the distribution and marketing. In many industries, these ventures offer low-cost entry into a market, achieve upstream economies, and leave local competition to firms who have established market positions. Yet, if joint ventures permit firms to concentrate their resources in upstream links, they also have the disadvantage of constraining the firm's ability to respond to the volatility of the global marketplace. An extensive strategy of joint ventures can lead not only to a division of profits between partners, but also to a potential reduction in profitability because of the loss of valuable options. Joint ventures are, thus, no panacea, but raise the fundamental issue in any strategy: namely, what price is the firm willing to pay in order to lay off some of the risk and forego flexibility?

Political Risk

The final point of leverage gained by being global is the bargaining power captured by operating dispersed operations. The key to this power is the leverage that different links of the international value-added chain exercise on enforcing equity claims or contracts in national markets. The classic case has been the petroleum industry. When the industry norms broke down and competition increased between the majors in terms of marketing, the OPEC countries nationalized the upstream production in order to sell the oil to the highest bidder. In many cases, however, the leverage is weighted toward the multinational corporation. Expropriations have been less frequent in high-technology industries since the value of the local subsidiaries depends on future technology flows.

CREATING COMPATIBLE INCENTIVES

The benefits of flexibility depend upon the extent to which the firm creates the organizational resources to exploit these arbitrage and leverage opportunities. Whether the costs of centralizing the above tasks are warranted will vary according to the uncertainty confronting the individual firms. But firms that have centralized these functions still confront a formidable challenge in terms of creating the appropriate incentive system. Consider the following cases. A large European multinational corporation continued to pour new investments into a hyperinflationary Latin American country and only realized its competitive position had consistently deteriorated subsequent to a long overdue devaluation of the local currency. A large American corporation was pleased at headquarters that one of its subsidiaries in Asia had won a major order, eventually to learn that the only significant competition was its Japanese subsidiary. A division of another large American corporation recently agreed to an overseas joint venture to offset its perceived weakness in international marketing despite the fact that a second division in the corporation had several decades of experience selling to the targeted market segments.

The multinational corporation faces, therefore, a fundamental dilemma. On the one hand, its multinationality creates valuable opportunities to arbitrage markets and to exercise competitive leverage. The exploitation of these opportunities rests on the efficiency of the organization to coordinate its overseas operations and subsidiaries. On the other hand, the centralized coordination of these activities entails significant fixed costs and variable costs in communicating information from subsidiaries to corporate headquarters. Changes in environmental and competitive conditions may only be evident at the local subsidiary level. As a result, the subsidiaries often possess the best knowledge concerning the country environment and the know-how for local adaptation.

Because of the limits on centralization and the need to maintain local adaptation, the realization of global benefits is significantly dependent upon the formalization of *integrative systems* to decentralize some of the responsibility for effective exploitation of these opportunities. Two of the most important systems are human resource management and planning and control. Curiously, there have been few studies which have linked these systems to decentralized mechanisms to enhance the strategic flexibility of the multinational corporation.

To the extent that studies have been carried out, the results have tended to show a surprising conflict between the corporate strategy and the embedded incentives of the two systems. Planning and control systems for American firms have tended to export the home organization

overseas.[11] Recently, a number of firms have tried to tackle the problem of setting targets and monitoring performance in a multiple currency world.

Very few firms have appeared to develop sophisticated systems that decouple the measurement of subsidiary from managerial performance. Yet, without such a decoupling, local managers are, for example, penalized for shifting production to plants in other countries. Furthermore, they are held responsible for exogenous shifts in exchange rates which affect the *competitive* position of the subsidiary but which are beyond their immediate control. A prerequisite to a planning and control system which provides incentives compatible with the overall strategy is the decoupling of exogenously caused competitive effects on the subsidiary from the measurement of managerial performance.[12] Only with such a decoupling can the inherent flexibility of the MNC be exploited without excessive centralization.

Another system to link managerial performance to strategy is human resource management. A few studies have found a tendency for career paths to be tied to frequent international reassignment when the effective deployment of strategies depended strongly on local subsidiaries.[13] Generally, though, evidence for American firms has tended to show significant failure rates for expatriate managers and the frequent use of local nationals.[14]

CONCLUSION

Global strategies, it was explained in the previous article, rest on the interplay of the competitive advantage of firms and the comparative advantage of countries. The decision of where to invest along a firm's value-added chain is a question of competitive advantage. The decision of where to place these activities internationally constitutes a question of comparative advantage. Except for trivial and uninteresting exceptions, these decisions are based upon considerable uncertainty over future costs, market developments, and technologies. They are also influenced by the willingness of firms to bear the risk of betting on a single sourcing platform, product market, or technology.

No matter what the risk profile, the firm that is able to exploit this volatility possesses a competitive advantage gained by its ownership of a global network. This advantage may be in the form of arbitraging markets. In the case of American multinational corporations, this arbitrage might potentially consist of production shifting. For a Japanese trading company, it might consist of the ability to respond quickly to new information due its ownership of an international purchasing and sales organization coupled with an extensive logistics capability. An advantage of being global also includes an enhanced leverage in local marketplaces or in negotiations with governments.

The capability to exercise these arbitrage and leverage opportunities rests on the existence of centralized task groups responsible for the coordination of the international activities of the firm. However, centralization is constrained by the need to maintain a careful balance between local subsidiary responsiveness and the coordination of these global benefits. From this perspective, the *structural* configuration of dispersed investment location and market penetration is a prerequisite to, but no less important than, the *operational* flexibility of the firm to respond to changes in the international environment.

For many firms, the failure to develop systems tied to the global strategy of the firm may well reflect the significant costs attached to a sophisticated information system that supports the management of planning and control and human resources. One suspects, however, that the benefits of such a system have not been fully specified in terms of balancing the centralized coordination of the multinational network against the maintenance of local subsidiary responsiveness. Where this balancing is critical,

the enhancement of integrative systems is invariably an integral element in the exploitation of the benefits gained by the global activities of the multinational corporation.

NOTES

1. Comparative advantage can also be defined in terms of the availability or abundance of factors of production. Thus, a country can be seen to have a comparative advantage in skilled workers by reason of their relative abundance, even though skilled wages may be the same for all countries.

2. Even here, though, a qualification must be added, for changes in exchange rates may attract the migration of foreign labor and interest rates may affect economic growth, the first affecting the supply, the second the demand of labor. Certainly, though, these second order effects are less strong than the immediate impact that exchange rate movements have on international competitiveness.

3. It would be wrong, however, to deduce from this single trend any conclusion on differences in risk tolerances between countries. The Japanese pattern might well reflect the avoidance of risk attached to operating overseas subsidiaries or the problems in transferring culturally bound practices and technologies to foreign countries. Our point here is that in terms of exchange rate exposure only, an export strategy is a high risk bet in the face of global competition.

4. The procurement patterns of Japanese overseas affiliates is given in Ministry of International Trade and Industry Survey (1980). K. Haberich kindly brought this data to my attention.

5. This latter option is suited also to a purely domestic setting. It has been argued, in fact, that the frontier of new technologies and industries is characterized by smaller scale or flexible manufacturing that is particularly well suited to the purported higher variance of the current marketplace. This argument is given by B. Kogut in the case of steel minimills, and, for flexible technologies, cursorily by K. Ohmae and in length in the impressive study by M. Piore and C. Sabel. See B. Kogut, "Steel and the European Economic Community," working paper, Sloan School of Management, MIT (1980); K. Ohmae, *The Mind of the Strategist: Business Planning for Competitive Advantage* (New York: McGraw Hill, 1982); and M. Piore and C. Sabel, *The Second Industrial Divide* (New York: Basic Books, 1985).

6. H. Perlmutter in a seminal work remarked upon several different cognitive orientations, naming them ethnocentric, polycentric, and geocentric. The first one refers to the condition of exporting the home organization; the second, to the treatment of each subsidiary separately; and the third

to the development of a global or cosmopolitan style. We develop the third cognitive orientation below. H. Perlmutter, "The Torturous Evolution of the Multinational Corporation," *Columbia Journal of World Business* (1969).

7. Of the many works, the book by Stopford and Wells was one of the earliest and remains one of the best studies of the transformation of American multinational corporations. Franko shows a similar trend for European firms toward more global structures. Root develops the notion of the multinational corporation as a network, which parallels our discussion below. See J. Stopford and L. Wells, *Managing the Multinational Enterprise* (New York: Basic Books, 1974); L. Franko, *The European Multinationals* (Stamford, Conn.: Greylock, 1977); and F. Root, *International Trade and Investment* (Cincinnati: Southwestern, 1984).

8. A discussion of valuation of such an option can be found in B. Kogut, "Foreign Direct Investment as a Sequential Process," in C. P. Kindleberger and D. P. Audretsch, eds., *The Multinational Corporation in the 1980s* (Cambridge, Mass.: MIT Press, 1983), and is the subject of current work.

9. For a discussion on the management of international and interdependent manufacturing operations, see B. Mascarenhas, "Coordination of Manufacturing Interdependence in MNCs," *Journal of International Business Studies* (1984).

10. The following discussion on remittance channels and financial market arbitrage draws substantially from work by D. Lessard. See his articles "Transfer Prices, Taxes and Financial Markets: Implications of Internal Financial Transfers within the Multinational Firm," in R. B. Hawkins, ed.,

Economic Issues of Multinational Firms, (Greenwich, Conn.: JAI Press, 1979), and "Finance and Global Competition," paper prepared for colloquium on Competition in Global Industries (Harvard University, April 26–27, 1984).

11. J. M. McInnes, "Financial Control Systems for Multinational Operations: An Empirical Investigation," *Journal of International Business Studies* (1971). Swedish studies show that weak control systems, true to the European pattern of loose headquarter/subsidiary ties, tend to prevail for Swedish multinational corporations. See G. Hedlund and P. Aman, *Managing Relationships with Foreign Subsidiaries: Organization and Control in Swedish MNCs* (Stockholm: Sveriges Mekanforbun, 1983).

12. Some recent work suggests possible ways to achieve this decoupling: D. Lessard and D. Sharp, "Measuring the Performance of Operations Subject to Fluctuating Exchange Rates," *Midland Corporate Journal* (1984). L. Jacque and P. Lorange, "Hyperinflation and Global Strategic Management," *Columbia Journal of World Business* (1984); and L. Jacque and B. Kogut, "The International Control Conundrum: A Multivariate Variance Smoothing Model," mimeo, The Wharton School (1984).

13. A. Edstrom and J. Galbraith, "International Transfer of Managers: Some Important Policy Considerations," *Columbia Journal of World Business* (1976), and Y. L. Doz and C. K. Prahalad, "Headquarters Influence and Strategic Control in MNCs," *Sloan Management Review* (Fall 1981), pp. 15–29.

14. R. Tung, "Selection and Training of Personnel for Overseas Assignments," *Columbia Journal of World Business* (1982).

9

▮▮▮ CHANGING PATTERNS OF INTERNATIONAL COMPETITION

Michael E. Porter

When examining the environmental changes facing firms today, it is a rare observer who will conclude that international competition is not high on the list. The growing importance of international competition is well recognized both

Source: California Management Review Vol. 28, no. 2 (Winter 1986), pp. 9–40. © 1986, The Regents of the University of California

in the business and academic communities, for reasons that are fairly obvious when one looks at just about any data set that exists on international trade or investment. Exhibit 1, for example, compares world trade and world GNP. Something interesting started happening around the mid-1950s, when the growth in world trade began to significantly exceed the growth in world GNP. Foreign direct invest-

Exhibit 1   Growth of World Trade

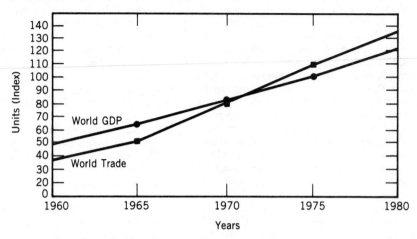

Source: United Nations, *Statistical Yearbooks*

ment by firms in developing countries began to grow rapidly a few years later, about 1963.[1] This period marked the beginning of a fundamental change in the international competitive environment that by now has come to be widely recognized. It is a trend that is causing sleepless nights for many business managers.

There is a substantial literature on international competition, because the subject is far from a new one. A large body of literature has investigated the many implications of the Heckscher-Ohlin model and other models of international trade which are rooted in the principle of comparative advantage.[2] The unit of analysis in this literature is the country. There is also considerable literature on the multinational firm, reflecting the growing importance of the multinational since the turn of the century. In examining the reasons for the multinational, I think it is fair to characterize this literature as resting heavily on the multinational's ability to exploit intangible assets.[3] The work of Hymer and Caves among others has stressed the role of the multinational in transferring know-how and expertise gained in one country market to others at low cost, and thereby offsetting the unavoidable extra costs of doing business in a foreign country. A more recent stream of literature extends this by

emphasizing how the multinational firm internalizes transactions to circumvent imperfections in various intermediate markets, most importantly the market for knowledge.

There is also a related literature on the problems of entry into foreign markets and the life cycle of how a firm competes abroad, beginning with export or licensing and ultimately moving to the establishment of foreign subsidiaries. Vernon's product cycle of international trade combines a view of how products mature with the evolution in a firm's international activities to predict the patterns of trade and investment in developed and developing countries.[4] Finally, many of the functional fields in business administration research have their branch of literature about international issues—for example, international marketing, international finance. This literature concentrates, by and large, on the problems of doing business in a foreign country.

As rich as it is, however, I think it is fair to characterize the literature on international competition as being limited when it comes to the choice of a firm's international strategy. Though the literature provides some guidance for considering incremental investment decisions to enter a new country, it provides at best a partial view of how to characterize a firm's overall international strategy and how such strategy should be selected. Put another way, the literature focuses more on the problem of becoming a multinational than on strategies for established multinationals. Although the distinction between domestic firms and multinationals is seminal in a literature focused on the problems of doing business abroad, the fact that a firm is multinational says little if anything about its international strategy except that it operates in several countries.

Broadly stated, my research has been seeking to answer the question: what does international competition mean for competitive strategy? In particular, what are the distinctive questions for competitive strategy that are raised by international as opposed to domestic competition? Many of the strategy issues for a company competing internationally are very much the same as for one competing domestically. A firm must still analyze its industry structure and competitors, understand its buyer and the sources of buyer value, diagnose its relative cost position, and seek to establish a sustainable competitive advantage within some competitive scope, whether it be across-the-board or in an industry segment. These are subjects I have written about extensively.[5] But there are some questions for strategy that are peculiar to international competition, and that add to rather than replace those listed earlier. These questions all revolve, in one way or another, around how a firm's activities in one country affect or are affected by what is going on in other countries— the connectedness among country competition. It is this connectedness that is the focus of this article and of a broader stream of research recently conducted under the auspices of the Harvard Business School.[6]

PATTERNS OF INTERNATIONAL COMPETITION

The appropriate unit of analysis in setting international strategy is the industry, because the industry is the arena in which competitive ad-

vantage is won or lost. The starting point for understanding international competition is the observation that its pattern differs markedly from industry to industry. At one end of the spectrum are industries that I call *multidomestic,* in which competition in each country (or small group of countries) is essentially independent of competition in other countries. A multidomestic industry is one that is present in many countries (e.g., there is a consumer banking industry in Sri Lanka, one in France, and one in the U.S.), but in which competition occurs on a country-by-country basis. In a multidomestic industry, a multinational firm may enjoy a competitive advantage from the one-time transfer of know-how from its home base to foreign countries. However, the firm modifies and adapts its intangible assets to employ them in each country and the outcome is determined by conditions in each country. The competitive advantages of the firm, then, are largely specific to each country. The international industry becomes a collection of essentially domestic industries—hence the term "multidomestic." Industries where competition has traditionally exhibited this pattern include retailing, consumer packaged goods, distribution, insurance, consumer finance, and caustic chemicals.

At the other end of the spectrum are what I term *global* industries. The term global—like the word "strategy"—has become overused and perhaps under-understood. The definition of a global industry employed here is an industry in which a firm's competitive position in one country is significantly influenced by its position in other countries.[7] Therefore, the international industry is not merely a collection of domestic industries but a series of linked domestic industries in which the rivals compete against each other on a truly worldwide basis. Industries exhibiting the global pattern today include commercial aircraft, TV sets, semiconductors, copiers, automobiles, and watches.

The implications for strategy of the distinction between multidomestic and global industries are quite profound. In a multidomestic industry, a firm can and should manage its international activities like a portfolio. Its subsidiaries or other operations around the world should each control all the important activities necessary to do business in the industry and should enjoy a high degree of autonomy. The firm's strategy in a country should be determined largely by the circumstances in that country; the firm's international strategy is then what I term a "country-centered strategy."

In a multidomestic industry, competing internationally is discretionary. A firm can choose to remain domestic or can expand internationally if it has some advantage that allows it to overcome the extra costs of entering and competing in foreign markets. The important competitors in multidomestic industries will either be domestic companies or multinationals with stand-alone operations abroad—this is the situation in each of the multidomestic industries listed earlier. In a multidomestic industry, then, international strategy collapses to a series of domestic strategies. The issues that are uniquely international revolve around how to do business abroad, how to select good countries in which to compete (or assess country risk), and mechanisms to achieve the one-time transfer of know-how. These are questions that are relatively well developed in the literature.

In a global industry, however, managing international activities like a portfolio will undermine the possibility of achieving competitive advantage. In a global industry, a firm must in some way integrate its activities on a worldwide basis to capture the linkages among countries. This will require more than transferring intangible assets among countries, though it will include it. A firm may choose to compete with a country-centered strategy, focusing on specific market segments or countries when it can carve out a niche by responding to whatever local country differences are present. However, it does so at some considerable risk from competitors with global strategies. All the important competitors in the global industries listed earlier compete worldwide with coordinated strategies.

In international competition, a firm always has to perform some functions in each of the countries in which it competes. Even though a global competitor must view its international activities as an overall system, it has still to maintain some country perspective. It is the balancing of these two perspectives that becomes one of the essential questions in global strategy.[8]

CAUSES OF GLOBALIZATION

If we accept the distinction between multidomestic and global industries as an important taxonomy of patterns of international competition, a number of crucial questions arise. When does an industry globalize? What exactly do we mean by a global strategy, and is there more than one kind? What determines the type of international strategy to select in a particular industry?

An industry is global if there is some competitive advantage to integrating activities on a worldwide basis. To make this statement operational, however, we must be very precise about what we mean by "activities" and also what we mean by "integrating." To diagnose the sources of competitive advantage in any context, whether it be domestic or international, it is necessary to adopt a disaggregated view of the firm. In my newest book, *Competitive Advantage,* I have developed a framework for doing so, called the value chain.[9] Every firm is a collection of discrete activities performed to do business that occur within the scope of the firm—I call them value activities. The activities performed by a firm include such things as salespeople selling the product, service technicians performing repairs, scientists in the laboratory designing process techniques, and accountants keeping the books. Such activities are technologically and in most cases physically distinct. It is only at the level of discrete activities, rather than the firm as a whole, that competitive advantage can be truly understood.

A firm may possess two types of competitive advantage: low relative cost or differentiation—

its ability to perform the activities in its value chain either at lower cost or in a unique way relative to its competitors. The ultimate value a firm creates is what buyers are willing to pay for what the firm provides, which includes the physical product as well as any ancillary services or benefits. Profit results if the value created through performing the required activities exceeds the collective cost of performing them. Competitive advantage is a function of either providing comparable buyer value to competitors but performing activities efficiently (low cost), or of performing activities at comparable cost but in unique ways that create greater buyer value than competitors and, hence, command a premium price (differentiation).

The value chain, shown in Figure 1, provides a systematic means of displaying and categorizing activities. The activities performed by a firm in any industry can be grouped into the nine generic categories shown. The labels may differ based on industry convention, but every firm performs these basic categories of activities in some way or another. Within each category of activities, a firm typically performs a number of discrete activities which are particular to the industry and to the firm's strategy. In service, for example, firms typically perform

such discrete activities as installation, repair, parts distribution and upgrading.

The generic categories of activities can be grouped into two broad types. Along the bottom are what I call *primary* activities, which are those involved in the physical creation of the product or service, its delivery and marketing to the buyer, and its support after sale. Across the top are what I call *support* activities, which provide inputs or infrastructure that allow the primary activities to take place on an ongoing basis.

Procurement is the obtaining of purchased inputs, whether they be raw materials, purchased services, machinery, or so on. Procurement stretches across the entire value chain because it supports every activity—every activity uses purchased inputs of some kind. There are typically many different discrete procurement activities within a firm, often performed by different people. Technology development encompasses the activities involved in designing the product as well as in creating and improving the way the various activities in the value chain are performed. We tend to think of technology in terms of the product or manufacturing process. In fact, every activity a firm performs involves a technology or technologies

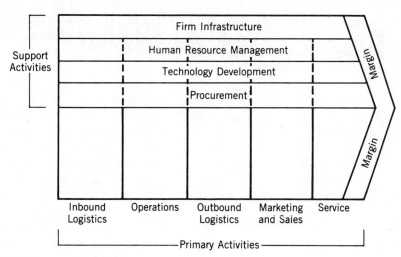

Figure 1 The Value Chain

which may be mundane or sophisticated, and a firm has a stock of know-how about how to perform each activity. Technology development typically involves a variety of different discrete activities, some performed outside the R&D department.

Human resource management is the recruiting, training, and development of personnel. Every activity involves human resources, and thus human resource management activities cut across the entire chain. Finally, firm infrastructure includes activities such as general management, accounting, legal, finance, strategic planning, and all the other activities decoupled from specific primary or support activities but that are essential to enable the entire chain's operation.

Activities in a firm's value chain are not independent, but are connected through what I call linkages. The way one activity is performed frequently affects the cost of effectiveness of other activities. If more is spent on the purchase of a raw material, for example, a firm may lower its cost of fabrication or assembly. There are many linkages that connect activities, not only within the firm but also with the activities of its suppliers, channels, and ultimately its buyers. The firm's value chain resides in a larger stream of activities that I term the value system. Suppliers have value chains that provide the purchased inputs to the firm's chain; channels have value chains through which the firm's product or service passes; buyers have value chains in which the firm's product or service is employed. The connections among activities in this vertical system also become essential to competitive advantage.

A final important building block in value chain theory, necessary for our purposes here, is the notion of *competitive scope.* Competitive scope is the breadth of activities the firm employs together in competing in an industry. There are four basic dimensions of competitive scope:

- *segment* scope, or the range of segments the firm serves (e.g., product varieties, customer types);

- *industry* scope, or the range of industries the firm competes in with a coordinated strategy;
- *vertical* scope, or what activities are performed by the firm versus suppliers and channels; and
- *geographic* scope, or the geographic regions the firm operates in with a coordinated strategy.

Competitive scope is vital to competitive advantage because it shapes the configuration of the value chain, how activities are performed, and whether activities are shared among units. International strategy is an issue of geographic scope, and can be analyzed quite similarly to the question of whether and how a firm should compete locally, regionally, or nationally within a country. In the international context, government tends to have a greater involvement in competition and there are more significant variations among geographic regions in buyer needs, although these differences are matters of degree.

International Configuration and Coordination of Activities

A firm that competes internationally must decide how to spread the activities in the value chain among countries. A distinction immediately arises between the activities labeled downstream on Figure 2, and those labeled upstream activities and support activities. The location of downstream activities, those more related to the buyer, is usually tied to where the buyer is located. If a firm is going to sell in Japan, for example, it usually must provide service in Japan and it must have salespeople stationed in Japan. In some industries it is possible to have a single sales force that travels to the buyer's country and back again; some other specific downstream activities such as the production of advertising copy can also sometimes be done centrally. More typically, however, the firm must locate the capability to perform downstream activities in each of the countries in which it operates. Upstream activities and support activities, conversely, can at least con-

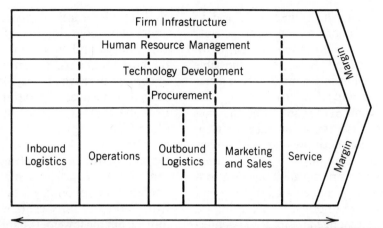

Figure 2   Upstream and Downstream Activities

ceptually be decoupled from where the buyer is located.

This distinction carries some interesting implications. The first is that downstream activities create competitive advantages that are largely country-specific: a firm's reputation, brand name, and service network in a country grow out of a firm's activities in that country and create entry/mobility barriers largely in that country alone. Competitive advantage in upstream and support activities often grows more out of the entire system of countries in which a firm competes than from its position in any one country, however.

A second implication is that in industries where downstream activities or buyer-tied activities are vital to competitive advantage, there tends to be a more multidomestic pattern of international competition. In industries where upstream and support activities (such as technology development and operations) are crucial to competitive advantage, global competition is more common. In global competition, the location and scale of these potentially footloose activities is optimized from a worldwide perspective.[10]

The distinctive issues in international, as contrasted to domestic, strategy can be summarized in two key dimensions of how a firm

competes internationally. The first is what I term the *configuration* of a firm's activities worldwide, or where in the world each activity in the value chain is performed, including in how many places. The second dimension is what I term *coordination,* which refers to how like activities performed in different countries are coordinated with each other. If, for example, there are three plants—one in Germany, one in Japan, and one in the U.S.—how do the activities in those plants relate to each other?

A firm faces an array of options in both configuration and coordination for each activity. Configuration options range from concentrated (performing an activity in one location and serving the world from it—for example, one R&D lab, one large plant) to dispersed (performing every activity in each country). In the latter case, each country would have a complete value chain. Coordination options range from none to very high. For example, if a firm produces its product in three plants, it could, at one extreme, allow each plant to operate with full autonomy—for example, different product standards and features, different steps in the production process, different raw materials, different part numbers. At the other extreme, the plants could be tightly coordinated by employing the same information system, the same production process, the same parts, and so forth. Options for coordination in an activity are typically more numerous than the configuration options because there are many possible levels of coordination and many different facets of the way the activity is performed.

Figure 3 lists some of the configuration issues and coordination issues for several important categories of value activities. In technology development, for example, the configuration issue is where R&D is performed: one location? two locations? and in what countries? The coordination issues have to do with such things as the extent of interchange among R&D centers and the location and sequence of product introduction around the world. There are configuration issues and coordination issues for every activity.

Figure 4 is a way of summarizing these basic choices in international strategy on a single diagram, with coordination of activities on the vertical axis and configuration of activities on the horizontal axis. The firm has to make a set of choices for each activity. If a firm employs a very dispersed configuration—placing an entire value chain in every country (or small group of contiguous countries) in which it operates, coordinating little or not at all among them—then the firm is competing with a country-centered strategy. The domestic firm that only operates in one country is the extreme case of a firm with a country-centered strategy. As we move from the lower left-hand corner of the diagram up or to the right, we have strategies that are increasingly global.

Figure 5 illustrates some of the possible variations in international strategy. The purest global strategy is to concentrate as many activities

Value Activity	Configuration Issues	Coordination Issues
Operations	• Location of production facilities for components and end products	• Networking of international plants • Transferring process technology and production know-how among plants
Marketing and Sales	• Product line selection • Country (market) selection	• Commonality of brand name worldwide • Coordination of sales to multinational accounts • Similarity of channels and product positioning worldwide • Coordination of pricing in different countries
Service	• Location of service organization	• Similarity of service standards and procedures worldwide
Technology Development	• Number and location of R&D centers	• Interchange among dispersed R&D centers • Developing products responsive to market needs in many countries • Sequence of product introductions around the world
Procurement	• Location of the purchasing function	• Managing suppliers located in different countries • Transferring market knowledge • Coordinating purchases of common items

Figure 3 Configuration and Coordination Issues by Category of Activity

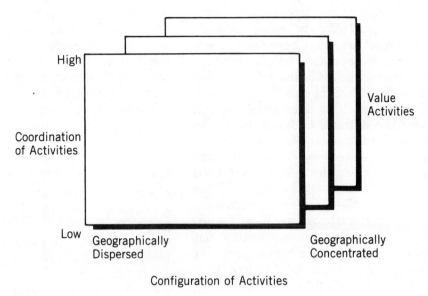

Figure 4   The Dimensions of International Strategy

	Geographically Dispersed	Geographically Concentrated
High	High Foreign Investment with Extensive Coordination among Subsidiaries	Purest Global Strategy
Low	Country-Centered Strategy by Multinationals with a Number of Domestic Firms Operating In Only One Country	Exposrt-Based Strategy with Decentralized Marketing

Coordination of Activities

Value Activities

Configuration of Activities

Figure 5   Types of International Strategy

as possible in one country, serve the world from this home base, and tightly coordinate those activities that must inherently be performed near the buyer. This is the pattern adopted by many Japanese firms in the 1960s and 1970s, such as Toyota. However, Figures 4 and 5 make it clear that there is no such thing as one global strategy. There are many different kinds of global strategies, depending on a firm's choices about configuration and coordination throughout the value chain. In copiers, for example, Xerox has until recently concentrated R&D in the U.S. but dispersed other activities, in some cases using joint-venture partners to perform them. On dispersed activities, however, coordination has been quite high. The Xerox brand, marketing approach, and servicing procedures have been quite standardized worldwide. Canon, on the other hand, has had a much more concentrated configuration of activities and somewhat less coordination of dispersed activities. The vast majority of support activities and manufacturing of copiers have been performed in Japan. Aside from using the Canon brand, however, local marketing subsidiaries have been given quite a bit of latitude in each region of the world.

A global strategy can now be defined more precisely as one in which a firm seeks to gain competitive advantage from its international presence through either concentrating configuration, coordination among dispersed activities, or both. Measuring the presence of a global industry empirically must reflect both dimensions and not just one. Market presence in many countries and some export and import of components and end products are characteristic of most global industries. High levels of foreign investment or the mere presence of multinational firms are not reliable measures, however, because firms may be managing foreign units like a portfolio.

Configuration/Coordination and Competitive Advantage

Understanding the competitive advantages of a global strategy and, in turn, the causes of industry globalization requires specifying the conditions in which concentrating activities globally and coordinating dispersed activities leads to either cost advantage or differentiation. In each case, there are structural characteristics of an industry that work for and against globalization.

The factors that favor concentrating an activity in one or a few locations to serve the world are as follows:

- economies of scale in the activity;
- a proprietary learning curve in the activity;
- comparative advantage in where the activity is performed; and
- coordination advantages of co-locating linked activities such as R&D and production.

The first two factors relate to *how many* sites an activity is performed at, while the last two relate to *where* these sites are. Comparative advantage can apply to any activity, not just production. For example, there may be some locations in the world that are better places than others to do research on medical technology or to perform software development. Government can promote the concentration of activities by providing subsidies or other incentives to use a particular country as an export base, in effect altering comparative advantage—a role many governments are playing today.

There are also structural characteristics that favor dispersion of an activity to many countries, which represent concentration costs. Local product needs may differ, nullifying the advantages of scale or learning from one-site operation of an activity. Locating a range of activities in a country may facilitate marketing in that country by signaling commitment to local buyers and/or providing greater responsiveness. Transport, communication, and storage costs may make it inefficient to concentrate the activity in one location. Government is also frequently a powerful force for dispersing activities. Governments typically want firms to locate the entire value chain in their country, because this creates benefits and spillovers to the country that often go beyond local content.

Dispersion is also encouraged by the risks of performing an activity in one place: exchange-rate risks, political risks, and so on. The balance between the advantages of concentrating and dispersing an activity normally differ for each activity (and industry). The best configuration for R&D is different from that for component fabrication, and this is different from that for assembly, installation, advertising, and procurement.[11]

The desirability of coordinating like activities that are dispersed involves a similar balance of structural factors. Coordination potentially allows the sharing of know-how among dispersed activities. If a firm learns how to operate the production process better in Germany, transferring that learning may make the process run better in plants in the United States and Japan. Differing countries, with their inevitably differing conditions, provide a fertile basis for comparison as well as opportunities for arbitraging knowledge, obtained in different places about different aspects of the business. Coordination among dispersed activities also potentially improves the ability to reap economies of scale in activities if subtasks are allocated among locations to allow some specialization—for example, each R&D center has a different area of focus. While there is a fine line between such forms of coordination and what I have termed configuration, it does illustrate how the way a network of foreign locations is managed can have a great influence on the ability to reap the benefits of any given configuration of activities. Viewed another way, close coordination is frequently a partial offset to dispersing an activity.

Coordination may also allow a firm to respond to shifting comparative advantage, where shifts in exchange rates and factor costs are hard to forecast. Incrementally increasing the production volume at the location currently enjoying favorable exchange rates, for example, can lower overall costs. Coordination can reinforce a firm's brand reputation with buyers (and hence lead to differentiation) through ensuring a consistent image and approach to doing business on a worldwide basis. This is particularly likely if buyers are mobile or information about the industry flows freely around the world. Coordination may also differentiate the firm with multinational buyers if it allows the firm to serve them anywhere and in a consistent way. Coordination (and a global approach to configuration) enhances leverage with local governments if the firm is able to grow or shrink activities in one country at the expense of others. Finally, coordination yields flexibility in responding to competitors, by allowing the firm to differentially respond across countries and to respond in one country to a challenge in another.

Coordination of dispersed activities usually involves costs that differ by form of coordination and industry. Local conditions may vary in ways that may make a common approach across countries suboptimal. If every plant in the world is required to use the same raw material, for example, the firm pays a penalty in countries where the raw material is expensive relative to satisfactory substitutes. Business practices, marketing systems, raw material sources, local infrastructures, and a variety of other factors may differ across countries as well, often in ways that may mitigate the advantages of a common approach or of the sharing of learning. Governments may restrain the flow of information required for coordination or may impose other barriers to it. The transaction costs of coordination, which have recently received increased attention in domestic competition, are vitally important in international strategy.[12] International coordination involves long distances, language problems, and cultural barriers to communication. In some industries, these factors may mean that coordination is not optimal. They also suggest that forms of coordination which involve relatively infrequent decisions will enjoy advantages over forms of coordination involving on-going interchange.

There are also substantial organizational difficulties involved in achieving cooperation among subsidiaries, which are due to the difficulty in aligning subsidiary managers' interests with those of the firm as a whole. The Germans do not necessarily want to tell the Americans about their latest breakthroughs on the production line because it may make it harder for them to outdo the Americans in the annual comparison of operating efficiency among plants. These vexing organizational problems mean that country subsidiaries often view each other more as competitors than collaborators.[13] As with configuration, a firm must make an activity-by-activity choice about where there is net competitive advantage from coordinating in various ways.

Coordination in some activities may be necessary to reap the advantages of configuration in others. The use of common raw materials in each plant, for example, allows worldwide purchasing. Moreover, tailoring some activities to countries may allow concentration and standardization of other activities. For example, tailored marketing in each country may allow the same product to be positioned differently and hence sold successfully in many countries, unlocking possibilities for reaping economies of scale in production and R&D. Thus coordination and configuration interact.

Configuration/Coordination and the Pattern of International Competition

When benefits of configuring and/or coordinating globally exceed the costs, an industry will globalize in a way that reflects the net benefits by value activity. The activities in which global competitors gain competitive advantage will differ correspondingly. Configuration/coordination determines the ongoing competitive advantages of a global strategy which are additive to competitive advantages a firm derives/possesses from its domestic market positions. An initial transfer of knowledge from the home base to subsidiaries is one, but by no means the most important, advantage of a global competitor.[14]

An industry such as commercial aircraft represents an extreme case of a global industry (in the upper right-hand corner of Figure 4). The three major competitors in this industry—

Boeing, McDonnell Douglas, and Airbus—all have global strategies. In activities important to cost and differentiation in the industry, there are compelling net advantages to concentrating most activities and coordinating the dispersed activities extensively.[15] In R&D, there is a large fixed cost of developing an aircraft model ($1 billion or more) which requires worldwide sales to amortize. There are significant economies of scale in production, a steep learning curve in assembly (the learning curve was born out of research in this industry), and apparently significant advantages of locating R&D and production together. Sales of commercial aircraft are infrequent (via a highly skilled sales force), so that even the sales force can be partially concentrated in the home country and travel to buyers.

The costs of a concentrated configuration are relatively low in commercial aircraft. Product needs are homogeneous, and there are the low transport costs of delivering the product to the buyer. Finally, worldwide coordination of the one dispersed activity, service, is very important—obviously standardized parts and repair advice have to be available wherever the plane lands.

As in every industry, there are structural features which work against a global strategy in commercial aircraft. These are all related to government, a not atypical circumstance. Government has a particular interest in commercial aircraft because of its large trade potential, the technological sophistication of the industry, its spillover effects to other industries, and its implications for national defense. Government also has an unusual degree of leverage in the industry: in many instances, it is the buyer. Many airlines are government owned, and a government official or appointee is head of the airline.

The competitive advantages of a global strategy are so great that all the successful aircraft producers have sought to achieve and preserve them. In addition, the power of government to intervene has been mitigated by the fact that there are few viable worldwide competitors and that there are the enormous barriers to entry created in part by the advantages of a global strategy. The result has been that firms have sought to assuage government through procurement. Boeing, for example, is very careful about where it buys components. In countries that are large potential customers, Boeing seeks to develop suppliers. This requires a great deal of extra effort by Boeing both to transfer technology and to work with suppliers to assure that they meet its standards. Boeing realizes that this is preferable to compromising the competitive advantage of its strongly integratⁿd worldwide strategy. It is willing to employ one value activity (procurement) where the advantages of concentration are modest to help preserve the benefits of concentration in other activities. Recently, commercial aircraft competitors have entered into joint ventures and other coalition arrangements with foreign suppliers to achieve the same effect, as well as to spread the risk of huge development costs.

The extent and location of advantages from a global strategy vary among industries. In some industries, the competitive advantage from a global strategy comes in technology development, although firms gain little advantage in the primary activities so that these are dispersed around the world to minimize concentration costs. In other industries such as cameras or videocassette recorders, a firm cannot succeed without concentrating production to achieve economies of scale, but instead it gives subsidiaries much local autonomy in sales and marketing. In some industries, there is no net advantage to a global strategy and country-centered strategies dominate—the industry is multidomestic.

Segments or stages of an industry frequently vary in their pattern of globalization. In aluminum, the upstream (alumina and ingot) stages of the industry are global businesses. The downstream stage, semifabrication, is a group of multidomestic businesses because product needs vary by country, transport costs are high, and intensive local customer service is required. Scale economies in the value chain are modest. In lubricants, automotive oil tends to be a country-centered business while marine motor oil is a global business. In automotive oil, countries have varying driving standards, weather conditions, and local laws. Production involves blending various kinds of crude oils and additives, and is subject to few economies of scale but high shipping costs. Country-centered competitors such as Castrol and Quaker State are leaders in most countries. In the marine segment, conversely, ships move freely around the world and require the same oil everywhere. Successful competitors are global.

The ultimate leaders in global industries are often first movers—the first firms to perceive the possibilities for a global strategy. Boeing was the first global competitor in aircraft, for example, as was Honda in motorcycles, and Becton Dickinson in disposable syringes. First movers gain scale and learning advantages which are difficult to overcome. First mover effects are particularly important in global industries because of the association between globalization and economies of scale and learning achieved through worldwide configuration/coordination. Global leadership shifts if industry structural change provides opportunities for leapfrogging to new products or new technologies that nullify past leaders' scale and learning—again, the first mover to the new generation/technology often wins.

Global leaders often begin with some advantage at home, whether it be low labor cost or a product or marketing advantage. They use this as a lever to enter foreign markets. Once there, however, the global competitor converts the initial home advantage into competitive advantages that grow out of its overall worldwide system, such as production scale or ability to amortize R&D costs. While the initial advantage may have been hard to sustain, the global strategy creates new advantages which can be much more durable.

International strategy has often been characterized as a choice between worldwide standardization and local tailoring, or as the tension between the economic imperative (large-scale efficient facilities) and the political imperative (local content, local production). It should be clear from the discussion so far that neither characterization captures the richness of a firm's international strategy choices. A firm's choice of international strategy involves a search for competitive advantage from configuration/coordination throughout the value chain. A firm may standardize (concentrate) some activities and tailor (disperse) others. It may also be able to standardize and tailor at the same time through the coordination of dispersed activities, or use local tailoring of some activities (e.g., different product positioning in each country) to allow standardization of others (e.g., production). Similarly, the economic imperative is not always for a global strategy—in some industries a country-centered strategy is the economic imperative. Conversely, the political imperative is to concentrate activities in some industries where governments provide strong export incentives and locational subsidies.

Global Strategy vs. Comparative Advantage

Given the importance of trade theory to the study of international competition, it is useful to pause and reflect on the relationship of the framework I have presented to the notion of comparative advantage. Is there a difference? The traditional concept of comparative advantage is that factor-cost or factor-quality differences among countries lead to production of products in countries with an advantage which export them elsewhere in the world. Competitive advantage in this view, then, grows out of *where* a firm performs activities. The location of activities is clearly one source of potential advantage in a global firm. The global competitor can locate activities wherever comparative advantage lies, decoupling comparative advantage from its home base or country of ownership.

Indeed, the framework presented here suggests that the comparative advantage story is richer than typically told, because it not only involves production activities (the usual focus of discussions) but also applies to other activities in the value chain such as R&D, processing orders, or designing advertisements. Comparative advantage is specific to the *activity* and not the location of the value chain as a whole.[16] One of the potent advantages of the global firm is that it can spread activities among locations to reflect different preferred locations for different activities, something a domestic or country-centered competitor does not do. Thus components can be made in Taiwan, software written in India and basic R&D performed in Silicon Valley, for example. This international specialization of activities within the firm is made possible by the growing ability to coordinate and configure globally.

At the same time as our framework suggests a richer view of comparative advantage, however, it also suggests that many forms of competitive advantage for the global competitor derive less from *where* the firm performs activities than from *how* it performs them on a worldwide basis; economies of scale, proprietary learning, and differentiation with multinational buyers are not tied to countries but to the configuration and coordination of the firm's worldwide system. Traditional sources of comparative advantage can be very elusive and slippery sources of competitive advantage for an international competitor today, because comparative advantage frequently shifts. A country with the lowest labor cost is overtaken within a few years by some other country—facilities located in the first country then face a disadvantage. Moreover, falling direct labor as a percentage of total costs, increasing global markets for raw materials and other inputs, and freer flowing technology have diminished the role of traditional sources of comparative advantage.

My research on a broad cross-section of industries suggests that the achievement of sustainable world market leadership follows a more complex pattern than the exploitation of comparative advantage per se. A competitor often starts with a comparative advantage-related edge that provides the basis for penetrating foreign markets, but this edge is rapidly translated into a broader array of advantages that arise from a global approach to configuration and coordination as described earlier. Japanese firms, for example, have done a masterful job of converting temporary labor-cost advantages into durable systemwide advantages due to scale and proprietary know-how. Ultimately, the systemwide advantages are further reinforced with country-specific advantages such as brand identity as well as distribution channel access. Many Japanese firms were fortunate enough to make their transitions from country-based comparative advantage to global competitive advantage at a time when nobody paid much attention to them and there was a buoyant world economy. European and American competitors were willing to cede market share in "less desirable" segments such as the low end of the producer line, or so they thought. The Japanese translated these beachheads into world leadership by broadening their lines and reaping advantages in scale and proprietary technology. The Koreans and Taiwanese, the latest low labor cost entrants to a number of industries, may have a hard time replicating Japan's success, given slower growth, standardized products, and now alert competitors.

Global Platforms

The interaction of the home-country conditions and competitive advantages from a global strategy that transcend the country suggest a more complex role of the country in firm success than implied by the theory of comparative advantage. To understand this more complex role of the country, I define the concept of a *global platform*. A country is a desirable global platform in an industry if it provides an environment yielding firms domiciled in that country an advan-

tage in competing globally in that particular industry.[17] An essential element of this definition is that it hinges on success *outside* the country, and not merely country conditions which allow firms to successfully master domestic competition. In global competition, a country must be viewed as a platform and not as the place where all a firm's activities are performed.

There are two determinants of a good global platform in an industry, which I have explored in more detail elsewhere.[18] The first is comparative advantage, or the factor endowment of the country as a site to perform particular activities in the industry. Today, simple factors such as low-cost unskilled labor and natural resources are increasingly less important to global competition compared to complex factors such as skilled scientific and technical personnel and advanced infrastructure. Direct labor is a minor proportion of cost in many manufactured goods and automation of non-production activities is shrinking it further, while markets for resources are increasingly global, and technology has widened the number of sources of many resources. A country's factor endowment is partly exogenous and partly the result of attention and investment in the country.

The second determinant of the attractiveness of a country as a global platform in an industry are the characteristics of a country's demand. A country's demand conditions include the size and timing of its demand in an industry, factors recognized as important by authors such as Linder and Vernon.[19] They also conclude the sophistication and power of buyers and channels and the product features and attributes demanded. Local demand conditions provide two potentially powerful sources of competitive advantage to a global competitor based in that country. The first is *first-mover advantages* in perceiving and implementing the appropriate global strategy. Pressing local needs, particularly peculiar ones, lead firms to embark early to solve local problems and gain proprietary know-how. This is then translated into scale and learning advantages as firms move early to compete globally. The other potential benefit of local demand conditions is a baseload of demand for product varieties that will be sought after in international markets. These two roles of the country in the success of a global firm reflect the interaction between conditions of local supply, the composition and timing of country demand, and economies of scale and learning in shaping international success.

The two determinants interact in important and sometimes counterintuitive ways. Local demand and needs frequently influence private and social investment in endogenous factors of production. A nation with oceans as borders and dependence on sea trade, for example, is more prone to have universities and scientific centers dedicated to oceanographic education and research. Similarly, factor endowment seems to influence local demand. The per capita consumption of wine is highest in wine-growing regions, for example.

Comparative disadvantage in some factors of production can be an advantage in global competition when combined with pressing local demand. Poor growing conditions have led Israeli farmers to innovate in irrigation and cultivation techniques, for example. The shrinking role in competition of simple factors of production relative to complex factors such as technical personnel seem to be enhancing the frequency and importance of such circumstances. What is important today is unleashing innovation in the proper direction, instead of passive exploitation of static cost advantages in a country which can shift rapidly and be overcome. International success today is a dynamic process resulting from continued development of products and processes. The forces which guide firms to undertake such activity thus become central to international competition.

A good example of the interplay among these factors is the television set industry. In the U.S., early demand was in large-screen console sets because television sets were initially luxury items kept in the living room. As buyers began to purchase second and third sets, sets became smaller and more portable. They were used increasingly in the bedroom, the kitchen, the car, and elsewhere. As the television set industry matured, table model and portable sets became the universal product variety. Japanese firms, because of the small size of Japanese homes, cut their teeth on small sets. They dedicated most of their R&D to developing small picture tubes and to making sets more compact. In the process of naturally serving the needs of their home market, then, Japanese firms gained early experience and scale in segments of the industry that came to dominate world demand. U.S. firms, conversely, cut their teeth on large-screen console sets with fine furniture cabinets. As the industry matured, the experience base of U.S. firms was in a segment that was small and isolated to a few countries, notably the U.S. Japanese firms were able to penetrate world markets in a segment that was both uninteresting to foreign firms and in which they had initial scale, learning, and labor cost advantages. Ultimately the low-cost advantage disappeared as production was automated, but global scale and learning economies took over as the Japanese advanced product and process technology at a rapid pace.

The two broad determinants of a good global platform rest on the interaction between country characteristics and firms' strategies. The literature on comparative advantage, through focusing on country factor endowments, ignoring the demand side, and suppressing the individual firm, is most appropriate in industries where there are few economies of scale, little proprietary technology or technological change, or few possibilities for product differentiation.[20] While these industry characteristics are those of many traditionally traded goods, they describe few of today's important global industries.

THE EVOLUTION OF INTERNATIONAL COMPETITION

Having established a framework for understanding the globalization of industries, we are now in a position to view the phenomenon in historical perspective. If one goes back far enough, relatively few industries were global. Around 1880, most industries were local or regional in scope.[21] The reasons are rather self-evident in the context of our framework. There were few economies of scale in production until fuel-powered machines and assembly-line techniques emerged. There were heterogeneous product needs among regions within countries, much less among countries. There were few if any national media—the *Saturday Evening Post* was the first important national magazine in the U.S. and developed in the teens and twenties. Communicating between regions was difficult before the telegraph and telephone, and transportation was slow until the railroad system became well developed.

These structural conditions created little impetus for the widespread globalization of industry. Those industries that were global reflected classic comparative advantage considerations—goods were simply unavailable in some countries (who then imported them from others) or differences in the availability of land, resources, or skilled labor made some countries desirable suppliers to others. Export of local production was the form of global strategy adapted. There was little role or need for widespread government barriers to international trade during this period, although trade barriers were quite high in some countries for some commodities.

Around the 1880s, however, were the beginnings of what today has blossomed into the globalization of many industries. The first wave of modern global competitors grew up in the late 1800s and early 1900s. Many industries went from local (or regional) to national in scope, and some began globalizing. Firms such as Ford, Singer, Gillette, National Cash Register, Otis, and Western Electric had commanding world market shares by the teens, and operated with integrated worldwide strategies. Early global competitors were principally American and European companies.

Driving this first wave of modern globalization were rising production scale economies

due to advancements in technology that outpaced the growth of the world economy. Product needs also became more homogenized in different countries as knowledge and industrialization diffused. Transport improved, first through the railroad and steamships and later in trucking. Communication became easier with the telegraph then the telephone. At the same time, trade barriers were either modest or overwhelmed by the advantages of the new large-scale firms.

The burst of globalization soon slowed, however. Most of the few industries that were global moved increasingly towards a multidomestic pattern—multinationals remained, but between the 1920s and 1950 they often evolved towards federations of autonomous subsidiaries. The principal reason was a strong wave of nationalism and resulting high tariff barriers, partly caused by the world economic crisis and world wars. Another barrier to global strategies, chronicled by Chandler,[22] was a growing web of cartels and other interfirm contractual agreements. These limited the geographic spread of firms.

The early global competitors began rapidly dispersing their value chains. The situation of Ford Motor Company was no exception. While in 1925 Ford had almost no production outside the U.S., by World War II its overseas production had risen sharply. Firms that became multinationals during the interwar period tended to adopt country-centered strategies. European multinationals, operating in a setting where there were many sovereign countries within a relatively small geographical area, were quick to establish self-contained and quite autonomous subsidiaries in many countries. A more tolerant regulatory environment also encouraged European firms to form cartels and other cooperative agreements among themselves, which limited their foreign market entry.

Between the 1950s and the late 1970s, however, there was a strong reversal of the interwar trends. As Exhibit 1 illustrated, there have been very strong underlying forces driving the globalization of industries. The important reasons can be understood using the configuration/

coordination dichotomy. The competitive advantage of competing worldwide from concentrated activities rose sharply, while concentration costs fell. There was a renewed rise in scale economies in many activities due to advancing technology. The minimum efficient scale of an auto assembly plant more than tripled between 1960 and 1975, for example, while the average cost of developing a new drug more than quadrupled.[23] The pace of technological change has increased, creating more incentive to amortize R&D costs against worldwide sales.

Product needs have continued to homogenize among countries, as income differences have narrowed, information and communication has flowed more freely around the world, and travel has increased.[24] Growing similarities in business practices and marketing systems (e.g., chain stores) in different countries have also been a facilitating factor in homogenizing needs. Within countries there has been a parallel trend towards greater market segmentation, which some observers see as contradictory to the view that product needs in different countries are becoming similar. However, segments today seem based less on country differences and more on buyer differences that transcend country boundaries, such as demographic, user industry, or income groups. Many firms successfully employ global focus strategies in which they serve a narrow segment of an industry worldwide, as do Daimler-Benz and Rolex.

Another driver of post–World War II globalization has been a sharp reduction in the real costs of transportation. This has occurred through innovations in transportation technology including increasingly large bulk carriers, container ships, and larger, more efficient aircraft. At the same time, government impediments to global configuration/coordination have been falling in the postwar period. Tariff barriers have gone down, international cartels and patent-sharing agreements have disappeared, and regional economic pacts such as the European Community have emerged to facilitate trade and investment, albeit imperfectly.

The ability to coordinate globally has also risen markedly in the postwar period. Perhaps the most striking reason is falling communication costs (in voice and data) and reduced travel time for individuals. The ability to coordinate activities in different countries has also been facilitated by growing similarities among countries in marketing systems, business practices, and infrastructure—country after country has developed supermarkets and mass distributors, television advertising, and so on. Greater international mobility of buyers and information has raised the payout to coordinating how a firm does business around the world. The increasing number of firms who are multinational has created growing possibilities for differentiation by suppliers who are global.

The forces underlying globalization have been self-reinforcing. The globalization of firms' strategies has contributed to the homogenization of buyer needs and business practices. Early global competitors must frequently stimulate the demand for uniform global varieties; for example, as Becton Dickinson did in disposable syringes and Honda did in motorcycles. Similarly, globalization of industries begets globalization of supplier industries—the increasing globalization of automotive component suppliers is a good example. Pioneering global competitors also stimulate the development and growth of international telecommunication infrastructure as well as the creation of global advertising media—for example, *The Economist* and *The Wall Street Journal*.

STRATEGIC IMPLICATIONS OF GLOBALIZATION

When the pattern of international competition shifts from multidomestic to global, there are many implications for the strategy of international firms. While a full treatment is beyond the scope of this paper, I will sketch some of the implications here.[25]

At the broadest level, globalization casts new light on many issues that have long been of interest to students of international business. In areas such as international finance, marketing, and business-government relations, the emphasis in the literature has been on the unique problems of adapting to local conditions and ways of doing business in a foreign country in a foreign currency. In a global industry, these concerns must be supplemented with an overriding focus on the ways and means of international configuration and coordination. In government relations, for example, the focus must shift from stand-alone negotiations with host countries (appropriate in multidomestic competition) to a recognition that negotiations in one country will both affect other countries and be shaped by possibilities for performing activities in other countries. In finance, measuring the performance of subsidiaries must be modified to reflect the contribution of one subsidiary to another's cost position or differentiation in a global strategy, instead of viewing each subsidiary as a stand-alone unit. In battling with global competitors, it may be appropriate in some countries to accept low profits indefinitely—in multidomestic competition this would be unjustified.[26] In global industries, the overall system matters as much or more than the country.

Of the many other implications of globalization for the firm, there are two of such significance that they deserve some treatment here. The first is the role of *coalitions* in global strategy. A coalition is a long-term agreement linking firms but falling short of merger. I use the term coalition to encompass a whole variety of arrangements that include joint ventures, licenses, supply agreements, and many other kinds of interfirm relationships. Such interfirm agreements have been receiving more attention in the academic literature, although each form of agreement has been looked at separately and the focus has been largely domestic.[27] International coalitions, linking firms in the same industry based in different countries, have become an even more important part of international strategy in the past decade.

International coalitions are a way of configuring activities in the value chain on a worldwide basis jointly with a partner. International coalitions are proliferating rapidly and are present in many industries.[28] There is a particularly high incidence in automobiles, aircraft, aircraft engines, robotics, consumer electronics, semiconductors and pharmaceuticals. While international coalitions have long been present, their character has been changing. Historically, a firm from a developed country formed a coalition with a firm in a lesser-developed country to perform marketing activities in that country. Today, we observe more and more coalitions in which two firms from developed countries are teaming up to serve the world, as well as coalitions that extend beyond marketing activities to encompass activities throughout the value chain.[29] Production and R&D coalitions are very common, for example.

Coalitions are a natural consequence of globalization and the need for an integrated worldwide strategy. The same forces that lead to globalization will prompt the formation of coalitions as firms confront the barriers to establishing a global strategy of their own. The difficulties of gaining access to foreign markets and in surmounting scale and learning thresholds in production, technology development, and other activities have led many firms to team up with others. In many industries, coalitions can be a transitional state in the adjustment of firms to globalization, reflecting the need of firms to catch up in technology, cure short-term imbalances between their global production networks and exchange rates, and accelerate the process of foreign market entry. Many coalitions are likely to persist in some form, however.

There are benefits and costs of coalitions as well as difficult implementation problems in making them succeed (which I have discussed elsewhere). How to choose and manage coalitions is among the most interesting questions in international strategy today. When one speaks to managers about coalitions, almost all have tales of disaster which vividly illustrate that coalitions often do not succeed. Also, there is the added burden of coordinating global strategy with a coalition partner because the partner often wants to do things its own way. Yet, in the face of copious corporate experience that coalitions do not work and a growing economics literature on transaction costs and contractual failures, we see a proliferation of coalitions today of the most difficult kind—those between companies in different countries.[30] There is a great need for researching in both the academic community and in the corporate world about coalitions and how to manage them. They are increasingly being forced on firms today by new competitive circumstances.

A second area where globalization carries particular importance is in *organizational structure*. The need to configure and coordinate globally in complex ways creates some obvious organizational challenges.[31] Any organization structure for competing internationally has to balance two dimensions; there has to be a *country* dimension (because some activities are inherently performed in the country) and there has to be a *global* dimension (because the advantages of global configuration/coordination must be achieved). In a global industry, the ultimate authority must represent the global dimension if a global strategy is to prevail. However, within any international firm, once it disperses any activities there are tremendous pressures to disperse more. Moreover, forces are unleashed which lead subsidiaries to seek growing autonomy. Local country managers will have a natural tendency to emphasize how different their country is and the consequent need for local tailoring and control over more activities in the value chain. Country managers will be loath to give up control over activities or how they are performed to outside forces. They will also frequently paint an ominous picture of host government concerns about local content and requirements for local presence. Corporate

incentive systems frequently encourage such behavior by linking incentives narrowly to subsidiary results.

In successful global competitors, an environment is created in which the local managers seek to exploit similarities across countries rather than emphasize differences. They view the firms's global presence as an advantage to be tapped for their local gain. Adept global competitors often go to great lengths to devise ways of circumventing or adapting to local differences while preserving the advantages of the similarities. A good example is Canon's personal copier. In Japan, the typical paper size is bigger than American legal size and the standard European size. Canon's personal copier will not handle this size—a Japanese company introduced a product that did not meet its home market needs in the world's largest market for small copiers! Canon gathered its marketing managers from around the world and cataloged market needs in each country. They found that capacity to copy the large Japanese paper was only needed in Japan. In consultation with design and manufacturing engineers, it was determined that building this feature into the personal copier would significantly increase its complexity and cost. The decision was made to omit the feature because the price elasticity of demand for the personal copier was judged to be high. But this was not the end of the deliberations. Canon's management then set out to find a way to make the personal copier saleable in Japan. The answer that emerged was to add another feature to the copier—the ability to copy business cards—which both added little cost and was particularly valuable in Japan. This case illustrates the principle of looking for the similarities in needs among countries and in finding ways of creating similarities, not emphasizing the differences.

Such a change in orientation is something that typically occurs only grudgingly in a multinational company, particularly if it has historically operated in a country-centered mode (as has been the case with early U.S. and European multinationals). Achieving such a reorientation requires first that managers recognize that competitive success demands exploiting the advantages of a global strategy. Regular contact and discussion among subsidiary managers seems to be a prerequisite, as are information systems that allow operations in different countries to be compared.[32] This can be followed by programs for exchanging information and sharing know-how and then by more complex forms of coordination. Ultimately, the reconfiguring of activities globally may then be accepted, even though subsidiaries may have to give up control over some activities in the process.

THE FUTURE OF INTERNATIONAL COMPETITION

Since the late 1970s, there have been some gradual but significant changes in the pattern of international competition which carry important implications for international strategy. Our framework provides a template with which we can examine these changes and probe their significance. The factors shaping the global con-

figuration of activities by firms are developing in ways which contrast with the trends of the previous thirty years. Homogenization of product needs among countries appears to be continuing, though segmentation within countries is as well. As a result, consumer packaged goods are becoming increasingly prone toward globalization, though they have long been characterized by multidomestic competition. There are also signs of globalization in some service industries as the introduction of information technology creates scale economies in support activities and facilitates coordination in primary activities. Global service firms are reaping advantages in hardware and software development as well as procurement.

In many industries, however, limits have been reached in the scale economies that have been driving the concentration of activities. These limits grow out of classic diseconomies of scale that arise in very large facilities, as well as out of new, more flexible technology in manufacturing and other activities that is often not as scale sensitive as previous methods. At the same time, though, flexible manufacturing allows the production of multiple varieties (to

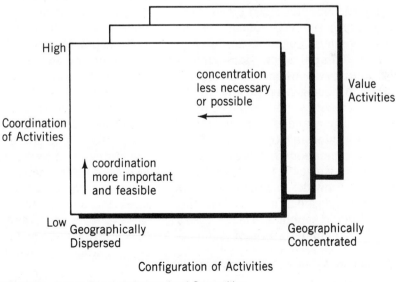

Figure 6 Future Trends in International Competition

serve different countries) in a single plant. This may encourage new movement towards globalization in industries in which product differences among countries have remained significant and have blocked globalization in the past.

There also appear to be some limits to further decline in transport costs, as innovations such as containerization, bulk ships, and larger aircraft have run their course. However, a parallel trend toward smaller, lighter products and components may keep some downward pressure on transport costs. The biggest change in the benefits and costs of concentrated configuration has been the sharp rise in protectionism in recent years and the resulting rise in nontariff barriers, harkening back to the 1920s. As a group, these factors point to less need and less opportunity for highly concentrated configurations of activities.

When we examine the coordination dimension, the picture looks starkly different. Communication and coordination costs are dropping sharply, driven by breathtaking advances in information systems and telecommunication technology. We have just seen the beginning of developments in this area, which are spreading throughout the value chain.[33] Boeing, for example, is employing computer-aided design technology to jointly design components on-line with foreign suppliers. Engineers in different countries are communicating via computer screens. Marketing systems and business practices continue to homogenize, facilitating the coordination of activities in different countries. The mobility of buyers and information is also growing rapidly, greasing the international spread of brand reputations and enhancing the importance of consistency in the way activities are performed worldwide. Increasing numbers of multinational and global firms are begetting globalization by their suppliers. There is also a sharp rise in the computerization of manufacturing as well as other activities throughout the value chain, which greatly facilitates coordination among dispersed sites.

The imperative of global strategy is shifting, then, in ways that will require a rebalancing of configuration and coordination. Concentrating activities is less necessary in economic terms, and less possible as governments force more dispersion. At the same time, the ability to coordinate globally throughout the value chain is increasing dramatically through modern technology. The need to coordinate is also rising to offset greater dispersion and to respond to buyer needs.

Thus, today's game of global strategy seems increasingly to be a game of coordination—getting more and more dispersed production facilities, R&D laboratories, and marketing activities to truly work together. Yet, widespread coordination is the exception rather than the rule today in many multinationals, as I have noted. The imperative for coordination raises many questions for organizational structure, and is complicated even more when the firm has built its global system using coalitions with independent firms.

Japan has clearly been the winner in the postwar globalization of competition. Japan's firms not only had an initial labor cost advantage but the orientation and skills to translate this into more durable competitive advantages such as scale and proprietary technology. The Japanese context also offered an excellent platform for globalization in many industries, given postwar environmental and technological trends. With home market conditions favoring compactness, a lead in coping with high energy costs, and a national conviction to raise quality, Japan has proved a fertile incubator of global leaders. Japanese multinationals had the advantage of embarking on international strategies in the 1950s and 1960s when the imperatives for a global approach to strategy were beginning to accelerate, but without the legacy of past international investments and modes of behavior.[34] Japanese firms also had an orientation towards highly concentrated activities that fit the strategic imperative of the time. Most European and American multinationals, conversely, were well established internationally before the war. They had legacies of local subsidiary autonomy that reflected the interwar environment. As Japanese firms spread internationally, they dispersed activities only grudgingly and engaged in extensive global coordination. European and country-centered American companies struggled to rationalize overly dispersed configurations of activities and to boost the level of global coordination among foreign units. They found their decentralized organization structures—so fashionable in the 1960s and 1970s—to be a hindrance to doing so.

As today's international firms contemplate the future, Japanese firms are rapidly dispersing activities, due largely to protectionist pressures but also because of the changing economic factors I have described. They will have to learn the lessons of managing overseas activities that many European and American firms learned long ago. However, Japanese firms enjoy an organizational style that is supportive of coordination and a strong commitment to introducing new technologies such as information systems that facilitate it. European firms must still overcome their country-centered heritage. Many still do not compete with truly global strategies and lack modern technology. Moreover, the large number of coalitions formed by European firms must overcome the barriers to coordination if they are not to prove ultimately limiting. The European advantage may well be in exploiting an acute and well-developed sensitivity to local market conditions as well as a superior ability to work with host governments. By using modern flexible manufacturing technology and computerizing elsewhere in the value chain, European firms may be able to serve global segments and better differentiate products.

Many Americans firms tend to fall somewhere in between the European and Japanese situations. Their awareness of international competition has risen dramatically in recent years, and efforts at creating global strategies are more widespread. The American challenge is to catch the Japanese in a variety of technologies, as well as to learn how to gain the benefits of coordinating among dispersed units instead of becoming trapped by the myths of decentralization. The changing pattern of international competition is creating an environment in which no competitor can afford to allow country parochialism to impede its ability to turn a worldwide position into a competitive edge.

NOTES

1. United Nations Center on Transnational Corporations, *Salient Features and Trends in Foreign Direct Investment* (New York: United Nations, 1984).

2. For a survey, see R. E. Caves and Ronald W. Jones, *World Trade and Payments,* 4th ed. (Boston: Little, Brown, 1985).

3. There are many books on the theory and management of the multinational, which are too numerous to cite here. For an excellent survey of the literature, see R. E. Caves, *Multinational Enterprise and Economic Analysis* (Cambridge: Cambridge University Press, 1982).

4. Raymond Vernon, "International Investment and International Trade in the Product Cycle," *Quarterly Journal of Economics,* Vol. 80 (May 1966): 190–207. Vernon himself, among others, has raised questions about how general the product cycle pattern is today.

5. Michael E. Porter, *Competitive Strategy: Techniques for Analyzing Industries and Competitors* (New York: The Free Press, 1980); Michael E. Porter, "Beyond Comparative Advantage," working paper, Harvard Graduate School of Business Administration, August 1985.

6. For a description of this research, see Michael E. Porter, ed., *Competition in Global Industries* (Boston: Harvard Business School Press, forthcoming).

7. The distinction between multidomestic and global competition and some of its strategic implications were described in T. Hout, Michael E. Porter, and E. Rudden, "How Global Companies Win Out," *Harvard Business Review* (September–October 1982): 98–108.

8. Howard V. Perlmutter, "The Tortuous Evolution of the Multinational Corporation," *Columbia Journal of World Business* (January–February 1969): 9–18. Perlmutter's concept of ethnocentric, polycentric, and geocentric multinationals takes the *firm* not the industry as the unit of analysis and is decoupled from industry structure. It focuses on management attitudes, the nationality of executives, and other aspects of organization. Perlmutter presents ethnocentric, polycentric, and geocentric as stages of an organization's development as a multinational, with

geocentric as the goal. A later paper (Yoram Wind, Susan P. Douglas, and Howard V. Perlmutter, "Guidelines for Developing International Marketing Strategies," *Journal of Marketing,* Vol. 37 (April 1973): 14–23) tempers this conclusion based on the fact that some companies may not have the required sophistication in marketing to attempt a geocentric strategy. Products embedded in the life style or culture of a country are also identified as less susceptible to geocentrism. The Perlmutter et al. view does not link management orientation to industry structure and strategy. International strategy should grow out of the net competitive advantage in a global industry of different types of worldwide coordination. In some industries, a country-centered strategy, roughly analogous to Perlmutter's polycentric idea, may be the best strategy irrespective of company size and international experience. Conversely, a global strategy may be imperative given the competitive advantage that accrues from it. Industry and strategy should define the organization approach, not vice versa.

9.   Michael E. Porter, *Competitive Advantage: Creating and Sustaining Superior Performance* (New York: The Free Press, 1985).

10.   Buzzell (Robert D. Buzzell, "Can You Standardize Multinational Marketing," *Harvard Business Review* (November–December 1980): 102–113; Pryor (Millard H. Pryor, "Planning in a World-Wide Business," *Harvard Business Review,* Vol. 23 (January–February 1965); and Wind, Douglas, and Perlmutter, "Guidelines," point out that national differences are in most cases more critical with respect to marketing than with production and finance. This generalization reflects the fact that marketing activities are often inherently country-based. However, this generalization is not reliable because in many industries, production and other activities are widely dispersed.

11.   A number of authors have framed the globalization of industries in terms of the balance between imperatives for global integration and imperatives for national responsiveness, a useful distinction. See C. K. Prahalad, "The Stategic Process in a Multinational Corporation," unpublished DBA dissertation, Harvard Graduate School of Business Administration, 1975; Yves Doz, "National Policies and Multinational Management," an unpublished DBA dissertation, Harvard Graduate School of Business Administration, 1976; and Christopher A. Bartlett, "Multinational Structural Evolution: The Changing Decision Environment in the International Division," unpublished DBA dissertation, Harvard Graduate School of Business Administration, 1979. I link the distinction here to where and how a firm performs the activities in the value chain internationally.

12.   See, for example, Oliver Williamson, *Markets and Hierarchies* (New York: The Free Press, 1975). For an international application, see Mark C. Casson, "Transaction Costs and the Theory of the Multinational Enterprise," in Alan Rugman, ed., *New Theories of the Multinational Enter-*prise (London: Croom Helm, 1982); David J. Teece, "Transaction Cost Economics and the Multinational Enterprise: An Assessment," *Journal of Economic Behavior and Organization* (1986).

13.   The difficulties in coordinating are internationally parallel to those in coordinating across business units competing in different industries with the diversified firm. See Michael E. Porter, *Competitive Advantage: Creating and Sustaining Superior Performance* (New York: The Free Press, 1985), Chapter 11.

14.   Empirical research has found a strong correlation between R&D and advertising intensity and the extent of foreign direct investment (for a survey, see Caves, *Multinational Enterprise*). Both these factors have a place in our model of the determinants of globalization, but for quite different reasons. R&D intensity suggests scale advantages for the global competitor in developing products or processes that are manufactured abroad either due to low production scale economies or government pressures, or which require investments in service infrastructure. Advertising intensity, however, is much closer to the classic transfer of marketing knowledge to foreign subsidiaries. High advertising industries are also frequently those where local tastes differ and manufacturing scale economies are modest, both reasons to disperse many activities.

15.   For an interesting description of the industry, see the paper by Michael Yoshino in Porter, ed., *Competition in Global Industries.*

16.   It has been recognized that comparative advantage in different stages in a vertically integrated industry sector such as aluminum can reside in different countries. Bauxite mining will take place in resource-rich countries, for example, while smelting will take place in countries with low electrical power cost. See Caves and Jones, *World Trade and Payments.* The argument here extends this thinking *within* the value chain of any stage and suggests that the optimal location for performing individual activities may vary as well.

17.   The firm need not necessarily be owned by investors in the country, but the country is its home base for competing in a particular country.

18.   See Porter, *Competitive Advantage.*

19.   See S. Linder, *An Essay on Trade and Transformation* (New York: John Wiley, 1961); Vernon, "International Investment"; W. Gruber, D. Mehta, and R. Vernon, "R&D Factor in International Trade and International Investment of United States Industries," *Journal of Political Economics,* 76/1 (1967): 20–37.

20.   Where it does recognize scale economies, trade theory views them narrowly as arising from production in one country.

21.   See Alfred Chandler in Porter, ed., *Competition in Global Industries,* for a penetrating history of the origins of the large industrial firm and its expansion abroad, which is consistent with the discussion here.

22. Ibid.
23. For data on auto assembly, see "Note on the World Auto Industry in Transition," *Harvard Business School Case Services* (#9-382-122).
24. For a supporting view, see Theodore Levitt, "The Globalization of Markets," *Harvard Business Review* (May–June 1983): 92–102.
25. The implications of the shift from multidomestic to global competition were the theme of a series of papers on each functional area of the firm prepared for the Harvard Business School Colloquium on Competition in Global Industries. See Porter, ed., *Competition in Global Industries.*
26. For a discussion, see Hout, Porter, and Rudden, "How Global Companies Win Out." For a recent treatment, see Gary Hamel and C. K. Prahalad, "Do You Really Have a Global Strategy?" *Harvard Business Review* (July–August 1985): 139–148.
27. David J. Teece, "Firm Boundaries, Technological Innovation, and Strategic Planning," in L. G. Thomas, ed., *Economics of Strategic Planning* (Lexington, Mass.: Lexington Books, 1985).
28. For a treatment of coalitions from this perspective, see Porter, Fuller, and Rawlinson, in Porter, ed., *Competition in Global Industries.*
29. Hladik's recent study of international joint ventures provides supporting evidence. See K. Hladik, "International Joint Ventures: An Empirical Investigation into the Characteristics of Recent U.S.-Foreign Joint Venture Partnerships," unpublished doctoral dissertation, Business Economics Program, Harvard University, 1984.
30. For the seminal work on contractual failures, see Williamson, *Markets and Hierarchies.*
31. For a thorough and sophisticated treatment, see Christopher A. Bartlett's paper in Porter, ed., *Competition in Global Industries.*
32. For a good discussion of the mechanisms for facilitating international coordination in operations and technology development, see M. T. Flaherty in Porter, ed., *Competition in Global Industries.* Flaherty stresses the importance of information systems and the many dimensions that valuable coordination can take.
33. For a discussion, see Michael E. Porter and Victor Millar, "How Information Gives You Competitive Advantage," *Harvard Business Review* (July–August 1985): 149–160.
34. Prewar international sales enjoyed by Japanese firms were handled largely through trading companies. See Chandler, in Porter, ed., *Competition in Global Industries.*

10

GLOBAL STRATEGIES: STANDARDIZATION VERSUS FLEXIBILITY
Lawrence H. Wortzel

Strategic management involves identifying and responding to opportunities as well as threats. Increasingly, both can originate from outside a firm's domestic market. More and more manufacturers in any country/market must now not only go head to head with domestic competitors, but must also face up to foreign multinationals. Furthermore, most of today's products have potential markets in several countries. Many argue, therefore, that markets and competitors are now global, and that firms should develop global strategies to survive and grow.[1] People, however, disagree about what a global strategy should actually look like.

INTERNATIONAL BUSINESS[2]

Firms of one kind or another have been operating across country borders for hundreds of years. Marco Polo was in the import/export business, and his writings are a by-product of his business travels. The current era of interna-

Source: 1989 International Business Strategy Resource Book. Strategic Direction Publishers, Inc.

tional business, marked by the burgeoning of multinationals, began after World War I, was interrupted by World War II, and accelerated rapidly when the war ended in 1945.

At first, multinationalization was primarily a trans-Atlantic phenomenon led by US-based firms. Many US manufacturing firms had subsidiaries in Europe well before World War II, and many others exported to Europe. US firms' penetration of European markets during the pre-war period depended on exploiting some ologopolistic advantages. These included such advantages as a technological lead enabling them to offer new products not yet available in Europe, an ability to mass-produce standardized products leading to a cost advantage, or the ability to develop and promote brand names.[3]

FROM INTERNATIONAL TO MULTINATIONAL

While war production during World War II sharpened US firms' abilities, Europe's production and marketing capacity was virtually destroyed. After the war, US firms once again quickly penetrated European markets, at first with exports, then with manufacturing subsidiaries. An environment in which both free trade and foreign direct investment were favored facilitated the spread of US firms into Europe. While US firms also entered markets in other parts of the world, Japan was the exception; few US firms successfully penetrated its domestic market. A cultural and language barrier, coupled with a centuries-old, highly insular and protectionist economy, made exporting to Japan extremely difficult and manufacturing there even more so.

After the war, Western Europe and Japan developed their own industries once again, and by the late 1960s, European and Japanese multinationals had begun competing with US multinationals in such industries as chemicals, automobiles, and consumer electronics. By the

1980s, multinational firms from the newly industrializing countries had entered the world market. And by mid-1988 the 500 largest non-US multinationals included 11 firms from South Korea, three from Taiwan, and six from Brazil.

Multinationals most often began their international activities with exports. They began exporting in response to opportunities in international markets, rather than in response to threats to their domestic businesses. But there were exceptions. Firms in the pharmaceutical industry, for instance, recognized the danger inherent in being smaller than their competitors. In the face of ever-mounting R&D costs, a firm in this innovation-dependent industry could survive only if it had a very large market in which to recoup its R&D investment. Similarly, Japanese auto and consumer electronics manufacturers, in particular Honda and Sony, entered international markets in order to provide enough volume to keep them cost-competitive in their respective domestic Japanese markets.

FROM MULTINATIONAL TO GLOBAL

Although their businesses were expanding horizontally into more and more markets, most European and US multinationals managed their business vertically, that is, coordinating the production, distribution, and marketing functions primarily within countries (or, less frequently, regions). Typically, they managed their business as a collection or portfolio of individual domestic entities, each with self-contained marketing and, often, manufacturing facilities. In many cases, national management led to significant differences in product lines across countries, as individual country managements reacted to specific threats and opportunities within their particular domestic markets.

By the 1980s, the competitive advantages that had produced success in the early post–

World War II period were no longer sufficient. Technological leads became much harder to sustain. Competitors became much more adept at copying each other's new products. An expanding number of firms across a wider spectrum of countries could be cost-competitive in manufacturing standardized products. Many more firms had the ability to promote brand names. And consumers had become much more receptive to new brands. Firms had to search for new sources of competitive advantage.

Many suggested that the multinational, with its vertical, country-focused management, inevitably faced a competitive disadvantage. They believed there were potentially important competitive advantages available to firms as a result of their being multinational. But multinationals, because of their country-focused organization and management, were not seizing these opportunities. While firms might be optimizing their businesses in terms of domestic market opportunities in each country, their country-by-country actions, taken together, were not optimal for the whole corporation. Critics pointed to the success of the leading Japanese multinationals in penetrating foreign markets. These Japanese firms employed large, highly coordinated, centralized manufacturing facilities located in Japan, from which they fanned out their products around the world.

Out of such arguments were born the concepts of the global firm and the global industry. Simply stated, a global industry is one in which a firm's activities in one country market can affect its competitive position in other country markets. A global firm is one that is organized and managed to take advantage of whatever synergies are available across country markets.[4] The global firm, many argue, will render both the multinational and the domestic firm obsolete by gaining insurmountable competitive advantage.[5] The differences they envision between the multinational and the global include the following:

- The global firm, like its predecessor the multinational, markets its products in many countries, and might also manufacture in many countries.
- Unlike the typical multinational, the global firm offers a standardized product in all country markets, perhaps also standardizing brand name, positioning, and advertising content.
- The global firm manufactures at whatever sites, and utilizes whatever plant sizes, that will minimize the cost of the delivered products across its country markets.
- The global firm organizes itself in a way that facilitates the efficient marketing, manufacture, and distribution of its standardized products.

In sum, a global firm has one global strategy rather than a series of national strategies.[6]

GLOBAL FIRMS, GLOBAL INDUSTRIES, AND GLOBAL STRATEGIES[7]

The notion of globalization—a global firm pursuing a global strategy—is very appealing to managers. In many industries, there are potential synergies in managing horizontally—that is, coordinating activities and functions across national boundaries. In these industries, global strategies—strategies that capitalize on the potential for synergy—offer the possibility of greater competitive advantage than national strategies. The easiest way to achieve the synergies is to standardize everything, and standardization is naturally attractive to managers. Standardizing the product makes it easy to standardize manufacturing and control systems, thus making the business easier to run and more amenable to control from headquarters.

Global standardization has its critics as well as its proponents. Proponents correctly perceive that the weakness in the country-specific strategies most multinationals pursue is that they may not be optimal for the corporation as a whole. But their critics say the proponents do not give enough weight to the greatest strength inherent in national strategies—the ability to tailor product, product line, and marketing efforts country-by-country to take best advantage of opportunities in each market. Flexibility, not standardization, the critics of standardization say, is the key to a successful global strategy.[8]

Critics of standardization believe that Japanese firms' successes were not due simply to the low-cost position they attained through long, high-volume production runs of standardized products. They note that many Japanese firms customize their products—autos and consumer electronics included—as necessary to best fit the requirements of specific country markets. Japanese firms have pioneered flexible manufacturing techniques that give them the ability to customize products and to quickly introduce new models in small quantities without incurring a significant cost penalty. Japanese firms' ability to identify opportunities to customize, and then to deliver to the market customized products at more or less the same cost, has sustained their success in world markets.

The major premises behind the argument for global standardization are that it has the potential for providing a cost advantage over both domestic firms and vertically managed multinationals, and that such cost advantages are an essential determinant of competitive advantage. The firm with a cost advantage can then either pass its cost savings on to customers in the form of lower prices or use the extra margin its low costs provide to enhance its R&D or marketing activities.

Implicit in these premises is the idea that cost savings are upstream (procurement, manufacturing) rather than downstream (distribution, marketing) activities. Firms can consolidate their upstream activities, but they must perform downstream activities country-by-country. Thus, a firm can best achieve cost savings by consolidating and rationalizing its upstream activities. The key to realizing these cost savings is producing standardized products and then marketing the same standardized products in each country.

Given the competitive situation that most firms face, no one can argue strongly against the importance of a favorable cost position as a key component in any strategy designed to produce significant volumes. What is questionable, however, is the viability of competitive strategies based on product standardization.

Critics argue that a global strategy based simply on offering a standardized product worldwide will not in all cases lead to a significant sustainable competitive advantage.[9] Global standardization, in fact, may result in a penalty rather than a bonus, because it locks the firm into a particular competitive posture, while sources of competitive advantage continually change. Where the sources of competitive advantage keep changing, sustainable competitive advantage is produced by flexibility, not standardization. The key is to constantly identify and capitalize on new sources of competitive advantage, and to be faster and more adept at identifying and implementing opportunities for change. Taking advantage of the opportunities requires a far more sophisticated and flexible strategy than simply standardizing.

ASSUMPTIONS BEHIND THE DEBATE

The major reason for the standardization/flexibility debate is that proponents of each strategy start from a different set of assumptions in three critical areas: country/market and product characteristics, determinants of a favorable cost position, and trade and investment barriers. Exhibit 1 identifies the key differences in the assumptions behind the standardization and flexibility strategies. To highlight the differences, I have drawn the characterization of each position as sharply as possible. Simply stated, the assumptions behind a standardization strategy are these:

- "One size fits all": the global consumer. Due mainly to technological advances in transportation

Exhibit 1   Global Strategy Assumptions

AREAS OF ASSUMPTION	Assumptions behind	
	Standardization	**Flexibility**
Country Market and Product Characteristics	Similar: not highly segmented. Stable: few changes or new products.	Different: highly segmented. Dynamic: constant change. New products.
Keys to Favorable Cost Position	Manufacturing costs are significant. Economies of scale in manufacturing. Experience-curve effects resulting from long runs of few products. Choice of production location(s) critical. Scale of economies of R&D.	Marketing costs are significant. Significant economies of scope as well as scale in manufacturing. Economies of scope in marketing and distribution. Market stimuli critical for new product development.
Trade & Investment Barriers	None. Invest, manufacture, procure where most advantageous. Ship anywhere.	Foreign direct investment regulated: nonregulatory investment barriers erected by host governments. Tariff and nontariff barriers to trade. Protectionism: nationalism; regionalism.

and communication, consumers worldwide—or at least in many countries—have become similar enough in their tastes and preferences that the same product will satisfy all of them. Where the standardized product might not be a consumer's ideal choice, if its price is sufficiently lower than that of the ideal product, the consumer will buy it.

• Product standardization leads to economies based on size. There are economies available in one or more of the business functions—manufacturing, procurement, distribution, R&D, management—as a result of marketing a standardized product across countries. Larger unit sales of the standardized product result in scale economies.

• Minimal trade barriers. Firms can freely ship merchandise across borders, tariffs are low or nonexistent, and nontariff barriers such as quotas or red tape do not exist, so a firm can manufacture wherever it is most advantageous.

In contrast, the assumptions behind a flexibility strategy are:

• Consumers in different country markets have different preferences, and if their preferences can be met without incurring a large cost penalty, customers will prefer a customized product.

• Manufacturing flexibility makes up for scale. By adopting flexible manufacturing techniques, the firm can produce small quantities of a wider range of products at costs approaching those obtained for a long run of a single product.

- Trade barriers exist that preclude freedom in choosing manufacturing sites.

CHOOSING THE RIGHT GLOBAL STRATEGY

Simply stated, setting a global strategy is a matter of adjusting as much as possible the business functions—manufacturing, procurement, marketing, distribution, and R&D—within the constraints of trade and investment barriers in a way that provides the best possible product/market fits. In some cases, the best fit is a standardized product; in others a customized product fits best. Setting a global strategy often involves following a zig-zag line between standardization and flexibility, trading off the costs and benefits of one against those of the other.

To identify the best product/market fit, first we have to identify salient product characteristics and then classify products according to these characteristics. Simply rating products as candidates for standardization (or for customization) is not sufficient. A second dimension—rate of change—is equally important.

Exhibit 2 arranges a sample of products along these two dimensions. The horizontal dimension, the consumers' preferred product, classifies products along a continuum from standardized to customized. The vertical dimension, rate of change in product, covers a spectrum from fast to slow. Let's examine some of the product examples in each of the four quadrants.

STANDARDIZED PRODUCTS

Many of the successful efforts at producing and marketing a standardized product across country markets have resulted from customers who demanded a standardized product. When customers demand standardization, standardizing does not lead to a competitive advantage; it is simply a competitive necessity. There are other cases in which standardization has come about through the efforts of marketers. We shall examine both cases.

RAPIDLY CHANGING STANDARDIZED PRODUCTS

The clearest cases of customer-demanded standardization occur where the customer is a multinational firm. Examples of standardized products include many OEM auto parts and telecommunications equipment used in transborder data networks. Although auto manufacturers may tailor the appearance and features of their cars to specific markets, many of the working parts they use are standardized. The objective is to use the identical part in every country in which they assemble autos. Multinational firms that have trans-border communications networks want standardized equipment at all sites to ensure network compatibility. To retain multinational customers, a supplier must not only offer a standardized product, but must be able to provide it globally, wherever its customers have operations.

Some rapidly changing consumer products, such as color snapshot and slide films, also require standardization. Here the impetus for standardization comes from both camera manufacturers with worldwide markets and traveling consumers. Even the simplest cameras now offer automatic light metering that requires standardized film in order to work properly. Consumers want to buy color film of a known brand and invariant characteristics wherever they go.

VCRs and compact disc players are two cases in which producers influenced consumers around the world to accept a standardized product. In the case of the VCR, at the beginning there were two competing systems, Beta and VHS. Matsushita, who championed VHS, marketed VCRs themselves, produced VCRs for resellers, and licensed the technology. VHS has

Exhibit 2 Market Requirements and Product Characteristics

RATE OF CHANGE OF PRODUCT

Fast

Computer chips: automotive electronics; color film; pharmaceutical chemicals; telecommunications; network equipment	Consumer electronics: automobiles; trucks Watch cases; dolls
	Toothpaste; shampoo Industrial machinery

Standardized in All Markets — **Customized Market-by-Market**

Steel; petrochemicals (e.g., polyethylene); cola beverages; fabric for men's shirts	Toilets; chocolate bars

CONSUMERS' PREFERRED PRODUCT

Slow

become the standard format for home videotape. Philips and Sony jointly championed the compact disc player, promoted it jointly, licensed the technology to others, and sold the necessary components to other manufacturers. As a result, the Philips/Sony compact disc is a worldwide standard for recorded music.

SLOWLY CHANGING STANDARDIZED PRODUCTS

Producers can standardize industrial products, such as steel and certain petrochemicals and fabrics, because customers, specifications for such products are similar in many countries. Among consumer products, cola beverages seem to be unique in having worldwide appeal. The leading producers—Coca-Cola and Pepsi-

Cola—have had little difficulty obtaining consumer acceptance for Coke and Pepsi virtually everywhere they have been available.

CUSTOMIZED PRODUCTS

While consumer durables such as automobiles and TV sets appear at first inspection amenable to standardization, there are subtle but significant differences in these products across country markets. Automobiles differ in their model names, in trim and headlights, engine sizes, safety equipment and accessories. TV sets must be manufactured to different broadcast standards (e.g., PAL in Great Britain, SECAM in France, NTSC in the US and Japan), and vary in external appearance. The most commonly sold sizes of refrigerators and washing machines in the US are much larger than those most commonly sold elsewhere. This means that, to gain a large share in diverse markets, automobile, TV, and appliance manufacturers must customize to at least some degree.

Differences in consumer packaged goods products across markets are legion. Colgate markets a toothpaste in England that is different from its US offering. Knorr customizes its line of dry soup and sauce mixes to the taste preferences of particular country markets. Even McDonald's does not offer a globally standardized product. Its menu includes beer in Germany and Rendang burgers (an indigenous spiced and stewed beef or buffalo) in Indonesia. And its "special sauce" varies from country to country.

Machinery sold in the US tends to be larger than machinery sold in Japan. Japanese firms prefer smaller equipment because factory space is limited and workers are generally smaller than their US counterparts. US firms also prefer machinery with more features. One observer, mixing metaphors in the process, has described US users' preference for machinery with "lots of bells and whistles," while the rest of the world prefers "plain vanilla." Similarly Komatsu's edge over Caterpillar in Asian markets is not due solely to its market proximity or its lower prices; the size and layout of the Komatsu cab fits its generally smaller Asian drivers better than Caterpillar's does.

Customizing is important in slowly changing products as well. As anyone who has traveled internationally can verify, flush toilets are very different across country markets. True, the international class hotels in many countries may install foreign toilets, but it is rare to see anything but the "national" toilet in any country's private homes.

Finally, chocolate is another example of a customized, slow-changing product. US chocolate bars (Hershey), British (Cadbury), Dutch (Droste), Swiss (Lindt), Mexican (Carlos Quinto) and Japanese (Lotte), all taste significantly different. Many chocolate candy produc-

ers sell their domestic product multinationally, with some success, but virtually none has achieved the level of penetration in foreign markets that it achieved at home. More often than not, the domestic market-share leader is a specialty product with a small market share in other countries. Consumer taste preferences for chocolate simply differ across countries.

SELECTING A STRATEGY: IDENTIFYING THE KEYS TO COMPETITIVE ADVANTAGE

Exhibit 3 shows the keys to competitive advantage for each of the product types presented in Exhibit 2. Each is discussed below, highlighting the most important elements of a strategy that best captures the competitive advantages available to that particular combination of product/market characteristics. We also look briefly at possibilities for gaining a better advantage by moving the product into a different quadrant, standardizing where everyone else is customizing, or vice versa.

STANDARDIZED, RAPIDLY CHANGING PRODUCTS: MAINTAINING DIFFERENTIATION

Although firms with products that fall into this category standardize them across country markets, they must at the same time try to differentiate their standardized offerings from those of competitors. Offering, for example, automobile electronics parts or telecommunications products demonstrably better than competitors, is a requirement for continued success. To maintain a product advantage, firms with products falling in this quadrant of Exhibit 3 must continually improve their products and supplement them with new products whenever possible. Competitive advantage lies in a firm's ability to:

Exhibit 3 Strategy Choices

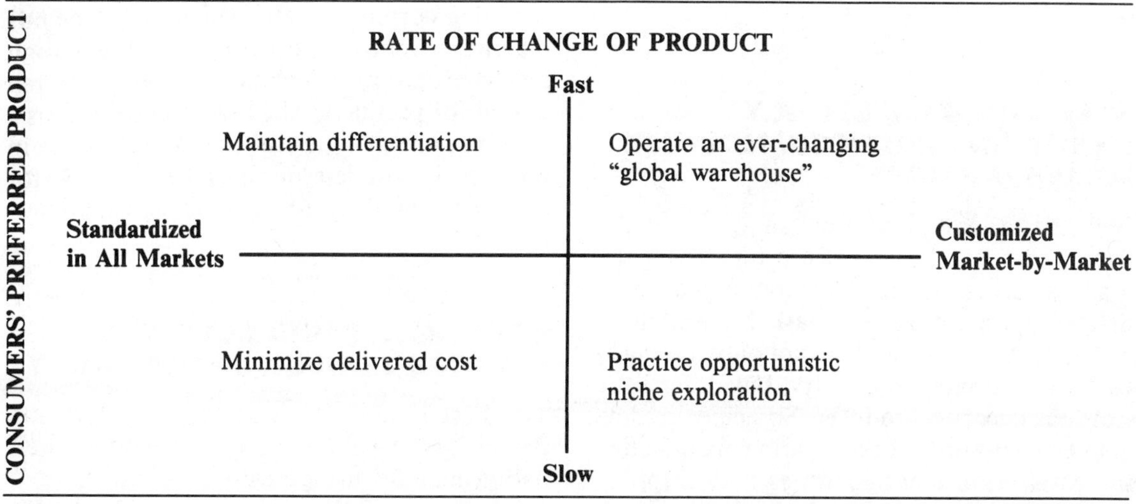

RATE OF CHANGE OF PRODUCT

Fast

| Maintain differentiation | Operate an ever-changing "global warehouse" |

Standardized in All Markets ——————————————— **Customized Market-by-Market**

CONSUMERS' PREFERRED PRODUCT

| Minimize delivered cost | Practice opportunistic niche exploration |

Slow

- Develop new products more quickly than the competition.
- Put them into production quickly.
- Produce them reliably and efficiently . . . and in quantity.

It is essential to locate R&D and production as close as possible to lead markets. New product development and product improvement are, most often, cut-and-try propositions. Success depends on understanding customer needs and an ability to translate those needs into product specifications. Innumerable studies, and the experience of a great many firms, confirm the importance of close and continuous contact with the market in order to anticipate and then successfully develop and commercialize new products. The process is most enhanced when the product developer is in close contact with lead users—those customers whose own needs require technological advances.

German automakers Mercedes Benz and BMW must offer high-performance cars. Fuel injection contributes to performance. Robert Bosch, because of its proximity to Mercedes and BMW's own R&D teams, has managed to develop and maintain a leadership position in

fuel injection. Similarly, the Eaton Corporation, working with US producers, has developed a leading position in truck transmissions and powertrains.

Firms should locate their manufacturing plants close to their R&D facilities (this means they will be de facto located close to their lead users). In this way, they can facilitate translation of R&D results into full-scale production and quickly make the changes usually required early in the commercial life of a new product.

Ideally, producers of standardized, quickly changing products should concentrate their manufacturing at the fewest possible locations. They can then take maximum advantage of scale and experience effects, and ensure conformance in manufacture. When concentration is not possible, they must set up mechanisms that ensure dissemination of information from R&D to plant, and from plant to plant.

When designing or upgrading their plants, manufacturers should aim for dynamic flexibility—that is, manufacturing systems that have the flexibility to quickly improve current products and also accomplish quick change-overs to newer, evolutionary products. Such flexibility gives firms the capability to bring innovations to market in the minimum possible time.

STANDARDIZED, SLOWLY CHANGING PRODUCTS: MINIMIZE DELIVERED COST

Here the key competitive advantage is low delivered cost. But, as we shall see, identifying the manufacturing sites that will produce the lowest delivered cost is not an easy task. Many of these products are mature and are not only standardized from country to country, but differ little from producer to producer. So achieving low delivered cost involves comparing manufacturing costs in different countries with shipping costs from those countries to destination markets. Because demand is relatively stable for many products in this classification, the task is apparently straightforward. In reality, however, it is excruciatingly complicated and full of uncertainty.

WHY UNCERTAINTY?

Uncertainties occur because the relative cost positions of different countries can—and do—change rapidly. One reason for the changes in relative cost positions is relative changes in manufacturing costs. Prices of raw materials and components can rise or fall more quickly in one country than another. And wage rates may increase more quickly (or less quickly) than productivity in some countries, changing country-to-country direct labor cost relationships.

Another factor affecting countries' relative cost positions is foreign exchange rates, which fluctuate even on a daily basis, and all too often do not reflect relative productivity across countries. The substantial appreciation of the Japanese yen as compared to the much smaller appreciation of the South Korean won, for example, has caused some Japanese firms to shift production to South Korea, even though pro-

ductivity may be higher in Japan. Because of changing currency relationships, the strategist may have trouble identifying the country that, given the pattern of demand, offers the most potential for producing the lowest delivered cost position. And selecting the right site can be even more critical in determining a firm's delivered cost position than either scale or experience factors.

SETTING A MANUFACTURING STRATEGY UNDER UNCERTAINTY

The best manufacturing strategy offers site flexibility—the ability to quickly shift to alternative manufacturing locations as cost relationships change. Such a strategy can be highly effective even without making the very best choices; one need only make better choices than one's competitors. First steps include identifying the most significant factors affecting production cost (e.g., raw materials, components, labor), producing a list of likely countries, and projecting the likely cost levels for each country.

In making cost projections, managers have to keep in mind that not all changes are linear. For example, in some countries, labor skill can increase faster than wages, for a time resulting in very high productivity. This was the case in South Korea, for instance, and the Korean experience could well be repeated in a country such as Thailand. Similarly, the sudden removal of barriers to raw material or component imports can make a heretofore high-cost country a low-cost producer. For example, a country such as Indonesia might be a highly attractive manufacturing site if components could be imported at lower prices.

All this adds up to one critical point: the most advantageous cost location can, and likely will, shift. Developing the ability to project sites with potential, and maintaining the flexibility to take advantage of them when they emerge, are an essential part of maintaining the key competitive advantage of low delivered cost.

CUSTOMIZED, RAPIDLY CHANGING PRODUCTS: THE EVER-CHANGING "GLOBAL WAREHOUSE"

Most consumer products, both packaged goods and durables, fall into the customized and rapidly changing quadrant of Exhibit 2. Global success within this quadrant requires:

- A broad product line.

- Constant innovation.

- Highly flexible manufacturing.

- Quick transmission and adoption of new product ideas across countries.

Markets for these products are highly segmented, and those segments, even if common across countries, are likely to vary significantly in size. Also, because products change so quickly, country customization rather than global standardization is almost always a better choice.

Consumer products usually have high marketing and distribution costs, so it is tempting to standardize products in the hope of saving manufacturing costs, and use the savings to cover marketing costs. But for a firm selling products in this category to adopt such a strategy is risky at best. A standardized version of any product is likely to have only limited appeal in some markets, thereby creating very high unit marketing and distribution costs.

THE PRODUCT LINE REQUIREMENT

In most cases a strategy based on covering marketing and distribution costs with money saved by achieving scale economies in manufacturing simply will not work. A better strategy is to cover marketing and distribution costs by seeking economies of scope, that is, economies based on offering broad product lines within

product categories, and on offering a range of related product categories. The range of categories offered should be capable of sharing marketing and distribution costs and, ideally, manufacturing costs as well. Japanese firms' successes in consumer durables are not simply the result of low-cost manufacturing. The economies of scope they achieve in marketing and distribution by offering broad product lines across the largest possible group of related product categories also have a lot to do with their success.

Firms that want to be successful with products that fall in this quadrant might well think of themselves as "global warehouses"—not edifices that stock physical products, but clearing houses for the collection, storage, exchange, and dissemination of product ideas, needs, and sources. Nestlé, for example, has a "warehouse" of over 200 products from which subsidiaries can choose. When a Nestlé subsidiary develops a new product for its country market, that product enters the warehouse and becomes available to other subsidiaries that want to manufacture or import it. The warehouse is a coordinating mechanism that encourages product development and sees that the firm, globally, takes maximum advantage of new ideas.

THE PRODUCT INNOVATION REQUIREMENT

Most products in the customized and rapidly changing quadrant are in a continuous state of evolution. Introduction of new models, in the case of durables, and new brands or flankers, in the case of packaged goods, occurs regularly. Firms competing in this sector must develop and maintain a capacity for innovation as a way of life. But maintaining this capacity is much more difficult than in the case of standardized products, because a new product idea can come from just about any country. The stimulus for instant noodles came from the Japanese market, for instance, and the product was first introduced there. ABS brakes, first introduced on German cars, were a response to the needs of northern European drivers. Fast-food hamburger restaurants were a US innovation. Such products have not only been successful in their country of origin, but have found markets, albeit of varying sizes, in many other countries of the world.

Ideally, firms should locate R&D units in several countries so as to be exposed to the maximum number of new product ideas. But they also need an integrating and rediffusing mechanism so that they can introduce new products or product improvements into other country markets as quickly as possible—modified, as required, for each.

THE MANUFACTURING REQUIREMENT

The key to manufacturing also is diffusion rather than concentration. To succeed, firms must support their broad product lines and innovation needs with a manufacturing capability that provides both dynamic and static flexibility. Dynamic flexibility is the ability to quickly put a new product into production, while static flexibility is the ability to easily switch production from product to product, and to economically produce small runs of a large number of products.

A customization strategy works best when manufacturing is located as close as possible to each country market. This facilitates the fast, successful commercialization of new product ideas, and speeds response to demand changes in existing products. The more flexibility—both static and dynamic—a firm can build into its manufacturing, the more production units it can support. The closer the manufacturing/country/market links, the faster the firm's response time.

TRANSMITTING AND ADOPTING NEW PRODUCT IDEAS

While close national links between manufacturing and marketing are essential, horizontal linkages across countries in R&D, manufacturing, and marketing are equally critical. Without such horizontal linkages, the global warehouse concept simply will not work well. Innovators and producers in one country market must have a means by which they can offer ideas (and product or production capacity) to subsidiaries in other country markets. And individual country subsidiaries need a place to shop for new product ideas and sometimes for sources of products that fill gaps in their existing lines.

CUSTOMIZED, SLOWLY CHANGING PRODUCTS: OPPORTUNISTIC NICHE EXPLOITATION

Here, the global strategy is to find and exploit niches. Products falling in this quadrant will typically have only one, or at best very few, markets in which they can earn a large share, and numerous markets in which they can, at best, gain a small share or niche. Many firms content themselves with being domestic because they do not believe they can profitably operate abroad with low volume. Small volumes offer profit potential only if the firm can obtain a premium price while holding costs down. For these products, the concern is not to develop an explicit global strategy as much as to develop a spirit of curious inquiry. The foreign market opportunities that may exist for customized, slowly changing products are not always easy to spot. Managers must uncover the opportunities and then find ways to use existing institutions and existing capabilities to exploit the opportunities.

Some Swiss chocolate-bar manufacturers, for example, retail their chocolate bars in the US at prices two to three times those of the leading domestic bar, Hershey's. They are able to hold expenses down because they use an established distribution channel that efficiently performs the required marketing and distribution tasks. They advertise very selectively to a small target audience, and depend for sales on the efforts of wholesalers who place their candy bars with point-of-sale displays selectively in targeted retail outlets.

CHANGING THE INDUSTRY'S RULES: STANDARDIZING THE CUSTOMIZED AND VICE VERSA

At times a firm might see a potential opportunity to set the rules for a new product line or to change the rules in an existing one. Philips and Sony, for example, established the rules for CD player components by pushing to standardize their system. A firm that considers a rule-changing move must first ensure that it can enforce the rule change and that it will, by changing the rules, improve its relative competitive position.

As a general proposition, moving from customization to standardization makes a business simpler and therefore easier to duplicate. The firm that does a good job of running a complex business well should think long and hard before making the rules of competition in its industry simpler. A firm should try to move its industry from customization to standardization only when it is positive that by so doing it can gain a highly significant, permanent cost advantage. The cost advantage must be large enough to make the standardized product substantially more attractive to consumers than the customized alternative. A better payoff for such firms, and at the same time a better insulation against a rival that could try to standardize, is to minimize the customization penalty by continually improving the product and by making manufacturing more flexible.

Similarly, the firm that can make a business more complex by moving from standardization to customization also stands to benefit if it can keep the customization penalty low enough. Consumers, after all, buy perceived value, not just price.

POLITICAL CONSTRAINTS ON GLOBAL STRATEGIES

The worlds of international trade and foreign investment are becoming increasingly constrained by conflicting national interest. All governments, it seems, want to maximize their country's exports and limit their imports. All governments want full employment, and many want to develop high-technology industries because their pay-off is higher than other types of industry. Business firms based in any country want as few competitors as possible in their own back yards, but at the same time want free access to world markets for themselves.

For these and related reasons, there is a political as well as an economic dimension to a global strategy. Governments by their actions influence the location of both manufacturing and R&D. Government regulations of product content, packaging, and labeling affect a firm's ability to standardize globally. Any global strategy, before being adopted, must be tempered by the reality of regulation. A government will be concerned primarily with the economic health of its own country, and will regulate to best serve its national interest, rather than to serve the global strategy needs of foreign firms. Rather than just thinking about global strategies, therefore—even where standardization is indicated—firms must in many cases think in terms of sets of regional or even country strategies.

NOTES

1. See, for example, 3, 5, 10, and 14 for contrasting views of global strategy.
2. This section, and the section to follow, are an interpretive synthesis of the work of many others.

3.   This history of the multinational enterprise is analyzed thoroughly in 33 and 34.

4.   See 15, 26, and 27, inter alia, for the elucidation of these definitions.

5.   This argument is made strongly in 22.

6.   These are a synthesis of points made by numerous writers, including, but not limited to, 4, 8, 13, and 16.

7.   The following two sections benefit from and synthesize published works listed in the references.

8.   See, for example, 1, 12, and 19.

9.   See 8 and 30 for summaries of such arguments.

REFERENCES

1.   Aaker, D. A., & B. Mascarenhas, "The Need for Strategy Flexibility," *Journal of Business Strategy,* 5(2) (Autumn 1984):74–82.

2.   Baden-Fuller, C., & John M. Stopford, "Why Global Manufacturing?" *Multinational Business* (Spring 1988):15–25.

3.   Barlett, Christopher, & Sumantra Ghosal, "Tap Your Subsidiaries for Global Reach," *Harvard Business Review* (November–December 1986):87–94.

4.   Barlett, Christopher A., & Sumantra Ghosal, "Managing across Borders: New Strategic Requirements," *Sloan Management Review* (Summer 1987):7–18.

5.   Chakravarthy, Balaji, & Howard V. Perlmutter, "Planning for a Global Business," *Columbia Journal of World Business* (Summer 1985):3–10.

6.   Cohen, Stephen S., & John Zysman, "The Emergence of a Manufacturing Gap," *Transatlantic Perspectives* (Autumn 1988):6–9.

7.   Domzal, Teresa, & Lynette Unger, "Emerging Positioning Strategies in Global Marketing," *Journal of Consumer Marketing* (Autumn 1987):23–24.

8.   Douglas, Susan P., & Yoram Wind, "The Myth of Globalization," *Columbia Journal of World Business* (Winter 1987):19–30.

9.   Doz, Yves L., "Managing Manufacturing Rationalization within Multinational Companies," *Columbia Journal of World Business* (Autumn 1978):82–94.

10.   Doz, Yves L., "Strategic Management in Multinational Companies," *Sloan Management Review* (Winter 1983):27–46.

11.   Doz, Yves L., & C. K. Prahalad, "Headquarters Influence and Strategic Control in MNCs," *Sloan Management Review* (Autumn 1981):15–29.

12.   Fannin, William R., "National or Global?—Control vs. Flexibility," *Long Range Planning* (October 1986):84–88.

13.   Ghoshal, Sumantra, "Global Strategy: An Organization Framework," *Strategic Management Journal* (1987):425–440.

14.   Hamel, G., and C. K. Prahalad, "Do You Really Have a Global Strategy?" *Harvard Business Review* (July–August 1985):139–148.

15.   Hout, Thomas, Michael E. Porter, & Eileen Rudden, "How Global Companies Win Out," *Harvard Business Review* (September–October 1982):98–108.

16.   Kiechel, Walter, "Playing the Global Game," *Fortune,* November 16, 1981, pp. 111–126.

17.   Kobrin, Steven J, *Managing Political Risk Assessment.* Los Angeles: University of California Press, 1982.

18.   Kogut, Bruce, "Designing Global Strategies: Comparative and Competitive Value-Added Chains," *Sloan Management Review* (Summer 1985): 15–28.

19.   Kogut, Bruce, "Designing Global Strategies: Profiting from Operational Flexibility," *Sloan Management Review* (Autumn 1985), 27–38.

20.   Kogut, Bruce, "Normative Observations on the International Value-Added Chain and Strategic Groups," *Journal of International Business Studies* (Autumn 1984): 151–167.

21.   Leontiades, James, "Market Share and Corporate Strategy in International Industries," *Journal of Business Strategy* (Summer 1984): 30–37

22.   Levitt, Theodore, "The Globalization of Markets," *Harvard Business Review* (May–June 1983): 92–102.

23.   Ohmae, Kenichi, *Triad Power.* New York: The Free Press, 1985.

24.   Porter, Michael, *Competitive Strategy: Techniques for Analyzing Industries and Competitors.* New York: The Free Press, 1980.

25.   Porter, Michael, *Competitive Advantage.* New York: The Free Press, 1985.

26.   Porter, Michael, ed., "Changing Patterns of International Competition," *California Management Review* (Winter 1986): 9–40.

27.   Porter, Michael, ed., *Competition in Global Industries.* Boston: Harvard Business School Press, 1986.

28.   Quelch, John A., & Edward J. Hoff, "Customizing Global Marketing," *Harvard Business Review* (May–June 1986): 59–68.

29.   Rapp, W. V., "Strategy Formulation and International Competition," *Columbia Journal of World Business* (Summer 1983): 98–112.

30.   Simon-Miller, Francoise, et al., "World Marketing: Going Global or Acting Local? Five Expert Viewpoints," *Journal of Consumer Marketing* (Spring 1986): 5–15.

31.   Stobaugh, Robert, & Piero Telesio, "Matching Manufacturing Policies and Product Strategy," *Harvard Business Review* (March–April 1983): 113–120.

32.   Vernon, Raymond, *Sovereignty at Bay.* New York: Basic Books, 1971.

33. Vernon, Raymond, *Storm over the Multinationals.* Cambridge, Mass.: Harvard University Press, 1977.
34. Vernon-Wortzel, Heidi, & Lawrence H. Wortzel, eds., *Strategic Management of Multinational Corporations: The Essentials,* 2nd ed. New York: John Wiley, 1989.
35. Vernon-Wortzel, Heidi, & Lawrence H. Wortzel, "Globalizing Strategies for Multinationals from Developing Countries," *Columbia Journal of World Business,* (Spring 1988): p. 27–35.

11

INTERNATIONAL JOINT VENTURES: A FRAMEWORK FOR ANALYSIS

Deepak K. Datta

Along with increased globalization of markets, the business world has, over the last decade, witnessed a considerable slackening of economic growth rates in major industrial nations. This has prompted many businesses in these countries to re-examine their fundamental assumptions on the definition of their current and future markets. There also seems to be an increasing awareness amongst businesses that, in order to achieve their corporate objectives, they need to recognize and avail of opportunities presented by potentially attractive and under-explored international markets, often in developing countries such as India, China or Brazil. However, while markets in these countries with increasing population and consumer demand offer substantial growth opportunities, traditional modes of entry can be difficult given the associated entry barriers. In this context, joint ventures provide multinational companies with an attractive strategic option—one that allows them to enter and function in markets where the complexity and the demand for local participation offer few other alternatives. Moreover, a situation of increased global competition, larger and riskier projects and R&D which is too

expensive to afford alone is forcing many managers to think in terms of joint ventures. They realize that, if effectively managed, drawbacks associated with joint ventures (e.g., reduction in control and the sharing of profits) are more than compensated by the benefits that such partnerships offer.

Joint ventures have been extensively studied by researchers in business administration—however, the focus of the past research has, unfortunately, been rather narrow. For example, although there is almost universal agreement that effective implementation plays a key role in determining joint venture success, very limited attention has been given to this important dimension. Moreover, the literature on joint ventures is rather fragmented, explained by the fact that no comprehensive framework currently exists for the study of joint ventures. A major objective of this article is to provide an analytical framework based on a critical examination and synthesis of the various tasks, activities and factors associated with and influencing joint ventures and their performance. The suggested framework should be useful not only in guiding and integrating future research but also from the managerial viewpoint in the analysis, planning, and implementation of such ventures.

Source: Journal of General Management, Vol. 14, no. 2 (Winter 1988), pp. 78–90.

EVALUATING THE INFLUENCE OF ENVIRONMENTAL FACTORS

For many corporations, joint ventures represent a substantial departure from their normal ways of doing business and, not surprisingly, many choose to avoid them. Yet, joint ventures, especially in the international arena, have been growing in number—a phenomenon which can be partially attributed to changes that have taken place in the business environment over the last couple of decades.

First, there has been a significant erosion in the bargaining power of multinationals, especially in terms of their technological knowhow. As a result, many host governments now insist that foreign companies form partnerships with local companies before being given the permission to set up operations in their country.[1] For example, India currently requires a minimum of 60 per cent local participation in any venture and similar restrictions have been imposed by governments in many other countries. Second, MNCs have begun to recognize that local firms can make a significant contribution to a venture through their intimate knowledge of, what is often, a complex and volatile local business environment.[2] Third, the recent increase in the overall joint venture activity has probably been the outgrowth of a growing awareness among organisations in developed countries that the continuing globalization of their markets requires them to be more cost-effective and efficient if they are to succeed in the global marketplace.[3] This, in turn, might require that operations be set up in other countries which provide cheaper raw materials and/or lower processing costs.

International joint ventures, however, are not limited to those in developing countries. Firms in developed countries too are entering into an increasing number of joint ventures, motivated, in part, by a need to share costs and risks in projects which are perpetually becoming larger, riskier and more expensive. For example, joint ventures have been recognized

as an attractive strategic option in the "telecommunications" industry, where the R&D costs incurred in developing a product are generally very high, while the product itself typically has a short life cycle. Others see joint ventures as providing competitive advantages through the realization of potential synergistic benefits in situations which allow the sharing of complementary skills and resources. Examples include, GM-Toyota, GTE-Fujitsu, Chrysler-Mitshubishi, all part of a recent spate of joint ventures among US and Japanese firms.

The feasibility and the desirability of a joint venture should, therefore, be assessed based on a careful analysis of these and other environmental forces (Figure 1). Forces in the economic and political environment are generally viewed by most managers as being the most influential; however, it is important that careful consideration also be given to forces in the social and the cultural environment. The influence of these forces can be particularly important in implementing and managing the venture. Also, while analysis of the impact of the various environmental forces undoubtedly plays a key role, a planned approach to joint ventures necessitates a thorough and careful evaluation of the multiple and, sometimes, diverse objectives of involved parties. As discussed in the following section, a concerted effort on their part is required if such differences are to be reconciled and mutually agreeable venture objectives developed.

ANALYZING JOINT VENTURE OBJECTIVES AND MOTIVES

While executives in transnational corporations often disparage joint ventures, there are a number of overriding economic and political reasons why they are being increasingly forced to accept and work with joint ventures. The reasons behind MNCs' decisions to enter into joint venture agreements include:

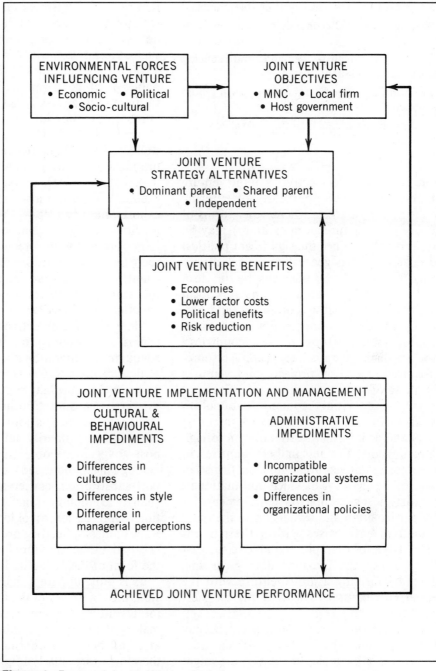

Figure 1 Framework for Joint Venture Analysis

- Entering new and potentially profitable markets
- Sharing heightened economic risks in new business ventures
- Satisfying nationalistic demands and reducing risks of expropriation
- Maintaining good relations with host governments
- Pooling organizational knowhow to realize synergistic benefits

From an MNC's perspective, a joint venture not only offers the opportunity of entering promising new markets where other forms of entry (e.g., as a foreign subsidiary) may be barred, it helps reduce the significant political and economic risks generally associated with foreign projects. These risks can be due to a variety of factors, including, unstable local governments, fluctuating currencies, and perennially strained communications and transportation infrastructures in host countries.[4] Also, by reducing the amount of capital resources required in a given project, joint ventures help an MNC reduce the element of financial risk. Moreover, rising economic nationalism has resulted in many host countries imposing formal and/or informal restrictions on foreign companies doing business in their countries. In this context, joint ventures with local firms can be one of the few ways in which multinationals can satisfy host governments' requirements for local participation and ownership in the management of enterprises within their boundaries.[5] IBM, for example, was able to successfully penetrate the Brazilian data processing market by forming a joint venture with the Gerdau Group, Brazil's leading private steel company.[6]

The *local partner,* on the other hand, usually enters a joint venture with a very different set of objectives. For example, such a venture might be attractive because it provides access to technology which would otherwise be very difficult to develop or buy.[7] In fact, transfer of technology probably constitutes the single most impor-tant reason why firms in developing countries seek joint ventures with organisations in technologically-advanced countries. An example of such a "technology transfer" joint venture is the Tianjin-Otis Elevator Co. in the People's Republic of China, a venture which provides the Chinese partner access to Otis technology and Otis access to the China market.[8] Joint ventures also provide the local firms access to the use of well-known brand names and trademarks of the products of the foreign partner. This not only makes the domestic marketing of the venture products easier but also facilitates subsequent exports, thereby helping the host country earn precious foreign exchange. Not surprisingly, joint ventures with foreign partners are often seen by many entrepreneurs in developing countries as important mechanisms by which they can achieve their corporate growth and diversification objectives.

Along with the objectives of the parent companies, analysis of a joint venture requires that adequate consideration also be given to the objectives of the *host government.* While the host government's role may be direct or indirect, one can rarely discount its influence; in fact, as previously mentioned, a joint venture strategy is often chosen primarily out of a need to satisfy host government objectives. These include, among others, increased local employment, import substitution, conservation of foreign exchange, technology transfer and the minimization of foreign control of local industry.[9] While some of these objectives are not always explicitly stated, others are more formally laid down in the form of local laws and regulations.

As is quite apparent from the above discussion, the objectives of the different parties in a joint venture are not necessarily congruent, making it, at times, very difficult to fund, operate, and benefit from such a venture. It is, therefore, particularly important that before a joint venture is actually formed the potential partners recognize the differences in their objectives and take necessary steps in reconciling them (Figure 2). Not doing so will inevitably re-

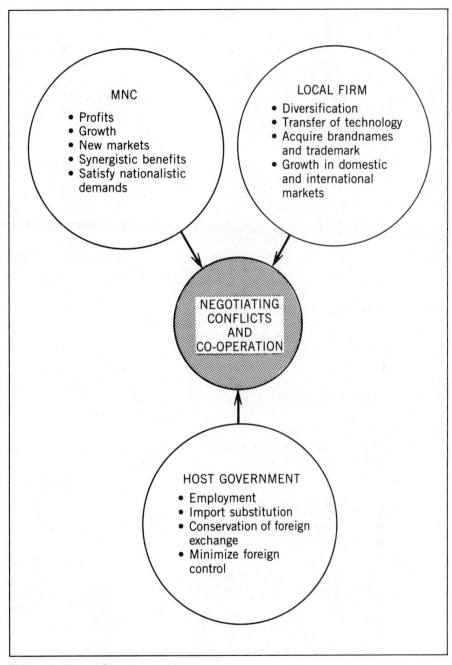

Figure 2 Diverse Objectives in Joint Ventures

sult in conflicts and misunderstandings, erosion of potential benefits and, might even lead to the ultimate demise of the joint venture. Unfortunately, such sophistication and flexibility do not always exist—there is often a desire by one or more of the parties to achieve their own objectives with little regard for the needs or values of the others, and such self-centredness can be extremely dysfunctional from the perspective of the joint venture.

The objectives of the joint venture partners (including those of the host government) are also reflected in their choice of the joint venture strategy. In the following section we discuss the alternative joint venture strategies and their respective characteristics.

JOINT VENTURE STRATEGIES

When executives speak of joint ventures, they usually have three definite attributes in mind:

- There is an acknowledged intent on the part of partners to share in the management of the resulting venture
- They are partnerships between legally incorporated entities (such as companies or chartered organisations), not between individuals, and,
- Equity positions are held by each of the partners.

Equity participation along with the degree of parental involvement and control forms the basis of the strategy typology developed by Killing.[10] He identified three joint venture strategies, namely, the dominant parent strategy, the shared management strategy and the independent joint venture strategy.

The *dominant parent strategy* comes closest to the concept of a wholly owned subsidiary with the dominant partner (generally the MNC) instrumental in the selection of most of the enterprise operational managers. In such ventures, the board of directors, while composed of executives from each parent, largely play a ceremonial role and virtually all the venture's strategic and operating decisions are made by the dominant partner's executives. From an MNC's viewpoint, this strategy is appropriate when it is forced to take on a partner solely in response to pressure from the host government or when the passive partner sees its involvement and participation as a purely financial investment with an acceptable rate of return. The second, and the more common form, is the *shared management venture.* Such ventures are managed by both parents and are most common in manufacturing situations where one parent supplies the technological knowhow and the other its knowledge of the local market. In such ventures both partners typically play an active role in the management of the joint business.

The third strategy, namely, the *independent joint venture,* involves ventures which are relatively free of the interference from either parent. While, in theory, joint ventures are often regarded as independent and autonomous businesses, numerous interdependences inevitably exist between the joint venture and the parent companies. Moreover, parents are generally reluctant in giving joint ventures the autonomy and freedom to develop as totally independent entities. Independent joint ventures, therefore, are fairly rare when compared to the other two, namely, dominant and shared management ventures.

Obviously, a multinational's choice of a joint venture strategy depends not only on its own objectives and the impact of environmental forces, but also on the objectives of its other partners. As suggested in the framework of Figure 1, the choice has important implications in terms of available benefits and the tasks associated with the implementation and the management of the venture—implications which need to be carefully considered in the analysis of any joint venture.

POTENTIAL BENEFITS IN JOINT VENTURES

Joint ventures offer a unique opportunity of combining the distinctive competences and the complementary resources of participating firms. Such combinations provide a wide range of benefits—benefits which neither participant might be able to attain on its own. These include, among others, economic benefits in the form of reductions in factor costs, transportation costs, overheads and taxes. Benefits might also result from increased economies of scale in areas such as manufacturing, R&D, sales and marketing. Therefore, joint ventures can be a particularly desirable alternative in situations and industries where the "critical mass" (the input activity level that has to be surpassed to obtain any significant output or result) is very high.[11] Moreover, the complementary needs, skills and expertise of the partners in joint ventures provide synergistic benefits as in the joint venture between Honda of Japan and Rover of UK. Honda gives Rover a wider model range; Rover gives Honda a "Trojan Horse"; and the venture provides customers with more choices.[12]

Along with those mentioned above, there are a number of benefits associated with joint ventures. For example, contributions from the local firm and the host government in a joint venture allows an MNC to enter a market with limited financial resources. Also, the funds provided by the local partner or government provide an important hedge against various political risks.[13] In fact, the biggest set of benefits in a joint venture are often "political" in nature. The local partner in the venture, in addition to contributing valuable market-related information, can be expected to bring to the partnership the benefits of its relations with local government authorities and institutions. The latter is particularly useful in obtaining privileged access to local resources and also in reducing specific discriminations in favor of local firms.

In brief, joint ventures offer significant potential economic and noneconomic benefits. However, the extent to which these benefits are actually realized depends largely on how well the joint venture is implemented and managed. Given the shared management concept, impediments to effective implementation are many

and, worse still, implementation issues often suffer from management neglect. The spotlight in joint ventures inevitably centers on the legal and economic aspects, and, consequently, issues relating to the implementation and management of the venture are often overlooked.[14] As discussed next, this lack of attention can have serious negative implications in terms of joint venture performance.

MANAGEMENT AND IMPLEMENTATION OF JOINT VENTURES

Joint ventures, while offering the promise of economic and other benefits, often entail significant costs in their implementation. Shared decision making makes them much more difficult to manage and, consequently, joint ventures tend to be fragile relationships with a high failure rate—45–50 per cent according to studies done by Beamish[15] and Reynolds.[16] Typically, a variety of behavioural, cultural, and administrative impediments makes the effective management of a joint venture quite a demanding task in terms of the executive time and effort. The nature of these impediments is briefly discussed in the following paragraphs.

Behavioural and Cultural Factors Influencing Joint Venture Management

Many of the problems and misunderstandings in joint ventures have their roots in the cultural differences that exist at both the national and the organisational level. Examples of the effect of cultural differences on joint venture performance have been documented by Peterson and Shimada[17] and Simiar[18] in their research on joint ventures in Iran and Japan, respectively. They found that cultural differences frequently led to failure on the part of parent company managers to "understand" one another. The resultant breakdown of communications generally had significant negative consequences, sometimes leading to the eventual dismemberment of the venture. However, the impact of cultural differences on performance is normally a function of the type of venture—the problems described above are more common in shared management ventures than in, say, dominant parent ventures, given that the former require greater involvement and interaction among parent company managers.

Along with cultural differences, existing differences in management styles across the two parent companies might constitute a major impediment to effective implementation. The "personal chemistry" between the management of the parent firms plays a key role both in the establishing of the joint venture and, also in its smooth functioning.[19,20] For example, management at the MNC might have a very different attitude towards risk than that in the smaller local partner. They may be willing to take more risks, be prepared to accept short-term losses in order to increase market share, take on higher levels of debt or spend more on advertising. Similarly, there could be differences in their approach to decision making—one might favor a participative style while the other believes in a more autocratic style of management. Conflicts and disagreements arising out of such differences obviously need to be resolved, and this often makes the process of decision making slow and frustrating. The resulting inefficiencies can easily erode many of the potential economic benefits that the joint venture initially had to offer.

Impediments to implementation and management can also arise out of incongruencies in the goals of the venture partners or differences in perceptions regarding the strategic importance of the joint venture project. The commitment of each partner is a function of the importance that the partner attaches to the project and, when such commitments differ significantly, management of the joint venture can be fraught with problems. Similar problems are associated with differences among parent companies on the extent of autonomy that should be given to the joint venture. This problem is especially acute if the multinational company attempts to integrate the joint venture's operations with its own against the wishes of the other partners.

Administrative Factors Influencing Joint Venture Management

Along with behavioural and cultural factors, various administrative factors play an important role in determining the extent to which performance expectations in a venture can eventually be realized. For example, incompatible administrative systems of the parent companies can prove to be a serious impediment to the effective implementation of the venture. Incompatibility makes the choices of the appropriate accounting, planning and control systems doubly difficult, with each company naturally favoring the system they use themselves. Problems in the managing of a joint venture also stem from incompatible organisational policies and strategies. The parent companies might have very different notions on the appropriate advertising-sales ratio, the nature of the markets served, the right distribution channels, the quality control standards to be adopted or the hiring and firing policy, all of which might generate potentially dysfunctional and damaging conflicts. "Shared management joint ventures," with operations managed by executives from both parents, are particularly vulnerable to such differences and, unless these differences are reconciled or equitable mechanisms developed to resolve resulting deadlocks, they can be extremely detrimental to the overall performance of the joint venture.

Proper management, therefore, is crucial to success in an international joint venture. The process starts in the negotiations phase itself—because such negotiations not only provide the substantial content of the formal agreement but also help in the establishment of a level of mutual trust and confidence between the involved parties.[21] Effective management entails the recognition and the analysis of the various impediments discussed above and the subsequent execution of necessary steps to minimize their negative effects. It also calls for an accommodation between the apparently conflicting administrative requirements for unified, unambiguous direction and control and the effective participation of partners. The greater the independences or linkages, the greater is the possibility of conflict, and it is important that these interdependences are recognized early on in the joint venture process and appropriate actions taken to minimize their negative consequences.

Effective management of a joint venture also requires that well defined reporting relationships and communication channels be established as early as possible. However, it may not be an easy task—in joint ventures, there is generally no "one best way" to organise or the one "best" organisational structure. Most successful ventures, therefore, use a mix of organisational and other managerial devices for promoting unified planning, partner participation and control. Janger[22] who studied the control systems used in 168 joint ventures, found the following to be some of the more commonly used mechanisms:

- Financial reports
- Informal visits by parent company executives
- Financial audits
- Formal planning systems
- Staff performance reviews
- Management audits.

However, as with any other aspect of joint venture management, the process of selecting a mutually acceptable control system in a joint venture can be a difficult one. Yet, it deserves critical attention especially when one considers the many differences that inevitably exist across the venture partners. Without an effective control system these differences and associated problems will invariably result in a quick demise of, what is often regarded as, an inherently fragile relationship.

CONCLUSION

In the 1970s, Peter Drucker had observed that joint ventures were fast becoming important mechanisms for diversification and growth.[23] His views find support in the recent survey conducted by the Conference Board, which found that "most of the Fortune 500 companies in the US and roughly 40 per cent of the industrial companies with more than 100 million dollars in sales engaged in one or more international joint ventures."[24] Increasingly, corporations have recognized that, while joint ventures might represent significant departures from their normal ways of doing business, they can be attractive strategic options in situations where high risks, scarce resources and various political factors offer very limited choices.

While many multinationals have found joint ventures to be beneficial partnerships, an examination of the high failure rates among joint ventures would suggest that this is not always the case. Executives contemplating such ventures should, therefore, make a careful analysis of the pros and cons of any venture in evaluating the probabilities of success. Actions which are likely to increase such probabilities include:

- Extensive discussions between potential partners to allow for exploration of mutual objectives and various technological and commercial issues
- A careful evaluation of the likely impediments in operating and managing the venture
- Getting the partners to specify mutual expectations of respective contributions and benefits.

While the risks associated with international joint ventures will always be substantial, they can certainly be minimized through careful planning and evaluation. It is hoped that the framework suggested in this article will provide managers with useful guidelines both in the assessment and the planning of joint ventures.

NOTES

1. S. G. Connolly, "Joint Ventures with Third World Multinationals: A New Form of Entry into International Markets," *Columbia Journal of World Business* (Summer 1984), pp. 18–22.

2. D. Hall, "International Joint Ventures: Pros and Cons," *SAM Advanced Management Journal* (Autumn 1984), pp. 4–11.

3. D. C. Shanks, "Strategic Planning for Global Competition," *Journal of Business Strategy,* Vol. 5, no. 3 (Winter 1985), pp. 80–89.

4. "Competing by Collaborating," *The Economist,* June 21, 1986, p. 19.

5. F. K. Berlew, "The Joint Venture—A Way into Foreign Markets," *Harvard Business Review* (July–August 1984) pp. 48–50, 54.

6. "The Steel Deal That Could Boost Big Blue in Brazil," *Business Week,* May 19, 1986, p. 66.

7. Berlew. "The Joint Venture."

8. S. R. Hendryx, "Implementation of Technology Transfer Joint Venture in the Peoples' Republic of China: A Management Perspective," *Columbia Journal of World Business,* Vol. 21 (Spring 1986), pp. 57–66.

9. W. W. Wright and S. S. Russel, "Joint Ventures in Developing Countries: Realities and Responses," *Columbia Journal of World Business,* Vol. 10, no. 2 (1975), pp. 74–80.

10. J. P. Killing, "How to Make a Global Joint Venture Work," *Harvard Business Review,* Vol. 61, no. 3 (May–June 1982), pp. 120–127.

11. Hall, "International Joint Ventures."

12. "Competing by Collaboration."

13. L. G. Franco, *Joint Venture Survival in Multinational Corporations* (New York: Praeger, 1971).

14. "Corporate Odd Couples," *Business Week,* July 21, 1986, pp. 100–105.

15. P. W. Beamish, "The Characteristics of Joint Ventures in Developed and Developing Countries," *Columbia Journal of World Business,* Vol. 20 (Fall 1985), pp. 13–19.

16. I. J. Reynolds, "The Pinched Shoe Effect of International Joint Ventures," *Columbia Journal of World Business* (Summer 1984), pp. 23–29.

17. R. B. Peterson and J. Y. Shimada, "Sources of Management Problems in Japanese-American Joint Ventures," *Academy of Management Review* (October 1978), pp. 796–804.

18. F. Simiar, "Major Causes of Joint Venture Failures in the Middle East: The Case of Iran," *Management International Review,* Vol. 23, no. 1 (1983) pp. 58–68.

19. R. E. Holton, "Making International Joint Ventures Work," in Lars Otterbeck (ed.), *Management of Headquarters-Subsidiary Relationships in Multinational Corporations* (New York: St. Martin's Press, 1981).

20. P. Scanlon, "Collaborative Ventures," *Journal of Business Strategy,* Vol. 6 (Winter 1986), pp. 81–83.

21. Peterson and Shimada, "Sources of Management Problems."

22. A. R. Janger, *Organization of International Joint Ventures.* Conference Board Report No. 787, New York, 1980.

23. P. Drucker, *Management: Tasks, Responsibilities, and Practices* (New York: Harper & Row, 1974).

24. Janger, *Organization of International Joint Ventures,* p. 1.

Section 3

THE POLITICAL ENVIRONMENT AND POLITICAL RISK

Managers of multinational corporations are acutely aware that they and their companies face political risks. Political risk is an issue whenever there are unanticipated changes in the political environment that interfere with managerial autonomy or the ability of the firm to carry out its objectives. For global corporations, the cost of uncertainty or interference may be unacceptably high. Therefore, whenever possible, managers try to anticipate and deal with political changes before they become crises.

While threats of war, large-scale nationalization of industry, and politically inspired kidnappings are dramatic media events, they are relatively rare occurrences. These substantial risks, often called "macrorisks," include events such as the Iranian revolution or Lebanese kidnappings. The impact of macrorisk may be different for individual firms, but every foreign and many domestic firms located in countries that experience political upheaval are affected to some degree.

The likelihood of any or all of these events taking place might constitute sufficient reason for a foreign company to decide not to invest in a country or even to withdraw established enterprises. On the other hand, present and potential benefits might be great enough to outweigh the risk.

In spring and summer 1989, Chinese students began to demonstrate in Beijing's Tiananmin Square. On June 4, soldiers marched into the square and brutally broke up the demonstrations. Although few foreigners were seriously hurt, investors concluded the events carried major political risks for their corporations. Companies that had considered political risk insurance wasteful and unnecessary rushed to brokers and underwriters but discovered it was nearly impossible to get political risk insurance. Corporations trying to buy coverage against such risks as an import/export embargo, expropriation, or nationalization of property in China found the market shut down. Political risk insurers compared managers' predemonstration attitude to the one that prevailed in Iran in the 1970s. In China, most foreign corporations adopted a "wait-and-see" strategy, postponing new investments but maintaining those already established.

Usually, companies do not face such dramatic events when they assess political risk. Multinational or global managers are much more likely to deal with sudden policy changes directed toward specific firms, industries, or projects. The degree of "microrisk," or impact on an individual firm, depends upon the industry the firm is in, its level of technology, managerial style, or corporate organization. When host nations promote their own political interests they usually do not jeopardize the continuation of foreign enterprises or seize their assets. Nevertheless, foreign firms may find their operations and global strategy compromised. Host countries may insist upon employment of greater numbers of locals in the work force or a greater proportion of locally made components. They may limit the repatriation of profits or demand other terms unacceptable to the multinational.

Beginning in 1987, many multinationals contemplated joint ventures in the Soviet Union. In 1988, several major U.S. multinationals, including Eastman Kodak, RJR Nabisco, Inc., Johnson & Johnson, Chevron Corp., and Archer-Daniels-Midland Co., formed a consortium to negotiate a trade agreement jointly. Several issues of political risk concerned negotiators. The most obvious was the political risk of doing business in a command economy in which a change in leadership might result in expropriation of foreign assets.

However, the the most troubling issue for potential investors was the provision of Soviet joint venture law stipulating that foreign companies could take profits in dollars only if the venture itself earned hard currency. It was unclear to potential investors whether that provision would be enforced, changed, or even eliminated. The stipulation was called the "killer clause" by some Western executives who wanted to tap the Soviet internal market but did not want to be compelled to export products for hard currency.[1] Another issue that carried microrisk was the Soviet government's insistence on a letter of credit to cover start-up costs. At any time, the Soviet government could increase the deposit needed by an investor. A Stamford, Connecticut, firm decided that a $500,000 to $1 million letter of credit was an unacceptable cash flow risk and made other investments instead.[2]

What can a company do to protect itself against political risk? In the case of macrorisk, it may decide to buy protection before a crisis occurs. In 1969, Congress created the Overseas Private Investment Corporation (OPIC). This company provides political risk insurance and financial services to American companies in less-developed countries (LDCs). In 1981, OPIC had record

[1]Peter Gumbel, "American Companies Form a Consortium to Cope with Soviet Trade Bureaucracy," *The Wall Street Journal,* April 14, 1988, p. 27.
[2]Taryn Toro, "Of Profit and Perestroika," *Fairfield County Advocate,* May 30, 1988, p. 8.

earnings of over $76 million through insurance sales that covered risk from expropriation, currency inconvertibility, wars, revolutions, and insurrections.

Insurance, however, cannot cover a firm for microrisk situations. Multinational companies planning to make a foreign investment may choose simply to stay out of potentially unstable environments or try to hedge their investment position by undertaking political risk analysis.

The three articles in this section look at the nature of political risk, the responses of organizations to risk, and the ways in which risk analysis can be integrated into the firm's strategic management.

READING SELECTIONS

Raymond Vernon's "Organizational and Institutional Responses to International Risk" examines risk-reducing strategies firms undertake when they invest abroad. While political risk is a central concern of foreign investors, other risks have an impact on their decision making. Risk of competition, risk of diminished cash flow, and risk of losing a technological lead are important considerations. Many firms use joint ventures to reduce risk.

These joint ventures take several forms. Foreign firms may form a consortium with each other, or they may go into partnership with a host country firm or with a state-owned enterprise. The risk of expropriation may be substituted for another risk, preemption by a competitor. To reduce preemption, foreign firms make arrangements such as long-term contracts or licensing agreements. Vernon asserts that individual firms have only limited power to affect prices and actions of rival, yet independent, firms. Although joint ventures may reduce the likelihood of expropriation, they cannot eliminate it. Investors respond both organizationally and institutionally to risk but the discipline of economics has not yet incorporated or formalized the concept.

Stephen Kobrin examines the literature to determine what elements constitute political risk. Events, however upsetting, are not political risks for a firm unless they can or do affect operations. Kobrin's usable definition of political risk is "the distribution of probable returns which is . . . a function of the probable impacts of political events on operations." As he points out, there has to be uncertainty for business risk to exist. Political events that do not subject the firm to that uncertainty do not constitute risk; they simply entail an assessment and evaluation of events on the company's well-being.

Kobrin finds that that most managers do not rigorously and systematically evaluate the impact of politics on operations. Instead, they rely on rather superficial and subjective perceptions of the degree to which they are likely to encounter risk. He recommends that much more work remains to be done to give managers a better definition of risk, a conceptual structure that will relate politics to the firm, and information about the impact of the political environment on the firm.

José de la Torre and David Neckar address the difficult task of forecasting political risk for international operations. They note that there are two different contingency losses associated with political risk: involuntary loss of control and reduction in expected value of return from foreign-controlled affiliates. The macro- and microrisks that we identified earlier can be divided into four types: massive expropriations, deterioration of the investment climate, selective nationalization, and restrictions of key sectors.

Since the mid-1970s, international banks, consultants, and companies themselves have developed models and techniques to forecast risk. Most of these models ignore the needs of firms for individually tailored instruments to measure project-specific risk. They are also based on historical data that may be partially or totally irrelevant for the future.

The authors note that any model designed to forecast risk must encompass all contingencies resulting from national policy changes and their effects on both countries and projects. They propose a model of political risk forecasting that begins by examining national characteristics. Stage I assesses the forces at work in a nation and will generate a set of outcomes or consequences unique to each project or affiliate. Stage II focuses on the features of the project and estimates conditional probabilities of various contingencies.

The macrorisk component of the analysis is based on huge data bases that can be standardized and manipulated. Only those familiar with a company's internal operations can perform the second part of the analysis. Modeling political risk at the corporate level demands good judgment and should be limited to countries or areas of the world where major investments of competitive positions are at stake.

12

ORGANIZATIONAL AND INSTITUTIONAL RESPONSES TO INTERNATIONAL RISK
Raymond Vernon

My mandate is to deal with the organizational and institutional responses that foreign direct investors have developed in their efforts to deal with international risk. The boundaries of that mandate are not very sharp.

One problem in drawing the boundaries is

Source: This article is reprinted from *Managing International Risk.* Essays commissioned in honor of the centenary of the Wharton School. University of Pennsylvania, ed. Richard J. Herring © Cambridge University Press. Reprinted by permission.

to define an institutional response. By implication, some responses to risk exist that are thought to be separable from institutions; I have had some difficulty in picturing what those responses may be. I hope I shall be forgiven therefore if, from time to time, this discussion wanders beyond the organizational and institutional dimensions into areas that some would regard as economics.

A second problem in drawing the boundaries of this chapter has been to decide which of the many different types of international risk could usefully be addressed. In one respect, the decision on boundaries is easy. This chapter is concerned both with the risks that arise from the investor's ignorance and with the risks that arise from random error. In other respects, however, the boundaries are less easily drawn. Direct investment internalizes a set of international transactions that otherwise would be conducted at arm's length with independent buyers or sellers, and one major purpose of this internalization is to avoid some of the risks that exist when dealing with such independent parties. Accordingly, a direct investment commonly represents a response to certain kinds of international risk. An exploration of this phenomenon seems almost indispensable as a preliminary for exploring the responses to the risks associated with the direct investment itself.

DIRECT INVESTMENT AS A RESPONSE TO RISK

The desire of managers to internalize certain transactions as a way of avoiding risk is a phenomenon that is encountered in domestic as well as international settings, occurring most commonly when the number of firms in the market is small, when the surrounding environment is uncertain, and when the representations or commitments of the parties concerned are difficult to verify or enforce.[1] Nevertheless, numerous writers have observed that the internalization of certain transactions is likely to be especially important as a risk-reducing measure when the transactions straddle national boundaries (Caves 1973, p. 117; Buckley and Casson 1976, pp. 33–59; Casson 1979, pp. 45–62).

Establishing the Foreign Subsidiary

The drive for internalization, it is generally agreed, stems from the firm's view that there is some marked imperfection in the market for the product or service concerned, a view that

stimulates the firm to create its own internal market and to accept the narrowing of choice that is commonly involved in that decision. Two types of industry in which such internalization is particularly common are the exploitation and processing of oil and minerals and the development and application of advanced technologies. Not surprisingly, therefore, these industries prove to be heavily overrepresented among foreign direct investors (Vernon 1971, pp. 4–17; United Nations 1978, pp. 45–46).

In the case of raw materials, large indivisible costs and high barriers to entry keep the numbers small. The entry barriers are created in part by the difficulties of achieving agreements with host countries on the terms of entry and in part by the size of the capital commitment needed to finance the extensive developmental work and infrastructure that go with the launching of large raw material projects.[2] Meanwhile, the dispersed location of overseas operations and the tenuous links among the participating parties create uncertainties and hamper fact finding to a degree that is especially acute.[3]

The entry barriers that are typical in the technologically advanced industries are of a different kind, but are commonly no less formidable. They are created by the fact that a considerable expenditure of money and time is commonly required while firms accumulate the necessary knowledge, skills, and reputation that may be necessary for the effective marketing of the product. Like the raw material industries, too, the high-technology firms typically incur developmental costs in the launching of new businesses that are relatively high when compared with the actual costs of production (Freeman 1974, p. 126; Hochmuth 1974, pp. 145–169; Brock 1975, pp. 27–41, 57; Measday 1977, pp. 266–268; Parker 1978, pp. 112–119). After beginning production, individual firms characteristically experience a persistent decline in production costs that appears to be a function of their accumulated production, a fact that represents an added deterrent for newcomers

(Hartley 1965, pp. 122–128; Abernathy and Wayne 1974, pp. 74–141; Conley 1981).

Both the firms in the raw materials industries and those in the high technology industries, then, begin with large sunk costs on which they hope for a return. The importance of reducing uncertainties in industries that have such a cost structure has been sufficiently explored. Firms in such industries place more than the usual stress on avoiding variations in output, inasmuch as small variations in output can generate disproportionate swings in their return on investment. But there are some differences in the two types of industry as well.

In the raw materials industries, the firm's problem of securing a stable return on its sunk commitments is exacerbated by the fact that a relatively high proportion of its operating costs is also fixed. Variations in output generate disproportionate fluctuations in net profits. Accordingly, a persistent objective in the strategy of firms in these industries has been to find ways of stabilizing the demand for their output and to safeguard themselves against interruptions in the supply of needed materials.

On the demand side, of course, the price elasticities of aggregate demand for an industrial raw material such as iron ore or crude oil are typically fairly low, especially in the short run. Individual firms, however, face a demand curve that is considerably more elastic than that of the industry as a whole, so that the risk of losing customers in a declining market can be fairly substantial. Insurance, in this case, takes the form of acquiring tied customers who do not have the option to shift their sources of supply.

On the supply side, the integrating imperative is just as obvious. Because of high barriers to entry, the suppliers are usually limited in number. For the processor that does not control its own source of supply, any large increase in price or outright interruption in supply, whatever its cause, can be dangerous. But a particularly disastrous type of price increase or supply interruption is one initiated by a supplier that also controls processing facilities downstream,

that is, a supplier that is also a competitor in the processor's market.[4] In that case, the supplier may be found taking over the customers of its unintegrated rival.

Events in the oil industry over the past decade have provided occasional illustrations of such a risk turned into reality. At various times during the 1970s, as multinational sellers were faced with reduced supplies of crude oil, they cut off practically all of the unintegrated processors that they had previously supplied, while continuing to supply their own downstream processing facilities and distributors (Commission of the European Communities 1975, pp. 144–145; OECD 1977a, pp. 23, 25; Levy 1982).

Nevertheless, the fact that such risks exist in the oligopolistic industries that process raw materials does not mean the risks always lead to vertical integration. Such integration has a cost. It requires an investment of capital, which has to be justified in terms of expected yield or an equivalent reduction in risk. Moreover, the capital investment entails risks of its own, which may outweigh the risk-reducing aspects of the investment. Besides, the flexibility of the integrated units is reduced as compared with unintegrated competitors; in times of easy supply, the integrated entity is inhibited from turning to cheaper sources of supply and in times of tight supply is restrained from abandoning its captive markets for markets in which profit margins are higher.

Why then is vertical integration so pervasive in the raw material industries? The strong tendency toward vertical integration seems to derive from the fact that, in an industry that is only partially integrated, there are always some participants who see themselves especially exposed by that fact; as long as partial state of integration exists in the industry, a new move toward vertical integration on the part of any firm withdraws a source of supply or a potential customer from the market and thereby increases the perceived risks of those that remain unintegrated. Accordingly, any movement toward integration seems likely to snowball, until all the actors have rendered themselves equally invulnerable by integration.[5] If the markets concerned are global in scope—a situation that clearly exists for oil and aluminum and exists in part for copper and steel—the interactions between the firms will also be global in their reach.

The high-technology industries, as I have already suggested, face a set of risks that differs somewhat from the raw materials industries. The challenge to the raw materials industries is to secure a firm link to supplies and markets, a challenge to which it commonly responds with vertical integration. The challenge to the high-technology firm is to secure a reliable return on its unique skills or knowledge. Unlike firms in the raw materials industries, however, those in the high-technology industries rarely exhaust the static and dynamic scale economies that can be exploited at any given production site, so that the costs of setting up another production point can sometimes be fairly high; besides, the relative unimportance of freight costs usually reduces the advantages of creating multiple production sites (Vernon 1977, p. 51). In addition, some high-technology firms such as those in the aircraft industry have been influenced in part by a desire to stay close to the military authorities in their own country, in order to avoid questions of divided loyalty or of security.

Nevertheless, risk-reducing considerations have pushed the firms in high-technology industries to set up overseas subsidiaries for a portion of their foreign business. The most obvious risk leading to direct investment has been that, as the technological edge of the firm is eaten away, foreign countries may begin to bar their products in favor of producers on their own soil.[6] Faced with that risk, firms in high-technology industries have commonly chosen the subsidiary alternative.[7]

But that response, as a rule, has not put an end to the risks to which the firms in high-technology industries have been exposed. The first move of such firms into foreign production sites has usually been limited, consisting of a facility designed to serve the local market. Countries with bargaining power, however, have sometimes obliged foreign firms to develop a more substantive response. In such cases, some firms have responded by establishing a world-scale plant in an important foreign market and shipping some of the output to other countries. That response has been particularly strong in the automobile industry, generating a shift in the location of production facilities, including a shift from the facilities at home; this development is very likely increasing the international flow of components and automobiles (Jenkins 1977, pp. 213–216; Bennett and Sharpe 1979, pp. 177–182; Frank 1980, pp. 102–105).

Once again, therefore, the avoidance of risk has contributed to the growth of foreign direct investment, as enterprises have shuffled their production facilities among countries in an effort to protect their access to the markets that otherwise might be denied to them.

Follow the Leader

What the discussion suggests so far is that the foreign direct investment of any firm may represent a response to threats of various kinds. One such risk is that competitors may imperil the foreigner's access to a raw material or a market by making investments of their own. That response, as it turns out, follows some predictable patterns.

Consider a world market, such as the market for nickel or aluminum, dominated by half a dozen leading firms, each capable of observing the main moves of the others. The price elasticity of aggregate demand for the final product, the processed metal, is low; the marginal cost of production in relation to full cost is also low. The challenge for the industry, therefore, is to ensure that no participating producer upsets the existing equilibrium by cutting its prices and enlarging its market share. If that should happen, there is a risk that other producers will also be obliged to cut their prices, thereby reducing the rent for the industry as a whole.

Now assume that in those circumstances, one of the participants, troubled by the risk of being cut off from its existing sources, nevertheless undertakes the development of some new mining properties in a remote corner of the world where no such mining had previously taken place. In circumstances of that sort, history suggests that the other members of the oligopoly are unlikely to be totally ignorant of the geological characteristics of the new areas. In the typical case, they will have some information based on local folklore, observation of outcroppings, or even systematic borings. But the information will be grossly incomplete, thus placing a heavy discount on the value of the most likely estimate. What is the optimum response of the other members of the oligopoly?

Consider the nature of the risk that the others face. The quality of the initiating firm's information is not clear; it may be good or bad. If bad, it may burden the firm with a cost that will have to be absorbed in the rent generated by its other operations. But if good, it may eventually arm the leader with a source of ore whose low cost or strategic geographical location poses a threat to the stability of the oligopoly. If other members of the oligopoly are risk avoiders, they will want to learn about the new location as rapidly as possible. If the acquisition and processing of information take time, the firm that is slow to respond faces the risk of being preempted by the hastier action of a rival firm. Accordingly, the risk avoiders are likely to turn their limited facilities for information-gathering to an examination of the new location, even if that means curtailing their search in other directions.[8] Indeed, some firms may want to commit themselves to the new territories even without all the requisite information. The propensity to move will be enhanced by the expectation that if a sufficient number of members of the oligopoly make a similar move

and if all of them eventually prove mistaken, the oligopoly will pass on part of the cost of the error to buyers in the form of higher prices. Hence, the follow-the-leader pattern.

On similar lines, risk-avoiding members of an oligopolistically structured industry will be expected to pursue one another into any substantial foreign market in which one of them has set up a producing subsidiary. In this case, the risk of preemption will be particularly great, inasmuch as the first entrant can be expected to urge the government to impose restrictions on any further imports and to limit the number of foreign producers allowed to set up production facilities in the country. The followers may possess little knowledge about the market's potential; projections about future demand may be inescapably subject to large error, but if the number of possible entrants is limited and if the aggregate demand for the product is thought to be inelastic, the followers can contemplate the possibility of cutting their collective losses by raising the prices.[9]

The urge of members in a tight oligopoly to maintain their relative positions in the industry, even if it entails some risky investments, stems in part from their desire to avoid what they perceive as an even greater risk. There is a common conviction among enterprises in oligopolistic industries that the enterprises is in special danger when its cash flow is diminishing in relation to that of its rivals. Behind that fear lie some strong assumptions about the efficiency of the capital markets. Internal capital is usually thought to be much cheaper than external capital; indeed, external capital is commonly viewed as a scarce, rationed commodity. (See Stigler 1967, pp. 287–292; Eiteman and Stonehill 1979, pp. 346–375. See also the various essays in Heslop 1977.) If oligopolists must match the moves of their rivals in order to maintain equilibrium, those with a reduced cash flow may therefore find themselves out of the competitive running. Worries such as these led a Ford executive to say:

If we don't spend the money, our products will not be competitive. We will not get 25 percent. We will get 20 percent. And if you fall back and take two or three years to recover, soon it will be 20 percent, then 18 percent. Then you can't spend money fast enough to catch up again. (The New York Times, December 4, 1975, pp. 1, 9)

Although the quotation goes back to 1975, it suggests a certain prescience regarding the conditions that would prevail in the automobile industry six years later.

The recognition that enterprises tend to move in unison in their foreign direct investments is hardly new, having been advanced as a behavioral proposition at least a quarter of a century ago (e.g., Barlow and Wender 1955, pp. 146, 149). In manufacturing, the evidence is quite extensive and systematic.[10] Now and then, the pattern is so pronounced that it pervades an industry. Outstanding examples have been the wave of investment in semiconductor and microcircuit production in Southeast Asia during the 1960s and the leapfrog patterns of investment among the soap companies and the soft drink companies in Latin American during the same period.

In the raw materials industry, the available data are only impressionistic, but cumulatively they carry some weight. In oil, a surge of investment in the years before the 1930s carried the leading British and American oil companies to the lands surrounding the Gulf of Mexico, from Venezuela to Texas. In the two decades after World War II, another surge of investment greatly expanded oil investments in the countries surrounding the Persian Gulf. Similar waves of investment were to be seen in metallic ores: bauxite investments in the Caribbean area from 1950 to 1965; copper investments in Chile from 1947 to 1958, and in Peru from 1955 to 1960; and iron ore in Venezuela from 1946 to 1960, and in Liberia from 1960 to 1965.

The fact that rival members of an oligopoly tend to move together into a new geographical area, of course, does not conclusively demonstrate that a follow-the-leader pattern exists. A rival possibility, not to be dismissed, is that all of them have been stirred to action by a common stimulus: by the pacification of a hitherto unsafe area, by the appearance of a new consumer market, or by some other such factor. But the empirical evidence is fairly strong for concluding that the follow-the-leader factor is important.

Some of the most obvious illustrations of linked behavior are found in the occasional agreements in the raw material industries under which rivals have explicitly given up the right to act independently. The red-line agreement of 1928 among the world's leading oil companies was one such case. This agreement covered a large portion of the Middle East and remained in force for a decade or two; under its terms, each enterprise undertook not to develop any new fields in the indicated territories except in partnership with the others (see U.S. Federal Trade Commission 1952, pp. 65–67; Jacoby 1974, pp. 29–30, 34–36).

In a very different time and place, other strong illustrations appear of the importance of linkage among members of an oligopoly, albeit not in the form of agreements or consortia. In many markets of the developing world during the 1960s, the leading automobile companies scrambled with one another to set up producing facilities. In at least two cases, that of Argentina and South Africa, the number of firms prepared to enter the scramble and the amount of capacity they were prepared to put in place were so far in excess of prospective market demand as to suggest strongly that some of the investors were reacting to the decisions of the others (Baranson 1969, pp. 46–47, 53; Sundelson 1970, pp. 243, 246–249; Jenkins 1977, pp. 39–42, 56–58). The seemingly nonrational behavior of the firms could be explained in a number of ways. The explanation I find most plausible, however, is that they were driven by a desire to hold down risk, defining that risk in the terms suggested earlier.

More systematic evidence that the follow-the-leader phenomenon reflects a risk-reducing reaction on the part of the participants in an oligopolistic industry is found in the Knickerbocker study mentioned earlier (1973, pp. 111–144). Knickerbocker found that the degree of the parallel behavior of U.S. firms in any industry was positively correlated with the degree of concentration in that industry—but only up to a point. The strongest patterns of parallel behavior were found in industries in which three or four near-equal firms were the leaders; in industries with an even higher concentration—say, one or two dominant firms, surrounded by a fringe of lesser enterprises—parallel behavior was not as strong. Knickerbocker also found that parallel behavior was a little less pronounced in firms with a relatively high level of technological inputs, where product differentiation was important, than in those with lower technological content. These added bits of information contribute marginally to the credibility of the follow-the-leader hypothesis as a factor in explaining foreign direct investment patterns.

The Exchange of Threats

Researchers also claim to see risk-reducing objectives in other seemingly imitative investments of the multinational enterprises. It has repeatedly been observed, for instance, that the U.S.-based industries that were generating the highest rates of foreign direct investments in Europe were much the same as the European industries that more or less simultaneously were investing in the United States (Hymer and Rowthorn 1970, pp. 80–82). One explanation for this behavior is provided by the so-called exchange-of-threat hypothesis. Threatened by the establishment of a foreign-owned subsidiary in their home market, the response of the leading firms in that market is to set up subsidi-

aries in the invader's home market. This cross-investment conveys a warning to the invading firm that any excessively energetic efforts to compete in the foreign market may be countered by similar efforts in the home market of the invader.[11]

The two-way flows of foreign direct investment in the same set of industries, moreover, may serve to reduce a somewhat different kind of risk, namely, the risk of lagging behind in the global technological race. In many oligopolistic industries, a limited number of multinational enterprises encounter each other in competition in many different national markets. In the computer mainframe industry, IBM, Fujitsu, and Siemens are world competitors; in chemicals, ICI, Dupont, and Rhone-Poulenc cross paths in international markets; and so on. Most multinational enterprises, however, do the bulk of their research and development within their home market (Samuelsson 1974; Ronstadt 1977, pp. xiii–xiv, 2; Lall 1980, pp. 102, 119–120); and, most of these enterprises are greatly influenced by the conditions of the home market as they develop the niche that differentiates their products and processes (Davidson 1976, pp. 207, 216; Franko 1976, pp. 27–44). The U.S. stress on labor-saving, mass-produced products, for instance, was traditionally based on the high cost of labor and the absolute scarcity of artisan skills (see Habakkuk 1962, Ch. 3 and 4; Rosenberg 1976, Ch. 1 and 3; also Rosenberg 1969, pp. 17–18).

One risk for multinational enterprises in industries with rapid innovational change is that their rivals in other countries, exposed to different conditions in their home markets, may develop a technological lead that will eventually prove threatening elsewhere. American automobile manufacturers, for instance, were eventually threatened by the Japanese mastery of small fuel-saving automobiles, a capability that the Japanese originally developed largely in response to the special needs of their own market. Aware of the risk of falling behind, some multinational enterprises have maintained a constant surveillance over their rivals in other countries and have sought licenses for foreign technology whenever they felt the need (Abegglen 1970, pp. 117–128; Ozawa 1974, pp. 52–56, 67–80). But some have preferred to acquire subsidiaries as a technological listening post in the territory of their rivals (Franko 1971, pp. 8, 14–15, 23; Michalet and Delapierre 1975; see also Vernon 1980, pp. 150, 153–154, and *Business Week* 1980, pp. 55, 59, 121). When that has occurred, the multinationalizing process has been the firm's response to a risk generated by the action of its competitors.

JOINT VENTURES AS RISK REDUCERS

Once a firm has determined that an international investment may be desirable as a means of reducing risk, it is still faced at times with the possibility of going it alone or investing in partnership with others. The choice among the various alternatives is commonly affected by questions of risk. But once again, the risks to be avoided are of various kinds.

Consortia of Foreigners

For reasons already discussed, firms in the raw material industries typically place a high premium on reducing the risks of the unforeseen, such as wars, strikes, and earthquakes. But in operations in which scale economies are large, such diversification can be costly, especially on the part of the smaller firms in the oligopoly. The solution is for such firms to multiply their sources by joining others in a number of consortia. (For aluminum, the subject is fully explored in Stuckey 1981.) That response has had the effect of producing various consortia composed of firms engaged in the common exploitation of a raw material in a country that is foreign to all of them.

Consortia of this sort in raw materials industries, however, also respond to another risk that

has already been noted: the risk that a rival firm might be in a position to upset the stability of an oligopoly by securing its materials at an especially advantageous cost. This second motive is, of course, difficult to distinguish from the first.

Some consortia in the raw materials industries, however, are formed with still a third group of risks in mind, namely, the category that is usually described as political risk. In practice, political risk can be of many different types. It can arise because of a host country's hostility to some specific foreign country and its nationals; or because of a host country's hostility to foreigners in general, irrespective of nationality; or because of a host country's efforts, without hostility to any foreigners in particular or in general, to improve an existing bargain.[12]

Whatever the variety of political risk may be, a consortium composed of foreigners of different nationalities is ordinarily seen as reducing the risk. If the risk to be reduced is a host country's hostility to one country, the consortium can be seen as diluting the exposure of any firm that is based in that country. If the risk is a deterioration in the position of foreigners in general, without regard to any particular country, the consortium can be seen as a counterforce that may be able to enlist the support of a number of different governments.

Although consortia among foreigners also are to be found in the manufacturing industries, especially those that require large-scale and heavy investment, such consortia are relatively uncommon. Occasionally, consortia of this type are imposed on the manufacturing firms by host governments. Foreign automobile producers in Peru and Mexico, for instance, have been compelled to merge their production activities in order to reduce the number of automobile types in the country and to achieve some obvious economies of scale.[13] But the reduction of risk is also a factor in such consortia.

One reason why consortia among foreign firms are less common in manufacturing than in mining or oil production is that manufacturing firms generally have better ways of diversifying their portfolios of direct investment. Although some foreign-owned manufacturing subsidiaries produce goods for export from the countries in which they are located, most market the bulk of their production within the host country (Vaupel and Curhan 1973, pp. 376–377; Curhan, Davidson, and Suri 1977, pp. 392–393, 398–399, Tables 7.2.1 and 7.2.6; U.S. Department of Commerce 1977, pp. 318–319, Tables III.H.1 and III.H.2). Firms in manufacturing, therefore, can often diversify their market risks by setting up subsidiaries in a number of different countries, relying on transportation costs or protective devices in each market to buffer them from outside competitors. Firms engaged in extractive activities, however, typically sell their products in world markets, so that high-cost production sites represent a real handicap. With fewer locations from which to choose, the raw materials firms find themselves obliged to turn more often to the consortium possibility in achieving adequate diversification.[14]

Finally, if the factors specified thus far were not enough to explain the lesser use of consortia by manufacturing firms, the nature of their strategies would provide a sufficient explanation. Unlike the raw materials producers, manufacturers commonly build such strategies on product differentiation, building up distinctive trade names and unique services to customers as their route to success. The consortium approach in any market, combining the offerings of rival producers, would be incompatible with a product-differentiating strategy.

Joint Ventures with Local Firms

When manufacturing firms take local partners with an eye to reducing risk, the risk they generally have in mind is political risk. To be sure, multinational enterprises have a number of other reasons for setting up joint ventures with local stockholders. In some cases, they have no

choice; host governments lay down and enforce a joint venture requirement (Turner 1973; United Nations 1973, pp. 83–84; Robinson 1976; United Nations Economic and Social Council 1978, pp. 22–23). In other instances, the decision to take a local partner may free the subsidiary of various discriminatory restrictions, such as disqualification from selling to government enterprises or borrowing from local banks. In still other cases, the joint venture may represent the right decision on the part of both partners simply on the basis of the classic choice of a profit-maximizing firm. It may allow both partners to put slack resources to work in a single entity; it may allow each of the partners to earn returns on their investments that were higher than their respective opportunity costs; and it may reduce the risks to the multinational enterprise of securing local distribution channels, while reducing the risks to the local distributor of securing assured supplies (Dubin 1976, pp. 27–43; Radetzki and Zorn 1979, pp. 57–61). The objective of reducing political risk, however, is ordinarily of some importance in such arrangements (see especially Franko 1977, p. 29; Pfeffer and Nowek 1976, p. 332; Caves 1970, pp. 283–302; Hogberg 1977, pp. 6–25; Tomlinson 1970, p. 5).

Apart from the direct testimony of businesspeople, the sense that risk reduction must be playing some significant role in the decision to set up joint ventures is supported by a number of studies of the behavioral patterns of the multinational enterprises. Two analyses, when interpreted in tandem, point in that direction. One of these studies offers strong evidence for the view that, as manufacturing firms gain experience in manufacturing in any market, they tend to assign a lower level of risk to that market. The second study concludes that the less experienced the firm, the higher its propensity for entering into joint ventures with local partners.

The first study, linking experience to perceived risk, covered the introduction and subsequent dissemination of 406 new products by fifty-seven large U.S.-based multinational enterprises during the period from 1945–75 (Vernon and Davidson 1979). In the early decades of that period, the firms were slow to establish production units for these products abroad. But the products introduced in the latter decades were produced abroad with much greater alacrity and in many more locations. By breaking down the data by firms and products, the factors that contribute to this trend became more evident. For instance, firms with a high proportion of exports transferred more rapidly and more extensively than those with a low proportion; firms with several different product lines established production sites abroad more rapidly in their principal product lines than in less important lines; firms that had made many prior transfers responded more rapidly than those that had made only a few; and all firms responded more rapidly in countries to which they had made many previous transfers than in countries to which they had made a smaller number.

The study that links experience levels with the propensity to enter into joint ventures consists of an exhaustive analysis of the behavior of the 2,800 foreign manufacturing subsidiaries of 186 U.S.-based multinational enterprises over a fifty-year period. In various ways, the data linked increased foreign experience with a decline in the propensity of the firm to use joint ventures (Stopford and Wells 1973, p. 99).

More suggestive evidence on the connection between risk and joint ventures comes from another direction. It has been commonly observed that for any foreign-owned enterprise the risk of nationalization rises as the firm loses its capacity to offer a scarce resource to the host country, such as technology, capital, or access to foreign markets (Vernon 1971, pp. 46–52; Krasner 1978, pp. 138–142; Jodice 1980, pp. 204–205; Kobrin 1980, pp. 65–88). At the same time, several studies suggest that firms that appear to be in a relatively weak bargaining position in relation to host governments, that is, firms that have little to offer the coun-

try, tend to use joint ventures more than firms in a strong bargaining position (Stopford and Wells 1972, pp. 120, 150–156; Fagre and Wells in press).

Most of the studies cited here are less than conclusive, being dogged by difficult problems of multicollinearity and multiple causation. But cumulatively they lend a considerable degree of plausibility to the hypothesis that risk avoidance is a substantial factor in the decision of foreign-owned enterprises to take local partners.

Joint Ventures with State-Owned Enterprises

A special category of joint venture that has grown somewhat in recent years is partnerships between foreign firms and enterprises owned by the state. The oil-processing industries of the oil-exporting countries contain numerous examples of such enterprises (Ghadar 1977, pp. 17–46; Turner and Bedore 1979, pp. 13–36). But they are found in many other industries as well.

The reasons for such arrangements have been fairly well studied.[15] From the viewpoint of foreign partners, many of the reasons for entering into agreements with state-owned enterprises are the same as those that argue for local private partners; freedom from special restrictions, access to local resources, and protection from political risk. Foreign firms generally assume, however, that each of these factors gains a little strength when the partner is a state-owned enterprise. Whether the foreigner actually acquires greater immunity from political risks by entering into partnership with the state, however, seems quite uncertain; when enough experience develops for researchers to explore the question adequately, the likelihood is that a complex answer will emerge.

One difference between partnerships with private local firms and partnerships with the host state lies in the evolution of the local partner's interests over time. In a significant proportion of the joint ventures, the private partnership interest is held by a large number of local stockholders,[16] who commonly have even less power than public stockholders in the United States. In other cases, local stockholdings are more highly concentrated and fewer in number, but many of these stockholders, having received their equity interests as a gift, are content to play a passive role and to provide the protective coloration the foreigner has bargained for. Only a fraction of these joint ventures, therefore, represent active partnerships.

Managers of state-owned enterprises, on the other hand, generally find themselves much more actively involved in their partnerships with foreigners. Being exposed to the political process in the home country, state managers are often torn between buffering the foreign partner against political pressures in order to maintain the partnership, or swallowing up the foreign partner's interest in order to demonstrate their national commitment. In the Middle East oil industry, according to one study, those motivations have shifted over time in predictable patterns, ending characteristically in the nationalization of the foreigner's interest (Bradley 1977, pp. 75–83; Ghadar 1977, pp. 25–27).

To be sure, oil may not prove to be a representative case, especially because of the period covered in existing studies. In other times and other industries, state-owned enterprises may see advantages in clinging to a foreign association, especially if technology or foreign market access is needed. But the recent history of the oil industry does suggest some of the difficult judgments that foreigners have been obliged to make when contemplating the use of joint ventures as insurance against risk.

OTHER ARRANGEMENTS FOR AVOIDING RISK

In an effort to reduce some of their various risks, firms have often been pushed to establish foreign subsidiaries, and, in an effort to reduce the risk to their subsidiaries, they have sometimes been compelled to enter into joint ventures. But there have been instances in which no subsidiary, whether joint venture or wholly owned, has seemed able to reduce their risks on balance. Such subsidiaries simply appeared to be substituting one set of risks for another—the risk of expropriation, for instance, for the risk of preemption by a competitor. Faced with such unpalatable alternatives, enterprises have sometimes groped toward some intermediate arrangement hoping to minimize both kinds of risks. These intermediate arrangements have commonly involved long-term contracts of various sorts.

Such contracts have taken a variety of forms. In both raw materials and high-technology industries, some long-term contracts have authorized and obligated foreign firms to exercise managerial functions over extended periods (Bostock and Harvey 1972; Fabrikant 1973; Smith and Wells 1976, pp. 45–49; Zorn 1980, Ch. 12). Some of these arrangements have contemplated cash flows for the foreign firm whose discounted value was not very different from the expected stream generated by an analogous direct investment. In fixing the appropriate discount rate, of course, either stream would have to be recognized as subject to risks of various sorts. But in some of these cases, one would probably have been justified in discounting the anticipated income from fees paid under managerial contracts at lower rates than those applicable to the streams anticipated from foreign direct investments.[17]

Yet long-term contracts simply substitute one set of risks for another. In practice, long-term contracts for the sale of raw materials have often turned out to be nothing much more than a statement of intentions on the part of the parties. Critical elements of the contract, such as prices and quantities, have been subject to repeated renegotiations. In their efforts to reduce uncertainties of this kind, one party or another has sought to introduce various kinds of sanctions. Buyers of raw materials, for instance, have made loans to raw materials producers with provisions for immediate repayment whenever the producers failed to deliver specified quantities, and producers have insisted that buyers must forfeit their rights to interest on such loans whenever the buyers failed to accept specified quantities.

Despite such provisions, large elements of uncertainty have remained. Buyers have been accused of delaying the arrival of their vessels in order to avoid picking up shipments of bulk cargoes; sellers have been accused of stimulating their governments to impose export embargoes in order to avoid delivering their products. Moreover, businesspeople have had reservations about the enforceability of their contracts, especially when enforcement could only be achieved through the use of foreign courts.

For firms in the high-technology industries, long-term contracts have typically taken the form of a licensing agreement with independent producers in foreign countries. Such licenses have normally been written with various restraints. These restraints have sought to ensure that the licensee would not impart the information acquired under the license to an unauthorized third person; that the licensee would confine its use of the information to some specified geographical territory; and finally, especially when the licensee was authorized to use the licenser's trademark, that the licensee would produce the product in accordance with some specified standards. Each of these conditions, it is apparent, is aimed at reducing the licenser's risks: the risk of unauthorized appropriation, the risk of competition among license holders, and the risk of impairment of a valued trademark through inadequate quality control.

But long-term licenses, like long-term bulk purchase contracts in the raw materials industries, have had their limitations. Licensers have been aware that licensees can often disregard the contract because the sanctions for violation are notoriously limited. Information that has once been divulged cannot be retrieved; the licensee, therefore, may have little or nothing to fear from losing the licenser's goodwill. On top of that, if the foreign licenser is obliged to pursue its remedies in the home courts of the licensee, court orders directing the licensee to observe the terms of the contract and money damages for breach of contract may prove difficult to obtain.

Apart from the possibility that the courts may not be blind to the foreign nationality of the licenser, there is also the possibility that the underlying legal position of the licenser may be weak. A licenser that holds a strong patent position on an invention in its own home market will sometimes find that the patent protection on the same invention issued by foreign governments is much less secure (Maier 1969, pp. 207–231; Horowitz 1970, p. 539; Penrose 1973, p. 768; Scherer 1976). Moreover, in recent years, various developing countries have adopted laws outlawing the geographical restraints and other restraints that licensers have heretofore found useful to impose on their foreign licensees, further reducing the usefulness of that approach (OECD 1977b; UNCTAD 1979, pp. 24–39; Naryenya-Takirambudde 1977, pp. 71–73).

Perhaps the most tenuous arrangements for the avoidance of risks in host countries entail payments that in U.S. law and practice would be classified as bribes. The justification for condemning bribes can sometimes be couched in rational terms. In a country whose officials do not solicit bribes, for instance, the foreign offerer of a bribe contributes to the destruction of a public good—the competitive market—an act that could conceivably be costly to all those in the market, including the offerer. But arguments of that sort are not the real stuff of the debate. One side finds bribery prima facie offensive and refuses to use it, whatever the consequences; the other thinks it totally entrenched, presenting an inescapable hurdle for those who wish to operate in certain foreign markets.[18] Any "rational" discussion of the use of bribes as a risk-insuring device is therefore likely to be offensive to one side of the debate and unsatisfying to the other. It is almost inescapable, too, that such a discussion will be seen as an apologia for the practice.

There is perhaps one point worth making nevertheless. The problem of bribery is either a smaller one or a bigger one than is ordinarily described. In the interest of reducing their risk in various developing countries, foreign investors are often obliged to make various payments that are not labeled as bribes. Influential local figures are commonly offered blocks of stock in what is then dubbed a joint venture, at prices well below their reasonable value. Local government officials are appointed to directorships in the enterprise, with appropriate emoluments. Ironically, such measures are often applauded as a sign of the foreign investor's responsiveness to local sensibilities. In this shadowy area of risk avoidance, the line between international chicanery and local adaptation will never be clearly drawn.

THE ANALYTICAL CHALLENGE

The avoidance of risk is a quintessential element in the strategy of foreign investors. As a rule, the decision to invest is motivated by a desire to reduce risks of various sorts: the risk of government restrictions on foreign imports, the relative unenforceability of the investor's rights under law or contract, and above all, the risk of preemptive action on the part of a competitor. Risk avoidance also affects the form of the investment; some forms of joint venture help the investor with limited resources to diversify more widely, whereas other forms of joint venture are thought to reduce political risk. On the other hand, even as a direct investment reduces one set of risks, it exposes the investor to another set, including the risk of expropriation. Accordingly, firms often attempt to establish a firm link with foreign markets or foreign sources of materials by long-term arrangements short of investment, but these too produce uncertain results.

The firms involved in the making of these complex judgments come predominantly from industries that are oligopolistic in structure. Because their risks are those that arise in the never-never land of oligopoly, where individual firms can affect prices and the actions of rival firms are interdependent, the analytical power of our microeconomic concepts proves somewhat limited. Those risks are often more easily analyzed in game-theoretic terms than in the familiar paradigms of systematic and random variance. To add to the difficulties, foreign direct investors are not usually investors in the usual sense; a critical portion of their investments commonly takes an intangible form, entailing assets that have no ready market price. Even the cost of such assets offers little help; such assets as technology or access to markets are provided at near-zero marginal cost.

As a result, the role that risk plays in international direct investment cannot be captured by minor addenda to the principles of finance, such as calculating the appropriate risk adjustment for a target rate of return or computing the appropriate price to be paid for a hedge. Foreign direct investors will resort to a series of stratagems for reducing the uncertainty in their environment that do not fit easily into the mainstream discussions of risk. Faced with that fact, this chapter has discussed, for want of a better term, the "organizational and institutional" responses of such investors to risk. But it is only a matter of time before the economics profession will formalize those responses in ways that incorporate them within the discipline. Indeed, that process is already well under way.

NOTES

1. See Williamson (1975, pp. 82–131), Bernhardt (1977, pp. 213, 215), Porter (1980, pp. 306–307), and Scherer (1980, pp. 78, 89–91, 302–304). For a survey of recent literature on the incentives for vertical integration, see Kaserman (1978, pp. 483–510); also Jensen, Kehrberg, and Thomas (1962, pp. 378–379, 384).

2. On the economics of backward integration in the raw materials industries, see for instance, Gort (1962, Ch. 6) and Teece (1976, pp. 105, 115–118).

3. For descriptions of the international oil industry, especially in relation to the issue of vertical integration, see Adelman (1972, pp. 318–319), Cooper and Gaskel (1976, pp. 72–74, 188), Teece (1976, pp. 83–89, 116–117). Mansvelt Beck and Wiig (1977), and Levy (1982). For the nonferrous metals, Charles River Associates, Inc. (1970, pp. 51–57). Bosson and Varon (1977, pp. 46–47), Duke et al. (1977), Banks (1979, pp. 21, 27, 45), Mikesell (1979a, pp. 108–109), and Goohs (1980).

4. For a basic statement of this problem, see Caves (1977, pp. 43–45), Porter (1980, pp. 308, 317), and Scherer (1980, pp. 90–91).

5. For an effort to demonstrate in theoretical terms that equilibrium exists only at the extremes of full integration or full nonintegration, see Green (1974).

6. On "buy-at-home" policies as a nontariff barrier to international trade, see Curtis and Vastine (1971, pp. 202–204), and Cline, Kawarabe, Kronojo, and Williams (1978, pp. 189–194). On the attempts of European governments to set up and protect national champions in the aerospace and computer industries, see Hochmuth (1974, pp. 145–170) and Jéquier (1974, pp. 195–255). On the restrictions of developing countries, see Robinson (1976, pp. 169–238).

7. For a discussion of the factors in high-technology industries, such as computers, tending toward vertical integration, see Katz and Philipps (in press). An econometric demonstration that firms in high-technology industries favor subsidiaries over independent licensees to a greater degree than in other industries is presented in Davidson and McFetridge (1981); the analysis is based on data presented in Vernon and Davidson (1979).

8. See, for instance, Cyert and March (1963, Ch. 6) and Cyert, Dill, and March (1970, pp. 87–88, 94–95, 107). The effort going into search can be considered a significant investment by the firm, as discussed generally in Arrow (1974, pp. 39–43).

9. The perceptions of prospective lenders in such oligopolistic situations are described in Stiglitz and Weiss (1981, pp. 393–411). These perceptions tend to favor follow-the-leader investors by increasing their ability to borrow.

10. The leading work on this point is Knickerbocker (1973). See also Aharoni (1966, pp. 55, 65–66) and Gray (1972, pp. 77, 96–98).

11. Koninklijke Nederlandsche Petroleum Maatschappij (1950, p. 18), *Forbes* (1964, pp. 40–41), Graham (1974, pp. 33–34, 75), Michalet and Delapierre (1975, p. 44). But rival explanations are also offered to explain the cross investment phenomenon; see, for instance, Franko (1976, pp. 166–172).

12. For illustrations, see Moran (1974, pp. 110–136), Thunell (1977, p. 99), Krasner (1978, p. 117), Radetzki and

Zorn (1980, p. 186); also Zorn (1980, pp. 225–226).

13. Pressures of this sort are usually applied informally by administrative means and so are difficult to document. But see Turner (1973, p. 101). For data on the trend to greater concentration of automobile producers in Latin American countries, see Jenkins (1977, pp. 145–150).

14. Indicative of the more limited opportunities of the raw materials firms are data in Vernon (1971, pp. 39, 62).

15. The subject is dealt with in Vernon (1979, pp. 7–15) and Aharoni (1981, pp. 184–193).

16. For detailed data see Vaupel and Curhan (1973, pp. 309–319).

17. See, for example, Mikesell (1979b, pp. 52, 56–57). OPEC members' purchases of petroleum management services are generally at a price approaching the return on an equivalent direct foreign investment by the oil companies; see Eiteman and Stonehill (1979, p. 242).

18. For some of the more serious explorations of this subject see Kobrin (1976, pp. 105–111), U.S. Securities and Exchange Commission (1976), U.S. Senate (1976), Jacoby et al. (1977, pp. 125–145), Kugel and Gruenberg (1977, pp. 113–124), Kennedy and Simon (1978, pp. 1–5, 118–120).

REFERENCES

Abegglen, J. C. (ed.). *Business Strategies for Japan.* Tokyo: Sophia University, 1970.

Abernathy, W. J., and Kenneth Wayne. *The Bottom of the Learning Curve: The Dilemma of Innovation and Productivity.* Boston: Division of Research, Graduate School of Business Administration, Harvard University, 1974.

Adelman, M. A. *The World Petroleum Industry.* Baltimore, Md.: Johns Hopkins University Press, 1972.

Aharoni, Yair. *The Foreign Investment Decision Process.* Boston: Division of Research, Graduate School of Business Administration, Harvard University, 1966, and "Managerial Discretion." In Raymond Vernon and Yair Aharoni (eds.), *State-Owned Enterprise in the Western Economies.* London: Croom Helm, 1981.

Arrow, K. J. *The Limits of Organization.* New York: W. W. Norton, 1974.

Banks, F. E. *Bauxite and Aluminum: An Introduction to the Economics of Nonfuel Minerals.* Lexington, Mass.: Lexington Books, 1979.

Baranson, Jack. *Automotive Industries in Developing Countries.* Baltimore, Md.: Johns Hopkins University Press, 1969.

Barlow, E. R., and I. T. Wender. *Foreign Investment and Taxation.* Englewood Cliffs, N.J.: Prentice-Hall, 1955.

Bennett, David, and K. E. Sharpe. "Transnational Corporations and the Political Economy of Export Promotion: The Case of the Mexican Automobile Industry." *Interna-*

tional Organization, Vol. 33, no. 2 (Spring 1979), pp. 177–201.

Bernhardt, I. "Vertical Integration and Demand Variability." *Journal of Industrial Economics,* Vol. 25, no. 3 (March 1977), pp. 213–229.

Bosson, Rex, and Bension Varon. *The Mining Industry and the Developing Countries.* New York: Oxford University Press, 1977.

Bostock, Mark, and Charles Harvey (eds.). *Economic Independence and Zambian Copper: A Case Study of Foreign Investment.* New York: Praeger, 1972.

Bradley, David. "Managing Against Expropriation." *Harvard Business Review* (July–August 1977), pp. 75–83.

Brock, G. W. *The U.S. Computer Industry.* Cambridge, Mass.: Ballinger, 1975.

Buckley, P. J., and M. Casson. *The Future of Multinational Enterprise.* New York: Holmes and Meier, 1976.

Business Week. "The Reindustrialization of America," June 30, 1980, pp. 55–146.

Casson, M. *Alternatives to the Multinational Enterprise.* London: Macmillan, 1979.

Caves, R. E. "Uncertainty, Market Structure and Performance: Galbraith as Conventional Wisdom." In J. W. Markham and G. F. Papenek (eds.), *Industrial Organization and Economic Development.* Boston: Houghton Mifflin, 1970. Also see "Industrial Organization." In J. M. Dunning (ed.), *Economic Analysis and the Multinational Enterprise.* New York: Praeger, 1973 and *American Industry: Structure, Conduct, Performance.* Englewood Cliffs, N.J.: Prentice-Hall, 1977.

Charles River Associates, Inc. "Economic Analysis of the Copper Industry." Prepared for the General Services Administration, March 1970.

Cline, W. R., Noboru Kawarabe, T. O. M. Kronojo, and Thomas Williams. *Trade Negotiations in the Tokyo Round: A Quantitative Assessment.* Washington, D.C.: The Brookings Institution, 1978.

Commission of the European Communities. *Report by the Commission on the Behavior of the Oil Companies in the Community during the Period from October 1973 to March 1974.* EEC Studies on Competition-Approximation of Legislation, no. 26. Brussels: European Economic Communities, December 1975.

Conley, Patrick. "Experience Curves as a Planning Tool." In R. R. Rothberg (ed.), *Corporate Strategy and Product Innovation.* New York: The Free Press, 1981.

Cooper, B., and T. F. Gaskell. *The Adventure of North Sea Oil.* London: Heinemann, 1976.

Curhan, J. P., W. H. Davidson, and Rajan Suri. *Tracing the Multinationals: A Source Book on U.S.-Based Enterprises.* Cambridge, Mass.: Ballinger, 1977.

Curtis, T. B., and J. R. Vastine, Jr. *The Kennedy Round and the Future of American Trade.* New York: Praeger, 1971.

Cyert, R. M., W. R. Dill, and J. G. March. "The Role of Expectations in Business Decision Making." In L. A. Welsch and R. M. Cyert (eds.), *Management Decision Making.* London: Penguin Books, 1970.

Cyert, R. M., and J. G. March. *A Behavioral Theory of the Firm.* Englewood Cliffs, N.J.: Prentice-Hall, 1963.

Davidson, W. H. "Patterns of Factor-Saving Innovation in the Industrialized World." *European Economic Review,* Vol, 8, no. 3 (October 1976), pp. 207–217.

Davidson, W. H., and D. G. McFetridge. "International Technology Transactions and the Theory of the Firm." Unpublished, Amos Tuck School, Dartmouth College, 1981.

Dubin, Michael. "Foreign Acquisitions and the Spread of the Multinational Firm." Unpublished DBA thesis, Harvard School of Business Administration, 1976.

Duke, R. M., R. L. Johnson, H. Mueller, P. D. Quaffs, C. T. Roush, Jr., and D. G. Tarr. *Staff Report on the United States Steel Industry and International Rivals.* Bureau of Economics, Federal Trade Commission, Washington, D.C., November 1977.

Eiteman, D. K., and A. I. Stonehill. *Multinational Business Finance,* 2nd ed. Reading, Mass.: Addison-Wesley, 1979.

Fabrikant, Robert. *Oil Discovery and Technical Change in Southeast Asia: Legal Aspects of Production-Sharing Contracts in the Indonesian Petroleum Industry.* Singapore: Institute of Southeast Asian Studies, 1973.

Fagre, Nathan, and L. T. Wells, Jr. "Bargaining Power of Multinationals and Host Governments." *Journal of International Business Studies,* in press.

Forbes. "The Game that Two Could Play." Vol. 94, no. 11, December 1, 1964, pp. 40–41.

Frank, Isaiah. *Foreign Enterprise in Developing Countries.* Baltimore, Md.: Johns Hopkins University Press, 1980.

Franko, L. G. *The European Multinationals, European Business Strategies in the United States.* Geneva: Business International, 1971. Also see *The European Multinationals.* Stamford, Conn.: Greylock Publishers, 1976; and *Joint Venture Survival in Multinational Corporation.* New York: Praeger, 1977.

Freeman, Christopher. *The Economics of Industrial Innovation.* London: Penguin Books, 1974.

Ghadar, Fariborz. *The Evolution of OPEC Strategy.* Lexington, Mass.: Lexington Books, 1977.

Goohs, C. A. "United States Taxation Policies and the Iron Ore Operations of the United States Steel Industry." Unpublished, J. F. Kennedy School, Cambridge, Mass., Spring 1980.

Gort, Michael. *Diversification and Integration in American Industry.* Princeton, N.J.: Princeton University Press, 1962.

Graham, E. M. "Oligopolistic Imitation and European Direct Investment in the United States." Unpublished DBA thesis, Harvard School of Business Administration, 1974.

Gray, H. P. *The Economics of Business Investment Abroad.* New York: Crane, Russak, 1972.

Green, J. R. "Vertical Integration and the Assurance of Markets." Harvard Institute of Economic Research, Discussion Paper 383, October 1974.

Habakkuk, H. J. *American and British Technology in the Nineteenth Century.* Cambridge: Cambridge University Press, 1962.

Hartley, Keith. "The Learning Curve and Its Application to the Aircraft Industry." *Journal of Industrial Economics.* Vol. 13, no. 2 (March 1965), pp. 122–128.

Heslop, Alan (ed.). *The World Capital Shortage.* Indianapolis: Bobbs-Merrill, 1977.

Hochmuth, M. S. "Aerospace." In Raymond Vernon (ed.), *Big Business and the State.* Cambridge, Mass.: Harvard University Press, 1974.

Hogberg, Bengt. *Interfirm Cooperation and Strategic Development.* Ghoteborg: b BAS ek. fhoren, 1977.

Horowitz, Lester. "Patents and World Trade." *Journal of World Trade Law,* Vol. 4, no. 4 (July–August 1970), pp. 538–547.

Hymer, Stephen, and Robert Rowthorn. "Multinational Corporations and International Oligopoly: The Non-American Challenge." In C. P. Kindleberger (ed.), *The International Corporation: A Symposium.* Cambridge, Mass.: MIT Press, 1970.

Jacoby, N. H. *Multinational Oil.* New York: Macmillan, 1974.

Jacoby, N. H., Peter Nehemkis, and Richard Eells. *Bribery and Extortion in World Business: A Study of Corporate Political Payments Abroad.* New York: Macmillan, 1977.

Jenkins, R. O. *Dependent Industrialization in Latin America: The Automobile Industry in Argentina, Chile, and Mexico.* New York: Praeger, 1977.

Jensen, H. R., E. W. Kehrberg, and D. W. Thomas. "Integration as an Adjustment to Risk and Uncertainty." *Southern Economics Journal,* Vol. 28, no. 4 (April 1962), pp. 378–384.

Jéquier, Nicolas. "Computer." In Raymond Vernon (ed.), *Big Business and the State.* Cambridge, Mass.: Harvard University Press, 1974.

Jodice, D. A. "Sources of Change in Third World Regimes for Foreign Direct Investment, 1968–1976." *International Organization,* Vol. 34. no. 2 (Spring 1980), pp. 177–206.

Kaserman, D. L. "Theories of Vertical Integration: Implications for Antitrust Policy." *The Antitrust Bulletin,* Vol. 23, no. 3 (Fall 1978), pp. 483–510.

Katz, B. G., and Almarin Phillips. "Government, Technological Opportunities, and the Emergence of the Computer Industry." In Herbert Giersch (ed.), *Emerging Technology.* Kiel: Institute of World Economics, in press.

Kennedy, Tom, and C. E. Simon, *An Examination of Questionable Payments and Practices.* New York: Praeger, 1978.

Knickerbocker, F. T. *Oligopolistic Reaction and Multinational Enterprise.* Boston: Division of Research, Graduate School of Business Administration, Harvard University, 1973.

Kobrin, S. J. "Morality, Political Power and Illegal Payments." *Columbia Journal of World Business,* Vol. 11, no. 4 (Winter 1976), pp. 105–110; and "Foreign Enterprise and Forced Divestment in LDCs." *International Organization,* Vol. 34, no 1 (Winter 1980), pp. 65–88.

Koninklijke Nederlandsche, Petroleum Maatschappij, N. W. *The Royal Dutch Petroleum Company 1890–1950.* The Hague, 1950.

Krasner, S. D. *Defending the National Interest.* Princeton, N. J.: Princeton University Press, 1978.

Kugel, Yerachmiel, and G. W. Gruenberg. "Criteria and Guidelines for Decision Making: The Special Case of International Payoffs." *Columbia Journal of World Business,* Vol. 12, no. 3 (Fall 1977), pp. 113–123.

Lall, Sanjaya. "Monopolistic Advantages and Foreign Involvement by U. S. Manufacturing Industry." *Oxford Economic Papers,* Vol. 32, no. 1 (March 1980), pp. 102–122.

Levy, Brian. "World Oil Marketing in Transition." *International Organization,* Vol. 36, no. 1 (Winter 1982), pp. 113–133.

Maier, H. G. "International Patent Conventions and Access to Foreign Technology." *Journal of International Law and Economics,* Vol. 4, no. 2 (Fall 1969), pp. 207–231.

Mansvelt Beck, F. W., and K. M. Wiig. *The Economics of Offshore Oil and Gas Supplies.* Lexington, Mass.: Lexington Books, 1977.

Measday, W. S. "The Pharmaceutical Industry." In Walter Adams (ed.), *The Structure of American Industry.* New York: Macmillan, 1977.

Michalet, C. A., and Michel Delapierre. *The Multinationalization of French Firms.* Chicago: Academy of International Business, 1975.

Mikesell, R. F. *The World Copper Industry: Structure and Economic Analysis.* Baltimore, Md.: Johns Hopkins University Press, 1979a; and *New Patterns of World Mineral Development.* New York: British-North American Committee, 1979b.

Moran, T. H. *Multinational Companies and the Politics of Dependence: Copper in Chile.* Princeton, N.J.: Princeton University Press, 1974.

Naryenya-Takirambudde, Peter. *Technology Transfer and International Law.* New York: Praeger, 1977.

The New York Times. "Ford Regroups for the Minicar Battle." December 4, 1975, pp. 1, 9.

Organization for Economic Cooperation and Development (OECD). *Restrictive Business Practices of Multinational Enterprises.* Report to the Committee of Experts on Restrictive Business Practices, Paris, 1977a; and *Transfer of Technology by Multinational Corporations.* Paris, 1977b.

Ozawa, Terutomo. *Japan's Technological Challenge to the West, 1950–1974: Motivation and Accomplishment.*

Cambridge, Mass.: MIT Press, 1974.

Parker, J. E. S. *The Economics of Innovation,* 2nd ed. New York: Longman, 1978.

Penrose, E. T. "International Patenting and the Less-Developed Countries." *Economic Journal,* Vol. 83, no. 331 (September 1973), pp. 768–786.

Pfeffer, Jeffrey, and Philip Nowek. "Patterns of Joint Venture Activity: Implications for Antitrust Policy." *The Antitrust Bulletin,* Vol. 21, no. 2 (Summer 1976), pp. 315–339.

Porter, M. E. *Competitive Strategy: Techniques for Analyzing Industries and Competitors.* New York: The Free Press, 1980.

Radetzki, Marion, and Stephen Zorn. *Financing Mining Projects in Developing Countries.* London: Mining Journal Books, 1979; "Foreign Finance for LDC Mining Projects." In Sandro Sideri and Sheridan Johns (eds.), *Mining for Development in the Third World: Multinational Corporations, State Enterprises and the International Economy.* New York: Pergamon Press, 1980.

Robinson, R. D. *National Control of Foreign Business Entry: A Survey of Fifteen Countries.* New York: Praeger, 1976.

Ronstadt, R. C. *Research and Development Abroad by U.S. Multinationals.* New York: Praeger, 1977.

Rosenberg, Nathan. "The Direction of Technological Change: Inducement Mechanisms and Focusing Devices." *Economic Development and Cultural Change,* Vol. 18, no. 1, pt. 1 (October 1969), pp. 1–24; *Perspectives on Technology.* Cambridge: Cambridge University Press, 1976.

Samuelsson, H. F. "National Scientific and Technological Potential and the Activities of Multinational Corporations: The Case of Sweden." Mimeographed. Report to the OECD Committee for Scientific and Technological Policy, 1974.

Scherer, F. M. "Antitrust and Patent Policy," Mimeographed. Seminar on Technological Innovation, sponsored by U.S. National Science Foundation and the Government of the Federal Republic of Germany, Bonn, April 1976; and *Industrial Market Structure and Economic Performance.* Skokie, Ill.: Rand McNally, 1980.

Smith, D. M., and L. T. Wells, Jr. *Negotiating Third World Mineral Agreements: Promises as Prologue.* Cambridge, Mass.: Ballinger, 1976.

Stigler, G. J. "Imperfections in the Capital Market." *Journal of Political Economy,* Vol. 75, no. 3 (June 1967), pp. 287–292.

Stiglitz, J. E., and Andrew Weiss. "Credit Rationing in Markets with Imperfect Information." *American Economic Review,* Vol. 71, no. 3 (June 1981), pp. 109–393.

Stopford, J. M., and L. T. Wells, Jr. *Managing the Multinational.* New York: Basic Books, 1972.

Stuckey, J. A. "Vertical Integration and Joint Ventures in the International Aluminum Industry." Unpublished doctoral thesis, Harvard University, 1981.

Sundelson, J. W. "U.S. Automotive Investments Abroad," in C. P. Kindelberger (ed.), *The International Corporation.* Cambridge, Mass.: MIT Press, 1970.

Teece, D. J. "Vertical Integration in the U.S. Oil Industry," in E.J. Mitchell (ed.), *Vertical Integration in the Oil Industry.* Washington, D.C.: American Enterprise Institute, 1976.

Thunell, L. H. *Political Risks in International Business: Investment Behavior of Multinational Corporations.* New York: Praeger, 1977.

Tomlinson, J. W. C. *The Joint Venture in International Business.* Cambridge, Mass.: MIT Press, 1970.

Turner, Louis. *Multinational Companies and the Third World.* New York: Hill and Wang, 1973.

Turner, Louis, and J. M. Bedore. *Middle East Industrialization: A Study of Saudi and Iranian Downstream Investments.* Westnead, Farmborough, Hants, UK: Saxon House, 1979.

UNCTAD. *The Role of Trade Marks in Developing Countries.* New York: United Nations, 1979.

United Nations Economic and Social Council, Commission on Transnational Corporations. *Transnational Corporations in World Development: A Reexamination.* New York: United Nations, 1978.

United Nations, Department of Economic and Social Affairs. *Multinational Corporations in World Development.* New York, 1973.

U.S. Department of Commerce, Bureau of Economic Analysis. *U.S. Direct Investment Abroad, 1977.* Washington, D.C.: U.S. Government Printing Office, 1981.

U.S. Federal Trade Commission. *The International Petroleum Cartel.* Washington, D.C.: U.S. Government Printing Office, 1952.

U.S. Securities and Exchange Commission. *Report on Questionable and Illegal Corporate Payments and Practices.* Washington, D.C.: U.S. Government Printing Office, May 12, 1976.

U.S. Senate Committee on Banking, Housing and Urban Affairs. "Prohibiting Bribes to Foreign Officials." *Committee Hearings.* Washington, D.C.: Committee Print, May 18, 1976.

Vaupel, J. W., and J. P. Curhan. *The World's Multinational Enterprises: A Source Book of Tables.* Boston: Division of Research, Graduate School of Business Administration, Harvard University, 1973.

Vernon, Raymond. *Sovereignty at Bay.* New York: Basic Books, 1971. *Storm over the Multinationals.* Cambridge, Mass.: Harvard University Press, 1977; and "The International Aspects of State-Owned Enterprises." *Journal of International Business Studies* (Winter 1979), pp. 7–15;

and "Gone Are the Cash Cows of Yesteryear." *Harvard Business Review* (November–December 1980), pp. 150–155.

Vernon, Raymond, and W. H. Davidson, "Foreign Production of Technology-Intensive Products by U.S.-Based Multinational Enterprises." Report to the National Science Foundation, no. PB 80 148638, January 1979.

Williamson, O. E. *Markets and Hierarchies: Analysis and Antitrust Implications.* New York: The Free Press, 1975.

Zorn, Stephen, "Recent Trends in LDC Mining Agreements," in Sandro Sideri and Sheridan Johns (eds.), *Mining for Development in the Third World: Multinational Corporations, State Enterprises and the International Economy.* Elmsford, N.Y.: Pergamon Press, 1980.

13

▮▮▮▮▮▮▮ POLITICAL RISK: A REVIEW AND RECONSIDERATION
Stephen J. Kobrin

When you enter an endeavor unsuccessfully then the planning was incorrect. The risk was above the gains and you stumble along the way . . . Sagacity, ingenuity, planning . . . it involves much weighing, odds against failure, odds against gain.

INTRODUCTION

While there has been increasing academic interest in the intersection of politics and international business, it is still a relatively new and loosely defined field. It would appear worthwhile to review and summarize what has been accomplished thus far and to look toward future needs. This paper will attempt to serve that end by focusing upon one of the more salient issue areas: the political risk associated with foreign investment. It has three specific objectives: to review the existing literature, to build upon this literature by attempting to define more precisely the concept of political risk, and to suggest fruitful directions for future research.

Source: Journal of International Business Studies (Spring–Summer 1979), pp. 67–80. Copyright © 1979. Reprinted by permission.

POLITICAL RISK

Although the term "political risk" occurs frequently in the international business literature, agreement about its meaning is limited to an implication of unwanted consequences of political activity. It is most commonly conceived of in terms of (usually host) government interference with business operations. Weston and Sorge's [64] definition is representative: "[P]olitical risks arise from the actions of national governments which interfere with or prevent business transactions, or change the terms of agreements, or cause the confiscation of wholly or partially foreign owned business property" (p. 60). Similarly, Aliber [2], Baglini [4], Carlson [11], Eiteman and Stonehill [16], Greene [23], *The Journal of Commerce* [28], Lloyd [41], and Smith [56] all explicitly or implicitly define political risk as governmental or sovereign interference with business operations. This rather widespread conception of political risk in terms of government interference with private investment has important normative implications which will be discussed in the next section.

A second major cluster of authors defines political risk in terms of events—either political acts, constraints imposed upon the firm, or some combination of both. While there are differences among them, Greene [19, 20], Hershbarger and Noerager [27], Nehrt [44], Rodriguez and Carter [47], Van Agtmael [62], and Zink [66] all equate political risk with either environmental factors such as instability and direct violence or constraints on operations such as expropriation, discriminatory taxation, public sector competition, and the like. Others—such as, Daniels [13], Dymsza [14], and Brooke and Remmers [9]—do not explicitly define the concept but rather note that the political environment (or the environment in general) is a source of business risk for the firm.

Robock, Root, and Haendel and West have considered the concept of political risk in considerable detail. Robock [46] suggests the following operational definition:

. . . political risk in international business exists (1) when discontinuities occur in the business environment, (2) when they are difficult to anticipate and (3) when they result from political change. To constitute a "risk" these changes in the business environment must have the potential for significantly affecting the profit or other goals of a particular enterprise. (p. 7)

The concepts of discontinuity and direct effects on the enterprise are central to Robock's definition. He notes that while all political environments are dynamic, changes which are gradual and progressive and are neither unexpected nor difficult to anticipate do not constitute political risk. He then clearly differentiates between political instability and political risk: ". . . political fluctuations which do not change the business environment significantly do not represent risk for international business. . . . Political instability, depending upon how it is defined, is a separate although related phenomenon from that of political risk" (p. 8). Robock also distinguishes between "macro risk" where political events result in constraints on all foreign enterprise (for example, Cuba in 1959–1960) and "micro risk" which affects only "selected fields of business activity or foreign enterprises with specific characteristics" (p. 9).

Root [50] defines political risk in terms of the:

. . . possible occurrence of a political event of any kind (such as war, revolution, coup d'etat, expropriation, taxation, devaluation, exchange controls and import restrictions) at home or abroad that can cause a loss of profit potential and/or assets in an international business operation. (p. 355)

Root emphasizes the difference between uncertainty and risk (drawing both normative and positive implications), attempts to separate political from other environmental risks, and develops several useful taxonomies. In a second paper [51] Root concludes that the distinction between political and economic risks breaks down at the experiential level as a result of the ". . . interdependence of economic and political phenomena: (p. 3). Still, an attempt at that distinction is made: [A]n uncertainty is political if it relates to (a) a potential government act . . . , or (b) general instability in the political/social system" (p. 4).

Root also categorizes political uncertainties in terms of the manner in which they affect the firm: (1) transfer—uncertainty about flows of capital, payments, technology, people, etc.; (2) operational—uncertainties about policies that directly constrain local operations; and (3) ownership/control—uncertainties about policies relating to ownership of managerial control (p. 357). He suggests that transfer and operations uncertainties flow primarily from political/economic events and ownership/control from political/social.

Haendel and West [24] focus upon a distinction between risk and uncertainty: between "the probability of occurrence of an undesired political event[s] and the uncertainty generated by inadequate information concerning the occurrence of such an event[s]" (p. 44). Thus, political risk is defined as the "risk or probability of occurrence of some political event[s] that will change the prospects for the profitability of a given investment" (p. xi). (They later note explicitly that political risk is both investor and investment specific.)

The crux of their argument is that information—in this case information about the political environment—can help bridge the gap; it can enable investors to convert uncertainty to risk that is, at least potentially, "measurable, insurable and avoidable" (p. 46).

POLITICAL RISK: A RECONSIDERATION

One of the conclusions of this paper is that most managers' understanding of the concept of political risk, their assessment and evaluation of politics, and the manner in which they integrate political information into decision making are all rather general, subjective, and superficial. We would argue that while the literature reflects substantial progress in a relatively short period of time, it still does not provide an analytic framework which can adequately contribute—in either a taxonomic or an operational sense—to improved practice.

As noted above, many authors simply view political risk in terms of an event occurring either in the environment (for example, instability) or at the junction of environment and enterprise (for example, a nationalization), typically associated with an act of government that has unfavorable consequences for the firm. Scholars who have explored the issue in more depth [24, 44, 46, 50] clearly distinguish between the political event[1] and the actual loss or gain to the firm. They note that the consequences of any given political event for the foreign investor depend upon its nature, the conditions under which it occurs, and the characteristics of the specific investment in question.

However, the existing state of the art limits operationalization in the context of the investment (or reinvestment) decision process. First, the phenomenon is not defined in a manner that allows for unambiguous classification of environmental events: that is, which are of concern and which are not. Second, while all of these authors deal with uncertainty in terms of both environmental processes (continuous versus discontinuous change) and decision makers' perceptions (uncertainty versus risk), the two processes are not explicitly linked in a manner that facilitates integration into investment decision making. Third, the concentration on discontinuous change or uncertainty limits unnecessarily the scope of political analysis. Last, the emphasis on the negative consequences of government intervention entails an implicit normative assumption that may not be universally valid.

The Political Environment

Root is correct when he claims that the analytical distinctions of the social scientist break down at the experiential level; society exists in the entirety. This most certainly applies to economics and politics. Gilpin [17], among others [8, 40], has argued that the relationship between the two is not at all distinct, but rather interactive and reciprocal. Lindblom [40] goes so far as to suggest that differences may be entirely perceptual.

It appears reasonable to ask whether there is any cause to consider the political environment separately—to distinguish between sources of business risk. There appear to be very pragmatic reasons for doing so. Economics and politics are sufficiently distinct, both as abstract phenomena and in terms of their impact upon the firm, to require separate analysis and managerial response. For example, it should be obvious that a Japanese producer's response to the U.S. imposition of steel trigger prices in 1977 would be quite different if analysis indicated that the primary motivation for trigger prices was the need to prevent the alienation of important domestic interest groups rather than strict balance of payments concerns.

Defining politics in terms of power or authority relationships exercised in the context of society at large [15, 39] can usefully distinguish it from economics. This paper is concerned with events, whether they appear to be political or economic (that is, directly concerned with the production and distribution of wealth), that are motivated by attempts to gain, maintain, or increase power at the state level, "to influence significantly the kind of authoritative policy adopted for society" [15, p. 127].

Although we can distinguish between economic and political determinants of events, they are obviously interrelated. First, at least in the short run, "politics largely determines the framework of economic activity" [17]. A change in regime can result in a change from a market to a socialist economy (Cuba in 1959) or the reverse (Chile in 1973). Second, and following from the first, political or power concerns often influence economic policy. The converse is, of course, equally true. The production and distribution of wealth directly affect the distribution of power; however, the distinction has heuristic value and can be applied in practice.

We would not, for example, consider a strike, or even a general strike, a political event if its motivation results from dissatisfaction over work-related issues. However, widescale strikes in Nicaragua in January 1978 protesting the Somoza regime were clearly political. Similarly, a general strike in Tunis at about the same time began as an economic event—a protest against wage restraints—and ended as a full challenge to the Bourguiba government.

The Environment and the Firm: Perceptions and Impact

The firm exists as a system within an environment. How do political events, which occur in the environment, affect the firm? The answer depends, to a large extent, on the nature of the world facing the firm. Three states of affairs—

in terms of managerial perceptions of events and outcomes—are of interest.

If a single outcome can be unambiguously associated with a given event, certainty exists. The distinction between the second and third states, which Knight [34] called risk and uncertainty, depends upon whether probabilities can be associated with outcomes. In the former, one has perfect knowledge of both all possible outcomes associated with an event and the probability of their occurrence, either "through calculation a priori or from statistics of past experience" [34, p. 233]. In the latter, neither knowledge of all possible outcomes nor "objective" probabilities (in the sense used earlier) exist. However, uncertainty is, following Shackle [54], bounded. Decision makers can make judgments about most of the important outcomes and their likelihood of occurrence. (Complete uncertainty is not of interest; it entails what Shackle calls a "powerless decision.")

To avoid semantic confusion (for example, political risk, business risk, systematic risk) the first state may be called certainty; the second, objective uncertainty; and the third, subjective uncertainty. The distinction between objective and subjective uncertainty is quite important, particularly in international business. Uncertainty is subjective in the sense that opinions about the relative likelihood of events are based upon perceptions that are a function of the available information, previous experience, and individual cognitive processes which synthesize both into an imagined future.

It is clear that for virtually all business decisions of the type discussed here both certainty and objective uncertainty are ideal constructs. As the decisions can neither be repeated nor divided—that is, treated as one of a series of experiments and pooled (as can both deaths and auto accidents)—they are unique events. Perhaps, more importantly, the decisions are made by human beings in a very complex environment which makes it difficult to specify all possible, or even all important, alternatives. Since decisions are taken in the present, possible outcomes must be imagined outcomes, existing subjectively in the mind of the decision maker; however, both certainty and objective uncertainty can be approximated.

Certainty can be approximated by situations when one outcome dominates all others. Thus, the probability that the next President of the United States will be selected by a constitutional process and that he (or she) will not institute a program of broadscale nationalization of industry is so high as to be virtually certain. Certainty may also be approximated in situations that Robock [46] described as gradual change, which one can anticipate, based upon current trends. Objective uncertainty can be approximated by situations where, while one outcome does not dominate, all feasible outcomes are known, information is readily available, and all (or almost all) observers agree upon probabilities. Again, an example would be the outcome of most U.S. presidential elections.

We can now return to the question of the impact of politics upon the firm. Several preliminary points are in order. First, one can say only that political events may affect the firm; whether they do so is a function of both environmental conditions and industry- and firm-specific factors. A coup, for example, may place a radical socialist government in power which expropriates all foreign-owned firms (as in Ethiopia); it may result in a conservative government which actually returns expropriated property (as in Chile in 1973), or it may simply replace governing elites without affecting foreign investors at all. Furthermore, as many authors have noted (for example, [46] and [50]), vulnerability is a function of enterprise-specific characteristics. Natural resource–based investment is generally more vulnerable, ceteris paribus, than are manufacturing firms producing essential products.

Second, one must clearly distinguish between the environment and the firm. Instability is a property of the environment and risk of the firm. It is the possible variation of a firm-specific variable (for example, returns) from its

expected value that can be caused by environmental events. Last, risk may imply positive as well as negative variation about the mean; it can result in gains as well as losses. The distinction between pure risk, which involves only a chance of loss or no loss (for example, a fire or fraud), and speculative risk, which involves the possibility of both gain and loss [31], is useful.

Given certainty, the firm does not face business risk; both outcomes of events and their impact upon the firm are known; however, political events can still affect returns. As an example, assume it is absolutely certain that a new government will come to power in one month and that it will force a firm to divest 100 percent of equity in five years at present book value. Although the political event will reduce the value of future returns, it will not in any way contribute to their variation. There is no business risk associated with the change in government.

However, once uncertainty is introduced, political events can both affect the expected value of returns and contribute to their variation. Political events are now a source of business risk. Whereas their impact upon the value of returns is not dependent upon whether the uncertainty is objective or subjective, the nature and extent of their contribution to risk clearly is. If uncertainty is objective, the contribution of political events to business risk is a function of only the events themselves. Risk, then, is the distribution of probable returns which is, ceteris paribus, a function of the probable impacts of political events on operations.

If uncertainty is subjective, the contribution of business risk is a function of both the events themselves and the fact that decision makers' perceptions of those events are inherently subjective—distorted by past experience, cognitive processes and the nature of the organization. This subjectivity factor is particularly important in international business operations where decisions are often taken in one sociopolitical environment based upon stimuli arising in another. As will be discussed later, the survey data indicate that managerial evaluations of political risk are typically subjective and ethnocentric.

A better understanding of the political process in general, the political environment in the country in question, and the potential impact of politics upon the firm's operations can thus obviously reduce risk by reducing the uncertainty about the actual probability distribution. However, the crucial point, one which forces us to take issue with the existing literature (for example, Haendel and West [24]), is that while better information can help eliminate misconceptions about both the political environment and its impact upon the firm, it can seldom convert uncertainty into risk or what we have called objective uncertainty. Opinions formed about future events (and particularly events which will take place in another culture) are inherently subjective. Hannah Arendt [3] put it well:

The world appears in the mode of it-seems-to-me, depending on particular perspectives determined by location in the world as well as by particular organs of perception. Not only does this produce error, which I can correct by changing my location, drawing closer to what appears, or by improving my imagination to take other perspectives into account; it also gives birth to true semblances—that is true deceptive appearances, which I cannot correct like an error. (pp. 108–109)

The term "political risk" thus appears overly constrained from both an analytical and operational viewpoint. What we are, or should be, concerned with is the impact of events which are political in the sense that they arise from power or authority relationships and which affect (or have the potential to affect) the firm's operations. Not the events, qua events, but their potential manifestation as constraints upon foreign investors should be of concern. Furthermore, although the same constraint (for example, restrictions on profit repatriations or a forced divestment of ownership) could be motivated by economic as well as political factors (or

both) depending upon the circumstances, the two may be differentiated to facilitate analysis and response. Last, political events may affect only the value of returns, or they may also contribute to business risk depending upon whether outcomes are evaluated under conditions approximating certainty or uncertainty. If that uncertainty is subjective, as it is likely to be in an international business decision, the contribution to risk will be greater because one is uncertain about both outcomes and the probabilities associated with them. Integration of the assessment of political risk into the investment decision process will be discussed next.

Integration into Decision Making

The integration of political assessments into decision making is not a subject that has been widely discussed. The literature focuses typically upon deriving probabilistic estimates of political events and their impact upon the firm rather than how the estimates are utilized; this study conforms to that tradition.

Most authors who have considered the problem assume that decision makers will utilize political analysis to adjust either cash flows or the discount rate. Robock [46], for example, shows how risk analysis can be used to determine the political risks likely to arise during specific time periods and then suggests that "the present value of expected cash flows, or the internal rate of return from the investment project under consideration can be adjusted to reflect the timing and magnitude of risk probabilities" (p. 17). (In the example that follows, however, only cash flows are adjusted.)

After reviewing evidence showing how most firms analyze political and economic stability, Stobaugh [57] suggests two more "sophisticated techniques": range of estimates and risk analysis. However, while both provide probability distributions as well as expected values of cash flows, Stobaugh's examples entail only the adjustment of the level of cash flows.

Stonehill and Nathanson [58] object to simple discount rate adjustments to reflect political and foreign exchange uncertainties. They suggest that "A better way to allow for uncertainty in the multinational case would be to charge each period's incremental cash flows the cost of a program of uncertainty absorption for that period, whether or not the program was actually undertaken" (p. 46). The program of uncertainty absorption could entail the purchase of additional information, insurance (including investment guarantees), hedging, and the like. They, in essence, recommend using a market-determined approximation of a certainty equivalent.

Shapiro [55] deals with political and economic risk, and specifically with expropriation in the context of the capital budgeting process. He notes that neither of two methods (a higher discount rate or a shorter payback period) commonly used to account for political or economic risk "lends itself to a careful evaluation of a particular risk's actual impact on investment returns. A thorough risk analysis requires an assessment of the magnitude of the risk's effect on cash flows as well as an estimate of the true pattern of the risk." (p. 6)

Shapiro then develops sophisticated techniques for adjusting cash flows given the probability of expropriation at a point in the future. However, he assumes that (1) the assumptions of the Capital Asset Pricing Model are relevant; and (2) the risks in question are nonsystematic in nature. Thus, the cash flow adjustments reflect only changes in expected values resulting from the impact of a given risk.

Although agreeing with Shapiro that, in evaluating the impact of the political environment on the firm, both the effect upon the magnitude of cash flows and on their distribution (that is, risk) must be taken into account, we would like to avoid entering the lists on the question of whether the firm should be viewed as a social organization reflecting managerial utilities (and risk preferences) or as an agent of the stockholders. Instead, we suggest that the potential effect of politics be evaluated in terms of the continu-

um discussed earlier. Under conditions giving rise to risk, whether one actually adjusts the discount rate or not will be determined by one's judgment as to (1) the applicability of the Capital Asset Pricing Model and (2) whether the risk is systematic or not.

Under conditions approximating certainty, decision makers should be concerned only with determining the effect of political events on the magnitude of cash flows. Risk clearly is not a relevant concern; however, political assessment and evaluation is still necessary. Certain outcomes are not inherently obvious; they are certain, given sufficient information about the environment and the firm.

Under conditions approximating objective uncertainty, the decision maker must consider the impact of politics on both the expected value of cash flows and their distribution (or business risk). The estimate of the contribution to risk will flow solely from the distribution of the joint probability of a political event taking place and affecting cash flows. Last, under conditions of subjective uncertainty, the decision maker is again concerned with the effect of political events upon both expected values and risk. However, in this instance risk is increased because one is uncertain about the shape of the probability distribution. In fact one knows one's estimate is inherently distorted due to subjective factors and that the distortion can never be completely eliminated.

One additional point entails an implicit normative assumption which is counterproductive in terms of the very issue of concern:[2] the tendency to view political risk in terms of government interference with one's operations.

Much of the discussion of political risk appears to assume that governmental restrictions on FDI—such as, partial divestment or local content regulations—involve economically inefficient and perhaps even irrational tampering with flows of direct investment that provide net benefits to their recipients. It is obvious that this viewpoint is less than universally accepted and that what appears as economic nationalism[3] to an investor may be regarded as an attempt to implement a policy of indigenous industrialization by the host. In short, company and host country objectives differ and neither has a monopoly on goodness and light. A perception to the contrary, whether explicit or implicit, may well increase the risk one is attempting to evaluate.

POLITICAL EVENTS AND FOREIGN DIRECT INVESTMENT

A number of empirical studies have attempted to analyze the relationship between FDI and environmental factors—typically measures of political instability and market size and potential. With some relatively minor exceptions the results are consistent. The overwhelmingly important determinant of manufacturing investment is the size and potential of the market [20, 35, 61]. A direct or simple relationship cannot be found between a general notion of instability and stocks or flows of FDI [7, 19, 20, 35]. For example, in an early study Green [7] regressed stocks of U.S. FDI in manufacturing and trade on an index of political instability while controlling for gross national product per capita across 46 countries. He concluded that political instability did not affect the overall allocation of U.S. marketing FDI. In a 62-country cross-sectional study Kobrin [35] analyzed the relationship between flows of U.S. manufacturing FDI and seven indicators of economic, social, and political factors. While the environmental factors accounted for 64 percent of the variance of FDI, only market size, growth, and a measure of prior U.S. export involvement were significant.

There have been several exceptions to the overall pattern of results. Green and Smith [22] established a weak but statistically significant relationship between profitability of U.S. FDI and instability. However, methodological problems cloud interpretation of the results. Root

and Ahmed [52] used discriminant analysis to attempt to account for differences between three groups of countries based upon per capita inflows of nonextractive FDI. While regular executive transfers was found to be a significant discriminator, it was the fifth variable selected by the stepwise procedure (the other five were market related), and its explanatory power, therefore, appears weak. Last, Knickerbocker [33], in his study of oligopolistic reaction, found a significant relationship between a measure of entry concentration and an index of stability across 21 countries. He concluded that "oligopolists were not inclined to make defensive investments in unstable markets" (p. 184).

At least two studies suggest a complex and indirect relationship between FDI and instability. Thunell [61], in a longitudinal study, attempted to analyze the relationship between major "trend" changes in the flow of FDI (the second derivative) and a number of indicators of elite and mass stability. An asymmetrical relationship was observed. A high level of mass violence precedes negative trend changes, whereas it takes both a low level of violence and a government transfer (which Thunell speculates implies a shift in policy) to generate a positive change. It should be noted that, although interesting, Thunell's results must be regarded as quite tentative due to problems of comparability and the absence (with one exception) of statistical analysis.

In a study of 48 countries, Kobrin [36] found a significant relationship between flows of FDI (controlling for market-related factors) and one dimension of intrastate conflict; focused anti-regime violence. The relationship is intensified at higher levels of development and when host country administrative capacity is strong. That study concluded that political conflict has the highest probability of affecting foreign investors when it is of a nature and occurs under conditions which are likely to motivate relevant changes in government policy.

It would thus appear that political factors are

not a major determinant of FDI. To the extent that a relationship does exist, it is rather complex and depends upon the probability that instability or conflict will result in changes in policy rather than in direct effects upon investors.

It should be obvious that all of the studies summarized have several glaring defects. First, they all focus upon instability when it is clear that political instability is neither a necessary nor a sufficient condition for changes in policy relevant to foreign investment. Second, they all utilize aggregate (typically cross-national) analysis when the risk posed by politics is markedly affected by industry, firm, and even project-specific factors. (This problem is somewhat alleviated by the focus of most of the studies on the manufacturing sector.) Last, all the studies entail major data and methodological problems ranging from the use of composite indices of instability to the almost universal use (with one exception) of cross-sectional techniques to investigate what is obviously a longitudinal phenomenon. In summary, while the results are useful and interesting, they must be taken as tentative.

THE POLITICAL ENVIRONMENT: ASSESSMENT AND RESPONSE

Surveys of managerial assessment and evaluation of the political environment consistently reveal an interesting paradox. With very few exceptions, managers rate political instability (or political risk) as one of the major influences on the foreign investment decision. Yet, again with very few exceptions, the same surveys report the absence of any formal or even rigorous and systematic assessment of political environments and their potential impact upon the firm.

Two early studies—those of Aharoni [1] and Basi [5]—found that political or economic stability was the first factor considered in the foreign investment decision. A second conclu-sion of Aharoni's described the assessment process: "Risk is not described in terms of the impact on a specific investment. It is, rather, described in general terms and stems from ignorance, generalizations, projection of U.S. culture and standards to other countries and on unqualified deduction from some general indicator to a specific investment" (p. 94). As we shall see, little can be found in reports of more recent surveys to support a challenge to Aharoni's conclusions.

Several other important studies were conducted (or reported) in the late 1960s. In two separate studies [48 and 49], Root surveyed executives in a large number of U.S. firms selected from the *Fortune 500* list. He reported that while executives indicated political risks and market opportunities are "the dominant factors in most (foreign) investment decisions ... no executive offered any evidence of a systematic evaluation of political risks, involving their identification, their likely incidence, and their specific consequences for company operations" [49, p. 75]. Furthermore, it is quite clear that executives' subjective perceptions of political instability were highly instrumental in shaping their attitudes toward the safety and profitability of investment climates.

A 1967–1968 Conference Board survey of investors in twelve countries [43] confirmed the earlier findings. First, estimates of political risk were typically based upon subjective perceptions: "The study makes it clear that obstacles to investment exist in the mind of the investor ... certain countries are dismissed from consideration as investment sites on the basis of information that is incomplete, outdated or in some cases even erroneous" (p. 2). Second, politics is perceived as an important determinant of foreign investment, and a common response to perceived political risk is avoidance. Studies reported in the early 1970s—[45, 59, 66]—added little new information. While political or quasi-political factors continued to be of major concern to investors, few U.S. companies had as yet developed techniques for assessing the political environment or evaluating its impact upon operations.

The most recent studies reported are monotonously consistent with previous findings. In two Conference Board reports [37 and 38] LaPalombara and Blank conclude that while some sort of environmental analysis exists in most firms, it is typically rather loose and casual, developing and utilizing a subjective "feel for the political situation." During the course of the study, various planning materials and documents were reviewed. The conclusion drawn is to the point: "More often than not, the few paragraphs devoted to a host country's social and political dynamics is not better than one might find in leading parent country newspapers" (p. 65).

Drawing on his experience as a Vice President of a major bank, Van Agtmael [62] concluded that even large and active MNCs do not analyze political risk in a very sophisticated manner; and he agrees with other authors that the typical response to political risk is avoidance. "Even those corporations which have made commitments overseas, by and large, try to avoid political risk by investing in 'safe' countries" (p. 26). There remains one, somewhat specialized, area of the political environment assessment literature—that dealing with the sovereign (or country) risk inherent in private bank lending to LDCs. Rather than extend what is already a rather lengthy paper, the reader may be referred to the following: Goodman [18], Mueller [42], Van Agtmael [63], and Yassukouich [65].

Last, a brief review of the findings of the literature on managers' sources of information about politics shows that the earliest findings still stand. In a classic study, which while dealing primarily with trade certainly has broader implications, Bauer, de Sola Pool, and Dexter [6] concluded that, to businessmen, knowledge of the "outside world" came in a number of ways:

it came in part through the printed word, but what came that way was surprisingly general and unfocused. Our respondents read Time, Business Week, The Wall Street Journal, The New York Times, *and other such journals. They read a great deal. They also read trade papers. But, in making specific business decisions, they did not do research in published sources. . . . Knowledge of foreign economic affairs came either from the most general news sources or, more vividly, from correspondence and personal experience. (p. 470)*

Zink [66] found that managers' major sources of political information were reports from host country employees, general news sources, and financial institutions (in that order). Only 23 percent of respondents considered internal political staff as an important source, and only 9 percent so rated outside consultants on a continuous retainer. Keegan [30] concluded that his study of managers at MNC headquarters emphasized "how little the systematic methods of information scanning have become a part of the way in which executives learn about their business environments" (p. 420). Executives stationed abroad (but not lower level employees), banks, and the public press were the most important sources of information for headquarters managers.

The findings reviewed here are impressively consistent. First, it is clear that managers consider political instability or political risk, typically quite loosely defined, to be an important factor in the foreign investment decision. Second, it is just as clear that rigorous and systematic assessment and evaluation of the political environment is exceptional. Most political analysis is superficial and subjective, not integrated formally into the decision-making process and assumes that instability and risk are one and the same. The response frequently is avoidance; firms simply do not get involved in countries, or even regions, that they perceive to be risky. Last, managers appear to rely for environmental information primarily on sources internal to the firm. When they look for outside data, they are most likely to go to their banks or the general and business media.

ENVIRONMENTAL ASSESSMENT METHODOLOGIES[4]

Existing screening models fit into two general categories: those aggregating subjective assessments (typically via a Delphi method) and those relying on quantified indicators of economic, social, and political factors. (A "soft/hard" distinction is not appropriate.) The best known examples of the former are Haner's "Business Environmental Risk Index" or BERI [25 and 26] and the Business International Index of Environmental Risk [10]. Both attempt to assess the general investment climate in a number of countries by using the Delphi technique to poll a panel of experts. Haner [26] states that the objective of BERI is to assess the business environment in a country from the viewpoint of a foreign investor six months to one year in the future.

BERI's panel assesses fifteen environmental factors quarterly (for example, political stability, attitude toward foreign investors, and economic growth). Each panelist scores each factor and the responses are then aggregated with the factors not equally weighted. The aggregate index and political, operations, and financial subindices are available. The BI system is quite similar.

While both indices attempt to screen the environment systematically, their usefulness is somewhat limited. First, they provide holistic rankings which are inherently independent of firm or industry factors. More importantly, they rely on a panel who may differ widely not only in terms of rankings, but in how they conceptualize the phenomena being evaluated. Last, while panel members are non-U.S. nationals, they also tend to be employees of industrial firms or financial institutions and their funda-

mental viewpoints are not likely to differ greatly from the users of the service. The net result, is, as Haner himself notes [25], that the index cannot forecast sudden changes in the political and economic environment. Again, however, both indices may be useful for general prescreening.

A second set of methodologies utilizes quantitative indices. Several authors [21] and [56] simply review existing indicators (or models) of political instability in terms of their managerial utility. There have also been attempts to develop more sophisticated quantitative indices of political risk. For example, Haendel and West [24] suggest what they call the Political System Stability Index (PSSI) which is composed of fifteen indicators of the system's stability/adaptability grouped into three subindices: socioeconomic, governmental processes, and societal conflict. A score and an estimate of confidence in that score (1–5) are provided for the overall index and each of the three major subindices. Rummel and Heenan [53] suggest integrating qualitative assessments (such as, reliance on "old hands," or Delphi techniques) with quantitative assessments. As an example, they utilize multivariate analysis to predict two components of intrastate conflict—turmoil and rebellion—in Indonesia through 1980.

Juhl [29] compares a number of environmental indicators, including four measures of political instability and BERI. The results are of interest. First, while the relationships (rank order correlation) between the various indices are typically significant, they are rather weak. Second, none of them account for more than 25 percent of the variance of any of three indices of nationalization. Last, with one exception, the author could not establish a significant relationship between the BERI Nationalism subindex and flows of FDI.

Although there are inherent limits of aggregate quantitative analysis—as with the Delphi techniques, it ignores industry and firm specific factors—it does offer a great deal of potential as a basis for systematic and rigorous assessment of the political environment. (However, that it can now, or at any point in the future, be utilized independently of qualitative judgments is not suggested.) In spite of the fact that most of the methodologies discussed were developed to aid in international firms' assessment of the political environment, they still measure political instability rather than the potential impact of politics upon the firm.

The problem transcends that of index development. While most authors reviewed agree that political instability and political risk are distinct phenomena, the fact of the matter is that enough is not known about how the former (and the political environment in general) affects the latter to construct reasonable predictive models.

CONCLUSIONS

Managers use a wide variety of techniques to reduce and cope with uncertainty in many areas of business operations. Most firms, for example, would not even consider basing a major new product introduction on a generalized feel for the market. Rather, they typically utilize a battery of relatively sophisticated research techniques to aid in reaching a judgment about both the product's potential and how to market it. Yet, judgments about the impact of politics upon operations appear, at least from the sources reviewed in this paper, to be rather superficial and typically based almost entirely on subjective perceptions.

To be absolutely clear, "sophisticated analysis" is not equated here with a complex mathematical model, but rather, what is suggested is a systematic and relatively rigorous approach to data gathering and problem solving. While stereotypes are admittedly unfair, the all too typical process, where political instability is equated with a poor investment climate and the market avoided, is a long way from that ideal. The literature reviewed in this paper reflects the substantial growth and development of a rela-

tively new area; however, some fairly major gaps must be filled if it is to contribute to more systematic and rigorous assessment and evaluation of politics by managers of international firms and to the effective integration of the information into the decision-making process. The lacunae that exist are both conceptual and empirical. We need better definitions of the phenomena, a conceptual structure relating politics to the firm, and a great deal of information about the impact of the political environment. The three are, of course, related.

Although this paper represents a preliminary attempt to redefine the concept of political risk, much work obviously remains. In fact, the term "political risk" might well be dropped from usage. (This suggestion, however, is probably a futile one.) It is overly confining and confusing. Rather, the area of interest should be defined in terms of the current and potential impact(s) of the political environment upon the operations of the firm where:

1. The political environment is circumscribed in terms of events which, however they are manifest, are motivated by or have as their objective the maintenance or modification of power or authority relationships at the governmental level.
2. The impact of political events upon the firm is defined in terms of both effects upon the magnitude of cash flows or returns and upon the business risk associated with them in the context of a specific project.
3. A significant impact on business operations cannot be assumed to be an inherent property of any political event.

In operational terms we are concerned with the probability that changes in the political environment will reduce returns to the point where the project would be no longer acceptable on the basis of ex ante criteria. Changes in the political environment can affect returns directly through damage to plant and equipment and degradation of the economy as a result of conflict. Returns can also be affected indirectly through changes in government policy such as expropriation, local content regulations, and restrictions on the remittance of dividends.

Last, research might be focused on the following areas:

1. *Empirical analyses of the conditions under which, and the process through which, political events affect the firm.* Further work (both theoretical and empirical) is needed to identify the types of environmental events likely to affect operations, the conditions under which they are most likely to do so, and the nature of the specific process through which effects are transmitted.

2. *More data on the effects themselves.* Aside from some limited data on nationalization, we really know very little about the relative importance of actual constraints imposed upon firms. Have, for example, pressures for local ownership, exchange controls, direct limits on operations, or restrictions on fees and royalties resulted from political change and how have they affected firms?

3. *Additional and more systematic studies of the assessment and evaluation of the political environment by multinational firms.* What factors affect the way the assessment and evaluation process is organized and executed? Where is it located in the organization? How is the resulting information integrated into decision making? Importantly, how does the process affect strategic decision making? Are there industrial or national differences? What affects managers' subjective perceptions or political environments? How does information act upon them?

4. *In-depth case studies.* Most of the research described in this paper is quantitative and cross-national. While it has been a valuable aid in mapping out the nature of relationships between variables, thorough case studies are needed to flesh out the skeleton. For example, a case study of the impact of a deteriorating political environment (Argentina in the late 1960s) on foreign investors could aid in understanding the exact nature of the impact of political events on foreign firms. Case studies could also help compensate for the lack of time-series data.

5. *Interdisciplinary research.* Work in this area, by definition, implies that one draw upon previous efforts in both management and political science; however, it is clear that efforts involving a number of the social sciences such as economics, organizational psychology, and anthropology are likely to bear fruit.

NOTES

1. As Baglini [4] notes, the political event is a cause of loss or a peril.
2. Bernard Mennis brought this point to my attention.
3. For a discussion of "economic nationalism," see Harry Johnson, "A Theoretical Model of Economic Nationalism in New and Developing States," *Political Science Quarterly* (June 1965), pp. 169–185.
4. While it could not be reviewed in this paper, the extensive literature on international business government relations is obviously relevant. For example, see Jack N. Behrman, J. J. Boddewyn, and Ashok Kapoor, *International Business—Government Relations* (Lexington, Mass.: Lexington Books, 1975), and Business International, *Corporate External Affairs* (New York: Business International, 1975).

REFERENCES

1. Aharoni, Yair. *The Foreign Investment Decision Process.* Boston: Division of Research, Graduate School of Business Administration, Harvard University, 1966.
2. Aliber, Robert Z. "Exchange Risk, Political Risk and Investor Demands for External Currency Deposits." *Journal of Money, Credit & Banking* (May 1975), pp. 161–179.
3. Arendt, Hannah. "Reflections (Thinking—Part 1)." *The New Yorker,* November 21, 1977, pp. 65–140.
4. Baglini, Normon A. *Risk Management in International Corporations.* New York: Risk Studies Foundation, 1976.
5. Basi, R. S. *Determinants of United States Private Direct Investment in Foreign Countries.* Kent, Ohio: Kent State University, 1963.
6. Bauer, Raymond A., Ithiel de Sola Poor, and Lewis A. Dexter. *American Business and Public Policy,* 2nd ed. Chicago: Aldine-Atherton, 1972.
7. Bennett, Peter D., and Robert T. Green. "Political Instability as a Determinant of Direct Foreign Investment in Marketing." *Journal of Marketing Research* (May 1972), pp. 182–186.
8. Bergsten, C. Fred, Robert O. Keohane, and Joseph S. Nye. "International Economics and International Politics: A Framework for Analysis." In *World Politics and International Economics,* edited by C. Fred Bergsten and Lawrence B. Krause, pp. 3–36. Washington, D.C.: Brookings Institute, 1975.

9. Brooke, Michael, and H. Lee Remmers. *The Strategy of Multinational Enterprise.* London: Longman Group, 1970.

10. *Business International.* New York: Business International Corporation, 1969.

11. Carlson, Sunne. *International Financial Decisions.* Uppsala: The Institute of Business Studies, 1969.

12. CitiBank. "The Multinational Corporation: An Environmental Analysis." Investment Research Department, New York, unpublished, April 1976.

13. Daniels, John D., Ernest W. Orgram, Jr., and Lee H. Radebaugh. *International Business: Environments and Operations.* Reading, Mass.: Addison-Wesley, 1976.

14. Dymsza, William A. *Multinational Business Strategy.* New York: McGraw-Hill, 1972.

15. Easton, David. *The Political System.* New York: Alfred A. Knopf, 1968 (1953).

16. Eiteman, David K., and Arthur I. Stonehill. *Multinational Business Finance.* Reading, Mass.: Addison-Wesley, 1973.

17. Gilpin, Robert. *U.S. Power and the Multinational Corporation.* New York: Basic Books, 1975.

18. Goodman, Stephen. "How the Big Banks Really Evaluate Sovereign Risks." *Euromoney,* February 1977, pp. 105–110.

19. Green, Robert T. *Political Instability as a Determinant of U.S. Foreign Investment.* Austin: Bureau of Business Research, Graduate School of Business, University of Texas at Austin, 1972.

20. Green, Robert T., and William H. Cunningham. "The Determinants of U.S. Foreign Investments: An Empirical Examination." *Management International Review,* Vol. 3 (February 1975), pp. 113–120.

21. Green, Robert T., and C. M. Korth. "Political Instability and the Foreign Investor." *California Management Review* (Fall 1974), pp. 23–31.

22. Green, Robert T., and Charles H. Smith. "Multinational Profitability as a Function of Political Instability." *Management International Review,* Vol. 6 (1972), pp. 23–29.

23. Greene, Mark K. "The Management of Political Risk." *Best's Review (Property/Liability ed.),* July 1974, pp. 71–74.

24. Haendel, Dan H., Gerald T. West, and Robert G. Meadow. *Overseas Investment and Political Risk.* Philadelphia: Foreign Policy Research Institute, 1975.

25. Haner, F. T. "Business Environmental Risk Index." *Best's Review (Property/Liability ed.),* July 1975, pp. 47–50.

26. Haner, F. T. "General Assessments of the Foreign Environment." Unpublished, 1975.

27. Hershbarger, Robert A., and John P. Noerager. "International Risk Management: Some Peculiar Constraints." *Risk Management,* April 1976, pp. 23–34.

28. "Risk Management." *Journal of Commerce,* December 14, 1977.

29. Juhl, Paulgeorg. "Prospects for Foreign Direct Investment in Developing Countries." In *Reshaping the World Economic Order,* edited by Herbert Giersch. Kiel: Tubingen, 1976.

30. Keegan, Warren J. "Multinational Scanning: A Study of the Information Sources Utilized by Headquarters Executives in Multinational Companies." *Administrative Science Quarterly* (September 1974), pp. 411–421.

31. Kelley, Margaret. "Evaluating the Risks of Expropriation." *Risk Management* (January 1974), pp. 23–43.

32. Kissinger, Henry A. Speech before the Future of Business Project of the Center for Strategic and International Studies, Georgetown, Virginia, Washington, D.C.: June 28, 1977.

33. Knickerbocker, Frederick T. *Oligopolistic Reaction and Multinational Enterprise.* Boston: Division of Research, Graduate School of Business Administration, Harvard University, 1973.

34. Knight, Frank H. *Risk Uncertainty and Profit* (1921). Chicago: University of Chicago Press, 1971.

35. Kobrin, Stephen. "The Environmental Determinants of Foreign Direct Manufacturing Investment: An Ex-Post Empirical Analysis." *Journal of International Business Studies* (Fall–Winter 1976), pp. 29–42.

36. Kobrin, Stephen. "When Does Political Instability Result in Increased Investment Risk." *The Columbia Journal of World Business,* October 1978.

37. LaPalombara, Joseph, and Stephen Blank. *Multinational Corporations and National Elites: A Study in Tensions.* New York: The Conference Board, 1976.

38. LaPalombara, Joseph, and Stephen Blank. *Multinational Corporations in Comparative Perspective.* New York: The Conference Board, 1977.

39. Lasswell, Harold D., and Abraham Kaplan. *Power and Society.* New Haven, Conn.: Yale University Press, 1950.

40. Lindblom, Charles E. *Politics and Markets.* New York: Basic Books, 1977.

41. Lloyd, B. *Political Risk Management.* London: Keith Shipton Developments, 1976.

42. Mueller, P. H., et al. "Assessing Country Exposure." *The Journal of Commercial Bank Lending,* December 1974, pp. 28–43.

43. National Industrial Conference Board. *Obstacles and Incentives to Private Foreign Investment, 1967–68,* Volume 1: *Obstacles.* New York: National Industrial Conference Board, 1969.

44. Nehrt, Lee Charles. *The Political Environment for Foreign Investment.* New York: Praeger, 1970.

45. Piper, James R. "How U.S. Firms Evaluate Foreign Investment Opportunities." *MSU Business Topics* (Summer 1971), pp. 11–20.

46. Robock, Stefan H. "Political Risk: Identification and Assessment." *Columbia Journal of World Business,* July–August 1971, pp. 6–20.
47. Rodriguez, Rita M., and E. Eugene Carter. *International Financial Management.* Englewood Cliffs, N.J.: Prentice-Hall, 1976.
48. Root, Franklin R. "Attitudes of American Executives Towards Foreign Governmental Investment Opportunities." *Economics and Business Bulletin* (January 1968), pp. 14–23.
49. Root, Franklin R. "U.S. Business Abroad and Political Risks." *MSU Business Topics* (Winter 1968), pp. 73–80.
50. Root, Franklin R. "Analyzing Political Risks in International Business," in *The Multinational Enterprise in Transition,* edited by A. Kapoor and Philip D. Grub, 354–365. Princeton, N.J.: Darwin Press, 1972.
51. Root, Franklin R. "The Management by LDC Governments of the Political Risk Trade-off in Direct Foreign Investment." Paper presented to The International Studies Association, Toronto, February 1976.
52. Root, Franklin R., and Ahmed A. Ahmed. "Empirical Determinants of Manufacturing Direct Foreign Investment in Developing Countries." Forthcoming, *Economic Development and Cultural Change.*
53. Rummel, R. J., and David A. Heenan. "How Multinationals Analyze Political Risk." *Harvard Business Review* (January–February 1978), pp. 67–76.
54. Shackle, G. L. S. *Decision, Order, and Time in Human Affairs,* 2nd ed. Cambridge: Cambridge University Press, 1969.
55. Shapiro, Alan C. *Capital Budgeting for the Multinational Corporation. Financial Management,* (Spring 1978).
56. Smith, Clifford Neal. "Predicting the Political Environment of International Business." *Long Range Planning* (September 1971), pp. 7–14.
57. Stobaugh, Robert B., Jr. "How to Analyze Foreign Investment Climates." *Harvard Business Review* (September–October 1969), pp. 100–107.
58. Stonehill, Arthur, and Leonard Nathanson. "Capital Budgeting and the Multinational Corporation." *California Management Review* (Summer 1968), pp. 39–54.
59. Swansborough, Robert H. "The American Investor's View of Latin American Economic Nationalism." *Inter-American Economic Affairs* (Winter 1972), pp. 61–82.
60. Terkel, Studs. *Hard Times.* New York: Avon Books, 1971.
61. Thunell, Lars H. *Political Risks in International Business.* New York: Praeger, 1977.
62. Van Agtmael, Antoine. "How Business Has Dealt with Political Risk." *Financial Executive* (January 1976), pp. 26–30.
63. Van Agtmael, Antoine. "Evaluating the Risks of Lending and Developing Countries." *Euromoney* (April 1976), pp. 16–30.
64. Weston, V. Fred, and Bart W. Sorge. *International Managerial Finance.* Homewood, Ill.: Richard D. Irwin, 1972.
65. Yassukovich, S. M. "The Growing Political Unrest and International Lending." *Euromoney* (April 1976), pp. 10–15.
66. Zink, Dolph Warren. *The Political Risks for Multinational Enterprise in Developing Countries.* New York: Praeger, 1973.

14

FORECASTING POLITICAL RISKS FOR INTERNATIONAL OPERATIONS

José de la Torre
David H. Neckar

Political risk forecasting has attracted considerable business and academic attention in the last decade. This paper starts with a review of the major findings and approaches to the assessment of political risk in foreign investment situations, particularly in terms of the specification of relevant causal relationships between the sources of risk and corporate contingencies. Next, a comprehensive model of general applicability incorporating these findings is outlined. Finally, we conclude with a few comments on the dynamics of political change and corporate strategy that make any such model subject to constant review and evaluation.

INTRODUCTION

In 1985, the world's stock of foreign direct investment (defined as those firms where 25% or more of the equity was in foreign hands) approached a value of $900 billion. If other assets owned abroad by non-financial corporations, such as bank deposits, securities, inventories and minority (less than 25%) interests, were added to this figure the total may very well exceed $1,500 billion. In addition, world trade in goods and services amounted to more than $2,000 billion in 1985. Given that a significant proportion of these assets are exposed to expropriation, war, terrorism or discriminant government intervention at any point in time, the implications for the management of global operations are rather sobering.

The authors wish to express their appreciation to Ms. Dorothea Bensen for her valuable assistance in the preparation of this paper. We are also grateful to Fariborz Ghadar, Stephen Kobrin and Jeffrey Simon for their critical comments and suggestions, while we exonerate them from any responsibility for the final product.

Source: International Journal of Forecasting, Vol. 4 (1988), pp. 221–241. North-Holland.

Surely there is nothing new in this. Trade and investment have been exposed to political risks ever since the first caravans ventured across the Middle East several millennia ago. It is rather the magnitude of the exposure, and the much publicized losses associated with the nationalizations which followed regime changes in post-colonial Africa, Cuba, Iran and Nicaragua, that have thrust the issue of political risks to the forefront of business and academic concern.

Political change and instability per se do not necessarily affect the international investor; change may be abrupt and yet leave the fabric of society basically untouched, or gradual but with profound effects. Instead, what must concern the international investor is the impact that any environmental shock, whether the result of a violent change in political regime or of a gradual process of social and political evolution is immaterial, may have on the value of its operations in that country. For this we can distinguish two generally different contingency losses. The first we may define as the involuntary loss of control (generally meaning property rights) over specific assets located in a foreign country, typically without adequate compensation. Expropriation, nationalization, the ravages of civil war and wanton destruction by terrorists are all examples of such losses. In fact, much of the literature and analysis on political risks has focused on specific instances of this type of loss, and particularly on the frequency and extent of expropriations.[1]

A second, perhaps more important, yet less well understood contingency concerns a reduction in the expected value of the returns from a foreign-controlled affiliate due to discriminatory actions taken against it, either because of its foreign nature or as part and parcel of a general tightening on free-market prerogatives. Some authors (e.g., Kobrin 1984) argue that the frequency of expropriation has declined dramatically since 1976, replaced almost universally by increased regulatory controls over investment behavior. Included here are various forms of discriminatory controls and restrictions often imposed by governments in times of domestic crisis (including foreign exchange and remittance restrictions), limitations on access to factor markets (financial, labor or raw materials), and on outputs (e.g., on prices or diversification possibilities), as well as changing rules on domestic value added, taxation or export performance requirements.

Another dimension of the exposure to political risks concerns the proximate cause. One possibility is to distinguish between the actions undertaken by legitimate (if not necessarily representative or democratically elected) governments in the exercise of their national prerogatives, and those which are the result of actions undertaken by actors outside the direct control of governmental authorities.[2] Figure 1 summarizes the first level of classification. Alternatively, one can define the horizontal dimension of the matrix in terms of the indiscriminant or selective nature of the actions. This difference between "macro" risks, that is, those which affect all foreign (and, for that matter, many

Contingencies May Include:	Loss May Be the Result of:	
	The actions of legitimate government authorities	Events caused by actors outside the control of government
The involuntary loss of control over specific assets without adequate compensation	• Total or partial expropriation • Forced divestiture • Confiscation • Cancellation or unfair calling of performance bonds	• War • Revolution • Terrorism • Strikes • Extortion
A reduction in the value of a stream of benefits expected from the foreign-controlled affiliate	• Non applicability of "national treatment" • Restriction in access to financial, labor or material markets • Controls on prices, outputs or activities • Currency & remittance restrictions • Value-added and export performance requirements	• Nationalistic buyers or suppliers • Threats and disruption to operations by hostile groups • Externally induced financial constraints • Externally imposed limits on imports or exports

Figure 1 Exposure to Political Risks

national) corporations in the country in question, and "micro" risks, defined as those which target a single or a few companies for intervention on the basis of specific arguments about their relative contributions to national welfare, is one that has been made repeatedly in the literature (e.g., Robock 1971, Kobrin 1979 and 1981, and Simon 1982).

Consider the four types of risks illustrated in Figure 2. Type A consists of the potential for massive expropriations of foreign properties typically related to drastic changes in government, such as those following decolonialization or the triumph of a Marxist revolutionary rebel force. They are often associated with closed systems in developing countries, which explode after a long period of national frustration or discontent, followed by growing repression and a collapse of authority. All foreign investors are subject to the same treatment with rare exceptions as they are closely identified with the previous regime and offer a ready source for the re-birth of national pride. Type B risks, on the other hand, can occur more gradually and in both industrial or developing economies. They consist of sector-specific or company-specific exposure which can be traced to the particular characteristics of the industry in question (e.g., its degree of technological sophistication or its oligopolistic nature) as well as to the current situation in the host country with regards to the saliency of the investment relative to national priorities and objectives. Thus, drastic changes in governments or political regimes may or may not result in massive expropriations, just as the gradual evolution of national goals and industry characteristics may bring certain sectors of economic activity under sudden scrutiny by non-radical government authorities eager to bring key economic sectors under national control for what appear to be legitimate objectives.[3]

On a less dramatic level, a change in government orientation, either in the course of a freely-held election or in response to external threats, can result in increases in taxation, new requirements in terms of domestic equity participation, lower remittance allowances, and so on, all or any of which can substantially alter the post-tax, home-currency present value of the benefits realized by the firm's foreign affiliate (Type C risks). Similarly, Type D risks entail considerable potential for loss. As LDC governments strive for a greater share of the fruits derived from foreign company operations in their territory, case-by-case analysis and lengthy negotiation on domestic value added, export performance, ownership limitations and the like will be more and more the rule than the exception. Of course, the evaluation of the potential benefits of the investment and the split of the spoils will be greatly dependent on the sector and the company involved, and not only on what the country has to offer, as has been argued elsewhere (de la Torre 1981). It is this latter category that we believe may be most prevalent in the future.

Political risk can then be defined as "the probability distribution that an actual or opportunity loss will occur due to the exposure of foreign affiliates to a set of contingencies that range from the total seizure of corporate assets without compensation to the unprovoked interference of external agents, with or without governmental sanction, with the normal operations and performance expected from the affiliate." Whether the loss is caused by legitimate government acts or not, whether it is the result of forces acting internally within the host country or emanating from the home or global environment, and whether all foreign companies are equally affected or not, are important methodological questions. The next section reviews some of the major findings and approaches to the assessment of political risk, particularly in terms of the specification of relevant causal relationships between the sources of risk and corporate contingencies. Next, a comprehensive model of general applicability which incorporates these findings is outlined. Finally, we conclude with a few comments on the dy-

Loss Contingencies An involuntary loss of control over specific assets without adequate compensation	Type A Massive expropriations	Type B Selective nationalizations
Value Contingencies Reduction in the expected value of the benefits to be derived from the foreign affiliate	Type C General deterioration of the investment climate	Type D Restrictions targeted to key sectors
	Macro Risks Sudden convulsive chances that threaten most of the population of foreign direct investors within the country	Micro Risks Interventions generally motivated by specific consideration closely related to the economic and social conditions prevailing at the time, and to specific industry and firm characteristics

Figure 2 The Nature of Political Risks

namics of political change and corporate strategy that make any such model subject to constant review and evaluation.

EMPIRICAL EVIDENCE AND PRACTICE

Empirical data on socio-political events and their impact on international business are hard to come by (for recent summaries see Kobrin 1982, Simon 1982, and Robock and Simmonds 1984). First, the collection of data over long time periods and covering a sufficiently large number of countries presents substantial problems of accuracy, validity and comparability. Second, while the most dramatic impacts are readily reported in the press (e.g., major nationalizations and confiscation of assets), the quality of the reporting is not always homogeneous or reliable. Third, there are no time series or data banks that report on the multitude of minor inconveniences and obstacles imposed on foreign companies on a daily basis by governments and other environmental actors. In fact, this information is seldom collected sys-

tematically by individual corporations, thus limiting the possibilities of case study methodologies. Fourth, the application of quantitative methodologies to political phenomena is a relatively new development, as attested by Gillespie and Nesvold (1971), Armstrong (1978), Choucri and Robinson (1978), Heuer (1978) and Simon (1982). Finally, and perhaps most critically, there has not been sufficient theoretical work until recently that allowed for the specification of causal relationships between political, social, and economic data, and the contingencies faced by firms.

Expropriation

There have been a number of serious studies attempting to explain the incidence of expropriation across countries, time and industries (see Burton and Inoue 1984). Truitt (1970 and 1974) and Hawkins et al. (1976) concluded, inter alia, that the extractive and service sectors were more vulnerable to expropriation, that certain organizational characteristics, such as size and ownership structure, were associated with a higher frequency of takeover, and that economic motivations, and not the ideological rhetoric designed for public consumption, dominated public policy as expropriations were directed at controlling economic activities vital to the nation. Bradley (1977) cast doubts on the widely held belief that joint ventures reduced political risks, and showed that very high and, surprisingly, very low levels of technological complexity seem to be a deterrent against expropriation. Bradley's data also indicated that those affiliates which were highly integrated into a multinational system were less likely to suffer expropriation, particularly if cutting them off from the parent company network would render them of little value.

Four more recent studies have covered some of the same ground as those above using larger data bases, and have tested for further hypothesized relationships among country, corporate and contingency variables. Jodice (1980) found little evidence that willingness to expropriate was associated with the level of economic development of the host country, but instead confirmed that the "capacity" of the state [as measured by the ratio of central government revenue to GDP] was strongly correlated with the incidence of expropriation. In addition, he established that governing elites tend to use expropriation as a mean of distracting attention from their own shortcomings in times of increasing political turmoil.[4] Kobrin (1980), using the same data base, focused on industry and corporate specific factors associated with the incidence of forced divestment. He found that in most instances of "selective" (as opposed to wholesale) expropriations, countries acted mainly in the more highly sensitive sectors, that is, those such as agriculture, mining and petroleum where national priorities and sensibilities were the largest.[5] He also confirmed that technological complexity and global integration of the subsidiary help reduce vulnerability to takeovers, while the level of industry maturity encourages it in the case of manufacturing affiliates.

Burton and Inoue (1984) examined an even larger data base consisting of 1857 cases of expropriation which included for the first time the experience of Japanese investors. Their findings related sectoral patterns of expropriation to the country's stage of economic development. Their analysis, however, is limited by the fact that no relative intensity of expropriation can be determined by the lack of base data on the stock of investment by region and sector, and by the distorting effect of several large scale takings in Cuba and Africa. Finally, a study by Juhl (1985), whose sources and data base are not specified, supported many of these findings, particularly the view that vulnerability increases with the host country's capacity to assume responsibility for the affiliate.

Bargaining Power

The dearth of evidence on contingencies other than expropriation make it practically impossible to confirm the existence of causal relationships with the confidence of the studies cited above. The literature on foreign investment in developing countries, however, provides ample basis for specifying hypothetical relationships (e.g., Vernon 1971 and 1977, Reuber 1973, Robinson 1976, Penrose 1976, Lall and Streeten 1977, and Frank (1980). Two basic models can be used to do this. First, there is the series of propositions deriving from the relative bargaining power model and its corollary, the obsolescent bargain paradigm. The second concerns the dependencia model and its assumptions about relative gains and losses to the host country from dependency on foreign investment. The former attempts to judge optimal policy on the basis of social cost-benefit analysis, subject to the existence of both firm- and country-specific advantages and to the opportunities for internalizing transactions within the firm. The latter, on the other hand, places a premium on non-economic factors such as national identity and self-reliance.

Four recent studies bring to bear some of these hypotheses to narrowly defined areas in the relationship between host country and multinational investor, and do so in a way which is consistent with the above conclusions. Fagre and Wells (1982) focused on the ownership policies of multinational companies in Latin America. They concluded that technology (R&D/sales), product differentiation (advertising/sales), and market access (both intra-corporate transfers and export volume) are significantly correlated with corporate bargaining power. Poynter (1982) examined a sample of 104 foreign subsidiaries operating in Tanzania, Zambia, Indonesia and Kenya, which had experienced government intervention ranging from expropriation to minor forms of harassment between 1970 and 1975. His findings confirm the propositions that control over sourcing of production inputs and sales to associated companies are a deterrent to host government intervention. A high level of operational and managerial complexity of the subsidiary also seems to provide insurance against interference. On the other hand, large firms operating in strategically important fields (to the host country) were found to experience above-average intervention. Finally, Poynter discovered that managers of foreign firms who pursue aggressive policies of lobbying for their causes, not only were better informed of the political winds, but succeeded in lowering the level of intervention by the government.

Lecraw (1984) tested the impact of firm-specific advantages (technology leadership, advertising intensity, asset size and export intensity) as well as country-specific advantages (market attractiveness and industry competition) on three sets of dependent variables: actual equity ownership held by the foreign firm, bargaining success (a firm- and country-corrected ownership variable) and "effective control." He confirmed and extended the previous findings on the impact of unique corporate resources on bargaining strength, but went further in concluding that the same firm-specific advantages are positively correlated with the exercise of effective control (that is, control by the parent over key aspects of the venture) even in the absence of majority ownership. Furthermore, he found a strong linear relationship between the success of the venture (a composite variable which included profitability, management satisfaction with results and performance relative to other companies in the same industry and country) and the degree of effective control the parent exercised over the affiliate. In contrast, the relationship between ownership and success was J-shaped, with 50/50 arrangements faring the worst. Finally, Kim (1985) extended Poynter's analysis with a detailed look at the level of industry competition and the "political responsiveness" of the subsidiary relative to the degree of government intervention in the firm's operations.

Political Assessment Models

Until very recently, most international firms limited their analysis of the political climate in a country to casual observations by "local experts" or corporate "old hands" sent in for this purpose, and to such occasions when a particular new investment or financial commitment was being considered. If management perceived political risks to be high, the investment would be cancelled or postponed, or a "risk premium" would be added to the calculations to account for the higher probability of loss. Seldom was this exercise conceived as an ongoing proposition; unless a major catastrophe occurred, the country's political rating was unlikely to be reassessed.

In one of the earliest surveys of corporate practice in this area, Stobaugh (1969) reported a prevalence for the "go/no go" or "premium for risk" methods involving little quantification or sophistication. Root (1968) also showed the lack of systematic approaches to risk assessment by U.S. multinationals, as did Marois

(1981) for French companies. Finally, Rummel and Heenan (1978) confirmed the use of casual observation by trusted corporate officials as a preferred method of assessment. It goes without saying that these idiosyncratic/impressionistic approaches suffer from excessive subjectivity that can be dangerous and misleading. Old stereotypes of foreign societies, rooted in either the corporate or individual mind, can play a vital and often distorting role in the decision-making process.

General/Broadly-based Models

Much formalization and modelling of macro political and economic risks has occurred in the last fifteen years.[6] The major international banks, spurred by dramatic increases in lending to less developed countries since 1974, were primarily concerned with what they called sovereign country risk, essentially the prospects for default or rescheduling of external debt by the borrowing nation. The specific nature of the risks involved lend itself to systematic analysis of macroeconomic data, although there was general recognition that some subjective of judgmental elements needed to be included as well. Van Agtmael (1976) reported on some early efforts in this direction involving both quantitative and qualitative measures. More recently, Nagy (1979 and 1984) proposed a "structured qualitative approach to the quantification of country risk" that combines an assessment of the size of loss with the probability of occurrence for different types of borrowers over time in a discounted present value model. Krayenbuehl (1985) suggests that the global assessment be divided into a political component (i.e., the will to honor external obligations) and a "transfer" risk consisting of a solvency and a liquidity measure of the ability to pay. Finally, Mascarenhas and Sand (1985), in a comprehensive review of U.S. bank practices, identified four major organizational approaches to country risk assessment which varied in technical and structural sophistication and which produced significantly different results.

A second group of these general surveys consist of a number of "expert" assessments, typically obtained as the end product of a multistage consultation process that may or may not involve Delphi methods. Some of these reports might include econometric data as well, but their major characteristic is the progressive ranking of a large number of countries according to a more or less explicit logic of analysis. The BERI (Business Environment Risk Index) service is the oldest of these, and consists of a rating system that ranks countries on the basis of four sub-categories highlighting political, operational, financial, and nationalistic factors. Judgments on 48 countries are made by a panel of experts located throughout the world, processed and sent back for another iteration. BERI also produces detailed forecast reports for certain countries and a lending risk rating evaluating a country's credit worthiness over the following five years.

Competing rating systems utilizing similar methodology have been developed by Frost & Sullivan (the World Political Risk Forecast), Business International and Data Resources Inc. (Policon). Most of these are available to users on-line and, at least in the case of Policon, users may alter the weight of different variables or include their own judgmental information whenever considered superior to the model's. Two financially oriented rating systems worth noting are the Institutional Investor's Country Credit Rating and Euromoney's Country Risk Index covering 109 and 116 countries respectively. The latest entry to the "expert" assessment rating field is by the Futures Group; their Political Stability Prospects reports combine observational data in formal models with expert generated opinions to produce a stability index on a probabilistic distribution.

These and other similar techniques have the advantage of permitting rank ordering of different environments on a fairly comparative basis.

They also allow, in some cases, for a significant degree of flexibility since the weight associated with the various criteria can be modified to suit different circumstances. However, the ranking can be only as good as the judgments which go into their components, and several observers have noted the tendency to utilize "establishment" private sector experts that may not necessarily view events dispassionately. Furthermore, these ratings are static by definition; they represent a view of past events and conditions that may bear no relationship to the future. The most serious criticism in this sense is that as long as the relationship between socio-economic factors and political risk remains implicit in the experts' minds no evaluation of the rating's utility for a specific application can be made.

Two models developed in the 1970s are based on such explicit causal relationships and rely primarily on econometric and other objective data. Perhaps the best known of these is the Political System Stability Index first described by Haendel et al. (1975) and later elaborated in Haendel (1979). By measuring directly a series of discrete components of the political and social environment (e.g., number of riots, ethnolinguistic fragmentation, and legislative effectiveness, among others), the resulting index is claimed to be free of judgmental inferences or distortions. One cannot escape, however, the model's implicit assumption that it accurately represents reality in both its structure and the choice of variables. In this sense, a major innovation of the model was the addition of confidence estimates which were assigned to the index scores for each component and each country. The second model, the Knudsen (1974) "ecological" approach, is based on the notions first put forth by Gurr (1971) that a high level of national frustration will exist whenever there is a gap between the aspirations of a people and their welfare, both dynamic concepts. If combined with a visible foreign-owned sector, such frustration may lead to intervention or ex-propriation, as foreign firms serve as useful scapegoats to the failure of the existing political order to satisfy the economic and political yearnings of the people.

Regardless of the thoroughness of the model's specifications or the accuracy of its measures, all these methods of estimating environmental risk share two unavoidable drawbacks. First, they are macro-risk oriented and largely ignore the need of the individual firm for custom-tailored measurement of project-specific risks. Although useful as a first-order indicator of the potential dangers threatening a given investment (a "red flag" function as Kobrin calls it), exclusive reliance on broad measures of risk would tend to overstate the threat to specific projects that may be immune to intervention under most circumstances, and may fail to anticipate the partial losses that would result from a gradual tightening of operating freedom facing foreign firms in many developing and developed countries.

Second, these models are based on historical data that may be totally or partially irrelevant for future conditions. For example, recent high levels of political turmoil leading to a radical change in government may appear under various quantitative indices as evidence of a high degree of political instability. While this may be undeniable for the immediate past, does it signify that instability will continue into the future? Or is the new government more likely to address the root causes of past instability and lead the nation to a new era of prosperity and tranquility? Obviously, no time series analysis can answer these questions adequately. Furthermore, to the extent that the data fed into the analysis are not entirely current, there will be a potentially significant gap between the last period for which data were available and current conditions. Given the rate of change of political and social phenomena in the less developed countries, and the difficulties and commensurate delays in generating reliable data in many of them, this is not a trivial problem.

In-house Models

The environmental turbulence that character-ized most of the 1970s, culminating with the fall of the Iranian monarchy in 1979, gave extraor-dinary impetus to the development of in-house capabilities in political and economic assess-ment among the world's largest international corporations. A survey conducted on behalf of the U.S. Conference Board (Blank et al. 1980) confirmed the rise in corporate interest in polit-ical risk analysis during the decade. It conclud-ed, however, that most of these efforts consisted of intuitive and unsystematic attempts to trans-late vague notions of the "quality of the investment climate" into recommendations for investment policy.

A good example of an extensive corporate model is the ESP (for economic, social and po-litical) system developed by Dow Chemical for their Latin American operations (Miquel 1978 and 1980). Dow's approach has the advantages that it is specifically tailored to their needs and that it involves line and senior corporate offi-cials in the assessment, thus assuring that the results will be taken relatively seriously. It does not deal, however, with the need for clear speci-fication of causality, relying instead on the experience of the leaders of the assessment teams to interpret events correctly and consist-ently. It also implies high costs and a large time commitment, thus limiting its applicability to a few countries per year at best.

Other companies have made use of scenario methodologies in an attempt to deal with socio-political projections (Raubitschek 1983 and Wack 1985). A related approach, much cited in the literature, is that developed by Shell Oil to assess the probability that contracts for the ex-ploration, development and production of oil in a certain country will be maintained on an equi-table basis for a period of up to ten years. As described by Bunn and Mustafaoglu (1978) and Gebelein, Pearson and Silbergh (1978), the Shell approach and its subsequent variants (e.g., the models developed by Risk Insights,

Inc. of New York) include a formal specifica-tion of the relationships involved, expert opinions constrained in a fashion designed to limit judgment errors, and a sophisticated sta-tistical algorithm to combine the results of both aggregate econometric data and individual as-sessments. As Kobrin (1981) views it, this is one of "the most sophisticated and effective ap-proaches to political risk assessment" that existed at that time. Its major limitation is again the cost issue. To apply the methodology to a large number of countries, or, for that matter, to a number of industries with different character-istics and risk profiles, would be extremely costly and cumbersome.

Summary

The multitude of studies and models described above are indicative of the complexity and multidimensionality implied in measuring po-litical risk which are specific to the foreign activities of individual firms across many coun-tries. The various analyses of the expropriation experience of foreign investors have yielded sig-nificant evidence of the importance of consid-erations rooted in both the national environ-ment (cultural, political, social and economic) as well as in industry, firm, and project (struc-tural) characteristics. The latter have been confirmed by the more recent studies on the de-terminants of bargaining power. The general thrust of practice in the field, however, tends to be polarized between those models and tech-niques aimed at measuring macro political risks on a comparative basis for a large number of subject countries, and those which are specific to a firm's needs but which are limited in their geographic scope. Figure 3 illustrates this di-chotomy, where the search for the ideal approach obviously leads to the bottom right-hand corner of the figure without much success to date.

Macro models must play an important role in this search. While it is true that political stabili-

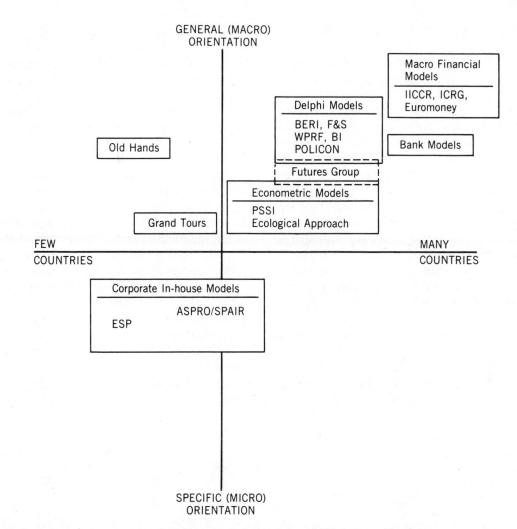

Figure 3 Political Forecasting Models Classified by Their Orientation and Their Geographic Scope

ty is no guarantee of the absence of potential exposure to loss, nor is instability necessarily associated with the probability of loss, it remains that 75% of all instances of expropriation have been linked to regime changes. The preferred approach must therefore have the capability of measuring macro risks and the ability to interpret them in terms of project-specific considerations.

Methodologically, all existing models have certain strengths and limitations. Expert-based systems can be criticized for not always making causal relationships explicit and for their potential bias in the judgments of its members. Econometric models often suffer from the difficulty of securing current sources of data for many of the important independent variables necessary for the analysis. In-house methods can be expensive, time consuming and of limited geographic coverage. It follows that what is needed is an eclectic approach that combines the best each method has to offer and includes both macro and micro judgments on the risks faced by specific foreign affiliates.[7]

MODELLING POLITICAL RISKS

Since risk is both a country and project dependent concept, any model designed to forecast the probability of loss must encompass both elements, and assess all contingencies that can result from changes in national policy. It is this ability to predict an emerging situation before it is fully manifested, in order to circumvent the crisis, that is essential for the survival and prosperity of many foreign operations.

Figure 4 summarizes the structure of the recommended framework for analysis. Its logic is rather simple and straightforward, although its implementation is another matter. It begins by examining a series of national characteristics—economic, social and political forces at work—that may or may not be critical to the issue of political stability. Whether such is the case or not will depend on the importance of the particular factor, on its relationship to others and on the magnitude of any changes or discontinuities involved. Furthermore, the source of trouble could be internal (e.g., political repression) or external (e.g., a drastic fall in commodity export prices). It is important to note, however, that these forces may, when activated, have dramatically different impacts depending, to a large extent, on the maturity and absorptive capacity of national institutions. A country where political parties, the press, the educational establishment, the financial system, et cetera, have achieved high levels of development should be able to withstand greater shocks to the system without precipitating drastic change in the social fabric or in the institutions themselves. The institutional framework, therefore, acts as a filter for the environmental forces in softening their impact on events.[8] An accurate judgment on the qualities of this filter is then as necessary to good political risk forecasting as an understanding of the underlying forces themselves. In the end, any number of political events can be the result of these conditions, each with its own probability distribution, as well as a probable timetable.

Stage I of political risk forecasting consists, therefore, of an assessment of the forces at work

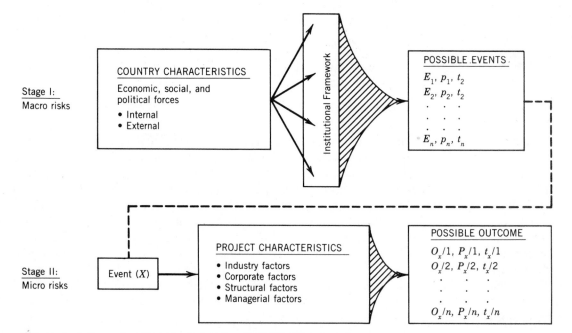

Figure 4 A Conceptual Model for Project-Specific Political Risk Analysis

in the nation and without, the institutions tempering their effectiveness, and the likely events that they may precipitate. This is the realm of "country" risk analysis. Much of it is amenable to econometric modelling and to the use of expert methods similar to those described earlier. In the corresponding section below we shall illustrate the variables that ought to be included in this analysis. The output should establish some basic measures of reference comparable across countries, it should identify current trends and any potential breaks in them, and it should delimit the areas of concern that may harbor the seeds of potential threats to foreign investors.

Not all events, however, will have similar consequences for different projects. As established in the above review, industry and corporate factors, as well as a number of characteristics of the structure of the investment, will play a determinant role in the likelihood and probable extent of any potential losses. Thus,

for each project or affiliate, every possible event can be seen as having a set of outcomes or consequences which are unique to it. These alternative outcomes have each a certain probability distribution and time horizon. Stage II of the political risk forecast consists of bringing into sharper relief the features of the project that either increase or diminish the possible negative consequences of each event. In this sense it is akin to estimating the conditional probabilities of various contingencies given a number of possible events. Since the latter may or may not be mutually exclusive, final estimates of the likelihood of loss can be arrived at by the proper mathematical manipulation of the probability estimates.

What follows is not a specification of such a comprehensive model, since obviously that would require considerable more space than available here and an intimate knowledge of the circumstances applicable to a specific investment project.[9] Figure 5 summarizes the ap-

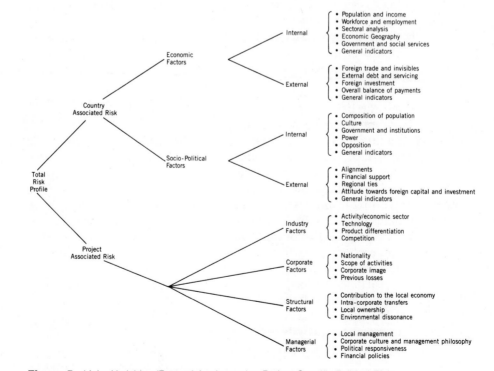

Figure 5   Major Variables (Factors) for Assessing Project Specific Political Risk

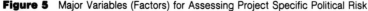

proach. The country associated risk analysis involves a total of 22 sets of variables or composite factors that must be monitored on an ongoing basis, yielding estimates of possible events, their probability of occurrence and the expected timetable. The project associated risk examines an additional 16 variables that are likely to have a major impact on the consequences of political change on a given foreign affiliate.

Country Associated Risk

An arbitrary but useful distinction can be made between economic and socio-political factors on the one hand, and between internal and external sources of risk on the other. The division is arbitrary because developments in all four areas have interactive effects on the other variables under scrutiny. It is important for the analyst to be sensitized to this web of hidden relationships and not follow the simple structure blindly. Also, it should be noted that many external influences, particularly in the economic sphere, can be systemic to the world. It is in such cases that the institutional elements of the analysis can serve to distinguish between countries in terms of expected impacts.

Economic Factors—Internal The analyst must first understand the basic components of the host nation's economy, its rate of development, and its vulnerability in order to anticipate factors that can affect the general business environment. Six major headings may be useful to organize the data as illustrated in Figure 6a. After this stage of the process, the analyst should have a reasonable picture of which economic variables are critical for continuity in the country's current economic development strategy, the vulnerability of the strategy to failure in any of these critical links, the likelihood of such failures and, as a result, the probability that performance will fall short of expectations. The objective is not economic analysis per se, but a search for what one might call the potential for trouble.

Economic Factors—External In order to gain a better understanding of the nation's economic conditions, the analyst must next turn to its external payments position. What are the country's international obligations, the extent of foreign indebtedness and servicing requirements, its level of diversification of export earnings, the exposure to commodity price fluctuations, the ridigity of import requirements, et cetera. Five headings would be helpful in organizing the analysis of these issues (Figure 6a).

This set of questions serves to determine to what extent external constraints will dictate domestic economic policy. A high degree of dependency and instability together with external debt servicing difficulties will substantially increase the risk of host government interference with foreign investors in the country, both in terms of expropriation and convertibility. In Mozambique, shortly after the revolution, the government, faced with severe external payment difficulties, nationalized those enterprises that consumed significant amounts of foreign exchange. Likewise in Nicaragua, the grave shortage of foreign exchange after Somoza's ouster prompted the new revolutionary government to take control of the main sources of foreign earnings. And the frequent use of "temporary" suspensions of dividend convertibility during difficult times in countries like Brazil underscore the need for such analysis.

Socio-Political Factors—Internal To understand the political situation of the host country and its potential for inspiring change one needs to begin with the cohesiveness of the social structure, the disparity between people's beliefs and aspirations on the one hand and the quality of leadership on the other, the relative power of government and opposition groups and the strength and traditions of national institutions. Again, Figure 6a illustrates six major headings that will guide the analysis. It should be evident that most of the information sought under these various headings is highly judgmental and difficult to evaluate objectively. Sources intimately familiar with local conditions are essential to

COUNTRY ASSOCIATED RISK

ECONOMIC FACTORS	POLITICAL FACTORS

INTERNAL

ECONOMIC FACTORS	POLITICAL FACTORS
Population and income • Size and sectoral distribution • Economic growth and per capita income • Population growth and contro • Income distribution	*Composition of population* • Ethnolinguistic, religious, tribal or class heterogeneity • Relative shares in economic and political power • Immigration and outmigration
Workforce and employment • Size and composition • Sectoral and geographic distribution • Productivity • Migration and urban unemployment	*Culture* • Underlying cultural values and beliefs • Religious and moral values • Sense of alienation with foreign or modern influences
Sectoral analysis • Agriculture and self-sufficiency • Industrial growth and distribution • Size and growth of the public sector • National priorities and strategic sectors	*Government and institutions* • Constitutional principles and conflicts • Resilience of national institutions • Role and strength of the army, church, parties, press, educational establishment, etc.
Economic geography • Natural resources • Economic diversification • Topography and infrastructure	*Power* • Key leaders' background and attitudes • Main beneficiaries of the staus quo • Role and power of the internal security apparatus
Government and social services • Sources and structure of government revenues • Sectoral and geographic pattern of expeditures • Size and growth of the budget deficit • Rigidities in spending programs • Regional dependency on central revenue sources	*Opposition* • Strength, sources of support, effectiveness *General indicators* • Level and frequency of strikes • Riots and terrorist acts • Number and treatment of political prisoners • Extent of official corruption
General indicators • Price indices • Wage rates • Interest rates, money supply, etc.	

EXTERNAL

ECONOMIC FACTORS	POLITICAL FACTORS
Foreign trade & invisibles • Current account balance and composition • Income and price elasticity of exports and imports • Price stability of major imports and exports • Evolution of the terms of trade • Geographic composition of trade	*Alignments* • International treaties and alignments • Position on international issues, UN voting record
External debt and servicing • Outstanding foreign debt, absolute and relative levels • Terms and maturity profile • Debt servicing to income and exports	*Financial support* • Financial aid, food and military assistance • Preferential economic and trade linkages
Foreign investment • Size and relative importance • Sectoral distribution • Geographic (by origin) and regional distribution • Court proceedings in disputes	*Regional ties* • Border disputes • External military threat or guerrilla activities • Nearby revolution, political refugees
Overall balance of payments • Trends in the capital account • Reserve position • Capital flight and "errors and omissions"	*Attitude towards foreign capital and investment* • National investment codes • Polls of local attitudes towards foreign investors
General indicators • Exchange rates (official and unofficial) • Changes in international borrowing terms	*General indicators* • Record on human rights • Formal exiled opposition groups • Terrorist acts in third countries • Diplomatic or commercial conflict with home country

Figure 6a Content of Country Risk Variables

the analysis. Therefore, it is advisable that external expert opinion be obtained and that their views be crossexamined by on-the-field assessments carried out to a large extent by the firm's own local staff.

Socio-Political Factors—External Political instability is often externally induced. At best, external influences can exacerbate internal conditions by playing on the fears or frustrations of the local population, or by lending moral, financial or ideological support to opposition groups. Five such problem areas deserve close scrutiny as indicated in Figure 6a. As with the section above, the knowledge and data sources required to complete this part of the analysis are highly specialized. A similar conclusion is thus warranted as to the utility of seeking expert advice supplemented by the views of those in the field.

Project Associated Risk

As noted in the literature review and as we have gleaned from practice, industry and corporate characteristics have a major influence on the level of risk. Both of these sets of factors are generally exogenously determined and can be altered only over long periods of time, if at all. Structural and managerial factors, however, are subject to management action and can be tailored to meet local circumstances in such a way that the risk/return trade-off is optimized for the foreign investor. It is in the context of these last two sets of variables that the concept of managing political risks takes a realistic meaning.

Industry Factors It has been obvious from the early days of political risk analysis that different economic sectors experienced different propensity to expropriation and government intervention in general. Four industry characteristics cited in Figure 6b seem to be closely associated with this: the economic sector, technology, product differentiation, and the level of competition.

PROJECT ASSOCIATED RISK

INDUSTRY FACTORS

Activity/economic sector
- Higher exposure in primary and infrastructure projects
- Size of project, relative importance, monopoly power
- National priorities, e.g., high technology sectors

Technology
- R&D intensity and rate of change of technology
- Alternative suppliers, relative quality

Product differentiation
- Specialized inputs, distinctiveness
- Service industry

Competition
- Largest risk when competition is non-existant or very active

CORPORATE FACTORS

Nationality
- Ex-colonial relationships
- Home/host country diplomatic and commercial relations

Scope of activities
- Sectoral nature of corporate activities
- Geographic distribution of affiliates

Corporate image
- Corrupt payments scandals
- Previous involvement in political subversion
- Past record as corporate citizen

Previous losses
- Patterns of bargaining and losses
- Instances of survival

STRUCTURAL FACTORS

Contribution to the local economy
- Positive factors include capital, employment creation, income and tax revenues, reinvestment, substitution effects, export generation, local industrial development, etc.
- Negative effects are dividends and capital repatriation, licensing, management and technical fees, transfer pricing, import generation, competitive effects, etc.
- Social cost/benefit analysis (14)
- Special agreements and investment code exceptions
- Timing, the obsolescing bargain

Intra-corporate transfers
- Degree of integration with parent company network
- Local-for-local affiliate

Local ownership
- Share and nature of domestic partners

Environmental dissonance
- Geographic location
- Ethnic, environmental and linguistic risks
- Cultural compatibility

Local management
- Extent and positions of local managers

Corporate culture and management philosophy
- Experience, training and sensitivity of expatriates
- Headquarters respect for local opinion, decentralization

MANAGERIAL FACTORS

Political responsiveness
- Degree of activism by local management
- Local contacts, lobbying, public affairs

Financial policies
- Exposure reduction vs. provocation (15)

Figure 6b   Content of Project Risk Variables

Corporate Factors   A number of characteristics of the investor are in themselves associated with the level of risk, and can be represented by the four factors which are included in Figure 6b: nationality, scope of activities, corporate image, and previous losses.

Structural Factors   Irrespective of the quality of its industrial and corporate characteristics, how the project or investment is structured will have a major impact on its risk profile. Again, four aspects of the structure should be analyzed as indicated in Figure 6b: contribution to the local economy, intra-corporate transfers, local ownership, and environmental dissonance.

Managerial Factors   In the end, it is up to management to reduce the level of risk associated with their foreign operations by pursuing prudent policies of limiting exposure while attending to the national and corporate interest. While conflict is unavoidable, the four policy areas

outlined in Figure 6b offer significant latitude for reducing risks consistent with minimum sacrifice in profitability: local management, corporate culture and management philosophy, political responsiveness, and financial policies.[10]

Summary

It is obvious from the preceding list that the cost in time and money of carrying out such detailed analysis for each country and each operation throughout the world would be prohibitive for any moderately large multinational corporation. Thus, any corporate system of forecasting political risks ought to strive for a compromise between the general and broadly based information available from multi-country rating and evaluation services, and the provision of case-by-case specific inputs from internal and contractual sources.

The macro or country risk component of the analysis is particularly suited to standardization and the systematic manipulation of large time series data bases. No individual firm, except perhaps the very large, can hope to duplicate the resources available to specialized agencies for collecting, processing and analyzing macroeconomic and socio-political data on a global basis. There are significant economies of scale from operating across multiple countries, and specialized agencies can amortize the cost of developing and constantly up-dating their forecasting systems over a large customer base. There remains, however, a genuine requirement for an internal function in assessing macro risks. Corporate executives familiar with the content of the models used by external analysts (i.e., the internal logic, sources of data, assumptions and specifications) should perform a control function which is free from any loyalty or commitment to the model itself or to its component parts. Their task is to make sure that the externally supplied assessments are suitable to the company's needs and acceptable to those who have to act on the basis of the information provided. Furthermore, specific project characteristics may limit the scope of the macro political environment which is of concern. If a given project or affiliate can be affected only by a narrow range of political events, it would facilitate the internal control function accordingly.

The second part of the analysis, that is, once the probability and time horizon of certain events have been established, can only be performed by those intimately familiar with the company's operations. How will certain events affect the profitability of, or the capacity to repatriate funds from, a given project or subsidiary needs to be determined on the basis of data only available to management. Therefore, a second role for the function of political risk assessment within the corporation consists of interpreting the results of the country risk forecasts in terms of the realities of industry, corporate, structural and managerial factors only known internally.

There is, however, an important qualitative difference between these two roles. Monitoring the quality and accuracy of country risk forecasts provided by external services and adapting them to the corporate reality should be a function performed and coordinated centrally. While operational management can and should have an input to the process, the modification of the model's specifications and the interpretation of their biases can only be appropriately conducted after considerable experience with such a system over relatively long time periods. Given the value of institutional memory in this process, it would be logical to centralize responsibility accordingly. The second role, that of evaluating micro risks from a given set of country risk forecasts, has to be carried out at the local level. Obviously, corporate involvement may be essential to assure impartiality and comparability across countries and projects, but since local management will be called upon to act on the results of the analysis, they must be party to its conclusions.

CONCLUSIONS

In assessing whether to set up, expand or contract operations in a given country one should distinguish between two sets of issues. The first has to do with the contribution the project or the affiliate is likely to make to the corporation's global strategy, including the returns from the venture proper as well as any synergistic or competitive contributions to other units in the corporate system. Such an assessment of "strategic attractiveness" will be based on a number of factors such as the degree of global competition prevalent in the industry (as opposed to competition based on fragmented national markets), the size and importance of the market, the fit with the company's long term strategic priorities, and so forth. This should result in a differentiated approach to global opportunities. The more attractive a particular location and the more critical to the achievement of corporate objectives, the more willing the company should be to undertake a high level of risk and to commit the necessary resources. It follows that the higher the priority accorded to a particular subsidiary in the company's global strategy, the greater the firm's need for management integration and control with respect to that subsidiary.

These views ought to be tempered by a second set of assessments concerning the quality of the "investment climate" in the country in question. To the extent that the risk of political upheaval and intervention is high, the expected returns may not materialize, or they may be significantly reduced, irrespective of the market's attractiveness. As the investment climate deteriorates, the foreign investor will attempt to reduce its financial, technological and human resource commitments (and exposure) while attempting to retain a measure of market presence as allowable under the circumstances. This may call for unorthodox approaches to ownership and control which take into account the need to minimize exposure consistent with preserving a position in the market. In contrast, an excellent investment climate is no substitute for market potential. Joint ventures and other independent arms-length transactions provide a useful vehicle to gain a foothold in such markets without unduly committing scarce corporate resources. Where poor market prospects coexist with a bad investment climate, it is clear that the firm will tend to limit both its commitments and exposure by resorting to independent market transactions, if at all. Figure 7 summarizes these choices.

It should have become clear by now that there exists such a diversity of factors impinging on an evaluation of the risk profile of a particular corporate project that the challenge of constructing a single model that will faithfully and accurately represent their interaction and complexity is monumental. Rough rankings of countries in terms of their relative political stability have limited use as predictors of potential losses in specific situations. The facts that causality is not easily determined in political phenomena, that up-to-date information is difficult to obtain, and that stability in itself is not necessarily a good measure of risk, all contribute to the many doubts often expressed about existing methods. Furthermore, the nature of the industry and the investor, and the timing and characteristics of the project are critical variables that alter significantly the risk profile within the same set of economic and political conditions.

Yet, no human being could possibly master this complexity for more than just a handful of countries. Unaided by standardized quantitative tools, the political risk analyst would drown in a sea of information. Judgment can best be applied when the range of variables to consider has been reduced to a manageable set. Herein lies the challenge. Modelling political risk at the corporate level must make use of good measures of quantifiable variables and systematic analysis that can reduce large quantities of data, according to accepted causal models, to probabilistic estimates of possible events in an efficient fashion. Secondly, it must call for many qualitative assessments of elusive trends, such as levels of national aspirations and frustration, that can only be obtained through intimate knowledge of the terrain. Thirdly, it must make all of this relevant to the particular project at hand. And finally, it demands good judgment above all, to mix the many inputs in a coherent manner so as to spot, as Holmes, the

Assessment of Political/Investment Climate

Market Attractiveness or Degree of Fit with Corporate Strategy		Good	Unstable	Poor
	High	Maximum commitment of human and financial resources and high tolerance for commercial risks: wholly owned affiliates preferred.	Limit financial exposure while sustaining market and human investments; accept normal commercial risks; majority-owned affiliate preferred.	Minimize financial exposure consistent with market presence; aim for minority position with licensing as a long-term hedge.
	Medium	Maintain high resource commitment and risk tolerance subject to better alternative investment opportunities.	Unwilling to commit significant resources; prefer to act through joint venture if necessary or appropriate.	Little interest in market presence; pursue only if possible without financial exposure of any consequence.
	Low	Indifferent to market opportunities; token financial or human commitment possible; independent distributor or joint venture.	Little if any resource commitment desirable; export sales agents preferred vehicle for any market activity; licensing possible.	No interest except for occasional exports or limited licensing agreements.

Figure 7 Preferred Strategic Posture in Foreign Markets according to Strategic Attraction and Political Climate

dog that did not bark in the night. It follows that a systematic approach such as is proposed here must be limited to those countries or areas of the world where major investments or competitive positions are at stake.

A final question that may be asked is how best to incorporate this analysis into the strategic planning process. The lack of accepted standards has resulted in significant disenchantment and skepticism with political risk analysis among many multinational corporations. Is political risk forecasting one more short-lived corporate fad? Most executives would readily agree with the desirability of having such an input available to the planning function, but not many firms have made the necessary investments in terms of both staff and administrative systems to generate the information and incorporate it into the decision process. As existing models are perfected, one might hope that the required commitment and organizational linkages will emerge.

NOTES

1. There is no denying the importance of these losses. As summarized by Burton and Inoue (1984), the expropriation risk has been variously estimated to affect 1 percent per year of the number of foreign affiliates active in less developed countries (LDCs) during the 1960–1977 period, represent cumulatively over the 1956–1972 period a total of 18.8 percent of the stock of foreign direct investment in 1972 plus the value of the expropriated assets (William 1975), amount to 1.6 percent of the total value of U.S. investments in LDCs during 1960–1974 (Hufbauer and Briggs 1975), and account for a cumulative (1960–1976) 4.4 percent of the 1976 stock of wholly and partially owned firms in LDCs plus the value of the seized assets (Kobrin 1980).

2. Simon (1982) makes a similar distinction between "societal" forces (i.e., those that emerge from general social phenomena) and government-inspired actions. It is also important to make a distinction between sudden changes in governments, government policies, or externally induced events, and a gradual evolution along a more or less predictable socio-political pattern. For more on this, see Kobrin (1979).

3. For a more elaborate approach that adds whether the actors' impacts on the firm are direct or indirect (that is, they influence those that can impact directly), and whether these impacts are caused by internal (within the host country) or external (originating in the home country or elsewhere in the world) forces, see Simon (1984).

4. The Jodice (1980) and Kobrin (1980) papers have a wealth of data on the history and regional distribution of expropriations in recent years. They show, among other things, that some of the smaller countries, for example, Italy, the Netherlands, Belgium and Canada, have suffered a much higher ratio of share of expropriations to share of FDI than the United States, Britain or France. Also, Africa and the Middle East show a greater relative propensity to expropriate than Asia or (the lowest!) Latin America.

5. An interesting divergence between the Kobrin (1980) and Burton and Inoue (1984) (discussed below) studies concerns this point. While the former argues that mass expropriations account for slightly over 10 percent of all takings in his sample, the latter, using essentially the same data base, conclude that large-scale nationalizations account for more than 70 percent of all firms taken. The discrepancy arises from the use of acts (by Kobrin) versus firms (by Burton and Inoue), although in both analyses it appears that selectivity is on the rise.

6. A recent survey by Blank et al. (1980) revealed that by 1979, 55 percent of the firms surveyed had taken some steps to establish formal responsibility for political assessment. For a review and classification of recent approaches and methodologies see Kobrin (1981) and Simon (1985).

7. Ascher (1982) provides a thorough discussion of the applicability of econometric and other forecasting methodologies to political analysis. His views differ somewhat from those expressed here in that he argues for less emphasis on forecasting techniques versus the development of systematic analytical approaches.

8. Katzenstein (1978) argues in an analogous fashion that the domestic structure of a nation-state (the filter in our case) "is a critical intervening variable without which the interrelation between international interdependence and political strategies cannot be understood." Although focused on the advanced countries, the concept of national institutional relationships being partially responsible for differing responses to common external shocks, is equally applicable to the problem at hand.

9. For a more detailed description of each set of variables see de la Torre and Neckar (1987). A similar approach is suggested by Austin and Yoffie (1984).

10. For some of the policies in question see Bradley (1977), Doz and Prahalad (1980), Gladwin and Walter (1980), Shapiro (1981), Eiteman and Stonehill (1982), Ghadar, Kobrin and Moran (1983), Ghadar and Moran (1984), and Encarnation and Vachni (1985).

REFERENCES

Armstrong, J. Scott. 1978. *Long range forecasting* (Wiley, New York).

Ascher, William. 1982. Political forecasting: The missing link. *Journal of Forecasting* 1, 227–239.

Austin, James E., and David B. Yoffie. 1984. Political forecasting as a management tool. *Journal of Forecasting* 3, 395–408.

Bassiry, G. R., and R. Hrair Dekmejian. 1985. MNCs and the Iranian revolution: An empirical study. *Management International Review* 25, 67–75.

Blank, Stephen, et al. 1980. Assessing the political environment: An emerging function in international companies, Report no. 794 (Conference Board, New York).

Bradley, David G. 1977. Managing against expropriation. *Harvard Business Review,* July–August, 75–83.

Bunn, D. W., and M. M. Mustafaoglu. 1978. Forecasting political risk. *Management Science,* November, 1557–1567.

Burton, F. N., and Hisashi Inoue. 1984. Expropriations of foreign-owned firms in developing countries: A cross-national analysis. *Journal of World Trade Law,* September–October, 396–414.

Choucri, Nazli, and Thomas W. Robinson, eds. 1978. *Forecasting in international relations: Theory, methods, problems, prospects* (Freeman, San Francisco, Calif.).

De la Torre, Jose. 1981. Foreign investment and economic development: Conflict and negotiation. *Journal of International Business Studies,* Fall, 9–32.

De la Torre, Jose, and David H. Neckar. 1987. Forecasting political risk. In Spyros Makridakis and Steven C. Wheelwright, eds., *The handbook of forecasting: A manager's guide,* 2nd ed. (Wiley, New York).

De St. Jorre, J. 1983. IRIS: A study of how to fail in business, *The International Herald Tribune,* April 20.

Doz, Yves, and C. K. Prahalad. 1980. How MNCs cope with host government intervention. *Harvard Business Review,* March–April, 149–157.

Eiteman, David K., and Arthur I. Stonehill. 1982. Reacting to political risk. In *Multinational Business Finance,* Ch. 6 (Addison-Wesley, Reading, Mass.).

Encarnation, Dennis J., and Sushil Vachani. 1985. Foreign ownership: When hosts change the rules. *Harvard Business Review,* September–October, 152–160.

Fagre, Nathan, and Louis T. Wells, Jr. 1982. Bargaining power of multinational and host governments. *Journal of International Business Studies,* Fall, 9–23.

Frank, Isaiah. 1980. Foreign enterprise in developing countries (Johns Hopkins University Press, Baltimore, Md.).

Gebelein, C. A., C. E. Pearson, and M. Silbergh. 1978. Assessing political risk of oil investment ventures. *Journal of Petroleum Technology,* May, 725–730.

Ghadar, Fariborz, and Theodore H. Moran, eds. 1984. *Political risk management: New dimensions* (Georgetown University, Washington, D.C.).

Ghadar, Fariborz, Stephen J. Kobrin, and Theodore H. Moran, eds. 1983. *Managing international political risk:*

Strategies and techniques (Georgetown University, Washington, D.C.).

Gillespie, John V., and Betty A. Nesvold, eds. 1971. *Macro quantitative analysis: Conflict, development and democratization* (Sage, Beverly Hills, Calif.).

Gladwin, Thomas N., and Ingo Walter. 1980. *Multinationals under fire: Lessons in the management of conflict* (Wiley, New York).

Gurr, Ted Robert. 1971. *Why men rebel* (Princeton University, Princeton, N.J.).

Haendel, Dan. 1979. *Foreign investments and the management of political risk* (Westview, Boulder, Colo.).

Haendel, Dan, Gerald T. West, and Robert G. Meadow. 1975. Overseas investment and political risk, Monograph series no. 21 (Foreign Policy Research Institute, Philadelphia).

Hawkins, Robert G., Norman Mintz, and Michael Provissiero. 1976. Government takeovers of U.S. foreign affiliates. *Journal of International Business Studies,* Spring, 3–15.

Heuer, Richard J., Jr., ed. 1978. *Quantitative approaches to political intelligence: The CIA experience* (Westview, Boulder, Colo.).

Hufbauer, Gary C., and P. H. Briggs. 1975. Expropriation losses and tax policy. *Harvard International Law Journal,* Summer, 553–564.

Jodice, David A. 1980. Sources of change in Third World regimes for foreign direct investment: 1968–1976. *International Organization,* Spring, 177–206.

Juhl, P. 1985. Economically rational design of developing countries' expropriation policies towards foreign investment. *Management International Review* 25, 45–52.

Katzenstein, Peter J. 1978. *Between power and plenty: Foreign economic policies of advanced industrial states* (University of Wisconsin Press, Madison, Wisc.).

Kim, W. Chan. 1985. The dynamic bargaining power position of multinationals: Managing competition and host government intervention in developing countries, Working paper, Dec. (University of Michigan, Ann Arbor, Mich.).

Knudsen, Harald. 1974. Explaining the national propensity of expropriate: An ecological approach. *Journal of International Business Studies,* Spring, 51–71.

Kobrin, Stephen J. 1979. Political risk: A review and reconsideration. *Journal of International Business Studies,* Spring–Summer, 67–80.

Kobrin, Stephen J. 1980. Foreign enterprise and forced divestment in LDCs. *International Organization,* Winter, 65–88.

Kobrin, Stephen J. 1981. Political assessment by international firms: Models or methodologies? *Journal of Policy Modeling* 3, 2, 251–270.

Kobrin, Stephen J. 1982. *Managing political risk assessment: Strategic response to environmental change* (University of California, Berkeley).

Kobrin, Stephen J. 1984. Expropriation as an attempt to control foreign firms in LDCs: Trends from 1960 to 1979. *International Studies Quarterly* 28, 329–348.

Krayenbuehl, Thomas E. 1985. Country risk: Assessment and monitoring (Woodhead-Faulker, Cambridge).

Lall, Sanjaya, and Paul Streeten. 1977. Foreign investment, trans-nationals, and developing countries (Macmillan, London).

Lecraw, Donald J. 1984. Bargaining power, ownership, and profitability of transnational corporations in developing countries. *Journal of International Business Studies*, Spring–Summer, 27–43.

Marois, Bernard. 1981. Comment les entreprises francaises gerent le risque politique. *Revue Francaise de Gestion*, May–August, 4–9.

Mascarenhas, Briance, and Ole Christian Sand. 1985. Country-risk assessment systems in banks: Patterns and performance. *Journal of International Business Studies*, Spring, 19–35.

Miquel, Rafael. 1978. The case for ESP studies. Unpublished manuscript, June.

Miquel, Rafael. 1980. Some comments on ESP analysis and its uses by management. Unpublished manuscript, Feb.

Nagy, Pancras. 1979–1984. Country risk. *Euromoney* (London).

Penrose, Edith. 1976. Ownership and control: Multinational firms in less developed countries. In G. K. Helleiner, ed., *A world divided—The less developed countries in the international economy* (Cambridge University, Cambridge), 147–174.

Poynter, Thomas A. 1982. Government intervention in less developed countries: The experience of multinational companies. *Journal of International Business Studies*, Spring–Summer, 4–23.

Raubitschek, Ruth S. 1983. Scenarios and strategy formulation, Research paper, June (Harvard Business School, Cambridge, Mass.).

Reuber, Grant L. 1973. *Private foreign investment in development* (Clarendon, Oxford).

Robock, Stefan H. 1971. Political risk: Identification and assessment. *Columbia Journal of World Business*, July–August, 6–20.

Robock, Stefan H. and Kenneth Simmonds. 1983. *Assessing political risk and national controls, international business and multinational enterprises*, Ch. 15 (Irwin, New York).

Root, Franklyn R. 1968. U.S. business abroad and political risk. *MSU Business Topics*, Winter, 73–80.

Rummel, R. J., and David R. Heenan. 1978. How multinationals analyze political risk. *Harvard Business Review*, January–February, 67–76.

Shapiro, Alan C. 1981. Managing political risk: A policy approach. *Columbia Journal of World Business*, Fall, 63–70.

Simon, Jeffrey D. 1982. Political risk assessment: Past trends and future prospects. *Columbia Journal of World Business*, Fall, 62–71.

Simon, Jeffrey D. 1984. A theoretical perspective on political risk. *Journal of International Business Studies*, Winter, 123–143.

Simon, Jeffrey D. 1985. Political risk forecasting, *Futures*, April, 133–147.

Stobaugh, Robert B., Jr. 1969. How to analyze foreign investment climates. *Harvard Business Review*, September–October, 100–108.

Truitt, J. Frederick. 1970. Expropriation of foreign investment: Summary of the post World War II experience of American and British investors in less developed countries. *Journal of International Business Studies*, Fall, 21–34.

Truitt, J. Frederick. 1974. *Expropriation of private foreign investment* (Indiana University, Bloomington, Ind.).

Van Agtmael, Antoine W. 1976. Evaluating the risks of lending to developing countries. *Euromoney*, April, 16–30.

Vernon, Raymond. 1971. *Sovereignty at bay* (Basic Books, New York).

Vernon, Raymond. 1977. *Storm over the multinationals: The real issues* (Harvard University, Cambridge, Mass.).

Wack, Pierre. 1985a. Scenarios: Uncharted waters ahead. *Harvard Business Review*, September–October, 72–89.

Wack, Pierre. 1985b. Scenarios: Shooting the rapids. *Harvard Business Review*, November–December, 139–150.

Williams, M. I. 1975. The extent and significance of the nationalization of foreign-owned assets in developing countries. *Oxford Economic Papers*, July, 268–273.

Section 4

FINANCE AND CONTROL

Finance and control are, of course, concerned, respectively, with allocating and investing funds, and with measuring and evaluating performance. These are much more complex activities in both the multinational and the global firm, simply because managers must deal with more than one currency. National currencies fluctuate, and an investment or holding denominated in a foreign currency can appreciate or depreciate against the currency in which a firm keeps its accounts and reports its results.

Many financial activities may involve foreign currency. Borrowing is one, and there are alternative ways to borrow. For example, a foreign subsidiary might borrow in its local currency or the parent might borrow for it in a different currency and relend the proceeds to the subsidiary. Because of currency fluctuations, different borrowing choices carry different risks, even if interest rates are the same. In choosing a borrowing alternative, the firm must balance several factors, including currency convertibility, relative interest rates, and expected future currency relationships.

Valuing earnings is more difficult. The multinational or global firm has a plethora of subsidiaries, each earning money denominated in a different foreign currency. Managers must question whether "a dollar earned" is "a dollar earned" regardless of the currency in which it is earned, especially if the earnings in that currency are not repatriated. They must consider the relationship between the sources of their earnings and how the market values their firms.

Capital budgeting presents complicated problems. Managers must consider a greater number of variables. They must estimate, then balance, the risks and returns expected from investments in different countries. Managers must consider future currency relationships, profit repatriation risks, and in some cases even expropriation risks.

Cash management is also more difficult. In a world of free-floating currencies, relationships can change quickly. Therefore, managers must be able to change almost instantly the makeup of their cash portfolios. The effective cash manager must be able to anticipate as well as make portfolio changes.

Asset management is another complex task. Currency depreciation can drive the book value of a fixed asset, such as a plant, down to virtually nothing while its economic value remains unimpaired. Similarly, valuing inventory, say, at cost, can significantly misstate its economic value when currency relationships change. The manager must understand both the accounting valuation and the economic value of assets, and be able to distinguish between the two.

Changing currency relationships make control and performance measurement more difficult. Firms use balance sheet and income statement data to evaluate the performance of a business unit and its management. To assess the performance of a foreign subsidiary, the assessor must distinguish dimensions truly reflective of management performance from those reflecting only changed currency relationships.

READING SELECTIONS

Donald Lessard follows up the Kogut articles in Section 2 with a broader, deeper look at the effects of exchange rates and how to cope with them. Lessard first points out the significant changes that have taken place in international financial markets as firms have become global. While financial markets have become more linked internationally, interest rates and exchange rates have become more volatile. These conditions present both threat and opportunity to the firm, and provide means for the finance function to contribute significantly to the firm's profits. In this article, Lessard discusses how finance can contribute through exploiting exchange and interest rate differentials and reducing the firm's financial risk and its taxes.

Marjorie Stanley addresses two key strategic finance issues, capital structure and cost of capital. Her article analytically reviews concepts and models proposed to deal with these issues in multinational and global firms. She focuses on financing rather than on investment decisions, but the material she reviews should be useful in predicting, for example, the effect of a particular investment on the value of the firm. Stanley organizes her review around two widely cited corporate finance frameworks, the Modigliani-Miller and the capital asset pricing models. She first reviews and analyzes separately work using each framework and then points out conflicts and knowledge gaps in the two frameworks. Her discussion of the Modigliani-Miller model and its extensions, in particular, illustrates even further some of the points Lessard makes in the previous article.

She notes, for example, that when a firm borrows in two or more countries, its cost of capital is affected by foreign exchange gains and losses as well as by interest rates. Problems in forecasting foreign exchange rates underline questions of the applicability of the model when extended to the multinational or global firm.

Stanley also discusses problems with the capital asset pricing model. For example, the model assumes perfect markets, but there are good reasons to suspect imperfect markets. She asks, in this context, whether the multinational or global corporation might, itself, be an instrument of financial integration. If so, the capital asset pricing model could be a useful analytical tool.

Vinod Bavishi compares theory and practice among U.S. multinationals in handling the investment side of finance, illuminating further some of its complications. He notes, for example, that the literature describes alternative means for evaluating the cash flows expected from an investment; in practice, different firms use different methods. Similarly, he observes that there is no agreement in either theory or practice in firms' choice of discounted cash flow methods or in establishing a discount rate. He then discusses the ramifications of different choices and recommends those he considers most useful.

Gunter Dufey and Ian Giddy focus on the forecasts of currency movements multinational and global firms must make in their financial planning. They identify as major financial planning decisions those affecting the choices of timing, maturity, and currency of denomination. Making the best choices requires forecasting interest and exchange rates.

Dufey and Giddy believe financial and currency markets implicitly provide such forecasts, and that we can understand these implicit forecasts by studying the proper indicators. This is not, however, a matter of simply using the present price of futures to predict the actual future value of, say, a currency. To forecast with maximum accuracy, the forecaster must make some careful adjustments. Managers can use the adjustment techniques the authors suggest in a variety of forecasting situations, not just those connected with investment decisions. Dufey and Giddy suggest applications in areas such as budgeting and performance evaluation.

Joseph Ganitsky and Gerardo Lema discuss a new and growing foreign investment vehicle, the transnational debt-equity swap. Opportunities for these swaps arise from less-developed countries' foreign bank debt. The debtor countries give their lender banks equity rights in exchange for part (or all) of the debt they owe. The lender banks can then sell these equity rights if they wish. Firms, through buying equity rights, may gain better or less expensive access to markets in developing countries than they could obtain by other means.

In their article, Ganitsky and Lema explain why the practice is growing. They detail the costs and benefits of equity swaps and show how to analyze potential equity acquisition opportunities. In doing so, they identify many of the problems attendant to making foreign investments in developing countries. The framework they present may be useful not only in analyzing equity swaps but more generally in analyzing developing country acquisition or even investment opportunities.

John Dyment's article changes the focus from investment to management control. He argues that the management control system a global, or highly coordinated, firm requires is much different from the system required in uncoordinated multinational or domestic firms. The global corporation should discard, he says, the concept of measuring the business in each country as though it were a separate entity. Management should evaluate each business unit based on its contribution to the firm's global strategy rather than on the specific profit it may earn.

W. M. Abdallah discusses a specific tool for motivating and evaluating managers, the transfer price. He argues that multinational firms design their transfer pricing systems based on currency flow and tax minimization considerations. He shows how the transfer price can affect managers' behavior under different circumstances and suggests how transfer prices can be used to influence the behavior of country managers. It may be a worthwhile exercise to compare Abdallah's perspective with the views on control systems Dyment expresses in the previous article.

15

FINANCE AND GLOBAL COMPETITION: EXPLOITING FINANCIAL SCOPE AND COPING WITH VOLATILE EXCHANGE RATES
Donald R. Lessard

INTRODUCTION

The emergence of global competition represents a major threat to firms that have gained competitive advantage under the previous largely multidomestic rules. However, it also creates new opportunities for firms that can reconfigure their operations to exploit the leverage provided by global scope with managers who can shift their perspectives to cope with this more complex environment.

Finance plays a critical role in a firm's adaptation to this new competitive environment. In discussing finance under global competition, we define its role broadly,

I am grateful to Carliss Baldwin, Gene Flood, Sumantra Ghoshal, Bruce Kogut, John Lightstone, Tom Piper, Michael Porter, David Sharp, Mark Trusheim, and Louis T. Wells for comments on earlier drafts; Alberto Boiardi, Yongwook Jun, Chartsiri Sophonpanich, David Sharp, and Mark Trusheim for allowing me to draw on their unpublished thesis research; and Nancy Dallaire for editorial assistance.

Source: Michael E. Porter, ed., *Competition in Global Industries.* Boston, Mass.: Harvard Business School Press, 1986.

- to provide a yardstick for judging current and prospective operations;

- to raise the funds required for these operations; and

- to add value in its own right by exploiting distortions in financial markets, reducing taxes, and managing the risks inherent in the firm's activities.

The larger stakes associated with world-scale operations require greater financial resources and flexibility. Further, global competition in product and factor markets reduces the ability of a firm to pass through to their customers any financing or tax costs in excess of those facing the lowest-cost producers. Thus, the firm must match its global competitors on these terms. Finally, volatile exchange rates create much greater challenges for a firm facing global competition than one operating largely in a multidomestic mode.

Under global competition, exchange rate fluctuations not only change the dollar value of the firm's foreign profits and foreign currency-denominated contractual assets and liabilities, such as accounts receivable and debt, they also alter the firm's competitive position and often call for changes in operating variables including pricing, output, and sourcing. These decisions are complicated by the fact that volatile exchange rates distort traditional measures of current and long-term profitability, creating illusions that depend on the currency in which alternatives are weighed and a manager's performance is judged.

A firm wearing "dollar-colored" eyeglasses or, for that matter, "yen-colored" eyeglasses will have a distorted view of its competitive position and is likely to make costly mistakes. A firm that sees through these effects will be in a much better position to judge its evolving competitive strengths. As a result, it will be more likely to make appropriate pricing, output, and sourcing choices in response to exchange rate shifts and will be in a better position to measure management's contribution to current performance, controlling for the macroeconomic situation.

These views are borne out by the experiences of 1978–79, when the weak dollar favored global competitors with U.S. production, and from 1981 through the present, when the strong dollar has had the opposite effect. In the first period, many firms were lulled into a false sense of security because the margins were holding up in the face of increasing Japanese competition, when in fact they should have been doing much better than normal. As a result, they were poorly prepared for the shift in competitive position vis-à-vis non-U.S. firms resulting from the dollar shock of late 1980. While it is impossible to forecast exchange rate movements, it is likely that extreme shifts such as these will reoccur, again altering international competitive positions and requiring major adjustments by firms.

This chapter is organized in four parts. In the first part I characterize changes in financial markets that have accompanied the shift to global competition. In the second I describe the changing role of finance in the context of global competition, and contrast it with finance under multidomestic competition. In the third I explore in greater depth the implications for the finance function of volatile exchange rates coupled with global competition, as well as the implications of a firm's financial perspectives for its competitive behavior under these circumstances. Finally, in the fourth part I summarize the themes developed in this chapter, briefly outline their implications for management practice, and suggest further lines of research.

THE NEW FINANCIAL ENVIRONMENT

The emergence of global competition has coincided with major changes in the international financial environment. These changes include an increased linkage of major financial markets, a counteracting increase in the use by governments of financial instruments in industrial policy, and a substantial increase in macroeconomic volatility as reflected in exchange and interest rates.

Increased International Linkage of Financial Markets

A major characteristic of the current financial environment is the increased linkage of national money and capital markets as the result of a variety of factors.[1] These include the dismantling of many restrictions on financial flows across national borders,[2] the deregulation of financial institutions both at home and abroad,[3] financial innovations that allow a separation of the choice of currency and other attributes of contracts from the jurisdiction in which they take place,[4] and increased corporate awareness of the intricacies of international finance.

This integration of financial markets is not universal, though. Many less-developed countries, in response to foreign exchange crises brought about by their own external borrowing coupled with the world recession, have imposed new or tighter exchange controls and other measures that isolate the domestic financial markets from world markets.[5] As a result, private firms based in these countries have seen their access to international financial markets cut back to pre-1970 levels. Nevertheless, financial markets are considerably more integrated on balance than they were in 1970.

This increased integration of financial markets, of course, implies an evening of the cost of funds in various countries and a consequent reduction in the benefits accruing to a firm from spanning national financial markets.[6] Increased global competition, though, puts more pressure on firms to take advantage of the remaining gains from global financial scope.

Increased Financial Intervention in Domestic Economies

Counteracting this trend toward a level international financial playing field are the increased uses by governments of financial interventions to favor home firms or home production. Credit allocation, with its implicit subsidies to firms with access to credit, continues in several industrialized countries and is the rule in most developing countries.[7] Many governments also offer concessional loans and explicit or implicit guarantees, to the point that these have become a major source of contention in international trade. Finally, most governments modify their basic tax structures by providing tax holidays, special deductions or credits, or the ability to issue securities exempt from personal tax to favor particular activities.[8]

These interventions lead to intense "shopping" for tax and financing benefits by firms . . . and increasing competition among governments for projects. . . . In many cases, access to these financial benefits is linked to performance requirements such as the location of the plant or the level of employment or exports.[9] However, the value of these incentives to the firm often depends on how it arranges its internal and external finances. For example, a firm with no need for borrowing in a country with cheap credit can shift its interaffiliate accounts so as to increase its apparent local borrowing requirements, while a firm investing in a start-up venture that will not break even for several years in a country offering a tax holiday can use transfer prices to shift profits from related operations to the tax-sheltered unit. Similarly, a firm engaged in overseas oil exploration may obtain a tax benefit from having operations in the United States because it can deduct these expenses from taxable profits in the United States, but not from profits in most other countries.[10] In the second section I show that the ability of the firm to exploit these conditions will depend on how many options it has for shifting funds and/or profits among subsidiaries across national boundaries, which in turn will depend on the number of places it operates and the magnitude and richness of the ongoing real and financial interactions among its component corporations. Thus, a firm's international financial scope is likely to be an important factor in its competitiveness.

Exchange and Interest Rate Instability

A major characteristic of the current world economy involving both the financial and real spheres is the extreme volatility of exchange and interest rates. This volatility is inextricably linked to differing degrees of integration internationally of finance, industry, and politics. Because of the high degree of integration among financial markets in major industrialized countries, factors influencing interest rates are readily transmitted across national boundaries. Given the lesser degree of integration in markets for goods and real factors of production, and the almost total lack of coordination in macroeconomic policies among nations, the result has been a high degree of volatility in nominal and real exchange rates.[11] This volatility, in turn, has led to sharp swings in the competitiveness of production facilities based in different countries.

In the short run, the volatility of exchange rates dominates longer-term trends, yet these trends are critical in the evolution of competitiveness. Over time, nominal exchange rates tend to adjust so as to offset cumulative differences in rates of inflation among countries.[12] Changes in real exchange rates—defined as changes in nominal exchange rates relative to cumulative inflation differences—therefore, do not cumulate to nearly the same extent. As a result, in the long run, the competitive effects of cumulative movements in real exchange rates are likely to be swamped by microeconomic factors such as the firm's productivity growth compared to that of its host economy.[13]

This long-run tendency for exchange rates and inflation differentials to offset each other is illustrated by the circles in Figure 1, which depict cumulative changes in nominal (vertical axis) and real exchange rates (horizontal axis) from 1973 through the end of 1980. In the short run, though, when inflation differentials are small, both real and nominal exchange rates move together as shown by the points represented by squares (June 1982) and triangles (September 1983) in Figure 1.

Resulting Threats and Opportunities

Global competition coupled with an increasingly integrated and volatile financial environment gives rise to both threats and opportunities for firms whose activities span real and financial markets in various countries. A major threat is the exposure to exchange rate volatility and its impact on the firm's competitive position. A closely related threat, which is more subtle and therefore more difficult to address, is the potential for management error due to illusions associated with short-run movements in exchange rates.

On the positive side, . . . exchange rate volatility provides an opportunity to exploit relative price shifts, but this requires production flexibility that is costly and organizational flexibility that is difficult to sustain.[14] Further, with the less than complete integration of financial markets and the significant degree of govern-

ment intervention, firms continue to face opportunities to engage in arbitrage across financial markets and tax regimes via internal financial transactions. While there is reason to believe that these arbitrage opportunities may be more limited than before, global competition creates more pressure to exploit them because it shifts the incidence of differential taxes and financing costs to the firm. Thus, finance not only comes into play in addressing issues that arise because of global competition in product markets, but also becomes a direct factor in that competition.

Each of these threats and opportunities has significant implications for the finance function and its interaction with other aspects of the firm. In order to trace these implications I will review the role of finance in the corporation and then consider how this role is or should be changed in the context of global competition.

THE ROLE OF FINANCE IN THE CONTEXT OF GLOBAL COMPETITION

Notwithstanding the periodic attempts of conglomerateurs or asset strippers to create values by repackaging financial claims, finance derives most of its value from the real business operations it makes possible. In an idealized world characterized by complete information, perfect enforceability of all contracts, and neutral taxation, the role of the finance function would be to provide a yardstick for judging business options to insure that they meet the "market test" for the use of resources, raise sufficient funds to enable the firm to undertake all projects with positive present values, and return funds to shareholders when they cannot be reinvested profitably.

Of course, the world does not match this idealization. Managers often possess information that they cannot or will not disclose to investors, and investors often disagree among them-

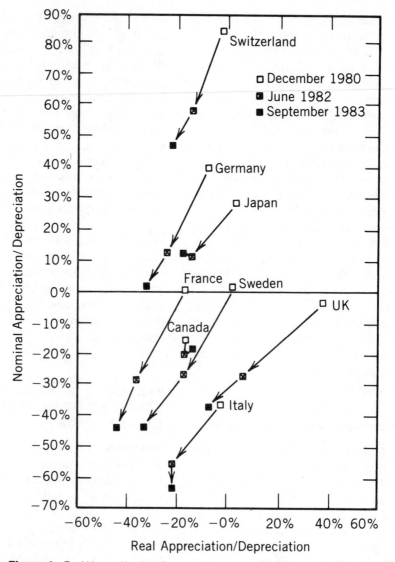

Figure 1 Real Versus Nominal Currency Movements Relative to U.S. Dollar, 1973 Base

selves as well as with managers regarding future prospects. As a result, defining and monitoring contractual relationships between managers and various classes of claimants is extremely complex and imperfect.[15] Further, taxes are not neutral and access to particular capital markets is often restricted in a discriminatory fashion. As a result, financial contracts at times are not fairly priced.

In such an environment, finance can contribute to the firm's value[16] in several ways in addition to its basic role of evaluating and funding investment opportunities. Finance can add value by permitting the firm to

- exploit pricing distortions in financial markets,
- reduce taxes, and

- mitigate risks and allocate them among different parties in order to:
    a. maximize diversification benefits,
    b. create appropriate managerial incentives, and
    c. reduce costs of financial distress.

What is of interest in this chapter is how the nature and potential contribution to value of each of these functions differ under conditions of global as opposed to multidomestic competition. Are the two environments really different from a financial perspective? Does finance play a different role in the two contexts? The nature and potential contribution of many of these functions would appear to depend on the firm's multinationality, that is, the extent to which it spans different currency areas or tax jurisdictions, rather than the degree of integration or coordination of the firm's primary activities such as manufacturing or marketing. Even the distinction of global versus multidomestic is vague from a financial perspective.

The finance function is an excellent example of the global-multidomestic continuum. Although much discussion treats the two as mutually exclusive categories, in practice firms can be a little bit global. A firm is global to the extent that it is structured and operates so as to realize benefits from international integration of particular activities (scale economies), coordination of activities (scope economies), and transnational learning. . . . Any multinational must achieve some such cross-border benefits to overcome the costs of operating at a distance.[17] At the multidomestic extreme of the continuum, integration typically is limited to indirect overhead functions including research and development and finance. At the global extreme, substantial portions of the direct value activities also are integrated or coordinated across borders. Further, it is likely that in such cases the indirect activities represent a larger fraction of value than in the multidomestic case. Thus, a multinational firm may be global in finance but not in other activities. On the other hand, merely being multinational does not guarantee that it will realize the benefits of global scope in even this one function. However, there are many reasons why the nature and potential contribution of the multinational financial function will differ in the context of global competition.

As noted in the introduction, the global operating environment is complicated by firms' differing exposures to volatile exchange rates, by the possibility that one firm will obtain a competitive advantage through access to favorable financing or fiscal arrangements, and by the proliferation of modes of international production accompanied by a veritable explosion of financing vehicles. Thus, finance not only comes into play in addressing issues that arise because of increased global competition in product markets, but also becomes a direct factor in that competition. Table 1 provides an overview of the changing nature of the finance function and its linkages to the firm's overall competitive position under international, multidomestic, and global competition.[18] I include tactical pricing and output changes to exchange rate changes, not strictly finance functions, because they are closely linked to exchange risk management and strongly influenced by a firm's currency perspective.

In the remainder of this section I review the implications of increased global competition coupled with the increased integration of financial markets for each of the major functions of finance identified earlier. In each case, I contrast this new context with the previous, largely multidomestic era, using the study of multinational finance by Robbins and Stobaugh (1973) as a base for comparison.

Evaluating Investment Opportunities

A clear implication of the current competitive and financial environment is an increase in the complexity of investment opportunities and the corresponding increase in the potential for

Table 1   Implications of Global Competition for Finance Function

Nature of International Competition Function	Export/Import	Multidomestic	Global
Investment evaluation	Domestic perspective, few "foreign" considerations	Yes/no decision to enter market or change mode to serve local market	Mutually exclusive global choices, currency, tax issues central
Funding operations*	Meet domestic norms	Meet local norms	Match global competitors' cost of capital
Exchange risk management	Focus on exposure of foreign currency contracts	Focus on exposure of converting foreign profits into dollars	Focus on exposure of home and foreign profits to competitive effects of exchange rate shifts
Output/pricing responses to exchange rate movements	No change in home currency price	No change in local currency price	Change in home, local price to reflect global competitive position
Performance measurement	Measure all operations in dollars at actual rates	Measure foreign operations in local currency	Measure all operations relative to standard that reflects competitive effects of exchange rate changes

*The entries in this row reflect typical behaviors of firms. Clearly, firms can and some do pursue global cost-minimizing financing strategies regardless of global linkage of operations.

management error. The estimation of incremental benefits from resource outlays must take into account increased international interdependence among the various activities of the firm in terms of the benefits of scale, scope, learning, and hence, future opportunities.

In analyzing alternative plant locations, for example, the firm must evaluate not only differences in the direct costs of operating in each location, but also the impact of different choices on other strategic factors such as access to particular markets and the scale and experience "platforms" that each alternative provides for future operations. Consider the case of the Korean consumer electronics industry whose U.S. operations appear to break even at best.[19] This poor financial performance is often taken as evidence of uneconomic behavior on the

part of Korean firms or of extensive Korean government subsidies of its firms' operations abroad. Another explanation, though, is that the financial performance of the U.S. operations is only one component of their contribution to Korean firms' value. Others include the impact of unit cost reduction due to the scale made possible by entering the U.S. market on the profits of these firms in Korea, where they are oligopolists with substantial market power and the impact of learning from present U.S. operations on future investment opportunities in the United States and elsewhere. Choices among alternative product and marketing programs are even more complex, because gains in some product market segments will result in erosion in others, while in other cases there may be positive carryover.

Given the varying patterns of government intervention, choices among strategic alternatives are further complicated by the need to trade these direct and indirect benefits off against alternative packages of investment incentives and performance requirements, where the present value of each package will depend on the corporation's anticipated cash flow and tax position in various jurisdictions. While similar complications existed under multidomestic competition, in general they were less central because they influenced whether a firm should enter a particular national market rather than which (mutually exclusive) way they should serve a world market.

A further complication is the problem of the "bent measuring stick" identified by Robbins and Stobaugh. They noted that unless the firm conducts all interaffiliate transactions at "arm's-length," the profits (incremental cash flows) of any activity to any corporate unit will not equal the incremental flows to the corporation as a whole. They further noted that there are many reasons, such as minimizing taxes which I discuss later, that a firm will not want to adopt arm's-length transfer pricing as well as reasons why it may not be able to compute such prices even if it wants to. Under global competition, this problem is exacerbated not only by the increased interdependencies among the firms' operations, but by the overwhelming impact of exchange rate fluctuations on revenues, costs, and profits, a point I develop in greater detail in the section "Coping with Exchange Rate Volatility." In projecting future profits and cash flows, firms must see through the short-term impacts on profits of currency movements to focus on their evolving microcompetitiveness.

These complexities have contributed to a general view that discounted cash flow (DCF) techniques are no longer valid and that their use by U.S. management has contributed to the decline in America's competitive position.[20] Nothing could be farther from the truth. It is probably true that U.S. managers' overreliance on short-term return on investment (ROI)

goals, coupled with a simplistic use of DCF techniques, result in a bias against projects with indirect future benefits.[21] When properly employed, however, DCF measures provide a powerful framework for combining the effects of scale, scope, and learning on present and future activities.[22] What is needed is a closer linkage of competitive analysis and DCF techniques rather than discarding these techniques in favor of more subjective approaches.

Funding Business Requirements

The increased scope of the competitive arena implies larger stakes for most major business gambles.[23] However, the increased integration of financial markets in different countries has enhanced firms' external financing capacity as well, especially for firms based in smaller countries with isolated capital markets.[24] Firms that consider themselves global competitors are broadening their funding bases to insure that they will not find themselves at a competitive disadvantage in this regard.[25] Even a multidomestic competitor is not safe; the emergence of a firm with a global financial advantage will alter the terms of competition in much the same way as would the emergence of a firm with globally integrated production in an industry hitherto characterized by production on a national scale.

Exploiting Financing Bargains

To the extent that financial markets are not fully integrated or that financing concessions differ among countries, multinational firms' ability to span these markets will not only increase [their] ability to fund global operations but also increase the likelihood that they can identify and exploit financing bargains.

If a firm can identify financial investment or borrowing opportunities that are mispriced, it can add value by engaging in arbitrage or speculation. In general, opportunities for such gains are rarer than for gains arising from real market advantages that are protected by barriers to entry, because there are likely to be fewer such barriers to financial transactions. This is the basis for Baldwin's skepticism regarding the alleged cost of capital advantages of Japanese firms. . . . However, such opportunities do exist from time to time, especially in capital markets that are distorted and isolated by controls on credit and exchange market transactions.

Because they are at once domestic and foreign, multinational firms are more likely to encounter exploitable distortions in financial markets than firms operating in single countries. They can often circumvent the credit market and exchange market controls that create these profit opportunities.[26] Firms' internal financial networks provide them with considerable latitude in the choice of *channels* through which they transfer cash and/or taxable profits among their various national corporate components as well as in the *timing* of interaffiliate transfers. A firm, for example, can advance funds to a subsidiary through an injection of funds in the form of equity or a loan, through a transfer of goods or intangibles such as technology at less than an arm's-length price,[27] or by providing it with a guarantee that enables it to borrow locally. Depending on how the subsidiary is funded, the firm then has a similar array of channels through which it can withdraw funds. It can accelerate or delay transfers by leading or lagging interaffiliate settlements relative to their scheduled dates, or if such behavior is prohibited, by shifting the timing of the shipment of goods within the corporation.

This discretion over the channels and timing of remittances among related corporations is of little value within a single tax and monetary jurisdiction, because transfers among units typically involve little cost and have no tax consequences. However, when the firm operates across jurisdictions, certain channels may be restricted by virtue of exchange controls and the use of others will trigger additional tax liabilities. Under these circumstances, the firm benefits from "internalizing" these transactions.[28]

Robbins and Stobaugh, studying a set of multidomestic multinationals, showed that the gains from exploiting internal financial systems were often significant. However, they also found that larger firms tended not to fully exploit this potential because of external constraints (or self-policing to avoid sanctions) and organizational limitations. I suspect that the pressure to pursue such gains is much greater with global competition because it drastically reduces the ability of a firm to pass through any financing costs in excess of those facing the industry cost leaders. In a multidomestic context, in contrast, the competitive impact of these costs depends on the relative position of firms in each country.

Reducing Taxes

By appropriately "packaging" the cash flows generated by business operations, firms often can substantially reduce the present value of governments' tax take.[29] The simplest example in a single-country setting is the use of debt as a way to reduce corporate income taxes. Firms operating internationally may be in a position to shift income into jurisdictions with relatively low rates and/or relatively favorable definitions of income. While some of these profit shifts occur through transfer prices of real inputs and outputs, the pricing of interaffiliate financial transactions often provides the greatest flexibility.[30] In the current global competitive environment, though, a new factor is coming into play. As governments seek to actively manipulate their fiscal systems for nationalistic and/or distributional gains, firms "shop" fiscal regimes and actively bargain over the distribution of rents resulting from a given activity. This is especially true of facilities on a world scale which, by definition, are not premised on access to any single market.[31] In these cases, tax system arbitrage becomes an area of active bargaining as well as gaming of passive fiscal systems.

A final way that an international firm can reduce (the present value of expected) taxes is to structure interaffiliate commercial and financial dealings, as well as hedging the risks of individual units through external transactions, in order to minimize the chance that any of its corporate components will experience losses on its tax accounts and, as a result, have to carry forward some of its tax shields. Virtually all corporate income tax regimes are asymmetric in that they collect a share of profits but rebate shares of losses only up to taxes paid in the prior, say, three years. Otherwise, the losses must be carried forward with an implied reduction in the present value of the tax shields. In essence, the tax authorities hold a call option on profits. As a result, the expected tax rate is an increasing function of the variability of the taxable profits of each entity that comprises the firm.[32]

As with financing costs, global competitors will be under much greater pressure than multidomestic competitors to match the lowest tax burden obtainable by any firm in the industry while increasing their flexibility in where to locate and how to coordinate value activities. Thus, tax and financial management aimed at minimizing the firm's cost of capital will no longer be an optional activity pursued by a handful of sophisticated firms, but an integral element of global competitive strategy.

Managing Risks

A final, often critical role of finance in a firm is to mitigate particular risks inherent in its undertakings and/or shift them to other firms or investors. Global competition, for example, increases firms' exposure to exchange rate volatility, but the firm can to a large extent lay off this risk through hedging transactions including currency futures, swaps, options, or foreign currency borrowing. Some aspects of exchange risk can also be shifted to suppliers or customers through the choice of invoicing currencies. Alternatively, the firm can retain this risk and, implicitly, pass it on to its shareholders.

An important result in financial theory is that in an idealized perfect capital market the allocation of risks among firms, as well as the form in which it is passed on to investors, does not matter because investors can completely diversify their holdings and hence will be affected only by undiversifiable risks. Under these circumstances, hedging does not add value and, as long as prices are "fair," contractual risk sharing with suppliers or customers is of no consequence. However, in practice, firms devote a great deal of effort to risk allocation in the form of hedging and risk sharing. While much of this behavior can be traced to attempts by managers to look good within imperfect control systems, several recent analyses provide a rigorous basis, consistent with shareholder value maximization, for hedging under some circumstances.[33] In particular, as we have seen earlier, it can reduce the (present value of) taxes. It can also increase diversification benefits, improve managerial incentives, and reduce the costs of financial distress.

Although capital markets are becoming more integrated, there are barriers to cross-border investment in the form of taxes, controls on foreign investment, and political risks that have different impacts on domestic and foreign investors, particularly transfer risks. Because of these barriers, investors in various countries will differ in their scope for diversifying particular risks and, hence, will place different values on particular securities.[34] They may also differ in their ability to mitigate those risks that are at least in part the result of choices by governments or other firms. A firm may exploit this comparative advantage in risk bearing by issuing securities either directly or indirectly, that is, by contracting with a firm with a different set of investors, to the investor group who will value them most highly. A global firm will not constrain itself to any particular capital market base and, hence, will exploit this potential to the fullest.

Volatile earnings and cash flows may reduce a firm's ability to compete by distorting management information and incentives, hindering access to capital markets, and threatening the continuity of supplier and customer relationships. In the case of risks that are outside the control of individual firms, but that affect many firms, such as exchange rates or relative prices of key commodities, firms with large specific exposures will benefit by laying off these risks to other firms or investors that have smaller or perhaps even opposite exposures. To the extent that the risks affecting particular business undertakings are at least partially controllable by one or more potential participants, risk allocation to create appropriate strategic stakeholdings is likely to mitigate risk.[35]

Organizational Implications

Global competition results in a blurring of the boundaries between finance and operations. Investment choices involve tax and financing considerations that depend on the firm's overall cash and profit position. Exchange rate impacts, typically the realm of the treasury function, are critical factors in the shifting competitiveness of the firm's operations. Operating profitability cannot be separated from financing considerations and must be judged relative to the macroeconomic environment.

Further, just as global competition blurs national product market boundaries, it also blurs national boundaries in finance. The use of finance to offset exchange exposures and exploit distortions in financial markets requires a high degree of global coordination and centralization of decision making, and may interfere with the management of operations sensitive to local conditions, especially in cases where global optimization reduces the profits of a local affiliate. Already bent, measuring sticks used in evaluating the performance of operations in a multidomestic context will be further distorted.

A further consequence of global management of the finance function is that it may require affiliates to act in conflict with local national interests.[36] Robbins and Stobaugh, following the theme of Vernon's *Sovereignty at Bay,* cited the firm's ability to bypass financial controls by using its internal network as a key element in the weakening of sovereign control. In recent years, governments of major industrialized countries appear to have conceded the battle over the control of international capital flows and, as a result, have found themselves severely constrained in terms of policies to stabilize currency values. The battle is still being fought on fiscal terrain, but the advent of global competition and the resultant aggressive tax shopping by firms and fiscal promotion by particular countries is transforming the conflict from one between firms and nation-states to one among states. Attempts at cooperation (cartelization?) by governments, such as the EC code on investment incentives, will undoubtedly increase, but whether they succeed is an open question.

The Bottom Line

Many of the differences between finance under global and multidomestic competition are of degree rather than kind. Multinationality in terms of being able to span national financial markets confers financial benefits on firms whether they compete globally or multidomestically. However, the ability of the firm to pass on differential financing costs and taxes is reduced by global competition. Thus, to compete it will have to match its competitors' "cost of capital" and, as a result, the value of an effective finance function to a global firm is overwhelming.

Further, the greater currency volatility of the current period and its greater proportionate effect on firms' cash flows and profits, given global competition, increase the importance of effective foreign exchange management, both in terms of limiting risks and providing management information for tactical and strategic choices.

The biggest differences appear to lie in this latter area, the role of finance in evaluating business options. The boundaries between finance and competitive behavior are blurred, and appear to be becoming even more so.

COPING WITH EXCHANGE RATE VOLATILITY

Given the vital importance of exchange rate volatility in the new global environment, it is necessary to examine in greater depth how exchange rate volatility affects firms engaged in global competition and how these firms cope with this volatility. I focus on three specific issues arising from the coincidence of volatile currencies and global competition. These are (1) the impact of exchange rate fluctuations on competitiveness, (2) corporate management of exchange risk, and (3) the impact of firms' currency perspectives on their strategic and tactical choices.

The Impact of Exchange Rate Shifts on Competitiveness

A major difference between multidomestic and global competition is the impact of exchange rates on the competitiveness and, hence, profitability of a multinational firm. Under multidomestic competition, markets are national in scope and, typically, a substantial proportion of value added is local. Thus, exchange rate shifts do not significantly change the relative costs of firms operating in a particular market. As a result, firms' revenues and costs move together in response to shifts in exchange rates, and profits from foreign operations, when converted into dollars, move roughly proportionally with exchange rates.[37]

In contrast, under global competition, there will be a tendency toward world prices and larger proportions of firms' value added are likely to be concentrated in particular countries.[38] Thus, unless all firms have the same geographic patterns of value added, shifts in exchange rates will change their relative costs

and profit margins. With the emergence of non-U.S. global competitors, this is almost bound to be the case.[39] In this case, the profits of foreign operations may respond either more or less than one for one with shifts in exchange rates, and the profits of operations in the United States will be affected as well.

The responsiveness of operating profits to shifts in exchange rates, then, is comprised of two effects: a *conversion effect* and a *competitive effect*. The conversion effect is the proportional adjustment of foreign currency operating profits into dollars. By definition, it applies only to foreign operations. The competitive effect, in contrast, is the response of local currency operating profits to exchange rate shifts resulting from the interaction of the various competitors' supply and price responses. It applies to both domestic and overseas activities.

These *operating exposures*—the sensitivity of a firm's operating profits (margins) measured in the parent currency to exchange rate movements—differ from *financial exposures*—the sensitivity of the parent currency value of its money-fixed assets and liabilities—in several ways. First, they are exposures to shifts in real exchange rates rather than in nominal exchange rates. Further, these operating exposures depend on the structure of the markets in which the firm operates and not necessarily on the country or currency in which the firm purchases or sells its product.

Consider the case of Economy Motors, a hypothetical U.S. manufacturer of small cars. Economy produces components and assembles its products in the Midwest and sells them throughout the United States. Its products sell in direct competition with Japanese imports, which dominate the market and are the price leaders. The shifting competitive position of Economy under different real exchange rate scenarios is illustrated in Figure 2.

In the base year, when the yen and dollar are "at parity," the Japanese set U.S. prices so that they (and Economy) earn normal margins. In some later year, if the yen strengthens in line

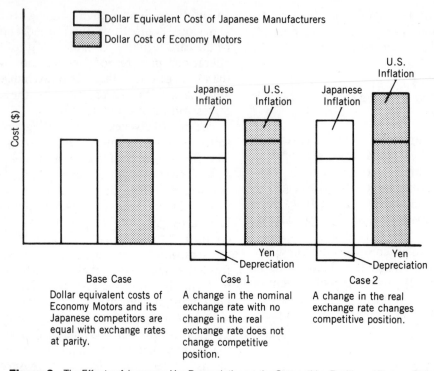

☐ Dollar Equivalent Cost of Japanese Manufacturers

▨ Dollar Cost of Economy Motors

Base Case

Dollar equivalent costs of Economy Motors and its Japanese competitors are equal with exchange rates at parity.

Case 1

A change in the nominal exchange rate with no change in the real exchange rate does not change competitive position.

Case 2

A change in the real exchange rate changes competitive position.

Figure 2   The Effects of Japanese Yen Depreciation on the Competitive Position of Economy Motors

with the difference in inflation between the two countries, Economy remains on par with the Japanese. However, if the yen weakens while Japan's inflation remains below that of the United States, the Japanese firms have lower dollar costs, they cut prices to gain share, and Economy faces reduced profits.

The reason Economy faces an operating exposure even though it operates entirely in its domestic market is that the market in which it sells its output is much more integrated globally than the markets in which it purchases its inputs.

The sensitivity of a firm's profits to shifts in exchange rates under global competition may be greater than one for one. Extending the Economy Motors example, assume that the operating margin under normal (parity) conditions is 15 percent, that all costs are in U.S. dollars, but that a 1 percent change in the real yen/dollar rate results in a .5 percent change in

dollar prices of small cars in the United States. In this case, assuming that the optimal response to exchange rate changes involves matching price and holding volume constant, the sensitivity of profits would be 3.33 to 1.[40] In other words, a 10 percent change in the exchange rate would result in a 33 percent change in operating profits!

A useful way to think of the price effects of exchange rate changes is in terms of a currency habitat for each product or input. This *currency habitat* is defined as the currency in which the price of the good tends to be most stable.[41] The determinants of the currency habitat can be summarized in two dimensions illustrated in Figure 3: (1) the geographical scope of the product market, and (2) the relative influence of producer costs and characteristics of consumer demand on price in a given market.

The geographic scope of the market will depend on the ability of the firm, or its suppliers

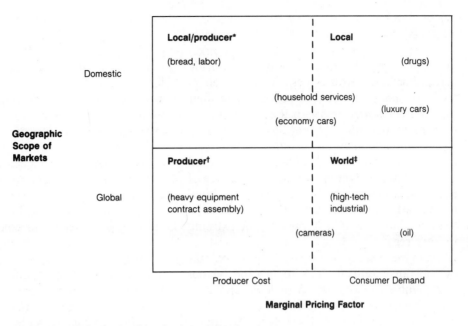

*Local if recurring costs of production are local.
†Currency of marginal firm/price leader depending on industrial structure.
‡Basket weighted by relative importance (income and elasticity) of consumers. As a
first approximation, this is the basket comprising special rights (Special Drawing Rights).

Figure 3 Determinants of Currency Habitat of Cost/Price

in the case of inputs, to segment national markets, either by limiting transshipment or by differentiating the products it sells in various markets. As product markets become more globally integrated, prices in various national markets tend toward a world price. The marginal pricing factor captures the relative importance of supply and demand considerations, which reflect among other things the competitive structure of the industry, the price elasticity of demand, the existence of complements and substitutes, and the structure of costs, in particular the level of nonrecurring costs.[42]

The two dimensions are not entirely independent because firms with significant market power will be able to discriminate among national market segments by "bundling" local services (e.g., warranties) with products or otherwise precluding transshipment by distributors or customers. The recent collaboration of Mercedes Benz and other luxury auto manufac-

turers with the U.S. government in requiring the stamping of various component parts to reduce theft was squarely aimed at stamping out the gray market, as were MBZ's ads stressing that while they stood behind all their cars, they could only promise exceptional service to owners who had purchased their cars from authorized U.S. dealers. Quotas have performed the same role for Japanese manufacturers. An additional dimension that is important when there are few global producers is the level of operating margins (quasi-rents) in the industry, reflecting the relative importance of nonrecurring (capital and R&D) and recurring costs.

In the case of local markets (the upper half of Figure 3), the currency habitat will clearly be the local currency if costs are local as well, because in this case international supply and demand will play little or no role. The more interesting case for our purposes, though, is where a significant proportion of value added is global in nature, that is, where the degree of global configuration and coordination is high, but where producers have sufficient market power to engage in some price discrimination across borders. Because these firms can effectively segment national markets through their own market power and with the collaboration of regulatory authorities, they face local currency-denominated marginal revenue curves. If recurring costs are low, therefore, they will tend to maintain constant local prices in the face of exchange adjustments. If these costs are high, in contrast, they will adjust both local price and volume. Patented drugs represent one extreme in this regard, with local currency habitats, while in the absence of quotas, the price habitat of mid-range autos such as Toyota and Nissan will involve a combination of local and producer currencies. The currency habitat for luxury cars, which face less elastic demand because of greater product differentiation, and with higher margins of sales price over recurring costs, will also involve a mix of local and producer currencies, but with a much greater weight on the local currency.

In those cases where transshipment cannot be barred, in contrast, either because of the portability of the product, the inability of manufacturers to control distribution channels, or the power of key customers, prices will tend to a single world level (lower half of Figure 3). The camera industry is a case in point, with gray marketeers denying manufacturers the ability to fully segment national markets. The same is true of industrial equipment and components that are sold to sophisticated buyers who themselves are multinational. The currency habitat of these world prices will depend on the weighted importance of demand from various countries and the currency habitat of the costs incurred.

Foreign Exchange Risk Management under Global Competition[43]

Exposure to exchange rate movements is a serious problem for firms in the current environment, especially those that are global competi-

tors. However, foreign exchange management as currently practiced is unlikely to help firms compete effectively and, in fact, is likely to provide misleading signals. There are two reasons for this. First, foreign exchange risk management is concerned primarily with deciding whether to hedge or retain particular exposures arising from operations rather than seeing to it that this exposure and its impact on expected operating profits have been factored into operating decisions. In fact, as practiced, it differs little from staking the assistant treasurer with a sum of money to be used to speculate on stock options, pork bellies, or gold. Second, it tends to focus on exposures that lead to identifiable foreign exchange gains or losses, contractual items as opposed to operating profit impacts.

Foreign exchange exposure can be defined as the sensitivity to shifts in exchange rates of either a firm's cash flows or its reported profits, or some subset thereof. While the cash flow perspective makes more economic sense, the reporting perspective also matters to the extent that it affects managerial decisions or financial market reactions.[44] Figure 4 shows the major categories of foreign exchange exposures on these two dimensions. Accounting impacts are classified in terms of their recognition in accounting reports.

Under current rules, transaction gains or losses are separately identified in earnings, translation adjustments bypass earnings and go directly to net worth, while operating impacts are mixed in with all other sources of variation in profits. Cash flow impacts are classified in terms of the nature of the cash flows in question, whether they are contractually fixed in some money or whether they depend on competitive interactions. The fictitious category refers to those accounting adjustments that have no cash flow counterpart.

The category that differs most under global, as opposed to multidomestic, competition is the operating/noncontractual cell that reflects the impact of exchange rate fluctuations on operating profits via adjustments in revenues and costs that have not been contracted for.

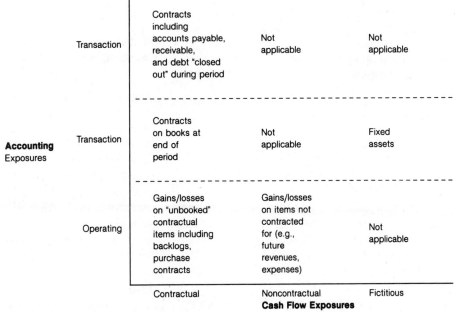

		Contractual	Noncontractual	Fictitious
	Transaction	Contracts including accounts payable, receivable, and debt "closed out" during period	Not applicable	Not applicable
Accounting Exposures	Transaction	Contracts on books at end of period	Not applicable	Fixed assets
	Operating	Gains/losses on "unbooked" contractual items including backlogs, purchase contracts	Gains/losses on items not contracted for (e.g., future revenues, expenses)	Not applicable
		Contractual	Noncontractual **Cash Flow Exposures**	Fictitious

Figure 4 Types of Foreign Exchange Exposures

This is what we refer to as operating exposure, consisting of both a conversion and a competitive effect. The conversion component is readily identifiable. However, the competitive component is much more difficult to isolate because it is mixed in with a host of other variables, both macroeconomic and microeconomic, that affect local operating profits. As a result, few firms have fully incorporated it into their foreign exchange management function, and they often do not take into account the impacts of these exposures on current and projected operating profits in making strategic and tactical choices. I will review each of these points in turn.

Measuring Operating Exposures While most firms are aware of their operating exposures, it appears that few have defined or estimated them very carefully or developed explicit procedures for dealing with them. In reviewing the 1982 and 1983 annual reports of thirty firms, Trusheim (1984) found that while twenty-two mentioned the impact of the strong dollar, sixteen of them focused on the reduced dollar value of foreign revenues and only six discussed impacts of the strong dollar on their margins or overall competitive position.

While these external reports do not provide a full picture of internal procedures, they do show that the treatment of operating exposure by U.S. firms is less than complete. This is corroborated by more detailed reviews of the practices of a few firms. In in-depth interviews with three firms, Boiardi (1984) found that all three had a rough notion of their operating exposures, but none had acted on this estimate. In discussions with six firms, we have found the same thing, a growing awareness of the general concept, but little or no progress in addressing it.[45] One reason for this is the relative difficulty of assessing operating exposures. The second is the difficulty of managing them appropriately in the typical firm.

Managing Operating Exposures Firms have both business and financial options for reducing exchange rate exposures. Three kinds of business options are available to the firm in managing operating exposure. These are:

1. configure individual businesses to have the flexibility to increase production and sourcing in countries that become low cost due to swings in exchange rates,
2. configure individual businesses to reduce operating exposure by matching costs and revenues, and
3. select a portfolio of business with offsetting exposures.

The first option, that of configuring operations to increase flexibility, can actually increase a firm's expected operating profits as well as reduce their variability. The other two can at best reduce variability with no reduction in expected operating profits and, often, will result in some reduction in expected operating profits. The reason for this in the case of configuring individual businesses to match the currency habitats or revenues and costs is that such matching typically will require some departures from the optimum configuration in terms of scale and locational advantages. In the case of selecting a portfolio of businesses with offsetting exposures, this is likely to be the case because of the increased administrative costs and reduced efficiency associated with managing diverse businesses without other synergistic linkages.

The firm also has several financial options available to it. These include long-dated forwards, swaps, or borrowing in foreign currencies as well as long-dated currency options. None of these is exact, because they are keyed to nominal rather than real exchange rates, but they have the advantage that when competitively priced they reduce the variability of operating profits with little or no reduction in the anticipated level of such profits.[46]

Given the magnitude of operating exposures and the fact that they do not necessarily have even the same sign as contractual exposures, firms that hedge only their contractual exposures may actually increase their total exposures.[47] If a firm does not understand its operating exposure, its best policy is not to hedge at all.

Strategic and Tactical Responses to Exchange Rate Volatility

Volatile exchange rates create havoc for operations in a globally competitive industry. Shifts in rates require decisions regarding pricing, output, and sourcing, and these decisions typically will involve a balancing act between vaguely understood limits to sustainable price differentials across countries and the impact of local currency price shifts on demand and hence profits. Further, given the emergence of global oligopolies in many industries, pricing decisions must reflect anticipations of competitor actions or reactions. Estimating these reactions is likely to be complicated by the fact that competitors differ significantly in the currency composition of their costs and, perhaps more importantly, in the currency eyeglasses they wear. Currency fluctuations also introduce noise into measures of current performance, reducing the firm's ability to monitor its evolving competitive position and distorting its results-based managerial incentives. If these distortions are significant, and if many key decisions are made on a decentralized basis, the firm's choices are likely to be distorted as well. Finally, the impact of currency fluctuations on current operations is likely to distort the perceived long-term profitability of strategic choices.

The finance function plays a key role in terms of the perspective it provides on these choices, though none involve finance in the classic sense of raising funds. This financial perspective on operating choices, and the rules of thumb that follow from it, are part of a firm's culture. The perspective is the result of corporate experience and is unlikely to change rapidly. Thus, given the drastic change in the competitive and financial environment over the last ten years, I expect that this perspective is only now catching up with the new reality.

This is clearly borne out in the relatively slow evolution of corporate management of exchange risk, and I expect it to have major operational implications as well.

Currency Illusions and Pricing/Output Choices   A perennial pricing error that results from a currency illusion is the practice of setting foreign currency prices by multiplying the domestic price by the spot rate and, perhaps, adding an "uplift" for the extra costs of doing business overseas. The illusion is that the foreign currency proceeds can be converted into dollars at the spot rate, whereas in fact the prices quoted are for future payment and, hence, can be converted only at the forward rate (or expected future spot rate) corresponding to the time of cash payment.[48] Foreign currency receivables are often "booked" at spot rather than forward rates, with the result that operating profits are initially overstated in the case of strong currencies or understated in the case of weak and subsequently exposed to potentially large transaction gains or losses that on average will offset the initial error. Depending on when and at what rate these receivables are "handed off" to treasury, the true profitability of one or both functions will be misstated and management decisions are likely to be distorted.[49] If operating managers are not held responsible for the ultimate exchange gains or losses, their contribution will be systematically misstated; if they are held responsible, their contribution is likely to be buried in the noise created by exchange rate movements.

This illusion can be readily overcome by valuing all contracts at forward rates, but this requires an explicit recognition that generally accepted accounting rules are misleading and therefore require a shift in procedures.[50] While many firms have changed procedures to do this, what is surprising is how many have not. A survey of practices conducted by Czechowicz, Choi, and Bavishi (1982), for example, found that 55 percent of all firms included transac-

tion gains and losses in measures of managers' performance.[51] This illusion affects all international transactions and is not unique to global competition. It does, however, illustrate how traditional perspectives can interfere with appropriate choices in a changing environment.

With global competition, the problem is compounded by the fact that pricing not only must take into account the relative value of future claims in various currencies, but also the possibly asymmetric impact of exchange rate shifts on the firm's costs and prices relative to competitors. If prices in local currencies are left unchanged subsequent to an exchange rate shift, prices will differ across countries, inviting transshipment and entry by competitors in "high-priced" markets. On the other hand, if prices in the parent currency are maintained by "passing through" the exchange rate variations to local customers, sales volumes may react abruptly.

Even with full information and a "rational" economic perspective, therefore, pricing adjustments to exchange rates will be extremely complex. In practice, though, I expect that choices will be strongly influenced by the firm's view of the world. The easiest response to a change with complex implications is to do nothing. Doing nothing, however, can be defined in many different ways. In the case of pricing responses to exchange rate changes, it could be either (1) maintaining parent currency (dollar) prices, or (2) maintaining local prices. Active responses, in turn, could involve either (3) maintaining market share, or (4) adjusting both price and volume to maximize long-term profit.

Under multidomestic competition, with its largely autonomous national operating units, the likely choice is for the firm to "do nothing" by maintaining local prices, although, as we see later in our discussion of control systems, the parent currency may play a role as well. With global competition though, firms' activities are more integrated or coordinated across national boundaries and, therefore, they are more likely to "do nothing" in terms of maintaining parent currency prices. This may be a reasonable approximation to the correct response for a firm that dominates world markets, but it will not be for a member of a global oligopoly with players based in several different countries and with different currency perspectives and exposures.

The heavy construction equipment industry, once dominated by a handful of U.S. firms but now including major Japanese and European players in global markets, is an excellent case in point. Sharp (1984) found that distributor prices of construction equipment sold in the United Kingdom by U.S. firms tended to remain stable in dollars through 1980, when they shifted abruptly in response to Japanese inroads, and subsequently appear to be sensitive to the dollar-yen relationship as well. His finding of different pricing responses to exchange rate changes for virtually identical products produced and sold in the United Kingdom by a U.S.- and a U.K.-based firm support the view that at least some of this effect can be traced to organizational factors rather than to technical demand or cost considerations.

An ironic example of this type of pricing is the reported satisfaction of many U.S. firms with their ability to hold their own and maintain dollar prices during the 1978–79 period, when in fact they should have been able to raise dollar prices given the general weakness of the dollar in that period. U.S. firms are not alone in this type of illusion. The Swedish auto firms, especially Volvo, nearly priced themselves out of U.S. markets in this same period. They apparently attempted to pass through to U.S. customers most of the appreciation of the krona, while they should have maintained relatively stable dollar prices.[52]

The picture is not all bleak, of course, Sharp's findings do suggest an awakening of U.S. firms to the realities of global pricing and Boiardi (1984) found that pricing decisions were consistent with market structures, although two of the three firms he studied faced multidomestic product market competition.

Interaffiliate Pricing   A large proportion of the production of firms engaged in global competition move through interaffiliate sales on their way to the final customer. Apart from their impact on taxes and tariffs, the transfer prices on these sales have no economic impact except through their effect on the behavior of managers. These behavioral impacts, though, are often substantial and represent a key determinant of the firm's pricing of final sales.

Firms with strong, centralized (or coordinated) production units often apply transfer pricing rules based on standard costs measured in the parent currency, imposing the full impact of currency swings on the downstream stages of the value-added chain. The shift to global competition strengthens this effect because the pursuit of global scale and scope economies requires greater integration and coordination of production.

There are several different ways to address this problem. The first is to create a mechanism whereby transfer prices are negotiated to approximate arm's-length prices, in essence forcing production and marketing to share the exchange rate impact. This clearly is most feasible where there are alternative sources of supply. The second is to leave the transfer prices as they are, but adjust the performance standards (margin or ROI) of the marketing units to reflect the baseline impact of the exchange rate shifts. This requires substantial prior analysis of exchange rate impacts and appropriate operating responses at the corporate and business unit levels. A third is to substitute narrower performance standards, for example, market share or some measure of production efficiency, for profits at one or more stages in the value-added chain. This approach, however, presupposes that the firm can specify such standards appropriately, which may be as complex as solving the cross-unit profit conflicts. This clearly is one of the most challenging issues arising in global competition and is likely to push key operating responsibilities up to higher levels within the firm.

Measurement of Current Performance Currency fluctuations clearly have an impact on measured performance, and these measures presumably feed back to a host of operating choices. While there are many technical issues in measuring performance in the face of fluctuating exchange rates, the debate among practitioners appears to be centered on whether performance should be measured in local currency or parent currency terms. Under conditions of global competition, neither is appropriate.

An ideal performance measurement system should hold managers responsible for those aspects of performance over which they have substantial control, but should limit responsibility for performance shifts due to factors largely beyond their control. Of course, this ideal is seldom met because, for example, fluctuations in aggregate demand are inextricably linked with managerial success in producing and selling a product. The emphasis of many firms on market share, however, is an attempt to separate these two effects. In the case of currency fluctuations, some aspects of the problem are easily separable while others are not. Gains or losses on accounts receivable resulting from currency surprises, for example, are outside the control of operating managers and can be split out by transferring these claims to treasury at forward rates. If this is done, treasury's contribution through "selective hedging," actually speculation in the form of market timing, is fairly measured as well.

In contrast, with the competitive component of operating exposures, such a clear separation is not possible because managers can and should react to exchange rate shifts by altering prices, output, and sourcing. However, so long as there is some degree of global competition it should be recognized that profits in either local or parent currency should fluctuate in line with real exchange rates. A failure to incorporate this in the control system is likely to lead managers to "leave money on the table" when they are favored by exchange rates, and to sacrifice too much market share by attempting to hold constant dollar margins when exchange rates work against them.

What is required is a budgetary standard that adjusts for exchange rate impacts. The process of developing such a budget should involve a joint exploration by corporate and business unit managers of the impacts of and appropriate responses to exchange rate movements, thus providing a dress rehearsal of future tactics as well as a standard against which future performance can be judged.[53]

The controller of a U.S. firm's U.K. plant, in an interview with Sharp, stated that he would have no trouble in meeting his firm's goal of "cutting real *dollar* costs by x percent" because in the period since the program was announced the pound had already fallen by a large fraction of that amount relative to the dollar. His response would have been quite different if the corporation had demanded an x percent cut relative to costs *normalized* for exchange rate circumstances.

Assessment of Strategic Options Just as currency fluctuations affect current performance, they also alter the attractiveness of the firm's strategic options. The long-run profitability of a given business unit will depend on its evolving competitive advantage, but in the short run its advantage can be swamped by exchange rate impacts. In some cases, the firm will be able to enhance its average profitability over time by building a degree of flexibility that allows it to shift sourcing and value-added activities as exchange rates move.[54] In general, though, it will have to look past the current circumstances to assess its long-run competitiveness. This requires a multistage procedure:

1. assess future expected cash flows conditional on purchasing power parity,[55] concentrating on

microcompetitive factors such as the firm's likely experience gains relative to anticipated wage increases,

2. assess how these (conditional expected) cash flows would differ under alternative exchange rate scenarios, and

3. estimate expected cash flows across scenarios given their relative likelihood.

In general, it should choose the alternative with the highest (net present value of) expected cash flows, without regard for exposure to exchange rate movements, because as noted earlier these exposures can be offset by financial hedges that have little or no cost in present value terms.

While there have been several recent surveys of capital budgeting practice,[56] none have focused on this issue, so it is not clear whether academic observers are lagging behind practice or whether practice is lagging behind changes in the competitive environment. I suspect some of both.

CONCLUSIONS: IMPLICATIONS FOR MANAGERS AND FUTURE RESEARCH

The emergence of global competition, coupled with both increased integration of financial markets and continued exchange rate volatility represents a major threat and challenge to U.S. firms that have been accustomed to world market leadership under multidomestic competition.

I have argued that the finance function plays a critical role in meeting the challenge of global competition, both because of the demands globalization places on the finance function per se and its requirement for a much more sophisticated financial perspective on strategic and tactical choices. Because a firm's financial eyeglasses are part of its culture, these changes in outlook lag changes in the competitive environment. However, it does appear that many firms are rapidly moving down the "financial learning curve" and changing their standard operating procedures to accommodate global competition.

Within the traditional realm of finance—the treasury functions of raising funds externally and maneuvering them efficiently within the corporation—firms will find that, in order to compete globally, they must fully exploit the benefits of multinational financial scope to match their competitors' costs of capital and effective rates of taxation. The structure of external financing will have to become more global, shifting from primarily home currency borrowing at the parent level and local currency borrowing on the part of foreign subsidiaries to a more complex pattern recognizing the interaction between minimizing taxes, exploiting financial incentives and distortions in financial markets, and offsetting exchange rate exposures.

Even greater changes will be required in areas where finance interacts more closely with operations. One such area is in the management of foreign exchange exposures. Financial managers, with their knowledge of the dynamics of foreign exchange, must assist operating managers in configuring operations to cope with exchange rate volatility and responding to shifts as they occur. They also should provide internal hedging facilities (or contingent performance standards) to insulate operating managers from the inevitable exposures resulting from strategic bets to the fullest extent consistent with maintaining incentives for proper operating responses. At the same time, they must expand the scope of corporate exchange risk management to include operating exposures.

Another such area is the measurement of business unit performance. Not only must each unit's performance be measured relative to a standard that takes into account key changes in the macroeconomic environment, including but not limited to shifts in exchange rates, but also adjust for tradeoffs that improve corporate profits at the expense of one or more units.

Firms will have to redefine business units along the dimensions where greatest coordination is required. However, because no structure can simultaneously capture geographic, product, and stage of value-added leverage points, they will also have to create more effective processes for mediating conflicts among units. This will, among other things, involve the substitution of relatively narrow measures of business performance, such as market shares and unit costs, for the bottom-line measures of financial profitability favored by most U.S. firms.

Regarding future research, we need to learn much more about how firms have reacted to the changed competitive and financial conditions and, especially, how these reactions have been colored by financial perspectives developed under other circumstances. Most normative statements regarding financial management assume that these perspectives play a critical role, but there is little sound evidence that they do.

Most recent academic research in finance has focused on the interplay between firms and capital markets. This research has provided a much better understanding on how investors value securities and hence how managers should judge whether their decisions add value. This valuation-based research must be extended in the international dimension to capture potential cost of capital differences due to differing institutional arrangements. However, most corporate decision makers operate in "internal capital markets" where there can be no direct capital market feedback. While research in the control area does focus on the organizational considerations that come into play in these internal systems, it often proceeds without a rigorous basis for judging value creation. Corporate finance should cover both aspects, linking capital market-based valuation theory with an understanding of the types of incentive and control mechanisms necessary so that managers will make appropriate decisions. How corporations cope with exchange rate volatility is a promising area for such boundary-crossing research. I hope that this discussion of some of the issues involved will be a useful starting point.

NOTES

1. For an overview of recent evidence on financial market integration, see Kohlhagen (1983).
2. For recent studies of border controls and their effects on financial markets, see Dooley and Isard (1980) and Otani and Tiwari (1981).
3. The deregulation of financial institutions first took the form of an escape from national regulations by banks operating "offshore" as described by Dufey and Giddy (1981), Grubel (1977), Kindleberger (1974), Tschoegl (1981), and others. Subsequently, partly in response to this offshore competition and partly to shifts in domestic considerations, it has taken the form of reduced regulation of financial intermediation within individual national markets.
4. For a review of recent financial innovations, see Dufey and Giddy (1981) and Antl (1984).
5. For a review of exchange restrictions, see International Monetary Fund (1985). Rosenberg (1983) discusses the (in)effectiveness of these controls given the mechanisms firms can use to circumvent them.
6. For overviews of the benefits to a firm of spanning national financial markets, see Robbins and Stobaugh (1973) and Lessard (1979a).
7. There is an extensive literature on interest rate repression in developing economies (for example, McKinnon 1973), but less in the context of industrialized countries.
8. These include the ability to make use of tax-exempt bond issues, "80/20" offshore financing in the United States and similar measures in most other industrialized countries.
9. See Guisinger et al. (1985).
10. This has been given as one explanation of BHP's (Australia) recent acquisition of a U.S. exploration company.
11. For recent views of the determinants of exchange rates, see Dornbusch (1983), Frenkel and Mussa (1980), and Stockman (1980).
12. This tendency, known as purchasing power parity, was first outlined by Cassel (1923). For a recent review of its various meanings, see Shapiro (1983). For evidence on how well it holds, see Roll (1979), Frenkel (1981), and Adler and Lehman (1983).
13. For a discussion of the strategic implications of purchasing power parity in the long run, see Kiechel (1981).
14. Also Kogut (1983).
15. Myers (1984) and Barnea, Haugen, and Senbet (1981) discuss the impact of these agency effects on financing choices.

16. Here we refer to the warranted (present discounted) value of the firm's shares, the most complete financial measure of a firm's performance.

17. This point was made as early as 1960 by Hymer; see Kindleberger (1985). It was further developed in Kindleberger (1969) and remains one of the central tenets of the theory of the multinational firm.

18. Export/import—predominately domestic value added in home country with some international sales and/or sourcing. Multidomestic—substantial value added in each country, little cross-border integration or coordination of primary value activities. Global—substantial cross-border integration and coordination of primary value activities.

19. This discussion draws on Jun (1985).

20. This theme is developed by Hayes and Abernathy (1980) and echoed by Hout, Porter, and Rudden (1982). Donaldson (1972) provides an earlier indictment of DCF techniques, but also indicates where the problems lie and suggests ways to overcome them.

21. Surveys by Schall, Sundem, and Geijsbeek (1978), Wicks (1980), and Oblak and Helm (1980) show that managers continue to favor DCF-rate of return calculations in spite of the clear superiority of additive present value calculations when a project gives the firm access to significant future growth options. Hodder and Riggs (1985) discuss how methodological biases distort decisions. Hodder (1984) finds substantial differences between the capital budgeting practices of U.S. and Japanese firms. U.S. firms appear to be more "number driven," but devote much less attention to alternative scenarios and strategic options.

22. One line of development of DCF techniques that is capable of taking many of these effects into account is the valuation by components method. Under this approach, cash flows are segregated into equity equivalents, debt equivalents, and option equivalents and each component is valued using techniques most appropriate to its characteristics. Developed by Myers (1974), it has been extended to the international context by Lessard (1979b, 1981). Recent work on valuing option equivalents in investment decisions by Brennan and Schwartz (1985) and Myers and Majd (1983) is particularly promising in the treatment of future options to invest, abandon, or receive various forms of government support. Booth (1982) and Lessard and Paddock (1986) discuss the advantages of valuation by components relative to the more traditional single discount rate approach.

23. Vernon (1979) argues that, in contrast to the 1960s, a much larger proportion of new product launches will be on a global scale with correspondingly larger outlays.

24. An interesting case in point is the Danish firm Novo whose entry into U.S. equity markets is chronicled by Stonehill and Dullum (1982). Firms such as Schlumberger and Ciments LaFarge have also shifted their funding from small home markets to integrated world markets and, most recently, Jardine-Mathieson is shifting its "window" on world capital markets from Hong Kong to Bermuda. Adler (1974) and Agmon and Lessard (1977) discuss the basis for such capital-market-seeking behavior of firms.

25. Hitachi, for example, recently announced the creation of five offshore financing centers for its worldwide business.

26. For a discussion of the relationship between credit market and exchange controls and pricing distortions in financial markets, see Dooley and Isard (1980) and Otani and Tiwari (1981).

27. The source of profit shifting in this case comes from manipulating the transfer prices among affiliates. See Brean (1985) for an in-depth discussion of financial transfer prices.

28. The concept of internalization has been extended to many other aspects of multinational firms' activities. See in particular, Buckley and Casson (1976), Hennart (1982), and Rugman (1981).

29. Packaging can involve setting up tax-minimizing ownership chains as discussed by Rutenberg (1970) or choosing the nature of the parent's financial claim—equity, debt, or a claim on royalties—as discussed by Horst (1977) and Adler (1979).

30. Examples of the impact of interaffiliate financial transactions on a firm's taxes are presented by Horst (1977) and Brean (1985).

31. The industry studies in Guisinger et al. (1985) confirm that fiscal incentives are most important when several alternative sites provide access to the same (common or world) market.

32. This point is developed in Smith and Stulz (1985).

33. See for example, Barnea, Haugen, and Senbet (1985), Shapiro and Titman (1985), and Smith and Stulz (1985).

34. For an introduction to the impact of cross-border barriers on the valuation of securities, see Stulz (1985).

35. See Blitzer, Lessard, and Paddock (1984).

36. See Robbins and Stobaugh (1973) for an early discussion of this point.

37. In more technical terms, given a change in the real exchange rate, the demand and supply curves facing the firm will remain unchanged in the local currency (adjusted for inflation). Hence the optimal output and local currency price will remain unchanged, as will local currency profit. From a dollar perspective, of course, both curves will shift by the same amount, and the dollar profit will change in proportion to the change in the exchange rate.

38. An exception may be IBM, which, because of its very large scale and its responsiveness to national goals, is able to balance global scale production of specific products with a matching of value added and sales in most major markets.

39. Under these circumstances, a change in the real exchange rate will result in a *relative* shift of demand and sup-

ply curves, regardless of the reference currency of the firm. This implies that the optimal price and volume will change as well.

40. If volume does not change, the sensitivity of operating profits can be defined as:

$$\text{sensitivity (profits)} = \frac{\text{sensitivity (revenues)}}{} \times \frac{\text{revenues}}{\text{profits}} - \frac{\text{sensitivity}}{\text{(costs)}} \times \frac{\text{costs}}{\text{profits}}$$

See Levi (1982) and Flood and Lessard (1986) for a fuller explanation.

41. The term currency habitat is introduced by Flood and Lessard (1986). It has also been defined as the "currency of price (cost) determination." It may differ from the currency in which prices are quoted, invoices issued, or transactions settled. For example, the prices of various products are quoted in particular currencies (e.g., crude oil in dollars, certain chemicals in DM, etc.) and as shown by Grassman (1973), Magee (1974), and McKinnon (1979), certain currencies are favored in invoicing, but the prices of the products in these currencies are not necessarily independent of the exchange rate.

42. If nonrecurring costs (e.g., "up-front" capital investment including R&D and capital equipment) are a large proportion of total costs, then the marginal unit costs of production will be small and pricing will be dictated primarily by demand considerations.

43. This section draws substantially on Lessard and Lightstone (1986).

44. For a discussion of why a firm should concern itself with managing foreign exchange risk, see Logue and Oldfield (1977), Wihlborg (1980), Dufey and Srinivasulu (1984), Lessard and Shapiro (1984), and the references cited in note 33.

45. The same point is made by Waters (1979) and several corporate finance officers interviewed in "Coping with Volatile Currencies: Multinationals Go for Safety First," *Business Week,* January 30, 1984.

46. Lessard and Lightstone (1986) describe an alternative hedge that is keyed to real exchange rates and, hence, is more appropriate for operating exposures.

47. This is especially likely for firms facing global competition that hedge their translation as well as transaction exposures, because under FAS 52 a foreign plant is often classified as a foreign asset, without regard to whether the prices of its inputs and outputs are determined locally, the prices of its inputs are determined locally but its outputs are priced internationally, or vice versa. While this contradiction can be resolved to some extent by clever choices of functional currencies, it is unlikely that any translation scheme will capture the exposure of a firm's future operating profits that is so important in the context of global competition.

48. For a recent example, see Hintz-Kessel-Kohl, a Harvard Business School case (#9-284-019) prepared by Professor Thomas Piper.

49. See Lessard and Lorange (1977) and Lessard and Sharp (1984) for further discussion of this point.

50. Strictly speaking, valuing contracts at forward rates only makes them comparable to contracts for future payment in the home currency. Both should still be discounted to reflect the time value of money measured in that currency.

51. The question asked does not quite address the issue I raised, because transaction gains/losses include anticipated gains/losses and surprises. I would contend, however, that neither component should be included in a manager's evaluation. See Lessard and Sharp (1984) for further discussion.

52. The reason why the dollar/krona relationship should have had little or no impact on dollar prices of Saabs or Volvos was that transshipment was limited and demand, presumably, relatively price elastic. Further, the effect of the exchange rate on short-run variable costs measured in dollars was quite small given that under Sweden's labor policies, wages are a fixed cost in the short run, and most other inputs are internationally sourced.

53. Lessard and Sharp (1984) discuss alternative ways that this recognition of exchange rate effects can be incorporated in the control system.

54. This point is discussed by Kogut (1983, 1985) and Baldwin (chap. 6 of this book [i.e., Competition in Global Industries—eds.]).

55. As might be expected, there is no unambiguous measure of purchasing power parity. An instructive attempt to estimate parity rates, though, is provided by Williamson (1983). A further issue that has not been resolved in the literature is whether real exchange rates tend to return to parity or to move randomly. The results of Adler and Lehman (1983) and Roll (1979) support the latter view, but the macroeconomic models of Dornbusch (1983) and others suggest that there must be some type of adjustment over time.

56. See note 21.

REFERENCES

Adler, M. "The Cost of Capital and Valuation of a Two-Country Firm." *Journal of Finance* 29 (1974): 119–137.

Adler, M. "U.S. Taxation of U.S. Multinational Corporations." In M. Sarnat and G. Szego, eds., *International Trade and Finance,* Vol. 2. Cambridge, Mass.: Ballinger, 1979.

Adler, M., and B. Dumas. "International Portfolio Choice and Corporate Finance: A Survey." *Journal of Finance* 38 (1983): 925–984.

Adler, M., and B. Lehman. "Deviations from Purchasing Power Parity in the Long Run." *Journal of Finance* 38 (1983): 1471–1487.

Agmon, T., and D. Lessard. "Financial Factors and the International Expansion of Small Country Firms." In Agmon and Kindleberger, eds., *Multinationals from Small Countries.* Cambridge, Mass.: MIT Press, 1977.

Antl, B. *Swap Financing Techniques.* London: Euromoney Publications, 1984.

Barnea, A., R. A. Haugen, and L. W. Senbet. "Market Imperfections, Agency Problems, and Capital Structure: A Review." *Financial Management* 10, no. 2 (Summer 1981): 7–22.

Barnea, A., R. A. Haugen, and L. W. Senbet. "Management of Corporate Risk." *Advances in Financial Planning and Forecasting,* Vol. 1. Greenwich, Conn.: JAI Press, 1985.

Blitzer, C., D. Lessard, and J. Paddock. "Risk-Bearing and the Choice of Contract Forms for Oil Exploration and Development." *The Energy Journal* 5 (1984): 1–28.

Boiardi, A. "Managing Foreign Subsidiaries in the Face of Fluctuating Exchange Rates." Master's thesis, MIT Sloan School of Management, 1984.

Booth, L. D. "Capital Budgeting Frameworks for the Multinational Corporations." *Journal of International Business Studies* 8, no. 2 (1982): 113–123.

Brean, D. J. S. "Financial Dimensions of Transfer Pricing." In Rugman and Eden, eds., *Multinationals and Transfer Pricing.* London and Sydney: Croom Helm, 1985.

Brennan, M. J., and E. S. Schwartz. "Evaluating Natural Resource Investments." *Journal of Business* 58, no. 2 (1985): 135–158.

Buckley, P., and M. Casson. *The Future of Multinational Enterprise.* London: Macmillan, 1976.

Carsberg, B. "FAS #52—Measuring the Performance of Foreign Operations." *Midland Corporate Finance Journal* 1, no. 2 (1983): 47–55.

Cassel, G. *Money and Foreign Exchange after 1914.* London: Macmillan, 1923.

Cornell, B., and A. C. Shapiro. "Managing Foreign Exchange Risk," *Midland Corporate Finance Journal* 1, no. 3 (Fall 1983).

Czechowicz, J., F. Choi, and V. Bavishi. *Assessing Foreign Subsidiary Performance: Systems and Practices of Leading Multinational Companies.* New York: Business International, 1982.

Donaldson, G. "Strategic Hurdle Rates for Capital Investment." *Harvard Business Review* 50 (March–April 1972): 50–55.

Dooley, M., and P. Isard. "Capital Controls, Political Risks and Deviations from Interest Rate Parity." *Journal of Political Economy* 88 (1980): 370–384.

Dornbusch, R. "Exchange Rate Economics: Where Do We Stand?" *Brookings Papers on Economic Activity* 1 (1980): 143–185.

Dornbusch, R. "Equilibrium and Disequilibrium Exchange Rates." *Zeitschrift für Wirtschafts und Sozialwissenschaften* 102 (1983): 573–599.

Dufey, G., and I. Giddy. *The International Money Market.* Englewood Cliffs, N.J.: Prentice-Hall, 1978.

Dufey, G., and I. Giddy. "Innovation in the International Financial Markets." *Journal of International Business Studies* 7, no. 2 (1981): 33–52.

Dufey, G., and S. L. Srinivasulu. "The Case for Corporate Management of Foreign Exchange Risk." *Financial Management* 12, no. 4 (1984).

Dukes, R. "Forecasting Exchange Gains (Losses) and Security Market Response to FASB 8," in Levich and Wihlborg, eds., *Exchange Risk and Exposure.* Lexington, Mass.: Heath Lexington, 1980.

Flood, E. "Global Competition and Exchange Rate Exposure." Research Paper #837, Graduate School of Business, Stanford University, September 1985.

Flood, E., and D. Lessard. "On the Measurement of Operating Exposure to Exchange Rates: A Conceptual Approach." *Financial Management* 15, no. 1 (Spring 1986): 25–36.

Frenkel, J. A. "The Collapse of Purchasing Power Parities During the 1970's." *European Economic Review* 16, no 1. (1981): 145–165.

Frenkel, J. A. "Flexible Exchange Rates, Prices and the Role of 'News': Lessons from the 1970's." *Journal of Political Economy,* no. 4 (August 1983): 665–705.

Frenkel, J. A., and M. Mussa. "The Efficiency of Foreign Exchange Markets and Measures of Turbulence." *American Economic Review* 70 (1980): 374–381.

Grassman, S. "A Fundamental Symmetry in International Payment Patterns." *Journal of International Economics,* no. 2 (May 1973): 105–116.

Grubel, H. "A Theory of International Banking." *Banca Nazionale del Lavoro Quarterly Review,* no. 123 (1977): 349–364.

Guisinger, S. E., et al. *Investment Incentives and Performance Requirements: Patterns of International Trade, Production, and Investment.* New York: Praeger, 1985.

Hayes, R., and W. Abernathy. "Managing Our Way to Economic Decline." *Harvard Business Review* 58, no. 4 (July–August 1980): 67–77.

Hennart, J.-F. *A Theory of Multinational Enterprise.* Ann Arbor: University of Michigan Press, 1982.

Hodder, J. E. "Evaluation of Manufacturing Investments: A Comparison of U.S. and Japanese Practices." Technical Report 84-8, Department of Industrial Engineering and Engineering Management, Stanford University, November 1984.

Hodder, J. E., and H. E. Riggs. "Pitfalls in Evaluating Risky Projects." *Harvard Business Review* 85, no. 1 (January–February 1985): 128–135.

Horst, T. "American Taxation of Multinational Firms."

American Economic Review 67 (1977): 376–389.

Hout, T., M. Porter, and E. Rudden. "How Global Companies Win Out." *Harvard Business Review* 60, no. 5 (September–October 1982): 98–108.

Hymer, S. *The International Operations of Multinational Firms.* Cambridge, Mass.: MIT Press, 1960.

Ijiri, Y. "Foreign Exchange Accounting and Translation." In R. J. Herring, ed., *Managing Foreign Exchange Risk.* New York: Cambridge University Press, 1983.

International Monetary Fund. *Annual Report on Exchange Arrangements and Exchange Restrictions,* 1985.

Jun, Y. W. "The Internationalization of the Firm: The Case of the Korean Consumer Electronics Industry," unpublished Ph.D. diss. Cambridge, Mass.: MIT Sloan School of Management.

Kiechel, W., III. "Playing the Global Game." *Fortune* 104 (November 16, 1981): 111–126.

Kindleberger, C. P. *American Business Abroad.* New Haven, Conn.: Yale University Press, 1969.

Kindleberger, C. P. *The Formation of Financial Centers: A Study in Comparative Economic History.* Princeton Studies in International Finance, no. 36, 1974.

Kindleberger, C. P. "Plus Ça Change—A Look at the New Literature." In Kindleberger, ed., *Multinational Excursions.* Cambridge, Mass.: MIT Press, 1985.

Kogut, B. "Foreign Direct Investment as a Sequential Process." In Kindleberger and Audretsch, eds., *The Multinational Corporation in the 1980's.* Cambridge, Mass.: MIT Press, 1983.

Kogut, B. "Designing Global Strategies: Profiting from Operating Flexibility." *Sloan Management Review* (Fall 1985): 27–38.

Kohlhagen, S. "Overlapping National Investment Portfolios: Evidence and Implications of International Integration of Secondary Markets for Financial Assets." In R. Hawkins, R. Levich, and C. Wihlborg, eds., *Research in International Business and Finance.* Greenwich, Conn.: JAI Press, 1983.

Lessard, D. "Transfer Prices, Taxes and Financial Markets: Implications of Internal Financial Transfers within the Multinational Firms." In R. B. Hawkins, ed., *Economic Issues of Multinational Firms.* Greenwich, Conn.: JAI Press, 1979a.

Lessard, D. "Evaluating Foreign Projects: An Adjusted Present Value Approach." In D. R. Lessard, ed., *International Financial Management.* New York: Warren, Gorham, and Lamont, 1979b.

Lessard, D. "Evaluating International Projects: An Adjusted Present Value Approach." In R. Krum and F. Derkindiren, eds., *Capital Budgeting under Conditions of Uncertainty.* Hingham, Mass.: Martinus Nijhoff, 1981.

Lessard, D., and J. Lightstone. "Volatile Exchange Rates Can Put Operations at Risk." *Harvard Business Review* (July–August 1986): 107–114.

Lessard, D., and P. Lorange. "Currency Changes and Management Control: Resolving the Centralization/Decentralization Dilemma." *Accounting Review* 52, no. 3 (1977): 628–637.

Lessard, D., and J. Paddock. "Evaluating International Projects: Weighted-Coverage Cost of Capital versus Valuation by Components." *Journal of International Business Studies,* 1986 forthcoming.

Lessard, D., and A. Shapiro. "Guidelines for Global Financing Choices." *Midland Corporate Finance Journal* 1, no. 4 (1984): 68–80.

Lessard, D., and D. Sharp. "Measuring the Performance of Operations Subject to Fluctuating Exchange Rate." *Midland Corporate Journal* 2, no. 3 (1984): 18–30.

Levi, M. *International Finance.* New York: McGraw-Hill, 1982.

Logue, D., and G. Oldfield. "Managing Foreign Assets When Foreign Exchange Markets Are Efficient." *Financial Management* 7, no. 2 (1977): 16–22.

Magee, S. "U.S. Import Prices in the Currency Contract Period." *Brookings Papers on Economic Activity,* no. 1 (1974): 303–323.

Magee, S., and R. Rao. "Vehicle and Nonvehicle Currencies in Foreign Trade." *American Economic Review* 70 (1980): 368–373.

Mason, S., and R. C. Merton. "The Role of Contingent Claims Analysis in Corporate Finance." In Altman and Subrahmanyan, eds., *Advances in Corporate Finance.* Homewood, Ill.: Dow Jones-Irwin, 1985.

McKinnon, R. *Money and Capital in Economic Development.* Washington, D.C.: The Brookings Institution, 1973.

McKinnon, R. *Money in International Exchange: The Convertible Currency System.* New York: Oxford University Press, 1979.

Myers, S. "Interactions of Corporate Finance and Investment Decisions." *Journal of Finance* 29 (1974): 1–25.

Myers, S. "The Capital Structure Puzzle." *Journal of Finance* 39 (1984): 575–592.

Myers, S., and S. Majd. "Calculating Abandonment Value Rising Option Pricing Theory," MIT Sloan School of Management, Working Paper #1462–83, August 1983.

Oblak, D. J., and R. J. Helm, Jr. "Survey and Analysis of Capital Budgeting Methods Used by Multinationals." *Financial Management* 9, no. 2 (Winter 1980): 37–40.

Otani, I., and S. Tiwari. "Capital Controls and Interest Rate Parity: The Japanese Experience 1978–1980." *Staff Papers* 28 (1981): 798–815.

Robbins, S., and R. Stobaugh. *Money in the Multinational Enterprise.* New York: Basic Books, 1973.

Roll, R. "Violations of Purchasing Power Parity and Their Implications for Efficient International Commodity Markets." In M. Sarnat and P. Szego, eds., *International*

Finance and Trade, Vol. 2. Cambridge, Mass.: Ballinger, 1979.

Rosenberg, M. "Foreign Exchange Controls: An International Comparison." In A. George and I. Giddy, eds., *International Finance Handbook,* Vol. 1. New York: John Wiley, 1983.

Rugman, A. *Inside the Multinationals: The Economics of Internal Markets.* New York: Columbia University Press, 1981.

Rutenberg, D. "Maneuvering Liquid Assets in a Multinational Company: Formulation and Deterministic Solution Procedures." *Management Science* 16, no. 10 (1970): B671–684.

Schall, L. D., G. L. Sundem, and W. R. Geijsbeek, Jr. "Survey and Analysis of Capital Budgeting Methods." *Journal of Finance* 33, no. 1 (1978): 281–287.

Schydlowsky, D. "Simulation Model of a Multinational Enterprise." In S. Robbins and R. Stobaugh, *Money in the Multinational Enterprise.* New York: Basic Books, 1973.

Shapiro, A. "What Does Purchasing Power Parity Mean?" *Journal of International Money & Finance* 2 (1983): 295–318.

Shapiro, A., and S. Titman. "An Integrated Approach to Corporate Risk Management." *Midland Corporate Finance Journal* 3, no. 2 (1985): 41–56.

Sharp, D. "Organization and Decision Making in U.S. Multinational Firms: Price Management Under Floating Exchange Rates." Diss., MIT Sloan School of Management, 1985.

Smith, C. W. Jr., and R. Stulz. "The Determinants of Firms Hedging Policies," *Journal of Financial and Quantitative Analyses* 20, no. 4 (December 1985): 391–405.

Sophonpanich, C. "Exchange Rates and Corporate Performance." Master's thesis, MIT Sloan School of Management, 1984.

Stockman, A. "A Theory of Exchange Rate Determination." *Journal of Political Economy* 88 (1980): 673–698.

Stonehill, A., and K. Dullum. *Internationalizing the Cost of Capital.* New York: John Wiley, 1982.

Stulz, R. "Pricing Capital Assets in an International Setting: An Introduction." *Journal of International Business Studies* 15, no. 3 (1985): 55–73.

Tobin, J. "A Proposal for International Monetary Reform." Cowles Foundation Discussion Paper 506, Yale University, New Haven, Conn., 1978.

Trusheim, M. "An Exploration of Foreign Exchange Operating Expense." Master's thesis, MIT Sloan School of Management, 1984.

Tschoegl, A. *The Regulation of Foreign Banks: Policy Formation in Countries Outside the United States.* NYU Monograph series in Finance and Economics (1981–82).

Vernon, R. "The Product Cycle Hypothesis in a New International Environment." *Oxford Bulletin of Economics & Statistics* 41, no. 4 (1979).

Vernon, R. *Sovereignty at Bay: The Multinational Spread of U.S. Enterprises.* New York: Basic Books, 1971.

Waters, S. "Exposure Management Is a Job for All Departments." *Euromoney* (December 1979): 79–82.

Wicks, M. E. *A Comparative Analysis of Foreign Investment Evaluations Practices of U.S.-based Multinational Companies.* New York: McKinsey and Co., 1980.

Wihlborg, C. "Economics of Exposure Management of Foreign Subsidiaries of MNCs." *Journal of International Business Studies* 6, no. 3 (1980): 9–18.

Williamson, J. *The Exchange Rate System.* Washington, D.C.: Institute for International Economics, 1983.

16

CAPITAL STRUCTURE AND COST-OF-CAPITAL FOR THE MULTINATIONAL FIRM

Marjorie Thines Stanley

INTRODUCTION

The objective of this paper is to review recent developments in models dealing with capital

Source: Journal of International Business Studies (Spring–Summer 1981), pp. 103–120. Copyright © 1981. Reprinted by permission.

structure and cost of capital as these have been extended to the multinational case. The models address a number of issues which bear upon the financing decisions of the multinational firm. The questions relating to capital structure include: Is there an optimal capital structure for the multinational firm? How does multinationality affect this question? Does subsidiary capital structure "matter"? The questions relating to cost of capital include: What is the effect, if any, of multinationality upon parent cost of equity? Is the multinational firm's cost of capital affected by its debt financing decisions? Does currency of denomination exert an influence of its own which is relevant to debt financing decisions? If so, what is the nature of this influence? Is it possible for the multinational firm to benefit from international differentials in nominal interest rates? Do firms attempt to do so? Underlying these specific issues is the basic theoretical and empirical question of the degree of segmentation or integration of international money and capital markets and a related question with regard to the efficiency of the foreign exchange market.

The models employed in research dealing with cost of capital and capital structure for the multinational firm are themselves a subject of controversy. Partially for this reason, the review of the literature has been organized on the basis of the models employed, in each case attempting to point out the specific problems addressed in individual studies, subsequent critiques of the studies, and the nature of the evolution of the theoretical and empirical research. The paper will be concerned not only with the contribution which the individual research studies may make to a resolution of the earlier enumerated questions related to the financial policy of the multinational firm, but will seek to comment also upon the realism and relevance of the models' theoretical assumptions and the practicability of empirical testing of the theoretical constructs.

The scope of the paper has been limited, perhaps somewhat arbitrarily, so as to exclude detailed examination of the issue of the separation/integration of the financing decision and the investment decision, and only tangential consideration will be given to the foreign investment decision itself. Reference to the comprehensive literature on foreign exchange market efficiency and to the extensive literature on international integration of financial markets which has a primarily macro thrust will be limited to conclusions drawn from selected studies which have direct relevance to issues of capital structure or cost of capital for the multinational firm. In short, the articles reviewed will be selected and evaluated primarily on the basis of their relevance to the financing decisions of the multinational firm, with occasional reference to closely related capital budgeting and international investment decisions.

Because the extension of domestic models to the multinational case has been done within or disputing the Modigliani-Miller framework and within the capital asset pricing model framework, the next section of the paper will examine models within or disputing the Modigliani-Miller framework [3, 34, 44, 45, 59, 66, 85, 98]. This will be followed by a section addressing research conducted within or disputing the capital asset pricing model framework [1, 6, 11, 14, 28, 32, 37, 40, 52, 57, 86, 87–91]. The paper will conclude with two sections summarizing the current state of knowledge—the first will emphasize current areas of conflict, data problems which hamper resolution of these conflicts, and areas for future research; the final summary will emphasize the financial policy prescribed or suggested for the firm by the current state of knowledge.

MODELS WITHIN OR DISPUTING THE MODIGLIANI-MILLER FRAMEWORK

Within the Modigliani-Miller framework, Krainer presented an extension analyzing the question of the capital structure and valuation of the multinational firm [44]. Abstracting from corporate income taxes and beginning with "a world where firms make physical investments and finance within a single capital market but portfolio investors are free to make investments in different national capital markets," Krainer explored the question of whether a firm can be in the same risk class in two different national capital markets. He concluded that, in a world where currencies are convertible into one another at varying rates and in varying degrees, the claimants to the uncertain earnings stream of foreign firms face currency risks that cause the risk/return relationship to differ as between a firm's foreign and domestic claimants, so "there is no reason to expect the level or structure of capitalization rates appropriate to (a firm's) securities to be the same in two different countries;" that is, arbitrage, though operative, will not completely eliminate a difference in capitalization rates associated with currency rate and repatriation risks. Krainer then argued that this result may enable a firm that invests and finances in several national capital markets to influence the cutoff rate at which it accepts new capital projects by altering its capital structure, given the condition that domestic portfolio investors are not "preferred borrowers" in foreign capital markets; that is, for the M-M results to hold for the multinational firm, portfolio investors must be able to issue personal debt in national capital markets open to the firm. Krainer concluded that financial planners for MNCs should study capital market conditions in "the larger national capital markets in order to take advantage of possible opportunities to reduce the average cost of capital" [44, p. 563].

Dropping the no-tax assumptions, Krainer concluded that the tax deductibility of interest payments and the associated "rebate" to the shareholders of the levered firm, when capitalized at a favorable foreign rate, provide an incentive for the multinational firm to issue debt up to its maximum debt limit [44, p. 564], imposed by either the firm itself or its creditors. Presumably, the self-imposed limit would be "prudential" in nature or, perhaps, be influenced by finance managers' perceptions of the effect of leverage upon expectations [54, pp. 40–42].

A critique of Krainer by Adler [3] raised several theoretical issues. Basically, these amounted to a criticism of the choice of the M-M model as opposed to a portfolio diversification approach and an emphasis upon default risk rather than foreign exchange risk as the relevant question to ask in extending the M-M model [3, pp. 850–851]. Adler reached this conclusion by assuming riskless and costless forward exchange transactions and uniform investor expectations with regard to security returns and exchange rate changes. Krainer found the first assumption unacceptable: "Where there is a real risk, it will not do . . . to ignore the cost of insuring against that risk" [45, p. 861]. In part, then, the issue between Krainer and Adler is one of choice of models and realism and relevance of assumptions. (Note that recent foreign exchange market research models have explicitly introduced transaction costs and diverse expectations on the part of market participants [25, 21].)

Krainer stressed [45, pp. 859, 861] that Adler's comment did not note that Krainer had mentioned degrees of currency convertibility, as well as changing exchange rates, as a reason for a possible breakdown of international arbitrage or for a redefining of risk classes [44, p. 555]. In later literature inconvertibility seems to have been relegated to the category of political risk and thus often excluded from financial models. Potential currency inconvertibility is nevertheless a factor likely to influence financial decisions of the firm and the security investor in ways relevant to the financial structure issue; it enters the literature at the financial management textbook level as a factor influencing planning [18, pp. 413–424]. Further empirical study of this issue is needed.

Another point mentioned but not pursued by Adler is that exchange risk affects expected returns on equities differently from the way it affects fixed-income bonds [3, p. 850]. This point, assumed away by Krainer [44, p. 556; 45, p. 862], relates to the economic effects of exchange rate risk. The distinction among translation, transactions, and economic effects of exchange risk has been receiving increased attention from financial managers since the advent of floating exchange rates and the adoption in the U.S. of Financial Accounting Standard No. 8 [95]. The economic effects of exchange rate fluctuations upon the corporation and its security holders are an area for future research.

Clearly, several issues raised or assumed away by Krainer's pioneering extension of the M-M model to the international case remain to be resolved.

Naumann-Etienne has dismissed "Krainer's findings that exchange rate and repatriation risk are sufficient to invalidate the Modigliani-Miller theorem in an otherwise perfect world capital market," because "the world-wide existence of corporate income taxes . . . achieves the same result" [61, p. 860]; however, the many reasons for international validity of the M-M theorem may be of practical importance to the financial policy of the multinational firm.

A critique of Krainer by Severn [81] raised questions relevant to Krainer's original empirical testing of his theoretical constructs. Krainer had attempted to test whether U.S.-based multinational firms had altered the magnitude of their foreign debt financing in response to changes in relative borrowing costs. Three tests were conducted: the results of these tests tended to support Krainer's hypothesis that multinational firms alter the country source of their debt financing in response to what Krainer perceived to be changes in relative borrowing costs. Severn's criticism was primarily centered on the influence of OFDI regulations on financing decisions during the 1965–1970 period; regressing the ratio of international bond issues of U.S. firms to domestic and international bond issues on the rates of European to U.S. interest rates, he obtained a positive, not negative, relationship over the 1968–1972 period. In response, Krainer took the ratio of foreign currency bond issues of U.S. firms (rather than the formerly employed total international bond issues of U.S. firms) to domestic offerings as it related to the ratio of European interest rates to U.S. Aa corporate bond yields and concluded that cost minimization was an important con-

sideration in the formation of financial policy of U.S.-based multinational firms [45].

It should be noted that if U.S. multinationals were indeed changing the source and currency mix of their financing in response to what Krainer perceived as changes in borrowing costs, the "fact" that they were doing so does not necessarily make such behavior normative. Apropos of this and of Severn's point with regard to the influence on financing decisions of the U.S. OFDI regulations, a study of U.S. firms that issued international and foreign bonds in the first half of 1968, following the imposition of compulsory regulations, indicated that 60 percent of the issuing firms found cost to be higher than U.S. borrowing would have been [96, p. 58]. Of those who found it to be lower, one noted it to be so, "providing foreign exchange risk is contained." With the benefit of hindsight we now know that, for those firms whose financing was denominated in the deutschmark or Swiss franc, relative nominal interest rates prevailing at the time of issue were an inadequate measure of ultimate cost of matured debt in dollar terms. A major data problem, then, for empirical studies relative to multinational cost of capital and financing behavior of the multinational firm is the inability to measure directly expectations with regard to foreign exchange rate changes for relevant currencies over the time periods involved in long-term financing, and the rarity of a spectrum of market conditions which might allow one to infer such expectations from interest rate differentials on differently denominated long-term issues [15, pp. 77–106; 92; 63, pp. 169–171].

Other weaknesses of Krainer's data certainly included such items as: (1) the use of an "average European" nominal interest rate (even if weighted, does it have economic content and significance?—it is easy to imagine funds flowing from the U.S. to a particular European country, and to the U.S. from another European country); (2) the use of a U.S. vs. Europe dichotomy in the debt categories employed (is lira-denominated debt equivalent to deutschemark-denominated debt?—data presented by Rugman reveal a correlation of Italian with West German long-term interest rates of .5903 for quarterly data, 1954–1973 [77, p. 40]); (3) the use of heterogeneous debt measures, for example, inclusive of trade credit (adjusted for intracompany debt?); (4) the inclusion of convertible debt with straight debt (perhaps necessitated by the fact that, at a certain time under OFDI, convertible debt was "about the only thing that could be sold" [96, p. 60]). In short, the use of such data leads to conclusions which fail to convince and satisfy.

An inevitable result of data problems is that researchers are likely to shun a topic. Stevens is one who did otherwise and attempted to develop and test a theoretical model, consistent with maximization of the market value of the firm, with the goal of explaining capital flows associated with the financing of foreign asset accumulations by international firms [98]. Relying on the M-M thesis, he stated that "it does not matter how the firm divides the financing of its foreign assets between capital flows from the United States and foreign sources" [98, p. 327],[1] but postulated a secondary goal for the firm in the form of minimization of risk of losses due to exchange rate fluctuations. Stevens' goal in developing the model was to examine the impact of voluntary and mandatory controls on foreign direct investment; his efforts received faint praise from Robbins and Stobaugh, who referred to his "imaginative use of the statistics that are available" and expressed their reservations with regard to the relevance of M-M for the international firm: "in the very real world of the multinational firm, the distribution of the subsidiaries' capital structure has a very real influence on the level of after-tax earnings" [66, p. 356].

Hirshleifer has also challenged the relevance of M-M to the international firm and has provided an analysis which underscores the importance of complete markets [34], as opposed to the market imperfections stressed by other writers. Thus, Hirshleifer noted that the M-M equation depends upon an assumption of complete markets, as well as the absence of taxes, bankruptcy, and transactions costs, so that individuals and firms together form a "closed system, with no losses to the outside" [34, p. 264]. With incomplete markets, he argues, the arbitrage opportunities necessary to equate the sum of the market value of the securities issues with the present certainty equivalent value of the income stream are not present, leaving open possibilities at the margin for profitable financing decisions [34, pp. 271–272]. Inasmuch as capital markets are not highly developed in many countries which host subsidiaries of MNCs, a major proportion of foreign debt financing is in the form of private placements or bank loans [93], and Hirshleifer's position is particularly relevant.

An examination of financing decisions and the cost of capital to be used in appraising the profitability of foreign investments was the goal of Shapiro in a recent paper [85]. He began by extending the weighted cost of capital concept to the multinational firm. While noting the M-M position that leverage is irrelevant in the absence of taxes, Shapiro assumed the marginal cost of capital to be constant and thus equal to the cost of new funds, minimized by choosing an appropriate capital structure and, following Adler [1, p. 120], assumed that suppliers of capital to the MNC would associate the risk of default with the MNC's consolidated worldwide debt ratio. In his conclusions, however, he noted that investor perceptions of the riskiness of MNCs are likely to be affected by the location as well as the percentage of foreign source earnings [85, p. 224]. Such a conclusion would appear to be consistent with the possibility that perceived risk of default may be affected by the location of sources as well as uses of funds, in addition to being affected by the ratio of total debt to assets.

Given his assumption to the contrary, Shapiro proceeded with the costing of various sources of funds and provided a formula for the incremental weighted cost of capital. This employs: (1) the parent's marginal cost of capital ("provided that the foreign investments undertaken do not change the overall riskiness of the MNC's operations"); (2) the cost of retained earnings abroad, using the cost of parent equity here unless tax and transfer costs are significant (which they may be [78, p. 671], but potential for misspecification of cost of subsidiary retained earnings also exists [62]); (3) the cost of depreciation-generated funds, equal to the firm's incremental average cost of capital, and (4) the after-tax dollar cost of borrowing locally, equal to "the sum of interest expense and the exchange gain or loss" [85, p. 214]. The incremental weighted cost of capital can then be calculated including a term for over- or underleveraging abroad which is associated with the opportunity cost of additional equity needed to restore the consolidated target debt ratio. If the foreign investment changes the parent risk characteristics, then the parent's cost of equity must be adjusted.

A major problem in making the formula operational is of course the determination of the after-tax dollar cost of borrowing locally, which, as noted, Shapiro defined as being equal to "the sum of interest expense and the exchange gain or loss" [85, p. 214]. Because the exchange gain or loss cannot be known in advance, expectations must be introduced into the cost of capital formulation. These expectations are not necessarily adequately observable in market-determined prices and/or rates. Thus, excluding such considerations as those associated with inflation-adjusted accounting and legally required indexing—for example, of bond principal and interest payments—the introduction of such expectations represents a fundamental change in the nature of the concept of cost of capital generally associated with single-currency financing.

When foreign-currency financing is employed, exchange rate expectations not only enter into the calculation of the cost of capital, but they do so in a much more complex way than in Shapiro's cost of capital formula, because the direction, amount, and timing of foreign exchange changes are all relevant. Shapiro employed the expected rate at the end of one year. This has the major advantage of being objectively observable in the form of forward market quotations for currencies for which uncontrolled forward markets exist. In fact, for a one-year period forward cover could be purchased and cost of capital could include this actual known cost, rather than the expected one as revealed by the forward rate. Unfortunately, forward markets for many currencies are nonexistent, thin, or subject to intervention or control, and the corporation is thrown back upon its own internally generated forecasts or those of an advisory service. Furthermore, a cost of capital formula which employs expectations of future exchange rates only one year forward is inadequate, while one that employs expectations of future exchange rates and their time path from date of debt issue to date of debt maturity is highly dependent upon forecasting and probability analysis. Unless international financial markets are perfectly integrated, and the expectations theory of the term structure, international interest rate parity, and purchasing power parity, or the international Fisher effect prevail, the extension to the multinational firm of the concept of weighted average cost of capital entails this difficulty of forecasting and quantifying expected changes in the exchange rate over the maturity of long-term debt.

On the other hand, to the extent that the forward premium and, thus, the short-term interest rate differential provide unbiased estimates of the expected rate of change of the exchange rate, the currency of denomination of short-term debt is a matter of indifference to borrowers. To the extent that the international Fisher effect holds, expected changes in exchange rates are reflected in international interest rate differentials, and changes in exchange rates offset differential inflation rates, thereby tending to keep relative purchasing power costs of debt denominated in different currencies constant. Then, the currency of denomination per se is a matter of indifference, and such factors as availability and tax effects become predominant in the debt financing decision; that is, the firm's cost of local-currency borrowing will be equivalent in an expected value sense to the cost of dollar borrowing, provided that the tax system does not discriminate in its treatment of interest costs on the basis of currency of denomination; such as, by virtue of its treatment of foreign exchange gain or loss. (Shapiro explicitly noted the importance of the latter factor [85, p. 214]).

The work of a number of researchers is relevant to the question of foreign exchange rate behavior and forecasting. First, about the international Fisher effect, Dufey and Giddy note that "by comparing the term structure of interest rates in two Eurocurrency markets, one may readily derive the term structure of exchange-rate expectations" [15, p. 79]. However, a number of studies show poor correlations between exchange rate changes and relative interest rates in the short run [26, 48]. Giddy found that the relationship held better over a three-year period than over three-month periods [26, p. 28]. He also observed that there were persistent small deviations from the international Fisher effect in long as well as short periods but noted that deviations might stem from errors in expectations rather than from interest rates incorrectly reflecting the expectations [26, p. 30].

In a test of forecasting models, Levich [48] found that Fisher external outperformed other forecasting models, judging "performance" on the basis of the mean squared error of forecasts for one-month, three-month, and six-month forecasting horizons for nine currencies in the period 1967–1975. For 27 country-horizon episodes, the Fisher external model had the lowest mean squared error on 13 episodes, followed closely by a lagged-spot model which was lowest on 12 episodes [48, pp. 134–137]. Forecast er-

rors tended to be smaller during pegged rate periods, except when there was a discrete change in the rate; forecast errors became larger and more volatile during the manager-float period, with some evidence that they are becoming smaller as the managed float continues [48, pp. 146–147]. As in Levich's study, most empirical tests of foreign exchange rate forecasting models have stressed relatively short forecasting horizons.

Solnik and Grall have suggested that market-implied expectations of exchange rate fluctuations are revealed by the currency structure of yield differentials in the new-issue Eurobond market [92, p. 225]. From end-of-quarter variables from October 1967 to March 1973, the data implied an average annual rate of devaluation of .7 percent for the dollar vis-à-vis the deutschemark [92, pp. 219, 227]; in the period March 1973 through December 1978, the actual average annual rate of devaluation was in excess of 5.5 percent [38]. Thus, the actual rate of change far exceeded the expected rate of change implied by Eurobond yield differentials.

Similarly, Quinn has cited the segmented secondary-market price behavior of deutschemark- and dollar-denominated Eurobond issues as indicators of expectations of devaluation, although emphasizing a relatively short time horizon [63, pp. 169–172]; expected dollar devaluation was imminent; large differentials in yield to maturity in dollar versus deutschemark bonds appeared: "In terms of the immediate exchange rate changes that transpired the market overreacted" [63, p. 171]. The practical import of this particular market overreaction for cost of capital expectations was probably small, however, because, given the market conditions studied, new-issue activity by foreign borrowers tended to dry up.

Note that these researchers focused upon the Euromarkets, not the domestic markets, as being likely to reflect, in interest differentials on like maturities, expected foreign exchange rate changes. The studies indicate that neither new-issue nor secondary-market

Eurobond yield and price behavior would have proved very useful as a means of correctly quantifying future exchange rates. The studies were, however, quite limited in scope. Other studies have noted that a risk factor may be embodied in the term structure of exchange rate expectations [15, p. 105]. This is an area for future research.

Miller and Whitman, working with macroeconomic models concerned with monetary and fiscal policy and the balance of payments, reported that no statistically significant proxy for expected spot exchange rates had been found [58, p. 276]. Financial managers report a short-term emphasis in foreign exchange risk management because "it is too difficult to predict beyond one year" [95]. Perhaps even a year is too long: "advisors who were offering year-long forecasts were doing so because clients were asking for it, rather than because such forecasts were worth giving" [7, p. 38].

Tests of foreign exchange forecasting models, even for short periods, show conflicting results. The managed-float "system" of foreign exchange has displayed increased volatility of exchange rates and concomitant decrease in the forecasting accuracy of the forward rate [49, pp. 244–245, 262–271]. Studies by Levich of the period 1967–1978 indicated that the model stating that the forward rate is an unbiased predictor of future exchange rate change could not be rejected, but that the prediction power of the relationship, measured by R^2, was very low [49, p. 271]. Other research by Levich on foreign exchange forecasting models, noted earlier, had indicated that the international Fisher effect regularly outperformed the forward rate, but the difference was "generally small enough to be explained by transaction costs or sampling errors" [48, p. 137].

Giddy and Dufey, testing models for predicting future spot rates, found that the forward rate was consistently the poorest predictor [27]; but Aliber concluded that the forward rate was a somewhat better predictor of the subsequent spot rate over the long run than either relative interest rates or purchasing power parity [42, p. 28]; and Kohlhagen concluded that "in the long run, even with floating and volatile markets, the forward rate has in general been an unbiased predictor of the future spot rate" [42, p. 29].

With regard to purchasing power parity, characterized as "the ideological antecedent of the current monetary approach" [35, p. 98], there is an extensive body of literature [42]. This literature indicates that purchasing power parity seems to hold in the long run [42, pp. 3, 43], and there is some evidence that it held quite well during the pegged rate period, 1959–1970 [42, p. 3]. However, there have been short-run deviations from purchasing power parity in both fixed and floating rate periods [42, pp. 3–4, 43], and a number of recent research studies indicate that it has not prevailed during the period of dirty floating exchange rates [42, p. 3].

One empirical study covering six countries during the period 1920–1924 and Canada during 1953–1957 indicates that freely floating foreign exchange markets respond almost if not immediately to changes in relative inflation rates, but it also notes that central bank intervention appears to reduce the impact of differential rates of inflation and to introduce inefficiencies into the foreign exchange markets [70]. Central bank foreign exchange market intervention is then a possible channel of influence upon equity and debt costs of the multinational firm.[2]

In summary, tests of foreign exchange forecasting models, even for short periods, show conflicting results, and the research suggests that a satisfactory proxy for long-term exchange rate expectations remains to be discovered. Given such conditions, the borrowing source decision appears to be an important one for the multinational firm, and the use of external local-currency long-term debt financing by foreign subsidiaries seemingly leads to possibilities for foreign exchange gain/loss in real terms for the multinational firm and to possible wealth transfers between bondholders and parent-company stockholders.

Despite the lack of a satisfactory proxy for long-term exchange rate expectations, which constitutes a major problem in making Shapiro's formula operational, he claimed that a simplified version of the formula—ignoring the possibility that the optimal D/E ratio may itself be dependent upon the relative costs of debt and equity—makes it possible to settle "one controversy in the literature," that between Zenoff and Zwick, who argued for the use of the company-wide marginal cost-of-capital as the discount factor to be used in multinational capital budgeting [102, pp. 186–190], and Stonehill and Stitzel, who argued for the use of the cost-of-capital appropriate to local firms operating in the same industry [100]. Shapiro characterized both as incorrect, because they "ignore the factor of multinationality" [85, p. 216]. Zenoff and Zwick defined the company-wide cost-of-capital as

a normative cost measure which reflects what overall financing costs would be if the firm obtained its debt and equity capital in the least expensive markets in ideal proportions. It is . . . used as the discount rate for capital budgeting decisions unless the proposed project under consideration is expected to change the business risk complexion of the firm as a whole. [102, pp. 188–189]

Zenoff and Zwick went on to consider the possibility that financing for particular foreign affiliates might be more expensive than the company-wide cost-of-capital; they would consider such cost premia as part of project outflows and would base debt policy on a consideration of cash flow characteristics in each local environment. Why? Because "the financial markets are segmented, precluding the selection of an optimal mix for the firm as a whole" [102, p. 189]. Thus, they took a partially negative view of the effects of market segmentation,

in contrast to the possible oligopsonistic advantages posited by Shapiro.

The Stonehill and Stitzel recommendation was based upon consideration of environmental factors, including concern over misallocation of resources in the host country, not upon a shareholder wealth maximization goal [100, pp. 92–95]. Eiteman and Stonehill, referring to the Stonehill and Stitzel recommendation, argued that optimal global financial structure would be different for all multinational firms because of their geographical diversity and that optimal structure from a cost-of-capital point of view can best be decided upon when comparisons can be made among firms in the same country, industry, and risk class [18, p. 225].

Turning to the question of appropriate subsidiary financial structure, Shapiro concluded that this should vary, so as to take advantage of opportunities to minimize the cost of capital [85, p. 216]; this assumed explicitly that capital markets are at least partially segmented and that the subsidiary's capital structure is relevant only insofar as it affects the consolidated worldwide debt ratio [85, pp. 217–218]. Shapiro then considered the related issues of company guarantees and nonconsolidation and decided that they are largely false issues [85, pp. 218–219, 224]. Shapiro also briefly mentioned taxes and regulatory factors, riskiness of foreign operations, political risk, inflation and exchange risk, diversification, investor perceptions, and joint ventures, concluding that a great deal of empirical testing remains to be done [85, p. 226]. The multiplicity of issues raised is in itself evidence of the complexities and data problems involved, and of some directions which further research might take in an effort to provide more definitive answers as a guide to policy and action.

INTERNATIONAL CAPITAL ASSET PRICING MODELS

The extension of the capital asset pricing model to the international case has been advanced by several researchers; here, we shall be concerned primarily with the implications of this work for multinational financing decisions and cost of capital, including both equity and debt capital, but with emphasis upon cost of equity.

Imperfections in international financial markets and their theoretical implications for risk premia and the cost of capital to firms were explored by Cohn and Pringle [11]. Their analysis emphasized that to the extent that economic activity in different economies is less than perfectly correlated, a lessening of restrictions on international portfolio diversification would affect risk-return relationships and security prices in two ways. The broadening of the market portfolio to include more (internationally traded) securities would reduce the nondiversifiable risk of each security and, given logarithmic or exponential utility functions, the slope of the capital market line—that is, the marginal rate of substitution of risk for return—would decline [11, pp. 60–62]. These two effects would act to reduce the risk-premium component of the cost of capital for firms [11, p. 63] and thereby to improve the efficiency of real capital allocation.

Solnik [88, 89] tested empirically an international market structure consistent with the International Asset Pricing Model and found that "national factors are quite important . . . violating the simple international market structure postulated in the single index market model" [88, p. 552]. After diversifying away the domestic factors in international portfolios, it was possible to show a strong relation between realized returns and international systematic risk. Solnik concluded that the true meaning of risk should be the international risk of an investment, not its national "beta," and that "the international capital market seems to be sufficiently integrated and efficient to induce an international pricing of risk for common stocks" [88, pp. 552–553].

Citing statistical problems in Solnik's procedures, Stehle provided an alternative approach, testing both a segmented markets hypothesis and an integrated markets hypothesis and concluding that neither could be rejected in favor of the other but finding some empirical support for the international model [97].

The question of the extent or degree of international market integration is an important one and other researchers have also addressed it [37, 57]. Noting that, if capital markets are perfect, the multinational firm does nothing for investors that they could not do for themselves, but that, if markets are not internationally integrated and the domestic market is efficient, multinational firms are performing a valuable function for investors which should be reflected in the pricing of equities of multinational firms, Hughes, Logue, and Sweeney studied 46 multinational and 50 domestic firms, characterized by them as roughly comparable in size and diversity of product lines,[3] for the period January 1970 through December 1973. They found that the "average returns for [the] multinational firms were higher than the average returns on [the] domestic firms," although "their betas were considerably lower," suggesting "some economies achieved by international diversification. . . . The distribution of measures of unsystematic risk [were] significantly lower for multinational firms than for domestic firms," supporting "the view that investors perceive multinational firms as providing substantial diversification benefits" [37, p. 633]. When the domestic market index was used, the performance of multinational firms was significantly superior to that of domestic firms, but when the world index was used the difference in performance was not statistically significant; the authors interpreted this as lending "some support albeit marginal to the view that assets are priced internationally rather than domestically and that international financial markets are indeed integrated" [37, p. 633]. Further, they concluded that multinational firms assist in this process and that "investors correctly perceive the diversification benefits of shares of multinational firms and that such firms do something for investors" [37, p. 636].

These conclusions are consistent with those of Agmon and Lessard whose empirical results supported their hypothesis that "U.S. investors recognize the international composition of the activities of U.S.-based corporations" when geographical diversification of these activities is represented by percentage of foreign sales [6, p. 1055]. Coupling this conclusion with the observation that capital flows forming part of direct investment by the multinational corporation may have lower cost or barriers than portfolio flows of individual investors, Agmon and Lessard suggested that the diversification motive, while difficult to isolate empirically, should be given more consideration than has been the case, because it appears to be relevant at the corporate as well as the investor level [6, pp. 1049, 1055].

Rugman has also emphasized diversification through foreign direct investment rather than portfolio investment. Because statistical tests show that international goods and factor markets are less correlated than international financial markets, Rugman suggested that the individual risk averter should purchase shares of the multinational firm as an indirect route to the risk reduction effects of international diversification [77, p. 33].

Lee and Sachdeva have provided a theoretical proof of this for home country investors under conditions of perfect competition and assumptions of equal risk-free rates in the home and host country, a nonstochastic foreign exchange rate, and a constant market price of risk [46, pp. 482–484, 490–491].

In a related empirical study, however, Jacquillat and Solnik found that investing in U.S. multinational firms could not be regarded as a good direct substitute for international portfolio diversification; foreign influence on stock prices was "unexpectedly limited" compared to the extent of the firm's foreign investment [39].

Hughes, Logue, and Sweeney suggested that a fruitful area for further research would be why the appearance and actuality of international market integration diverge. They posited that

the higher (risk-adjusted) returns available in countries other than the U.S. may be illusory because they may merely compensate for higher transaction costs. If netting these out were to result in similar risk/return tradeoffs among countries, markets would be shown to be highly integrated internationally [37, p. 636].

Hughes, Logue, and Sweeney repeatedly suggested that one source of advantage for the multinational firm may be higher debt capacity, reflected in stock-market–assigned measures of risk [37, pp. 628, 630] and owed to the diversifications of the MNC's activities among semi-independent economies [37, pp. 631, 633].[4]

Rugman has tested risk reduction by international diversification, using earnings variance as a proxy for risk, and foreign sales/total sales as a measure of international diversification, with earnings defined as net income/net worth. His empirical results showed that the foreign operations variable (foreign sales/total sales) was statistically significant and inversely related to variance of profits [77, pp. 11–13, 16–17]. Thus, Rugman's results would tend to support the suggestion of Hughes, Logue, and Sweeney with regard to investor perceptions of higher debt capacity for multinational firms. However, Rugman was specifically interested in examining the risk reduction attendant upon diversification via foreign direct investment and regarded the CAPM (used by Hughes, Logue, and Sweeney) as inappropriate for such tests because of the CAPM's perfect-markets assumptions that are inconsistent with direct investment motivated at the level of the firm by market imperfections [76; 77, p. 12].

Mehra, examining the influence of exchange risk on both the investment and financing decisions of multinational firms within the CAPM framework (and with its perfect-markets assumptions) concluded that alterations of the firm's capital structure do not change its value, even in the presence of exchange risk [57, p. 240]. Mehra employed a two-country model and assumed nonsegmented capital markets with individuals free to invest in the stock and bond markets of both countries. He showed that in this case a firm's beta consists of two terms, involving covariance of the security with the world market portfolio and with a position in foreign exchange [57, pp. 227, 235]. For country A firms, risk was shown to be understated (overstated) by the Sharpe-Lintner-Mossin CAPM depending, for example, upon whether their returns were likely to increase (decrease) due to devaluation (revaluation) by country A and whether country A was a surplus (deficit) country in terms of its net investment position [57, pp. 235–237].

There are capital budgeting implications here; that is, "if the effects of exchange risk are not considered explicitly in capital budgeting decisions, a systematic bias will develop" [57, p. 239]. The effect upon cost of capital of project covariance with the exchange rate will depend upon the net investment position of the country; in a country with a surplus investment position, a project whose returns decrease due to a devaluation of that country's currency will have a lower cost of capital, ceteris paribus; in a deficit country the project favored by a devaluation will have a lower cost of capital. Acceptance criteria for a project were shown to be the same for both countries' firms [57, pp. 238–239].

It should be emphasized, however, that all of these "normative implications" of Mehra's model for the "value-maximizing firm" ultimately depend upon the model's assumptions of nonsegmented markets in which individuals are free to borrow and invest.

A main issue, then, is whether the degree of market segmentation is sufficient to make segmented markets models the relevant ones for decision-makers, or whether the degree of market integration is sufficient to make integrated markets models the relevant ones. In the absence of governmental controls, growing individual investor sophistication and evolving financial institutions would be expected to contribute to greater market integration. How much is "enough" seems to underlie much of

the disagreement in the literature. The multinational firm itself may tend to reduce the practical managerial importance of this issue, achieving through its use of intracompany funds transfers and transfer pricing many of the effects of market integration [67, pp. 161–171; 61, pp. 863–864].

Apropos of the multinational firm's financing decisions, Jucker and deFaro have considered the problem of selecting a foreign borrowing source within a portfolio diversification framework, assuming a one-year time period, no use of forward markets, spot exchange always available when needed, and a pure financing problem, without consideration of other changes that a firm may face as a result of currency devaluations. Jucker and deFaro concluded that: "The principal difference between the (borrowing) source selection problem and the portfolio selection problem is the source of uncertainty" [40, p. 406]; namely, currency fluctuations. They therefore presented a model to aid in estimating characteristics of the random variables that express his uncertainty, making it possible to assess the necessary probability distributions. The exposition was developed assuming conditions prevailing under the Smithsonian Agreement, but the basic model is applicable to a managed floating rate system. The paper is useful by virtue of its emphasis upon the applicability of portfolio selection techniques to the borrowing source problem.

In an earlier related paper deFaro and Jucker dealt with both inflation and exchange risk, concluded that only exchange risk matters, and presented a decision criterion calling for comparison of interest differentials and expected foreign exchange rate changes over the duration of the loan [14, pp. 97–104], a conceptually obvious criterion with the previously noted operational problems associated with quantifying the direction, magnitude, and timing of expected foreign exchange rate changes.

Folks, noting [23, p. 246] that he was building upon work of Jucker and deFaro [40], developed an approach applicable to the selection of an optimal currency source for a short-term loan when it is possible for the borrowing unit to enter the forward exchange market for a term equivalent to the maturity of the loan. His approach emphasizes not only that the relevant cost of funds is the cost of covered borrowing in each currency but also emphasizes the tight relationship between the money market and the foreign exchange market, by showing that the optimal sourcing problem may be transmuted into an optimal forward exchange purchase problem [23, p. 252]. Folks himself notes that this probably has limited practical application because of the "currency speculation" label that would likely be attached to the prescribed actions [23, pp 252–253], but the point undoubtedly has educational shock value for financial policy. It also serves to emphasize again the exchange risk aspects of the long-term foreign borrowing source problem.

CURRENT STATE OF KNOWLEDGE: CONFLICTS, DATA PROBLEMS, AREAS FOR FUTURE RESEARCH

The review of recent literature which extends to the multinational case financial theory relevant to capital structure and cost-of-capital for the domestic firm reveals the substantially greater complexity of the international case and various areas of conflict in the literature. Data problems contribute to the continuation of the conflict, because definitive empirical testing of certain theoretical constructs is, at best, difficult.

There has been, for example, substantial testing of equity pricing and risk/return relationships in international extensions of the capital asset pricing model, but there is still disagreement on the basic ICAPM to be employed; controversy surrounds "the" world market model, and there is no commonly accepted definition of the world market factor. There is a basic questioning of the applicability of the CAPM, with its assumption of perfect markets

and market participants able to borrow or lend at the pure rate, to the question of international diversification of risk, particularly to the case of diversification effects of foreign direct investment which rest upon market imperfections [89, 80, 77]. There is also detailed questioning of statistical methodology and judgment solutions to problems involved [76; 77, p. 44; 97].

Conflict over Modigliani-Miller varies from that over the best reason for declaring it invalid at the international level (for example, exchange risk, repatriation risk, taxes and tax differentials [44, 45, 61]), to a thesis extending it to the borrowing source decision [98], implicitly disputed by researchers concerned with the substance of that decision [83, 85, 23, 40].

There is basic disagreement as to how foreign exchange risk should be treated: is it a real factor stemming from (nationally differentiated) consumption preferences, or a monetary factor? [89, 29, 26] Related to this issue is the fact that empirical evidence with regard to the international Fisher effect, purchasing power parity, and forward rate bias and predictive power is mixed [15, 42, 70, 26, 27, 48, 49].

Conflict over the degree and relevance of international market segmentation versus market integration is unresolved [98, 66, 67, 8, 11, 87–91, 55, 37, 46, 47]. The main problem is the lack or inadequacy of data, particularly with regard to the testing of M-M models and related financing policies and decisions. The problem is well illustrated by the nature and criticism of the data employed by Krainer and Stevens [44, 45, 98, 3, 81, 66]. The available data are inadequate at both the macro and micro levels. Flow of funds and international financial statistics simply do not provide desired detail by country, currency of denomination, or type of financial instrument; data that do exist are often not homogeneous (for example, with reference to default risk characteristics, marketability, tax status), and/or are flawed proxies for desired data (such as, discount and bank rates in lieu of bond market rates) [15, pp. 90, 96; 77, pp. 38, 41].

At the level of the firm, disclosure requirements are not such that information on amount, denomination, and maturity of foreign currency debt is available from corporate financial statements. Indeed, Robbins and Stobaugh have stated that "the parent firm, itself, may not be fully aware of the total amount of over-all system borrowing" [66, p. 355]. Data problems, then, include not only those facing the researcher, but those facing the security market participant whose perception of risk and response to perceived risk/return relationships is fundamental to financial market theory.

The measurement of multinationality itself presents problems. In the absence of data on foreign investment by individual firms, the most frequently used measure is that of foreign sales/ total sales; this measure includes both foreign production and home-produced exports and thus mixes international trade (including final sales of export goods as well as intracompany transactions) with international investment.

Data problems make us aware of the fact that empirical research results must be greeted with caution. Can the CAPM and M-M theorems be applied realistically and relevantly to multinational enterprise? The financial theory in question has been developed by theorists in industrialized countries with highly developed financial infrastructures, and empirical testing has been limited largely to such countries. The applicability of such work to the multinational enterprise operating in less developed countries is questionable, because the requisite characteristics of capital, money, and foreign exchange markets may not obtain. Thus, the case of the multinational firm operating in less developed countries is one open to both theoretical development and empirical research.

The financial models reviewed here have thus far largely explicitly or implicitly excluded the joint venture case. Both developed and developing countries may seek to control foreign direct investment by requiring that it be done in the form of a joint venture with a local partner, perhaps a controlling partner; this raises related questions about dividend policy and the interaction between real and financial investment decisions. The interrelationship between the investment decision and the financing decision, still much disputed in the literature with regard to the domestic firm [56, 10, 65], is more complex at the multinational level. Thus, both the joint venture case and the interrelationship between the investment decision and the financing decision in the general multinational case are top candidates for future research.

Another important area for future research is the question of the degree to which the multinational corporation itself serves as an instrument for market integration and greater market efficiency; for example, through intracompany transactions. Further foreign exchange market research is needed to guide multinational corporations' decisions with regard to capital structure, borrowing sources, denominating currencies, and hedging policy. Specific research might be directed to central bank foreign exchange market intervention as a potential channel of influence upon equity and debt costs of the multinational firm. This is part of the broader question of the economic effects of exchange rate fluctuations upon the multinational enterprise and its security holders.

CURRENT STATE OF KNOWLEDGE: FINANCIAL POLICY PRESCRIBED FOR THE FIRM

What policy is prescribed for the firm by the international extensions of theoretical financial models? The basic question to be answered concerns the effect of multinationality upon cost of capital. Several studies of equity pricing employing an international extension of the capital asset pricing model indicate that the common stock of the multinational firm is priced so as to reflect international diversification of risk. The domestic firm if it goes multinational can do so without adverse effect upon its cost of equity; indeed, it may expect a reduction in its cost of equity, ceteris paribus. Although both theoretical and empirical difficulties exist, and none of the studies is without critics, none presents evidence indicating that cost of equity capital is higher for the multinational than for the purely domestic firm, ceteris parabus.[5]

The international extensions of the Modigliani-Miller theorem tend to emphasize reasons for its inapplicability to the multinational firm and lend support to analyses employing the traditional approach that there is an optimal debt/equity ratio or range thereof for the multinational firm. The subject is more complex for the multinational firm than for the domestic firm because of the influence of such factors as international diversification of risk, foreign exchange risk, inconvertibility risk, subsidiary capital structures, tax differentials, and multiple market environments. Existing research does not provide a definitive answer to the question of optimum capital structure for the multinational firm, nor to how it is determined.

Whereas financial markets are more highly internationally integrated than are product and factor markets [77, pp. 33–42], various researchers [34; 66, pp. 356; 102, p. 189] characterize them as incomplete and imperfect, and several researchers believe them to be sufficiently so as to offer possibilities for reduction of cost of debt capital by appropriate choice of borrowing source and currency [14; 40; 66, p. 356; 34, pp. 271–272]. Whether this is approached in a portfolio context [40] or in a weighted cost of capital context [85], the operational problem involved in quantifying expected changes in exchange rates is a major one.

Although quantification of expected foreign exchange risk is important for the determination of ex ante cost of debt, it may be argued that the currency in which debt is denominated is irrelevant if, for example, the international Fisher effect holds. Given imperfect foreign exchange markets, the parent is faced with both translation exposure on long-term debt and economic exposure of interest payments and ultimate repayment of principal if local-currency-denominated debt is used. Evidence on this question of foreign exchange risk is mixed.

One policy alternative would be that of using short-term local-currency borrowing to hedge current assets, while financing foreign fixed assets with parent equity and/or intracompany debt. This would avoid translation exposure for the parent under FAS No. 8, while the economic exposure accompanying the equity in fixed assets could be regarded as hedged by an assumed long-run tendency toward purchasing power parity, the receptivity of multinational firms to this policy prescription might well depend upon the ratio of fixed assets to total assets in their industry and their evaluation of their degree of exposure to political risk. An alternative policy would be the use of local-currency–denominated long-term debt within a portfolio diversification approach to foreign exchange risk [18, p. 359; 93]. This alternative has the advantage of retaining for the firm the greater capital availability associated with use of local borrowing sources. However, the advisability of use of local-currency–denominated long-term debt in the financial structure of the multinational firm remains a controversial question.

NOTES

1. A comparable statement might be made with regard to debt financing, relying not on the M-M thesis but on the international Fisher effect in foreign exchange rate determination. This will be discussed later in the paper.

2. Here, a recent suggestion by Elliott is of interest. In an empirical study of the relationship between cost of capital and aggregate investment, Elliott found that 75 percent of the fluctuation in his weighted average cost of capital measure was due to the fluctuations in tax-adjusted equity costs while only 25 percent was due to fluctuations in debt costs [19, p. 994]. Accordingly, he suggested that "monetary policy efforts to influence investment by changing the cost of capital will have a much greater impact if they succeed in influencing equity costs than if they are primarily confined to debt markets influences" [19, p. 994].

3. This characterization was disputed by Rugman [76; 77, p. 44].

4. There is an extensive literature concerned with the effect of conglomerate diversification upon valuation and

debt capacity of the domestic firm; it has been excluded from consideration here.

5. However, in a study of the effects of statement of Financial Accounting Standard No. 8 on security return behavior, multinationals with relatively large investments in foreign assets were shown to have had lower returns than multinationals with relatively low investments in foreign assets in the period 1975–1977 [16, pp. 99–102].

REFERENCES

1. Adler, Michael. "The Cost of Capital and Valuation of a Two-Country Firm." *Journal of Finance*, (March 1974), pp. 119–132.

2. Adler, Michael. "The Cost of Capital and Valuation of a Two-Country Firm: Reply." *Journal of Finance* (September 1977), pp. 1354–1357.

3. Adler, Michael. "The Valuation of Financing of the Multi-National Firm: Comment." *Kyklos,* Vol. 26, no. 4 (1973), pp. 849–851.

4. Adler, Michael, and Bernard Dumas. "Optimal International Acquisitions." *Journal of Finance* (March 1975), pp. 1–19.

5. Agmon, Tamir. "The Relations among Equity Markets: A Study of Share Price Co-Movements in the U.S., U.K., Germany and Japan." *Journal of Finance* (September 1972), pp. 839–855.

6. Agmon, Tamir, and Donald R. Lessard. "Investor Recognition of Corporate International Diversification." *Journal of Finance* (September 1977), pp. 1049–1055.

7. "A Guide to the Banks and Firms in the Foreign Exchange Advisory Business." *Euromoney* (August 1978), pp. 25–41.

8. Black, F. "International Capital Market Equilibrium with Investment Barriers." *Journal of Financial Economics,* Vol. 1 (1971), pp. 337–352.

9. Chen, Andrew H. "Recent Developments in the Cost of Debt Capital." *Journal of Finance* (June 1978), pp. 863–877.

10. Ciccolo, John, and Gary Fromm. " 'Q' and the Theory of Investment." *Journal of Finance* (May 1979), pp. 535–547.

11. Cohn, Richard A., and John J. Pringle. "Imperfections in International Financial Markets: Implications for Risk Premia and the Cost of Capital to Firms." *Journal of Finance* (March 1973), pp. 59–66.

12. Cooley, Philip L., Rodney L. Roenfeldt, and It-Keong Chew. "Capital Budgeting Procedures Under Inflation." *Financial Management* (Winter 1975), pp. 18–35.

13. Dawson, Steven M. "Eurobond Currency Selection: Hindsight." *Financial Executive* (November 1973), pp. 72–73.

14. deFaro, Clovis, and J. V. Jucker. "The Impact of Inflation and Devaluation on the Selection of an International Borrowing Source." *Journal of International Business Studies* (Fall 1973), pp. 97–104.

15. Dufey, Gunter, and Ian H. Giddy. *The International Money Market.* Englewood Cliffs, N.J.: Prentice-Hall, 1978.

16. Dukes, Roland E. *An Empirical Investigation of the Effects of Statement of Accounting Standards No. 8 on Security Return Behavior.* Stamford, Conn.: Financial Accounting Standards Board, 1978.

17. Dumas, Bernard "The Theory of the Trading Firm Revisited." *Journal of Finance* (June 1978), pp. 1019–1030.

18. Eiteman, David K., and Arthur I. Stonehill. *Multinational Business Finance,* 2nd ed. Reading, Mass.: Addison-Wesley, 1979.

19. Elliott, J. Walter. "The Cost of Capital and U.S. Capital Investment: A Test of Alternative Concepts." *Journal of Finance* (September 1980), pp. 981–999.

20. Fama, Eugene F. "The Effects of a Firm's Investment and Financing Decisions on the Welfare of Its Security Holders." *American Economic Review* (June 1978), pp. 27–284.

21. Figlewski, Stephen. "Market 'Efficiency' in a Market with Heterogeneous Information." *Journal of Political Economy* (August 1978), pp. 581–597.

22. Findlay, M. Chapman, III, Alan W. Frankle, et al. "Capital Budgeting Procedures under Inflation: Cooley, Roenfeldt and Chew vs. Findlay and Frankle." *Financial Management* (Autumn 1976), pp. 83–90.

23. Folks, William R., Jr. "Optimal Foreign Borrowing Strategies with Operations in Forward Exchange Markets." *Journal of Financial and Quantitative Analysis* (June 1978), pp. 245–254.

24. Fremgen, James M. "Capital Budgeting Practices: A Survey." *Management Accounting* (May 1973), pp. 19–25.

25. Frenkel, Jacob A., and Richard M. Levich. "Transactions Costs and Interest Arbitrage: Tranquil versus Turbulent Periods." *Journal of Political Economy* (November–December 1977), pp. 1209–1226.

26. Giddy, Ian H. "Exchange Risk: Whose View." *Financial Management* (Summer 1977), pp. 23–33.

27. Giddy, Ian H., and Gunter Dufey. "The Random Behavior of Flexible Exchange Rates: Implications for Forecasting." *Journal of International Business Studies* (Spring 1975), pp. 1–32.

28. Goldberg, Michael A., and Wayne Y. Lee. "The Cost of Capital and Valuation of a Two-Country Firm: Comment." *Journal of Finance* (September 1977), pp. 1348–1353.

29. Grauer, F. L. A., R. H. Litzenberger, and R. H. Stehle.

"Sharing Rules and Equilibrium in an International Capital Market under Uncertainty." *Journal of Financial Economics,* Vol. 3 (1976), pp. 233–256.

30. Grubel, H. G. "Internationally Diversified Portfolios: Welfare Gains and Capital Flows." *American Economic Review,* (December 1968), pp. 1299–1314.

31. Grubel, H. G., and K. Fadner. "The Interdependence of International Equity Markets." *Journal of Finance* (March 1971), pp. 89–94.

32. Hamada, Robert S. "Portfolio Analysis, Market Equilibrium, and Corporation Finance." *Journal of Finance* (March 1969), pp. 13–31.

33. Hartman, David G. "Foreign Investment and Finance with Risk." *Quarterly Journal of Economics* (May 1979), pp. 213–232.

34. Hirshleifer, J. *Investment, Interest and Capital.* Englewood Cliffs, N.J.: Prentice-Hall, 1970.

35. Hodrick, Robert J. "An Empirical Analysis of the Monetary Approach to the Determination of the Exchange Rate." In Jacob A. Frenkel and Harry G. Johnson, eds., *The Economics of Exchange Rates,* pp. 97–116. Reading, Mass.: Addison-Wesley.

36. Hufbauer, G. C. "The Multinational Corporation and Direct Investment." In Peter B. Kenen, ed., *International Trade and Finance,* pp. 253–319. Cambridge: Cambridge University Press, 1975.

37. Hughes, John S., Dennis E. Logue, and Richard James Sweeney. "Corporate International Diversification and Market Assigned Measures of Risk and Diversification." *Journal of Financial and Quantitative Analysis* (November 1975), pp. 627–637.

38. *International Letter.* Federal Reserve Bank of Chicago.

39. Jacquillat, Bertrand, and Bruno Solnik. "Multinationals Are Poor Tools for Diversification." *Journal of Portfolio Management* (Winter 1978), pp. 8–12.

40. Jucker, James V., and Clovis deFaro. "The Selection of International Borrowing Sources." *Journal of Financial and Quantitative Analysis* (September 1975), pp. 381–407.

41. Kohers, Theodor. "The Effect of Multinational Operations on the Cost of Equity Capital of U.S. Corporations: An Empirical Study." *Management International Review,* nos. 2–3 (1975), pp. 121–124.

42. Kohlhagen, Steven W. *The Behavior of Foreign Exchange Markets: A Critical Survey of the Empirical Literature.* Monograph 1978–3, New York University Graduate School of Business Administration, Salomon Brothers Center for the Study of Financial Institutions.

43. Kornbluth, J. S. H., and Joseph D. Vinso. "Financial Planning for the Multinational Corporation: A Fractional Multiobjective Approach." Working Paper No. 5, Graduate School of Business Administration, University of Southern California, October 1979.

44. Krainer, Robert E. "The Valuation and Financing of the Multi-National Firm." *Kyklos,* Vol. 25 (1972), pp. 553–573.

45. Krainer, Robert E. "The Valuation and Financing of the Multi-National Firm: Reply." *Kyklos,* Vol. 26 (1973), pp. 857–865.

46. Lee, Wayne Y., and Kanwal S. Sachdeva. "The Role of the Multi-National Firm in the Integration of Segmented Capital Markets." *Journal of Finance* (May 1977), pp. 479–492.

47. Lessard, Donald R. "World, Country, and Industry Relationships in Equity Returns: Implications for Risk Reduction through International Diversification." *Financial Analysts' Journal,* (January–February 1976), pp. 2–8.

48. Levich, Richard M. "Tests of Forecasting Models and Market Efficiency in the International Money Market." In Jacob A. Frenkel and Harry G. Johnson, eds., *The Economics of Exchange Rates,* pp. 129–158. Reading, Mass.: Addison-Wesley, 1978.

49. Levich, Richard M. "The Efficiency of Markets for Foreign Exchange: A Review and Extension." In Donald R. Lessard, ed., *International Financial Management,* pp. 243–276. Boston and New York: Warren, Gorham and Lamont, 1979.

50. Levy, H., and M. Sarnat. "International Diversification of Investment Portfolios." *American Economic Review* (September 1970), pp. 668–692.

51. Lewellen, Wilbur G. "A Conceptual Reappraisal of Cost of Capital." *Financial Management* (Winter 1974), pp. 63–70.

52. Lintner, John. "Security Prices, Risk, and Maximal Gains from Diversification." *Journal of Finance* (December 1965), pp. 587–615.

53. Linnter, John. "The Valuation of Risk Assets and the Selection of Risky Investments in Stock Portfolios and Capital Budgets." *Review of Economics and Statistics* (February 1965), pp. 13–37.

54. Logue, Dennis E., and Larry J. Merville. "Financial Policy and Market Expectations." *Financial Management* (Summer 1972), pp. 37–44.

55. Logue, Dennis E., Michael A. Salant, and Richard James Sweeney. "International Integration of Financial Markets: Survey, Synthesis, and Results." In Carl H. Stem, John H. Makin, and Dennis E. Logue, eds., *Eurocurrencies and the International Monetary System,* pp. 91–137. Washington, D.C.: American Enterprise Institute for Public Policy Research, 1976.

56. McCabe, George M. "The Empirical Relationship Between Investment and Financing: A New Look." *Journal of Financial and Quantitative Analysis* (March 1979), pp. 119–135.

57. Mehra, Rajnish. "On the Financing and Investment Decisions of Multinational Firms in the Presence of Exchange Risk." *Journal of Financial and Quantita-*

tive Analysis (June 1978), pp. 227–244.

58. Miller, Norman C., and Marina V. N. Whitman. "The Outflow of Short-Term Funds from the United States: Adjustments of Stocks and Flows." In Fritz Machlup, Walter Salant, and Lorie Tarshis, eds., *International Mobility and Movement of Capital,* pp. 253–286. New York and London: Columbia University Press for National Bureau of Economic Research, 1972.

59. Modigliani, Franco, and Merton H. Miller. "The Cost of Capital, Corporation Finance, and the Theory of Investment." *American Economic Review* (June 1958), pp. 261–297.

60. Myers, Stewart C. "Interactions of Corporate Financing and Investment Decisions: Implications for Capital Budgeting." *Journal of Finance* (March 1974), pp. 1–25.

61. Naumann-Etienne, Ruediger. "A Framework for Financial Decisions in Multi-National Corporations: A Summary of Recent Research." *Journal of Financial and Quantitative Analysis* (November 1974), pp. 859–874.

62. Ness, Walter L. "A Linear Programming Approach to Financing the Multinational Corporation." *Financial Management* (Winter 1972), pp. 88–100.

63. Quinn, Brian Scott. *The New Euromarkets.* New York: Halsted Press, 1975.

64. Rendleman, Richard J., Jr. "The Effects of Default Risk on the Firm's Investment and Financing Decisions." *Financial Management* (Spring 1978), pp. 45–53.

65. Reinhart, Walter J. "Discussion of 'The Channels of Influence of Tobin-Brainard's Q on Investment,'" *Journal of Finance* (May 1979), pp. 561–564.

66. Robbins, Sidney, and Robert B. Stobaugh. "Comments." In Fritz Machlup, Walter Salant, and Lorie Tarshis, eds., *International Mobility and Movement of Capital,* pp. 354–357. New York and London: Columbia University Press for National Bureau of Economic Research, 1972.

67. Robbins, Sidney, and Robert B. Stobaugh. *Money in the Multinational Enterprise.* New York: Basic Books, 1973.

68. Robichek, Alexander A., and Mark R. Eaker. "Debt Denomination and Exchange Risk in International Capital Markets," *Financial Management,* Autumn 1976, pp. 11–18.

69. Robichek, Alexander A., and Mark R. Eaker. "Foreign Exchange Hedging and the Capital Asset Pricing Model." *Journal of Finance* (June 1978), pp. 1011–1018.

70. Rogalski, Richard J., and Joseph D. Vinso. "Price Level Variations as Predictors of Flexible Exchange Rates." *Journal of International Business Studies* (Spring–Summer 1977), pp. 71–81.

71. Roll, Richard. "A Critique of the Asset Pricing Theory's Tests." *Journal of Financial Economics* (March 1977), pp. 129–176.

72. Roll, Richard, and B. H. Solnik. "A Pure Foreign Exchange Asset Pricing Model." *Journal of International Economics,* Vol. 7 (1977), pp. 161–179.

73. Ross, Stephen A. "The Current Status of the Capital Asset Pricing Model (CAPM)." *Journal of Finance* (June 1978), pp. 885–901.

74. Rudd, Andrew, and Wilson Chung. "Implementation of International Portfolio Diversification: A Survey." Mimeographed. September 1978.

75. Rugman, Alan M. "A Note on Internationally Diversified Firms and Risk Reduction." *Journal of Business Administration* (Fall 1975), pp. 182–184.

76. Rugman, Alan M. "Discussion: Corporate International Diversification and Market Assigned Measures of Risk and Diversification." *Journal of Financial and Quantitative Analysis* (November 1975), pp. 651–652.

77. Rugman, Alan M. *International Diversification and the Multinational Enterprise.* Lexington, Mass.: D.C. Heath, 1979.

78. Rutenberg, David P. "Maneuvering Liquid Assets in a Multinational Company: Formulation and Deterministic Solution Procedures." *Management Science* (June 1970), pp. 45–49.

79. Scott, Davis F., Jr. "Evidence on the Importance of Financial Structure," *Financial Management* (Summer 1972), pp. 45–50.

80. Severn, Alan K. "Investor Evaluation of Foreign and Domestic Risk." *Journal of Finance* (May 1974), pp. 545–550.

81. Severn, Alan K. "The Financing of the Multi-National Firm: Comment." *Kyklos,* Vol. 26, no. 4 (1973), pp. 852–856.

82. Shapiro, Alan C. "Capital Budgeting for the Multinational Corporation." *Financial Management* (Spring 1978), pp. 7–16.

83. Shapiro, Alan C. "Evaluating Financing Costs for Multinational Subsidiaries." *Journal of International Business Studies* (Fall 1975), pp. 25–32.

84. Shapiro, Alan C. "Exchange Rate Changes. Inflation and the Value of the Multinational Corporation." *Journal of Finance* (May 1975), pp. 485–502.

85. Shapiro, Alan C. "Financial Structure and the Cost of Capital in the Multinational Corporation." *Journal of Financial and Quantitative Analysis* (June 1978), pp. 211–226.

86. Sharpe, William F. "Capital Asset Prices: A Theory of Market Equilibrium under Conditions of Risk." *Journal of Finance* (September 1964) pp. 425–442.

87. Solnik, Bruno H. "An Equilibrium Model of the International Capital Market." *Journal of Economic Theory,* Vol. 8 (1974), pp. 500–524.

88. Solnik, Bruno H. "An International Market Model of Security Price Behavior." *Journal of Financial*

and Quantitative Analysis (September 1974), pp. 537–554.

89. Solnik, Bruno H. *European Capital Markets.* Lexington, Mass.: D. C. Heath, 1973.

90. Solnik, Bruno H. "Testing International Asset Pricing: Some Pessimistic Views." *Journal of Finance* (May 1977), pp. 503–512.

91. Solnik, Bruno H. "The International Pricing of Risk: An Empirical Investigation of the World Capital Market Structure." *Journal of Finance* (May 1974), pp. 365–378.

92. Solnik, Bruno H., and Jean Grall. "Eurobonds: Determinants of the Demand for Capital and the International Interest Rate Structure." *Journal of Banking Research* (Winter 1975), pp. 218–230.

93. Stanley, Marjorie Thines. "Local-Currency Long-Term Debt in the Multinational's Financial Structure." *Atlantic Economic Review* (December 1979), p. 80.

94. Stanley, Marjorie Thines, and Stanley B. Block. "Portfolio Diversification of Foreign Exchange Risk: An Empirical Study." *Management International Review,* Vol. 20 (1980/1), pp. 83–92.

95. Stanley, Marjorie Thines, "Response by United States Financial Managers to Financial Accounting Standard No. 8." *Journal of International Business Studies* (Fall 1978), pp. 85–99.

96. Stanley, Marjorie Thines, and John D. Stanley. "The Impact of U.S. Regulation of Foreign Investment." *California Management Review* (Winter 1972), pp. 56–64.

97. Stehle, Richard. "An Empirical Test of the Alternative Hypothesis of National and International Pricing of Risky Assets." *Journal of Finance* (May 1977), pp. 493–502.

98. Stevens, Guy V. G. "Capital Mobility and the International Firm." In Fritz Machlup, Walter Salant, and Lorie Tarshis, eds., *International Mobility and Movement of Capital,* pp. 323–353. New York and London: Columbia University Press for National Bureau of Economic Research, 1972.

99. Stonehill, Arthur, Theo Beekhuisen, Richard Wright, Lee Remmers, Norman Toy, Antonio Pares, Alan Shapiro, Douglas Egan, and Thomas Bates. "Financial Goals and Debt Ratio Determinants: A Survey of Practice in Five Countries." *Financial Management* (Autumn 1975), pp. 27–41.

100. Stonehill, Arthur, and Thomas Stitzel. "Financial Structure and Multinational Corporations." *California Management Review* (Fall 1969), pp. 91–96.

101. Vickers, D. "The Cost of Capital and the Structure of the Firm." *Journal of Finance,* (March 1970) pp. 35–46.

102. Zenoff, David B., and Jack Zwick. *International Financial Management.* Englewood Cliffs, N.J.: Prentice-Hall, 1969.

17

CAPITAL BUDGETING PRACTICES AT MULTINATIONALS

Vinod B. Bavishi

What is the theory of capital budgeting for multinational corporations? Do the current capital budgeting practices of U.S.-based multinational corporations coincide with the theory?

To find out I sent a questionnaire survey to the top financial executives of the 306 largest U.S.-based MNCs. The companies were selected from *Fortune* Magazine's "500 largest

Source: Management Accounting (August 1981), pp. 32–35. Copyright © 1981 by National Association of Accountants. Reprinted by permission.

United States Industrial Corporations for 1978." Overseas assets for each company in the survey accounted for 10% or more of its total assets and each company was operating in at least four countries as of December 31, 1978. One hundred and fifty-six (156) companies completed and returned the questionnaire—a response rate of 51%, which is unusually high for a voluntary survey and reduces the likelihood of nonresponse bias.

A synthesis of capital budgeting techniques for analysis of the overseas investment described in the literature includes these practices:

1. *Cash flows* should be evaluated from either the parent's or the subsidiary's perspective as long as the underlying assumptions are satisfied. If the foreign subsidiary's viewpoint is used, it should be assumed that unremitted earnings will be reinvested in the host country and eventually be available to the U.S. parent. If some portion of the earnings are blocked (i.e., cannot be remitted in the foreseeable future), then whatever is remittable under the host country laws (i.e., maximum amount of dividend, management fees and royalties allowed), which is the U.S. parent company's viewpoint of cash flow measurement, should be used.

2. *Discounted cash flow methods,* that is, Internal Rate of Return (IRR) or Net Present Value (NPV) should be used for analyzing project cash flows.

3. *MNCs should use their marginal worldwide weighted average cost of capital* for evaluating investment projects. The formula for this computation includes all sources of long-term financing, including the U.S. parent company's domestic liabilities as well as debts of all foreign subsidiaries. All debt of foreign subsidiaries, whether guaranteed by the parent or not, is included because the debt is, in the long run, that of the parent.

4. The *allowance for risk* in analyzing capital budgeting projects should be done in either of two ways. One approach would be to compute certainty equivalent cash flow in which project cash flows are adjusted for appropriate risk and then discounted at a risk-free discount rate to arrive at NPV. Another method is to use risk-adjusted discount rates to reflect the relative uncertainty of the project's cash streams.

THE NATURE OF THE RESPONSE

Table 1 provides a breakdown of responses by the Fortune 500 companies divided into five groups of 100 each. The highest response rate of 67% was in the first group of 100, possibly indicating their greater interest in the study. Another possible explanation for this distribution may be that the large MNCs have more time and resources available to respond to the questionnaire than do the smaller MNCs.

Table 2 shows a breakdown of sample companies as well as useful responses by industries. The Standard Industrial Classifications (SIC Code) established by the U.S. Office of Management and Budget is used here to group companies into industry groups. A review of the table reveals that major industries are well represented in the study.

A summary of the respondents' departments is presented in Table 1. Their actual titles below the treasurer's level are not summarized here since there was a wide variation (i.e., director, manager, supervisor, coordinator), but almost all of these respondents are in a managerial position in the financial staff function, either in the corporate group or in the international group. It can be safely assumed that respondents are fully conversant with their respective companies' overseas capital budgeting practices.

CURRENT PRACTICE DISCLOSED

The respondents were asked to identify the cash flow used in evaluating overseas investments. Five choices were provided:

1. Before tax cash flow to the foreign subsidiary;
2. After tax cash flow to the foreign subsidiary;
3. Earnings remitted to the U.S. parent;
4. Total cash flows to the U.S. parent, and
5. Total cash flows to the U.S. parent plus reinvested (or remitted) earnings.

The results showed that cash flow from the foreign subsidiary's viewpoint is preferred by 42% of the respondents while cash flow from the U.S. parent's viewpoint is preferred by 21% and the remaining 37% of the respondents are using both perspectives together in one form or another (Table 3). Based on this survey, cash flow from the foreign subsidiary's viewpoint is used most.

Then I asked MNC managers which capital

Table 1 Number of MNCs in the Sample and Responses Received

By *Fortune* Rank

Fortune Rank	Sample	Useful Responses Received	% of Sample	% of Total Useful Responses
1–100	82	56	68	36
101–200	70	36	51	23
201–300	63	23	37	15
301–400	47	18	38	11
401–500	44	19	43	12
Unidentified	—	4	—	3
Total	306	156	51	100

Analysis of Respondents' Department

Department (title)	Corporate Group	International Group	Total
Vice president, finance	13	4	17
Controllers/asst. controllers	17	7	24
Treasurers/asst. treasurers	8	6	14
Financial planning	18	3	21
Financial analysis	23	4	27
Capital budgeting	18	4	22
Budgets/costs	6	—	6
Accounting	7	5	12
Administration	—	2	2
External financial communications	2	—	2
Total	112	35	147
Unidentified			9
Total responses			156

budgeting techniques (CBT) they used in analyzing overseas investment projects: Payback Period (PBK), Profitability Index (PI), Return on Investments (ROI), Internal Rate of Return (IRR), or Net Present Value (NPV). Responses were returned from 155 MNCs.

The most popular CBT is PBK, used by 76% of the respondents (but only 1% use it as the sole CBT). PI is used by 10% (none use it as the only CBT), ROI by 63% (4% use it as the only CBT), IRR by 69% (7% use it as the only CBT), and NPV by 40% (2% use it as the only CBT). See

Table 4. From the total number of responses to the question, it can be seen that the use of two or more capital budgeting techniques is very common (85% of the respondents use two or more CBTs). The most popular combinations of CBTs are PBK-ROI-IRR (used by 26 respondents), PBK-ROI-IRR-NPV (by 21 respondents), and PBK-ROI (by 21 respondents).

In a comparison of the use of traditional and discounted capital budgeting techniques, 67% of the respondents said they use both traditional and discounted techniques, 21% of the respon-

Table 2 Useful Responses Received by Industry

SIC Code	Industry Titles	MNCs in Sample	Useful Responses Received	% of Sample
10	Mining, crude oil	7	3	43
20	Food	31	17	55
21	Tobacco	4	2	50
22	Textiles, vinyl flooring	2	1	50
23	Apparel	6	3	50
25	Furniture	1	—	0
26	Paper, fiber, wood products	13	6	46
27	Publishing, printing	3	1	33
28	Chemicals	31	17	55
29	Petroleum and refining	22	13	59
30	Rubber, plastic products	7	5	71
32	Glass, concrete, abrasives, gypsum	8	6	75
33	Metal manufacturing	13	5	38
34	Metal products	16	5	31
36	Electronics, appliances	23	7	30
37	Shipbuilding, railroad and transportation equipment	3	2	67
38	Measuring, scientific, photo-graphic equipment	15	6	40
40	Motor vehicles	18	12	67
41	Aerospace	6	3	50
42	Pharmaceuticals	17	8	47
43	Soaps, cosmetics	7	4	57
44	Office equipment (includes computers)	11	8	73
45	Industrial and farm equipment	31	11	35
47	Musical instruments, toys, sporting goods	4	3	75
48	Broadcasting, motion picture production and distribution	4	2	50
49	Beverages	3	2	67
	Unidentified	—	4	—
	Total	306	156	51

Table 3 Cash Flow Measurement

Method	For All Responses N = 155	
	Number	Percent
Cash flow: foreign subsidiary's viewpoint	65	42
Cash flow: U.S. parent's viewpoint	32	21
Cash flow: both foreign subsidiary's and U.S. parent's viewpoint	58	37
Total	155	100

Table 4 Capital Budgeting Techniques

| | All Responses *(155 companies responding)* | | | | | |
| | Use Technique Exclusively | | Use in Combination with Others | | Total | |
Technique	Number	%	Number	%	Number	%
Payback period	2	1	116	75	118	76
Profitability index	0	0	15	10	15	10
Return on investments	6	4	91	59	97	63
Internal rate of return	11	7	96	62	107	69
Net present value	3	2	59	38	62	40

dents use only traditional capital budgeting techniques, and 12% of the respondents use only discounted techniques.

The MNCs were asked to identify which rate they use as a base discount rate, or alternatively, how the cost of capital is determined for evaluation of overseas investments. Four choices were given:

1. Determined subjectively;
2. Cost of capital for financing only overseas projects used;
3. Weighted average cost of capital for financing all overseas projects used, and
4. Weighted average cost of capital for worldwide financing used.

One hundred thirty-six out of 155 respondents answered this question (88% of the total respondents). Of those MNCs which indicated that a discount rate is used, 30% determine it subjectively, 27% use only overseas financing cost (either of individual projects or of total overseas financing), and 43% use weighted average cost of capital for worldwide financing. See Table 5.

As for the methods used in adjusting for project risks, of the 153 companies responding to the question, 14% made no allowance for risks in capital budgeting analysis. Most respondents (70%) stated that subjective adjustment is made by either shortening the minimum payback period, raising the required rate of return or

adjusting project cash flows subjectively. Only 16% use a certainty equivalent cash flow concept.

ASSESSMENT OF CURRENT PRACTICE

Survey results indicate that current method used (i.e., total cash flow to the foreign subsidiary and the U.S. parent company) for the measurement of project's cash flow coincide with the theoretically prescribed techniques.

Most of the respondents use discounted cash flow methods (along with traditional methods or separately) for analyzing project cash flows. Therefore, it can be said that the theory and practice are alike in this area. The results also show, however, that a majority of the respondents use two or more techniques. This fact raises a question concerning the use of numerous techniques which may result in a confused ranking. Also there are inefficiencies inherent in computing two or more measures when one measure can easily provide sufficient decision criteria. It appears that the traditional methods (i.e., payback method and rate of return on investments) are still widely used, more as secondary indicators for risk and/or profitability. These traditional methods are also used for smaller projects in which detailed analysis may not be justified.

MNC managers might well undertake an

Table 5 Methods of Establishing Discount Rate

Method	All Responses (136 companies responding)	
	Number	Percent
Determined subjectively	41	30
Overseas cost of capital for overseas financing (either project or all overseas financing considered)	36	27
Weighted average cost of capital for both domestic and overseas financing	59	43
Total	136	100

evaluation of the techniques they currently use with the objective of eliminating techniques that provide duplicate results.

The results indicated that there is a substantial difference between theory and practice in the area of determination of the discount rate. Theory prescribes use of the MNC's marginal worldwide weighted average cost of capital as a discount rate, while in practice MNCs determine discount rate either subjectively or based upon overseas cost of capital. The difficulties in computing their worldwide weighted average cost of capital, the availability of overseas financing for a specific project (the project would not be undertaken if the financing were not available), and a corporate policy to use a high enough discount rate to allow for errors and uncertainties—all were offered by the interviewed respondents as possible explanations for the differences between theory and practice.

It appears that the gap between theory and current practice can be easily bridged in this area because theory provides workable procedures to compute weighted average cost of capital. MNC managers should consider modifying their current practices to incorporate this calculation in evaluating all investment projects worldwide. Researchers could facilitate this modification by developing case studies using the variety of different financing sources available to today's multinationals and include

a step-by-step illustration of the weighted average cost computation.

The majority of respondents adjust for a risk subjectively either by raising the minimum payback period and/or by raising the discount rate. The use of either of these two techniques distorts the project's cash flows because such adjustments are made arbitrarily and the time pattern of the risk variables is not considered. For example, if expropriation is expected at the end of the fifth year, the use of the higher discount rate for all cash flows would penalize cash flow for the first four years.

The respondents expressed dissatisfaction with present methods for adjusting project risks, which they described as too judgmental and arbitrary. The interviewed respondents stated that a possible reason for the gap between theory and practice is that, at present, there are as yet no theoretical models or techniques available which would incorporate all the risk variables involved in the overseas project.

It seems the gap between theory and practice will not be easy to reconcile. But new developments in the theory of finance, especially the capital asset price model (CAPM), have potential for further refinement and may be able to be used by MNCs to evaluate overseas investments.

These findings provide another perspective on the difference between theory and current practice because there are two possible reasons why a particular aspect of overseas investment is difficult to evaluate. First, it may be difficult to evaluate because of unavailability of theoretically prescribed techniques as is the case of adjusting cash flow for project risks. Second, the difficulty may be in evaluation because of the nonutilization of currently available theoretical concepts as is the case with discount rate computations where worldwide weighted average cost of capital is not used.

18

INTERNATIONAL FINANCIAL PLANNING: THE USE OF MARKET-BASED FORECASTS

Gunter Dufey
Ian H. Giddy

Corporate planning is an integrated effort by all levels of management to achieve the firm's strategic objectives under future conditions of opportunity, risk, and uncertainty through established forecasting, planning, and budgeting procedures on a regular basis. International corporations face greater risks than domestic ones but also have wider opportunities, and therefore they require a planning system specifically adapted to international market uncertainties.

The formal planning and budgeting process is similar in all large corporations. Based on overall strategic business objectives, operating plans originate from product groups or regional business units. These plans are then coordinated at the corporate level and are adjusted in a process of give and take with financial management, which in turn provides information about the availability of funds at various cost levels. Once an agreement has been reached on the volume of assets to be financed, work can begin on a detailed financing plan.

PLANNING AND BUDGETING IN INTERNATIONAL COMPANIES

In multiunit, multijurisdiction organizations such as international corporations, this process is an involved one, since it must be done for every corporate entity. In the end, financial planners in such firms must make decisions about the following issues:

• Should funds be obtained in the form of equity or debt and, if the latter, for which maturity? Alternatively, in which financial instruments should excess funds be invested?

• In which market (and which currency) should funds be raised (invested)?

• What legal entity is to raise (invest) the funds?

• How should funds be transferred from the corporate entity that raises them from third parties to the entity(ies) that need them for investment in productive assets and working capital?

The primary task of international financial management is to minimize the cost of funds and to maximize the return on investment over time, by means of the best combination of currency of denomination and maturity characteristics of financial assets and liabilities. The implementation of these choices, however, requires the formulation and revision of capital structure decisions for various units and budgets for intercompany funds transfers. Only to the extent that financial managers have some influence over these decisions will they be able to take full advantage of the firm's financial planning and forecasting tools described in this article.

FORECASTING REQUIREMENTS OF FINANCIAL PLANNING

The international corporate planning process relies heavily on forecasts of prices, availability of supplies, government actions, competitors' responses, labor conditions, technological development, and so forth. We can conveniently identify three categories of forecasts necessary for corporate planning: (1) forecasts of product market and industry conditions: product demand, industrial activity, and so on: (2) forecasts of conditions within the firm: technical changes in production, labor relations, management needs, and so on, and (3) forecasts of conditions in financial markets: interest rates, funds availability, and so on.

In this article we are concerned chiefly with the forecasts necessary for financial planning. How are such forecasts used? We take as given the timing, amount, and currency of cash outflows and the needs of the firm during the planning period. The financial manager's role is that of planning for the transfer of funds within the firm and for international working capital and funding decisions. Undoubtedly, a large part of this task is to devise the legal entities and arrange the form of international transactions so as to maximize flexibility for corporate funding and transfer needs. Yet we take these as given too, focusing specifically on the decisions that remain when institutional and legal opportunities and constraints have been identified.

What decisions are left? Given the anticipated cash needs or surpluses of various operating units at various dates in the future, and given the constraints on how and where funds can be moved, the financial planners have to decide on the timing, maturity, and currency of denomination that will minimize funding costs, and on the timing and maturity of investments in financial assets.

Decisions about when funds should be raised, and at what maturity, depend on anticipated interest rate movements or changes in the availability of funds, as well as the timing of cash needs. Decisions on the currency of debt depend on expected exchange rate changes, as well as the currency of denomination of funds needs and flows. The million-franc needs of a French subsidiary six months from now, for example, could be met by borrowing French francs when the funds are required. Depending on forecasts of credit and currency market conditions, on the other hand, financial planners may recommend the issuance of long-term debt now (if interest rates are lower than expected in the future) instead of later, or borrowing in dollars instead of francs (if the French franc is regarded as a strong currency).

To summarize: financial planning decisions on timing, maturity, and currency of denomination of financial assets and liabilities require interest rate and exchange rate forecasts. In the next section we shall describe the rather wide range of implicit forecasts provided by the financial and currency markets themselves, and how they relate to one another. Later we suggest the use of such forecasts in financial planning.

THE MARKET'S FORECASTS OF FINANCIAL CONDITIONS

The traditional theory of markets views the price of any good or service (a bicycle or a haircut), and of any financial asset (a bond or a pound sterling), as the outcome of the forces of supply and demand. While few would dispute this basic contention, in recent years the focus of theoretical and empirical research has emphasized the role of *market expectations,* rather than current supply and demand, as the prime determinant of prices and interest rates in financial markets. This fact is of great interest to forecasters, because if present prices and yields embody the market's expectations of future prices and interest rates, it may be possible to determine the market's forecast by looking at competitively determined prices and rates.

Futures prices in commodity markets provide the best available information about the market's forecasts of spot prices. For example, market participants who believe that they have better information about future spot prices of soybeans than do other market participants will attempt to make profits by buying or selling futures contracts. The result is that new information is quickly incorporated into the prices of futures contracts, and the pattern of futures prices reflects the best guesses of well-informed market participants about the path of future spot prices.

We can go further: according to the "efficient market" hypothesis, the market's forecast is *rational,* in the sense of being a function of the true determinants of future spot prices, and utilizes all available information in the most efficient way possible. If this is true, the market forecast, and hence the futures price, is the best available estimate of the future price of a commodity.[1] While many do not accept this argument in its pure form, the bulk of evidence in recent years supports the notion that futures prices are unbiased predictors of subsequent spot prices.

While futures prices exist in some uniform raw materials and agricultural commodity markets, these are too few and far between to be of much use to operating management. The market for labor, for example, is too diverse and inefficient for a futures wage rate (if it existed) to be of much use in forecasting labor costs. In contrast, the markets for many currencies and financial instruments are highly efficient and standardized and numerous traders stand ready to exploit perceived profit opportunities whenever they arise.

In the currency market, the market's forecasts are embodied in the forward exchange rate (futures prices). Of course, the forward exchange rate is not an *accurate* forecast, because traders' buy or sell decisions are only based on information available *now.* Not only will the market-based forecast be continually revised as new information reaches the market, right up to the date of the maturity of the futures contract, but the *actual* future price will also deviate from the predicted price because of new information that reaches the market. In fact, even over long periods the forecasting error of the forward rate is not likely to average out to zero.[2]

Thus, over any given period the actual price will turn out to differ from the futures price. The amount C in Figure 1 will usually be positive or negative. But the chances that the actual price will be above or below the futures price are equal. Because price changes result from new information reaching the market, and because new information is by its nature unpredictable, the deviation C tends to be randomly distributed about zero. In other words, the *expected value* of the forecasting error C is *zero.*

For financial planning purposes, the forecaster should consider three differences (illustrated in Figure 1). Amount A, the difference between today's exchange rate and the actual

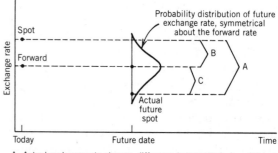

A—Actual exchange rate change: difference between today's and the actual future exchange rate.
B—Anticipated change: difference between today's spot rate and the forward rate.
C—Unanticipated change: difference between the forward rate and the actual future exchange rate.

Figure 1 Exchange Rate Forecasting Using the Forward Rate

future rate, is often thought of as the possible exchange risk. However, by calculating amount B, the difference between today's rate and the market-expected future rate, we are usually able to *anticipate* much of the exchange rate change. Hence, what matters to the planner is amount C, the *unanticipated* exchange rate change; and, as we have seen, this can be positive or negative, and has a zero expected value.

If the forward exchange rate equals the expected future spot rate, we may assume that forward rates for various maturities trace the expected movement of the spot exchange rate in the future. By expressing the forward rate as an annualized discount or premium from the spot rate, as in Figure 2, we can estimate the market forecast of the rate of change of the exchange rate for any period in the future.

We have thus far linked the forward premium or discount to exchange rate expectations. But exchange rate expectations themselves are linked to inflationary expectations, or rather, expectations about *relative* inflation rates in the two countries. This so-called purchasing power parity relationship simply states that the rate of change of the exchange rate tends over time to equal the difference between inflation rates in two countries.

Further, covered interest arbitrage between two currencies creates a linkage between interest rates and the forward premium or discount. That is, the forward premium or discount tends always to equal the interest rate differential between financial assets denominated in different currencies. The relative interest rates are themselves also linked more or less directly to exchange rate and inflation rate expectations, for one would expect that the country with the higher inflation rate and whose currency is expected to depreciate would also have a higher interest rate.

All these relationships are summarized diagrammatically in Figure 3. As the diagram suggests, while market-based forecasts of expected exchange rate changes can be obtained most directly from spot and forward exchange rates, they can also be obtained from the interest rate differential. By subtracting the domestic from the foreign interest rate we obtain the expected rate of change, and hence the expected path, of the foreign currency's value, as Figure 4 illustrates.

So far, we have talked only of market forecasts of exchange rates (and inflation rates) based on the term structure of forward ex-

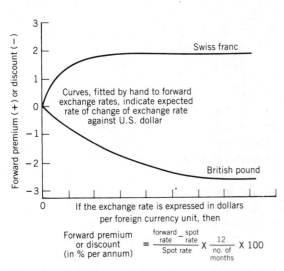

Figure 2 Market-Implied Exchange Rate Expectations, August 1977

Figure 3 Equilibrium Relationships among Exchange Rates, Inflation Rates, and Interest Rates

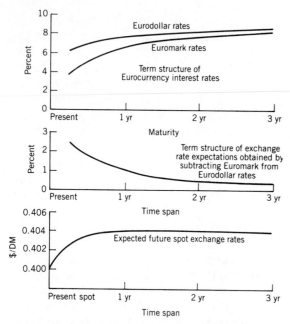

Figure 4 Market-based Forecast of Exchange Rate Changes, from Interest Rate Differential (*Source:* from Gunter Dufey and Ian Giddy, *The International Money Market,* Englewood Cliffs, N.J.: Prentice-Hall, 1978, section on "The Term Structure of Eurocurrency Interest Rates." Used with permission.)

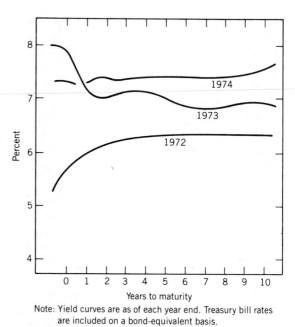

Note: Yield curves are as of each year end. Treasury bill rates are included on a bond-equivalent basis.

Figure 5 Recent Yield Curves for U.S. Government Securities. (*Source:* From Morgan Guaranty Trust Co., *The Morgan Guaranty Survey,* July 1977, p. 11.)

change rates.[3] Can interest rates be forecasted in the same way? In principle, the answer is yes, although the technique for discovering the market's interest rate forecast is usually a little more subtle than that for exchange rates. Nevertheless, the market's forecast for interest rates at almost any date in the future can be estimated by looking at the yield curve on, say, government bonds. The yield curve is a chart that plots the current yields to maturity of a group of securities of various maturities, but which are all equivalent as to credit quality. This "term structure of interest rates" is often upward-sloping, but can also be flat, downward-sloping, or even humped. Figure 5 illustrates three such curves.

In an efficient market, the shape of the yield curve is determined largely by expectations about future interest rates. An upward-sloping curve means interest rates are likely to rise; a downward-sloping one, that a fall is expected.

Long-term rates tend to equal the average of expected future short-term rates; if that were not the case, investors would take speculative actions tending to bid long-term rates up or down until they fulfilled that condition. For example, if interest rate expectations rise so that the average of expected intervening short-term rates is higher than long-term rates, investors will sell long-term bonds and buy short ones, in the expectation of reinvesting the money in short-term securities. This will continue until long rates are bid up to the point of reflecting expected future short-term rates.

More specifically, the rate on a nine-month Treasury bill tends to approximately equal the average of today's rate on a three-month bill and the market-expected rate on a six-month bill issued three months from now. If today's three-month rate is 4 percent and the nine-month rate 6 percent, the implied forecast for the six-month rate three months from now is 7 percent. This is because the weighted average of 4 percent for three months and 7 percent for six months is 6 percent. The general method for calculating the market interest rate forecast is shown in Figure 6 (see appendix for formula).

The method just described is the traditional approach and will work whenever rates are free to reach their competitive levels. Recently, however, the development of interest rate futures markets has provided a more direct gauge of interest rate expectations. The prices of futures contracts for three-month Treasury bills and government securities provide a set of market forecasts of near-term interest rate prospects parallel to those available from yield curves. The two approaches should provide identical forecasts. Since contracting to buy a three-month Treasury bill six months from now is exactly equivalent to borrowing at a fixed rate for six months and investing the proceeds in a nine-month Treasury bill, interest rate expectations have the same effect on financial futures as they do on the term structure of interest rates. Futures prices for financial instruments are quoted on a discount basis; hence the interest rate forecast implied by a Treasury bill futures contract priced at 96 is $100 - 96 = 4$ percent.

In conclusion, we find that in reasonably efficient and competitive markets for uniform goods or assets, today's prices and rates are strongly influenced by forecasts of future market conditions, and that the term structures of commodity futures prices, forward exchange rates and interest rates provide good readings of the market's forecasts.

At this point, we must address the possibility that market prices of futures, both interest rate futures or forward exchange rates, may not predict future rates in an unbiased fashion. Put differently, the question is whether there is reason to expect that the rate predicted by the forward instrument will be systematically over- or underestimated. Two possible sources of bias may exist.

First, a bias may result from obvious market imperfections. For example, the existence of extensive credit allocation, heavy-handed administrative barriers to borrowing and lending, and tight exchange controls would provide prima facie evidence for the argument that forward rates may deviate systematically from the expected future exchange rate. On the other hand, the mere presence of controls does not necessarily imply that forward rates or interest rate differentials are biased, for many and devious are the paths of arbitrage. Only when controls on both the credit and foreign exchange markets are effective is a systematic bias likely to be evident. In such cases, forward rates or interest rate differentials provide a good starting point for forecasting and for the identification of profit opportunities, as we shall see below.

More difficult to deal with is the claim of the existence of systematic ex ante deviations, when no such barriers exist. The best known source of biases of this kind is the presence of a liquidity premium inherent in the prediction of short-term interest rates by long-term rates. According to this view, the yields on long-term instruments overestimate future short-term interest rates, just as yields on financial futures contracts are upward biased estimates of ex-

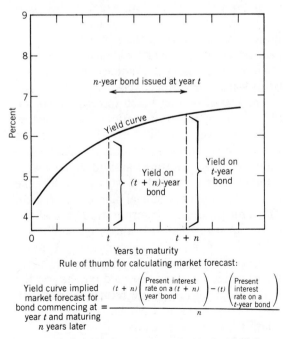

Figure 6 The Market Forecast Implied in the Yield Curve

pected future interest rates. The empirical evidence on the existence of liquidity premiums is not altogether clear, partially because of the statistical measurement difficulties. More important for our purposes, however, is the fact that estimates of such liquidity premiums have been quite small when they were found at all.[4]

In the case of foreign exchange rates the issue is a bit more difficult, if only because the evidence of market imperfections is more pervasive. Several strands of reasoning can be distinguished. One hypothesizes that because currencies are financial assets issued by different countries, they differ in terms of "political risk": countries can deprive holders of the use of their money balances, or can otherwise restrict their ultimate use to settle claims.[5]

Another argument supporting systematic forecasting errors has been based on the notion that yield differentials on the same assets denominated in different currencies reflect not only expected exchange rate changes but also a risk premium arising from the possibility that exchange rate changes may be correlated with returns on other assets, creating a systematic risk for speculators that cannot be diversified away.[6] The prevailing conclusion of researchers, however, is that such a "covariance term" is probably small, and that for practical purposes it is virtually impossible to identify any ex ante bias in the absence of specific market imperfections.[7] The equilibrium relationships presented in this section probably provide the most reliable framework for planning purposes.

HOW CAN FINANCIAL PLANNERS USE MARKET-BASED FORECASTS?

We have argued that, in the absence of a systematic bias, the forecasts of interest rates and exchange rate changes contained in the term structure of interest rates and forward rates represent the most realistic point estimate of market expectations. We shall now show why such forecasts should not be used in isolation, but rather as a *benchmark* against which to judge the firm's own ability to forecast or to exploit market imperfections. Given the market-based forecasts, we can distinguish three situations each with distinct implications for the maturity and currency aspects of financial planning.

Situation 1. *When the financial markets in question are reasonably efficient, and financial planners know of no systematic biases or constraints on market rates, then market-based forecasts should be accepted as valid.* Under these conditions, which probably hold for most financial decisions involving the U.S. and major international financial markets, no expected gain will result from manipulating the timing or currency of borrowing or investing, and financial management's energies should be directed toward matching borrowings and investments with the timing and currency of the funds needed or generated by the firm's operations.

Although this is a simple principle, its implementation requires a fairly detailed analysis of the firm's cash flows. The application of the above principle to financial planning must begin with the recognition that it is likely that the market's expected value will seldom be attained; indeed every *actual* interest rate and each *actual* exchange rate will be likely to differ from the value that was predicted by the futures or forward rate, respectively.

The use of market-based forecasts then implies planning for the deviations, or forecasting errors, that we know will occur. The first step in the planning process is to obtain a forecast that indicates how deviations around the expected interest rates or exchange rates will affect the entity for which a financial plan is established. This entity can be the corporation as a whole, or one of its affiliates. In the latter case, however, it is imperative to assess not the effects on the operating unit per se, but rather the effect that the change in the expected rate has on the unit's contribution to the return (or net cash flow) of the firm as a whole. In other words, marginal analysis is required.

Specifically, what we want to know is how cash flows from operations (return on assets) will change for any given deviation of the interest or exchange rate from the value predicted. As long as the return on assets is contractually fixed and denominated in a particular currency, as would be a portfolio of bonds or loans, the analysis is quite straightforward. A rise in interest rates will cause a proportional fall in the value of such a fixed-interest portfolio; and a given fall in the exchange rate will lead to an equal drop in the dollar value of the portfolio. Protecting the value of such assets, therefore, simply requires funding the liabilities of the firm in the same currency and maturity as the assets.

Unfortunately, this simple procedure is not applicable to multiunit international manufacturing operations. In such a firm, unexpected exchange rate and interest rate changes cause changes in prices, volumes, cost of inputs and similar factors in complex ways. Net cash flows and, therefore, return on assets can be affected positively, negatively, or not at all by a given exchange rate, according to its dependence on imports, its volume of export sales, its ability to raise prices and so forth. Similarly, an interest rate change may be associated with a rise or reduction in demand for the firms' products and have other indirect effects on operating cash flows. It is one of the most important functions of the financial planner to identify the specific cash flow effects that unanticipated interest or exchange rate effects may have for his particular firm. This, of course, is not an easy task.

Apart from the complexity of the analysis, there are technical issues of measurements that must be resolved. Should "return on assets" be measured in accounting terms, or in terms of expected future cash flows?

In periods of inflation, the valuation of assets at historical cost distorts accounting results. When foreign exchange rate changes combine with different rates of inflation and valuation principles based on historical cost, the resulting data differ substantially from those obtained by analyzing the impact of an unexpected exchange rate change on the operating results. The cash flow approach is the correct one; but financial planners who have faced the task of recasting data in pro forma accounting statements will recognize the difficulty of doing so. And if management compensation is tied to accounting results ("the bottom line"), the implementation of financial plans founded on market-based forecasts and deviations from expected cash flow becomes a heroic task. Finally, as to whether stock prices are affected by accounting results that do not reflect the cash flow effect of exchange rate changes, the empirical evidence is at present too scanty to draw conclusions one way or another.

Under the assumption that the market forecasts are the best available, no anticipated gain can be had by changing the maturity or currency mix of liabilities. Hence, the only rational purpose of financial planning in an efficient market is *to structure the firm's liabilities in such a way that any unanticipated change in the return on assets is offset, as far as possible, by a change in the effective cost of liabilities.*

Let us examine the basis for this principle more closely. Manufacturing and other nonfinancial enterprises expect a net profit because they have a competitive advantage in providing goods and services by managing real assets. The role of financial management is to protect this expected profit from unexpected fluctuations in financial market conditions. Since the structure of real assets is determined by fundamental business strategy considerations, the adjustment to offset financial risk must, therefore, occur on the liability rather than the asset side of the firm. We can illustrate the general principle with a few simple examples.

1. A firm operating only in one currency, whose operating cash flows fluctuate with inflation, can afford to fund itself largely with short-term debt, assuming that inflation is also the major influence on short-term rates.

2. On the other hand, a corporation whose operating return is uncorrelated or negatively corre-

lated with short-term interest rates is well advised to borrow long-term at fixed interest rates in order to stabilize its funding costs and thereby reduce the impact of unanticipated interest changes on final net cash flows.

3. Since the cost of foreign currency debt is directly correlated with unexpected exchange rate changes, the application of our general principle to foreign cash flows is quite straightforward. When a unit's operating returns are positively correlated with a currency's value, that unit should be funded in the same currency, because any unanticipated depreciation of the currency reduces not only returns from operations, but also the effective cost (interest rate plus/minus exchange rate change) of the liabilities.

It is, of course, very rare that the change in the net cash flow on the asset side will be completely offset by a change on the liability side; hence, a residual risk will always remain. However, it is an essential part of the task of financial planning management to gauge the magnitude of such risks and to communicate it effectively to top management. The function of top management is to decide whether this risk is tolerable, or whether operations must be restructured to reduce the basic sensitivity of the corporation to unanticipated changes in interest and exchange rates. Such operational adjustments often involve far-reaching strategic decisions: a change of markets and marketing (long-term contractual sales), a change in sources of supplies, the degree of in-house production versus purchases from outside suppliers, and perhaps even a change in the choice of technology to be employed in the production process.

The financial planning framework laid out above assumes the market's forecasts are unbiased predictions of future interest and exchange rates. Often, specific market imperfections will not allow this assumption to hold. The next two sections consider the implications of such biases.

Situation 2: *When the term structure of interest or exchange rates deviates in a systematic way from the*

market's actual expectations because of government controls on interest rates and exchange rates, or because of other specific market imperfections, financial management has profit opportunities. The exploitation of these opportunities requires (a) a flexible legal and operational structure, and (b) an explicit trade-off function that permits management to decide whether the gains are worth the increase in risk that the exploitation of market imperfections may involve.

Government intervention in credit and foreign exchange markets through administrative action, such as interest rate ceilings, quantitative credit allocation, or selection restrictions on international fund transfers tends to keep both interest rates lower and exchange rates higher than market participants think they should be. By the same token, such administrative controls imply that government limits access to credit and foreign exchange markets, thereby deciding who obtains credit and foreign exchange and the profits that are inherent in such favored positions. It is here that international firms as producing, job-creating enterprises with legal entities operating in many countries, centrally coordinated by corporate financial planning, have an advantage in arbitraging between actual rates and expected rates.

Unlike pure financial operators who could exploit profit opportunities only by contravening government laws and regulations, international firms can legally circumvent these restrictions, provided their financial activities are properly coordinated—and this is what financial planning is all about. Government controls tend to be always partial, never comprehensive. The reason is simple: controls on *all* borrowing or lending, and *all* international transfers of funds would cause economic activity to come to a grinding halt. Therefore, with regulations permitting certain transactions, and funds being fungible, international firms with diverse legal structures and a multitude of intercompany links usually are in a privileged position to exploit the financial windfalls that government actions provide by keeping interest rates low and preventing exchange rates from adjusting to market pressures.

Sometimes the maturity and currency of debt that will best capitalize on such market opportunities is close to that which would have been chosen merely in order to offset fluctuations in asset returns. However, decisions become complicated when the financial management must consider a maturity or currency structure that would increase the overall risk of the firm, but whose cost is less than the risk-minimizing alternative because of government controls of the type described above. In this case, top management must provide indications of how much more risk it is willing to accept in return for the lower cost of funds. Again, the task of financial planning is to clearly communicate the dimensions of the choice to top management in order to aid it in this crucial decision.

In many respects, situation 2—where market-based forecasts deviate from forecasted rates because of specific market imperfections—is similar to the situation which we discuss next.

Situation 3: *When the market-based forecasts deviate from forecasted rates, not because of market imperfections but because the firm has some proprietary information or unusual forecasting ability, then financial managers should act on their forecasts only when the risks of doing so are offset by the expected gains.* When financial planners can confidently answer the question. "Why do we believe we can predict interest or exchange rates better than the market?" their focus should be on the proper perspective on the risks involved in speculative actions, and on a rapid response to opportunities when action is warranted.

Few financial managers can consistently resist the temptation to base financing decisions on their own judgments rather than those of the market. In most cases little harm is done, for unless the firm really goes out on a limb, positive and negative forecasting errors tend to cancel out over time. But the mark of a good financial manager is not his knack for occasion-

ally outguessing the market's forecasts, but rather his ability to obtain the highest return on invested assets, for a given level of risk, and the best long-run terms and conditions on debt, *irrespective* of the trend of interest rates or exchange rates. It is important for the integrity of the financial management process to keep these aspects of the function strictly separate. Otherwise, the inability of financial management to outperform the markets tends to be hidden in the results of the risk-management function.

Speculative actions in financial markets should be vigorously segregated from the other functions of financial managers, and subjected to separate policy guidelines and scrutiny. A strategy for performance evaluation of the financial forecasting abilities of financial management is suggested in the next section.

MARKET-BASED FORECASTS AS YARDSTICKS FOR BUDGETING AND PERFORMANCE EVALUATION

We began this article with a discussion of corporate planning and budgeting; in this last section we shall try to show how market-based forecasts of financial data have applications in operating budgets and management control as well as in financial planning.

For multinational corporations with decentralized operating units, Robbins and Stobaugh have argued cogently that the prime tool for goal-setting and performance evaluation should be the periodic budget that is set jointly by financial planners and operating managers, and revised in the light of changing conditions.[8] On the other hand, few dispute the gains to be had from a centralized control of intracompany cash flows in order to respond to changing currency, interest rate, taxation, and exchange control developments. For our purposes, this means that operating units, such as foreign subsidiaries, should not be held responsible for interest rate or exchange rate developments.[9] Yet all budgets must explicitly or implicitly incorporate a cost of funds, and budgets for foreign operations must be translated at some exchange rate. What interest and exchange rates should be used?

Most corporations calculate the cost of funds using a standard interest rate based on past borrowing costs and translate foreign subsidiaries' cash flow projections at the exchange rate prevailing at budget date. That approach would be fine if the firm were somehow guaranteed the same interest rate and exchange rate for the entire budget period. When subsidiary managers are not held responsible for the impact of deviations from the budgeted exchange and interest rates, it surely makes more sense to use projected interest costs and exchange rates for budget preparation and performance evaluation than to use past rates. In the past, firms without access to a reliable exchange rate and interest rate forecasting service may have been reluctant to make such projections. The availability of costless market-based forecasts of interest and exchange rate trends, however, leaves them with no such excuse.

The market's forecasts may not be very accurate, but they will certainly result in fewer errors than the implicit assumption that today's rate is the appropriate projection. In addition, market rates have the virtue of being objective.

If operating managers are not held responsible for deviations of the actual cost of funds and exchange rate from the budget rates, then the financial managers whose task is to manage intercompany cash flows and transactions in the credit and foreign exchange markets must be made accountable for the impact of unanticipated interest rate and exchange rate changes. Here we find an additional virtue to the use of market-based forecasts for budgeting and performance evaluation purposes. We have argued that if financial managers choose to reject the market forecasts as a basis for financing, investment and currency decisions, they are implicitly asserting their own ability to "beat the market."

Can they do so? Only time will tell, but it will tell very explicitly if the consequences of actions based on the financial managers' *own* forecasts are consistently evaluated against the results of actions based on the *market's* forecasts. Either method of forecasting will result in errors, but the financial decision maker is justified in relying on his own forecasts only if doing so results in a superior average track record than would reliance on the market-based forecasts.

No financial manager can reasonably be blamed for being unable to predict unanticipated events in the financial system, but all managers should be evaluated against the dual criteria that (a) the cost of any effort to forecast interest and exchange rates should be justified on the basis of better-than-market performance and (b) the recognition that forecasting errors are inevitable and that the prime task of financial management is to structure the firm's cash flows in such a way that the impact of such errors is minimized.

CONCLUSIONS

The message of this article is as follows: corporate planning and budgeting relies in large part on projections of conditions in various markets, including those for the firm's products and services, labor and other inputs, credit, and foreign currencies. Management attention, we argue, should be concentrated on those markets in which the firm has a competitive advantage. Since the market's forecasts—implicit in the term structure of interest rates and of forward exchange rates—are readily available in the financial markets, which are both competitive and efficient, and in which the firm is unlikely to have a particular advantage, there is an a priori rationale for making borrowing and investment decisions based on these forecasts.

On the other hand, where financial managers feel they have a peculiar advantage in such financial markets, resulting from the firm's legal structure, geographical locations or because of an unusual forecasting ability, then the timing, maturity, and currency of borrowing and investment decisions should be based on the firm's own forecasts whenever the expected gains justify the risks. However, the risks and ex post performance of the decisions taken should always be compared against the outcomes of decisions based on market-based forecasts. The market's projections constitute the best benchmark for the evaluation of financial management's performance.

NOTES

1. To be precise, market efficiency need not imply that future prices are unbiased forecasts. For an exposition of the efficient markets argument, see Aldich A. Vasicek and John A. McQuown, "The Efficient Market Model," *Financial Analysts Journal* (September–October 1972), pp. 71–82.
2. See, for example, Robert Ankrom, "Among Their Hedges, Treasurers May Miss the Obvious," *Euromoney* (December 1977), p. 99.
3. The precise formulas for these linkages between interest rates, forward exchange rates, and currency and inflation rate expectations may be found in Ian H. Giddy, "An Integrated Theory of Exchange Rate Equilibrium," *Journal of Financial & Quantitative Analysis* (December 1976).
4. See studies cited in A. E. Burger, R. W. Lang, and R. H. Rasche, "The Treasury Bill Futures Market and Market Expectations of Interest Rates," *Federal Reserve Bank of St. Louis—Monthly Review* (July 1977), p. 5.
5. R. Z. Aliber, "Exchange Risk, Political Risk, and Investor Demand for External Currency Deposits," *Journal of Money, Credit and Banking* (May 1975), pp. 161–179.
6. Versions of this idea can be found in Michael C. Adler and Bernard Dumas, "Portfolio Choice and the Demand for Forward Exchange," *American Economic Review* (May 1976), pp. 332–339, and Bruno H. Solnik, "The International Pricing of Risk: An Empirical Investigation of the World Capital Market Structure," *Journal of Finance* (May 1974), pp. 365–379.
7. See Jeffrey A. Frankel, "On the Mark: A Theory of Floating Exchange Based on Real Interest Differentials," unpublished manuscript, Massachusetts Institute of Technology, October 1977, Appendix A.
8. Sidney M. Robbins and Robert B. Stobaugh, "The Bent Measuring Stick for Foreign Subsidiaries," *Harvard Business Review* (September–October 1973).
9. These issues are discussed in some detail in Donald R. Lessard and Peter Lorange, "Currency Changes and Management Control: Resolving the Centralization/Decentralization Dilemma," *Accounting Review* (July 1977).

APPENDIX

The exact formula for the term structure implied interest rate forecast is

$$_t r_{t+n} = \left[\frac{(1 + {}_0R_{t+n})^{t+n}}{(1 + {}_0R_t)^t} - 1 \frac{1}{n} \right]$$

where $_t r_{t+n}$ is the implied interest rate on a bond starting at t and maturing at $t + n$, $_0R_{t+n}$ is today's interest rate on a bond of maturity $t + n$, and $_0R_t$ is today's interest rate on a bond of maturity t. All interest rates are expressed as decimal fractions rather than as percentages.

19

FOREIGN INVESTMENT THROUGH DEBT-EQUITY SWAPS

Joseph Ganitsky
Gerardo Lema

Debt-equity swaps (DES) are becoming a popular mechanism for corporate investment in less developed countries. This article examines the historical background of DES, participants' typical costs and concerns, and factors to consider when analyzing a DES opportunity. The authors advise managers to base a decision on the merits of the project itself, and to be sure that a DES's benefits are in line with the firm's overall global strategy.

Managers of firms conducting business in less developed countries (LDCs) in the late 1980s must be familiar with and ready to use transnational debt-equity swaps. DES are financial transactions in which LDCs exchange part of their debt with foreign banks for equity rights to be sold to an interested party. The purchasers of these equity rights can be either the same lenders or else firms who pay lenders for these rights.

Debt-equity swaps can be a profitable source of competitive advantage for firms that exploit their key benefits. Notable advantages of DES include the following:

• Access to local currency at exchange rates more favorable than the official rates; this lowers the discount rate used in calculating the U.S. dollar net present value of possible investments in LDCs;

• Access both to previously protected markets and to less stringent profit remittance regulations;

• A basis for more harmonious relations with host governments; and

• An improved ability either to circumvent existing barriers to entry in global markets or to erect new ones.

Substantial benefits are available to firms capable of foreseeing, for each less developed

Source: Sloan Management Review (Winter 1988), pp. 21–29.

country, the likely evolution of the factors affecting both debt-equity swaps and their associated discounts. This article provides conceptual and pragmatic assistance to decision makers considering incorporating DES into their international investment process. We review the nature and historical background of debt-equity swaps and discuss motivations, benefits, costs, and concerns of DES participants. We then consider trends that support corporate interest in using debt-equity swaps. We conclude with an overview of the financial, operational, and strategic factors that maximize DES benefits.

NATURE OF DEBT-EQUITY SWAPS

Historical Background

Debt-equity swaps have surged as a short-term solution to the international debt crisis confronted by debtor nations, banks, and the international financial community.[1] U.S. banks are swapping their problem loans into equity investments because the debtors have insufficient hard currency to make interest payments, let alone to pay back principal. They make the swaps either directly, as an exchange for other loans with which the bank invests abroad, or indirectly, by selling the loan in the secondary market. Debt-equity swaps contrast with initiatives that address the debt crisis from a long-term perspective and demand continued support from banks and international organizations: DES rely solely on immediate market valuations.

Two factors have lured U.S. banks into direct investments. First, swaps outside the U.S. do not produce accounting losses, whereas the write-offs that would be taken against the loans in question exceed the financial capabilities of most banks. Second, losses from direct swaps tend to be smaller than those from a cash sale. On the other hand, banks have sold their debt in the secondary market in response to several factors: the risks associated with operating in unfamiliar businesses and turbulent environments; the bank's limited role as passive investor; and the 19.9 percent ceiling on the ownership of nonfinancial companies imposed by U.S. banking regulators. (This was abolished recently.[2])

Evolution

DES volume in the secondary market has grown from almost nothing two years ago to two billion dollars in 1985, and five billion dollars in 1986. (Most of the growth has been in Chile, the Philippines, Mexico, Turkey, Brazil, and Argentina.)[3] Decisions by other debtors to engage in DES transactions, and by U.S. money center banks to increase loan loss reserves on LDCs' loans (thus affecting their short-term profitability), are facilitating DES negotiations.[4] Even if DES volume were to reach fifty billion dollars in five years, as some analysts forecast, it would represent only a fraction of the half-trillion-dollar debt held in 1986 by LDCs.[5,6] There are, in any event, already indications in several countries that these forecasts are ambitious and may not materialize. Thus DES may be only a short-term opportunity for corporate investors.[7]

Role of the Participants

There are four major participants in the transnational debt-equity swap: the lending bank, the investor, the broker, and the debtor country.

The *lending bank* evaluates the possibility of unloading one or more problem loans. This evaluation considers the loan, the country, the impact of unloading on the bank's bargaining power with that and other debtors, and the evolution of discounts in related DES markets. If the bank decides to sell, it defines a negotiation discount range that will satisfy its own financial requirements.

When the bank's discounted loan is matched by an offer from a *corporate investor,* the loan is sold. In some cases the investor may be a domestic corporation in the LDC that has access to hard currency sources, often as a result of previous capital flight.

The *debtor country* redeems the debt in local currency after defining its procedures and policies for debt-equity swaps. Of particular importance to the debtor country are the following: areas of activity in which swaps are allowed; sources of soft currency to be tapped in reducing the nation's foreign debt (i.e., currency printing or internal debt), which ideally should be consistent with monetary policies to minimize inflationary effects; administrative processes used in reviewing and approving swaps; redemption rates; and restrictions on both profit remittance and capital repatriation.

The *broker* links these participants, and, through competitive bidding, helps disseminate financial and market information. Some brokers will purchase the loans in the event of failure by the corporate investor to fulfill the financial agreement. DES brokerage services are provided by traditional financial brokers, such as Merrill Lynch and Shearson Lehman Brothers, and by investment bankers themselves, such as Citicorp's 5,000-person Latin American investment network.[8] The role and the fees commanded by brokers decline as public officials, banks, and corporations learn the ins and outs of debt-equity swaps. Already some firms have successfully bypassed these brokers and so reduced costs.[9]

Financial Transactions

Several financial transactions make up each DES. Figure 1 depicts these transactions and the relations among participants. The example shows hard and soft currencies, fees, and obtained yield for a typical DES transaction.

The first transaction is a debt sale in hard currency. Lending banks sell debt obligations in hard currency from foreign debtors (whether central governments, their agencies, or private firms) in the U.S. secondary loan market, at a lower price than their nominal (or face) value. In the summer of 1987 average discounts of LDCs' debt ranged from Venezuela's 28 percent to Peru's 87 percent.[10] Debt obligations are usually purchased by brokers on behalf of investors, other banks, or corporations.

Next, a currency exchange takes place. The acquired hard-currency debt is presented by the purchaser to the country's central bank, which redeems it for local currency. The redemption rate is roughly equal to the debt's original face value (i.e., computed at the official exchange rate minus a transaction fee). However, some countries may attempt to capture a greater share of DES margins by lowering the redemption rates.[11]

The DES is concluded by the corporate investors who purchase, in local currency, equity rights to existing ventures or invest in the startup of new ones.[12]

Value of DES

The *net value* at which a corporation exchanges currencies through debt-equity swaps is obtained by subtracting the broker's discounts and the administrative or governmental fees from the proceeds paid in the secondary market adjusted by the redemption exchange rate. The *yield* is computed by dividing the net value

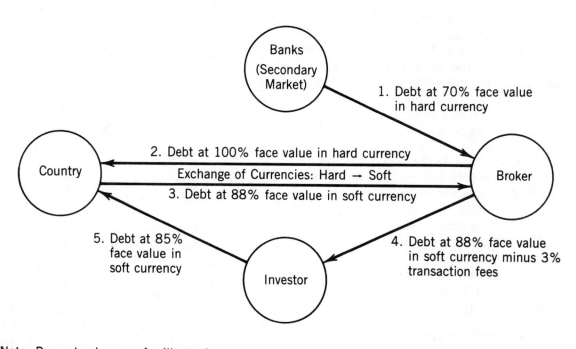

Note: Percent values are for illustrative purposes only.

Figure 1 Participants and Their Relationships in Transnational Debt-Equity Swaps

by the nominal value and subtracting one. The net value, the discounts, and the yield are immediate valuations in international financial markets of the LDC's long-term political and economic risks, its immediate ability to service its debt, and its capacity to generate a favorable investment climate.[13] If the country's long-term outlook is gloomy, the short-term discount tends to be high, and vice versa.

Managers can assess the value to the corporation of each DES from the perspective of either the increased positive cash flows, or the lowered discount rate used in calculating the net present value of the proposed investment. Both analyses will highlight a lower initial hard-currency requirement in any investment project. Moreover, managers should add a broader perspective (i.e., country-, industry-, and firm-risk profiles) to their immediate financial assessments. Once a DES is completed, the debtor country's old debt is replaced with a piece of ownership by the investing corporation in the debtor country. At that time, the outlook for the invested funds changes significantly. The corporation has modified the default risk of the investment by adding the industry and company risks to the country's economic/political risk. The corporate investor's resulting risk profile will depend on its ability to profit from the opportunities and resources at hand.

The value of DES to some corporations has been enhanced through expedient analysis of other, nontangible factors. Four factors have favored corporations willing to assume long-term commitments when debt-equity swaps were less popular, more uncertain, and less regulated.

First, debt-equity swaps' high net discounts generate political and economic forces in the debtor country oriented toward reducing them. These forces have already been incorporated into market perceptions that, in turn, will eventually be reflected in adjusted discounts. Although there is clear evidence that in early 1987 such forces existed in some nations, DES net discounts have not narrowed yet.[14] This sit-

uation seems to confirm Abell's notion that "the time to invest in a product or market is when a 'strategic window' is open."[15] That is, the period of time for debt-equity swaps' more favorable discounts to investors is expected to be short. This probability provides financial benefits of strategic significance.

Second, based on the fact that there is far more bad debt than there are good investment opportunities, markdowns could be expected to increase as banks try to dump more debt onto the DES market. In turn, host governments may attempt to limit markdowns either by imposing new restraints and rules or by appropriating some of the added discount through lower redemption rates. Hence, debt-equity swaps are more valuable for firms and banks capable of identifying opportunities that (a) have not been and are not likely to be regulated by governments, and (b) are consistent with the corporation's expertise, risk, and competitive profile.

Third, given that some swap discounts incorporate heavy penalties for short-term difficulties in the LDC, DES are more valuable to investors capable of identifying countries and industries with profiles brighter in the long rather than the short term. DES will be a less risky speculation to the corporate investor who is knowledgeable about improved long-term prospects for the country or industry.[16] For example, some investors in Mexico's swaps profited greatly as a result of recent, expected rises in oil prices that fueled an increase in Mexico's secondary market debt from 56 percent to 58 percent of face value between November 1986 and May 1987.[17]

However, most firms are not in a position to outpredict the market on average, nor can they do it for all countries, nor are they constantly shopping across countries to find the best DES deal. Thus most DES markets tend to balance and incorporate short- and long-term considerations.

Fourth, the country's economic and political risks may decline once the positive impact of initial swaps is felt. These risks can be reduced further when other investors decide to join in the recuperative process. This snowball effect, however, has lateral repercussions in the country's economic and political climate. Subsequent discounts of new swaps will tend to be lower and less advantageous to followers. For example, the average discount on Chilean debt paper has increased from 68 percent to 70 percent during the last year.[18]

Motivations

There must be a balance between the benefits and costs to all participants (summarized in Table 1) and the strategic and operational objectives of corporate investors. Nowadays, bankers and government officials understand that if this is not the case, then debt-equity swaps will not take place. Hence corporations, as new players in the negotiation between banks and countries, have great bargaining power before the deal goes through. By transforming the problems of banks and foreign governments into opportunities for growth, corporations perform a crucial catalytic role. By being sensitive to the motivations and costs of the other participants, corporate managers can further strengthen the firm's negotiating leverage.

BROAD TRENDS ATTRACT CORPORATE INVESTORS TO DES

During the late 1980s, managers responsive to the following three trends can use debt-equity swaps to enhance the value of their investments in LDCs.

Reduced Role of the Public Sector

In response to the growing problems associated with the debt crisis, governments have encouraged both the privatization of state-owned companies and the existence of free, unregulated, and nonsubsidized markets. As part of this trend, previous barriers to entry are being

eliminated. In addition, established firms may rationalize their operations, perform new functions, abandon old ones, merge with competitors, suppliers, or distributors, or redefine their missions.

As a by-product, industries in LDCs face numerous opportunities to restructure themselves. Established firms will have to change to survive, while newcomers—including foreign firms previously banned or discouraged— capable of competing will enjoy advantages.[19] Nissan, for example, spent fifty-four million dollars to update and expand warehouses and other facilities in Mexico. This investment, partially oriented to serving the U.S. market by exploiting Mexico's favorable labor costs, benefited from huge DES discounts: 42.5 percent from bank to government and 12 percent from government to Nissan.[20]

Global Competition

The globalization of industries has induced firms to broaden their scope and to be more aggressive in their search for competitive advantage and unique expertise.[21] Most investors— regardless of origin, size, or field—have recognized a strategic need to develop strengths in LDC markets that until recently were not considered vital.

Within this global perspective, some companies use debt-equity swaps to comply with local debt covenants, such as the maintenance of certain debt-to-equity ratios. For example, in 1985 Abbott Laboratories bought 6.2 million dollars of Philippine debt to improve its subsidiary's working and investment capital; that purchase was reflected in the company's debt-to-equity ratio.[22]

Reduced Prices as a Result of Oversupplied Markets

Lower prices have generated huge challenges to the public and private sectors. Several LDC governments, unable to maintain previous sub-

Table 1 Benefits and Costs of Debt-Equity Swaps to Participants

Participants	Strategic Benefits	Operational Benefits	Costs
Countries	• Reduce debt in hard currencies and services costs. • Encourage foreign investment and repatriation of capital flight. • Regain ability to borrow again in hard currencies at competitive rates. • Improve economic climate and utilization of resources and opportunities.	• Improve balance of payments and reduce strain on export earnings. • Encourage exports through use of investors' resources. • Focus investments in selected industries. • Reduce interest payments on existing loans.	• Sovereignty at stake. • Lose control of state-owned companies. • Capital inflow increases inflationary pressures. • Official recognition of unfavorable international rating, if discount is large. • Unfair precedent for established companies not benefiting from new DES.
Banks	• Change composition of loan portfolio. • Reassess risk/return assumptions on loans. • Focus lending strategy toward healthier and more promising opportunities. • Increase bank's short-term liquidity.	• Reduce exposure to default/currency risks. • Confront the problem: reduce management time on dubious loans and invest it in more rewarding activities. • Avoid increased lending as part of "rescue" packages.	• Potential downgrade of bank's entire loan portfolio. • Increase reserves at the expense of dividends/investments for growth. • Heavy cash losses due to loan discounting. • Establish undesirable precedent for other loans to same/other customers.
Investors	• Convenient/unique source of low-cost financing. • Expedite stalled and new projects fitting with global competitive strategy. • Increase bargaining power and recognition of strengths by host government.	• Lower cost than traditional investments. • Achieve strategy at a lower cost and facilitate market entry. • Gain access to activities/resources banned previously.	• Increase exposure to foreign, political, and economic risks. • Adjust policies and administrative systems to those of partners in case they are needed for successful operations in new environment. • Adaptation of investor's organization to country's legal, political, cultural, and ethical frameworks.
Brokers	• Expand financial services' assortment to customers. • Profit from developed trust between DES participants in the short and long term.	• Receive substantial commission fees from customers. • Develop broader skills to facilitate transactions.	• Risk credibility by failing to solve conflicts of interest among country, bank, and investor. • Managerial resources strained as a result of underestimating demands of the swap.

sidies, yet pressed to generate sources of employment, have modified their policies. For example, Bolivia's decision to cut price subsidies in the exploitation of its tin mines resulted in a major reallocation of workers and a redefinition of the country's international trade policies. As a result, Bolivia's currency value was strengthened in international financial markets. Businesses in LDCs have become better at (a) developing ways to deliver better-quality products at a lower cost, and (b) finding new products and markets.

Many LDC governments have concluded that their best bet for achieving long-term goals is to encourage firms to transfer and adapt new technologies, to develop new markets, and to use the country's resources efficiently and creatively. *Most governments of LDCs now have favorable attitudes toward potential foreign investors, and some have already enacted schemes to lure them.* These schemes include innovative variations of the debt-equity swaps described here.[23]

ANALYZING DEBT-EQUITY SWAPS

Decision makers can and should analyze any swap from three parallel perspectives: financial, strategic, and operational.

Estimating the Financial Advantages of DES

The project's viability *without* DES low-cost financing advantages should be examined first. If the forecasted return on investment, cash flow, market share, or any other measure used meets the firm's investment criteria, the project is viable. If the criteria are *not* met, though, the swap may improve the attractiveness of the project. Thus a similar analysis *including* DES benefits should follow. Debt-equity swaps' benefits could become a key parameter in the decision. (This approach is similar to looking at leverage considerations in any project.) Once

the project passes the firm's threshold financial criteria, analysts can examine it from operational and strategic perspectives.

Managers need to *assess* the likely evolution of *DES discounts* for each country considered. These assessments allow firms to decide how much discount to offer—and when to offer it—in the secondary loan market. For this purpose, decision makers should gather information concerning:

- Relevant international market fluctuations of discounts for each country;
- Factors influencing the bank's loan unloading records and future intentions; and
- Social, economic, and political forces affecting the LDC's government.

Given that the costs of gathering this information are high, a systematic internal approach seems to be justified only for very large and frequent investors. Other firms might prefer to make spot estimates when they consider entering the market. For both types of firm, the information provided by specialized brokers is valuable and should be considered by analysts.

Corporations estimating the financial advantages of debt-equity swaps find that their *lower costs yield shorter payback periods and higher return rates.* This outcome could favorably influence a firm's decision to carry out new or formerly rejected projects, to expand into target markets that suddenly seem more attractive, and to gain control of ventures previously beyond its realm. These multiple goals can be integrated in a single project, as exemplified by New Zealand's Tasman Bio purchase of 50 percent ownership in the Chilean company Papeles Bio-bio for 61.5 million dollars.[24]

Firms using DES lower costs enjoy significant cash-flow advantages over established competitors. These advantages can be used to buy market share, reap profits more quickly, or invest surplus cash flows in other projects.

To determine the impact of debt-equity swaps' financial advantages, managers must incorporate into their analysis the soft currency obtained at its effective exchange rate (lower than the official one), which adds a positive financial incentive to the opportunity. This incentive may be estimated by either altering the operational cash flows or reducing the cost of capital. Since the methods offer identical results, we present the simplest—altering the operational cash flows—below.

When starting to evaluate any investment project, financial managers estimate cash flows based on inflows and outflows during the life of the project, and then discount those cash flows at the project's cost of capital. If the project is of a similar nature and risk to others implemented by the company, decision makers will use the firm's cost of capital. If the project is of a different nature or risk, managers will define a specific cost of capital for the project. The company then discounts the cash flows at the cost of capital and usually compares the net present value (NPV) of the investment opportunity with other available investment projects. Subsequently, the company makes its investment decisions choosing the highest NPV in conjunction with capital rationing or any other corporate constraint.

In the calculation of the project's NPV, the presence of financial benefits is viewed as a *positive addition* to the operational cash flows. This addition varies with the type and source of financing. In the case of debt-equity swaps, the additional component comes from the cheaper funds available because of lower exchange rates. Thus the investment amount is lower when the hard currency is exchanged for soft currency at a lower rate. Accordingly, the NPV analysis can be defined as:

$$NPV = Base\ NPV + NPV\ of\ financial\ decisions.[25]$$

For example, a company plans to invest $1,000,000 in Mexico, which will generate $250,000 per year for a period of ten years, the life of the project. The company's assumed cost of capital for this project type (i.e., nature and risks) is 15 percent. Therefore the base NPV is

$254,692. Since the NPV is positive, the project is a good investment. However, the company can make it more attractive by using DES. If the company obtains an effective 20 percent discount (after government and broker's fees) on the initial investment of $1,000,000, the NPV of the swap is $200,000 (i.e., $1,000,000 × 0.2), which is what the company saves on the initial investment. Thus, the total NPV is $454,692 (i.e., $254,692 + $200,000). This enhanced total NPV makes the investment still more attractive.

To appreciate even more the financial benefits of DES, let's assume that the project's higher risk calls for a higher cost of capital (20 percent instead of 15 percent). At that cost of capital the base NPV is $48,118 and the total NPV is $248,118. The project is still very attractive, though more dependent on DES net discount. This example illustrates the increasing importance of debt-equity swap's discounts as the risks of potential investments increase—which happens often in LDCs.

In summary, the financial advantages of DES are additional cash flows that increase the attractiveness of the NPV's base (operational) cash flows.

Strategic Considerations for Investors

While financial analysis is being carried out, corporate managers also examine strategic factors in the context of the firm's global competitive profile. The swap's strengths are identified more easily than its weaknesses, but the latter require greater consideration. DES risks and the environmental threats magnify the vulnerability of the firm. Nationalist sentiments, rampant inflation partially fueled by other swaps, currency swings, and uncertainty about how the host government will manage its economy in the future are a few of the risks to be evaluated by decision makers before any swap is approved.

DES projects that imply a diversification in either products or markets, as most do, must pass three essential tests recently advanced by Michael Porter.[26]

- The industries chosen must be structurally attractive or capable of being made attractive.
- The costs of entry must not capitalize all the future profits.
- Either the new investment must gain competitive advantage from its link with the corporation, or vice versa.

Even those projects that do not call for diversification of the firm's operations must pass the industry-attractiveness test both in global and local contexts. Figure 2 shows four investment scenarios and their respective strategic decisions.

The following examples will clarify the four scenarios of Figure 2. Sugar cane processing is by all accounts a mature industry facing serious problems. Thus, attractiveness using either a local or a global perspective is very low (scenario 1). In this case DES benefits would not be enough to change that lack of attractiveness.

On the other hand, numerous products within the chemical industry, though mature and less attractive in most of the world, still have good opportunities in most LDCs (scenario 2). A decision to invest in this industry could be facilitated by DES benefits, if a swap increased the NPV of the project. These bene-

fits can switch a project from being unattractive to being attractive.

The optical fiber industry, as a third example, is attractive globally, but is at an early stage of maturity in most LDCs (scenario 3). Investors would be well advised to wait for the expansion of that industry in the LDC under consideration. Otherwise, they may suffer the consequences of small markets and slow growth for several years.

Finally, if Brazil were to open its reserved computer market through swaps, several firms would enter almost at once, considering the profits they can reap from Brazil's huge domestic consumer and institutional markets (scenario 4). However, this is unlikely to happen, given Brazil's policy of developing strong and sovereign computer and defense-related industries.

DES would not protect firms investing under *any* scenario from reversals in host government policies, but heightened rewards would make the risk of this eventuality more palatable to decision makers.

Managers usually have difficulty evaluating the relationship between resources and expectations at the global and local levels. Such issues as how to transfer the investor's global strengths (for example, technology or managerial systems) to the new venture without weakening the corporation's long-term competitive position are not easily addressed. The firm's

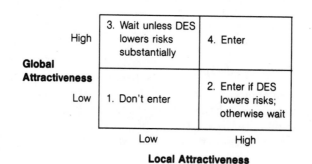

Figure 2 Strategic Decisions in Four Scenarios Based on Industry Attractiveness

decision to use DES should reflect an integrated analysis of both DES opportunities and the firm's global strategy.

Operational Considerations for Investors

Managers responsible for determining whether a specific DES makes sense must look beyond strategic and financial attractiveness. The firm's operational and managerial fundamentals, as well as its capacity to support the investment implicit in a given swap, are critical to the swap's success.[27] They should be examined from both a global and a country perspective.

Firms must be willing to meet the requirements of the host country. If the two parties cannot reconcile their differences, there is no point in pursuing swap options any further.[28] As project analysis proceeds, corporate decision makers should be especially receptive to the debtor country's

- Managerial processes unique to DES transactions, which must be fulfilled by the firm's representatives (see Appendix); and
- Perspectives and priorities in regard to DES, usually targeted at specific projects such as privatization or job creation. Such projects may not offer reasonable profit potential, or focus on economic sectors likely to generate stable revenues.

The firm's capacity to favorably influence the governmental review process and perspectives for DES projects is especially critical in cases where limitations to profit remittance and capital repatriation can be imposed.

CONCLUSION

It is too early to assess debt-equity swaps' long-term impact on corporate performance. However, there have been a sufficient number of swaps that comprehensive descriptions of corporate experiences should be forthcoming. Until such research is completed, corporations aiming to maximize the benefits of debt-equity swaps may benefit from the following guidelines.

- Make the investment decision based on the firm's risk and strategic profiles, the industry's attractiveness, and the host country's political and economic outlook.
- Consider joint venture arrangements; invest substantial energy in choosing a reliable local partner knowledgeable about market and governmental operations.
- Deploy resources sufficient to improve the chances of project success.
- Invest in economic sectors likely to offer steady sources of revenue; for example, exports or low-cost and well-differentiated goods and services for the local market.
- If the project represents substantial diversification for the corporation, make sure that it passes Porter's three tests, mentioned earlier.
- Invest preferably only if the project is within a highly attractive industry both at the global and local levels.

APPENDIX: CORPORATE RESPONSES TO LDC-GOVERNMENT PROCESSES

First, a substitution-of-debt proposal must be presented to the host government's ministry of finance or central bank and to the agency regulating foreign investments. This proposal, signed by the firm's representative and the bank(s) selling the rights on the debt, details the following: purposes of the proposed arrangement; actions to be taken by the participants on the closing day of the operation; and instructions for disposition and disbursement of the various moneys derived from the operation.

The prospective investor must also obtain an official letter of conformity from the ministry or bank. This includes, among other items: amount; term; origin of the paper; redemption rate; manner in which the agreed-upon amount for the issuance of the company to be capitalized will be paid by the public-sector debtor whose paper is used for the operation;[29] interest rates earned and other terms regulating the funds not used by the capitalized company, administrative discounts; and restrictions (if any) on either capital repatriation or profit remittances.

In addition, approval of the DES must be obtained from the governmental agency controlling foreign investments. This agency will examine the proposal in terms of the benefits the specific project will bring to the national economy. In the event that the project is authorized, the redemption rate and the fees charged, if variable, will be a function of these benefits.

NOTES

1. The international debt crisis was discussed at length in the Fall 1986 *Columbia Journal of World Business.*

2. See P. Truell, "Fed Agrees to Let U.S. Banks Acquire Nonfinancial Firms in Debtor Nations," *The Wall Street Journal,* August 13, 1987.

3. J. Newman and K. Fogerty, "Silent Revolution in Bank Portfolio," *FT Euromarket Report,* June 9, 1986; and B. Hannon and M. Haugen, "Latin America: Debt Conversion Proliferates," *Business America,* June 22, 1987.

4. See L. Berton, "Auditors Press Banks to Bite Bullet on Foreign Loans," *The Wall Street Journal,* June 8, 1987; P. Truell an C. F. McCoy, "Banks Try Debt-Equity Swaps in Crisis," *The Wall Street Journal,* June 11, 1987; and J. Fierman, "John Reed's Bold Stroke," *Fortune,* June 22, 1987.

5. "A Way to Turn Debt from a Burden to a Boom," *Business Week,* December 22, 1986.

6. K. S. Witcher and R. B. Schmitt, "Growing Market in Third World Debt Raises Questions in Loans' Value," *The Wall Street Journal,* October, 1986.

7. W. A. Orme, "Swaps Said to Have Little Impact on Mexico Debt," *International Herald Tribune,* December 1986; and E. W. Desmond, "Whittling Away at Debt," *Time,* October 13, 1986.

8. S. Bartlett, "The Citi Squeezes Its Lemons," *Business Week,* June 15, 1987.

9. "How One MNC Handles Debt-Swap Paperwork In-House to Cut Costs," *Business Latin America,* February 23, 1987.

10. Bartlett, "The Citi Squeezes Its Lemons."

11. "What to Expect from Latin America after Citicorp's Debt Move," *Business Latin America,* June 8, 1987.

12. For an overall look at LDCs and DES, see R. W. Boatler and M. T. Stanley, "Latin American Equities and International Portfolio Diversification," paper presented at the Conference of Business Association for Latin American Studies, April 1986; S. E. Halliwell, "Could Debt-Equity Swaps Make Global Debt Manageable?" *ABA Banking Journal,* April 1984; and R. M. Lipton, "Debt-Equity Swaps for Parent Subsidiary," *Journal of Taxation,* Vol. 59 (December 1983), pp. 406–413.

13. For a discussion of the political and economic risks, see R. B. Stobaugh, "How to Analyze Foreign Investment Climates," *Harvard Business Review* (September–October 1969), pp. 100–108.

14. See, for example, "Debt Equity: Strike While the Iron Is Hot," *Business Latin America,* January 8, 1987.

15. D. F. Abell, "Strategic Windows," *Journal of Marketing* (July 1978), pp. 21–26.

16. Though banks may now invest in some of these opportunities, most do not have the operational expertise or the resources to manage them. They prefer to pass the opportunities on to others.

17. Bartlett, "The Citi Squeezes Its Lemons."

18. "Focus on Finance," *Business Latin America,* May 18, 1987.

19. Two recent examples of this trend in Latin America are Mexico's and Chile's privatization efforts, which follow similar ones in Ecuador, Brazil, Argentina, and Venezuela. See J. E. Austin et al., "Privatizing State-Owned Enterprises: Hopes and Realities," *Columbia Journal of World Business* (Fall 1986), pp. 51–60; "Mexico Modifies Investment Rules," *Business Latin America,* September 8, 1986; and "Chile's Goals for Privatization," *Business Latin America,* February 16, 1987.

20. B. Hannon and S. Gould, "Debt-Equity Swaps Help Latin America out of Its Debt Dilemma," *Business America,* January 19, 1987.

21. See, for example, T. Levitt, "The Globalization of Markets," *Harvard Business Review* (May–June 1983), pp. 92–102.

22. "Debt Conversion Scheme Allows Low-Cost Investment in Philippines," *Business Asia,* September 1, 1986.

23. "Next Wave of Variations on Debt-Equity Swaps Offers Creative New Options," *Business Latin America,* April 6, 1987.

24. "New Zealand Expands Ties with Chile," *Chile Economic Report* (November 1986), pp. 3–4.

25. Many writers have addressed the components of NPV. See, for example, R. Brealey and S. Myers, *Principles of Corporate Finance,* 2d. ed. (New York: McGraw-Hill, 1984).

26. M. E. Porter, "From Competitive Advantage to Corporate Strategy," *Harvard Business Review* (May–June 1987), pp. 43–59.

27. Identifying the "right" people and what is expected from them usually becomes the focal point of analyzing op-

erational requirements. The new participant(s) assumes the critical role that in a different context is performed by the broker.

28. For a discussion of strategies and processes used to reconcile the conflicting economic and political imperatives between investing nations and host governments, see

Y. L. Doz, "Strategic Management in Multinational Companies," *Sloan Management Review* (Winter 1980), pp. 27–46.

29. If existing subsidiaries are being improved, or new ventures are being formed, corporations will obtain local currency for the release of debt rather than equity rights.

20

STRATEGIES AND MANAGEMENT CONTROLS FOR GLOBAL CORPORATIONS

John J. Dyment

A global corporation will have to be managed very differently than either a domestic or a multinational company. The management control system must be designed to suit the global strategy.

Companies evolve from domestic to multinational to global. Along the way, the management control systems must also change to reflect a dramatic change in the definition of the strategic business unit. If the old controls remain in place, the focus of management's actions may be misdirected and the advantages of going global may be lost.

A global corporation is one that gains a competitive advantage through a coordinated strategy that includes all the countries in which it operates. This contrasts with the multinationals that operate in each country with locally defined strategies and organizational structures.

The global corporation, for example, may have a product that was designed in a European country, with components manufactured in Taiwan and Korea. It may be assembled in Canada, and sold as a standard model in Brazil and as a model fully loaded with options in the United States. Transfer prices of the compo-

nents and assembled product may be determined with an eye to minimizing tax legally. Freight and insurance may be contracted for and relet through a Swiss subsidiary, which earns a profit subject only to the low cantonal taxes. The principal financing may be provided from the Eurodollar market based in London. Add the complication of having the transactions in different currencies, with foreign exchange hedging contracts gains and losses that sometimes offset trading losses or gains, and one has a marvelously complex management control problem.

Who earns the profit, how much was earned, and was this the planned result?

These questions reflect the standard approach to management control. Set an objective, assign responsibility for a result, compare what actually occurred with what was expected, and take corrective actions if needed.

In today's world of rapid communications, intensive competition, and dynamic technological change, a very different approach to management control is needed. One must change from what was considered appropriate for a

Source: The Journal of Business Strategy, Vol. 7 (Spring 1987), pp. 20–26.

stable economy (which proved not to be so stable, thanks to OPEC and other factors) to a radically different approach to management controls. For the global corporation, one needs a system that measures and rewards performance based on achieving strategic objectives that cross national borders, including the gains that come from intelligent selection of where in the world each value-added component should be located. This usually means that one needs to set aside the traditional management control systems that are much more appropriate to the management of a domestic, noninternational business unit. With few differences, the domestic control systems have also been adopted by most multinational or multidomestic corporations. These control systems should change when the strategy adopted is global.

MANAGEMENT CONTROL SYSTEMS

For *domestic corporations,* a sound management control system could consist of:

- *Standard costs* which serve as a yardstick against which to measure actual cost of operations;
- *Monthly budgets* and reporting of actual expenditures compared with budgets by area of organizational responsibility;
- A *long-range plan* that guides the allocation of the organization's resources; and
- A *strategic plan* that focuses all the activities of management toward achieving a distinctive advantage that is valued by a segment of the market.

For *multinational corporations,* the domestic information system is modified to meet the legal and managerial situation of operating in a number of countries. These modifications usually involve the following:

- *Reporting requirements for each country's fiscal and tax authorities.* These usually differ significantly from U.S. government or internal managerial reporting needs.

- *National budgets and five-year plans, against which actual results are compared.* These plans and results may be forwarded to regional and international headquarters where they are analyzed, additional information is often requested, and summary reports are prepared.

Despite the different market and technological situations in each country, and despite the transfer prices which are usually not controlled by the country's affiliate's chief executive, reports of each country's results are critically important to the career success of the expatriate executive. "My plan is my contract," said the chief executive for Italy of a major U.S. multinational. His bonus, and, indeed, his job, depended on the art of foreseeing the results of his actions, predicting foreign exchange shifts, and making decisions on where his material supplies should come from.

Typically, multinational management control reports are made using a worldwide uniform system of account classification, designed primarily to facilitate the consolidation of results at corporate headquarters. If the multinational is headquartered in the United States, the consolidation will produce reports for the SEC, stockholder reports based on Financial Accounting Board Standards, and data for the Internal Revenue Service.

It is probable that the global purpose of the multinationals could be better achieved by redesigning the management control reports to focus on strategic needs of local management rather than on requirements, of the parent company's legal and internal analysis reporting system. Because management control accounting should be fast and relevant to be useful, the multinational's domestic reporting often results in a dysfunctional system. Affiliate accountants' priorities are first; the reports to the parent company, second; the legal reports to the local fiscal and tax authorities, third; and last, if there is any time for it at all, information to assist the local resident management to control their actions and to improve the affiliate's strategic position against local competition. The management reporting systems of the multinational companies could often be improved by a process of recognizing the inconsistency in the objectives of reports for stockholders, tax authorities, and management.

Global corporations have needs that are different from those of multinationals. The strategic information needed by global corporations *must* cross international borders, whereas the strategic information needs of the multinational's foreign affiliate's managers are most often focused on the local environment, local competitors' capabilities, and the local organization's economic strength. The global corporation executive must make economic decisions involving all aspects of the value-added chain from research and development, through manufacturing to distribution, with an integrated, worldwide strategy. One should first look at the strategic advantage sought by the global corporation as the basis for determining the management controls it needs.

THE STRATEGIC ADVANTAGE OF THE GLOBAL CORPORATION

Today's technology has made communication and transportation accessible even to isolated parts of the world. The result has been a homogenization of demand. People everywhere want what they have heard is in demand elsewhere—from McDonald's hamburgers to CAT scanners. The homogenization of demand may be stratified by income level and may vary considerably in size among countries. For example, a product in demand by middle-income people in the United States may only have a market among upper-income people in India. Nevertheless, the result is global demand for globally standardized products, with corresponding economies of scale for the global supplier. The global company can select the location and management approach for each element in the value chain that gives it a strategic advantage. For example:

- Raw material may be purchased in business environments that support just-in-time inventory replenishment techniques.

- Computer-integrated manufacturing can be used where the skill base exists.

- Labor-intensive manufacturing can be located in low-labor-cost countries, and capital-intensive manufacturing can be established in locations with low financing costs.

- Transportation to the assembly plants or distribution warehouses can be planned in ways that add relatively little costs.

- A common sales force can be used to serve a number of countries, and proprietary marketing techniques can realize more scale cost reductions.

- Other advantages of lower costs due to scale may be achieved by centralized and vertically integrated manufacturing, centralizing purchasing, and being able to spread research and development costs and market research costs over larger product volumes.

Adopting the techniques of world-class manufacturing can give the global corporation an enormous cost advantage over domestic competitors. Modern inventory management can produce turnover rates of 80 to 100 times a year, in contrast to the two or three turnovers experienced by the typical U.S. manufacturer. Computer integrated manufacturing can cut the need for labor by a factor of ten.

And the labor that is used can cost less. Labor costs in Korea's auto plants average $3 per hour, those in Japan $12, and in the United States, over $20. It has been reported that attention to the methods of fully using cargo capacity allows the Japanese to ship from steel mills in Japan to Australia at the same cost for U.S. mills to ship from Pittsburgh to Detroit.

The overall economies of scale for a disposable syringe company that adopted a global strategy illustrate the extent of the advantage that may be expected. As reported in the Harvard thesis of Marquise Cvar, of the Cvar-Von Hapsburg Group, when this company went global it doubled the volume from its U.S. base and produced cost reductions of 20 percent in production, 15 percent in marketing, 5 percent in purchasing, and 50 percent in R&D (or 25 percent of total costs on a weighted average basis).

It is not only lower costs that are achievable. Automated manufacturing and rapid product enhancements from technological research may allow the global corporation to provide a higher product quality than competition, and when this quality advantage is combined with lower costs, the result is devastating to the non-global competitors. Two of the generic strategies to gain a competitive advantage are cost and differentiation. The Chevrolet, for years, was sold simply on the strategy of providing North Americans with reliable transportation at a lower cost than for most other cars. Rolls-Royce pursued a pure differentiation strategy, providing a car of luxury and immaculate quality, with little concern for the low cost of transportation. Then Toyota, with a global strategy, entered the market in the early 1970s with a car that embraced elements of both generic strategies. It was several thousand dollars cheaper than the Chevrolet yet was perceivably a higher-quality car. (See Exhibit 1.) In a few years, Toyota and then other Japanese cars cap-tured a large share of U.S. and the world's car markets, creating a crisis for the U.S. manufacturers from which they have still not recovered.

The global corporation may also differentiate itself through its international image. This is particularly evident in cosmetics and fashion clothing where awareness of a product's success in other countries enhances its image domestically.

THE MANAGEMENT CONTROL SYSTEM

The management control system needed for a global corporation should enable management to control the essential strategy of the company. This strategy will differ in fundamental characteristics from those of both a national and multinational corporation. The concept that business is a portfolio of separate businesses whose optimum strategies may be determined by their relative market shares and relative growth rates can be disastrous if applied to the global corporation. The global corporation requires a strategy that interrelates the use of all its resources.

The multinational corporation, with local strategies, may assign resources based on the relative success of each strategic business unit. For the global corporation, measurement of whether a business unit in a particular country is earning a superior return on investment relative to risk may be irrelevant to the contribution an investment may make to the worldwide, long-term results of the enterprise. The return earned in a country unit may even be negative, yet new investments may be justified by the contribution the unit can make to the worldwide strategy.

The global organization must be centrally managed, and the product managers must have worldwide authority. That is, the local results must not be the main measure of how well the planned results are being achieved. Local profit and loss results are important for fiscal tax and financial reports but do little to measure how

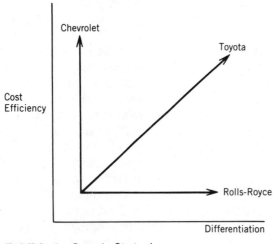

Exhibit 1 Generic Strategies

well management has been achieving strategic goals.

CHOOSING THE SUCCESSFUL GLOBAL STRATEGY

The corporation that wants to compete globally must define its strategic excellence positions (SEPs). These SEPs are the distinctive capabilities of a corporation, its product, or service that have special value to a particular part of the marketplace.

Examples of strategic positions of global corporations are:

Global Company	SEP
Gillette	Innovation and quality
IBM	Financial strength and customer service
Kodak	R&D and standard quality
L.M. Ericsson	Electronic telephone switching techology
Caterpillar	Wordwide distribution and service
McDonald's	Standard quality worldwide

Each of these companies has concentrated sufficient resources on its SEPs to achieve a preeminent competitive position.

To arrive at such a position, an organization needs first to agree on its mission, defining its vision of what it wants ultimately to become, its product or service scope, and the territory in which it wants to operate. The mission must be based on the beliefs and values of the operating executive responsible for implementation of the strategy, otherwise implementation will not be achieved. If the strategy is not implemented, performance will not result.

With the heavy involvement of the operating executives, the organization next needs to analyze systematically:

- *The environment.* What opportunities and risks will result from emerging trends, by segment of the market? What likely technological changes may take place? What is happening to the economy that will likely affect the company's strategies?
- *The competition.* Who are they, how big are they, and what are the strategic excellence positions of each?
- *The orgainzation's own capabilities.* What does the company do particularly well that has a value to an important segment of the market? What resources can the company use to improve each element of its value chain (from design, to manufacturing, to distribution, to after-sales service)?

Clearly, making this analysis for each potential market, and considering the host of options concerning where manufacturing facilities may be placed, could take an unreasonable amount of time. The company seeking a global strategy must structure the process to prioritize available options and then study only those with the highest priorities. Using the operating executives in this process greatly reduces the analysis time from what would be necessary using outside or even in-house consultants. Consultants are valuable for guiding the process to be followed, and for gathering facts, but they should not be asked to develop the strategies that operating management must later implement.

It may help for operating management to review, systematically, each of the sources of strategic excellence. A list of these sources may be found under each of the generic strategies of efficiency, differentiation, and time. (See Exhibit 2.)

The review should compare opportunities and competitors' positions of strength with the corporation's own capabilities. Then, the executive group should select and agree to focus on the few, key SEPs that will give the global company a competitive advantage.

Next, for each of these positions the company should decide upon long- and short-range objectives. Objectives are internally oriented, quantified, and time-related statements of what must be accomplished to achieve the strategic excellence position.

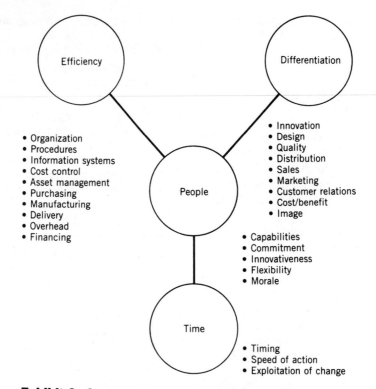

Exhibit 2 Sources of Strategic Excellence

The key to the management control system for the global corporation is to identify the *critically few objectives* that should be achieved next year, and those that will be achieved later. Next year's *critical few* are those objectives that *must* be accomplished and hence need special attention by top management. It is these critically few objectives that should form the nucleus of the global corporation's management control system.

CENTRALIZED INFORMATION

At the managerial headquarters, certain control information will be needed to measure progress toward achieving the global strategic goals so that, if necessary, corrective action may be taken or plans changed. The future environment and competitors' actions will rarely turn out as anticipated, so strategic plans need to be flexible and changed to take advantage of new opportunities and to avoid unexpected obstacles.

The information needed should consist primarily of:

- *Critical few objectives.* Data is needed to measure progress toward achieving the critical few objectives. These objectives will not be standard in format, differing by country and year as they are accomplished and renewed. For example, a manufacturing unit may report on its progress toward implementing just-in-time inventory management; another may report the progress on constructing an automated plant. A sales unit entering a new market may report on the number of qualified salespeople hired, while a sales organization in a developed market may report on total sales and margins by product line and customer type.

- *Financial control reports.* The information required to maintain overall control of the financial viability and profitability of the enterprise usually requires a lot less information than typically required by a multinational corporation. Consider the major items of a balance sheet. Most need to be managed through specific information reporting systems—usually on a close–to–real time basis:

- International cash management is a daily, even hourly activity in global corporations. Worldwide cash positions are so closely managed that additional reporting on a monthly basis is redundant.

- Receivables and inventories also use short-term controls for past-due accounts and inventory replenishment. These items can be reviewed on a monthly basis in ratio terms (i.e., number of days of sales in receivables, percentage receivables past due, days of costs in inventories, and percentage of inventory older than a specified number of months).

- Changes in fixed assets are usually controlled through reports that measure progress on capital expenditure programs. These are special, and important, and for major projects may require weekly reports of a technical nature on progress. The month-to-month change in the total fixed asset value is of little significance for control purposes.

- Current liabilities should be managed as part of the cash management controls and are therefore part of the daily, even hourly, reports of available cash and amounts due for payment. In the global corporation, it is important to borrow short-term funds in the country with the lowest cost, taking into account exchange risk and currency control restrictions. As this is written, commercial bank prime lending rates range widely among major countries (e.g., 3.75 percent in Japan, 7 percent in W. Germany, 12 percent in the United Kingdom, and 18.5 percent in Australia). The location of borrowing can make a significant cost difference. Monthly reporting on current liabilities is redundant except for reports required by creditors, and for shareholders.

- Significant changes in long-term debt and issued capital are the result of major, carefully considered decisions and are reported when they occur. Again, monthly reporting of the current balance adds little to management control.

In sum, financial control over the elements of a global corporation's balance sheet need specific systems, many requiring daily or hourly measurements of current positions. The traditional monthly reporting of balance sheets, profit and loss statements, and a multitude of supporting schedules provides very little additional control, and probably does not justify its cost in most global corporations.

- *Tax, legal, and administrative compliance.* Similarly, the information needed for tax, legal, and administrative purposes, if separated from the management control reporting requirements, may be kept to a minimum by focusing on only the critical information that is needed. The information needed will depend on each country's tax and regulatory reporting requirements, some of which will be monthly, some quarterly, and others once a year.

- *Tactical information.* An example of tactical information would be the worldwide foreign exchange position by currency, which is used to hedge exposed positions in the currencies deemed most likely to weaken in future. Long- and short-term raw material supply situations may also be coordinated and balanced centrally in some global corporations.

- *Management accounts.* Prepared primarily for determination of top management bonus compensation, accounts may be kept that measure, according to a set of agreed upon rules, the contribution various international transactions make towards the overall earnings of the enterprise. The staff that maintains these accounts is fully advised about the rules for recording the global profit contribution created by complex transactions, such as swaps, countertrade and multicountry transactions. Incentive bonuses for producing profitable business transactions are determined by the results of the management accounts.

MANAGEMENT COMPENSATION

The total compensation of a manager can consist of the following:

- A *basic salary,* independent of performance incentives.

- A *profitability bonus* based on the results shown in the management accounts. This will not apply to all positions or to all global corporations. The management profitability bonus is most appropriate in situations where the executives can take initiatives that result in a profit. Again, the profit may be made in the purchase or production and sale of the product itself, or from a gain on trading in the freight position, financing, insurance, and foreign exchange required to complete the transaction.

- A *performance bonus* based on achievement of the critically few objectives defined for each position.

As discussed, the weight given to achievement of the critical objectives should depend on what each organizational unit is expected to accomplish during the year and should be negotiated with each manager in advance. Similarly, the proportion of total compensation assigned to the basic salary, a profitability bonus, and performance bonus may vary depending on the functional roles assigned to the unit. These may be defined by the unit's role as either a sales center, a cost center, or a profit center. In the latter case, any simple calculation of an organizational unit's profit in a global corporation is not likely to be a useful measurement of the unit management's contribution, hence the need for special management accounts.

REDUCING REPORTING REQUIREMENTS

The purpose of management controls in the global corporation should be to see that the overall, worldwide strategies of the organization are being successfully implemented. Therefore the principal management reporting requirements should be about how the critically few objectives assigned to each unit are being accomplished. If the reports indicate that an objective is not being achieved, special attention can be given to correcting the out-of-line situation. Where the nonachievement of an objective is due to a condition that is out of the control of management, the global strategy itself will need to be reviewed and possibly amended. However, the reports on progress to-

ward achieving critical few objectives will normally not require much numerical data or extensive written commentary. A system of worldwide, hourly or daily reporting of cash, borrowing, and exchange positions will typically be needed so that the total currency exchange risk may be controlled and working capital obtained at the lowest financing rates that do not impair the exchange risk position.

The remaining financial reporting can be minimized. Total sales, gross and net profit, days of sales in receivables, days of costs in inventories, and total capital expenditures should give the essential information as to how the organization is doing overall. Although few companies will go to the extreme of eliminating all reporting except for these few numbers, the mass of detail submitted monthly to regional and world headquarters can usually be radically reduced. A good working rule is to obtain detailed reports on the results of the next lower organizational level, and to have summary data only on the levels below that. Information required for mandatory reports to government regulators or tax authorities may be reported and controlled separately from the management control system.

CONCLUSION

The decision to adopt a global strategy is a critical one. The corporation that becomes global should achieve a major competitive advantage. Failure to change from the controls appropriate for a domestic or multinational company will direct management to focus on the wrong elements and the strategic advantages will likely not be fully attained. A control system, with management incentives, that is designed to match the characteristics of the global corporation should be a key element in achieving the superior competitive position possible from using a global strategy.

21

HOW TO MOTIVATE AND EVALUATE MANAGERS WITH INTERNATIONAL TRANSFER PRICING SYSTEMS
W. M. Abdallah

Theoretically, MNEs have the ability to use their international transfer pricing policies to maximize their global profits. Practically, it is the toughest pricing problem and it is more complicated than developing domestic transfer pricing policies.

An MNE has to manage its production and marketing policies in a world characterized by different international tax rates, different foreign exchange rates, different governmental regulations, currency manipulation, and other economic and social problems. Such market characteristics create high transaction costs for an MNE when using its regular marketing policies. It is important for them to create an internal market if they want to avoid these problems and any costs associated with them.[1] Allocation of resources among domestic and foreign subsidiaries requires the central management of an MNE to set up the appropriate transfer price to achieve certain objectives.

Central top-management at the home country and subsidiary managers, both domestic and foreign, must understand the objectives for using transfer pricing policies within their organization. Those objectives are usually interrelated, top management and managers need to understand how they can affect each other.[2]

An International Transfer Pricing system should achieve two different groups of objectives, the first group includes: (a) the consistency with the system of performance evaluation, (b) motivation of subsidiary managers, and (c) achievement of goal congruence. The second group includes: (a) reduction of income

taxes, (b) reduction of tariffs on imports and exports, (c) minimization of foreign exchange risks, (d) avoidance of conflict with host governments, (e) management of cash flows, and (f) competition in the international markets. This paper will discuss only the first group of objectives.

An international transfer pricing system cannot achieve its full potential until it is integrated with other management control systems such as performance evaluation systems and reward (or motivation) systems.

MNEs set up their international transfer pricing policies at the central (or top) management level to facilitate cash movements where currency restrictions exist and to minimize taxes. It is more likely that a conflict between international transfer pricing techniques and performance evaluation measurement is to be expected, and, in general, transfer pricing policies are not complementary to the profit center concept.

The purpose of this paper is threefold: (a) identify, at the international level, different objectives of establishing transfer pricing systems; especially performance evaluation, motivation, and goal congruence, (b) to investigate how MNEs can achieve these objectives under their international transfer pricing systems, and (c) to point out significant problems MNEs might face when they try to achieve these objectives.

PERFORMANCE EVALUATION

The 1972 Committee on International Accounting of the American Accounting Association indicated that the traditional profit center concept for performance evaluation is inappro-

Source: Management International Review, Vol. 29 (1989/1), pp. 65–71.

priate for MNEs because there is no clear distinction between operating subdivisions of MNEs. With integrated, centrally coordinated operations, foreign subsidiary management does not have authority for major decisions which affect its reported profits.[3] The 1973 Committee on International Accounting of the American Accounting. Association agrees with the previously reported conclusions, and adds that the differences between countries such as social, economic, political, legal, and educational differences, have a considerable effect on manager performance. In conclusion, the Committee believes there is a need for further research to introduce additional elements into traditional management accounting evaluation techniques.[4]

In evaluating the performance of the foreign subsidiary, it is appropriate to evaluate its contribution to the objectives and goals of the whole MNE. It is also important to evaluate the contribution of foreign subsidiary managers to the performance of the MNE. Solomons has stated, "in the absence of evidence to the contrary, the presumption is that the success of one implies the success of the other. But circumstances outside a manager's control may dictate success or failure of the venture."[5]

The headquarters enforce a specific transfer price to be used by its own subsidiaries to achieve certain objectives such as domestic and foreign income tax minimization, foreign exchange risk reduction, and foreign exchange control avoidance among others. To achieve the above objectives, international transfer pricing may result in showing higher artificial profits of foreign subsidiaries, while others may show much lower artificial profits.

A foreign subsidiary manager may have the operations of his area being evaluated as if it were a completely autonomous and independent subsidiary. They may have the greatest degree of freedom in making decisions related to the short-run. However, they have lesser degree of freedom in making decisions directly affecting other foreign subsidiaries and the globe.

With the frequent fluctuations of currency values combined with the floating exchange rates system, MNEs face the problem of distorted performance measurements of their domestic and foreign subsidiaries as profit centers.[6]

Performance of foreign subsidiaries in U.S.-based MNEs is usually evaluated on the basis of reports stated in U.S. dollars. However, as the exchange rates fluctuate, performance evaluation of subsidiaries is not an easy task to be done. Using transfer pricing as a basis for performance evaluation under the floating exchange rates system makes it a much more complicated problem because international transfer prices are not usually adjusted for any fluctuations in currency exchange rates.[7]

At Honeywell Inc., Malmstrom implemented a simple solution for this problem. His technique is called "dollar indexing." This technique is used to have the same impact as local currency invoicing including two basic objectives: (a) to allow realistic or undistorted performance evaluation, and (b) to reflect the real economic cost of the product transferred.[8]

Malmstrom used an indexed formula for U.S.-dollar transfer prices as shown below:

$$NTP = OTP \times \frac{CER}{PER}$$

where:
NTP = New transfer price
OTP = Old transfer price
CER = Current exchange rate
PER = Planned exchange rate

Using this formula will result in applying a uniform transfer price for all goods transferred out of the same subsidiary.

For illustration, let us assume that subsidiary (A) in the U.K. transferred 16,000 units of its products at an established transferred price, by the parent U.S.-based MNE, $5.00 per unit to another foreign subsidiary (B) in Switzerland, owned by the same MNE. The foreign exchange rates were £1.00 = $1.63 and Swiss franc 1.00 = $1.49, respectively. As can be seen in Exhibit 1, subsidiary (A) achieves a net income of $6,700 or £4,010 (in the U.K. currency), while subsidi-

Exhibit 1   The Effect of Transfer Pricing on Performance Evaluation

	Subsidiary (A) (Seller)		Subsidiary (B) (Buyer)		The Global Income Statement U.S.D
	U.S.D	U.K.	U.S.D	SF	
Sales					
16,000 @ $5.00	$80,000	£49,080			
16,000 @ $12.00			$192,000	SF128,859	$192,000
Less CGS	(68,000)	41,718	(80,000)	(53,691)	(68,000)
Gross Profits	12,000	7,262	112,000	75,168	124,000
Less S & A Expenses	(5,300)	(3,252)	(75,000)	(50,336)	(80,300)
Net Income Before Taxes	6,700	4,010	37,000	24,832	43,700
Net Income as a Percentage of Sales	8%	8%	19%	19%	22.8%

ary (B) achieves a net income of $37,000 or 24,832 in Swiss francs.

If we assume that the U.S. dollar was depreciated against both of the British and the Swiss currencies to £1.00 = $2.188 and SF 1 = $2.00, respectively, the income statements for both subsidiaries and the MNE measured in U.S. dollars and local currencies are shown in Exhibit 2.

Since the transfer price ($5.00 per unit) was set centrally by the U.S.-based MNE, the operating results of the U.K. subsidiary would show net loss of $18,394 or £8,407, while the Swiss subsidiary would achieve net income of $77,046 or SF 38,523 because of the devaluation of the U. S. dollar in the international markets as can be seen in Exhibit 2.

The effect of using the $5.00 as a transfer price for international operations when there is devaluation in the parent's currency resulted in switching the operating results of the selling subsidiary from net income of 8% of sales to a net loss of 23% of sales. On the other hand, the operating results of the buying subsidiary would be in the opposite direction by switching from net income of 19% to a higher net income of 30%. That is, this transaction did not only transfer goods from the U.K. subsidiary to the Swiss subsidiary but also transferred $25,094 ($6,700 + $18,394) of profits and a translation gain of $14,952, with a total

of $40,042. In this case, the MNE as a whole would be $14,952 higher than before because of the translation gains resulting from the devaluation of the U. S. dollar.

For performance evaluation purposes, the manager of the British subsidiary was negatively affected by the change in the exchange rate and the imposed transfer price. While the Swiss subsidiary's manager did not do anything more than before to show a 30% net income (which is 11% higher than before the change occurred).

Using the indexed formula for U.S.-dollar transfer prices, suggested by Malmstrom, the adjusted transfer price would be:

$$NTP = OTP \times \frac{CER}{PER}$$

$$NTP = \$5.00 \times \frac{£2.188}{£1.630} = \$6.71$$

or

$$NTP = \$5.00 \times \frac{SF\ 2.00}{SF\ 1.49} = \$6.71.$$

Exhibit 3 shows the effect of transfer prices adjusted for changes in exchange rates. The new transfer price is $6.71, which is higher than the old one. For subsidiary A and B, the net income percentage as related to sales is the same as before any changes in the exchange rate, and both of them have the same measured performance as before. For the MNE, it has higher global

Exhibit 2   The Effect of Transfer Prices with Changes in Foreign Exchange Rates on Performance Evaluation

	Subsidiary (A) (Seller)		Subsidiary (B) (Buyer)		The Global Income Statement U.S.D
	U.S.D	U.K.	U.S.D	SF	
Sales					
16,000 @ $5.00	$80,000	£36,563	$257,718	SF128,859	$257,718
Less CGS	(91,279)	(41,718)	(80,000)	(40,000)	(91,279)
Gross Profits	(11,279)	(5,155)	177,718	88,859	166,439
Less S & A Expenses	(7,115)	(3,252)	(100,672)	(50,336)	(107,787)
Net Income Before Taxes	(18,394)	(8,407)	77,046	38,523	58,652
Net Income as a Percentage of Sales	(23%)	(23%)	30%	30%	22.8%

Exhibit 3   The Effect of Transfer Prices Adjusted for Changes in Exchange Rates

	Subsidiary (A)		Subsidiary (B)		The Global Results U.S.D
	U.S.D	U.K.	U.S.D	SF	
Sales					
(16,000 @ $6.71)	$107,360	£49,068	$257,718	SF128,859	$257,718
Less CGS	(91,279)	(41,718)	(107,360)	(53,691)	(91,279)
Gross Profits	16,081	7,350	150,358	75,168	166,439
Less S & A Expenses	(7,115)	(3,253)	(100,672)	(50,336)	(107,787)
Net Income	8,966	4,098	49,686	24,832	58,652
Net Income as a Percentage of Sales	8%	8%	19%	19%	22.8%

Exchange Rates:
£1.00 = $2.188 U.S.D
SF1.00 = $2.00 U.S.D
The New Transfer Price (Adjusted for Foreign Currency Fluctuations) = $6.71

profits with the dollar devaluation by $14,952 which is a translation gain. However, the translation gains were divided between the two subsidiaries as $2,266 to the U.K. subsidiary and $12,686 to the Swiss subsidiary.

The Swiss subsidiary has received $12,686 out of total translation gains of $14,952, while the British subsidiary has received $2,266 only due to how much was the U.S. dollar devaluated in relation to the local currency. In other words, Malmstrom's system does not work as it should as to the net income in dollars even though the ratios are the same as before; therefore, it still gives distorted financial results because of the foreign currency fluctuations.

MOTIVATION

Motivation is considered as one of the important objectives of setting international transfer pricing policies for domestic and foreign subsidiaries. Subsidiary managers need to be motivated to maximize (or increase) their divisional profits and transfer, in and out of their areas of responsibility within the MNE, their products or services at appropriate transfer prices. Transfer prices, in this case, can be used to motivate subsidiary managers to achieve their divisional goals (by maximizing their divisional profits) and at the same time achieving their MNE's goals (by maximizing the global profits).

However, the more autonomy the subsidiary managers have to decide on their transfer pricing to achieve their divisional profits, the more conflict may exist between achieving both MNE's and divisional profits. Also conflicts may arise between different objectives of using transfer pricing policies.

Higher transfer pricing for intracompany sales may help a subsidiary manager to show higher profits and be more motivated by doing his best efforts to achieve the MNE's goal. However, if the tax rate of the foreign country where that subsidiary located is very high, the global profits will be deteriorated, and a conflict of goal congruence exists between divisional and global goals.

For an international transfer pricing system to be a motivator, it must be tied to performance of subsidiary managers. In doing so, an international transfer price to be used as a measure of performance must meet the following four criteria:[9]

1. It must be a result of the manager's behavior.
2. It must include all the actions that need to be performed.
3. It must be accepted by subsidiary managers as valid measure of their performance.
4. It must include attainable goals for subsidiary managers.

Now, does the transfer pricing system reflect all the actions which should be performed by the foreign subsidiary manager in selling his products to another subsidiary? In other words, does the transfer price measure completely the foreign subsidiary manager's performance? Certainly, the answer is no, because a foreign subsidiary manager does not have control over the fluctuations of the exchange rate of the foreign currency of the country in which he is doing business. He can easily achieve translation gains or losses to be included in his performance report because of political, legal, economic, or social factors over which he does not have any degree of control. His profits can go up or down because of sudden increase in inflation rates and/or commodity or stock prices, and, consequently, the outcome will be an increase or decrease in the market price, when it is used as a transfer price.

MNEs must analyze the potential impact of using transfer pricing system as a motivator on foreign subsidiary managers' behavior. Actions or decisions, which are made by managers to improve their performance, can have a negative effect on the global goals or profits of the MNE as a whole.

GOAL CONGRUENCE

Goal congruence exists when the goals of subsidiary managers in the MNE are, so far as feasible, consistent with the global goals of the MNE. In establishing ITP policies, top management would like to motivate subsidiary managers to achieve their divisional goals by contributing toward the achievement of their MNE's goals.

It is almost impossible to achieve perfect congruence between subsidiary managers' goals and MNE's goals. However, at least the ITP policies should not motivate subsidiary managers to make decisions which may be in conflict with the MNE's goals.

Motivation and goal congruence are important factors in designing ITP systems. If a MNE desires to have its subsidiary managers to be strongly motivated toward achieving congruent goals, it is necessary to consider the effect of the transfer pricing on their divisional profitability or performance. However, if there is a conflict between subsidiary managers' goals and the global goals, it may be preferable to have as little motivation and autonomy of subsidiary managers as possible.

Generally, an ITP system should be designed in such a way that a foreign or domestic subsidiary manager is motivated to make decisions which are in the best interest of the MNE as a whole. When subsidiary managers increase their divisional profits and at the same time increase the global profits, then subsidiary managers are in the MNE interest if the ITP system does not mislead managers about what the MNE interests really are.

However, both subsidiary managers and central management must be aware that their divisional net income (or contribution) as measured under this ITP system are inherently imperfect, and the limited usefulness of that performance measure is further complicated by the existence of common resources used with the MNE.

SUMMARY AND CONCLUSION

This paper identified and discussed three different objectives of establishing an international transfer pricing policy. They are: (1) performance evaluation, (2) motivation, and (3) goal congruence.

Whenever performance evaluation systems are combined with the fluctuation in foreign exchange rates, transfer pricing policies will lead to presenting misleading and imperfect financial measures of performance. Malmstrom's system (dollar indexing technique) has been believed to give distorted financial results for performance evaluation.

Achieving motivation, goal congruence, and autonomy of foreign subsidiaries and their managers are always leading to conflicting results with performance evaluation, reduction of income taxes, reduction of tariffs, and avoid-

ance of foreign exchange risks. Whenever international transfer pricing objectives lead to conflicting consequences, MNEs are enforced to trade-off between achieving different objectives and must accept less global profits when one objective has a priority over others especially for achieving long-run objectives.

In designing an international transfer pricing policy, accounting literature does not provide MNEs with any unique technique or model to help them to arrive at the appropriate transfer price. Therefore, MNEs are in urgent need for a practical and objective technique or model, which can avoid conflicts between different objectives of the system, and, at the same time, achieve the global goals of MNEs to continue in doing their international business under different political, economic, and social environmental variables.

NOTES

1. Alan M. Rugman, "Internationalization Theory and Corporate International Finance," *California Management Review* (Winter 1980), p. 76.
2. Lynette L. Knowles, and Ike Mathur, "International Transfer Pricing Objectives, *Managerial Finance*, Vol. II (1985), p. 12.
3. *An Introduction to Financial Control and Reporting in Multinational Enterprises* (Austin: Bureau of Business Research, The University of Austin, 1973), pp. 71–73.
4. American Accounting Association, "Report of the Committee on International Accounting," *The Accounting Review*, 49 (1974), Supplement, pp. 252–257.
5. David Solomons, *Divisional Performance, Measurement and Control* (Homewood, Ill.: Richard D. Irwin, 1976), p. 59.
6. Duance Malmstrom, Accommodating Exchange Rate Fluctuations in Intercompany Pricing and Invoicing, *Management Accounting* (September 1977), p. 25.
7. Ralph L. Benke, Jr., and James Don Edwards, *Transfer Pricing Techniques and Uses* (New York: National Association of Accountants, 1980), p. 118.
8. Ibid., p. 25.
9. Edward E. Lawler, *Motivation in Work Organizations* (San Francisco: Wadsworth, 1973), p. 133.

SECTION 5

MARKETING

In the successful firm, whether domestic or global, marketing and strategic planning are closely related activities. Marketing helps to identify the best product/market foci for the firm and plays a key role in implementing strategic plans. As compared to the domestic marketer, the marketer in a multinational or global firm must deal with a much larger, much more diverse set of competitors, market conditions, and decision alternatives.

The multinational or global marketer's decisions include selecting markets, products with which to compete in them, and marketing strategies for the chosen countries. Entering a new country/market means dealing with an environment that can be considerably different from those already experienced. Even in a world that may be moving toward increasing similarities in consumer tastes, marketing methods, production processes, and business practices, differences (some subtle, some not) may persist.

There are many and growing examples of global products made possible by convergence in consumer taste, ranging from Coca-Cola to air travel. But consumers across the world are still different. In Japan, sales of rice still lead bread sales. In the United States the situation is reversed. As a result, rice cookers show a higher level of market penetration in Japan than in the United States, whereas a larger proportion of households in the United States as compared to those in Japan have toasters.

In many European countries per capita beer consumption is higher, and soft drink consumption lower than in the United States. But the Japanese do eat bread, people in the United States eat rice, and both Europeans and Americans drink beer and soft drinks. To complicate the matter still further, Japanese and American consumers do not like the same kinds of bread. And many Europeans' and Americans' beer preferences are different from each other.

These, and the multitude of other, similar, situations pose a question that has occupied marketers for some years: whether to standardize worldwide or customize on a market-by-market basis. We addressed this problem briefly in Section 2 of this book; we return to it now in more depth. There are three components of marketing that managers must decide to standardize or customize:

the marketing mix used; and the process, the activities that implement the program.

READING SELECTIONS

Theodore Levitt argues strongly for globally standardized products. He presents a variety of anecdotal evidence showing that national and regional differences in product preference have been steadily declining. As markets become global, a low-cost position will become more and more critical to success. Achieving this low-cost position, Levitt maintains, requires scale economies in manufacturing. In Levitt's world, the multinational (Porter's multidomestic) that modifies its products and practices on a country-by-country basis will not be able to compete. The global firm will take over.

Susan Douglas and Yorem Wind strongly disagree. In "The Myth of Globalization," they label the strategy of global standardization "naive and oversimplistic." Using both the marketing literature and their own reasoning, they examine critically the assumptions behind the global standardization argument presented by Levitt and others. They look at program and process as well as product. Douglas and Wind conclude there are certain situations that favor global standardization and present a framework for identifying them.

Subhash Jain presents a framework for determining the appropriate degree of product and marketing mix standardization. (His definition of program encompasses product as well.) He goes on to present and discuss specific propositions about the degree of standardization appropriate in different circumstances. These are grounded in an extensive review of the literature. While Jain formulates his hypotheses as proposals for research, they are also useful starting points for managerial decision making. It should be worthwhile to compare and integrate Jain's perspective with that of Douglas and Wind. The perspective and frameworks presented in these two articles may be useful in deciding what strategy to use in a specific country as well as what to do worldwide.

Sandra Huszagh moves us away from the standardize/customize debate, describing an important but not widely enough understood international marketing technique, countertrade. Countertrade encompasses a variety of techniques through which buyers can obtain foreign merchandise without using foreign currency to pay for it. As Huszagh's descriptions show, some of these techniques are quite complex and sophisticated. Many Third World and command economy countries make extensive use of countertrade, and firms desiring to market to these countries must understand such transactions.

22

THE GLOBALIZATION OF MARKETS
Theodore Levitt

Many companies have become disillusioned with sales in the international marketplace as old markets become saturated and new ones must be found. How can they customize products for the demands of new markets? Which items will consumers want? With wily international competitors breathing down their necks, many organizations think that the game just isn't worth the effort.

In this powerful essay, the author asserts that well-managed companies have moved from emphasis on customizing items to offering globally standardized products that are advanced, functional, reliable—and low priced. Multinational companies that concentrated on idiosyncratic consumer preferences have become befuddled and unable to take in the forest because of the trees. Only global companies will achieve long-term success by concentrating on what everyone wants rather than worrying about the details of what everyone *thinks* they might like.

A powerful force drives the world toward a converging commonality, and that force is technology. It has proletarianized communication, transport, and travel. It has made isolated places and impoverished peoples eager for modernity's allurements. Almost everyone everywhere wants all the things they have heard about, seen, or experienced via the new technologies.

The result is a new commercial reality—the emergence of global markets for standardized consumer products on a previously unimagined scale of magnitude. Corporations geared to this new reality benefit from enormous economies of scale in production, distribution, marketing, and management. By translating these benefits into reduced world prices, they can decimate competitors that still live in the disabling grip of old assumptions about how the world works.

Gone are accustomed differences in national or regional preference. Gone are the days when a company could sell last year's models—or lesser versions of advanced products—in the

Source: Harvard Business Review (May–June 1983), pp. 92–102.

less-developed world. And gone are the days when prices, margins, and profits abroad were generally higher than at home.

The globalization of markets is at hand. With that, the multinational commercial world nears its end, and so does the multinational corporation.

The multinational and the global corporation are not the same thing. The multinational corporation operates in a number of countries, and adjusts its products and practices in each—at high relative costs. The global corporation operates with resolute constancy—at low relative cost—as if the entire world (or major regions of it) were a single entity; it sells the same things in the same way everywhere.

Which strategy is better is not a matter of opinion but of necessity. Worldwide communications carry everywhere the constant drumbeat of modern possibilities to lighten and enhance work, raise living standards, divert, and entertain. The same countries that ask the world to recognize and respect the individuality of their cultures insist on the wholesale transfer to them of modern goods, services, and technologies. Modernity is not just a wish but also a widespread practice among those who cling, with unyielding passion or religious fervor, to ancient attitudes and heritages.

Who can forget the televised scenes during the 1979 Iranian uprisings of young men in fashionable French-cut trousers and silky body shirts thirsting with raised modern weapons for blood in the name of Islamic fundamentalism?

In Brazil, thousands swarm daily from pre-industrial Bahian darkness into exploding coastal cities, there quickly to install television sets in crowded corrugated huts and, next to battered Volkswagens, make sacrificial offerings of fruit and fresh-killed chickens to Macumban spirits by candlelight.

During Biafra's fratricidal war against the Ibos, daily televised reports showed soldiers carrying bloodstained swords and listening to transistor radios while drinking Coca-Cola.

In the isolated Siberian city of Krasnoyarsk, with no paved streets and censored news, occasional Western travelers are stealthily propositioned for cigarettes, digital watches, and even the clothes off their backs.

The organized smuggling of electronic equipment, used automobiles, western clothing, cosmetics, and pirated movies into primitive places exceeds even the thriving underground trade in modern weapons and their military mercenaries.

A thousand suggestive ways attest to the ubiquity of the desire for the most advanced things that the world makes and sells—goods of the best quality and reliability at the lowest price. The world's needs and desires have been irrevocably homogenized. This makes the multinational corporation obsolete and the global corporation absolute.

LIVING IN THE REPUBLIC OF TECHNOLOGY

Daniel J. Boorstin, author of the monumental trilogy *The Americans,* characterized our age as driven by "the Republic of Technology [whose] supreme law . . . is convergence, the tendency for everything to become more like everything else."

In business, this trend has pushed markets toward global commonality. Corporations sell standardized products in the same way everywhere—autos, steel, chemicals, petroleum, cement, agricultural commodities and equipment, industrial and commercial construction, banking and insurance services, computers, semiconductors, transport, electronic instruments, pharmaceuticals, and telecommunications, to mention some of the obvious.

Nor is the sweeping gale of globalization confined to these raw material or high-tech products, where the universal language of customers and users facilitates standardization. The transforming winds whipped up by the proletarianization of communication and travel enter every crevice of life.

Commercially, nothing confirms this as much as the success of McDonald's from the Champs Elysées to the Ginza, of Coca-Cola in Bahrain and Pepsi-Cola in Moscow, and of rock music, Greek salad, Hollywood movies, Revlon cosmetics, Sony televisions, and Levi jeans everywhere. "High-touch" products are as ubiquitous as high-tech.

Starting from opposing sides, the high-tech and the high-touch ends of the commercial spectrum gradually consume the undistributed middle in their cosmopolitan orbit. No one is exempt and nothing can stop the process. Everywhere everything gets more and more like everything else as the world's preference structure is relentlessly homogenized.

Consider the cases of Coca-Cola and Pepsi-Cola, which are globally standardized products sold everywhere and welcomed by everyone. Both successfully cross multitudes of national, regional, and ethnic taste buds trained to a variety of deeply ingrained local preferences of taste, flavor, consistency, effervescence, and aftertaste. Everywhere both sell well. Cigarettes, too, especially American-made, make year-to-year global inroads on territories previously held in the firm grip of other, mostly local, blends.

These are not exceptional examples. (Indeed their global reach would be even greater were it not for artificial trade barriers.) They exemplify a general drift toward the homogenization of the world and how companies distribute, finance, and price products.[1] Nothing is exempt. The products and methods of the industrialized world play a single tune for all the world, and all the world eagerly dances to it.

Ancient differences in national tastes or modes of doing business disappear. The commonality of preference leads inescapably to the standardization of products, manufacturing, and the institutions of trade and commerce. Small nation-based markets transmogrify and expand. Success in world competition turns on efficiency in production, distribution, marketing, and management, and inevitably becomes focused on price.

The most effective world competitors incorporate superior quality and reliability into their cost structures. They sell in all national markets the same kind of products sold at home or in their largest export market. They compete on the basis of appropriate value—the best combinations of price, quality, reliability, and delivery for products that are globally identical with respect to design, function, and even fashion.

That, and little else, explains the surging success of Japanese companies dealing worldwide in a vast variety of products—both tangible products like steel, cars, motorcycles, hi-fi equipment, farm machinery, robots, microprocessors, carbon fibers, and now even textiles, and intangibles like banking, shipping, general contracting, and soon computer software. Nor are high-quality and low-cost operations incompatible, as a host of consulting organizations and data engineers argue with vigorous vacuity. The reported data are incomplete, wrongly analyzed, and contradictory. The truth is that low-cost operations are the hallmark of corporate cultures that require and produce quality in all that they do. High quality and low costs are not opposing postures. They are compatible, twin identities of superior practice.[2]

To say that Japan's companies are not global because they export cars with left-side drives to the United States and the European continent, while those in Japan have right-side drives, or because they sell office machines through distributors in the United States but directly at home, or speak Portuguese in Brazil is to mistake a difference for a distinction. The same is true of Safeway and Southland retail chains operating effectively in the Middle East, and to not only native but also imported populations from Korea, the Philippines, Pakistan, India, Thailand, Britain, and the United States. National rules of the road differ, and so do distribution channels and languages. Japan's distinction is its unrelenting push for economy and value enhancement. That translates into a drive for standardization at high quality levels.

Vindication of the Model T

If a company forces costs and prices down and pushes quality and reliability up—while maintaining reasonable concern for suitability—customers will prefer its world-standardized products. The theory holds, at this stage in the evolution of globalization, no matter what conventional market research and even common sense may suggest about different national and regional tastes, preferences, needs, and institutions. The Japanese have repeatedly vindicated this theory, as did Henry Ford with the Model T. Most important, so have their imitators, including companies from South Korea (television sets and heavy construction), Malaysia (personal calculators and microcomputers), Brazil (auto parts and tools), Colombia (apparel), Singapore (optical equipment), and yes, even from the United States (office copiers, computers, bicycles, castings), Western Europe (automatic washing machines), Rumania (housewares), Hungary (apparel), Yugoslavia (furniture), and Israel (pagination equipment).

Of course, large companies operating in a single nation or even a single city don't standardize everything they make, sell, or do. They have product lines instead of a single product version, and multiple distribution channels. There are neighborhood, local, regional, ethnic, and institutional differences, even within metropolitan areas. But although companies customize products for particular market segments, they know that success in a world with homogenized demand requires a search for sales opportunities in similar segments across the globe in order to achieve the economies of scale necessary to compete.

Such a search works because a market segment in one country is seldom unique; it has close cousins everywhere precisely because technology has homogenized the globe. Even small local segments have their global equivalents everywhere and become subject to global competition, especially on price.

The global competitor will seek constantly to standardize his offering everywhere. He will digress from this standardization only after exhausting all possibilities to retain it, and he will push for reinstatement of standardization whenever digression and divergence have occurred. He will never assume that the customer is a king who knows his own wishes.

Trouble increasingly stalks companies that lack clarified global focus and remain inattentive to the economics of simplicity and standardization. The most endangered companies in the rapidly evolving world tend to be those that dominate rather small domestic markets with high value-added products for which there are smaller markets elsewhere. With transportation costs proportionately low, distant competitors will enter the now-sheltered markets of those companies with goods produced more cheaply under scale-efficient conditions. Global competition spells the end of domestic territoriality, no matter how diminutive the territory may be.

When the global producer offers his lower costs internationally, his patronage expands exponentially. He not only reaches into distant markets, but also attracts customers who previously held to local preferences and now capitulate to the attractions of lesser prices. The strategy of standardization not only responds to worldwide homogenized markets but also expands those markets with aggressive low pricing. The new technological juggernaut taps an ancient motivation—to make one's money go as far as possible. This is universal—not simply a motivation but actually a need.

ECONOMIES OF SCOPE

One argument that opposes globalization says that flexible factory automation will enable plants of massive size to change products and product features quickly, without stopping the manufacturing process. These factories of the future could thus produce broad lines of customized products without sacrificing the scale economies that come from long production runs of standardized items. Computer-aided design and manufacturing (CAD/CAM), combined with robotics, will create a new equipment and process technology (EPT) that will make small plants located close to their markets as efficient as large ones located distantly. Economies of scale will not dominate, but rather economies of scope—the ability of either large or small plants to produce great varieties of relatively customized products at remarkably low costs. If that happens, customers will have no need to abandon special preferences.

I will not deny the power of these possibilities. But possibilities do not make probabilities. There is no conceivable way in which flexible factory automation can achieve the scale economies of a modernized plant dedicated to mass production of standardized lines. The new digitized equipment and process technologies are available to all. Manufacturers with minimal customization and narrow product-line breadth will have costs far below those with more customization and wider lines.

THE HEDGEHOG KNOWS

The difference between the hedgehog and the fox, wrote Sir Isaiah Berlin in distinguishing between Dostoevski and Tolstoy, is that the fox knows a lot about a great many things, but the hedgehog knows everything about one great thing. The multinational corporation knows a lot about a great many countries and congenially adapts to supposed differences. It willingly accepts vestigial national differences, not questioning the possibility of their transformation, not recognizing how the world is ready and eager for the benefit of modernity, especially when the price is right. The multinational corporation's accommodating mode to visible national differences is medieval.

By contrast, the global corporation knows everything about one great thing. It knows about the absolute need to be competitive on a worldwide basis as well as nationally and seeks constantly to drive down prices by standardizing what it sells and how it operates. It treats the world as composed of few standardized markets rather than many customized markets. It actively seeks and vigorously works toward global convergence. Its mission is modernity and its mode, price competition, even when it sells top-of-the-line, high-end products. It knows about the one great thing all nations and people have in common: scarcity.

Nobody takes scarcity lying down; everyone wants more. This in part explains division of labor and specialization of production. They enable people and nations to optimize their conditions through trade. The median is usually money.

Experience teaches that money has three special qualities: scarcity, difficulty of acquisition, and transience. People understandably treat it with respect. Everyone in the increasingly homogenized world market wants products and features that everybody else wants. If the price is low enough, they will take highly standardized world products, even if these aren't exactly what mother said was suitable, what immemorial custom decreed was right, or what market-research fabulists asserted was preferred.

The implacable truth of all modern production—whether of tangible or intangible goods—is that large-scale production of stan-

dardized items is generally cheaper within a wide range of volume than small-scale production. Some argue that CAD/CAM will allow companies to manufacture customized products on a small scale—but cheaply. But the argument misses the point. (For a more detailed discussion, see the insert, "Economies of scope.") If a company treats the world as one or two distinctive product markets, it can serve the world more economically than if it treats it as three, four, or five product markets.

Why Remaining Differences?

Different cultural preferences, national tastes and standards, and business institutions are vestiges of the past. Some inheritances die gradually; others prosper and expand into mainstream global preferences. So-called ethnic markets are a good example. Chinese food, pita bread, country and western music, pizza, and jazz are everywhere. They are market segments that exist in worldwide proportions. They don't deny or contradict global homogenization but confirm it.

Many of today's differences among nations as to products and their features actually reflect the respectful accommodation of multinational corporations to what they believe are fixed local preferences. They *believe* preferences are fixed, not because they are but because of rigid habits of thinking about what actually is. Most executives in multinational corporations are thoughtlessly accommodating. They falsely presume that marketing means giving the customer what he says he wants rather than trying to understand exactly what he'd like. So they persist with high-cost, customized multinational products and practices instead of pressing hard and pressing properly for global standardization.

I do not advocate the systematic disregard of local or national differences. But a company's sensitivity to such differences does not require that it ignore the possibilities of doing things differently or better.

There are, for example, enormous differences among Middle Eastern countries. Some are socialist, some monarchies, some republics. Some take their legal heritage from the Napoleonic Code, some from the Ottoman Empire, and some from the British common law; except for Israel, all are influenced by Islam. Doing business means personalizing the business relationship in an obsessively intimate fashion. During the month of Ramadan, business discussions can start only after 10 o'clock at night, when people are tired and full of food after a day of fasting. A company must almost certainly have a local partner; a local lawyer is required (as, say, in New York), and irrevocable letters of credit are essential. Yet, as Coca-Cola's Senior Vice President Sam Ayoub noted, "Arabs are much more capable of making distinctions between cultural and religious purposes on the one hand and economic realities on the other than is generally assumed. Islam is compatible with science and modern times."

Barriers to globalization are not confined to the Middle East. The free transfer of technology and data across the boundaries of the European Common Market countries are hampered by legal and financial impediments. And there is resistance to radio and television interference ("pollution") among neighboring European countries.

But the past is a good guide to the future. With persistence and appropriate means, barriers against superior technologies and economics have always fallen. There is no recorded exception where reasonable effort has been made to overcome them. It is very much a matter of time and effort.

A FAILURE IN GLOBAL IMAGINATION

Many companies have tried to standardize world practice by exporting domestic products and processes without accommodation or change—and have failed miserably. Their deficiencies have been seized on as evidence of bo-

vine stupidity in the face of abject impossibility. Advocates of global standardization see them as examples of failures in execution.

In fact, poor execution is often an important cause. More important, however, is failure of nerve—failure of imagination.

Consider the case for the introduction of fully automatic home laundry equipment in Western Europe at a time when few homes had even semiautomatic machines. Hoover, Ltd., whose parent company was headquartered in North Canton, Ohio had a prominent presence in Britain as a producer of vacuum cleaners and washing machines. Due to insufficient demand in the home market and low exports to the European continent, the large washing machine plant in England operated far below capacity. The company needed to sell more of its semiautomatic or automatic machines.

Because it had a "proper" marketing orientation, Hoover conducted consumer preference studies in Britain and each major continental country. The results showed feature preferences clearly enough among several countries (see the *Exhibit*).

The incremental unit variable costs (in pounds sterling) of customizing to meet just a few of the national preferences were:

	£	s.	d.
Stainless steel vs. enamel drum	1	0	0
Porthole window		10	0
Spin speed of 800 rpm vs. 700 rpm		15	0
Water heater	2	15	0
6 vs. 5 kilos capacity	1	10	0
	£6	10s	0d

$18.20 at the exchange rate of that time.

Considerable plant investment was needed to meet other preferences.

The lowest retail prices (in pounds sterling) of leading locally produced brands in the various countries were approximately:

U.K.	£110
France	114
West Germany	113
Sweden	134
Italy	57

Product customization in each country would have put Hoover in a poor competitive position on the basis of price, mostly due to the higher manufacturing costs incurred by short production runs for separate features. Because Common Market tariff reduction programs were then incomplete, Hoover also paid tariff duties in each continental country.

How to Make a Creative Analysis

In the Hoover case, an imaginative analysis of automatic washing machine sales in each country would have revealed that:

1. Italian automatics, small in capacity and size, low-powered, without built-in heaters, with porcelain enamel tubs, were priced aggressively low and were gaining large market shares in all countries, including West Germany.
2. The best-selling automatics in West Germany were heavily advertised (three times more than the next most promoted brand), were ideally suited to national tastes, and were also by far the highest-priced machines available in that country.
3. Italy, with the lowest penetration of washing machines of any kind (manual, semiautomatic, or automatic) was rapidly going directly to automatics, skipping the pattern of first buying handwringer, manually assisted machines and then semiautomatics.
4. Detergent manufacturers were just beginning to promote the technique of cold-water and tepid-water laundering then used in the United States.

The growing success of small, low-powered, low-speed, low-capacity, low-priced Italian machines, even against the preferred but highly priced and highly promoted brand in West Germany, was significant. It contained a powerful message that was lost on managers confidently wedded to a distorted version of the marketing concept according to which you give the customer what he says he wants. In fact the customers *said* they wanted certain features, but their behavior demonstrated they'd take other features provided the price and the promotion were right.

In this case it was obvious that, under prevailing conditions, people preferred a low-priced automatic over any kind of manual or semiautomatic machine and certainly over higher priced automatics, even though the low-priced automatics failed to fulfill all their expressed preferences. The supposedly meticulous and demanding German consumers violated all expectations by buying the simple, low-priced Italian machines.

It was equally clear that people were profoundly influenced by promotions of automatic washers; in West Germany, the most heavily promoted ideal machine also had the largest market share despite its high price. Two things clearly influenced customers to buy: low price regardless of feature preferences and heavy promotion regardless of price. Both factors helped homemakers get what they most wanted—the superior benefits bestowed by fully automatic machines.

Hoover should have aggressively sold a simple, standardized high-quality machine at a low price (afforded by the 17% variable cost reduction that the elimination of £6–10-0 worth of extra features made possible). The suggested retail prices could have been somewhat less than £100. The extra funds "saved" by avoiding unnecessary plant modifications would have supported an extended service network and aggressive media promotions.

Hoover's media message should have been: *this* is the machine that you, the homemaker, *deserve* to have to reduce the repetitive heavy daily household burdens, so that *you* may have more constructive time to spend with your children and your husband. The promotion should also have targeted the husband to give him, preferably in the presence of his wife, a sense of

Exhibit Consumer Preferences as to Automatic Washing Machine Features in the 1960s

Features	Great Britain	Italy	West Germany	France	Sweden
Shell dimensions*	34" and narrow	Low and narrow	34" and wide	34" and narrow	34" and wide
Drum material	Enamel	Enamel	Stainless steel	Enamel	Stainless steel
Loading	Top	Front	Front	Front	Front
Front porthole	Yes/no	Yes	Yes	Yes	Yes
Capacity	5 kilos	4 kilos	6 kilos	5 kilos	6 kilos
Spin speed	700 rpm	400 rpm	850 rpm	600 rpm	800 rpm
Water-heating system	No†	Yes	Yes††	Yes	No†
Washing action	Agitator	Tumble	Tumble	Agitator	Tumble
Styling features	Inconspicuous appearance	Brightly colored	Indestructible appearance	Elegant appearance	Strong appearance

*34" height was (in the process of being adopted as) a standard work-surface height in Europe.
†Most British and Swedish homes had centrally heated hot water.
††West Germans preferred to launder at temperatures higher than generally provided centrally.

obligation to provide an automatic washer for her even before he bought an automobile for himself. An aggressively low price, combined with heavy promotion of this kind, would have overcome previously expressed preferences for particular features.

The Hoover case illustrates how the perverse practice of the marketing concept and the absence of any kind of marketing imagination let multinational attitudes survive when customers actually want the benefits of global standardization. The whole project got off on the wrong foot. It asked people what features they wanted in a washing machine rather than what they wanted out of life. Selling a line of products individually tailored to each nation is thoughtless. Managers who took pride in practicing the marketing concept to the fullest did not, in fact, practice it at all. Hoover asked the wrong questions, then applied neither thought nor imagination to the answers. Such companies are like the ethnocentricists in the Middle Ages who saw with everyday clarity the sun revolving around the earth and offered it as Truth. With no additional data but a more searching mind, Copernicus, like the hedgehog, interpreted a more compelling and accurate reality. Data do not yield information except with the intervention of the mind. Information does not yield meaning except with the intervention of imagination.

ACCEPTING THE INEVITABLE

The global corporation accepts for better or for worse that technology drives consumers relentlessly toward the same common goals—alleviation of life's burdens and the expansion of discretionary time and spending power. Its role is profoundly different from what it has been for the ordinary corporation during its brief, turbulent, and remarkably protean history. It orchestrates the twin vectors of technology and globalization for the world's benefit. Neither fate, nor nature, nor God but rather the necessity of commerce created this role.

In the United States two industries became global long before they were consciously aware of it. After over a generation of persistent and acrimonious labor shutdowns, the United Steelworkers of America have not called an industrywide strike since 1959; the United Auto Workers have not shut down General Motors since 1970. Both unions realize that they have become global—shutting down all or most of U.S. manufacturing would not shut out U.S. customers. Overseas suppliers are there to supply the market.

Cracking the Code of Western Markets

Since the theory of the marketing concept emerged a quarter of a century ago, the more managerially advanced corporations have been eager to offer what customers clearly wanted rather than what was merely convenient. They have created marketing departments supported by professional market researchers of awesome and often costly proportions. And they have proliferated extraordinary numbers of operations and product lines—highly tailored products and delivery systems for many different markets, market segments, and nations.

Significantly, Japanese companies operate almost entirely without marketing departments or market research of the kind so prevalent in the West. Yet, in the colorful words of General Electric's chairman John F. Welch, Jr., the Japanese, coming from a small cluster of resource-poor islands, with an entirely alien culture and an almost impenetrably complex language, have cracked the code of Western markets. They have done it not by looking with mechanistic thoroughness at the way markets are different but rather by searching for meaning with a deeper wisdom. They have discovered the one great thing all markets have in common—an overwhelming desire for dependable, world-standard modernity in all things, at aggressively low prices. In response, they deliver irresistible value everywhere, attracting people with products that market-research technocrats described with superficial certainty as being unsuitable and uncompetitive.

The wider a company's global reach, the greater the number of regional and national preferences it will encounter for certain product features, distribution systems, or promotional media. There will always need to be some accommodation to differences. But the widely prevailing and often unthinking belief in the immutability of these differences is generally mistaken. Evidence of business failure because of lack of accommodation is often evidence of other shortcomings.

Take the case of Revlon in Japan. The company unnecessarily alienated retailers and confused customers by selling world-standardized cosmetics only in elite outlets; then it tried to recover with low-priced world-standardized products in broader distribution, followed by a change in the company president and cutbacks in distribution as costs rose faster than sales. The problem was not that Revlon didn't understand the Japanese market; it didn't do the job right, wavered in its programs, and was impatient to boot.

By contrast, the Outboard Marine Corporation, with imagination, push, and persistence, collapsed long-established three-tiered distribution channels in Europe into a more focused and controllable two-step system—and did so despite the vociferous warnings of local trade groups. It also reduced the number and types of retail outlets. The result was greater improvement in credit and product-installation service to customers, major cost reductions, and sales advances.

In its highly successful introduction of Contac 600 (the timed-release decongestant) into Japan, SmithKline Corporation used 35 wholesalers instead of the 1,000-plus that established practice required. Daily contacts with the wholesalers and key retailers, also in violation of established practice, supplemented the plan, and it worked.

Denied access to established distribution institutions in the United States, Komatsu, the Japanese manufacturer of lightweight farm machinery, entered the market through over-the-road construction equipment dealers in rural areas of the Sunbelt, where farms are smaller, the soil sandier and easier to work. Here inexperienced distributors were able to attract customers on the basis of Komatsu's product and price appropriateness.

In cases of successful challenge to prevailing institutions and practices, a combination of product reliability and quality, strong and sustained support systems, aggressively low prices, and sales-compensation packages, as well as audacity and implacability, circumvented, shattered, and transformed very different distribution systems. Instead of resentment, there was admiration.

Still, some differences between nations are unyielding, even in a world of microprocessors. In the United States almost all manufacturers of microprocessors check them for reliability through a so-called parallel system of testing. Japan prefers the totally different sequential testing system. So Teradyne Corporation, the world's largest producer of microprocessor test equipment, makes one line for the United States and one for Japan. That's easy.

What's not so easy for Teradyne is to know how best to organize and manage, in this instance, its marketing effort. Companies can organize by product, region, function, or by using some combination of these. A company can have separate marketing organizations for Japan and for the United States, or it can have separate product groups, one working largely in Japan and the other in the United States. A single manufacturing facility or marketing operation might service both markets, or a company might use separate marketing operations for each.

Questions arise if the company organizes by product. In the case of Teradyne, should the group handling the parallel system, whose major market is the United States, sell in Japan and compete with the group focused on the Japanese market? If the company organizes regionally, how do regional groups divide their efforts between promoting the parallel vs. the sequential system? If the company organizes in

terms of function, how does it get commitment in marketing, for example, for one line instead of the other?

There is no one reliably right answer—no one formula by which to get it. There isn't even a satisfactory contingent answer.[3] What works well for one company or one place may fail for another in precisely the same place, depending on the capabilities, histories, reputations, resources, and even the cultures of both.

THE EARTH IS FLAT

The differences that persist throughout the world despite its globalization affirm an ancient dictum of economics—that things are driven by what happens at the margin, not at the core. Thus, in ordinary competitive analysis, what's important is not the average price but the marginal price; what happens not in the usual case but at the interface of newly erupting conditions. What counts in commercial affairs is what happens at the cutting edge. What is most striking today is the underlying similarities of what is happening now to national preferences at the margin. These similarities at the cutting edge cumulatively form an overwhelming, predominant commonality everywhere.

To refer to the persistence of economic nationalism (protective and subsidized trade practices, special tax aids, or restrictions for home market producers) as a barrier to the globalization of markets is to make a valid point. Economic nationalism does have a powerful persistence. But, as with the present almost totally smooth internationalization of investment capital, the past alone does not shape or predict the future. (For reflections on the internationalization of capital, see the insert, "The shortening of Japanese horizons.")

Reality is not a fixed paradigm, dominated by immemorial customs and derived attitudes, heedless of powerful and abundant new forces. The world is becoming increasingly informed about the liberating and enhancing possibilities of modernity. The persistence of the inherited

THE SHORTENING OF JAPANESE
HORIZONS

One of the most powerful yet least celebrated forces driving commerce toward global standardization is the monetary system, along with the international investment process.

Today money is simply electronic impulses. With the speed of light it moves effortlessly between distant centers (and even lesser places). A change of ten basis points in the price of a bond causes an instant and massive shift of money from London to Tokyo. The system has profound impact on the way companies operate throughout the world.

Take Japan, where high debt-to-equity balance sheets are "guaranteed" by various societal presumptions about the virtue of "a long view," or by government policy in other ways. Even here, upward shifts in interest rates in other parts of the world attract capital out of the country in powerful proportions. In recent years more and more Japanese global corporations have gone to the world's equity markets for funds. Debt is too remunerative in high-yielding countries to keep capital at home to feed the Japanese need. As interest rates rise, equity becomes a more attractive option for the issuer.

The long-term impact on Japanese enterprise will be transforming. As the equity proportion of Japanese corporate capitalization rises, companies will respond to the shorter-term investment horizons of the equity markets. Thus the much-vaunted Japanese corporate practice to taking the long view will gradually disappear.

varieties of national preferences rests uneasily on increasing evidence of, and restlessness regarding, their inefficiency, costliness, and confinement. The historic past, and the national differences respecting commerce and industry it spawned and fostered everywhere, is now subject to relatively easy transformation.

Cosmopolitanism is no longer the monopoly of the intellectual and leisure classes; it is becoming the established property and defining characteristic of all sectors everywhere in the world. Gradually and irresistibly it breaks down the walls of economic insularity, nationalism, and chauvinism. What we see today as escalating commercial nationalism is simply the last violent death rattle of an obsolete institution.

Companies that adapt to and capitalize on economic convergence can still make distinctions and adjustments in different markets. Persistent differences in the world are consistent with fundamental underlying commonalities; they often complement rather than oppose each other—in business as they do in physics. There is, in physics, simultaneously matter and anti-matter working in symbiotic harmony.

The earth is round, but for most purposes it's sensible to treat it as flat. Space is curved, but not much for everyday life here on earth.

Divergence from established practice happens all the time. But the multinational mind, warped into circumspection and timidity by years of stumbles and transnational troubles, now rarely challenges existing overseas practices. More often it considers any departure from inherited domestic routines as mindless, disrespectful, or impossible. It is the mind of a bygone day.

The successful global corporation does not abjure customization or differentiation for the requirements of markets that differ in product preferences, spending patterns, shopping preferences, and institutional or legal arrangements. But the global corporation accepts and adjusts to these differences only reluctantly, only after relentlessly testing their immutability, after trying in various ways to circumvent and reshape them as we saw in the cases of Outboard Marine in Europe, SmithKline in Japan, and Komatsu in the United States.

There is only one significant respect in which a company's activities around the world are important, and this is in what it produces and how it sells. Everything else derives from, and is subsidiary to, these activities.

The purpose of business is to get and keep a customer. Or, to use Peter Drucker's more refined construction, to *create* and keep a customer. A company must be wedded to the ideal of innovation—offering better or more preferred products in such combinations of ways, means, places, and at such prices that prospects *prefer* doing business with the company rather than with others.

Preferences are constantly shaped and reshaped. Within our global commonality enormous variety constantly asserts itself and thrives, as can be seen within the world's single largest domestic market, the United States. But in the process of world homogenization, modern markets expand to reach cost-reducing global proportions. With better and cheaper communication and transport, even small local market segments hitherto protected from distant competitors now feel the pressure of their presence. Nobody is safe from global reach and the irresistible economies of scale.

Two vectors shape the world—technology and globalization. The first helps determine human preferences; the second, economic realities. Regardless of how much preferences evolve and diverge, they also gradually converge and form markets where economies of scale lead to reduction of costs and prices.

The modern global corporation contrasts powerfully with the aging multinational corporation. Instead of adapting to superficial and even entrenched differences within and between nations, it will seek sensibly to force suitably standardized products and practices on the entire globe. They are exactly what the world will take, if they come also with low prices, high quality, and blessed reliability. The global company will operate, in this regard, precisely as Henry Kissinger wrote in *Years of Upheaval* about the continuing Japanese economic success—"voracious in its collection of information, impervious to pressure, and implacable in execution."

Given what is everywhere the purpose of commerce, the global company will shape the vectors of technology and globalization into its great strategic fecundity. It will systematically push these vectors toward their own conver-

---

TURTLES ALL THE WAY DOWN

There is an Indian story—at least I heard it as an Indian story—about an Englishman who, having been told that the world rested on a platform which rested on the back of an elephant which rested in turn on the back of a turtle, asked (perhaps he was an ethnographer; it is the way they behave), what did the turtle rest on? Another turtle. And that turtle? "Ah, Sahib, after that it is turtles all the way down." . . .

The danger that cultural analysis, in search of all-too-deep-lying turtles, will lose touch with the hard surfaces of life—with the political, economic, stratificatory realities within which men are everywhere contained—and with the biological and physical necessities on which those surfaces rest, is an ever-present one. The only defense against it, and against, thus, turning cultural analysis into a kind of sociological aestheticism, is to train such analysis on such realities and such necessities in the first place.

From Clifford Geertz, *The Interpretation of Cultures* (New York: Basic Books 1973). With permission of the publisher.

---

gence, offering everyone simultaneously high-quality, more or less standardized products at optimally low prices, thereby achieving for itself vastly expanded markets and profits. Companies that do not adapt to the new global realities will become victims of those that do.

NOTES

1. In a landmark article, Robert D. Buzzell pointed out the rapidity with which barriers to standardization were falling. In all cases they succumbed to more and cheaper advanced ways of doing things. See "Can You Standardize Multinational Marketing?" *Harvard Business Review* (November–December 1968), p. 102.

2. There is powerful new evidence for this, even though the opposite has been urged by analysts of PIMS data for nearly a decade. See "Product Quality, Cost Production and Business Performance—A Test of Some Key Hypotheses," by Lynn W. Phillips, Dae Chang, and Robert D. Buzzell, Harvard Business School, Working Paper No. 83-13.

3. For a discussion of multinational reorganization, see Christopher A. Bartlett, "MNCs: Get Off the Reorganization Merry-Go-Round," *Harvard Business Review* (March–April), p. 138.

23

▬▬▬▬▬ THE MYTH OF GLOBALIZATION

Susan P. Douglas
Yoram Wind

Considerable controversy has arisen in recent years concerning the most appropriate strategy in international markets. It has been cogently argued that a strategy of global products and brands is the key to success in international markets. This paper examines critically the key assumptions underlying this philosophy, and the conditions under which it is likely to be effective. Barriers to its implementation are highlighted. Based on this analysis, it is proposed that global standardization is merely one of a number of strategies which may be successful in international markets.

In recent years, globalization has become a key theme in every discussion of international marketing strategy. Proponents of the philosophy of "global" products and brands, such as professor Theodore Levitt of Harvard, and the highly successful advertising agency, Saatchi and Saatchi, argue that in a world of growing internationalization, the key to success is the development of global products and brands, in other words, a focus on the marketing of standardized products and brands worldwide (Levitt, 1983). Others, however, point to the numerous barriers to standardization, and suggest that greater returns are to be obtained from adapting products and marketing strategies to the specific characteristics of individual markets (Fisher, 1984; Kotler, 1985; Vedder, 1986).

The growing integration of international markets as well as the growth of competition on a worldwide scale implies that adoption of a global perspective has become increasingly imperative in planning marketing strategy. However, to conclude that this mandates the adoption of a strategy of universal standardization appears naive and oversimplistic. In particular, it ignores the inherent complexity of operations in international markets, and the

formulation of an effective strategy to penetrate these markets. While global products and brands may be appropriate for certain markets and in targeting certain segments, adopting such an approach as a universal strategy in relation to all markets may not be desirable, and may lead to major strategic blunders. Furthermore, it implies a product orientation, and a product-driven strategy, rather than a strategy grounded in a systematic analysis of customer behavior and response patterns and market characteristics.

The purpose of this paper is thus to examine critically the notion that success in international markets necessitates adoption of a strategy of global products and brands. Given the restrictive characteristic of this philosophy, a somewhat broader perspective in developing global strategy is proposed which views standardization as merely one option in the range of possible strategies which may be effective in global markets.

The paper is divided into four parts. First, the traditional perspective on international marketing strategy focusing on the dichotomy between "standardization" and "adaptation" is reviewed. The second part examines the key assumptions underlying a philosophy of global standardization, as well as situations under which this is likely to prove effective. In the

Source: Columbia Journal of World Business (Winter 1987), pp. 19–29.

third part, the constraints to the implementation of a global standardization strategy are reviewed, including not only external market constraints, but also internal constraints arising from the structure of the firm's current operations. Finally, based on this review, a more general approach is suggested, enabling consideration of a range of alternative strategies incorporating varying degrees of standardization or adaption.

THE TRADITIONAL PERSPECTIVE ON INTERNATIONAL MARKETING STRATEGY

Traditionally, discussion of international business strategy has been polarized around the debate concerning the pursuit of a uniform strategy worldwide versus adaptation to specific local market conditions. On the one hand, it has been argued that adoption of a uniform strategy worldwide enables a company to take advantage of the potential synergies arising from multi-country operations, and constitutes the multinational company's key competitive advantage in international markets. Others however, have argued that adaptation of strategy to idiosyncratic national market characteristics is crucial to success in these markets.

Fayerweather (1969) in his seminal work in international business strategy described the central issue as one of conflict between forces toward unification and those resulting in fragmentation. He pointed out that within a multinational firm, internal forces created pressures toward the integration of strategy across national boundaries. On the other hand, differences in the sociocultural, political and economic characteristics of countries as well as the need for effective relations with the host society, constitute fragmenting influences which favor adaptation to the local environment.

This theme has been elaborated further in subsequent discussions of international business strategy. Doz (1980), for example, characterizes the conflict as one between the requirements for economic survival and success, (the economic imperative), and the adjustments to strategy made necessary by the demands of host governments, (the political imperative). Economic success or profitability in international markets is viewed as contingent on the rationalization of activities across national boundaries.

The political imperative, on the other hand, implies a strategy of "national responsiveness" foregoing potential benefits of global integration and allowing local subsidiaries substantial autonomy to develop their own production policies and strategy. A third alternative, "administrative coordination" is, however, postulated. In this case, each strategic decision is made on its own merits, allowing flexibility either to respond to pressures for national responsiveness or alternatively to move toward worldwide rationalization.

Recent discussion of global competitive strategy (Porter, 1980, 1985) echoes the same theme of the dichotomy between the forces which have triggered the globalization of markets and those which constitute barriers to global competition. Factors such as economies of scale in production, purchasing, faster accumulation of learning from operating worldwide, decrease in transportation and distribution costs, reduced costs of product adaptation and the emergence of global market segments have encouraged competition on a global scale. However, barriers such as governmental and institutional constraints, tariff barriers and duties, preferential treatment of local firms, transportation costs, differences in customer demand, and so on, call for nationalistic or "protected niche" strategies.

Similar arguments have characterized the debate concerning uniformity vs. adaptation of marketing and advertising strategies. In this context, greater attention has generally been focused on barriers to standardization (Buzzell, 1968; Elinder, 1964). Differences in customer behavior and response patterns, in local competition, in the nature of the marketing infrastructure, as well as government and trade regulation have all been cited as calling for, and in some cases rendering imperative, the adaptation of products, advertising copy, and other aspects of marketing policy (Miracle, 1968; Dunn, 1966; Donnelly and Ryans, 1969; Ryans, 1969). Yet, some advocates of a uniform or standardized strategy worldwide, especially in relation to advertising copy, have emerged— who point to a growing internationalization of lifestyles, and increasing homogeneity in consumer interests and tastes (Britt, 1974; Fatt, 1967; Boote, 1967; Killough, 1978). They have, for example, noted benefits such as development of a consistent uniform image with customers worldwide, improved planning and control, exploitation of good ideas on a broader geographic scale, as well as potential cost savings.

Compromise solutions such as "pattern standardization" have also been proposed (Peebles, Ryans, and Vernon, 1978). In this case, a global promotional theme or positioning is developed, but execution is adapted to the local market. Similarly, it has been pointed out that even where a standardized product is marketed in a number of countries, its positioning may be adapted in each market (Keegan, 1969). Conversely, the positioning may be uniform across countries, but the product itself adapted or modified.

Although this debate first emerged in the 1960s, it has recently taken on a new vigor with the widely publicized pronouncements of proponents of "global standardization" such as professor Levitt and Saatchi and Saatchi. Levitt, for example, in his provocative article (1983) stated,

A powerful force (technology) now drives the world toward a single converging commonality. The result is a new commercial reality—the explosive emergence of global markets for globally standardized products, gigantic world-scale markets of previously unimagined magnitudes.

Corporations geared to this new reality generate enormous economies of scale in production, distribution, marketing, and management. When they translate these into equivalently reduced world prices, they devastate competitors that still live functionally in the disabling grip of old assumptions about how the world now works.

The sweeping and somewhat polemic character of this argument has sparked a number of counterarguments as well as discussion of conditions under which such a strategy may be most appropriate. It has, for example, been pointed out that the potential for standardization may be greater for certain types of products such as industrial goods or luxury personal items targeted to upscale consumers, or products with similar penetration rates (Huszagh, Fox, and Day, 1985). Opportunities for standardization are also likely to occur more frequently among industrialized nations, and especially the Triad countries where customer interests as well as market conditions are likely to be more similar than among developing countries (Hill and Still, 1983; Huszagh, Fox, and Day, 1985; Ohmae, 1985).

The role of corporate philosophy and organizational structure in influencing the practicality of implementing a strategy of global standardization has also been recognized (Quelch and Hoff, 1986). Here, it has been noted that few companies pursue the extreme position of complete standardization with regard to all elements of the marketing mix, and business functions such as R and D, manufacturing, and procurement in all countries throughout the world. Rather, some degree of adaptation is likely to occur relative to certain aspects of the firm's operations or in certain geographic areas. In addition, the feasibility of implementing a standardized strategy will depend on the autonomy accorded to local management. If local management has been accustomed to substantial autonomy, considerable opposition may be encountered in attempting to introduce globally standardized strategies.

An examination of such counterarguments suggests that there are a number of dangers in espousing a philosophy of global standardization for all products and services, and in relation to all markets worldwide. Furthermore, there are numerous difficulties and constraints to implementing such a strategy in many markets, stemming from external market conditions (such as government and trade regulation, competition, the marketing infrastructure, etc.), as well as from the current structure and organization of the firm's operations.

The rationale underlying the philosophy of global products and brands is next examined in more detail, together with its inherent limitations.

THE GLOBAL STANDARDIZATION PHILOSOPHY: THE UNDERLYING ASSUMPTIONS

An examination of the arguments in favor of a strategy of global products and brands reveals three key underlying assumptions:

1. customer needs and interests are becoming increasingly homogeneous worldwide.
2. people around the world are willing to sacrifice preferences in product features, functions, design and the like for lower prices at high quality.
3. substantial economies of scale in production and marketing can be achieved through supplying global markets. (Levitt, 1983)

There are, however, a number of pitfalls associated with each of these assumptions. These are discussed here in more detail.

Homogenization of the World Wants

A key premise of the philosophy of global products is that customers' needs and interests are becoming increasingly homogeneous worldwide. But while global segments with similar interests and response patterns may be identified in some product markets, it is by no means clear that this is a universal trend. Further-

more, there is substantial evidence to suggest an increasing diversity of behavior within countries, and the emergence of idiosyncratic country-specific segments.

Lack of Evidence of Homogenization In a number of product markets ranging from watches, perfume, handbags, to soft drinks and fast foods, companies have successfully identified global customer segments, and developed global products and brands targeted to these segments. These include such stars as Rolex, Omega and Le Baume & Mercier watches, Dior, Patou or Yves St. Laurent perfume. But while these brands are highly visible and widely publicized, they are often, with a few notable exceptions, such as Classic Coke or McDonald's targeted to a relatively restricted upscale international customer segment (Ohmae, 1985).

Numerous other companies, however, adapt lines to idiosyncratic country preferences, and develop local brands or product variants targeted to local market segments. The Findus frozen food division of Nestle, for example, markets fish cakes and fish fingers in the UK, but beef bourguinon and coq au vin in France, and vitello con funghi and braviola in Italy. Their line of pizzas marketed in the UK includes cheese with ham and pineapple topping on a French bread crust. Similarly, Coca-Cola in Japan markets Georgia, cold coffee in a can, and Aquarius, a tonic drink, as well as Classic Coke and Hi-C.

Growth of Intra-Country Segmentation Price Sensitivity Furthermore, there is a growing body of evidence which suggests substantial heterogeneity within countries. In the US, for example, the VALS study has identified nine value segments (Mitchell, 1983), while other studies have identified major differences in behavior between regions and subcultural segments (Kahle, 1986; Garreau, 1981; Wallendorf and Reilly, 1983; Saegert, Moore, and Hilger, 1985). Lifestyle approaches such as the Yankelovitch Monitor (Beatty, 1985) or the customized AIO approach (Wells, 1975) have also identified different lifestyle segments both generally and relative to specific product markets.

Many other countries are also characterized by substantial regional differences as well as different lifestyle and value segments. The Yankelovitch Monitor and AIO approaches have, for example, been applied in a number of countries throughout the world (Broadbent and Segnit, 1973; the RISC Observer No. 1 & 2, 1986). In some cases, this has resulted in the identification of some common segments across countries, but country-specific segments have also emerged (Douglas and Urban, 1977; Boote, 1982/3). Lifestyle segmentation studies conducted by local research organizations in other countries also reveal a variety of lifestyle profiles (Hakuhodo, 1985).

Similarly, in industrial markets, while some global segments, often consisting of firms with international operations can be identified, there also is considerable diversity within and between countries. Often local businesses constitute an important market segment and, especially in developing countries, may differ significantly in technological sophistication, business, philosophy and strategy, emphasis on product quality, and service and price, from large multinationals (Hill and Still, 1984; Chakrabarti, Feinman, and Fuentivilla, 1982).

The evidence thus suggests that the similarities in customer behavior are restricted to a relatively limited number of target segments, or product markets, while for the most part, there are substantial differences between countries. Proponents of standardization counter that the international marketer should focus on similarities among countries rather than differences. This may, however, imply ignoring a major part of a local market, and the potential profits which may be obtained from tapping other market segments.

Universal Preference for Low Price at Acceptable Quality

Another critical component of the argument for global standardization is that people around the world are willing to sacrifice preferences in product features, functions, design and the like, for lower prices assuming equivalent quality. Aggressive low pricing for quality products which meet the common needs of customers in markets around the world is believed to further expand the global markets facing the firm. Although an appealing argument, this has three major problems.

Lack of Evidence of Increased Price Sensitivity Evidence to suggest that customers are universally willing to trade-off specific product features for a lower price is largely lacking. While in many product markets there is invariably a price-sensitive segment, there is no indication that this is on the increase. On the contrary, in many product and service markets, ranging from watches, personal computers, household appliances, to banking and insurance, an interest in multiple product features, product quailty and service appears to be growing.

For example, findings from the PIMS project overwhelmingly suggest that product quality is the driving force behind successful marketing strategies not only in the US, but also in other developed countries (Douglas and Craig, 1983; Gale, Luchs, and Rosenfeld, 1986). In industrial markets insofar as global market segments consist of multinational corporations, they may be more concerned with the ability to supply and service their operations worldwide than with the price. Similarly, in consumer markets where global market segments consist of upscale affluent customers, they are likely to look for distinctive prestige, high quality products such as Cartier watches and handbags and Godiva chocolates. Consequently, it is arguable that world customers are less price sensitive than other customers.

Low Price Positioning Is a Highly Vulnerable Strategy Also, from a strategic point of view, emphasis on price-positioning may be undesirable especially in international markets, since it offers no long-term competitive advantage. A price-positioning strategy is always vulnerable to new technological developments which may lower costs, as well as to attack from competitors with lower overhead, and lower operating or labor costs. Government subsidies to local competitors may also undermine the effectiveness of a price-positioning strategy. In addition, price-sensitive customers typically are not brand or source loyal.

Standardized Low Price Can Be Overpriced in Some Countries and Underpriced in Others Finally, a strategy based on a combination of a standardized product at a low price, when implemented in countries which vary in their competitive structure, as well as the level of economic development, is likely to result in products which are overdesigned and overpriced for some markets and underdesigned and underpriced for others. There is, for example, substantial evidence to suggest that where markets in developing countries are price sensitive, a strategy of product adaptation and simplification may be the most effective (Hill and Still, 1984). Cost advantages may also be negated by transportation and distribution costs as well as tariff barriers and/or price regulation (Porter, 1980, 1985).

Economies of Scale of Production and Marketing

The third assumption underlying the philosophy of global standardization is that a key force driving strategy is product technology, and that substantial economies of scale can be achieved by supplying global markets. This does, however, neglect three critical and interrelated points: (a) technological developments in flexible factory automation enable economies of scale to be achieved at lower levels of output and do not require production of a single standardized product, (b) cost of production is only one and often not the critical component in determining the total cost of the product, and (c) strategy should not be solely product-driven but should take into account the other components of a marketing strategy, such as positioning, packaging, brand name, advertising, P.R. consumer and trade promotion and distribution.

Developments in Flexible Factory Automation Recent developments in flexible factory automation methods have lowered the minimum efficient scale of operation and have thus enabled companies to supply smaller local markets efficiently, without requiring operations on a global scale. However, diseconomies may result from such operations due to increased transportation and distribution costs, as well as higher administrative overhead, and additional communication and coordination costs.

Furthermore, decentralization of production and establishment of local manufacturing operations enables diversification of risk arising from political events, fluctuations in foreign exchange rates, or economic instability. Recent swings in foreign exchange rates, coupled with the growth of offshore sourcing have underscored the vulnerability of centralizing production in a single location. Government regulations relating to local component and/or offset requirements create additional pressures for local manufacturing. Flexible automation not only implies that decentralization of manufacturing and production may be cost-efficient but also makes minor modifications in products of models in the latter stages of production feasible, so that a variety of model versions can be produced without major retooling. Adaptations to product design can thus be made to meet differences in preferences from one country to another without loss of economies of scale.

Production Costs Are Often a Minor Component of Total Cost In many consumer and service industries, such as cosmetics, detergents, pharmaceuticals, or financial institutions, production costs are a small fraction of total cost. The key to success in these markets is an understanding of the tastes and purchase behavior of target customers distribution channels, and tailoring products and strategies to these rather than production efficiency. In the detergent industry, for example, mastery of mass-merchandising techniques, and an effective brand management system is typically considered the key element in the success of the giants in this field, such as Procter and Gamble (P&G) or Colgate-Palmolive.

For many products the establishment of an effective distribution network is often of prime importance in penetrating international markets. This is particularly the case for consumer products in countries where the absence or limited reach of mass-communication channels such as TV or magazines preclude the use of "pull" strategies. Distribution may also be crucial for products such as agricultural machinery, which require extensive after-sales service and maintenance. Furthermore, for some companies such as Avon with their Avon sales ladies network, or direct marketing insurance companies, distribution may constitute the crux of their marketing strategy and be a major component of their costs.

In these cases, the potential for scale economies arising from a standardization of operations may be negligible or non-existent. In some instances, greater efficiency in operational systems and procedure may result from experience in multiple country market environments, but as also noted previously, there may also be significant scale diseconomies.

The Standardization Philosophy Is Primarily Product Driven The focus on product and brand related aspects of strategy in discussions of global standardization is misleading since it ignores the other key marketing strategy variables. Strategy in international markets should also take into consideration other aspects of the marketing mix, and the extent to which these are standardized across country markets rather than adapted to local idiosyncratic characteristics. Thus, not only should the effectiveness of using standardized positioning strategy promotional and advertising campaigns be considered, but a standardized distribution system and uniforming pricing should be considered as well. There are, however, often formidable barriers to such a strategy which will be discussed subsequently.

REQUISITE CONDITIONS FOR GLOBAL STANDARDIZATION

The numerous pitfalls in the rationale underlying the global standardization philosophy suggest that such a strategy is far from universally appropriate for all products, brands or companies. Only under certain conditions is it likely to prove a "winning" strategy in international markets. These include: (a) the existence of a global market segment, (b) potential synergies from standardization and (c) the availability of a communication and distribution infrastructure to deliver the firm's offering to target customers worldwide.

Existence of Global Market Segments

As noted previously, global segments may be identified in a number of industrial and consumer markets. In consumer markets these segments are typically luxury or premium type products. Global segments are, however, not limited to such product markets, but also exist in other types of markets, such as motorcycle, record, stereo equipment, and computer, where a segment with similar needs and wants can be identified in many countries.

In industrial markets, companies with multinational operations are particularly likely to have similar needs and requirements worldwide. Where the operations are integrated or coordinated across national boundaries, as in the case of banks or other financial institutions, compatibility of operation systems and equipment may be essential. Consequently, they may seek vendors who can supply and service their operations worldwide, in some cases developing global contracts for such purchases. Similarly, manufacturing companies with worldwide operations may source globally in order to ensure uniformity in quality, service and price of components and other raw materials throughout their operations.

Marketing of global products and brands to such target segments and global customers enables development of a uniform global image throughout the world. In some markets such as perfume, fashions, et cetera, association with a specific country of origin or a foreign image in general may carry a prestige connotation. In other cases, for example, Sony electronic equipment, McDonald's hamburgers, Hertz or Avis car rentals, IBM computers, or Xerox office equipment, it may help to develop a worldwide reputation for quality and service. Just as multinational corporations may seek uniformity in supply worldwide, some consumers who travel extensively may be interested in finding the same brand of cigarettes and soft drinks, or hotels in foreign countries. This may be particularly relevant in product markets used extensively by international travelers.

While the existence of a potential global segment is a key motivating factor for developing a global product and brand strategy, it is important to note that the desirability of such a strategy depends on the size and economic viability of the segment in question, the strength of the segment's preference for the global brand, as well as the ability to reach the segment effectively and profitably.

Synergies Associated with Global Standardization

Global standardization may also have a number of synergistic effects. In addition to those associated with a global image noted above, opportunities may exist for the transfer of good ideas for products or promotional strategies from one country to another. For example, a new product or an effective promotional strategy developed in one country (not necessarily the country in which the product or brand originated) may be effectively exploited in other countries. For example, US detergent companies have acquired or developed new, more effective detergent formulas and fabric softeners to cope with harder water conditions in European markets. These have subsequently been introduced into the US home market. Similarly, promotional campaigns such as the Marlboro cowboy may also prove effective in several countries.

Global marketing also generates experience of operating in multiple and diverse environments. Experience gained in one foreign environment may thus be transferred to another country, or may facilitate more rapid adaptation to new environmental conditions, even if these have not been previously experienced. Consequently, the range of experience acquired may result in the introduction of operating efficiencies.

The standardization of strategy and operations across a number of countries may also enable the acquisition or exploitation of specific types of expertise which would not be feasible otherwise. Expertise in assessing country risk or foreign exchange risk, or in identifying and interpreting information relating to multiple country markets may, for example, be developed.

Such synergies are not, however, unique to a strategy of global standardization, but may also occur wherever operations and strategy are coordinated or integrated across country markets (Takeuchi and Porter, 1985). In fact, only certain scale economies associated with product and advertising copy standardization and the development of a global image as discussed earlier, are unique to global standardization.

Availability of an International Communication and Distribution Infrastructure

The effectiveness of global standardization also depends to a large extent on the availability of an international infrastructure of communications and distribution. As many corporations have expanded overseas, service organizations have followed their customers abroad to supply their needs worldwide.

Advertising agencies such as Saatchi and

Saatchi, McCann Erickson and Young and Rubicam now have an international network of operations throughout the world while many research agencies can also supply services in major market worldwide. With the growing integration of financial markets, banks, investment firms, insurance and other financial institutions are also becoming increasingly international in orientation and are expanding the scope of their operations in world markets. The physical distribution network of shippers, freight forwarding, export and import agents-customs clearing, invoicing and insurance agents is also becoming increasingly integrated to meet demand for international shipment of goods and services.

Improvements in telecommunications and in logistical systems have considerably increased capacity to manage operations on a global scale and hence facilitate adoption of global standardization strategies. The spread of telex and FACS systems, as well as satellite linkages and international computer linkages, all contribute to the shrinking of distances and facilitate globalization of operations. Similarly, improvements in transportation systems and physical logistics such as containerization and computerized inventory and handling systems have enabled significant cost savings as well as reducing time required to move goods across major distances.

OPERATIONAL CONSTRAINTS TO EFFECTIVE IMPLEMENTATION OF A STANDARDIZATION STRATEGY

While adoption of a standardized strategy may be desirable under certain conditions, there are a number of constraints which severely restrict the firm's ability to develop and implement a standardized strategy. These include both external or environmental constraints, the nature of the marketing infrastructure, resource market conditions or the type of competition, as well as internal constraints which stem from the firm's current strategy or organization of international operations.

External Constraints to Effective Standardization

The numerous external constraints which impede global standardization are well recognized, and have been clearly identified in the classic discussion by Buzzell (1968). Here, three major categories are highlighted, namely: (a) governmental and trade restrictions, (b) differences in the marketing infrastructure, such as the availability and effectiveness of promotional media, (c) the character of resource markets, and differences in the availability and costs of resources, and (d) differences in competition from one country to another.

Governmental and Trade Restrictions Government and trade restrictions, such as tariff and other trade barriers, product, pricing or promotional regulation, frequently hamper standardization of the product line, pricing or promotion strategy. Tariffs, or quotas on the import of key materials, components or other resources may, for example, affect production costs and thus hamper uniform pricing or alternatively result in the substitution of other components and modifications in product design. Local content requirements or compensatory export requirements, which specify that products contain a certain proportion of components manufactured locally or that a certain volume of production is exported to offset imports of components or other services may have a similar impact.

Regulation of business practices may also affect the feasibility of standardization. In Japan, for example, in many product markets such as electronics, and food, product design and composition must conform to standards established by the relevant trade body, necessitating adaptation by foreign companies. Similarly, severe advertising regulation in countries such as Germany and Switzerland, has restricted the use of many campaigns successful in other countries.

The existence of cartels such as the European steel cartel, or the Swiss chocolate cartel, may also impede or exclude standardized strategies in countries covered by these agreements. In particular, they may affect adoption of a uniform pricing strategy as the cartel sets prices for the industry. Cartel members may also control established distribution channels, thus preventing use of a standardized distribution strategy. Extensive grey markets in countries such as India, Hong Kong, and South America may also affect administered pricing systems, and require adjustment of pricing strategies. For example, Wilkinson's attempt to market its line of razor blades in India suffered greatly from price undercutting in the grey market.

The Nature of the Marketing Infrastructure
Differences in the marketing infrastructure from one country to another may hamper use of a standardized strategy. These may, for example, include differences in the availability and reach of various promotional media, in the availability of certain distribution channels or retail institutions, or in the existence and efficiency of the communication and transportation network. Such factors may, therefore, require considerable adaptation of strategy of local market conditions.

The type of media available as well as their reach and effectiveness differ from country to country. For example, TV advertising, while a major medium in the US, Japan and Australia, is not permitted in Scandinavian countries. Where TV advertising is permitted it may reach only a limited number of households due to limited ownership of TVs, as for example, in South Africa, Nigeria or Indonesia. Similarly, in countries with high levels of illiteracy the effectiveness of print media is severely limited. Conversely, in some countries certain media are particularly effective or unique to the country. These include the circular street advertising to be found in Paris, or the neon advertising common in Japan.

The nature of the distribution system and structure also differs significantly from one country to another. While in the US supermarkets account for the major proportion of food sales, in other countries there are virtually no supermarkets and Mom and Pop type stores predominate. This severely limits the effectiveness of a "pull" type strategy and ability to use "in store" promotions or display to stimulate customer interest. Even in industrialized nations such as Japan, Italy, Belgium, Portugal and Spain, more than 75% of retail sales are done through small retailers. Again, discount outlets common in many industrialized nations may not exist in other countries, which may restrict a company's ability to use an aggressive price penetration strategy.

The physical and communications infrastructure also varies from country to country. Inadequate mail service (as for example, in Brazil or Italy) will limit the effectiveness of direct mail promotion. A poor or ill-maintained road network may necessitate use of alternative modes of transportation such as rail or air. Inaccessibility of outlying rural areas due to the nature of the physical terrain in countries, such as Canada, Australia and Peru, may also require the design of logistical systems specifically adapted to their unique conditions.

Interdependencies with Resource Markets Yet another constraint to the development of standardized strategies is the nature of resource markets, and their operation in different countries throughout the world as well as the interdependency of these markets with marketing decisions. Availability and cost of raw materials, as well as labor and other resources in different locations, will affect not only decisions regarding sourcing of and hence the location of manufacturing activities but can also affect marketing strategy decisions such as product design. For example, in the paper industry, availability of cheap local materials such as jute and sugar cane may result in their substitution for wood fiber. Similarly, the relative cost of paper vs. plastic materials may affect product packaging decisions. In Europe, use of plastic rather than paper is more common than in the US due to differences in the relative cost of the two materials.

Cost differentials relative to raw materials, labor, management and other inputs may also influence the trade-off relative to alternative marketing mix strategies. For example, high packaging cost relative to physical distribution may result in use of cheaper packaging with a shorter shelf-life and more frequent shipments. Similarly low labor costs relative to media may encourage a shift from mass media advertising to labor intensive promotion such as personal selling, and product demonstration.

Availability of capital, technology and manufacturing capabilities in different locations will also affect decisions about licensing, contract manufacturing, joint ventures, and other "make-buy" types of decisions for different markets, as well as decisions about counter-trade, reciprocity and other long-term relations.

The Nature of the Competitive Structure Differences in the nature of the competitive situation from one country to another may also suggest the desirability of adaptation strategy. Even in markets characterized by global competition, such as agricultural equipment, and motorcycles, the existence of low-cost competition in certain countries may suggest the desirability of marketing stripped-down models or lowering prices to meet such competition. Even where competitors are predominantly other multinationals, pre-emption of established distribution networks may encourage adoption of innovative distribution methods or direct distribution to short-circuit an entrenched position. Thus, the existence of global competition does not necessarily imply a need for global standardization.

All such aspects thus impose major constraints on the feasibility and effectiveness of a standardized strategy, and suggest the desirability or need to adapt to specific market conditions.

Internal Constraints to Effective Standardization

In addition to such external constraints on the feasibility of a global standardization strategy, there are also a number of internal constraints which may need to be considered. These include compatibility with the existing network of operations overseas, as well as opposition or lack of enthusiasm among local management toward a standardized strategy.

Existing International Operations Proponents of global standardization typically take the position of a novice company with no operations in international markets, and hence, fail to take into consideration the fit of the proposed strategy with current international activities. In practice, however, many companies have a number of existing operations in various countries. In some cases, these are joint ventures, or licensing operations or involve some collaboration in purchasing, manufacturing or distribution with other companies. Even where foreign manufacturing and distribution operations are wholly-owned, the establishment of a distribution network will typically entail relationships with other organizations, as for example, exclusive distributor agreement.

Such commitments may be difficult if not impossible to change in the short run, and may constitute a major impediment to adoption of a standardized strategy. If, for example, a joint venture with a local company has been established to manufacture and market a product line in a specific country or region, resistance from the local partner (or government authorities) may be encountered if the parent company wishes to shift production or import components from another location. Similarly, a licensing contract will impede a firm from supplying the products covered by the agreement from an alternative location for the duration of the contract, even if it becomes more cost efficient to do so.

Conversely, the establishment of an effective dealer or distribution network in a country or region may constitute an important resource to a company. The addition of new products to the product line currently sold or distributed by this network may therefore provide a more efficient utilization of company resources, than expanding to new countries or geographic regions with the existing product line, as this would require substantial investment in the establishment of a new distribution network.

In addition, overseas subsidiaries may currently be marketing not only core products and brands from the company's domestic business, but may also have added or acquired local or regional products and brands in response to local market demand. P&G, for example, acquired Domestos, an established local brand of household cleanser in the UK, and added it to its product line in a number of other European markets. In some cases, therefore, introduction of a global product or brand may be likely to cannibalize sales of local or regional brands.

Advocates of standardization thus need to take into consideration the evolutionary character of international involvement, which may render a universal strategy of global products and brands sub-optimal. Somewhat ironically, the longer the history of a multinational corporation's involvement in foreign or international markets, and the more diversified and far-flung its operations, the more likely it is that standardization will not lead to optimal results.

Local Management Motivation and Attitudes
Another internal constraint concerns the motivation and attitudes of local management with regard to standardization. Standardized strategies tend to facilitate or result in centralization in the planning and organization of international activities. In particular, product development and positioning as well as key promotional themes are likely to be developed at corporate headquarters. Especially if input from local management is limited, this may result in a feeling that strategy is "imposed" by corporate headquarters, and/or not adequately adapted nor appropriate in view of specific local market characteristics and conditions.

Local management is likely to take the view—"it won't work here—things are different," which will reduce their motivation to implementing a standardized strategy effectively.

Standardization tends to conflict with the principal of local management responsibility. Emphasis on local management autonomy stems from the advantages traditionally associated with decentralization and a concern with encouraging local entrepreneurship. The establishment of a standardized strategy by corporate headquarters may therefore reduce the overall effectiveness of the firm. It also restricts local management's ability to adapt to local market competitive conditions for example, in promotion or distribution decisions which can result in sub-optimal reactions to competition.

A FRAMEWORK FOR CLASSIFYING GLOBAL STRATEGY OPTIONS

This review of the rationale underlying "global standardization" thus suggests that it's appropriate only in relation to certain product markets or market segments under certain market environment conditions, and dependent on company objectives and structure. The adoption of a global perspective should not therefore be viewed as synonymous with a strategy of global products and brands. Rather for most companies, such a perspective implies consideration of a broad range of strategic options of which standardization is merely one.

In essence, a global perspective implies planning strategy relative to markets worldwide rather than on a country by country basis. This may result in the identification of opportunities for global products and brands and/or integrating and coordinating strategy across national boundaries to exploit potential synergies operating on an international scale. Such opportunities should, however, be weighed against the benefits of adaptation to idiosyncratic customer characteristics.

The development of an effective global strategy thus requires a careful examination of all alternative international strategic options in terms of standardization vs. adaptation open to the firm. These are, however, vast in number given the range of possible geographic areas, countries, market segments, product variants, and marketing strategies to be considered. It is, therefore, helpful to classify these options based on the degree of standardization. A continuum can thus be identified, ranging from "pure standardization" to "pure differentiation," where most options fall into the intermediate category of mixed or "hybrid" strategies. This is shown in Chart 1.

In the extreme case of pure standardization, all dimensions of marketing strategy are standardized or uniform throughout the world. In practice, as noted previously, not only is such a strategy fraught with problems, but is rarely likely to be feasible in relation to all elements of the mix. The other extreme is that of totally differentiated strategy, in which each component of the mix is adapted to the specific idiosyncratic customer and environmental characteristics in each country. Management in each country thus develops its own strategy, independently with no coordination across countries, nor attempt to identify any commonality from one country to another.

In between these two extremes is a set of mixed or hybrid options including some standardized and some differentiated components. Here, a variety of different patterns may be identified. These include those in which some components of the mix are standardized, while others are adapted to local market factors; those where strategies are standardized across regions or clusters of countries; strategies standardized by market segment; as well as combinations of the above.

For example, as shown in Chart 2, some components of the marketing mix, product or advertising copy, are standardized across countries, but others, such as distribution policy or pricing, are adapted to specific country or environmental characteristics. For example, companies marketing global products or brands may pursue different distribution or pricing policies in each country. Apple Computers, for

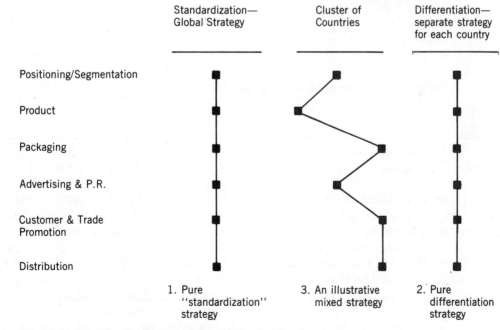

Chart 1 The Standardization-Differentiation Continuum

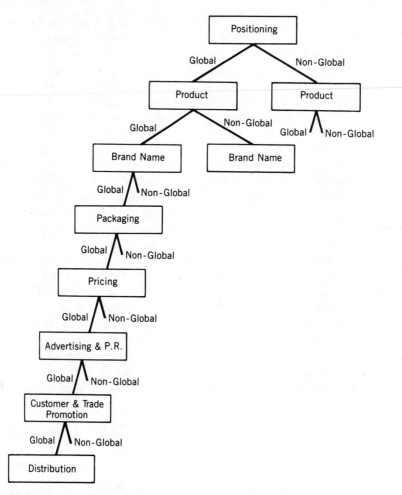

Chart 2 Key Dimensions of Global Marketing Strategy

example, while selling a standardized product line worldwide, has different positioning, promotional, and distribution strategies in each country.

Another option is to standardize strategy across regions or clusters of countries. Ford, for example, develops different models for its European operations as compared with the US market. The Fiesta, Granada, and Taurus models were all initially developed for the European market, as were the positioning strategy and promotional themes.

Alternatively, strategies might be standard-

example, while selling a standardized product line worldwide, has different positioning, promotional, and distribution strategies in each country.

Another option is to standardize strategy across regions or clusters of countries. Ford, for example, develops different models for its European operations as compared with the US market. The Fiesta, Granada, and Taurus models were all initially developed for the European market, as were the positioning strategy and promotional themes.

Alternatively, strategies might be standard-

Table 1 A Standardized Global Strategy Checklist

	YES Continue to Explore	NO Standardization Not Appropriate
1. Is there a global market segment for your product?	Yes	No
2. Are there synergies associated with a global strategy?	Yes	No
3. Are there no **external** constraints/government regulations on ability to implement a global strategy?	Yes	No
4. Are there no **internal** constraints to implementing a global strategy?	Yes	No
If yes to all 4 consider global	Yes	No

wide, but the promotional strategy is adapted to different geographic regions. Similarly, Kellogg's Corn Flakes is sold worldwide, but in some regions such as Latin America, and the Far East, promotional themes are standardized, while in other areas, such as Europe, promotional themes, packaging and distribution strategies are specific to each country. Again, Virginia Slims is targeted to "liberated" women throughout the world, but in Japan, the advertising copy is changed from "You've Come a Long Way Baby," to "Oh So Slim and Sexy," (translation from Japanese).

In addition to such options which all assume a worldwide strategy, companies may also target specific and unique product markets and segments in a given geographic region or country. In the detergent market, for example, a company may market its line of powdered detergents worldwide, its liquid detergents and softeners in industrialized countries, and for the developing countries, develop a line of synthetic detergents and bar soaps. Similarly in India, a major segment of the tooth cleansing market consists of black and white toothcleansing powders. Multinationals such as P&G and Colgate have each developed a brand of white tooth-cleansing powder to tap this market.

A firm's international operations are thus likely to be characterized by a mix of strategies, including not only global products and brands, but also some regional products and brands and some national products and brands. Similarly, some target segments may be global, others regional and others national. Hybrid strategies of this nature thus enable a company to take advantage of the benefits of standardization, and potential synergies from operating on an international scale, while at the same time not losing those afforded by adaptation to specific country characteristics and customer preferences. Guidelines and an approach for developing such a strategy based on a dynamic portfolio perspective have been proposed (Wind and Douglas, 1987). These take into consideration the company's existing network of operations, the current mix of products and brands, and their competitive positioning in each country, in designing an effective global marketing strategy.

CONCLUSION

The main thesis of this paper is that the design of an effective global marketing strategy does not necessarily entail the marketing of standardized products and global brands worldwide. While such a strategy may work for some companies and certain product lines, for other companies and other product markets adaptation to local or regional differences may yield better results. The key to success is rather a careful analysis of the force driving toward globalization as well as the obstacles to this approach, and to assess, based on the company's strengths and weaknesses, where the most attractive opportunities and the company's differential advantage in exploiting these appear to lie.

REFERENCES

Boote, Alfred S. (1982–83). "Psychographic Segmentation in Europe," *Journal of Advertising* (December–January).

Britt, Stewart Henderson. (1974). "Standardizing Marketing for the International Market," *Columbia Journal of World Business* (Winter), 39–45.

Buzzel, R. (1968). "Can You Standardize Multinational Marketing?" *Harvard Business Review* (November–December), 102–113.

Donnelly, James H., Jr., and John K. Ryans. (1969). "Standardized Global Advertising, A Call as Yet Unanswered," *Journal of Marketing* (April), 57–60.

Chakrabarti, Alok K., Stephen Feinman, and William Fuentivilla. (1982). "The Cross-National Comparison of Patterns of Industrial Innovations," *Columbia Journal of World Business* (Fall), 33–38.

Douglas, Susan P., and Christine Urban. (1977). "Life Analysis to Profile Women in International Markets," *Journal of Marketing*, 41 (July), 46–54.

Douglas, Susan P., and C. Samuel Craig. (1983). "Examining the Performance of U.S. Multinationals in Foreign Markets," *Journal of International Business Studies* (Winter), 51–62.

Doz, Yves. (1980). "Strategic Management in Multinational Companies," *Sloan Management Review*, 21 (Winter), 27–46.

Dunn, S. Watson. (1966). "The Case-Study Approach in Cross-Cultural Research," *Journal of Marketing Research*, (February), 26–31.

Elinder, Erik. (1965). "How International Can European Advertising Be?" *Journal of Marketing* (April), 7–11.

Fatt, Arthur C. (1967). "The Danger of 'Local' International Advertising," *Journal for Marketing* (January).

Fayerweather, John. (1969). *International Business Management: A Conceptual Framework*. New York: McGraw-Hill.

Fisher, Anne B. (1984). "The Ad Biz Gloms onto Global," *Fortune*, November 12.

Gale, Bradley, Robert Luchs, and Joel Rosenfeld. (1987). "Who Will Succeed in Europe's Changing Marketplace," *International Management Development Review* (to appear).

Garreau, J. (1981). *The Nine Nations of North America*. Boston: Houghton Mifflin.

Hakuhodo Institute of Life and Living. (1983). *Hitonami: Keeping Up with the Satos*. Tokyo: Hill.

Hill, J. S., and R. R. Still. (1984). "Adapting Products to LDC Tastes," *Harvard Business Review*, 62 (March–April), 92–101.

Huszagh, Sandra, Richard J. Fox, and Ellen Day. "Global Marketing: An Empirical Investigation," *Columbia Journal of World Business*, Twentieth Anniversary Issue, 31–43.

Kahle, Lynn R. (1986). "The Nine Nations of North America and the Value Basis of Geographic Segmentation," *Journal of Marketing*, 56 (April), 37–47.

Killough, James. (1978). "Improved Payoff from Transnational Advertising," *Harvard Business Review* (July–August), 103.

Kotler, Philip. (1985). "Global Standardization—Courting Danger," panel discussion, 23 American Marketing Association Conference, Washington, D.C.

Levitt, T. (1983). "The Globalization of Markets," *Harvard Business Review* (May–June), 92–102.

Miracle, Gordon. (1968). "Internationalizing Advertising Principles and Strategies," *MSU Business Topics* (Autumn), 29–36.

Mitchell, A. (1983). *The Nine American Lifestyles*. New York: Macmillan.

Ohmae, Kenichi. (1985). "Becoming a Triad Power: The New Global Corporation," *The McKinsey Quarterly* (Spring), 2–25.

Ohmae, Kenichi. (1985). *Triad Power*. New York: The Free Press.

Peebles, Dean M., John K. Ryans, and Ivan R. Vernon. (1978). "Coordinating International Advertising," *Journal of Marketing*, 46 (Winter), 27–35.

Porter, Michael. (1980). *Competitive Strategy: Techniques for Analyzing Industries and Competitors*. New York: The Free Press.

Porter, Michael. (1985). *Competitive Advantage*. New York: The Free Press.

Quelch, Joan A., and Edward J. Hoff. (1986). "Customizing Global Marketing," *Harvard Business Review* (May–June).

The RISC Observer, No. 1 and 2 (1986). Paris: RISC mimeographed.

Ryans, John K. (1969). "Is It Too Soon to Put a Tiger in Every Tank?" *Columbia Journal of World Business* (March), 69–75.

Saegert, Joel, Robert J. Hoover, and Marye Thorp Hilger. (1985). "Characteristics of Mexican American Consumers," *Journal of Consumer Research*, 12 (June), 104–109.

Segnit, Susanna, and Simon Broadbent. (1973). "Lifestyle Research," *European Research*, 1 (January).

Takeuchi, H., and M. E. Porter. (1985). "The Strategic Role of International Marketing: Managing the Nature and Extent of Worldwide Coordination." In Michael E. Porter (ed.), *Competition in Global Industries*. Cambridge, Mass.: Harvard Graduate School of Business Administration.

24

STANDARDIZATION OF INTERNATIONAL MARKETING STRATEGY: SOME RESEARCH HYPOTHESES
Subhash C. Jain

Two aspects of international marketing strategy standardization are process and program standardization. A framework for determining marketing program standardization is introduced. Factors affecting program standardization are examined critically. In an attempt to establish a research agenda on the standardization issue, the author develops research propositions for each factor.

Global marketing is much on the minds of academicians and practitioners today. It has been argued that the worldwide marketplace has become so homogenized that multinational corporations can market standardized products and services all over the world, by identical strategies, with resultant lower costs and higher margins. Interestingly, the standardization issue is not new. Whether to standardize or to customize has been a vexing question with which international marketers have wrestled since the 1960s. The world went on without the issue being fully resolved. Recent resurgence of interest in the international standardization issue is attributed to such global influences as TV, films, widespread travel, telecommunications, and the computer.

Though much has been said and written lately on globalization of marketing, we are nowhere close to any conclusive theory or practice. This situation is not surprising, as empirical studies in the area of international marketing are limited. Because empirical detection requires a theoretical base, this article is an attempt to provide a conceptual framework for gaining insights into the standardization issue. Hypotheses are presented in the form of propositions. Ideas for testing these hypotheses are given. In brief, an attempt is made to establish a research agenda on the standardization issue.

LITERATURE REVIEW

As used here, standardization of international marketing strategy refers to using a common product, price, distribution, and promotion program on a worldwide basis. The issue of standardization first was raised by Elinder (1961) with reference to advertising. He stressed that emerging similarities among European consumers make uniform advertising both desirable and feasible. Interestingly, advertising continues to be the leading standardization concern (Killough, 1978; Miracle, 1968; Peebles, Ryans, and Vernon, 1977, 1978). In the last 25 years, of the 34 major studies on the

Source: Journal of Marketing, Vol. 53 (January 1989), pp. 70–79.

subject, 14 have been on advertising. In addition, almost 55% of these studies have been conceptual. Though the subject of standardization has not been researched conclusively, an examination of these writings leads to the following conclusions.

- There are two aspects of standardization, process and program (e.g., Sorenson and Wiechmann, 1975).
- Across-the-board standardization is inconceivable (e.g., Killough, 1978).
- The decision on standardization is not a dichotomous one between complete standardization and customization. Rather, there can be degrees of standardization (e.g., Quelch and Hoff, 1986).
- A variety of internal and external factors impinge on the standardization decision. Among these, product/industry characteristics are paramount (e.g., Wind and Douglas, 1986).
- Generally standardization is most feasible in settings where marketing infrastructure is well developed (e.g., Peebles, Ryans, and Vernon, 1978).

The preceding observations, taken as a whole, seem to suggest that standardization at best is difficult and impractical. However, we do know that the marketplace is becoming increasingly global and indeed there are global products. Among consumer durable goods, the Mercedes car is a universal product. Among nondurable goods, Coca-Cola is ubiquitous. Among industrial goods, Boeing jets are sold worldwide as a global product. How do we explain this phenomenon conceptually?

This article is an attempt to establish a research agenda on the standardization issue. The article is organized into four sections. In the first section a framework for determining marketing program standardization is introduced. The next section critically examines various factors that affect standardization. Research propositions for establishing a research agenda on the standardization issue are developed around these factors. The degree of standardization feasible in a particular case and its impact on performance in program markets are

discussed in the third section. In the last section, managerial implications are provided.

STANDARDIZATION FRAMEWORK

As noted before, standardization has two aspects: marketing *program* and marketing *process*. The term "program" refers to various aspects of the marketing mix and "process" implies tools that aid in program development and implementation. A company may standardize one or both of these aspects. Inasmuch as the current controversy pertains to program standardization, this article addresses only that aspect.

Figure 1 is a framework for determining the degree of standardization feasible in a particular case. The following key concepts underlie the rationale for this framework.

- Likelihood of program standardization depends on a variety of factors identified as target market, market position, nature of product, and environment. Explanation of these factors is given in Figure 1.
- Effective implementation of standardization strategy is influenced by organization perspectives.
- Total standardization is unthinkable.
- The degree of standardization in a product/market situation should be examined in terms of its long-term advantage.

MARKETING PROGRAM STANDARDIZATION

With few exceptions, most of the literature on standardization, especially the earlier studies, addresses globalization/standardization of marketing program (Walters, 1986). The term "program" comprises various facets of marketing mix, which can be classified as product design, product positioning, brand name, packaging, retail price, basic advertising message, creative expression, sales promotion, media allocation, role of salesforce, management of salesforce,

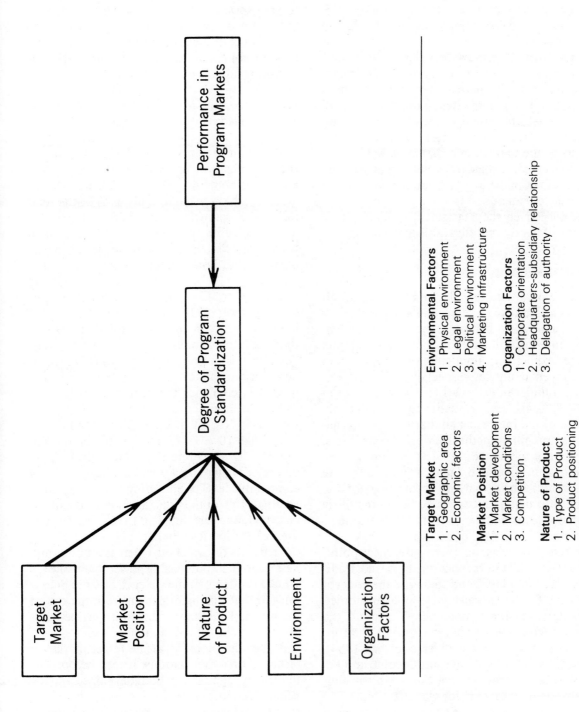

Figure 1 A Framework for Determining Marketing Program Standardization

Target Market
1. Geographic area
2. Economic factors

Market Position
1. Market development
2. Market conditions
3. Competition

Nature of Product
1. Type of Product
2. Product positioning

Environmental Factors
1. Physical environment
2. Legal environment
3. Political environment
4. Marketing infrastructure

Organization Factors
1. Corporate orientation
2. Headquarters-subsidiary relationship
3. Delegation of authority

Performance in Program Markets

Degree of Program Standardization

Target Market

Market Position

Nature of Product

Environment

Organization Factors

role of middlemen, type of retail outlets, and customer service (Quelch and Hoff, 1986; Sorenson and Wiechmann, 1975; Wind and Douglas, 1986).

Advertising (ad message and creative expression) and, to a lesser extent, product design are two aspects of the marketing program that have been examined more often than others, in both conceptual and empirical studies. Future research should explore globalization of other aspects of the marketing program as well.

Conceptually, standardization of one or more parts of the marketing program is a function of five factors identified in Figure 1. Individually and collectively these factors affect standardization differently in different decision areas.

Target Market

The standardization decision is situation-specific, requiring reference to a particular target market for a particular product. Researchers have examined the globalization issue, either explicitly or implicitly, with reference to advanced countries, especially Western Europe. Elinder (1961), Fatt (1964), and Roostal (1963) considered globalization feasible because of the increasing similarity and international mobility of the European consumers. According to Ohmae (1985), the United States, Western Europe, and Japan, which constitute the major world markets accounting for the bulk of product, appear to be becoming fairly homogeneous and hence fit for globalization.

Opponents of globalization also use advanced countries as their reference point. Fournis (1962) notes that customs and traditions tend to persist and therefore the concept of the "European consumer" is a misnomer. Scholars observe that as people around the globe become better educated and more affluent, their tastes actually diverge (Fisher, 1984). Boddewyn (1981) found sharp income and behavior differences between European consumers to be discouraging for globalization.

The studies cited raise an important research question: Does economic similarity (referring to per capita GNP, disposable income, quality of life) among nations foster market homogeneity in terms of specific product needs, opening the door for globalization? The following proposition is advanced.

P₁: In general, standardization is more practical in markets that are economically alike.

The point can be illustrated with reference to the Organization for Economic Cooperation and Development (OECD) countries. OECD nations, which make up only 15% of the total number of countries in the world, account for as much as 55% of the global GNP. Markets in these countries have similarities in consumer demand and commonalities in lifestyle patterns that are explained by several factors (Nissan Motor Company, 1984). First, the purchasing power of OECD residents, as expressed in discretionary income per individual, is more than eight to 15 times greater than that of residents of less developed countries (LDCs) and newly industrialized countries (NICs). Second, in OECD countries the penetration of television into households is greater than 75% whereas in NICs it is about 25% and in LDCs it is less than 10%. Third, more than one-third of the OECD consumers graduate from high school or higher educational institutions, but a comparable level of education still is offered to less than 15% of the population in NICs and to an even lower percentage in LDCs. Briefly, it is their education level (what they read and see), their television watching (their level of awareness), and their purchasing power that make the OECD residents similar to each other in behavior and that distinguish them from the rest of the world. Thus standardization may be feasible among the OECD nations.

Rather than looking at the target market in terms of rich/poor nations, it may be possible to identify segments, in both developed and developing countries, that are similar and represent a homogeneous market. Several scholars have explicitly endorsed this type of approach (Kale and Sudharshan, 1987; Levitt, 1983; Sheth, 1986; Simmonds, 1985). Levitt states (p. 92, 94),

The multinational corporation operates in a number of countries, and adjusts its products and practices in each at high relative costs ... [companies should] know that success in a world of homogenized demand requires a search for sales opportunities in similar segments across the globe in order to achieve the economies of scale necessary to compete. Such a segment in one country is seldom unique—it has close cousins everywhere precisely because technology has homogenized the globe.

Empirical evidence on the *intermarket segment concept* is provided by Hill and Still (1984), who found that greater product adaptation was required in rural areas than in urban areas in the LDCs. This finding can be interpreted to mean that the urban areas in developing countries may have segments that are similar in character to those in industrialized nations.

As a research idea, country markets can be segmented, say on the basis of occupation, and the needs and shopping traits of a particular segment can be examined on a worldwide basis. This suggestion leads to the following proposition.

P$_2$: Standardization strategy is more effective if worldwide customers, not countries, are the basis of identifying the segment(s) to serve.

The significance of the intermarket segmentation concept can be illustrated with reference to India and Kuwait. Kuwait's per capita GNP in 1983 was $18,000 and India's $260. On the basis of these figures, Kuwait is about 70 times more attractive than India. However, India's total GNP in 1983 was eight times greater than Kuwait's and its population was 400 times as large. If we assume that only 5% of the Indians

would have the purchasing power of a Kuwaiti, the Indian market would be 20 times as attractive as the Kuwaiti market. Thus segments for standardization may be present in both rich and poor countries.

Market Position

Segmenting world markets in isolation of market-specific contexts is insufficient. *Market development, market conditions,* and *competitive factors* must be considered.

Different national markets for a given product are in different stages of development. A convenient way of explaining this phenomenon is through the product life cycle concept. If a product's foreign market is in a different stage of market development than its United States market, appropriate changes in the product design are desirable in order to make an adequate product/market match (Jain, 1984; Kirpalani and MacIntosh, 1980). Polaroid's Swinger camera is claimed to have failed in France because the company pursued the same strategy there as in the United States when the two markets were in different stages of development. The United States market was in the mature stage, whereas the French market was in the introductory stage (de la Torre, 1975).

The three market conditions that influence the standardization decision are cultural differences (Arndt and Helgesen, 1981; Hall, 1959; Lee, 1966; Ricks, 1983, 1986; Terpstra and David, 1985), economic differences (Douglas, Craig, and Keegan, 1986; Henzler, 1981; Luqmani, Quraeshi, and Delene, 1980; Terpstra 1986), and differences in customer perceptions (Bilkey and Nes, 1982; Cattin, Jolibert, and Lohnes, 1982; Kaynak and Cavusgil, 1983; Nagashima, 1977; Narayana, 1981) in foreign markets.

Culture influences every aspect of marketing. The products people buy, the attributes they value, and the principals whose opinions they accept are all culture-based choices (Lipman, 1988). For example, different levels of awareness, knowledge, familiarity, and affect with people, products in general, and specific brands may result in differential attitudes toward similar products (Parameswaran and Yaprak, 1987). Cultural differences influence consumer acculturation which, in turn, affects acceptance of standardized products (Schiffman, Dillon, and Ngumah, 1981). Hence, where a product is culturally compatible with the society, it is likely to be more suitable for standardization (Britt, 1974; Keegan, 1969).

Poor economic means may prevent masses in LDCs from buying the variety of products that U.S. consumers consider essential. To bring such products as automobiles and appliances within the reach of the middle class in developing countries, for example, the products must be appropriately modified to cut costs without reducing functional quality. Finally, the decision on product standardization should be based on the psychological meaning of the product in different markets (Friedman, 1986). Foreign products in many cultures are perceived as high quality products. In such cases, standardization would be desirable (Aydin and Terpstra, 1981). In contrast, if the image of a country's products is weak, it would be strategically desirable to adapt a product so that it could be promoted as different from, rather than typical of, that country's products.

From the preceding discussion, the following propositions are presented as a research agenda.

P_3: The greater the similarity in the markets in terms of customer behavior and lifestyle, the higher the degree of standardization.

P_4: The higher the cultural compatibility of the product across the host countries, the greater the degree of standardization.

In the absence of current and potential competition, a company may continue to do well in a market overseas with a standard product. However, the presence of competition may necessitate customization to gain an advantage over rivals by providing a product that ultimately matches local conditions precisely. Similarly, if the competitive position of the firm does not vary among markets, pursuing a global strategy may be worthwhile (Henzler and Rall, 1986; Porter, 1986). For example, if a company has a "leadership" position (in terms of market share) in both the U.S. and select overseas markets, other things being equal, it can successfully standardize its marketing strategy in all those countries.

In addition, if the firm competes with the same rivals, with similar share position, in different markets, standardization would be more likely (Copeland and Griggs, 1985; Quelch and Hoff, 1986). Therefore:

P_5: The greater the degree of similarity in a firm's competitive position in different markets, the higher the degree of standardization.

P_6: Competing against the same adversaries, with similar share positions, in different countries leads to greater standardization than competing against purely local companies.

Nature of Product

Studies on the subject show that standardization varies with the nature of the product. Two product aspects are relevant, *type of product* (i.e., industrial vs. consumer product) and *product positioning*.

Standardization is more feasible for industrial goods than for consumer goods (Bakker, 1977; Boddewyn, Soehl, and Picard, 1986). Among consumer goods, durables offer greater opportunity for standardization than nondurables because the latter appeal to tastes, habits, and customs, which are unique to each society (Douglas and Urban, 1977; Hovell and Walters, 1972).

Empirical evidence in this matter comes from a recent study showing that industrial and high technology products (e.g., computer hardware, airliners, photographic equipment, heavy equipment, and machine tools) are considered most appropriate for global brand strategies. Confections, clothing, food, toiletries, and household cleaners are considered much less appropriate (Peterson Blyth Cato Associates, Inc., and Cheskin & Masten, 1985). Briefly, if a product meets a universal need, it requires little adaptation across national markets and standardization is facilitated (Bartlett, 1979; Levitt, 1988). Corning Glass Works, for example, considered its electronic and medical products to be universal products that did not vary by country. They tended toward standardization in product policy, product development, and pricing. Corningware, in contrast, is not a universal product. It must be adapted to suit various market needs. For example, the "oven-to-freezer" feature has been very popular in the United States but was not appropriate in France; a souffle dish was popular in France but did not have a big market in the U.S. (Yoshino and Bartlett, 1981).

"Positioning" refers to designing the product to fit a given place in the consumer's mind (Kotler, 1984). If a product is positioned overseas by the same approach as at home, standardization would be feasible (Sorenson and Wiechmann, 1975). Tang has been positioned in the United States market as an orange drink substitute, but not in France (where orange drink is not a breakfast staple), making standardization inappropriate (Grey Advertising, Inc., 1984). Phillip Morris, Inc., has been able to standardize Marlboro's marketing program because it has positioned the brand everywhere with the same emphasis, the Marlboro Country concept.

Future research can be planned around two propositions:

P_7: Industrial and high technology products are more suitable for standardization than consumer products.

P_8: Standardization is more appropriate when the home market positioning strategy is meaningful in the host market.

Environment

Global marketing decisions about product, price, promotion, and distribution are no different from those made in the domestic context. However, the environment within which these decisions are made is unique to each country. Hence differences in environment are an important concern affecting the feasibility of standardization (Britt, 1974; Buzzell, 1968; Cavusgil and Yavas, 1984; Donnelly, 1970; Donnelly and Ryans, 1969; Dunn, 1976; Green, Cunningham, and Cunningham, 1975). Operationally, four types of environments can be identified: *physical, legal, political,* and *marketing infrastructure.* (A fifth factor, culture, is also important, but it is examined under Market Position).

The *physical conditions* of a country (i.e., climate, topography, and resources) may affect standardization in various ways. In a hot climate, as in the Middle East, such products as cars and air conditioners require additional features for satisfactory performance (*World Business Weekly,* 1981). Differences in the size and configuration of homes affect product design for appliances and home furnishings.

Different countries have different *laws* about product standards, patents, tariffs and taxes, and other aspects (Buzzel, 1968; Hill and Still, 1984; Kacker, 1972; Rutenberg, 1982). These laws may necessitate program adaptation. Pricing decisions commonly involve localization because pricing elements such as taxes vary among countries (Sorenson and Wiechmann, 1975). Kacker's (1972, 1975) research showed that legal requirements forced a substantial proportion (45%) of the responding American firms operating in India to localize their products to meet pricing restrictions.

The perspectives of the *political environment* of a country may result in intervention in the affairs of foreign businesses. Political interference can be defined as a decision on the part of the host country government that forces a change in the operations, policies, and strategies of a foreign firm (Poynter, 1980). Political intervention may invalidate standardization even in carefully chosen overseas markets (Vernon, 1971). Doz and Prahalad's (1980) research showed that fear of political interference led many MNC affiliates to diversify into areas in which neither the parent nor the affiliate had core capabilities. Price guidelines in overseas markets may be based on political considerations rather than economic realities (Henley, 1976).

The *marketing infrastructure* consists of the institutions and functions necessary to create, develop, and service demand, including retailers, wholesalers, sales agents, warehousing, transportation, credit, media, and more. The availability, performance, and cost of the infrastructure profoundly affect standardization (Bello and Dahringer, 1985; Ricks, Arpan, and Fu, 1979; Shimaguchi and Rosenberg, 1979; Tajima, 1973; Thorelli and Sentell, 1982).

In terms of environmental factors, no two markets are exactly alike. However, the research question is, "What is the tolerable level of difference in physical, legal, and political environments and the infrastructure to permit standardization?" This question leads to the following propositions.

P_9: The greater the difference in physical, political, and legal environments between home and host countries, the lower the degree of standardization.

P_{10}: The more similar the marketing infrastructure in the home and host countries, the higher the degree of standardization.

Organization Factors

The preceding discussion explores the external imperatives that affect standardization. Examined in this section are the organizational aspects that create conditions for successful implementation of standardization strategy.

Effective standardization is accomplished through a tight linkage of the subsidiaries with the headquarters. The relevant factors are *corporate orientation, headquarters-subsidiary relationship,* and *delegation of authority.* The orientation of a company's managers toward the various aspects of doing business overseas includes such considerations as managers' attitudes toward foreigners and overseas environments, their willingness to take risks and seek growth in unfamiliar circumstances, and their ability to make compromises to accommodate foreign perspectives. Perlmutter (1969) has identified among international executives three primary orientations toward building multinational enterprises: ethnocentric (home-country-oriented), polycentric (host-country-oriented), or geocentric (world-oriented).

An organization having either an ethnocentric or a geocentric orientation is likely to standardize its program. However, in the former case the subsidiary managers may resist any sudden move toward increased standardization, considering it to be an imposition from headquarters. If the orientation is truly geocentric, however, a standardized program can be recommended without affecting the decision-making authority of the local managers. Geocentric perspectives provide flexibility sufficient to exploit standardization opportunities as they emerge and to react to unanticipated problems within the context of the overall corporate interest (Simmonds, 1985). If country managers consider headquarters' approaches to be mutually beneficial, they are least likely to resist accepting them (Quelch and Hoff, 1986).

The second organizational factor that influences standardization of marketing strategy is the headquarters-subsidiary relationship. In any organization, conflicts may arise between parent corporation and overseas subsidiaries because of their different points of view (Das, 1981; Nowakoski, 1982; Reynolds, 1978; Sim, 1977). If the conflict is excessive, it is likely to discourage program transfer. Opel, the German subsidiary of General Motors, is an example. Opel had developed into an independent organization that did things its own way. It developed its own product line and set its own policies. On every issue, Opel had an approach different from the parent's, making it difficult for General Motors to develop a *world car* using Opel as the base (Prahalad and Doz, 1987).

An interesting research question that can be raised here is whether the conflict is likely to be within tolerable limits if the organization is geocentrically oriented. Indirect evidence shows that these factors may not be related. For example, Wind, Douglas, and Perlmutter (1973) concluded that international orientation alone does not appear to provide sufficient guidelines for developing international marketing policies.

The final organizational factor that influences the standardization of marketing strategy is the extent to which decision-making authority is delegated to the foreign subsidiaries (D'Antin, 1971; Doz, 1980). Marketing is a polycentric function that is deeply affected by local factors. Primary authority for international marketing decisions therefore is decentralized in favor of host country managers. Aylmer (1970) found that local managers were responsible for 86% of the advertising decisions, 74% of the pricing decisions, and 61% of the channel decisions, but product design decisions were made primarily by the parent organization. A similar study by Brandt and Hulbert (1977) substantiates Aylmer's findings. Thus, the product decision seems to offer the most opportunity for standardization.

Effective implementation of strategy suggests the following propositions.

P_{11}: Companies in which key managers share a common world view, as well as a common view of the critical tasks flowing from the strategy, are more effective in implementing a standardization strategy.

P_{12}: The greater the strategic consensus among parent-subsidiary managers on key standardization issues, the more effective the implementation of standardization strategy.

P_{13}: The greater the centralization of authority for setting policies and allocating resources, the more effective the implementation of standardization strategy.

STANDARDIZATION AND PERFORMANCE

In the final analysis, the decision on standardization should be based on economic payoff, which includes financial performance, competitive advantage, and other aspects. Concern for financial performance, in the context of standardization, has been expressed for a long time (Buzzell, 1968; Keegan, 1969). In recent years, Hout, Porter, and Rudden (1982), Rutenberg (1982), Levitt (1983), and Henzler and Rall (1986) have emphasized the scale effects that transcend national boundaries and provide cost advantages to companies selling to the world market. As a matter of fact, it is the concern for financial performance that has led researchers to stress one marketing decision area over others for standardization (Hovell and Walters, 1972; Walters, 1986). Though concern for financial performance implications has been commonly expressed, few researchers have supported their viewpoint with hard data. Hence the topic affords an opportunity for future research.

The decision on standardization also should be examined for its impact on competition, measured in terms of competitive advantage that it may provide (Hamel and Prahalad, 1985; Porter, 1986; Robinson, 1984). In addition to financial performance and competitive advantage, Walters (1986) recommends standardization for coherent international image, rapid diffusion of products and ideas internationally, and greater central coordination and control. Clearly, the topic of performance criteria in the realm of marketing program standardization has not been thoroughly examined and warrants new investigation (Buzzell, 1968; Chase, 1984; Hamel and Prahalad, 1985; Hout, Porter, and Rudden, 1982; Huszagh, Fox, and Day, 1986; Keegan, 1969; Levitt, 1983; Rutenberg, 1982).

IMPLICATIONS AND CONCLUSIONS

A model for making the standardization decision is developed by synthesizing both theoretical and empirical works in marketing, international business, and strategic planning. A distinction is made between process and program standardization. Program standardization is proposed to be a function of several factors and can be reviewed with reference to product, price, promotion, and distribution decisions. The ultimate relevance of standardization depends on its real economic payoff. Previous research has focused primarily on program standardization; with emphasis on the product and advertising areas. A comprehensive framework such as the one proposed here has been lacking. This framework is likely to be useful in future studies in directing research attention to key variables and relationships.

The framework developed in this article has implications for domestic marketing decisions, as well as the actors involved in the standardization process—international corporate managers and subsidiary managers.

Domestic Marketing Decision Implications

What type of headquarters marketing perspective will help foster globalization? The framework discussed here can be used to seek answers to this question. For example, the propositions stated can be tested to determine whether a higher degree of similarity in competitive market shares offers greater opportunity for standardization. Likewise, one can test whether the similarity between markets (in development and conditions) is likely to lead to greater globalization.

An important aspect of standardization is the combination of common segments in different country markets to designate the target market. How a firm should go about recognizing identical segments throughout the world, coalescing them, and then serving them as one market is an interesting research question.

Corporate Management Implications

The framework implies that corporate managers can influence certain variables to create a climate in which a greater degree of standardization would be feasible. These variables include (1) establishing a geocentric orientation in the organization (which is conducive to achieving standardization), (2) balancing the objectives of the headquarters and large affiliates (because the presence of the latter affords greater opportunity for standardization), (3) providing opportunities for an ongoing parent-subsidiary dialogue for greater harmony (to avoid conflict between the two groups), and (4) encouraging an international outlook in general.

On a different level, corporate managers can reduce the detrimental effects of cultural differences between corporate and subsidiary marketing managers through a proper staffing/training system. For example, marketing managers with international back-ground can be hired at headquarters. Similarly, a common marketing program can be organized for managers from all over the world.

Implications for Subsidiary Managers

By conceptualizing standardization in terms of degree of involvement and information sharing in various stages of marketing decision making at headquarters, subsidiary managers can better understand their own role *vis-à-vis* the corporate managers. The proposed framework can be used to answer such questions as "Which group is most capable of providing authoritative information on what topics?" and "Which group should undertake what tasks?" Once respective areas of strength are established, the degree of standardization feasible in a particular case can be explored.

Instead of simply implying that multinational companies should aim at standardization, the framework helps in identifying the specific problem areas. Hence it should aid in resolving the controversy on the subject and provide a much-needed base for empirical research.

REFERENCES

Arndt, J., and T. Helgesen. (1981). "Marketing and Productivity: Conceptual and Measurement Issues." In *Educators' Conference Proceedings*, Series 47, Kenneth Bernhardt et al., eds. Chicago: American Marketing Association, 81–84.

Aydin, N., and Vern Terpstra. (1981). "Marketing Know-How Transfers by MNCs: A Case Study in Turkey," *Journal of International Business Studies*, 12 (Winter), 35–48.

Aylmer, R. J. (1970). "Who Makes Marketing Decisions in the Multinational Firm?" *Journal of Marketing*, 34 (October), 25–30.

Bakker, B. A. (1977). "International Marketing Standardization," presentation to European International Business Administration Annual Meeting (December), 1–21.

Bartlett, Christopher. (1979). "Multinational Structural Evolution: The Changing Decision Environment in International Divisions," doctoral dissertation, Harvard Business School.

Bello, Daniel C., and Lee D. Dahringer. (1985). "The Influence of Country and Product on Retailer Operating Practices: A Cross National Comparison," *International Marketing Review*, 2 (Summer), 42–52.

Bilkey, Warren J., and Eric Nes. (1982). "Country of Origin Effects on Product Evaluations," *Journal of International Business Studies*, 13 (Spring–Summer), 89–99.

Boddewyn, J. J. (1981). "Comparative Marketing: The First Twenty-Five Years," *Journal of International Business Studies*, 12 (Spring–Summer), 61–79.

Boddewyn, J. J., Robin Soehl, and Jacques Picard. (1986). "Standardization in International Marketing: Is Ted Levitt in Fact Right?" *Business Horizons*, 29 (November–December), 69–75.

Brandt, William K., and James M. Hulbert. (1977). "Headquarters Guidance in Marketing Strategy in the Multinational Subsidiary," *Columbia Journal of World Business*, 12 (Winter), 7–14.

Britt, Stuart H. (1974). "Standardizing Marketing for the International Market," *Columbia Journal of World Business*, 9 (Winter), 39–45.

Buzzell, Robert. (1968). "Can You Standardize Multinational Marketing?" *Harvard Business Review*, 46 (November–December), 102–113.

Cattin, Philippe, Alain Jolibert, and Colleen Lohnes. (1982). "A Cross-Cultural Study of 'Made In' Concepts," *Journal of International Business Studies*, 13 (Winter), 131–141.

Cavusgil, S. Tamer, and Ugur Yavas. (1984). "Transfer of Management Knowledge to Developing Countries: An Empirical Investigation," *Journal of Business Research*, 12 (January), 35–50.

Chase, Dennis. (1984). "Global Marketing: The New Wave," *Advertising Age* (June 25), 49.

Copeland, Lennie, and Lewis Griggs. (1985). *Going International.* New York: Random House, Ch. 3.

D'Antin, P. (1971). "The Nestle Product Manager as Demigod," *European Business*, 6 (Spring), 41, 49.

Das, Ranjan. (1981). "Impact of Host Government Regulations on MNC Operations: Learning from Third World Countries," *Columbia Journal of World Business*, 16 (Spring), 85–90.

de la Torre, Jose. (1975). "Product Life Cycle as a Determinant of Global Marketing Strategies," *Atlantic Economic Review*, 9 (September–October), 9–14.

Donnelly, James H., Jr. (1970). "Attitudes Toward Culture and Approach to International Advertising," *Journal of Marketing*, 34 (July), 60–63.

Donnelly, James H., Jr., and John K. Ryans, Jr. (1969). "Standardized Global Advertising, a Call as Yet Unanswered," *Journal of Marketing*, 33 (April), 57–60.

Douglas, Susan P., Samuel C. Craig, and Warren J. Keegan. (1986). "Approaches to Assessing International Marketing Opportunities for Small and Medium-Sized Companies." In *International Marketing: Managerial Perspectives*, Subhash C. Jain and Lewis R. Tucker, Jr., eds. Boston: Kent, 157–169.

Douglas, Susan P., and Christine D. Urban. (1977). "Life-Style Analysis to Profile Women in International Markets," *Journal of Marketing*, 41 (July), 46–54.

Doz, Yves L. (1980). "Strategic Management in Multinational Companies," *Sloan Management Review*, 22 (Winter), 27–46.

Doz, Yves L., and C. K. Prahalad. (1980). "How MNCs Cope with Host Government Intervention," *Harvard Business Review*, 58 (March–April), 147–157.

Dunn, S. Watson. (1976). "Effect of National Identity on Multinational Promotional Strategy in Europe," *Journal of Marketing*, 40 (October), 50–57.

Elinder, Erik. (1961). "How International Can Advertising Be?" *International Advertiser* (December), 12–16.

Fatt, Arthur C. (1964). "A Multinational Approach to International Advertising," *International Advertiser* (September), 17–20.

Fisher, Anne B. (1984). "The Ad Biz Gloms onto 'Global'," *Fortune* (November 12), 77–80.

Fournis, Y. (1962). "The Markets of Europe or the European Market?" *Business Horizons*, 5 (Winter), 77–83.

Friedman, Roberto. (1986). "The Psychological Meaning of Products: A Simplification of the Standardization vs. Adaptation Debate," *Columbia Journal of World Business*, 21 (Summer), 97–104.

Green, Robert T., William H. Cunningham, and Isabel C. Cunningham. (1975). "The Effectiveness of Standardized Global Advertising," *Journal of Advertising*, 4 (Summer), 25–30.

Grey Advertising, Inc. (1984). "Global Vision with Local Touch." New York: Gray Advertising, Inc. (report).

Hall, Edward T. (1959). *The Silent Language.* Garden City, N.Y.: Doubleday, pp. 61–81.

Hamel, Gary, and C. K. Prahalad. (1985). "Do You Really Have a Global Strategy?" *Harvard Business Review,* 63 (July–August), 139–148.

Henley, Donald S. (1976). "Evaluating International Product Line Performance: A Conceptual Approach." In *Multinational Product Management.* Cambridge, Mass.: Marketing Science Institute.

Henzler, Herbert. (1981). "Shaping an International Investment Strategy," *McKinsey Quarterly* (Spring), 69–81.

Henzler, Herbert, and Wilhelm Rall (1986). "Facing Up to the Globalization Challenge," *McKinsey Quarterly* (Winter), 52–68.

Hill, J. S., and R. R. Still. (1984). "Effects of Urbanization on Multinational Product Planning: Markets in LDCs," *Columbia Journal of World Business,* 19 (Summer), 62–67.

Hout, Thomas, Michael E. Porter, and Eileen Rudden. (1982). "How Global Companies Win Out," *Harvard Business Review,* 60 (September–October), 98–105.

Hovell, P. J., and P. G. Walters. (1972). "International Marketing Presentations: Some Options," *European Journal of Marketing,* 6 (Summer), 69–79.

Huszagh, Sandra, Richard J. Fox, and Ellen Day. (1986). "Global Marketing: An Empirical Investigation," *Columbia Journal of World Business,* 21 (Twentieth Anniversary Issue), 31–44.

Jain, Subhash C. (1984). *International Marketing Management.* Boston: Kent, 351.

Kacker, M. P. (1972). "Patterns of Marketing Adaptation in International Business," *Management International Review,* 12(4–5), 111–118.

Kacker, M. P. (1975). "Export-Oriented Product Adaptation," *Management International Review,* 15(6), 61–70.

Kale, Sudhir H., and D. Sudharshan (1987). "A Strategic Approach to International Segmentation," *International Marketing Review,* 4 (Summer), 60–71.

Kaynak, Erdener, and S. Tamar Cavusgil. (1983). "Consumer Attitudes Towards Products of Foreign Origin: Do They Vary Across Product Classes?" *International Journal of Advertising,* 2(3), 147–157.

Keegan, Warren J. (1969). "Multinational Product Planning: Strategic Alternatives," *Journal of Marketing,* 33 (January), 58–62.

Killough, James. (1978). "Improved Payoffs from Transnational Advertising," *Harvard Business Review,* 56 (July–August), 102–110.

Kirpalani, Vishnu H., and N. B. MacIntosh. (1980). "International Marketing Effectiveness of Technology-Oriented Small Firms," *Journal of International Business Studies,* 11 (Winter), 81–90.

Kotler, Philip. (1984). *Marketing Management,* 5th ed. Englewood Cliffs, N.J.: Prentice-Hall.

Lee, James A. (1966). "Cultural Analysis in Overseas Operations," *Harvard Business Review,* 44 (March–April), 108–116.

Levitt, Theodore. (1983). "The Globalization of Markets," *Harvard Business Review,* 61 (May–June), 92–102.

Levitt, Theodore. (1988). "The Pluralization of Consumption," *Harvard Business Review,* 66 (May–June), 7–8.

Lipman, Joanne. (1988). "Marketers Turn Sour on Global Sales Pitch Harvard Guru Makes," *The Wall Street Journal* (May 12), 1.

Luqmani, Mushtaq, Zahir A. Quraeshi, and Linda Delene. (1980). "Marketing in Islamic Countries: A Viewpoint," *MSU Business Topics,* 28 (Summer), 16–26.

Miracle, Gordon E. (1968). "International Advertising Principles and Strategies," *MSU Business Topics,* 16 (Autumn), 29–36.

Nagashima, Akira. (1977). "A Comparative 'Made In' Product Image Survey Among Japanese Businessmen," *Journal of Marketing,* 41 (July), 95–100.

Narayana, Chem L. (1981). "Aggregate Images of American and Japanese Products: Implications on International Marketing," *Columbia Journal of World Business,* 16 (Summer), 31–34.

Nissan Motor Company. (1984). *Automobile Industry Handbook.* Tokyo: Nissan Motor Company.

Nowakoski, Christopher A. (1982). "International Performance Measurement," *Columbia Journal of World Business,* 17 (Summer), 53–57.

Ohmae, Kenichi. (1985). *Triad Power: The Coming Shape of Global Competition.* New York: The Free Press.

Parameswaran, Ravi, and Attila Yaprak. (1987). A Cross-National Comparison of Consumer Research Measures," *Journal of International Business Studies,* 18 (Spring), 35–50.

Peebles, Dean M., Jr., John K. Ryans, and Ivan R. Vernon. (1977). "A New Perspective on Advertising Standardization," *European Journal of Marketing,* 11(8), 569–576.

Peebles, Dean M., Jr., John K. Ryans, and Ivan R. Vernon. (1978). "Coordinating International Advertising," *Journal of Marketing,* 42 (January), 28–34.

Perlmutter, Howard V. (1969). "The Tortuous Evolution of the Multinational Corporation," *Columbia Journal of World Business,* 4 (January–February), 9–18.

Peterson Blyth Cato Associates, Inc., and Cheskin & Masten. (1985). "Survey on Global Brands and Global Marketing," empirical report, New York.

Porter, Michael E. (1986). *Competition in Global Industries.* Boston: Harvard Business School Press.

Poynter, Thomas A. (1980). "Government Intervention in Less-Developed Countries: The Experience of Multinational Companies," Working Paper Series, No. 238,

School of Business Administration, University of Western Ontario.

Prahalad, C. K., and Yves L. Doz. (1987). *The Multinational Mission.* New York: The Free Press, 157–168.

Quelch, J. A., and E. J. Hoff. (1986). "Customizing Global Marketing," *Harvard Business Review,* 64 (May–June), 59–68.

Reynolds, John I. (1978). "Developing Policy Responses to Cultural Differences," *Business Horizons,* 21 (August), 30–34.

Ricks, David A. (1983). *Big Business Blunders: Mistakes in Multinational Marketing.* Homewood, Ill.: Dow Jones–Irwin.

Ricks, David A. (1986). "How to Avoid Business Blunders Abroad." In *International Marketing: Managerial Perspectives,* Subhash C. Jain and Lewis R. Tucker. Jr., eds. Boston: Kent, 107–121.

Ricks, David A., Jeffrey S. Arpan, and Marilyn Y. Fu. (1979). "Pitfalls in Overseas Advertising." In *International Advertising and Marketing,* S. Watson Dunn and E. S. Lorimer, eds. Columbus, Ohio: Grid, 87–93.

Robinson, Richard D. (1984). "New Factors in International Competition for Markets," paper presented at American Marketing Association International Conference, Singapore (March).

Roostal, I. (1963). "Standardization of Advertising for Western Europe," *Journal of Marketing,* 27 (October), 15–20.

Rutenberg, D. P. (1982). *Multinational Management.* Boston: Little, Brown.

Schiffman, Leon G., William R. Dillon, and Festus E. Ngumah. (1981). "The Influence of Subcultural and Personality Factors on Consumer Acculturation," *Journal of International Business Studies,* 12 (Fall), 137–143.

Sheth, Jagdish N. (1986). "Global Markets or Global Competition?" *Journal of Consumer Marketing,* 3 (Spring), 9–11.

Shimaguchi, Mistsuaki, and Larry J. Rosenberg. (1979). "Demystifying Japanese Distribution," *Columbia Journal of World Business,* 14 (Spring), 32–41.

Sim, A. B. (1977). "Decentralized Management of Subsidiaries and Their Performance," *Management International Review,* 17(2), 45–51.

Simmonds, Kenneth. (1985). "Global Strategy: Achieving the Geocentric Ideal," *International Marketing Review,* 2 (Spring), 8–17.

Sorenson, Ralph Z., and Ulrich E. Wiechmann. (1975). "How Multinationals View Marketing Standardization," *Harvard Business Review,* 53 (May–June), 38.

Tajima, Yoshihiro. (1973). *Outline of Japanese Distribution Structures.* Tokyo: Distribution Economics Institute of Japan.

Terpstra, Vern. (1986). "Critical Mass and International Marketing Strategy." In *International Marketing: Managerial Perspectives,* Subhash C. Jain and Lewis R. Tucker, Jr., eds. Boston: Kent, 93–106.

Terpstra, Vern, and Kenneth David. (1985). *The Cultural Environment of International Business,* 2nd ed. Cincinnati, Ohio: South-Western.

Thorelli, Hans B., and Gerald D. Sentell. (1982). "The Ecology of Consumer Markets in Less and More Developed Countries," *European Journal of Marketing,* 16(6), 53–62.

Vernon, Raymond. (1971). *Sovereignty at Bay: The Multinational Spread of U.S. Enterprises.* New York: Basic Books, 192–201.

Walters, Peter G. (1986). "International Marketing Policy: A Discussion of the Standardization Construct and Its Relevance for Corporate Policy," *Journal of International Business Studies,* 17 (Summer), 55–69.

Wind, Yoram, and Susan P. Douglas. (1986). "The Myth of Globalization," *Journal of Consumer Marketing,* 3 (Spring), 23–26.

Wind, Yoram, Susan P. Douglas, and Howard V. Perlmutter. (1973). "Guidelines for Developing International Marketing Strategies," *Journal of Marketing,* 37 (April), 14–23.

World Business Weekly. (1981). "Rolls-Royce Beaten by Canada's Winters" (April 6), 41.

Yoshino, Michael Y., and Christopher A. Bartlett. (1981). "Corning Glass Works International (B)," Case 9-381-161, Harvard Business School.

25

INTERNATIONAL BARTER AND COUNTERTRADE

Sandra M. Huszagh
Fredrick W. Huszagh

Barter and countertrade will be significant trade tools throughout the 1980s. Presently confronted by saturated established markets and debt-burdened new markets, firms of all sizes in all industry sectors must evaluate these trading approaches. This paper describes the forms of barter and countertrade, products typically traded, markets served, and objectives advanced by each form. The intent is to explore opportunities and problems accompanying each form, so that managers can assess the utilities of these transactions to their firms' international marketing strategies.

Barter and countertrade contributed approximately 28 per cent to total world trade in 1984.

Traditionally the domain of state trading organisations within Eastern Europe and the USSR, Western firms are now confronted by demands for these trading approaches from Third World markets. A total of 88 national government now require countertrade in major trade transactions.

Managers can expect barter or countertrade demands if any one of three conditions pertains: (a) the priority attached to the Western import is low; (b) the total value of the transaction is high; or (c) the trading country requires reciprocal purchases either to generate hard currencies needed for Western purchases or to reduce the impact of such purchases on the balance of trade. Obviously one or more of these conditions can apply in any market, which definitely expands the roster of countries beyond the Eastern European bloc.

Both the sizeable contribution to world trade and the numerous markets now active in its practice require a working understanding of the various forms of barter and countertrade, the marketing advantages each forms offers, and the precautionary measures management must initiate to advance corporate objectives.

Source: International Marketing Review (Summer 1986), pp. 7–19.

This paper (a) notes the disciplinary perspectives most relevant for analysing these trading approaches; (b) describes the seven forms of barter and countertrade, the typical products exchanged, markets served, and marketing objectives supported in each form; and (c) comments on the durability of these approaches through the 1980s.

Three disciplinary focuses are directly applicable to the practice of barter and countertrade—marketing, public administration, and finance.

Marketing principles are central to barter and countertrade. Each form represents special utilities in accessing new markets and expanding within established markets when the product offering of the company or the economic health of foreign markets require non-monetised trade.

On the product side, firms are now confronted by saturated traditional markets. This has propelled such firms into the search for new markets. However, on the market side many countries which have been untapped by Western firms are burdened by precariously high foreign debts. Thus both products and markets set the stage for barter/countertrade involvement by firms as they endeavour to accomplish marketing strategies and tactics.

Public administration also deserves attention because it best accounts for infrastructure changes within and between governments which have stimulated barter and countertrade developments. Since World War II, trade structures for managing relationships among governments have evolved from a predominantly bilateral to a multilateral trading system.

This system operates currently within the supervision of the General Agreement on Tariffs and Trade (GATT) and the International Monetary Fund (IMF). Both the GATT and the IMF generally interpret acceptable trade behaviours from a market perspective and espouse government disinvolvement in trade transactions. "Conduct codes" produced by the GATT and debtor-creditor negotiations led by the IMF demonstrate these institutions' efforts to minimise government involvement.

With lessened government involvement, trading parties have considerable latitude, particularly in Western, market-based economies. This freedom of action can be exercised by each trading firm on its own or delegated to large trading companies operating on an international basis. In essence, a privatisation of international trade transactions and diminished government responsibility have fostered the growth of barter and countertrade.

The basic tenets of the final disciplinary perspective, finance, are central to the dynamics of barter and countertrade due to the insights they shed on the medium of the exchange transaction. Since pre-history, traders have exchanged commodities with utility value. The industrial revolution brought the general monetisation of exchange and valuation in domestic and international trade transactions. Financial intermediaries also entered into and became integral to trade transactions. Since World War II, the dollar has emerged as the dominant instrument of and measure for exchange and valuation.

Similarly, US financial institutions have assumed world leadership as critical intermediaries in the value-exchange process and in reducing risk associated with volatility among world currencies. In fact, a major component of large banks' profits is associated with these trading activities. To the extent that these prof-

its relate to the provision of "transaction" services, critical to international exchanges of real assets, they may be deemed an enduring facet of international marketing. If, however, such profits relate primarily to reducing risk associated with the medium of exchange rather than the risk inherent in transfer of real wealth, they provide significant incentives for producers and consumers of real goods to resort to barter and countertrade.

The scope of this paper precludes treatment of how these perspectives of marketing, public administration and finance should be best integrated to meet the demand for non-monetised trade. A framework, however, is provided to demonstrate which marketing objectives can be best advanced by management when responding to barter or countertrade demands of trading partners.

In reflecting on the utility of this framework, the following financial issues suggest whether or not managers find barter and countertrade a comfortable trading approach:

• Fiscal and monetary policies of countries often have major impacts on international trade flows that are unrelated to the underlying real value of goods and services traded. Conversely, such policies often have major impacts on the perceived values of national currencies which are used daily as surrogate measures of values in real goods and services.

• As the guardian of one of the major instruments of contemporary, monetised trade, the United States is not prepared to coordinate its fiscal and monetary policies with most trading countries.

• Unsynchronised fiscal and monetary policies among trading countries will perpetuate currency instability through the 1980s. Therefore, money will be the most volatile commodity which every business person must buy to participate in conventional, monetised trade. This partly explains the rapid growth of futures instruments related to financial rather than physical commodities.

• Currently a significant component of the US dollar's relative value to other currencies is associated with speculation about future US fiscal and monetary policies and their relationship to inflation. As long as nominal interest on US dollar investments embodies an inflation expectation of more than five percentage points about real worldwide interest rates, the dollar cannot be viewed as a durable proxy for real wealth.

MARKETING IMPLICATIONS OF BARTER/COUNTERTRADE MECHANISMS

Within academic publications and the trade press, considerable confusion exists about how the categories of barter and countertrade differ and which forms represent each category. At least four features distinguish barter from countertrade.

First, barter transactions are exchanges of goods/services without money, while countertrade includes partial or full compensation in money and thus is still sensitive to currency swings in proportion to the monetary commitment. For example, in a countertrade transaction the supplier agrees to make reciprocal purchases from the buyer which are paid for in cash or credit. The intent is to reimburse the buyer partly or fully for the cash paid for the supplier's products or technology. Obviously countertrade transactions demand greater commitment by Western managers, especially if reciprocal purchases do not fit with the firm's existing marketing and distribution expertise. Countertrade thus differs from barter transactions in the marketing effort required by the Western supplier.

Second, one contract formalises a barter transaction while two or more contracts are generally required to consummate countertrade transactions. Of the two contracts in countertrade deals, the first represents the initial sales agreement between the supplier and the foreign customer and the second details the supplier's commitment to purchase goods from either the foreign customer or a designated industry. Thus, the negotiation process leading up to the resulting contracts will demand greater outlays of time and talent by management, particularly in accomplishing the necessary legalities.

Third, compared to barter, countertrade requires more commitment and hence more risk of the firm's resources. For example, some forms of countertrade require Western firms to provide licensing rights to technology and even capital investment in joint venture manufacturing.

Finally, barter's short time frame of generally one year or less contrasts with the longer time span of countertrade. In some countertrade transactions, arrangements may extend over several years, with contract provisions allowing adjustment in the exchange ratio as market prices change (Weigand, 1979).

The discussion of each transaction begins with definitions and diagrams of transaction flows. Based on empirical research and industry vignettes in the trade press, the discussion also includes a look at each transaction in terms of the typical products exchanged, the foreign markets served, and the company objectives supported.

Classic Barter

Also called straight, simple or pure barter, this transaction form is the simplest and oldest form of bilateral, non-monetised trade.

As diagrammed in Figure 1 the two parties directly exchange goods or services; both parties function as buyers and sellers. While no money changes hands, the parties construct an approximate shadow price for products flowing in each direction (Korth, 1981). Western suppliers may assign marketing responsibilities for goods received to trading companies or other trading specialists who in turn convert goods to cash.

This delegation of marketing responsibilities occurs when managers are unaccustomed to dealing with goods received in terms of their product characteristics, customer segment or distribution channels. Classic barter follows the

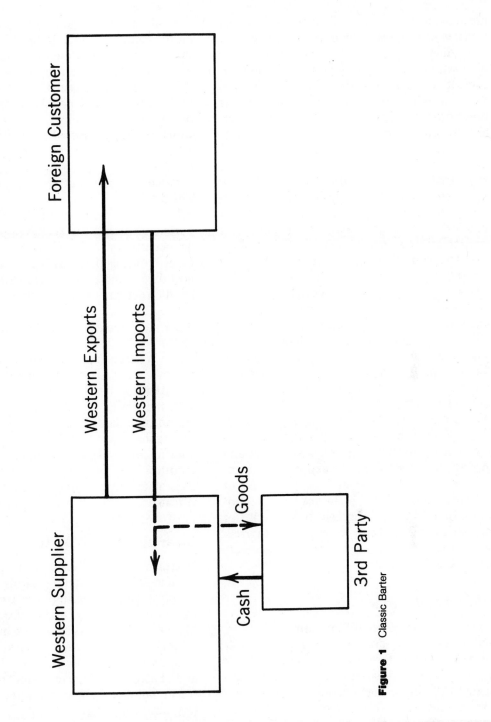

Figure 1 Classic Barter

norm with one contract formalising transactions, which typically span less than one year.

Products exported by Western suppliers are diverse, including capital goods, commodities subject to international standards, and consumer goods and services. Typical imports range from manufactured goods to internationally graded commodities.

Classic barter offers outlets for the widest, most diversified array of export product lines compared to all other transaction forms. Also a leader in market diversification, classic barter meets the needs of markets at all stages of economic development. Classic barter thus offers special utilities in trading with commodity-based economies where currency volatilities are extreme.

Marketing objectives supported by classic barter cluster around developing new markets and further penetrating existing markets. These objectives typically require less corporate resources and are implemented in a shorter time frame compared to corporate objectives like product development, integrative growth and diversified growth.

Considering classic barter's support for product and market diversification and shorter-term corporate objectives, frequency of use and growth in volume might be expected throughout the 1980s. However, the problems of matching both parties' input needs with product outputs in an acceptable time frame for deliveries may limit classic barter's use to irregular, infrequent, and short term arrangements on a periodic basis.

Closed-End Barter

This transaction form differs from classic barter since a third party buyer is found for imported goods before the contract is signed. Hence, closed-end barter reduces the risk associated with marketing of goods received by the Western supplier. Again, no money is involved in the exchange between the two principal parties. The typical time span is one year or less.

While minimal details are publicly available on the frequency of closed-end barter transactions, capital goods emerge as the typical product offering by Western firms. In general, Western suppliers receive in return commodities which are highly perishable or are currently in worldwide oversupply. These are conditions which certainly justify the need for guaranteed sales. As would be expected from the nature of the products, foreign customers are generally situated in commodity-based markets of the Third World.

Like classic barter, marketing objectives supported are mainly market development or market penetration. However, a recent study of US firms indicates that closed-end barter can support diversified growth when firms organise to handle such goods by setting up trading company subsidiaries which manage marketing to third party buyers (Huszagh and Barksdale, 1986).

For Western suppliers the major advantages of closed-end barter relate to reducing marketing risks associated with products received and with the timing of deliveries since these risks are normally assumed by the third party. Despite such advantages, its widespread use is questionable unless the markets and the commodities they offer present solid opportunities for the firm in product or market diversification.

Clearing Account Barter

In clearing account barter (also known as clearing agreements, bilateral clearing accounts, or simply bilateral clearing), the goal of trading parties is to exchange goods of equal value so that neither party has to acquire hard currency. Mainly practised between Third World markets, and occasionally between such markets and Eastern European countries, bilateral agreements are set up between the trading entities' national governments.

Figure 2 shows the typical transaction flows in clearing account barter. The main intent of

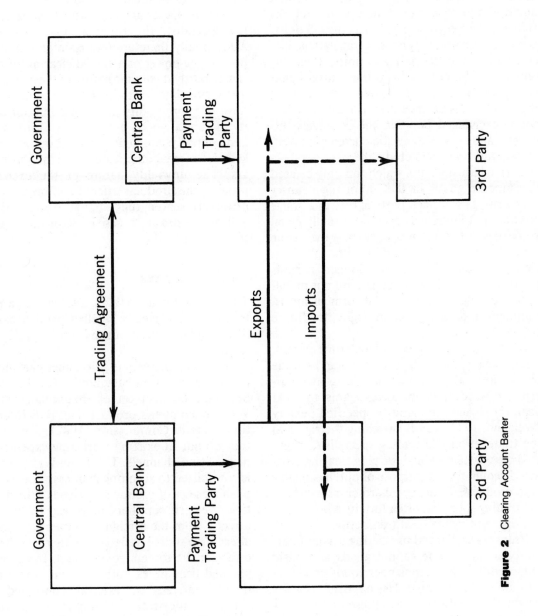

Figure 2 Clearing Account Barter

these agreements is to overcome foreign exchange controls and foreign currency shortages by valuing traded goods in clearing account units. While clearing account units may be stated in hard currencies, such as the US dollar or the Swiss franc, they are not translatable into currency (Welt, 1984). These units effectively represent a line of credit in the central banks which are managed by the governments of trading countries. A balance sheet is maintained on goods exchanged between the countries, exporters are paid in domestic currencies (Welt, 1984), and importers credit the exporters' accounts in clearing units which can only be used to purchase goods in the importing country (Verzarui, 1985). Each party agrees in a single contract to purchase a specified, usually equal value of goods and services, typically over a one year period (Weigand, 1977), although occasionally they extend over longer periods (Korth, 1981). When exchanges are not in balance, "payment" assumes the form of an assignment of clearing account rights for future purchases of goods.

At the close of the contracted time period, one of several methods is used to handle trade imbalances: (a) settlement in a designated currency, (b) crediting imbalances against the next year, (c) paying a previously specified penalty (Weigand, 1977), or (d) switching the rights to the trade surplus to trading specialists. These trading specialists "buy" surplus clearing units at a discount for the purpose of purchasing salable products. To achieve hard currency sales, the trading specialist often forfeits a portion of the discount in the final transaction.

Products exchanged in clearing account barter typically include capital goods and basic commodities. Since consumer goods and services are seldom offered, less opportunities for product diversification are presented than in classic barter. Limits on product diversification are partly explained by the markets involved whose economies are either industrialising or centrally planned.

Although clearing accounts offer trading parties the flexibility of a year's time for drawing on the lines of credit, if goods must be converted into hard currency by the firm or a trading specialist, the time lag may be costly. Additionally there are uncertainties about the purchasing power of assigned clearing account rights, partly due to the nature of the goods typically translated into clearing account units. Unstable commodity prices and inferior quality of capital goods produced in Third World and centrally planned Eastern European markets definitely complicate the valuation process. The unwieldy nature of the exchange process, the products offered and markets traditionally served suggest that Western firms will not be drawn to active use of this type of transaction.

Counterpurchase

This form of countertrade, also called parallel trading or incorrectly labelled parallel barter, differs from other forms on several key features.

First, each delivery is paid either partially or totally in cash or in bank credit (Korth, 1981). Second, products received are unrelated to the Western supplier's product lines (US International Trade Commission, 1982). Therefore, they do not fit existing marketing expertise or distribution channels. Third, the Western firm is committed to accomplish or assist in accomplishing sales of products received to third parties. Western suppliers may receive imports directly from the foreign customer or from an alternative source designated either by the customer or the foreign government. In centrally planned economies both the "customer" and the alternative source are state controlled.

Figure 3 illustrates counterpurchase arrangements. The Western supplier performs a "trade broker" role in-house or, given the demands of marketing unrelated goods, externalises that role to trade specialists. Firms can turn to a

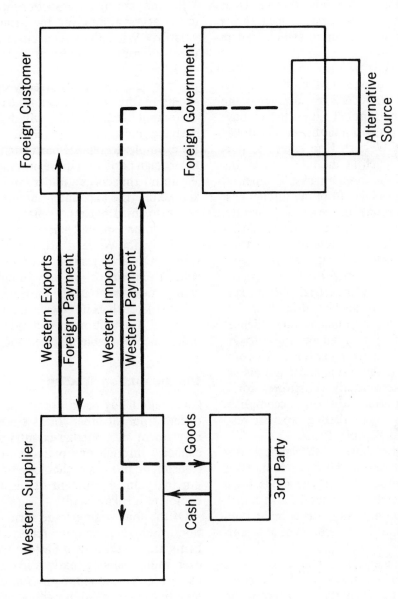

Figure 3 Counterpurchase

wide array of trading specialists including giant trading companies set up for commodities, large multinationals like General Electric and Control Data Corporation which handle diversified manufactured goods, thousands of small companies oriented for certain countries and/or products, or specialised switch traders or brokers.

In counterpurchase transactions, at least two contracts are signed, one in which the Western supplier's sale of products is consummated, the other in which the supplier agrees to purchase and market products from the buyer. The dollar amount that the Western firm agrees to purchase can be as much as the full value of the products sold to the foreign party. The period for taking back products from the foreign customer ranges from one to five years. When the Western supplier or a trade specialist designated by the supplier sells these goods, the trading cycle is complete (Kaikati, 1976).

Counterpurchase compares to reciprocal dealing used in many industrialized markets which suggests that such transactions are hardly unique to Western management (Schuster, 1980). The major advantage flows to the foreign customer since the net result is a committed market for the terms and amounts established. This essentially substitutes for a direct marketing effort, a worthy accomplishment considering the marketing expertise resident in successful Western firms.

Counterpurchase shares with classic barter opportunities for serving all types of markets with all types of products—capital goods, basic commodities, and consumer goods. Like classic barter, counterpurchase supports company objectives in both market development and market penetration.

However, managers using counterpurchase arrangements must resolve several inherent problems. First, the problem of synchronising multiple transactions, since of all forms counterpurchase can represent the most extensive number of parties: (a) Western seller, (b) foreign buyer, (c) alternative sources for Western imports designated in the foreign buyer's market, (d) third party customers for imports arranged by the Western principal, (e) trading specialists, and (f) banks.

Second, multiple transactions may be particularly aggravating given the issue of currency volatility. When the foreign customer's government imposes a countertrade requirement, the potential for currency fluctuations is high since trade imbalances, hard currency shortages, and extensive foreign debt often underlie such a requirement. Such volatility will degrade the underlying goal of counterpurchase requirements, for example, to replace hard currency used by the foreign party to acquire products. When the Western firm acts as a trader rather than a broker, taking title to counter-purchased goods for resale to third parties, exchange rate fluctuations can be especially risky.

Finally, for Western firms, successful counterpurchase arrangements require considerable trading experience not only in cushioning exchange rate risk, but also in protecting against other risks such as non-performance by parties involved, fluctuation in commodity prices or other uncontrollable market conditions.

Compensation Trading

Also called buy-back, compensation trading differs from all other forms since it requires investment in a foreign country's productive capacity through one or more approaches—transfer of process technology or capital, exporting plant equipment or installation of a complete turnkey facility.

Of the four countertrade forms, compensation trading is most often reported in Western firms' transactions with Eastern Europe. However, industrialising markets like South Korea have recently joined the ranks of countries demanding compensation trading. Such demands are occasionally tied to offset arrangements discussed below.

Two separate, and parallel contracts generally are involved. In the first contract, the supplier agrees to build a plant or provide plant equipment which is typically accompanied by technology transfer. The foreign party usually makes a hard currency down payment for a portion of the contract's value, upon delivery. In the second contract, the supplier commits to take back as payment products resulting from the production facility for up to as many as 20 years. This essentially means that the balance due the supplier is paid for by future delivery of resulting products. These products are most often used directly by the Western firm. The cash to goods ratio in recent East-West compensation contracts has averaged 20 per cent cash to 80 per cent goods—the inverse of the situation in the mid-1970s (Weigand, 1980).

The advantages to the host country are access to Western technology, capital, and/or equipment with only a partial down payment which diminishes the drain on foreign currency reserves. Also, if Western investment is part of the package, less capital is required from the foreign party while the production facility is developed.

During the 1980s trade partners' demands for capital flows through compensation trading are likely to increase for several reasons. First, many foreign governments and enterprises are already burdened by high interest rates and heavy debt service. Second, traditional financing may be unavailable due to the latter factor or prior creditors' claims. Third, when available, financing may be prohibitive in cost due to perceived and actual risks associated with countries undergoing financial restructuring to qualify for debt rescheduling.

For the Western firm, advantages include access to otherwise closed markets, such as the People's Republic of China and Eastern Europe. Also the firm achieves a better fit of products taken back with its marketing expertise and channels or compatibility with production when parts are received. Long-term arrangements usually establish a lower cost source of finished goods or parts, although managers must be cautious in assuring that the amount agreed upon does not exceed future requirements or costs as alternative sources develop. In arrangements with Eastern Europe and the USSR, special benefits accrue from dealing directly with the production unit rather than with the highly bureaucratic foreign trade organisations (FTOs).

The major disadvantages to the Western supplier include all risks associated with conventional, long-term investments such as political risk; the potential for creating eventual competitors which will cannibalise established markets (Kaikati, 1981); and disputes over product quality. The latter problem can be effectively managed if the Western supplier achieves the foreign partner's agreement to a system for monitoring output quality. Such a commitment is difficult to accomplish, however, particularly in the more closed markets of Eastern Europe and the USSR.

Company objectives supported by compensation trading are more extensive compared to other countertrade forms. In addition to providing opportunities for developing new markets and further penetrating existing markets, integrative growth also results as Western firms achieve long-term, guaranteed supplies for their own production facilities.

The success of these arrangements rests on their potential for reducing the volume of international cash transfers on the foreign party's side, and in overcoming disadvantages associated with balancing supply against demand, maintaining cost efficiencies, and assuring product quality on the Western manager's side. If Western suppliers can achieve market diversification outside Eastern Europe through arrangements with rapidly industrialising markets, the impact of these disadvantages may be partly mitigated.

Offset

Another form of countertrade, offset conforms with compensation trading in that reciprocal purchases are for the Western supplier's use.

As many as three contracts are negotiated to formalise (a) the Western supplier's export sales, (b) the Western supplier's import purchases from the foreign party, and (c) subcontracting by the foreign party when compensation trading is tied to the offset arrangement. Given the Western firm's direct consumption of imports, there is no trading specialist involved.

Typically, foreign buyers' offset requests range from 20–50 per cent of the value of the suppliers' products. In a highly competitive "buyers' market," demands for offset may climb to over 100 per cent. When the buyer's leverage is substantial, the Western supplier must also commit to compensation trading which involves local subcontracts for manufacturing parts which are incorporated in finished products received by the foreign customer. Usually there is an understanding between the two parties that capital or technology committed to local production will also satisfy offset obligations.

Foreign governments require offset arrangements to diminish capital outflows for large scale industrial or defense projects. Countries demanding offsets include highly developed nations such as Canada, Switzerland and Australia. Recently offset demands on US firms have been successfully mounted by industrialising countries like Israel and even by oil-rich Saudi Arabia. This strategy fits such countries' goals to access new products and new technologies.

During the 1980s Western firms will continue to experience offset demands due to the benefits such as (a) decreasing hard currency outlays by governments; (b) offering a financing alternative when interest rates and terms are exorbitant due to a lack of creditworthiness or prior creditors' constraints; and (c) when combined with compensation trading, providing access to technology and generating local employment.

From the Western supplier's perspective, offset arrangements support company objectives in market penetration and market development and, when joined with compensation trading, present opportunities for integrative growth. Western aircraft manufacturers have been active in utilising offsets as marketing tools, particularly in military sales. The risks and costs of currency volatility are diminished by the proportion of the trade in products, an attractive factor for large sales.

Two major risks stand outside the currency realm and demand special attention by management. The first relates to the problem of non-performance by the foreign party, which requires rigorous qualification of potential partners in advance. The second risk is whether by offset arrangements with rapidly industrialising nations Western firms may inadvertently create future competitors. As a case on point, the US defence industry's offsets in South Korea must be carefully weighed relative to the long-term impact on its competitive edge (*Wall Street Journal,* 1984). Up to the present time, leading firms in the aircraft industry have found offset combined with compensation trading an advantageous approach for discharging contract commitments when operations and investment philosophies mesh.

Co-operation Agreements

The major distinction between co-operation agreements and other forms of countertrade is that two Western parties are involved, with one Western firm specialised for selling and a second Western firm handling the buying function.

There are two basic form of co-operation agreements: (a) co-operation agreements and classic barter or triangular deals and (b) co-operation agreements combined with conventional trade financing. In both forms two contracts are required—a selling contract and a buying contract. Markets typically demanding co-operation agreements are centrally planned. Capital goods are usually offered by Western firms in return for raw materials.

With co-operation and classic barter, the parties to the transaction are a foreign principal and two unrelated Western firms. For example, a US firm may serve as the seller, delivering manufactured goods to an Eastern European FTO. In payment for these goods, the FTO delivers raw materials to a Western European firm which then functions as the buyer, but pays the US firm rather than the FTO for the raw materials. The value of the raw materials is equivalent to the value of manufactured goods originally sent to the Eastern FTO.

From the two Western firms' perspectives there are several advantages associated with this transaction form. The US firm is removed from the obligation to buy unwanted goods, particularly those goods unsuited to the firm's marketing and distribution know-how. The Western European firm realises a considerable reduction in transport costs. Advantages also relate to the lower probability of currency volatility since two Western currencies are generally involved in the cash transaction (from the Western European firm to the US firm in the example discussed), although time delays can impose exchange rate losses. Problems associated with these arrangements include finding two Western firms with the appropriate supply-demand fit, and with the flexibilities to handle time delays in receipt of payment and/or in delivery of goods.

Cash flow distinguishes conventional trade from the classic barter type of co-operation agreement. Modifying the example discussed above, when the US firm sells manufactured goods it is paid by the FTO on delivery. When the Western European firm receives raw materials from the FTO, it immediately remits payment for raw material deliveries. This arrangement obviously minimises currency volatility risk. As with cooperation agreements utilising classic barter, the cost of raw materials equals the cost of manufactured goods. The issue of finding Western partners again is critical, which stands out as another factor accounting for the growth of trading houses and dealers specialised in matching Western firms.

Compared to other forms of countertrade, Western firms can realise advantages in receiving only goods needed, and product quality is usually assured since raw materials are generally received from the foreign principal. With widely accepted grading standards in place, raw materials are far more attractive to the Western party compared to manufactured goods where it is difficult to predetermine quality before goods arrive.

In terms of disadvantages, Western suppliers are presented with limited product and market opportunities. The burden of finding two Western firms with the appropriate supply-demand fit also impairs growth of this transaction form. However, smaller markets with mounting foreign debts like Poland may continue to demand co-operation agreements. Western capital goods' manufacturers whose traditional markets both at home and abroad have reached saturation may willingly comply with such demands.

CONCLUSION

Major trading partners are not likely to co-ordinate fiscal and monetary policies throughout the 1980s. This lack of co-ordination and the dollar's pivotal role in international exchange set the stage for continued growth of barter and countertrade. Managers charged with international marketing responsibilities in firms of all sizes and product lines must understand these trading approaches.

Knowledge about the major distinctions between barter and countertrade can guide management in selecting the transaction form which will best serve the firm's objectives. Such distinctions demonstrate that compared to barter, countertrade requires more marketing effort by the Western firm, greater attention to legalities to protect the firm throughout multiple transactions, and a higher level and longer time span of involvement in the foreign customer's business, particularly when technology transfer occurs. The cash component of countertrade transactions also raises the additional burden of currency volatility.

Thus management's first step is to analyse whether marketing resources and personnel with the necessary skills are available. Answers to such questions can determine whether greater commitments and risks inherent in countertrade can be assimilated by the firm.

Compared to all other forms, classic barter and counterpurchase offer firms opportunities for the most extensive degree of product and market diversification. Both forms also support firms in market development and market penetration. However, these forms differ on two critical dimensions: (a) Counterpurchase carries with it a longer time frame and (b) trading experience is far more critical given multiple transactions and currency volatility likely to accompany counterpurchase.

Closed-end barter stands out as a transaction form uniquely suited to managing risks of goods unneeded or dissimilar to the firm's product mix; this form is similar to counterpurchase arrangements, although without a cash component. For firms with the organisational resources to set up trading company subsidiaries, the closed-end barter approach may be the least risky of all forms. Especially if the firm's major markets are commodity-producers based in the Third World, closed-end barter is an attractive approach for managing fluctuations in currency values.

Clearing account barter and co-operation agreements, while distinctively different regarding the degree of monetisation and government involvement, are similar in their limited product and market diversification. Both forms also achieve only one marketing objective—market penetration. On the advantage side, both clearing account barter and co-operation agreements have some utilities in reducing currency volatility, since trade balances in clearing account barter are kept in domestic currencies and currencies of Western parties are generally used in co-operation agreements.

However, the principal difference is that Western suppliers will be involved only on the outskirts of clearing accounts, using the agreements between Eastern bloc or developing markets to trade with a member of either of the two groups (Verzariu, 1985). Given the complexities of these two forms, along with their limited utilities in advancing marketing objectives, Western firms would be better served to focus attention on other transaction forms.

Compensation trading offers Western firms the best opportunities for integrative growth, since by the transfer of technology Western firms invest in a future source of products fitting their own production needs. Compensation trading is close to offsets in the structure of the transaction, however, only compensation trading involves technology transfer.

Both transaction forms support development of new markets and further penetration of existing markets. Compensation trading has typically been an East-West tradition; offsets appear to allow greater market diversification including industrialised and rapidly industrialising markets as well. The cash component in both transactions increases the potential for currency volatility; the longer time frame for compensation trading can aggravate not only currency volatility but also the reliability of estimates on future demand and costs of products taken back. From the Western manager's perspective, one of the most troublesome features of both arrangements is the potential for creating future competitors.

REFERENCES

Huszagh, Sandra M., and Hiram C. Barksdale. (1986). "International Barter and Countertrade: An Exploratory Study," *Journal of the Academy of Marketing Science,* 17 (Spring), 21–28.

Kaikati, Jack G. (1976). "The Reincarnation of Barter as a Marketing Tool," *Journal of Marketing,* 40 (April), 17–24.

Kaikati, Jack G. (1981). "The International Barter Room: Perspective and Challenges," *Journal of International Marketing,* 1, 29–38.

Korth, Christopher. (1981). "Barter—An Old Practice Yields New Profits," *Business,* 31 (September–October), 2–8.

Schuster, Falko. (1980). "Barter Arrangements with Money: The Modern Form of Compensation Trading," *Columbia Journal of World Business,* 15 (Fall), 61–66.

U.S. International Trade Commission. (1982). *Analysis of Recent Trends in U.S. Countertrade.* Washington, D.C.: USITC Publication 1237.

Verzariu, Pompiliu. (1985). *Countertrade, Barter, and Offsets.* New York: McGraw-Hill.

The Wall Street Journal. (1984, April 17). Section 2, 38.

Weigand, Robert E. (1977). "Barter Arrangements Can Overcome Barriers to Deals with Eastern Europe and the Third World," *Harvard Business Review,* 55 (November–December), 28.

Weigand, Robert E. (1979). "Apricots for Ammonia: Barter, Clearing, Switching, and Compensation in International Business," *California Management Review,* 22 (Fall), 33–41.

Weigand, Robert E. (1980). "Barters and Buy-Backs: Let Western Firms Beware!" *Business Horizons,* 23 (June), 54–61.

Welt, Leo G. B. (1984). *Trade Without Money: Barter and Countertrade.* New York: Harcourt Brace Jovanovich.

SECTION 6

PRODUCTION MANAGEMENT

In a world marked by increasing competition, production management takes on increased importance, not just to multinational and global firms, but to domestic firms as well. Domestic as well as global firms must search the world for the best possible production sites. No firm can automatically assume it will remain competitive simply by producing in the countries in which it markets. As readings in Section 2 have already pointed out, decisions as to the location, size, number, and configuration of a firm's manufacturing facilities are critical to the firm's success.

But the most basic decision, of course, is whether to make or buy. At the finished goods level, a firm can contract for local production of products it markets abroad or for offshore production of products it markets domestically (both "buy" decisions). Alternatively, it can produce at one location and export or produce in each country in which it markets ("make"). Similarly, the firm must decide the degree to which it wants to integrate vertically, making its own raw materials and components, or buying them.

An important consideration in the make or buy decision is comparative costs, both capital and operating costs; another is assuring quality and continuity of supply. In some circumstances, though, the most important consideration may be to keep proprietary a production process or some of its elements; in such circumstances, the firm would make even if the economics favored buy.

There are several plant configuration alternatives to consider. The simplest, of course, is to produce everything at one location and then export to other markets. In the past, Japanese firms followed this strategy very successfully in product lines ranging from TV sets to automobiles. But protectionist pressures have forced a number of Japanese manufacturers to produce (or at least assemble) in many of the countries in which they marketed. In the late 1980s, cost pressures forced some Japanese firms to shift a portion of their manufacturing from Japan to third countries.

Another possible configuration is an integrated network of plants sited strategically around the world. In such a network each plant might specialize in certain finished products which it ships to several markets. Or some plants may be primary manufacturers for particular components which these plants ship to a larger network of assembly plants. The pharmaceutical industry uses such two-stage production arrangements. Many global pharmaceutical firms produce active ingredients in a small number of plants. They then ship to a wider number of plants that add inert ingredients and fabricate dosage forms.

Some automobile manufacturers also use two-stage production processes. A plant producing complete automobiles might export some of its output as kits or knocked-down cars to assembly plants in other countries. Or one engine factory might supply auto manufacturing plants in several countries. Auto manufacturers' networks might be regional rather than worldwide.

In other industries, firms may have plants in almost every country in which they market, and make little or no attempt to integrate them; they dedicate each facility to serving a particular country or market. These arrangements are not necessarily inferior to an integrated network. There can be good reasons for maintaining independent production facilities in some circumstances.

Many multinational and globals have settled the question of production process in the simplest way—they try to use common production processes in all their plants. They make only the most necessary concessions required by different plant sizes, different materials and machinery availability, and different levels of labor skill. In many cases, this means using advanced capital-intensive or automated manufacturing processes in low-labor-cost countries, ignoring differences in factor costs.

There is justification for standardizing production processes even where factor costs might suggest otherwise. Standardizing facilitates cost and productivity comparisons across plants. More important, using machines increases control over product quality and uniformity by minimizing the chances for worker error. It also allows firms to use a less skilled work force.

READING SELECTIONS

John Dunning presents an extensively elaborated paradigm to explain three production phenomena: extent (the degree to which a firm expands its production internationally) form (essentially whether the firm owns its own international production operations or, for example, licenses or buys from others), and pattern (where it manufactures or sources). In his view, the explanation rests on the interplay of several factors, the most important of which are the reasons behind the firm's international expansion and the particular competitive advantages the firm might enjoy.

He identifies three reasons why a firm might consider expanding its production internationally or moving its production offshore: when seeking new markets (or protecting existing overseas markets), when seeking new sources of supply, or when seeking greater manufacturing efficiency. Similarly, he identifies three kinds of competitive advantages a firm might gain: ownership (of assets such as patents, trademarks, or facilities), location (where the firm operates or can operate), and internalization (the degree to which the firm is vertically integrated).

Dunning's paradigm can be of significant use as an analytical framework in several circumstances, in understanding why manufacturing in any given industry may have developed in a particular way, in evaluating specific countries as manufacturing sites, in predicting how manufacturing configurations may evolve in a particular industry, and in setting manufacturing strategy for a firm.

Charles Baden-Fuller and John Stopford question the wisdom of global manufacturing as a universal prescription. Based on their analysis of the European major appliance industry, they conclude that firms with nationally focused strategies were more profitable than were those pursuing global strategies. They ascribe these results to factors that have prevented the European market from becoming unified. Even if there are potential gains from larger-scale production, firms cannot realize those gains when there are barriers to distribution or differences in consumers' preferences across countries.

Yves Doz, in contrast, sees opportunities in rationalizing nationally focused manufacturing operations. He presents a framework for identifying opportunities to rationalize and for managing the rationalization process. Doz recommends considering rationalization in mature industries where price competition is pronounced. Firms should rationalize when the result will be lower unit costs after adjusting for transportation costs, tariffs, and the like.

Observation of the behavior of growth stage products such as microprocessor chips and VCRs suggests that price competition begins early in the product life cycle. Establishing and maintaining a low-cost position is such products is important from the very beginning, not just at maturity. Thus, firms might well consider rationalization for growth stage as well as mature products.

Ramchandran Jaikumar presents another manufacturing alternative, flexible automation. Flexible automation is an alternative to large-scale plants as a way of achieving low manufacturing costs. When employed correctly, it makes low costs achievable with small production volumes. Thus, flexible automation can be an alternative to production rationalization, and may even allow nationally focused strategies to succeed even in the absence of barriers.

In this article, Jaikumar reports on a study comparing U.S. and Japanese firms' experience with flexible automation. He finds that the Japanese firms he studied are far ahead of their U.S. counterparts. Flexible automation, rather than helping U.S. firms to catch up, has widened the gap between U.S. and Japanese productivity. The reason for the widened gap is not a difference in hardware so much as a difference in the way systems in the two countries are managed.

Christopher Gopal points out that global manufacturing requires a complex, sophisticated logistics system. This is especially the case when some plants produce components that feed into the manufacturing process of another plant located in a different country. In order to implement global manufacturing systems, he argues, managements will have to centralize their planning, purchasing, and distribution functions. To control, these functions, management will require an integrated information system. In this article, Gopal discusses many of the considerations key to developing such logistics and information systems.

26

THE ECLECTIC PARADIGM OF INTERNATIONAL PRODUCTION A RESTATEMENT AND SOME POSSIBLE EXTENSIONS

John H. Dunning

Abstract. This article reviews some of the criticisms directed towards the eclectic paradigm of international production over the past decade, and restates its main tenets. The second part of the article considers a number of possible extensions of the paradigm and concludes by asserting that it remains "a robust general framework for explaining and analysing not only the economic rationale of economic production but many organisational and impact issues in relation to MNE activity as well."

INTRODUCTION

The concept of the eclectic paradigm of international production[1] was first put forward by the present author in 1976 at a presentation to a Nobel symposium in Stockholm on *The International Allocation of Economic Activity*.[2] The intention was to offer a holistic framework by which it was possible to identify and evaluate the significance of the factors influencing both the initial act of foreign production by enterprises and the growth of such production. The choice of the word eclectic was an ambitious yet deliberate one. It was meant to convey the idea that a full explanation of the transnational activities of enterprises needs to draw upon several strands of economic theory; and that foreign direct investment is just one of a number of possible channels of international economic involvement, each of which is determined by a number of common factors.

It is accepted that, precisely because of its generality, the eclectic paradigm has only limited power to explain or predict particular kinds of international production; and even less, the behaviour of individual enterprises.[3] But this deficiency, if it is a deficiency, which some critics have alleged, could no less be directed at attempts to formulate a general but operationally testable paradigm of international trade. The classical and neoclassical theories of trade, for example, while still having wide explanatory powers for most kinds of inter-industry trade are quite inadequate to explain much of intra-industry trade.[4] Indeed it is perhaps worth emphasizing that the point at which the Heckscher-Ohlin-Samuelson (H-O-S) theory of trade fails is precisely that at which the modern paradigm of international production starts, namely the point at which there are positive transaction costs in intermediate goods markets.[5] The difference between the neo-technology and other modern theories of trade and those of international production is that, while the former *implicitly* assume that all goods are exchanged between independent buyers and sellers across national frontiers, the latter *explicitly* postulate that the transfer of intermediate products is undertaken within the same enterprises. In other words, without international market failure, the raison d'etre for international production disappears. But once it exists, explanations of trade and production may be thought of as a part of a general paradigm based upon the international disposition of factor endowments, and the costs of alternative modalities for transacting intermediate products across national boundaries. This is the central theme of this paper.

Source: *Journal of International Business Studies* (Spring 1988), pp. 1–31.

CRITICISMS OF THE ECLECTIC PARADIGM

Are Competitive or Ownership Advantages Necessary to Explain International Production?

In its original form, the eclectic paradigm stated that the extent, form, and pattern of international production was determined by the configuration of three sets of advantages as perceived by enterprises.[6] First, in order for firms of one nationality to compete with those of another by producing in the latter's own countries, they must possess certain advantages specific to the nature and/or nationality of their ownership. These advantages—sometimes called competitive or monopolistic advantages—must be sufficient to compensate for the costs of setting up and operating a foreign value-adding operation, in addition to those faced by indigenous producers or potential producers.

In our 1976 paper we identified three types of ownership-specific advantages: (a) those that stem from the exclusive privileged possession of or access to particular income generating assets, (b) those that are normally enjoyed by a branch plant compared with a de novo firm, and (c) those that are a consequence of geographical diversification or multinationality *per se*.[7] In a later typology (Dunning 1983a, 1983b), we distinguished between the *asset* (Oa) and *transaction* (Ot) advantages of multinational enterprises (MNEs).[8] While the former arise from the proprietary ownership of specific assets by MNEs vis-à-vis those possessed by other enterprises (i.e., of type (a) above, which can only occur in a situation of structural market distortions),[9] the latter mirror the capacity of MNE hierarchies vis-à-vis external markets to capture the transactional benefits (or lessen the transactional costs) arising from the common governance of a network of these assets, located in different countries.

The distinction between *structural* and *transactional* market imperfections is an important one (Dunning and Rugman, 1985). Clearly the relevance of each in determining the ownership advantages of MNEs will vary according to the characteristics of firms, the products they produce, the markets in which they operate, and whether the competitive process is viewed from a static or dynamic perspective. Certainly earlier analyses of foreign direct investment—particularly those of the Hymer (1960, 1976) tradition—tended to emphasize the former kind of imperfection; but, similarly, so do contemporary economists working in the area of innovation and technological development (e.g., Pavitt, 1987; Cantwell, 1986); and business analysts seeking to identify the systemic advantages of globally-oriented enterprises (e.g., Pralahad and Doz, 1987; Kogut, 1983, 1985a). By contrast, the modern theory of the MNE qua MNE (e.g., as summarized by Teece, 1986, and Casson, 1987) tends to emphasize transactional market failure as the main raison d'être for international production. The two kinds of imperfection are, of course, often interrelated, particularly in a dynamic market situation,[10] and there is a growing consensus that the most successful MNEs are those that are best able to nurture and exploit *both* asset and transactional ownership advantages.

The second condition for international production is that it must be in the best interests of enterprises that possess ownership-specific advantages to transfer them across national boundaries *within* their own organizations rather than sell them, or their right of use to foreign-based enterprises. This immediately suggests that MNEs perceive that the international market place is not the best modality for transacting intermediate goods or services. The reasons for the internalization of markets has been explored in considerable detail in the literature.[11] Suffice to reiterate here that three main kinds of market failure are usually identified as: (i) those that arise from risk and uncertainty as, for example, those succinctly analyzed by Vernon (1983); (ii) those that stem from the ability of firms to exploit the economies of large-scale production, but only in an imperfect market situation; and (iii) those that occur where the transaction of a particular good or service yields costs and benefits *exter-*

nal to that transaction, but that are not reflected in the terms agreed to by the transacting parties.[12] The desire by firms to integrate different stages of the value-added chain, to engage in product diversification, or to capture the economies of the use of complementary assets (Teece, 1986), originate from the presence of one or other of these forms of transactional market failure—even though the motives for internalization may be expressed rather differently (e.g., to safeguard supplies of essential inputs, to ensure the quality of end products, to guarantee markets, to protect property rights, to allow price discrimination, to spread the costs of shared overheads and so on). The greater the perceived costs of transactional market failure, the more MNEs are likely to exploit their competitive advantages through international production rather than by contractual agreements with foreign firms. By contrast, the higher the administrative costs of hierarchies and/or the external diseconomies (or disbenefits) of operating a foreign venture (e.g., as shown by the Bhopal disaster), the more probable the latter vehicle (or at least a jointly shared equity stake) will be preferred.

In such cases where there is no external market for the competitive advantages of MNEs, the distinction between ownership and internalization advantages may seem irrelevant. Indeed some writers (notably Buckley and Casson, 1985; and Casson, 1987) have argued that the failure of international intermediate product markets is both a necessary and sufficient condition to explain the *existence* of MNEs. Yet we believe it is not only useful but logically correct to distinguish between the capability of MNEs to internalize markets, and their willingness to do so. For while the latter may explain why hierarchies rather than external markets are the vehicle by which transactional ownership advantages (Ot) are transferred across national boundaries, it is the former which explains why these advantages are exploited by one group of MNEs rather than another, or by MNEs rather than firms indigenous to the country of production.[13] This point has in fact been acknowledged by Casson (1986a, p.46).

Certainly in the exploitation of specific intangible assets (Oa) (e.g., a patent or trade mark), firms often have a choice between using the external market or not. Here the distinction between asset *generation,* or *acquisition,* and asset *usage* is an important one. We would accept with Rugman (1981) that, if an ownership advantage is either created by or becomes the exclusive property of a particular enterprise, it has in some sense "internalized" the market for its use,[14] but we believe this to be a questionable extension of the interpretation of a term that originally and quite specifically was intended to convey a response to transactional rather than structural market failure.[15]

Locational Advantages: Structural and Transactional Market Failure

The third strand of the eclectic paradigm is concerned with the "where" of production. Enterprises will engage in foreign production whenever they perceive it is in their best interests to combine spatially transferable intermediate products[16] produced in the home country, with at least some immobile factor endowments or other intermediate products in another country. While, in the eclectic paradigm, the advantages or disadvantages of particular locations are treated separately from the ownership advantages of particular enterprises, and while the market for these advantages are internalized; the decision on where to site a mine, factory or office, is not independent of the ownership of these assets nor of the route by which they or their rights are transacted. Similarly, the choice of location may be prompted by spatial market failure: historically the imposition of trade barriers has led to a lot of foreign manufacturing investment by MNEs. At the same time a reduction in transport costs and the formation of customs unions or regional trading blocs (e.g., EEC and LAFTA) have prompted greater regional specialization of production by MNEs (Dunning, 1987b).

Once more a distinction needs to be drawn between the different kinds of market imperfections that may influence the locational decisions of MNEs. Structural market distortions—for example, those arising from some (but not all) kinds of government intervention,[17] which affect the costs and/or revenues of producing in different locations—may either encourage or discourage inward direct investment (Guisinger 1985). On the other hand, even without such distortions MNE activity would still occur wherever there are transaction gains likely to result from the common governance of activities in different locations. Such advantages include enhanced arbitrage and leverage opportunities, the reduction of exchange risks and better coordination of financial decision taking, the protection afforded by a hedged marketing or multiple sourcing strategy, and the possibility of gains through transfer price manipulation, leads and lags in payments, and so on (Kogut, 1985b; Dunning 1987a).

The ability to generate and sustain such ownership advantages itself strengthens the competitive position of MNEs vis-à-vis uninational firms. But because transactional market failure is sometimes country-specific, it has locational implications as well. To this extent, Rugman is on the right lines when he refers to the MNE as "internalising exogenous spatial imperfections" (Rugman, 1981); but his analysis better explains the common *ownership* of MNE subsidiaries in different locations, rather than why *particular* subsidiaries are located where they are.

Specific or General Theories of International Production?

It is then the juxtaposition of the ownership-specific advantages of firms contemplating foreign production, or an increase in foreign production, the propensity to internalize the cross-border markets for these, and the attractions of a foreign location for production which is the gist of the eclectic paradigm of international production. But the identification and value of the specific ownership, location and internalisation (OLI) parameters that will influence individual MNEs in any particular production decision will vary according to the motives underlying such production. The pa-

rameters influencing a MNE to invest in a copper mine in New Guinea are unlikely to be the same as those influencing investment by a Japanese color television company in the United States; while those determining the pattern of rationalized production in the EEC by a large and geographically diversified US motor vehicles MNE will be different from an investment by a Korean construction management company in Kuwait.

However, the eclectic paradigm does allow one to go a step further by relating the OLI configuration facing MNEs to a number of structural or contextual variables. We have previously identified the more important of these as *country, industry* (or activity) and *firm-specific* (Dunning, (1981). For example, the asset advantages (Oa) of particular MNEs may be expected to vary according to the factor endowments and other characteristics of the countries from which they originate, and/or in which they operate; and the technological and other features of the activities in which they engage. The fact that such assets may be the exclusive property of particular firms, and be mobile across national boundaries, does not negate the possibility that their source may be explained by the international disposition of country-specific and immobile endowments. To this extent, one is back to H-O-S–type trade theory, but with two differences. The first is that the goods and services traded are intermediate rather than final products, and the second is that the eclectic paradigm allows for the role of governments, in affecting, by the political systems they operate and the economic policies they pursue the real (as opposed to the potential) value of the resources contained within their jurisdictional areas.[18] Several writers, for example, Franko (1976), Ergas (1984), Davidson (1976), and Pavitt (1987), have demonstrated that the kind of innovatory advantages generated by MNEs reflect the resource endowments, markets, culture, attitudes and institutional framework of their home countries.[19]

It requires but a small modification of the factor endowment approach to explain why some types of economic activity are more prone to internalization than others. Again the spatial disposition of resource endowments and international transport costs are the key variables. If the capacity to create a particular asset is ubiquitous, and the right to its use can be disseminated at zero cost, then international production is unlikely; it is also improbable where the competitive advantages of firms rest not in the exclusive possession of specific assets, but in the access to immobile but nonspecific factor endowments on favorable terms. Thus, a combination of the resource requirements of particular economic activities, their geographical disposition, and the transfer costs of their output, helps to explain some of the operations of MNEs.

But only some! For example, it does little to explain the cross-hauling of investment in the same industries by MNEs of different nationalities; or the fact that some countries display similar patterns of international production. The explanation is limited because it ignores transactional market failure, which itself varies between countries and types of economic activities. Without such failure, but with an uneven distribution of resource endowments, trade in intermediate products would be conducted through external markets. With an even distribution of resource endowments, but with market failure, then the only advantage which MNEs qua MNEs possess is their capability to better overcome international transactional imperfections than their uninational rivals (Dunning, 1986c).

Does the Eclectic Paradigm Insufficiently Allow for Firm-Specific Behavioral Differences?

We now turn to consider a structural variable, which some business analysts regard as the most crucial of all in influencing the level and pattern of international production. This is the strategic response of decision takers within MNEs to a set of economic and other variables, and the way the idiosyncratic behaviour of firms might influence and respond to cross-border market failure.

A cursory review of the international profiles of the leading MNEs identified by Stopford

(1982) reveals that in some sectors (e.g., consumer electronics, motor vehicles, pharmaceuticals, etc.), there are as many differences between the characteristics of MNEs in the same sector as there are between MNEs in different sectors. Moreover, since these firms rarely supply identical products or the same range of products, or produce on the same (or similar) points of the value-added chain, or sell in the same markets, and since they have differing capabilities for, and a need of, international production; it follows that not only are they faced with a different set of strategic options, but that their evaluation of these options, and the risks attached to them, will vary. Indeed, the risk diversification thesis (Rugman, 1979) asserts that different firms may view identical investment opportunities offered by a particular country differently, inter alia, according to the distribution of their existing portfolios and their attitudes towards uncertainty. For these, and other reasons identified in the business literature, firm-specific characteristics may be a crucial determinant of the response by MNEs to any particular OLI configuration.

While there have been some attempts to model the strategic behaviour of firms towards their foreign operations,[20] they have not generally been incorporated into the mainstream of international production theory. The exceptions are the product cycle, oligopolistic strategy and risk minimization models. The first two (Vernon, 1974; Knickerbocker, 1973) look upon much of foreign production as a strategy by firms to protect or gain an ownership-specific advantage vis-à-vis their rivals, the implication being that, in a more competitive and less risky environment, firms would have less impetus to engage in international direct investment (Vernon, 1983). Evidence of such strategies of oligopolists include the bunching of the timing of foreign investment in some sectors (Dunning, 1986a; Knickerbocker, 1973; Graham, 1978, 1985; Lake, 1976a and b). The risk minimization hypothesis argues that, other things being equal, firms will prefer to diversify the geographical portfolio of their investments. This concept may be extended to incorporate nonfinancial portfolio behaviour. Clearly, whether or not a firm adopts a global product or marketing strategy, or chooses to engage in multiple sourcing (Kogut 1983, 1985b), reflects not only on its ability to do so (which inter alia will be function of its size, product structure and existing overseas commitments), but on its perceptions of the resulting costs and benefits.

To what extent can differences in the behaviour of firms be embraced by the OLI framework? The answer is they can, insofar as it is possible to identify and evaluate systematic patterns of such behavior. Purely random or idiosyncratic actions by particular MNEs cannot be so easily incorporated. But no less is this true if one was attempting a generalized theory of the uninational firm. Such theories as abound in the literature are really theories of the behavior of *firms* in the sense that it is not the behaviour of any particular firm they are trying to predict but that of a group of firms, or of a representative (or average) firm of that group. They usually assume two things. First, that firms have broadly similar goals; and second, that they respond to economic signals to advance these goals in a rational and consistent way. When neither condition exists, it is not possible to offer any generalized explanations of behaviour; which, indeed, is exactly what some business analysts would claim.

We do not accept that such a drastic course is either desirable or justifiable; indeed, we believe that, for most firms, that part of business conduct which is purely idiosyncratic is probably very small. However, we are persuaded that the interface between the economic and behavioral theories of the firm does need more explicit and systematic analysis. While there is general agreement about the main *country* and *industry* characteristics likely to influence each of the main components of the eclectic paradigm, much less attention has been given to identifying the key attributes of firms—and especially those that might be identified as operational or strategically based—that may affect their response to any particular configuration of OLI parameters.

There are now signs of this happening. Some

of the recent literature on global dimensions of business[21] is replete with attempts to identify the strategically-related characteristics of firms most likely to be associated with a robust international posture. These include their long-term goals and perspectives, the nature and scope of their core assets, their attitude to innovation and change (are they leaders or followers in their industry, are they innovators or imitators?), the range and segment of critical markets served, their attitude to risk and uncertainty, their operational flexibility, their organizational and cultural ethos, the entrepreneurial initiative of their chief decision takers and their willingness and capacity to conclude cross-border alliances.

There has been little empirical research on these and other behavioral-related variables in influencing the extent and pattern of international production. In 1972 Horst concluded that, apart from size, he could identify no firm-specific variable which satisfactorily explained the degree of multinationality of US-owned firms across industries and countries. More recently a study undertaken on the *modes* of transferring technology between countries but within firms (Davidson and McFeteridge, 1984, 1985) revealed that such variables as existing overseas commitment, research intensity, and degree of product diversification were positively and significantly correlated with the extent of a firm's internalization. Most recently of all, Porter (1986) has developed a model that relates the extent to which different types of firms seek to coordinate their cross-border value-adding investments, with the propensity to centralise or decentralize the location of these investments. Porter describes a globally or geocentrically-oriented MNE as one that operates an extensive network of foreign affiliates, the activities of which are subject to a high degree of centralized coordination. Such an MNE is to be distinguished from a multi-domestic company, that, through its loosely organised overseas subsidiaries, pursues a series of country centered strategies; or, indeed, from one that adopts a simple strategy with a geographically concentrated configuration of activities.[22]

In conclusion, it may well be that there are some behavioral-related variables of firms that have not been successfully incorporated into the eclectic paradigm. Insofar as it is possible to identify those that might influence the response of groups of enterprises to a given OLI configuration, there is no reason why this could not be done. But where no general systematic or consistent response of firms to changes in exogenous variables can be discovered, any attempt to generalize about the causes of international production is thwarted from the start.

The Aliber Theory of Foreign Direct Investment

Let us now briefly turn to Robert Aliber's (1983) dissatisfaction with the eclectic paradigm and, indeed, with all theories that take some measure of the foreign activities of enterprises as their starting point of interest. This reflects Aliber's view that the key attribute of a MNE is not the fact that it engages in foreign production, but that it finances at least part of this production in its home currency. He is, then, primarily interested in the export of direct investment as a means of financing foreign capital expenditure rather than as a channel by which an enterprise transfers nonfinancial resources between countries, and controls the use of such resources once transferred. He would appear to believe that the extraterritorial expansion of firms per se raises no issues not already addressed by the theory of the domestic firm. Rather, the uniqueness of the MNE is its ability to dominate its geographically dispersed assets in different currencies, and by so doing, to take advantage of structural or transactional imperfections in international capital and foreign exchange markets.

Inasmuch as scholars are entitled to study subjects of interest to them, we have no dispute with Aliber. We would, however, challenge his implicit assumption that while differences *in kind* exist between national and international financial markets, this is not the case for nonfinancial markets, such as these for technology and management services. Moreover, it seems to us that Aliber restricts his consideration of foreign direct investment to situations in which enterprises invest in different currency areas. While this may be usually the case, it is by no means universally so.

In any event, we do not find Aliber's thesis incompatible with the eclectic paradigm. The very fact that firms, by their presence overseas, may be able to denominat their assets and goods in different currencies, could give them a competitive of an ownership-specific edge over uninational firms. This advantage will be the more pronounced the greater the degree of structural or transactional failure in international capital and/or exchange markets, and the better equipped MNEs are to internalize these markets. Yet, by themselves, these advantages are not sufficient to explain either the amount or distribution of foreign direct investment. For example, expected profits (other than those resulting from the internalization of imperfect financial markets) are not independent of the locations in which investments are made nor of the ability of MNEs to appropriate economic rent by internalizing nonfinancial markets.

It is not our purpose to offer a detailed critique of the Aliber hypothesis,[23] but rather to suggest that, insofar as imperfections do exist in the markets in which he is interested, these may affect both the way in which capital expenditure by MNEs is financed, and the geographical distribution of international production. Similarly, the factors identified in the eclectic paradigm as influencing the foreign activities of firms, may directly, by their impact on capital and exchange markets, and/or, indirectly, by affecting the total capital expenditure by MNEs, have no less a bearing on their financing of these activities. We would then assert that, in support of his own theory, Professor Aliber must take cognizance of the nonfinancial aspects of the international operations of firms.

The Kojima Hypothesis[24]

As originally propounded (Kojima 1978, 1982), Professor Kojima's theory of foreign direct investment is an extension of the neoclassical theory of trade to embrace cross-border transactions of intermediate products (e.g., technology, management skills, etc.). It is primarily a normative theory, and views the MNE as an instrument by which the comparative trading advantage of nation states may be better advanced. Hence his prescription that a *home* country should invest abroad in sectors that require intermediate (but internationally mobile) products that it is comparatively well suited to supply, but that need to be combined with nontransferable inputs in which the *host* country is relatively well endowed. In this case, foreign direct investment acts both as a catalyst to trade and as an arbitrager for improving the international allocation of economic activity.

Kojima criticizes the eclectic paradigm for being too micro- or business-oriented, and claims it is of limited use for policy formation by home or host countries. But, as we have sought to demonstrate from the perspective of the United Kingdom (Dunning, 1981, chap. 6), many of the normative implications of our paradigm are entirely consistent with Kojima's recommendations. This is particularly the case for resource-based and import substitution investment, where the export of intermediate products by MNEs to countries best suited to engage in further value added activities, either circumvents artificially imposed impediments to trade, or better promotes the dynamic comparative advantage of the participating countries.

However, even as a prescriptive macroeconomic model, the Kojima approach is deficient in two major respects. First, since it is neoclassical in its stance, it can neither explain, nor evaluate the welfare implications of those types of foreign direct investment prompted by the desire to rationalize international production and to benefit from the common governance of cross-border activities (i.e., Ot advantages). The eclectic paradigm can and does embrace such international production. Second, and related to the first, Kojima largely ignores the essential characteristic of MNE activity— namely, the internalization of intermediate product markets, and where he does take this into account, he always seems to assume that

the resulting allocation of resources is less desirable to that which would have been dictated by the market (Kojima, 1978, chap. 9). This is because Kojima is locked into a neoclassical paradigm of perfect competition that negates the very possibility of market failure. In his scenario, the MNE can *never* be the most efficient agent for transferring resources across national boundaries, simply because its very existence implies a second-best transactional situation.

Again, this does not seem to be of much practical value to governments in their formulation of policy towards MNEs. Firms do not exist in a riskless or timeless vacuum; many individual transactions do give rise to external costs or benefits; the exploitation of economies of scale may not be possible without the presence of some structural market distortion; some product differentiation may be desirable; and some property rights may require, at least temporary protection against their infringement or dissipation, if they are to be supplied at all.[25] The question at issue is surely that, *given the viable alternatives, and over an appropriate time period,* can the resource allocation between countries be improved by foreign direct investment or the operation of MNEs?

Empirically, the alleged dichotomy between the patterns of Japanese and U.S. direct investment is a false one. As Mason (1980) has well argued, such differences as do exist reflect the different stages in the evolution of Japanese and American MNEs as much as anything else. The eclectic paradigm would suggest that, in a world free of trade restrictions, the initial act of foreign direct investment would normally occur in those sectors that use intermediate products in which the investing country has a comparative advantage. This act would be welfare-creating wherever the price charged for the intermediate output fairly reflected its social opportunity cost, and the resources released within the home country are deployed in a way consistent with the principle of comparative advantage. We would accept that most Japanese foreign investment of the 1960s and '70s was of this kind. However, as firms become more multinational and take a more global perspective of their foreign operations, their ownership advantages become less based on the exclusive possession of particular intangible assets, which are country-specific in origin, and more on their ability to successfully coordinate and manage a network of geographical activities. These transaction costs-minimizing advantages—which tend to be firm-rather than country-specific in origin—were largely the property of the larger US and European MNEs in the 1960s and 1970s; only now, in the later 1980s, are they beginning to be exploited by their Japanese counterparts.

A RESTATEMENT OF THE ECLECTIC PARADIGM

So much for some of the criticisms of the eclectic paradigm. In consideration of these, and on further reflection, we are now fully persuaded that any holistic theory of international production must draw upon two inter-related strands of economic analysis. The first is the neoclassical theory of factor endowments, extended to embrace intermediate products, and to allow for the possibility that some endowments are mobile across national boundaries. Ceteris paribus, the more uneven the geographical distribution of factor endowments, the more international production is likely to take place. The nature of such production will resemble that of H-O-S trade in that it is inter-industry in character. The second strand is the theory of market failure, which is relevant to explaining not only the location of some kinds of economic activity across national boundaries, but also the division of that activity between multinational and uninational firms.[26] Ceteris paribus, the higher the transaction costs of using the market as a transactional model, and the greater the efficiency of MNEs as coordinators of geographically dispersed activities, the more international production is likely to take place. Such production may be either inter- or intra-industry in character; but that based on Ot advantages alone is more likely to be of the latter kind (Dunning and Norman, 1985).

In Figure 1, we set out the relationship between these two intellectual strands and the analytical constructs set out in this paper. We believe this figure is self-explanatory and needs no further elaboration. Figure 2 illustrates the relevance of these two basic elements of the eclectic paradigm in explaining the three main kinds of international production. We also would reiterate an earlier observation, that as an enterprise develops a network of foreign affiliates, which it treats as part of a global system of activities, the relative importance of factor endowments in explaining changes in international production is likely to decrease; and that of market failure likely to increase.[27]

SOME POSSIBLE EXTENSIONS OF THE ECLECTIC PARADIGM

It is our contention that the eclectic paradigm provides a rich and robust framework not only for analyzing and explaining the determinants of international production and how this varies between firms, industries, and countries, and over time, but for our understanding of a wide variety of other MNE-related issues. In this paper, we will illustrate six possible directions in which work on the paradigm might be further developed.

A More Formal Modeling of the Paradigm

There is need for a more systematic and rigorous modeling of the explanation of different types of international production by the use of specifically and operationally testable OLI parameters.[28] Given these types, the variations within them may be explained by structural variables as identified by empirical research.[29] Some work by trade economists, notably Ethier (1986), Markussen (1984), and Helpman (1984), is currently proceeding in this direction. There is also need for formal modeling of the MNE as an organizational mechanism and/or choice of modality of resource transfer. Again some progress has been made by Grosse (1985), Casson (1985), and Horstman and Markussen (1986), but more work requires to be done. Finally, there is need for a more systemic approach to examining the strategic behavior of MNEs—using, for example, such tools as game theoretic and network analysis.

Dynamic and Development Aspects of International Production

Some commentators (e.g., Vernon, 1985) have alleged that the eclectic paradigm is couched in static terms and is unable to explain the dynamics or the process of change of international production. Dynamics can be interpreted and modeled in various ways; Vernon's particular concern is that the eclectic paradigm fails to allow for the behavioral interaction between international oligopolists, which both affect and is affected by their foreign activities. In other words, faced with the same set of OLI parameters, not only would the response of MNEs vary according to their strategic postures, but this response might trigger off reactions on the part of their competitors, that themselves may cause a change in one or other of these parameters. In the real world of uncertainty about future markets, the actions of government, the conduct of competitors, suppliers, consumers and labor unions, firms—and particularly those that are geographically or industrially diversified—have a variety of strategic options, simply because they do not know with certainty what is its best option. This is a very different scenario from the one assumed by the neoclassical models, where, once the value of the relevant parameters is known, the first best solution is both identifiable and assumed always to be adopted by MNEs.

The literature identifies various factors likely to influence the strategy of MNEs towards their foreign operations. These include the structure of their existing investment portfolios and risk exposures, their competitive strengths and weaknesses, their bargaining power with governments, their product portfolios, their liquidity position and so on. However, these are at best partial behavioral explanations. The crucial question is whether a general theory of business strategy can be devised that can be used alongside the eclectic paradigm to explain the actions of MNEs in a dynamic situation.

Perhaps the best hope for progress here lies in some of the concepts in industrial organization theory, example, that of dynamic market contestability,[30] and for the transactional model itself to embrace the type of market failure inherent in interactive behavioral situations.

A somewhat different but nonetheless related interpretation of dynamics might suggest that the eclectic paradigm should embrace the economics of entrepreneurship and technological innovation and change. Mark Casson (1986a) has forcibly argued that any satisfactory explanation of the dynamics of ownership advantage must rest on the reinstatement of the role of the entrepreneur to a central position in the theory of the firm. Like Casson, Cantwell (1986) and Dunning and Cantwell (1986) view the economy as an evolutionary system, and, have applied the eclectic paradigm to analyzing the way in which MNEs both generate and respond to technological change. Economic and business historians, too, are making a useful contribution to our understanding of the growth of international production, using especially a transaction cost approach (North, 1985; Nicholas, 1986).

Viewing growth and development from the perspective of countries rather than firms, more progress has been made, using mainly the tools of the development economist. Here, the concept of an investment development path or cycle, as first set out in Dunning (1979), subsequently extended in Dunning (1986c), and modified by Tolentino (1987) is especially relevant.[31]

The basic hypothesis of the investment development path or cycle is that a country propensity to engage in outward direct investment, or be invested in by foreign firms, will vary according to (i) its stage of economic development, (ii) the structure of its factor endowments and markets, (iii) its political and economic systems and (iv) the nature and extent of market failure in the transaction of intermediate products across national boundaries. It suggests that, as a country's economic development proceeds, its international direct investment position will pass through a number

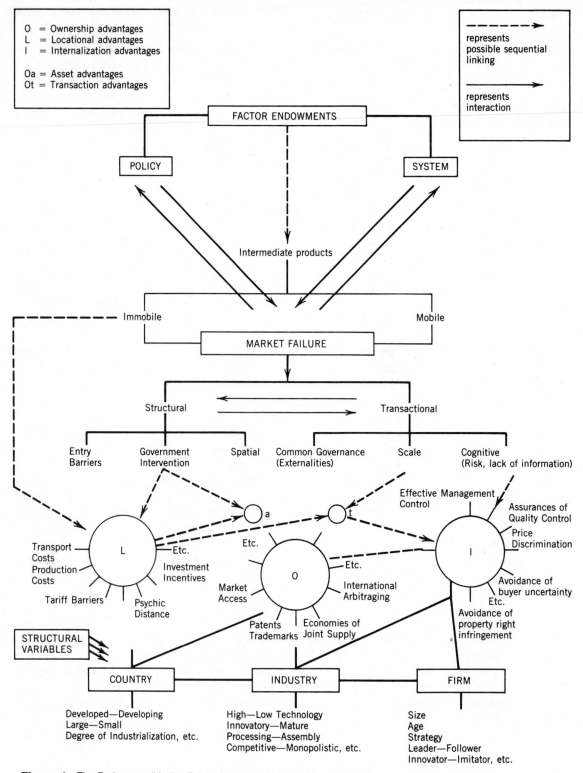

Figure 1 The Endowment/Market Failure Paradigm of International Production

Main Types of International Production	Factor Endowments (Affecting geographical distribution of L)	Market Failure	
		Structural (Affecting L and Oa)	Transactional (Affecting Ot, L and I)
1 Market Seeking (import substituting)	Home country for creation of Oa (= mobile endowments/ intermediate products) Host country advantage in immobile endowments with which Oa have to be used e.g., natural resources, some kinds of labour Market size & character	Firm specific = proprietary Oa (e.g., Knowledge) privileged access to inputs Restrictions on trade in goods (a)–natural (transport costs) (b) artificial (import controls) Oligopolistic market structure	Search and negotiating costs Protection against misrepresentation or infringement of property rights Economics of bulk purchasing Part of international portfolio to spread risks Protection against actions of competitors
2 Resource Seeking (supply oriented)	Home country—as above but also market size & character Host country. Availability of resources, natural, labour (export processing) technology (e.g., investment by ldcs in dcs)	As above, but also privileged access to markets Incentives offered by Government to fdi (also relevant for 1 & 3) Oligopolistic market structure	Avoidance of risks of breach of contract and interruption of supplies Absence of future markets Economics of vertical integration
3 Efficiency Seeking (rationalised investment) O = Ownership advantages L = Locational advantages I = Internalisation advantages Oa = asset advantages Ot = transaction advantages	VERTICAL Mainly as 1 & 2 above HORIZONTAL Usually distribution of factor endowments not very relevant, as international production in countries with similar resource structures LATERAL Of limited importance in effect	As above but as investment influenced more by supply than market considerations. Government induced structural imperfections likely to be of considerable importance (e.g., tax differentials, investment incentives, performance requirements etc.) Note that as above regional integration and reduction of trade barrier aids rationalised investment	As with 2 above Economies of scale and scope Risk reduction through product diversification As above, but in respect of ancillary activities (e.g., various services—shipping, consultancy etc.)

Figure 2   Illustration of Use of Factor Endowment/Market Failure Paradigm in Explaining Three Main Forms of International Production

of stages. In the first stage, there will be neither inward nor outward MNE activity, partly because its markets and factor endowments are insufficient to attract either import substituting or resource-based inward investment, and partly because its political, commercial and technological infrastructure is unable to generate the kind of support services required by foreign direct investors (or, for that matter by indigenous firms engaged in similar activities). As the infrastructure improves, then, depending on the economic structure of the country and government policy, intermediate products will start to be imported; however, because of the high transaction costs of using external markets, these will tend to be internalized by the foreign suppliers. In this first stage of inward investment, the ownership advantages of MNEs are more likely to derive from the possession of individual intangible assets (Oa) (vis-à-vis those of indigenous firms), rather than on the economies of coordinating multiple activities (Ot), but this will partly depend on whether the MNE already has related investment in other countries and the extent of its intra-firm trade (Dunning, 1986c).

The third stage of development is marked by the ability of a developing country's firms to generate their own ownership-specific advantages, which, initially at least, are likely to reflect the structure of the country's factor endowments. Depending on the nature of these advantages, the relative attractions of a foreign location, and their strategic priorities, these firms may go abroad as market or resource-seekers. However, whereas in their early ventures abroad, industrialized countries normally sought natural resources and low cost labor in which their home country was disadvantaged, those from developing countries are currently seeking to acquire technology (i.e., the resource in which they are comparatively poorly endowed).[32] Alternatively, developing countries may export the kind of intermediate products that require endowments in which they have comparative advantage. In the case of South Korea, Turkey and the Philippines, for example, this has sometimes involved the export of unskilled labor services—notably of construction workers—an intermediate product, traditionally thought to beimmobile across frontiers.

It should benoted that the point at which a country reaches the third stage of the investment development cycle—if indeed it is reached at all—rests largely on the structure of its resource endowments, and the attitudes of its government towards international economic involvement in general and inward and outward direct investment in particular.[33] A country such as India, with its sights set on industrial self-sufficiency, might well prefer to indigenize activities, initially undertaken by foreign affiliates, rather than to participate in an international division of labor in which its own firms become foreign investors. By contrast, economies such as Singapore, Hong Kong, and Taiwan, would seem to favor building up a comparative advantage in the production of intermediate products, that, in part at least, may best beused in conjunction with immobile resources in other countries; while, at the same time, they seek to foster inward investment in activities that require immobile resources in which they are evolving (e.g., by way of appropriate education, training and innovating policies) a comparative advantage.

The fourth stage of the investment development cycle occurs when a country becomes a net outward investor. Since by definition the outward capital stock or investment flows of all countries must equal the inward capital stock or investment flows of all countries, it follows that, at a given moment of time, only some countries can benet outward investors. Therefore, any correlation between net outward in-

vestment and economic development can only hold good when making cross-country comparisons. Using time-series data, the correlation may be positive for some countries but not for others. This problem, however, may be overcome by normalizing the per capita income of particular countries by the average per capita for all countries.

But how far can the eclectic paradigm predict *which* countries will become net outward investors, and/or the point on the investment development cycle that this will occur? And how far can it explain the *reduction* in the net outward position of some high (and rising) income countries (e.g., the U.S.) in recent years? The answers lie in the changing international distribution of factor endowments, especially those that are transferable across national frontiers; and in the changing efficacy of hierarchies and markets as transnational modes. As a general hypothesis, the less evenly assets (which help produce mobile intermediate products) are distributed across national boundaries, and the greater the transactional failure of markets in these products, the wider will be the dispersion of the net outward investment position of countries[34] (around a zero net outward investment position). The more evenly resources are distributed, and the less the transactional market failure, the narrower the dispersion in the net outward investment position of countries is likely to be.

The gradual convergence of per capita income levels and the economic structure of the advanced industrialized economies, together with some harmonization of government policies, is making for more symmetrical transborder direct investment patterns. This phenomena is associated with another, namely the growth of intra-industry production. Like intra-industry trade, such production reflects less the disposition of factor endowments and more the advantages of scale economies in production and marketing, and differences in consumer tastes between countries; although *within* some sectors (e.g., consumer electronics), there may continue to be some international division of labor based on the distribution of country-specific endowments.[35] Like inter-industry production, it sometimes replaces trade (e.g., where it is prompted by import restrictions); and sometimes complements or changes the pattern of trade (e.g., where there is specialization of products or production processes in different locations). Again in this latter case, the competitive advantages of the participating firms are less those of the rent-seeking kind, and more those that arise from the common oversight of complementary assets. The fact, too, that intra-industry production is largely in the hands of large and diversified multinational oligopolists adds further to this likelihood.

The case of Japan is a particularly interesting application of the investment development path, in spite of (or perhaps because of) the fact that government intervention by the Japanese government deliberately curtailed the role of inward investment for most of the second stage of the cycle. In terms of the OLI paradigm, Japan initially disallowed the internalization of most intermediate products (especially technology) markets by foreign MNEs; instead, it acquired these products in other ways, or promoted their indigenous production. This process continued until the Japanese economy had evolved a strong indigenous technological capability, and its firms, distinctive ownership advantages in world markets. At the same time, and partly as a consequence of this process, Japan's locational attractions began to change. Rising real wages reduced the competitive edge of its unit labor costs; technology-intensive and material-saving activities became comparatively more attractive. The net result of these changes was that Japan both needed to export mobile resources and intermediate products to help to relocate the kind of production that required immobile resources in which her comparative advantage was declining, while importing mobile resources and intermediate products that could be used with immobile resources in which her comparative advantage was rising. But for its own firms to become multinational, it also had to accept the presence of foreign MNEs. Moreover, the type of mobile re-

sources it required were not often forthcoming via the non-equity route; in consequence, over the years Japanese policy towards inward direct investment has been liberalized.

In the mid-1980s, Japan entered the fifth stage of development cycle.[36] This point is reached where two things happen. First the ownership-specific advantages of a country's MNEs become more *firm*-specific (i.e., of a transaction cost-minimizing kind) and less *country*-specific (i.e., asset-based); and second, the locational decisions by both foreign and domestic MNEs become less based on the comparative advantage of factor endowments, and more on the strategies of competitors supplying regional or global markets, the desire to fully exploit the economies of large-scale production, the need to reduce market instabilities and uncertainty, and the incentive to reap the gains from integrating related activities over space. To these features another may be added, which rests less on the development stage of a country and more on its economic position vis-à-vis that of other countries. Here, the proposition is that as countries converge in their income levels and economic structures, the more symmetrical cross-investment flows are likely to be. The relatively faster growth of European and Japanese direct investment in the U.S. than of U.S. direct investment in Europe and Japan in the 1970s and the early 1980s lends support to this proposition; while the dramatic improvement of U.S. economic performance in the mid-1980s, the accelerated path of technological advance, and the realities of global competition is causing a resurgence of foreign activity by U.S. MNEs.

The fact that Japanese participation in European and U.S. manufacturing industry is currently growing very quickly, and especially in those sectors (e.g., electronics and motor vehicles) that tend to bedominated by MNEs, and that European and U.S. firms in similar industries are forming alliances with the Japanese in their home markets (Ohmae, 1985), suggests that the structure of Japanese outward direct investment is now increasingly resembling that of the U.S. and European countries. And, indeed, it may bereasonably predicted that as the Japanese economy becomes an increasingly high-wage and technology-intensive economy, yet more internationally oriented, that the character of Japanese MNEs will change in two ways. First a higherproportion of their investments will bedirected to the developed world and bewithin similar sectors to those invested in by foreign companies in Japan. Second, their competitive strengths will come to depend more on their ability to operate successfully a global network of interrelated activities than on the favored possession of particular assets. At the same time, while there is some suggestion (Dunning, 1986a) that Japanese manufacturing MNEs are currently concentrating their high-value activities in their home plants, a need to tap and monitor the latest technological advances in such sectors as biotechnology and telematics is encouraging these same MNEs to set up (or share with local firms) research, development and design facilities in Europe and the U.S. (Ohmae, 1985).

Explaining Different Forms of International Economic Involvement

The third direction in which the eclectic paradigm of international production might be extended is for it to incorporate other forms of international business transactions, notably arm's-length trade, joint ventures and non equity contractual agreements. To date, however, while some progress has been made in embracing the latter two subject areas[37]—indeed, some authors (e.g., Casson, 1986d) would go so far to argue that the contractual relationship, be it part of an equity or non-equity form of business, association, is the key to our understanding of international business involvement—only limited headway has been made in unifying explanations of trade and production.[38] We suggest there are two main reasons for this. The first is that the modern theory of international production derives its analytical framework from the theories of the firm and industrial organization rather than from the theory of international trade; and, implicitly, at least, all tradeable activities are assumed to be conducted between independent buyers and sellers.[39] Secondly, while the latter theory takes as its unit of interest the nation state, the focus of interest of students of the MNE is the firm or groups of firms.

It is true that several of the modern theories of trade—particularly those designed to explain intra-industry transactions—explicitly acknowledge the role of market imperfections as determining factors; but the emphasis of interest is strongly directed to structural rather than transactional imperfections (Krugman, 1981, 1983). Much of neo-technology and monopolistic competitive trade may be explained by the spatial distribution of resources that gave rise to ownership-specific advantages, but which are used by firms in conjunction with immobile resources located in the *home* country. When a firm goes abroad, it exports these intangible assets or their rights, and uses them in conjunction with foreign resources that it can obtain at lower cost than at home. However, the implications of transactional market failure that make for the common ownership of assets across national boundaries, and which, in turn, may impinge on the trading competitiveness of firms, have been largely neglected by trade theorists. It is here that an integrated approach to production and trade offers particular promise (Dunning and Norman, 1985).

Historically, there are many parallels in the way in which the patterns of trade and international production have evolved. To start with, most trade was intersectoral and largely explainable by the international distribution of factor endowments. Likewise, as we have already suggested, although an element of market failure is necessary to explain the ownership of international production, its structure and location initially follow the dictates of the H-O-S paradigm as applied to intermediate products. Later as trade became more intrasectoral, new explanations were sought and found (Grubel and Lloyd, 1975; Tharakan, 1984). Intrasectoral production also possesses many of the attributes of intra-industry trade, but with additional market imperfections (notably those which are unique to the common ownership of assets in different countries and the internalization of trade in intermediate products). Moreover, unlike intra-industry trade, intra-industry production implies intra-*firm* trade as well. Indeed, the ability of a firm to trade internally may itself afford that firm certain advantages over its competitors (e.g., the possibility of gains from specialized sourcing or transfer price manipulation). It is, then, not surprising that the more multinational a firm becomes, the more it is inclined to engage in internalized trade (Dunning and Pearce, 1985).

The economic theory of intra-firm trade, and how it differs from inter-firm trade is now beginning to receive some attention in the literature, but again, mostly by scholars interested in the organization of transactions rather than the transactions *per se*. Normatively, insofar as intra-firm trade is market replacing, it has been viewed with some suspicion by welfare economists, and is commonly perceived as a means through which MNEs manipulate transfer prices in a way inimical to the interests to one or other (or both) of the trading countries. Though the organization of trade *need* not affect its extent, pattern, or terms, the country-specific differences in the perceived gains which transfer pricing manipulation may encourage MNEs to locate production in countries in which the gains are thought to be most likely. On the other hand, MNEs may engage in intra-firm international trade for exactly the same reason as domestic firms may engage in intra-firm national trade, namely, to internalize the external economies of individual transactions. Whether this benefits or adversely affects the distribution of international economic activity and/or the welfare of the participating countries, depends on the nature of the market failure being internalized, the consequences of such internalization, and how the gains or losses resulting from it are distributed. But there is no a priori reason to suppose that intra-firm trade in final goods products is less beneficial to international resource allocation than either *inter*-firm trade conducted in imperfectly competitive markets or *intra*-firm trade in intermediate products.

The fact that an optimum solution (in the Pareto sense) is so difficult to identify is that, because market failure exists, one is forced to compare a number of second best alternatives. Once matters such as the distribution of benefits over time, risk and government intervention enter the equation, one's criteria for judging optimality inevitably becomes multifaceted. While in principle, transactions between different parts of a domestic firm pose identical problems, the gains or losses resulting from the transactions are at least contained in that country. In the case of trade within hierarchies across national boundaries, inter-country distributional questions cannot be ignored; just as government may judge internal allocative efficiency in terms of their own economic and social goals, so they will evaluate the impact of MNEs on the extent and pattern of trade flows.

Before concluding this section, brief reference may be made to one of the fastest-growing forms of institutional arrangements, namely, the cross-border non-equity collaborative venture at a product or project level between MNEs, and particularly those operating in the OECD area. These have arisen for a variety of economic and strategic reasons, but as several contributors to a recent symposium on the subject (Contractor and Lorange, 1987) demonstrated, the exploitation of complementary ownership advantages by horizontal or vertical integration, is not only consistent with the premises of the eclectic paradigm, but points to a need for broadening its scope to embrace quite specific, and perhaps temporary, international alliances between enterprises, as part and parcel of their wider international strategies.

The Locus of Decision Taking

One subject area, normally considered outside the domain of the economist but one in which we believe the eclectic paradigm offers a useful conceptual framework, concerns the geographical locus of decision-taking within the MNE. Let us focus on the question, Why and under what conditions are decisions on the way in which resources are allocated by foreign affiliates of MNEs controlled or influenced by managers[40] located in the parent company? This question may be broken down into the "where" and "who" aspects of decision-taking. The former is mainly an issue of locational economics, and concerns the price and efficiency of decision-taking (including support) resources in different countries, and the costs of trans-border inter- and intra-firm transactions (e.g., especially administration and communication costs), in which managers are involved. Here a factor endowment model may be the appropriate tool of analysis.

The "who" aspect may be divided into two components that parallel two questions asked earlier in this paper: Why does a MNE undertake production in a foreign country rather than an indigenous firm in that country?, and, Why does a MNE choose to internalize the market for the cross-border transfer of intermediate products? The competitive advantage of centralized decision-taking rests in the capacity to take (what are perceived to be) the right decisions for the MNE as a whole. If, for one reason or another, such capacity cannot be efficiently transferred to foreign affiliates—either through the training of local managers or by exporting expatriates—then the decision-taking resources will be located in the home country. Clearly, the more the specificity, idiosyncrasy, or non-codifiable nature of information and related managerial assets, the more difficult it is to ensure an efficient use of them in a foreign affiliate. And the greater the advantages of scale economies or benefits of centralized decision-taking, that accrue to the MNE *in toto* then the less likely decision-taking is to be delegated. On the other hand, the more decisions required to be customized to local needs, or depend on indigenous support facilities and expertise for their efficient execution (e.g., with respect to personnel management, industrial relations, distribution and public relations), the more likely they are to be decentralized.

But even assuming there is capacity in the host country to assimilate the transfer of ownership-specific advantages, unless there is a mutuality of interests between managers at headquarters and their agents in the affiliates,

decision-taking may still be centralized. When might this occur? Two possibilities arise. The first is wherever, as a consequence of the actions of an affiliate, there are costs and benefits that accrue to the *rest* of the organization of which it is part, and the second is where there is a different perception of objectives and/or risks by local and central management. Take a simple example. Suppose an MNE operates two manufacturing plants, one in the U.S. and the other in France. Assume the aim of each is to maximize local profits, and that each acts as an independent decision-taking unit. Then as long as the locational advantages favor the siting of managerial resources in France, and these resources are efficiently used, decisions will be decentralized. Now suppose the parent plant adopts a new strategy aimed at maximizing *group profits*. To do so it *may* need (and the situation is comparable to a takeover by one firm of another) to centralize decisions so as to both rationalize resource allocation and capture any benefits external to either of the production units but internal to the organization as a whole. In this way, by centralizing decision-taking, the MNE is undergoing an hierarchical process very similar to that of the internalization of intermediate product markets.

Using the OLI framework, then, it may be possible to construct an economic theory of the locus of decision-taking (and as a variant of this, within a location, the nationality of the decision taker).[41] The hypothesis is that decision-taking will be more centralized: (i) the greater the uniqueness, specificity and non-codifiable nature of decision-taking advantages emanating from the home country; (ii) the greater the likelihood of a conflict of interests between the parent company and the subsidiary, with respect especially to (a) risk perception and (b) externalities; and (iii) the more the locational costs of decision-taking resources favors the home country, which might reflect both difficulties in transferring management attitudes and practices, and the price of management and management-related services.

These elements will clearly vary according to *country industry* and *firm*-specific factors, and also according to the decision-taking functions. The tendency to centralize decisions relating to research and development, capital budgeting and accounting methods, but to decentralize those relating to personnel matters and sourcing arrangements, might be explained in these terms. Some illustrations of the use of this approach is contained in Dunning (1986b), which examines the locus of decision-taking as between U.S. parent companies and their U.K. subsidiaries in the 1950s and their Japanese counterparts in the 1980s.[42]

Divestment by MNEs

A fifth possible area for further study relates to our understanding of divestment or a reduction of foreign production by MNEs. Some progress along these lines has been made by Boddewyn (1983) and Casson (1986d), but by and large, the literature has so far treated divestment as a discrete act of asset disposal (i.e., the reverse of acquisition) rather than part and parcel of a continual reappraisal of the amount and disposition of the assets a firm wishes to hold. The process of a reduction, or disintegration of foreign production, is different from an initial act of entry in two ways. First, it requires the absence of only one of the three OLI variables; and second, there may be certain barriers to exit that do not correspond to barriers to entry.[43]

Using the "Mark 2" version of the eclectic paradigm set out earlier in this paper, we might predict that MNEs would wish to reduce their presence in a particular country or sector under two circumstances. First, where a change in the distribution of factor endowments (or the efficiency with which these are used) (i) weakens their competitive advantages, relative to those of firms in host countries, or (ii) causes them to switch production from the host to home (or indeed, other host countries).[44] Second, where the net transactional benefits (costs) or using the external markets for the exploitation of these competitive advantages increase (fall) *relative* to those offered administered hierarchies.[45]

As a starting point for an integrated approach to an understanding of changes in international production, let us assume that once a firm is es-

tablished abroad, its sequential investment decisions are organically related to the size and pattern of its existing investments, and to its views about (a) its existing and likely future competitive strengths and weaknesses, (b) its expectations about technological and market opportunities, and (c) its perception of its competitors' reactions to (a) and (b). In a dynamic situation, this is likely to result in a continual reassessment, relocation and reorganization of activities. As a firm's competitive position changes; as new core skills replace existing ones; as new management strategies evolve; as new markets open up and others die; and as the balance of advantage between using internal and external markets shifts, so will the level and structure of its international production. Although in some cases, this may lead to a divestment of the entire foreign assets of a firm, more often, it will result in a restructuring of its portfolio, with a sale of assets in some countries or sectors helping to finance an increase of assets in others. Integration and disintegration within MNEs often go hand in hand with each other, just as do the birth and death of firms.[46]

The realignment of the OLI advantages of leading international investors in the last two decades provides ample confirmation of the relevance of the factor endowment model component of the eclectic paradigm. The emergence of Japan as a significant international investor has resulted in a fall of the share of U.S. and European MNEs in several industrial sectors, notably automobiles and consumer electronics. The growth of offshore manufacturing in some developing countries in the 1970s to take advantage of an apparently changing international division of labor helped accelerate the decline of labor-intensive domestic sectors (both of multinational and uninational companies) in developed countries. However, recent technological advances, while placing a premium on skilled labor, have at the same time reduced the significance of labor costs in many manufacturing processes. This has resulted in a return home of some of these activities.[47] Within some of the more rapidly developing industrializing developing countries (e.g., South Korea, Taiwan and

Singapore), one has also seen divestment in low value-added and new investment in high value-added activities. In some primary sectors, mainly at the insistence of host governments, one has witnessed a marked decline in inward investment; in others, and particularly in some service industries, domestic and/or international vertical integration has sharply increased. Just as the volume and pattern of trade of a firm or country is affected by changes in the distribution of factor endowments, so will that of international production.

The question of the changing *ownership* of assets in particular countries is perhaps more interesting. Why should MNEs sell assets and acquire others? Clearly, when there are changes in the relative transaction costs of individual capital and foreign exchange markets (not least due to uncertainties about interest and exchange rates), MNEs will reappraise their international financial portfolios. But what about longterm real forces? The answer must be that, where incentives for the direct investment are reduced or advantages of common governance disappear, so divestment will occur, *providing* that the exit costs (which themselves involve transaction costs) do not outweigh the savings of using the market. The transaction costs of exit require further study, but anything that reduces the risk and uncertainty of external markets, lessens the importance of scale economies in production, or reduces the externalities of particular transactions will make for divestment.[48]

This shifting of the balance of advantages of hierarchies and external markets for international transactions, together with the emergence of new contractual arrangements which possess some of the characteristics of each (Oman 1984, Casson 1986c), has led to frequent realignments of the functions and boundaries of MNEs. While vertical integration has noticeably increased in some sectors (e.g., vehicles and electronics) and fallen in others (e.g., hotels and shipping),[49] the general trend has been towards new collaborative arrangements built around a group of core technologies. This has elsewhere been termed quasi-integration (Contractor and Lorange 1987). At the same time, technological and organizational advances have increasingly linked investment in services with investment in goods; the information industry is a classic example. In secondary industry, new alliances between firms along the value-added chain have been fostered, to exploit complementary technologies and to link computer-aided design of components with that of later manufacturing processes (Hayes and Wheelright 1984). On the other hand, the sizeable amounts of capital involved and the danger of an integrated firm being locked into one particular source of supply increases the risk of internalization.[50]

Similarly, the raison d'etre of horizontal integration may change as the importance of synergistic ownership advantages shifts with advances in technology and information. The extent of cross-hauling of hierarchical or quasi-hierarchical arrangements in the technologically advanced sectors between the U.S. and Japan is testimony of this. Indeed the growth of global industries, characterized by a substantial amount of intra-industry and intra-firm production and an interlocking network of cross-border alliances is a feature that industrial organization economists and strategists are only just starting to get to grips with. But here too, an organic approach to both divestment and investment by MNEs is required.

The Consequences of MNE Activity

One final area in which the eclectic paradigm can be a useful framework for analysis is in examining the impact of MNE activity on home and host country economic goals. Let us illustrate from the viewpoint of a *host* country.

The argument runs something like this. Inward direct investment is welcomed for the resources and/or access to markets it brings to the recipient country, and the way it may promote the upgrading and better deployment of existing indigenous endowments. The concern over this particular vehicle of importing intermediate products is two-fold. First, that because of its strong bargaining power, the investing firm is able to capture an undesirably high share of the value added or created by its subsidiary in the host country, and second, that decisions taken about the amount and kind of resources transferred, and about the use of these resources, may yield less benefit to the recipient country than that which might arise from some other pattern of resource allocation.

In the one case, the MNE is regarded as an organizational mechanism by which intermediate products, which are unavailable or costly to produce in the host country, are efficiently acquired and used; in the other, as a vehicle of economic rationalization and economic power, which is uses to promote its global goals in a way which distorts or inhibits the desired disposition of resources by the host country.

The debate over the impact of inward direct investment on host countries is now entering a new phase as markets and production become increasingly internationalized. Moreover, not only are MNEs taking a global view of their strategies and view the locational attributes of countries from this perspective—but countries also are beginning to recognize that their industrial strategies and competitive postures must take on an international dimension. Since the industries which most countries view as strategically desirable are largely dominated by MNEs, it follows that conflict between multinational oligopolies pursuing global economic strategies and countries pursuing domestic political strategies—and both within a changing and increasingly competitive international environment—is inevitable, and, in part, irreconcilable. In the 1950s and '60s, the interest centered largely on whether the types of resources provided by MNEs were appropriate to needs of recipient countries; and if, compared with alternative routes of acquiring these resources, their benefits exceeded their costs. The debate in the 1980s has much more to do with the way in which MNEs use their worldwide assets to achieve their long-term economic goals; and whether the resulting allocation of activity is consistent with that which the countries in which they operate are seeking to achieve. As a framework for analyzing these questions, we believe that the eclectic paradigm has a great deal to offer.

CONCLUSIONS

This paper has sought to demonstrate that, a decade after its inception, the eclectic paradigm remains a useful and robust general framework for explaining and analyzing not only the economic rationale of international production but many organizational and impact issues relating to MNE activity as well. Conceptually, there are close parallels between the main tenets of the paradigm and that of modern theory of business strategy,[51] though neither approach is sufficient to explain the international profile of any particular MNE. It is likely, however, that new theorizing in the next decade will take a different form to that of the last ten years, if for no other reason than the character and organization of international production is itself undergoing fundamental change. More especially, we foresee a more systematic effort by trade economists to model transactional market failure into more general theories of international economic involvement, while industrial and business economists are likely to become more interested in the dynamics of the OLI configuration, and its impact on the strategy of individual firms, through such techniques as game theoretic analysis and network models (Johanson and Mattson, 1987). We expect more attention to be paid to the determinants and effects of collaborative ventures now being formed between MNEs from advanced countries (Contrator and Lorange, 1987), and between MNEs and their customers and suppliers.

We foresee a renewed interest in identifying and evaluating the ownership-specific advantages of firms, with particular focus on entrepreneurship, the ability of management to identify and coordinate a range of core skills and assets through a variety of organizational routes, and to promote operational flexibility in a volatile world environment; global marketing networks; the creation and use made of computer-related information and communications technology; and a variety of cross-cultural management-related issues. Finally, we would perceive a gradual interweaving of the approaches of the economist, business analyst and organizational theorist to our understanding of international production, although within these and related disciplines, theorizing and empirical work will become both more technically sophisticated and more policy oriented.

NOTES

1. Defined as production financed by foreign direct investment and undertaken by multinational enterprises.

2. The proceeds of which were published under the editorship of Ohlin et al. (1977)

3. But see our remarks in the second section of this paper.

4. For a recent review of the literature on intra-industry trade, see Tharakan (1984).

5. For an elaboration of this thesis see Dunning and Norman (1985).

6. A full account of the eclectic paradigm is given in Dunning (1981). See also Dunning (1983a and 1986d); Dunning and McQueen (1981); Dunning and Norman (1985); and Norman, Flanagan, and Seymour (1985) for some extensions and applications of the concept.

7. Dunning (1981), p. 27.

8. Teece (1983) uses a rather different terminology, namely *production and transaction advantages.*

9. For example, as identified by Bain (1956) as monopoly power, product differentiation, absolute cost barriers and government intervention.

10. See, for example, an interesting paper by Buckley (1986) presented to the London meeting of the Academy of International Business in November 1986.

11. See especially Casson (1979), Buckley and Casson (1985), Teece (1981 and 1985), Hennart (1986), and Rugman (1986). The word "failure" is an unfortunate one as it implies that there is an alternative transactional mechanism which is superior to the market. This is not necessarily the case.

12. As, for example, occurs in the case of "natural monopolies" and in industries with high sunk or developmental costs.

13. For example, in the United Kingdom, Japanese affiliates dominate the color TV sector partly because their parent companies prefer this route of entry rather than licensing their competitive advantages to U.K. producers; but partly too, because they are more successful at internalizing intermediate product transactions, than, for example are their U.S. counterparts.

14. In that what might be (or was) *exogenous* the firm is (or now becomes) *endogenous.*

15. We would also accept with Hennart (1982, 1986) that a privileged access to technology or capital may enable a firm to internalize cross-border intermediate product markets. We would, however, suggest that the privileged access per se arises because of an *operational* rather than an *organizational* failure of that market, in the sense that it discrimi-

nates in favor of particular groups of transactors, rather than it fails as a transactional mode, c.f. some other mode, for example, a firm.

16. For a useful distinction between transferable and nontransferable intermediate products, see Lall (1980).

17. It is possible for government intervention to be directed to counteracting or alleviating the affects of market failure as well as distorting the pattern of resource allocation to meet its social and strategic goals. See especially page 113, Table 5.2 in Dunning (1981).

18. The concept of 'induced' or 'managed' comparative advantage is gaining strength in the literature. (See for example Scott and Lodge, 1985; Teece, 1987.) It suggests that, at a given moment of time, a country's productive assets consist not only of the natural resources then available (defined in the H-O-S sense) but the accumulated manmade assets of the past; the way in which these are organized; and the attitudes of its people towards wealth creation and economic security, and towards the rest of the world. The literature further suggests that government may and does play a major role in fashioning the strategy for resource allocation and income distribution; the transaction costs of markets; and of the ideological, cultural and work ethic of its population.

19. Sometimes referred to as the environment, systems and policy (ESP) paradigm. See Koopman and Montias (1971) and Dunning (1981). See also a paper by Boddewyn (1986).

20. See, for example, Robock and Simmonds (1983) and Rugman, Lecraw, and Booth (1985).

21. See particularly Porter (1985) and (1986), Hamel and Prahalad (1987), Lahdepaa and Ansoff (1987). The difference between the firm-specific variables identified by these scholars and those of their predecessors is that the latter concentrated on the *structural* characteristics of firms, e.g., size, age, product composition, etc., while the former focused on *operational*, i.e., strategic-related characteristics, such as those identified by above.

22. It is one of the more irritating characteristics of academic researchers (and the present author is no exception!) for them to invent their own nomenclature for concepts that are familiar under different names to other researchers. Thus Porter's concept of configuration is for all intents and purposes the same as our location advantages; while his coordination dimension is similar to those aspects of internalization that relate to the common governance of value-adding activities. Finally Porter's competitive advantages make up a major part of our concept of ownership advantages. The only difference, as far as I can see, is that our concept of ownership advantages *may* include attributes of firms that more accurately reflect their monopolistic power than their competitive prowess.

23. Some of these were identified by the author when Aliber's thesis (Aliber, 1970) was first put forward (Dunning, 1971). See also more recent criticisms by Gray (1982) and Teece (1986).

24. For a more extended analysis of the differences and similarities between the Kojima and the eclectic and inter-

nalization paradigm, see Buckley (1983) and (1985) and Gray (1985).

25. Unless the asset is sold outright in the first place.

26. This suggests that economists interested in explaining the international allocation of activity both by firms and countries needed to be versed in modern trade and location theory, industrial organization theory and the theory of the firm, and on the way in which each interacts with the other. Both Casson (1985a), and Norman and Dunning (1984) take up and illustrate this point. See also page 000–000 of this reading.

27. See Kogut (1983). At the same time, the extent and pattern of market failure may itself be country-specific. Compare, for example, the organizational structures and subcontracting relationships of U.S. and Japanese firms (Imai 1985; Sullivan and Nonaka 1986).

28. A first attempt to do this by use of cluster analysis was made in Chapter 5 of Dunning (1981).

29. For example, while it may be possible to identify the major variables influencing all import substitution FDI, there may be additional factors specific to (say) Swedish investment in the Thai car industry.

30. See, for example, some work on these lines by Graham (1986) and Johanson and Mattson (1987).

31. For a full explanation, see Chapter 5 of Dunning (1981 and 1986c). The term "cycle" was used in that it was predicated that a country both started as a zero net outward and, at a later stage in its development, returned to that position when its inward direct investment stake was balanced by its (growing) outward direct investment stake. In retrospect, the term "path" might have been a better word to describe the process of change in a country's international direct investment position.

32. Hence the acquisition or part acquisition of European and U.S. high-technology firms (particularly those in difficult financial straits) by, for example, Indian, Middle Eastern, and Chinese firms.

33. The role of government is one of the most idiosyncratic to evaluate. In the 1970s and 1980s, for example, there have been quite dramatic swings in the policies of individual countries to inward investment, according to the government in power. Insofar as it is possible to generalize, the more right (left) wing a government is in relation to its predecessor, the more (less) liberal its attitude is likely to be towards inward and outward foreign direct investment and indeed to private enterprise as a whole.

34. Most countries are in fact negative net outward investors, that is, net inward investors.

35. For example, MNEs may continue to concentrate their high-value (e.g., research and development) activities in countries that have a comparative advantage in the supply of highly trained manpower, while locating the low-value-added activities in countries that have a comparative advantage in the supply of low- or semiskilled labor.

36. Not considered in the original version of the theory. For an elaboration see Dunning (1986c).

37. For a review of the literature see Oman (1984) and Buckley and Casson (1985).

38. With some noticeable exceptions, for example, the work of Hirsch (1976), Gray (1982), Ethier (1986), and Markusen (1986).

39. And no distinction appears to be made between multi-activity and single-activity trading firms.

40. Using managers as a generic term for decision takers.

41. For example, why are most Japanese manufacturing subsidiaries in the United Kingdom headed by a Japanese expatriate whereas most U.S. subsidiaries have a U.K. national as chief executive?

42. See also some interesting work on the structure of decision taking in U.K. subsidiaries in the 1970s by Young, Hood, and Hamill (1985).

43. Porter (1980) identifies six of these, namely, the presence of specialized assets, fixed costs, strategic exit barriers, information constraints, managerial emotions and pride, and government-related barriers.

44. The question of a reduction in foreign production in toto and that in a particular country and/or sector needs more careful distinction than it has been given up to now.

45. We use the term net benefits and costs because there are often costs *and* benefits of using both routes for transacting goods and services.

46. It is interesting that there is abundant literature on the theory of the growth of the firm (which, in practice, often occurs as a result of the expansion of *part* of a firm's activities), but very little on the decline of the firm. Yet particularly in times of rapid technological change, growth and decline are handmaidens to each other.

47. Ohmae (1985) suggests that while labor costs in many developing countries are only one-third of those in developed countries, the direct labor costs in the major competitive manufacturing companies represent less than 10 percent of total costs. The savings on costs in producing in developing countries is often more than outweighed by the transport costs between developing and developed countries. Moreover, as real wage costs rise in developing countries, these savings are likely to fall.

48. It is worth emphasizing at this point that internalization is not without its costs and multinationality may bring diseconomies, external to particular affiliates and internal to the MNE.

49. See Dunning and McQueen (1981) and Casson (1986b). In both these latter cases, contractual agreements of one kind or another have enabled the contractor to gain many of the benefits of integration without the costs.

50. For a summary of some interesting work on the integration of information systems in manufacturing see DeMeyer and Ferdows (1984). For a general view of changing corporate strategies in a time of technological change, see Ergas (1985) and Dunning (1986c).

51. As, for example, set out by Porter (1980, 1985 and 1986) and Kogut (1985a). The expression "competitive advantage" may be interpreted as ownership-specific advantage, while the comparative advantage of countries appears synonymous with our location advantage. While the business strategy approach gives more emphasis to the positioning of firms in the sectors in which they compete, the

eclectic paradigm places more stress on the organizational form of transactional relationships.

REFERENCES

Aliber, R. (1970). A theory of foreign direct investment. In C. P. Kindleberger, *The international corporation.* Cambridge, Mass.: MIT Press.

Aliber, R. (1983). Money, multinationals and sovereigns. In C. P. Kindlberger and D. B. Audresch, *The multinational corporation in the 1980s.* Cambridge, Mass.: MIT Press.

Bain, J. S. (1956). *Barriers to new competition.* Cambridge, Mass.: Harvard University Press.

Boddewyn, J. (1983). Foreign divestment theory: Is it the reverse of FDI theory? *Weltwirtschaftliches Archiv,* 119:345–355.

Boddewyn, J. (1986, November). International political strategy: A fourth "generic" strategy? Paper presented to the Academy of International Business Annual Meeting, London.

Buckley, P. J. (1983). Macroeconomic versus international business approach to direct foreign investment: A comment on professor Kojima's interpretation. *Hitosubashi Journal of Economics,* 24:95–100.

Buckley, P. J. (1985). The economic analysis of the multinational enterprise: Reading v. Japan. *Hitosubashi Journal of Economics,* 26:117–124.

Buckley, P. J. (1986, November). *The limits of explanation: Tests of the theory of the multinational enterprise.* Paper presented to Academy of International Business Annual Meeting, London, November.

Cantwell, J. A. (1986). *Technological innovation and international production in the industrial world: A study of the accumulation of capital in international networks.* Ph.D. thesis, University of Reading, England.

Casson, M. C. (1979). *Alternatives to the multinational enterprise.* London: Macmillan.

Casson, M. C. (1985). The theory of foreign direct investment. In P. J. Buckley and M. C. Casson, *The economic theory of the multinational enterprise.* London: Macmillan.

Casson, M. C. (1986a). General theories of the multinational enterprise: A critical examination. In P. Hertner and G. Jones, eds. *Multinationals: Theory and history.* Aldershot and Brookfield, Vt.: Gower.

Casson, M. C. (1986b, January). The role of vertical integration in the shipping industry. *Journal of Transport Economics and Policy,* 22:7–29.

Casson, M. C. (1986c, May). *Alternative contractual arrangements for technology transfer: New evidence from business history.* University of Reading Discussion Papers in International Investment and Business Studies No. 95.

Casson, M. C. (1986d). Foreign divestment and international rationalization: The sale of Chrysler (U.K.) to Peugot. In J. Coyne and N. Wright, eds., *Divestment and strategic change.* Oxford: Philip Allan.

Casson, M. C. (1987). *The firm and the market.* Oxford: Basil Blackwell.

Coase, R. H. (1937, November). The nature of the firm. *Economica,* 4:386–405.

Contractor F., and P. Lorange. (1987). *Cooperative strategies in international business.* Lexington, Mass.: Lexington Books.

Davidson, W. D. (1976). Patterns of factor saving innovation in the industrialized world. *European Economic Review,* 8:207–217.

Davidson, W. D., and D. G. McFeteridge. (1984). International technology transaction and theory of the firm. *Journal of Industrial Economics,* 32:253–264.

Davidson, W. D., and D. G. McFeteridge. (1985, Summer). Key characteristics in the choice of international transfer mode. *Journal of International Business Studies,* 16.

DeMeyer, A., and K. Ferdows. (1984, December). *Integration of information systems in manufacturing.* INSEAD Research Working Papers No. 13.

Dunning, J. H., ed. (1971). *The multinational enterprise.* London: Allen & Unwin.

Dunning, J. H. (1981). *International production and the multinational enterprise.* London: Allen & Unwin.

Dunning, J. H. (1982). International business in a changing world environment. *Banco Nazionale del Lavoro Quarterly Review,* 143:351–373.

Dunning, H. J. (1983a). Changes in the structure of international production: The last 100 years. In M. C. Casson, ed., *The growth of international business.* London: Allen & Unwin.

Dunning, J. H. (1983b). Market power of the firm and international transfer of technology. *International Journal of Industrial Organisation,* 1:333–351.

Dunning, J. H. (1986a). *Japanese participation in British industry.* London: Croom Helm.

Dunning, J. H. (1986b). *Decision-making structures in U.S. and Japanese manufacturing affiliates in the U.K.: Some similarities and contrasts.* Geneva: ILO Working Paper No. 41.

Dunning, J. H. (1986c). The investment development cycle and third world multinationals. In K. M. Khan, ed., *Multinationals of the south.* London: Francis Porter.

Dunning, J. H. (1987a). International business and economic restructuring. In N. Hood and J. E. Vahlne, eds., *Strategies in global competition.* London: Croom Helm.

Dunning, J. H. (1987b, July). *Cross-border corporation integration and regional integration.* University of Reading Discussion Papers in International Investment and Business Studies No. 105.

Dunning, J. H., and J. Cantwell. (1986, December). *The changing role of multinational enterprises in the international creation, transfer and diffusion of technology.* University of Reading Discussion Papers in International Investment and Business Studies No. 101.

Dunning, J. H., and M. McQueen (1981, December). The eclectic theory of international production: A case study of the international hotel industry. *Managerial and Deci-*

sion Economics. 2:197–210.

Dunning, J. H., and R.D. Pearce. (1985). *The world's largest industrial enterprises 1962–83.* Aldershot: Graver.

Dunning, J. H., and G. Norman, (1985). Intra-industry production as a form of international economic involvement. In A. Erdilek, ed., *Multinationals as mutual invaders.* London: Croom Helm.

Dunning, J. H., and A. Rugman. (1985, May). The influence of Hymer's dissertation on theories of foreign direct investment. *American Economic Review,* 228–232.

Ergas, H. (1984). *Why do some countries innovate more than others?* Brussels: Center for European Policy Studies.

Ergas, H. (1985). Corporate strategies in transition. In A. Jacquemin, *Industrial policy and international trade.* London: Cambridge University Press.

Ethier, W. J. (1986). The multinational firm. *Quarterly Journal of Economics,* 101:805–833.

Franko, L. (1976). *The European multinationals.* New York: Harper.

Graham, E. M. (1978). Transatlantic investment by multinational firms: A rivalistic phenomenon. *Journal of Post Kevnesian Economics,* I (Fall).

Graham, E. M. (1985). Intra-industry direct investment, market structure, firm rivalry and technological performance. In A. Erdilek, ed., *Multinationals as mutual invaders.* London. Croom Helm.

Graham, E. M. (1986). *Internal economics, oligopoly reaction and dynamic contestability in global industries: A first cut at synthesis.* Mimeo.

Gray, H. P. (1982). Towards a unified theory of international trade, international production and direct foreign investment. In J. Black and J. H. Dunning, eds., *International capital movements.* London: MacMillan.

Gray, H. P. (1985, December). Multinational corporations and global welfare: An extension of Kojima and Ozawa. *Hitosubashi Journal of Economics,* 26:125–132.

Grosse, R. R. (1985, Spring). An imperfect competition theory of the MNE. *Journal of International Business Studies,* 16:57–80.

Grubel, H. G. And P. J. Lloyd. (1975). *Intra-industry trade, the theory and measurement of international trade in differentiated products.* London: Macmillan.

Guisinger, S. (1985). *Investment incentives and performance requirements.* New York: Praeger.

Hamel, G. and C. K. Prahalad. (1987). Creating global strategic capability. In N. Hood and J. E. Vahne, eds., *Strategies in global competition.* London: Croom Helm.

Hayes, R. H. and S. C. Wheelwright. *Restoring our competitive edge: Competing through manufacturing.* Chichester and New York: John Wiley.

Helpman, E., (1984). A simple theory of international trade with multinational corporations. *Journal of Political Economy,* 92:447–51.

Hennart, J. F. (1982). *A theory of multinational enterprise.* Ann Arbor: University of Michigan Press.

Hennart, J. F. (1986). What is internalization? *Weltwirt-*

schaftliches Archiv, 122:791–804.

Hertner, P., and G. Jones. (1986). *Multinationals: Theory and history.* Aldershot and Brookfield, Vt.: Gower.

Hirsch, S. (1976). An international trade and investment theory of the firm. *Oxford Economic Papers,* 28:258–70.

Horst, T. O. (1972, August). Firm and industry determinants of the decision to invest abroad. *Review of Economics and Statistics,* 54.

Horstman, I., and J. R. Markusen. (1986). *Licensing v direct investment: A model of internalization by the multinational enterprise.* University of Western Ontario, mimeo.

Hymer, S. (1960). *The international operations of national firms: A study of direct investment.* Ph.D. thesis, MIT (published by MIT Press under the same title in 1976).

Imai, K. (1985, July). Network organization and incremental innovation in Japan. Institute of Business Research, Hitotubashi University. Discussion Paper No. 122, July.

Johanson J. and L. G. Mattsson. 1987. Internationalization in industrial systems. A network approach. In N. Hood and J. E. Vahne, ed., *Strategies in global competition.* London: Croom Helm.

Knickerbocker, F. T. (1973). *Oligopolistic reaction and the multinational enterprise.* Cambridge, Mass.: Harvard University Press.

Kogut, B. (1983). Foreign direct investment as a sequential process. In C. P. Kindleberger and D. Audretsch, eds., *The multinational corporation in the 1980s.* Cambridge, Mass.: MIT Press.

Kogut, B. (1985a, Summer). Designing global strategies: Corporate and competitive value added chain. *Sloan Management Review,* 25:15–28.

Kogut, B. (1985b, Fall). Designing global strategies: Profiting from operational flexibility. *Sloan Management Review,* 26:27–38.

Kojima, K. (1978). *Direct foreign investment.* London: Croom Helm.

Kojima, K. (1982). Macroeconomic versus international business approach to foreign direct investment. *Hitosubashi Journal of Economics,* 23:1–19.

Kojima, K. and T. Ozawa. (1984). Micro and macro-economic models of direct foreign investment: Towards a synthesis. *Hitosubashi Journal of Economics,* 25 (2): 1–20.

Kojima, K. (1985). Towards a theory of industrial, restructuring and dynamic comparative advantage. *Hitosubashi Journal of Economics,* 26 (December):135–145.

Koopman, K, and J. M. Montias. (1971). On the description and comparison of economic systems. In A. Eckstein, *Comparison of economic systems.* Berkeley: University of California Press.

Krugman, P. M. (1981). Intra-industry specialization and the gains from trade. *Journal of Political Economy,* 89.

Krugman, P. M. (1983). The new theories of international trade and the multinational enterprise. In C. P. Kindleberger and D. Audretsch, eds., *The multinational corporation in the 1980s.* Cambridge, Mass.: MIT Press.

Lahdepaa, J., and K. Ansoff. (1987). A network analysis of international transactions. In N. Hood and J. E. Vahne, eds., *Strategies in global competition*. London: Croom Helm.

Lake, A. W. (1976a, March). *Transnational activity and market entry in the semi-conductor industry*. NBER Working Paper 126.

Lake, A. W. (1976b, March). Foreign competition and U.K. pharmaceutical industry. NBER Working Paper 127.

Lall, S. (1980). Monopolistic advantages and foreign involvement by U.S. manufacturing industry. *Oxford Economic Papers*, 32:102–122.

Markusen, J. R. (1984). Multinationals, multi-plant economies and the gain from trade. *Journal of International Economics*, 16:205–216.

Mason, R. H. (1980). A comment on professor Kojima's Japanese type versus American type of technology transfer. *Hitosubashi Journal of Economics*, 20:242–252.

Nicholas, S. (1986). The theory of multinational enterprise as a transactional mode. In P. Hertner and G. Jones, eds., *Multinationals: Theory and history*. Aldershot: Gower.

Norman, G., R. Flanagan, and H. Seymour. (1985). *A theory of international production in the international construction industry*. University of Reading Discussion Papers in International Investment and Business Studies No. 87.

Norman, G., R. Flanagan, and J. H. Dunning. 1985. Intra-industry foreign direct investment: Its rationale and trade effects. *Weltwirtschaftliches Archiv*, 120:522–540.

North, D. C. 1985. Transaction costs in history. *Journal of European Economic History*, 14:557–574.

Ohlin, B., P. O. Hesselborn, and P. M. Wiskman, eds, 1977. *The international allocation of economic activity*. London: MacMillan.

Ohmae, K. (1985). *Triad power*. New York: The Free Press.

Oman, C. (1984). *New forms of international investment in developing countries*. Paris: OECD.

Pavitt, K. (1987). International patterns of technological accumulation. In N. Hood and J. E. Vahne, eds., *Strategies in global competition*. London: Croom Helm.

Porter, M. F., (1980). *Competitive strategy*. New York: The Free Press.

Porter, M. F., (1985). *Competitive advantage*. New York: The Free Press.

Porter, M. F., ed. (1986). *Competition in global industries*. Boston: Harvard Business School Press.

Pralahad, C. K., and Y. L. Doz. (1987). Quality of management: An emerging source of global competitive advantage. In N. Hood and J. E. Vahne, eds., *Strategies in global competition*. London: Croom Helm.

Robock, S. F., and K. Simmonds. (1983). *International business and the multinational enterprise*, 3rd ed. Homewood, Ill.: Richard D. Irwin.

Rugman, A. M. (1979). *International diversification and the multinational enterprise*. Farnborough: Lexington.

Rugman, A. M. (1981). *Inside the multinationals: The economics of internal markets*. London: Croom Helm.

Rugman, A. M. (1986). New theories of multinational enterprises: An assessment of internalisation theory. *Bulletin of Economic Research*, 38:101–118.

Rugman, A. M., D. J. Lecraw, and I. D. Booth. (1985). *International business: Firm and environment*. New York: McGraw-Hill.

Scott, B. R. and G. R. Lodge, eds. *U.S. competitiveness in the world economy*. Boston: Harvard Business School Press.

Stopford, J. (1982). *The world directory of multinational enterprises*. Basingstoke: Macmillan.

Sullivan, J. J., and I. Nonaka. (1986, Fall). The application of organizational learning theory to Japanese and American management. *Journal of International Business Studies*, 127–147.

Teece, D. J. (1981). The multinational enterprise: Market failure and market power considerations. *Sloan Management Review*, 22:3–17.

Teece, D. J. (1983). Technological and organizational factors in the theory of the multinational enterprise. In M. C. Casson, ed., *Growth of international business*. London: Allen & Unwin.

Teece, D. J. (1986). Transaction cost economics and the multinational enterprise. *Journal of Economic Behavior and Organization*. 7:21–45.

Teece, D. J., ed. (1987). *The competitive challenge*. Cambridge, Mass.: Ballinger.

Tharakan, P. K. M. (1984). *The economics of intra-industry trade*. Amsterdam: North-Holland.

Tolentino, P. (1987). The global shift in international production: The growth of multinational enterprises from the developing countries: The Philippines. Ph.D. thesis, University of Reading.

Vernon, R. 1974. The location of economic activity. In J. H. Dunning, *Economic analysis and the multinational enterprise*. London: Allen & Unwin.

Vernon, R. (1983). Organizational and institutional responses to international risk. In R. J. Herring, ed., *Managing international risk*. Cambridge: Cambridge University Press.

Vernon, R. (1985). Comment on chapter by J. H. Dunning and G. Norman. In A. Erdilek, ed., *Multinationals as mutual invaders*. London: Croom Helm.

Williamson, O. (1981). The modern corporation: Origins, evolution, attributes. *Journal of Economic Literature*, 19:1537–1568.

Young, S., N. Hood, and J. Hamill. (1985). Decision making. In *Foreign owned multinational subsidiaries in the United Kingdom*. Geneva: ILO Working Paper No. 35.

27

WHY GLOBAL MANUFACTURING?

C. BADEN-FULLER AND J. M. STOPFORD

The division of labour is limited by the extent of the market.

Adam Smith, Wealth of Nations, *1776*

Nothing it seems is new in the arguments about how firms can serve their markets. As markets have become more international the current debate is about how firms may create advantages from exploiting the division of labour in new ways. Production, research, design, marketing and other functions in a firm's value-adding activities all have the potential for enhancing competitiveness if they are specialised and concentrated in one location to serve multiple national markets. Border-crossing specialisation in a wide variety of innovative ways has been loosely labelled as 'global strategy." The alternative approach is to adopt a "country-centred" approach whereby the multinational firm replicates its business structure in each market: local production, marketing and sales are combined within a national profit centre. The question then, is under what conditions will a global approach provide for gains greater than those of a country-centred one?

To confront this question we examined the record of the major domestic appliance industry ("white goods") in Europe. It is commonly accepted that the success of the Italian major appliance industry was based on adopting a European strategy as opposed to a national one. Decreasing costs of transport, communications and tariffs taken together with assertions of convergence in national taste seemed to point to an inexorable trend towards global strategies. Yet it is by no means clear that the trend is one way. Persistent differences in national income levels and taste, combined with changing economics of supply as more flexible manufacturing systems are introduced, can halt and even reverse the trend. We set out to establish whether nationally focused companies such as Hotpoint and Thomson could compete against large multinationals adopting global, or export-oriented, strategies.

The authors are grateful to the Economic and Social Research Council, UK, for generous financial support and to executives in the industry for their time and patience in supplying them with data and opinions. They are also grateful for the research assistance of P. Nicholaides (on pricing), L Forlai, S. Evans and B. Rimmer (on profitability), and to colleagues at London and elsewhere for comments and encouragement.

Source Multinational Business, No. 1. (1988), pp. 15–25.

THE EVIDENCE

Intra-industry Trade

The substantial volume of intra-European trade is strong evidence that the European major appliance industry in general, and washing machines in particular, *has been* fairly global. In the 1960s, the Italian producers Zanussi, Zoppas, Indesit, Ignis (IRE) and Candy captured a large share of the European market by providing a low-cost, well designed range of appliances aimed at the mass market. In the late 1970s and early 1980s more than one-third of the European consumption of major appliances (re-frigerators, freezers, washing machines, dishwashers) was produced by Italian manufacturers. West German companies also exported a substantial part of their output, principally to their close neighbours Austria, Switzerland and Northern Europe. Figure 1

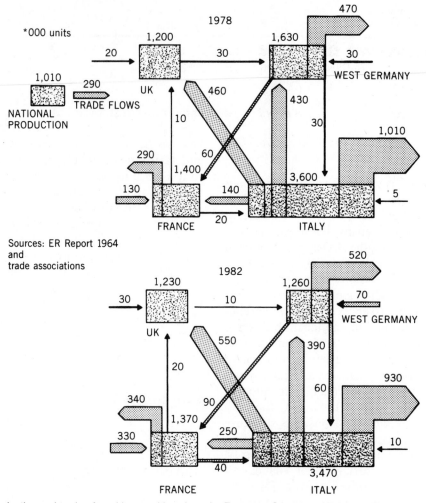

Figure 1   Production and trade of washing machines in major European Countries, 1978 and 1982

shows the patterns of trade for washing-machines between the UK, France, West Germany and Italy for the years 1978 and 1982. These four countries are Europe's major producers.

From this diagram it can be seen that Italy accounts for more than 45 percent of the production of these four countries, and that West Germany is the next largest with more than 25 per cent, followed by France and the UK. The extent of trade is considerable: more than 40 per cent of all washing machine production in

these four countries is transported across national boundaries.

The Competitive Structure

As might be expected in a heavily traded industry, the appliance industry has a high degree of concentration of competitors. About two-thirds of the production and sales of major appliances in general (particularly washing machines) is accounted for by a dozen large companies. The other association often made with extensive trade, the prevalence of global strategies, is not however encountered in this industry. Table 1 lists all the major European appliance producers and divides this list into three strategic categories:

- companies with plants and sales in several countries adopting a global strategy (global players)
- companies with a large production base in one country, but involved in substantial exports (exporters)
- nationally focused companies (national players).

The two global players, Electrolux and Philips, are the largest firms and together supply more than 28 per cent of Europe's major appliances and 22 percent of Europe's washing machines.

Electrolux, the Swedish-based multinational, has its strength in the Scandinavian market and the North European countries. Its principal plants are in Sweden, with other plants in the UK and France. Recently it acquired Italy's Zanussi, Europe's largest appliance producer. Zanussi's principal plants are located in Italy, with additional manufacturing in Spain. Electrolux-Zanussi produces the full range of major appliances, selling the greater part under a wide variety of brand names, as well as supplying "own-label" products for other producers and retailers. Electrolux has also acquired White, the third largest US producer of appliances, and the appliance divisions of Thorn, a British producer of refrigerators and cookers.

Acquisition has also been important in the expansion of Philips, the Dutch multinational. In the early 1970s it acquired the Italian company Ignis (now called IRE), then Europe's second largest producer of appliances. Nearly a decade later Philips bought Bauknecht, the

Table 1 Leading European Major Domestic Appliance Producers with Approximate Market Shares

	All Appliances (%)	Washing Machines (%)
Global players		
Electrolux-Zanussi	15	11
Philips-IRE-Bauknecht	13	11
Exporters		
Bosch-Siemens	8	6
AEG	4	4
Indesit	4	4
Ariston Merloni	3	3
Candy	3	4
Miele	3	3
Hoover	2	5
National players		
Thompson	6	7
Hotpoint	3	6
Lec	2	—
Thorn[a]	2	—
Creda[b]	1	—
Others (mainly national)	30	35

[a]Now part of Electrulux, Thorn does not make washing machines. [b]Now Hotpoint
Source: Industry estimates based on market surveys.

bankrupt West German appliance producer. Today, most of Philips major appliance European production capacity is in Italy and West Germany, with some additional capacity in France. Philips also has plants outside Europe and is negotiating links with Whirlpool, the largest US producer of appliances.

Both Philips and Electrolux are involved in extensive European trade, producing appliances in one country (typically Italy), and selling them not only in the country of production, but also other European countries. Philips is truly a global player rather than a series of nationally focused companies grouped under common ownership. Though we label Electrolux a global player, its strategy is not uniform. It adopts national strategies in North America, but more global strategies elsewhere in Europe.

The second group, the exporters, consists of those companies which have production located in a single country but which sell a substantial amount of their output in other European markets. These companies include: Bosch-Siemens (a joint venture between Bosch and Siemens), AEG and Miele, all of which have plants located in West Germany and export up to half of their production; Candy, Indesit and Ariston Merloni, which are based in Italy and export nearly 60 per cent of their output; and Hoover, the US-owned British manufacturer which exports 30 per cent of its output. (Candy and Merloni have some overseas production but it is quite small.) Together, these companies account for 27 per cent of all of Europe's production in domestic appliances and 29 per cent of all washing machine production.

There is a third group of companies, the national players, which produce and sell primarily in their local country-market, exporting less than 10 per cent of their output. Of interest are the French company Thomson, with about 6–7 per cent of the European market, and the British companies Hotpoint, Lee and Creda. Hotpoint and Thomson are the two largest na-

Table 2 Leading Companies' Market Shares, Washing Machines, 1984 (per cent)

UK

Hotpoint	25
Hoover	20
Indesit	9
Servis	8
Zanussi	8
Thorn (Bendix)	8
Philips	6
Candy	3
Ariston Merioni	2
Others	11

France

Thomson (Brandt, Thomson)	41
Philips (Philips, Radio La, Laden)	20
Electrolux (Arthur Martin, Zanussi)	14
Bosch-Siemens	4
Hoover	2
Miele	2
AEG	2
Others	15

West Germany

Bosch-Siemens (Bosch, Siemens)	25
Quelle	20
Miele	16
AEG	14
Bauknecht (Philips)	7
Zanker	4
Others	14

Italy

Electrolux-Zanussi (Rex, Zoppas, etc.)	28
Candy	15
SMEG	12
San Giorgio	7
Indesit	6
AEG	5
Merioni (Ariston)	5
Siemens	4
Philips (Ignis)	3
Others	15

Note: Names in parentheses are the leading brand names where different from company names. Quelle is a department store brand.

Source: Estimates from industry executives and market surveys.

tional producers of washing machines, having 15 per cent of the European market between them. There is also a fourth group which we do not discuss here: low-cost exporters from the East bloc and some small specialist exporters from Italy and Spain.

Marketing and Consumer Preferences

As might be expected, the exporters have tended to use a single name for all their markets and many have also adopted common marketing themes. By contrast, the global players use multiple brands, largely because they have retained the brands of the companies they acquired. In some cases multiple names are used in the same market. Philips, for example, sells in France under the Radio La and Laden brands as well as the international brand of Philips (using the same logo as for its many other products), and the Bauknecht label for much of its German-sourced output.

Overall the penetration of international brands has been limited. Although these brands are *available* in all countries, in many countries they command only small shares in comparison with the local national firms. German brands have, however, had greater success in penetrating the adjacent but small markets in Austria and Switzerland.

Limited penetration by the international brands is one measure of the fragmentation of demand. Another is consumers' preference for different product features. Take the case of washing machines. Of all the product variations possible, two features—spin-speed and method of loading—show how widely based are consumer preferences. Spin-speeds range from 400 revolutions per minute to 1,200 revolutions per minute. Some machines are loaded from the top, others from the front. There are additional variants such as "economy" for water and detergent, and there is a combination machine: the washer-drier.

There are striking differences in the sales patterns in the four major markets. In France, top-loading machines account for about 70 per cent of the market. Front-loading machines typically sell at a small discount to top-loaders, despite the fact that the production cost of a top-loading machine is about the same as that of a front-loading machine. West German consumers prefer machines which are front-loaders and have high spin-speeds of 800 rpm or more. Italian consumers prefer front-loaders with low spin-speeds, typically 400–600 rpm. The long hot summers seem to make high spin-speed machines less valuable in Italy. UK consumers lie between the West Germans and Italians, having a preference for 600–800 rpm, front-loading machines. In the much more homogeneous UK market, regional and climatic differences have much less impact on purchasing behavior.

For Europe, the distinctions are deeply ingrained in cultural behaviour to the extent that a machine which is a popular seller in one market may have only a relatively small potential sale in another market. Curiously, these cultural distinctions have not been static. In the mid-1960s, when automatic machines were in the early phase of their life cycle, French and British preferences appeared to be reversed. At that time the British were buying a large proportion of their automatic machines as top-loaders, and the French as front-loaders. Between the mid-1960s and the end of the 1970s the patterns changed but did not converge.

Such evidence from the market place strongly suggests that Europe cannot be considered as an homogeneous market. The sense of fragmentation is enforced when one considers the required tailoring of machines to fit national tastes (hence diminishing economies of scale), entry barriers and differences among national channels of distribution.

Costs

The traditional view has been that, providing output is homogeneous, there are significant scale economies up to and perhaps above a capacity of 1 mn units per year. This view seems to be confirmed by the policies of Japanese and US manufacturers, all of which operate such large plants, and by the policies of Zanussi and Bosch-Siemens who built large plants in Europe during the 1960s and 1970s.

Other producers have, however, taken a different view. Today, the typical plant size in Europe is quite small, about 250,000 units per year. Given that the combined production of the producers in the UK, France, West Germany and Italy exceeds 7 mm units a year for all major appliances, the obvious question arises: is the European configuration inefficient?

Comparisons of productivity among assembly lines shows that until recently the highest productivity, 600–1,000 units per worker per year, is achieved in plants whose scale is 200,000–300,000 units a year. Large plants rarely achieve an output per man greater than 400 units per year.

This is because large plants typically serve many countries and must produce a wide range of models; small plants typically produce for one or two countries. Though large plants do not suffer tariff penalties within the EC and transport costs are relatively insignificant—about 5 per cent of the wholesale price—they necessarily incur cost penalties when products need adaptation to different local needs. Some of these differences are minor, such as fascia plates bearing instructions in the local language. Other differences, such as spin-speed and method of loading, are more major and more expensive.

Barriers to Entry

The UK washing machine market provides a clear illustration of the barriers to entry under today's conditions. The height of that barrier goes a long way to explaining why it has become much more difficult to create an international brand presence in a national market.

Two major factors impede the establishment of a new brand on an existing market: the high sunk costs (that is, non-recoverable costs) of advertising and other selling costs; and the need for after-sales service. Gaining access to distribution is also a problem as there are no distributors of importance which span the national boundaries, and outside the UK most of the distribution of appliances is undertaken by a large number of independently owned retailers (called independents). Retailers in general, and independents in particular, have a limited capacity for stocking and displaying major appliances. A new brand needs to create an awareness in the market to persuade retailers to stock the item, and this awareness can be created by advertising and the use of sales staff who visit retailers.

We can summarise the above by comparing the costs of a British manufacturer with 25 per cent of the home market with a continental manufacturer holding 5 per cent of the British market, and a second continental manufacturer with 1 per cent of the market—see Table 3. We assume, for convenience, that all companies have the same basic production costs of £150 a unit and are producing 500,000 units a year in a standard-size plant of minimum efficient scale. A UK producer faces distribution costs of, say, £6 a unit, and after-sales service costs of £3 a unit. Small-market-share foreign companies are estimated to face higher production costs due to smaller model runs, higher distribution costs because of greater distance, and higher service costs due to their small market share; these raise their costs before promotion by 10 per cent and 14 per cent.

Taking into account both kinds of promotion costs—advertising and sales office expenses—we estimate that an incumbent might spend £1 mn, and the two entrants £500,000 and £300,000 respectively. Thus, after promotion costs, the entrants face even more substantial cost penalties of 11 and 20 per cent, respectively.

The significance of the cost penalties is increased by the retaliation a prospective entrant

Table 3 Cost Structure of Incumbent and Entering Companies in the UK Washing Machine Market

	Incumbent[a]	Entrant A	Entrant B
Sales (units)	500,000	100,000	20,000
Market share	28%	5.5%	1%
Basic cost	£150	£155	£160
Transport	£6	£10	£15
Service costs	£3	£10	£6
Total	£159	£175	£181
Total promotional costs	£1 mn	£500,000	£300,000
Unit promotional costs	£2	£5	£12
Total unit cost	£161	£180	£193

[a]Incumbent is assumed to be an established U.K. company. Entrants A and B are assumed to be established continental companies.

can expect from the incumbents. Because of the static nature of the market, demand is inelastic, so that an entrant cannot expect to expand the market sufficiently to accommodate its entry, either by cutting prices or by spending money on advertising. Any successful entrant is likely to reduce the sales, and profits, of its rivals.

Incumbent companies have a variety of ways of retaliating. Advertising is one method, starting a price war is another, and launching new products or new brands is a third. UK companies have undertaken all three activities. The best known example was the retaliation against Rolls Bloom in the 1960s. The dangers of retaliation may be overrated, however. Although our earlier analysis of advertising shows the expenditure in the UK market over recent years has not been stable year on year, the changing patterns of expenditure cannot be linked directly to entry attempts. Rather, over the years, Hotpoint, the lead UK manufacturer, has increased its advertising significantly in a successful attempt to increase market share.

Are Global Producers More Profitable than Nationally Focused Companies?

Most export-oriented manufacturers have only a small share in their export markets, at least in comparison with leading national players. The consequent short production runs push up production costs, while dis-economies of local scale force up marketing costs. Additionally, companies need far more sophisticated information systems in order to serve multiple markets. Offsetting these higher costs are the potential benefits of large scale and scope. In this industry, however, economies of scale and scope appear to be of little importance, and if this holds true then exporters and global companies would be expected to have higher costs than national producers focusing on one market. This means that global and export-oriented companies operating in highly priced countries may not be more profitable.

And indeed we found this to be the case. We collected data on the profitability of the assembly and marketing divisions of the appliance business units of most of the major producers in the UK, Italy, Sweden and USA from publicly available records. We cross-checked our data with discussions with executives and, in some cases, sight of confidential management accounts. Three measures of profitability were used:

- return on sales (ROS)
- return on capital employed (ROCE)
- adjusted return on capital employed.

Table 4 shows the profitability of the major UK, Swedish and US appliance manufacturers for the years 1974 to 1985. The European companies account for almost half the European market, and the US companies for over 80 per cent of the US market. Generally, the global companies and exporters in the table have performed badly, both absolutely and compared with the nationally focused companies. Hotpoint, Lee and Creda, however—three nationally focused UK companies—have done well both absolutely and in comparison with US companies. Hotpoint is especially remarkable, as this company has increased its size, its UK market share and its profitability over the last ten years.

The profitability of the global player Philips has been particularly poor. Electrolux has fared better, but its accounts do not reflect the acquisition of Zanussi. The bulk of Electrolux's profits come from the Scandinavian plant, which has more than 70 per cent of the local market. The French operation is said to be unprofitable; nor is the British operation (shown in Table 4) very profitable. The Italian companies Indesit, Candy and Ariston Merloni have not performed as well as Hotpoint in recent years. The figures for Candy are not considered to be reliable, but Candy's management acknowledges that "Hotpoint has performed better than us."

Data on profitability of the French and West German manufacturers are not shown. We have discussed the profitability of appliances with Thomson, Bosch-Siemens, AEG and Bauknecht, and in some cases have seen and examined their accounts. Confidentially precludes us from revealing these in detail, but we are in a

Table 4 Profitability of Major Western Applicance Manufacturers (per cent)

Company	ROS			ROCE			Adjusted ROCE		
	1974–79	1980–84	1985	1974–79	1980–84	1985	1974–79	1980–84	1985
Global players and subsidiaries									
Electrolux AB	8.1	7.5	7.9	27.8	18.2	—	—	—	—
Electrolux UK	11.1	6.1	4.2	20.7	9.4	4.7	21.3	8.4	4.5
Zanussi	9.6	0.5	5.5	14.3	1.5	8.0	12.9	(2.0)	12.6
Philips IRE	4.2	3.6	1.5	11.4	10.1	4.2	7.3	7.0	5.3
Exporters									
Indesit	8.4	(5.2)	—	16.0	(10.0)	—	14.8	(21.6)	—
Merloni	9.1	9.0	5.1	17.7	13.0	8.3	16.1	12.5	10.5
Candy	4.3	5.5	3.3	11.4	12.2	8.9	10.0	29.9	12.1
Hoover	6.2	1.3	5.5	11.8	3.5	14.7	10.6	1.0	12.7
Nationals									
Hotpoint	2.3	8.9	12.5	6.6	23.2	37.9	7.3	19.0	34.7
TI Creda	8.4	11.9	9.1	35.1	34.7	11.8	35.0	35.7	23.1
Lee	7.4	7.6	5.7	21.7	21.1	14.6	19.4	20.9	14.8
USA									
GE	—	10.4	12.9	—	28.7	33.3	—	—	—
Whirlpool	9.8	10.1	9.3	20.0	19.8	18.3	—	—	—
White	—	6.4	—	—	13.5	—	—	—	—
Maytag	—	19.3	20.0	—	36.6	37.5	—	—	—

Note: Bracketed figures indicate a loss.

Sources: Published records.

position to observe that, taking the last ten years, the profitability of Thomson (a national player) has been greater than that of the three West German companies Bosch-Siemens, AEG and Bauknecht (all exporters). However, Thomson's performance has been uneven, and in 1985 it only broke even. Bosch-Siemens, in contrast, has consistently made a profit. AEG and Bauknecht have sustained periods of losses. This partly confirms the proposition that national companies have been more profitable over the long run than multinational companies and exporters.

Since 1980 the national players, Hotpoint and Creda, have been more profitable than any other European manufacturer in our survey, including the West German producers Bosch-Siemens, Bauknecht and AEG. Their profit records are in the same league as the three major American appliance producers, GE (General Electric), Whirlpool and White, Hotpoint's performance is especially impressive when one considers that it makes and sells refrigerators, washing machines and driers for the "middle market" of the UK, and these are sold in direct competition with machines produced by Hoover, Indesit, Candy, Ariston Merloni, Philips (which exports machines from its Italian plants), Bosch-Siemens and Bauknecht. Our analysis shows that a nationally focused strategy can be very profitable even where the company operates in a low priced country.

Global or National?

The European market for washing machines is mature and subject to extensive international trade. Despite this, the market has not become unified because there are strong and increasing barriers to gaining access to local distribution. These barriers are not accounted for by local government regulations, nor by tariffs, but rather they are a combination of factors: local consumer preference; sunk costs and scale economies in advertising, promotion and product development; and the necessity of manufacturing for local market needs.

As a consequence of these non-tariff barriers to trade, wholesale and retail prices of washing machines differ among European countries. The differences observed are large, with French retail prices nearly 50 per cent higher than those of the UK, and West German and Italian prices about 40 per cent higher than UK prices. Wholesale prices also differ substantially across countries.

The evidence is that in recent years nationally focused strategies have been successful. Globally organised and export-oriented manufacturers such as Philips, Electrolux, Candy, Merloni and Bosch-Siemens, operating in several high-priced countries, are less profitable than the large, nationally oriented companies in the UK and France. To fully understand these profitability differences we are undertaking further research into the costs of operating an integrated system across countries in this industry.

The evidence so far shows the power of Adam Smith's proposition. The market for domestic appliances in Europe is not unified—and so the international division of labour does not yield great rewards. For global strategies to become profitable in the future, the economies of the market (either on the demand or the supply side) must change so as to allow greater overall gains from policies of specialisation.

28

MANAGING MANUFACTURING RATIONALIZATION WITHIN MULTINATIONAL COMPANIES

Yves L. Doz

Reduction of tariffs and other trade barriers and the emergence of free trade areas in Western Europe have provided an opportunity to multinational companies (MNCs) manufacturing in several countries to have each of their plants specialize and ship production to other subsidiaries for sale or integration into finished products. Instead of multiproduct-multistage plants autonomously serving a national market, it has become feasible and economically attractive to develop plants that manufacture only one model or one product line, or are involved in only certain stages of the production process for the worldwide market.

Rationalization means shifting from a set of local-for-local plants, each serving its own national market with a broad product range, to an integrated network of large-scale production-specialized plants serving the world market. Only a few products, or some components, are made in each plant, but in very large numbers. Rationalization also involves the development of a single worldwide product line and the integrated management of product engineering activities to avoid duplications and to maintain production specialization.

Not all companies can benefit equally from rationalizing their production. In some cases transportation costs would be disproportionate: in others, economies of scale beyond the current plant sizes do not warrant rationalization; in still others, customers' tastes and preferences differ sufficiently between countries to jeopardize any attempt to rationalize.

Nevertheless, many companies, with less-differentiated products where economies of scale are important and where making a full line of sizes or models or types is critical for successful competition, can derive immense benefits from rationalization, particularly when their production costs are important in relation to total costs.

For mature industries in developed countries, rationalization must be seriously considered. Multinationals face more and more competition from Japan, whose industry is very efficient; from lesser developed countries who have lower labor or energy costs; and from competitors who do not follow usual trade practices or pricing policies (e.g., the Soviet bloc). Given the extreme concern that governments show toward maintaining employment, a multinational can hardly shrink its activities in developed countries and move them to lower cost countries without social upheavals that can damage its prospects permanently. The issue then often becomes how to increase production efficiency inorder to maintain or restore competitiveness. Probably the greatest untapped source of efficiency is rationalizing production (and often product engineering) activities between several countries.

Despite its economic advantages, rationalization seldom is implemented as part of a new opportunity-seeking strategy. Rather, it emerges as a response to serious difficulties. According to a survey[1] taken in 1974, a number of years after trade barriers were reduced, few of the companies who had been expected to rationalize their manufacturing operations had done so. In many cases companies had invested into new subsidiaries abroad rather than serve foreign markets through exports. Only in a few industries that were subjected to very severe Far Eastern competition had multinationals rationalized their European operations. And, even then, the process of rationalization was often slow, difficult, and not always successful. Most managers attributed the difficulties of the rationalization process to administrative and managerial issues that made implementation difficult. There was no dearth of analytical studies calling of rationalization, but few of them had been followed by actual implementation.

RATIONALIZATION: NECESSARY BUT DIFFICULT TO DIAGNOSE

This paper, based on clinical research into the management of a number of large diversified MNCs over the last two years, proposes a framework for diagnosing the need for rationalization and for managing the rationalization process. The paper first suggests how to determine whether a MNC should rationalize production and what difficulties are likely to interfere with an objective diagnosis; it then analyzes problems of implementation and suggests administrative measures that can facilitate the rationalization process.

The difficulties of rationalization begin when analytical and behavioral issues conflict. The purely analytical issues are simple: rationalization is needed when product market maturity leads to price competition and product standardization on a worldwide basis. Rationalization is possible when product unit costs are sensitive to scale of manufacture, that is, when longer series or larger plants result in lower unit costs.

Table 1 A Framework for Managing the Rationalization Process

Diagnosis	Start-up	Changes in the Management Process	Corporate Management Options Support Rationalization
Product market maturity Price competition Unexploited scale economies	Product type inventory Coordination group Staff experts Coordinators	Marketing coordination Export coordination and sourcing control Logistics Overall market-share Production programming Technical coordination Funding: R&D capital	Communication of purpose Planning integration Changes in measurement, evaluation and reward systems Changes in career paths and management development
Pitfalls Lack of perception of new competition Autonomous subsidiary structure favors national responses rather than rationalization need diagnosis Rationalization may be opposed by national subsidiary managers' slanted diagnosis	Too assertive coordinator Too little top management support to coordinators Coordinators subordinate to group of subsidiary managers Too many subsidiaries Joint ventures	Wrong timing Inappropriate sequencing Poor choice of coordinators	Lack of top management visible support Continuation of country based evaluation and compensation schemes Poor choice of country managers

Yet, social and political difficulties within the multinational corporation often hinder an objective diagnosis and delay the start of rationalization. If we pause to consider the structure of the MNC prior to rationalization, the difficulties become clear. In all likelihood the relative self-sustenance of national subsidiaries primarily geared to their domestic market has led over time to separate management of the various national companies. In such a fragmented setting there are obvious barriers to the emergence of multicountry rationalization as a strongly supported proposal. First, the significance of new competition is often difficult to recognize rapidly. Second, the decentralized management characteristic of local-for-local operations make national managers look for local-for-local solutions first. Finally, because rationalization threatens their power and identity, managers approach it with great reluctance.

PRODUCT MARKET MATURITY AND PRICE COMPETITION

Rationalization is most needed in mature industries whose customers use precise, hard criteria based on product price performance relationships in their purchasing decisions. For instance, European consumers have developed an increasingly discriminating attitude toward cars and hi-fi sets since the 1950's; they now require high quality, low price, no-nonsense products. The same tendency is seen in the U.S. computer industry where, as products have matured and become better known, customers have become more price sensitive. In response to customers' shifts, suppliers can put more emphasis on cost reduction rather than product differentiation or new innovative products. Products innovations become harder to come by because most aspects of the technology, functions and possible variations of the product itself have already been explored by one competitor or another. Innovative efforts are

now geared to low cost production processes rather than new products.[2]

Such conditions usually lead competitors to strive for low production costs through extensive rationalization in high cost areas, through sheer size, and through production in lower cost countries. Warning signals to MNCs in developed countries can come from low cost imports taking a growing market share in home markets, other MNCs rationalizing their activities, or large scale national producers exporting aggressively. When such signals appear, rationalization is usually urgently needed or profits may soon tumble. In the free trade environment of the western world, products such as cars, trucks, bearings, electrical motors, and consumer electronics are obvious candidates for rationalization.

ECONOMICS OF MANUFACTURE

Rationalization can bring great benefits only if the production process is highly sensitive to scale economies. Although there are no fast rules, it is generally accepted that production cost decreases depend on two major variables:

1. The size of a given operation. A 500,000 unit per year capacity automobile plant will have lower unit costs than, say, a 200,000 unit per year plant, for example.[3]
2. The number of units produced by a given operation since it started, that is, accumulated experience.[4] To some extent this applies both to particular products (i.e., Volkswagen production) and to more general experience in a given industry (refrigeration real costs fall for any given manufacturer, with a product range evolving over time).

An analysis of the sensitivity of unit costs to scale of production is a key part of diagnosing a need for rationalization. If higher production volumes will yield much lower production costs, rationalization is highly desirable. As much as feasible, one must be careful (particularly for multiproduct, multistage-related activities) to identify what cost decreases derive from longer individual production series, overall accrued experience, or sheer size of the plant, as these differences imply different rationalization patterns. For instance, in consumer good production, audio products are easier to rationalize than video products. Radio and hi-fi production costs are mostly sensitive to individual production series, of which there are many different types. Existing small plants in various countries can specialize without too much difficulty. In TV tube production, on the other hand, there are few types and individual plants need to be very large; hence, it is very difficult for a large number of existing plants to specialize without many factory closings that are, at best, difficult and slow to implement in most developed countries.

Furthermore, more efficient manufacturing processes often require larger production volumes in a single site to reach their full efficiency. For instance, a variety of ball bearings can be produced on the same set of machines, each type in relatively small numbers. Bearings can also be produced on highly efficient fully automated transfer lines. Each line produces only one type, but in extremely large quantities. Concentrating all production of one type in one location often permits the adoption of more efficient production processes leading immediately to a spectacular drop in manufacturing costs. This was a key to SKF's rationalization success within its five main European subsidiaries.

Finally, economies of scale can affect various stages in the production process differently. Some stages can be very scale sensitive (for instance wafer production in semiconductors), others very labor intensive but not much affected by scale (semiconductor packaging), still others both scale sensitive and labor intensive (semiconductor testing). These differences are reflected by the patterns of production rationalization of the U.S. semiconductor companies: wafer manufacture in very large plants in the U.S., assembly and packaging farmed out to the Far East and Latin America, and testing in various locations.

POTENTIAL PITFALLS IN DIAGNOSIS

In an analytical perspective, diagnosing the need for rationalization is relatively simple: product standardization and price competition in mature product markets and the existence of further economies of scale are the key elements. Why, then, is diagnosis so difficult to carry out? Information difficulties may delay the perception of new competition, national subsidiary autonomy makes a worldwide diagnosis most difficult, and national managers see rationalization cutting across their power base.

Information Difficulties

It is difficult to detect an overall threat to the company's competitive position. Acute competitive pressures are seldom felt in all countries simultaneously. New, low price competitors adopt a gradual approach, seldom storming a whole continent at once. They may strike first where established manufacturers have lesser stakes, as did the importers of Japanese cars in Europe by first penetrating countries such as Belgium, Denmark or Portugal, where no home-based European manufacturer felt the pinch immediately. Delays in building distribution networks and a fragmented users' market may further blur the perception of new competition.

The company itself is often in a poor position to detect overall competitive pressures. Over the years, predominance of a national orientation can lead to decay of central management. Lean (or sometimes non-existent) corporate staffs, the absence of systematic exchange of information about specific products and markets between national subsidiaries, and the lack of worldwide product management all add to the difficulties of synthesizing a global view of competitors from the fragmentary glimpses provided by the subsidiaries.

Structural Difficulties

Often the wide-ranging operational decentralization granted to national subsidiary managers is compensated with tight profit and loss accountability. Such a control mechanism reinforces the desire of a national subsidiary manager to feel responsible and usually prompts him to reach for solutions he can first implement by himself. Faced with deteriorating profits, he is more likely to react by cutting costs and trimming employment that he can control than by calling for a companywide strategic and structural change.

Furthermore, the national subsidiary structure favors the development of commitments by managers. Other researchers[5] have shown the importance of these commitments in delaying and weakening management intervention into crisis situations, and in stalling strategic changes. A firm belief, shared by a whole organization, that operational responsibility and accountability are better placed at the national level, is difficult to change. This is particularly true of European top managers whose formative years witnessed a breakdown of international relations (protectionism in the Great Depression, immediately followed by World War II) and who may be reluctant to take advantage of conditions of free trade which they regard as vulnerable and of institutions they consider fragile (the EEC administrative regulatory machinery).

Such beliefs are sometimes reinforced by the incomplete state of free trade. In some industries, scale economies of production and price competition would dictate rationalization but the strategic importance of the products prompts national governments to prevent or limit international trade and rationalization of production, as with telecommunication equipment and electrical power systems.[6] In some other cases employment considerations or technological and financial factors prompt governments to prevent rationalization, through financial incentives, export subsidies, research grants, and other benefits, made contingent upon full local production. For many industries the extent of rationalization may thus be informally limited by national subsidiary managers who are more attuned to the possible national government desires for full local production than to the benefits of rationalization.

Delegation of responsibility to the national level may prevent top management from developing a clear-cut overall proactive view of the evolution of the company in response to worldwide competition. Without a will to develop global strategies for dealing with the changing environment it is unlikely that sufficient energy can be mustered to seriously question past commitments to national subsidiary, autonomy.

Power Base Difficulties

The power of the national subsidiary manager is based upon his control of the activities of the company in the host country. Coordination and integration of the activities of various functions and product lines within his domain are his key prerogatives and provide the base for his power. Rationalization, with its central management of investments, production scheduling and logistics, cuts at the heart of that power base. The manager's feeling of overall responsibility is threatened. A national subsidiary manager of a recently rationalized company once confided, "Now I am no more than a building superintendent." This is one of the central problems of rationalization: how to lead national or regional managers who were "kings in their fiefdoms" to relinquish their power for the good of the whole company.

National managers are likely to defend against rationalization by overplaying the importance of direct links with customers and the need to customize their products, in order to make rationalization seem undesirable. Corporate management is often ill-placed to assess the righteousness of their claims, particularly when government relations or employment issues are raised.

When these claims are well-founded, they may justify a partial rationalization only. Entire responsibility is left to the national subsidiaries for products that need local design and for which local production *does* matter to customers.[7] Sometimes corporate management may offer commitments to labor unions to not cut employment in the rationalization process, in order to gain their support and cut one possible objection by the subsidiary managers.

It is seldom possible to specify in great detail the exact benefits than can be brought by rationalization. The economies of production are not known in sufficient detail to make very precise cost projections. Some market share may be lost in one country, some gained in another, prices may be reduced, profits increased—but to assess precisely what the economic consequences of rationalization will be for each product in each country in terms of sales and contribution is next to impossible. Because of this fuzziness, national managers may slant a diagnosis or oppose necessary rationalization of part of their product line for fear of "what comes next."

These are the major problems that must be overcome in the diagnosis of a need for rationalization. They are not insurmountable but they must be carefully considered. Their existence explains why it is only in the face of the most pugnacious competition that rationalization is undertaken. It took intense Japanese and Eastern bloc competition to prompt European electrical motor and bearing manufacturers to rationalize their European manufacturing activities around common models. It is only when the need is blatant, and where sometimes the survival of the company (or one of its major subsidiaries) is at stake that rationalization is undertaken.

Rationalization: Managing the Process

From the experiences of a few multinationals that were subjects of clinical research, some common characteristics and "do's" and "don'ts" emerge. The activities involved in a rationalization process fall into two broad stages: "start up" and reorganization of the production system. The rationalization process itself must, of necessity, span a period of several years (a) because implementation needs to proceed in several steps and (b) because the physical tasks themselves take much time (relocation of production equipment, changes in production methods, closing of old lines, opening of new ones, training of workers and supervisors, etc.). Here I shall focus on the management process rather than on the physical process, and assume that the latter can be designed and carried out technically without major difficulties.

START UP

The diagnostic difficulties outlined above suggest the need to gain early commitment from subsidiary managers. A simple way to begin is to make an inventory of redundant product types. Such redundancies can be dramatically presented to national managers. For example, Philips' Radio, Gramophone and Television product group convened all its national subsidiary managers to show them hundreds of similar radio and television sets spread out on tables covering the ballroom of a large hotel, all made by one or another national subsidiary because it was "necessary for the market." In most cases the diagnosis can be expressed simply: the inventory shows obvious duplications and overlapping product ranges. SKF, the world's largest ball bearing manufacturer, with manufacturing operations in most European countries, concluded that the 50,000 different types of bearings produced in its five major national subsidiaries could easily be reduced to 20,000; a "core product line" of 7,000 types could be rationalized and made for inventory: and 13,000 other types could be made by one or another national subsidiary for domestic customers only.

Once the inventory of product types is completed, a business strategy analysis is undertaken to assess the special competencies of the various subsidiaries and to guide their specialization. This often is the first opportunity to consider the firm's business in a global perspective. Again, active cooperation with the national subsidiary managers is needed. To make the rationalization diagnosis part of an existing ongoing management process, where cooperation is already developed between subsidiaries, alleviates the fears of national managers and facilitates the evolution of their commitments. Often an established structure of technical coordination committees provides such an opportunity. Opportunities may also appear at times of broad strategic reassessment, when rationalization can be expected to dawn upon the participating managers as a solution to overall strategic problems. Direct, active involvement of the management of national subsidiaries in the process is a prerequisite for the shifts in commitments required by a successful rationalization. Reliance on functional staff experts whose influence is based on recognized competence, rather than direct control or responsibility, to guide the diagnosis, first addressing the least controversial questions such as common nomenclature, product specifications, quality standards and manufacturing methods, helps to loosen former commitments and to start a cooperative process between subsidiaries. Similarly, first initiating rationalization of products identified as losers and of which no subsidiary is committed to production can provide a start for the process.

Potential Pitfalls in Start-up

At this early stage, there are several pitfalls to avoid. First, the development and acceptance of an overall blueprint is not as critical as the start of a cooperative process between subsidi-

aries and the affirmation that rationalization efforts are worth pursuing. These can be hampered by early formalization of the process or by the appointment of corporate coordinators or their equivalents who have undertaken exhaustive analytical studies to be used as blueprints. Powerful "coordinators" appearing as first signs of a strong central product management could stifle the process by taking it out of the hands of the national subsidiaries' managers, who would then resist it. The appointment of coordinators by the subsidiaries may also prove a hindrance: by creating a permanent but subordinate structure, the group of national subsidiaries may well prevent further implementation. A rationalization committee chaired by a straw man and where real power would lie with subsidiary managers can easily lead to inaction because of haggling between subsidiaries or a consensus to do nothing. There is a difficult balance to be sought by top management: provide enough impetus to keep the process on its track; avoid pressure that may scare subsidiary managers.

Getting into complex and ill-defined products is another pitfall. Product design and manufacturing simplicity, well-defined customer groups and functions, low diversity within the product line, well-known distribution characteristics facilitate the emergence of a common appreciation of competition and make it more difficult for national managers to retrench behind technical and marketing differentiation arguments. In this sense it is much easier for a company such as SKF to reach a common rationalized "European" product line by 1981 that it is, say, for a Honeywell Information Systems.

A third potential pitfall to avoid is including too many subsidiaries in the process. Some countries discourage certain rationalization schemes for antitrust reasons (SKF left its U.S. subsidiary out of its rationalization plan), others are adamant in closing their borders to imports and promoting autarky (Philips left its Indian subsidiary out of its Radio plan), and others have many constraints and regulations that often discourage rationalization (e.g., Brazil, Mexico). Some of the autonomous subsidiaries are joint ventures, whose partners may be dismayed by rationalization and may strongly oppose it. Franko[8] found that the emergence of a regional structure in MNCs (which usually accompanies, with some lag, a rationalization process) was the single most important cause of joint venture problems in a rationalization. These problems should be closely studied before the attempt is made to bring a part-owned subsidiary into a rationalization plan. Finally, adding smaller subsidiaries to the scheme may well multiply administrative problems and diminish economic returns.

IMPLEMENTATION OF CHANGES IN THE MANAGEMENT PROCESS

The very nature of the rationalization process is self-defeating: if left to the national managers, implementation may stop short of expectations as there is no overall institutionalized way of managing the rationalized system, and because national managers are not likely to relinquish power voluntarily once the sorest points have been dealt with.

At some point a centralized management body must be appointed, without, at the same time, reducing the strength of national subsidiary management. Most often the increasing sensitivity of host governments, and the internal trauma caused by sweeping reorganization, would rule out a complete sudden overall structural change which would suddenly replace national subsidiary preeminence with worldwide (or regional) management of all activities. Again, the problem to avoid is ruling by diktat and building an entirely new corporate architecture; one wishes instead to manage a smooth transition to a structure in which the central management body would acquire an increasing influence, but not absolute power.

The form taken by the new centralized management body may vary. In some cases it may

be a new staff service, such as SKF's "General Forecasting and Supply System," based in the neutral ground of Brussels and organized to administer the rationalization. In other cases, such as the International Telecommunications Division of GTE, product vice presidents may be appointed at headquarters. In still other companies, the expansion of corporate headquarters or regional manufacturing staff may serve the same function. The form this reinforcement of central management takes will vary according to the idiosyncrasies of each company and the products it manufactures.

Whatever its form, this new management is likely to be confronted with the same set of issues: how to gain influence over subsidiary activities without usurping the power of their managers in too brutal a fashion. Several problems of intersubsidiary coordination appear in the rationalization process; they cannot be easily solved by the subsidiaries independently, and so are likely to be brought to headquarters where top management can give them to the new product management unit to solve.

Marketing Coordination

Once each subsidiary no longer manufactures a full product line, coordination of export marketing becomes important. Export orders have to be directed to the center and then allocated to the appropriate subsidiary. Beyond the mechanistic elements, there often remains a latitude of choice as to the source subsidiary, either because the order is not extremely specific or because several subsidiaries still manufacture comparable products. In some cases part of the rationalization design is to arrange for two or more sources so as to decrease vulnerability to strikes or other supply disruptions in any one of the subsidiaries. The ability to control allocation of export orders to the subsidiaries confers power over the subsidiaries to the central allocator.

The overall volume of activities of individual subsidiaries is also increasingly affected by export orders coming from the product management unit. Naturally, coordination of intersubsidiary shipments, production scheduling, and short-term logistics have to be managed jointly, particularly when the rationalization involves both segments of the product line and stages in the production process. The ability to expand or contract the volume of export business of particular subsidiaries, and thus affect their profitability, becomes a strong incentive for subsidiaries to fall in line.

Finally, both the global perspective of the product management unit and the lower costs yielded by rationalization may increase the worldwide overall market share of the company. Thus the slice of the cake offered to each subsidiary increases in size. In businesses where selling is an important, costly activity which requires much competence and intensive effort, a central unit is often better able to increase the overall return from the world market than a collection of autonomous subsidiaries competing against one another.

From the viewpoint of worldwide management, the maintenance of allocation flexibility in source and export markets constitutes a particularly powerful influence over the subsidiaries. For instance, the stable a priori allocation of geographic markets to certain subsidiaries in case of duplication effectively reduces the influence of product management. Similarly, the existence of only one source for one product effectively confers power on that source. So beyond the safety of supply questions, it is ironical to conclude that in order to be managed smoothly it may well be that rationalization has to remain incomplete!

Production Programming Coordination

Usually concurrent with control over export marketing is the development of a central worldwide market analysis and forecasting system. The subsidiaries learn to depend on the central system for their own forecasting and planning as the share of exports (to other sub-

sidiaries and possibly to third parties) in the sales of each subsidiary increases. Simultaneously, particularly when rationalization involves multistage production processes, production programs must be coordinated between the various subsidiaries—and the central management unit can become a broker and an arbitrator for the planning of intersubsidiary transactions.

Technical Coordination

Regrouping the technical coordination structures with the new management unit may also provide the latter with a measure of control over the transfer of product and process technology between the subsidiaries. Linkages with the central research and development laboratories can also provide much influence. Controlling the transfer of new technology from the United States to European subsidiaries was a major source of influence of the product vice presidents at GTE.

Investment and R&D Coordination

Control over capital and R&D expenditure can be delegated by top management to the worldwide product management unit. Because investments are now made with the aim of serving a worldwide market, individual national companies cannot be left in full control. Given their worldwide perspective combined with an in-depth knowledge of the business, product managers are best able to check, evaluate, and integrate into a coherent whole the investment proposals of the subsidiaries. This control was the single strongest source of influence for the corporate product directors at Dow Chemical.

Difficulties and Pitfalls

The issues of export allocation, joint production programming, technical coordination, and capital and R&D fund appropriation have been found to provide a basis for establishing central coordination in order to complete the rationalization process. These issues enable the coordination center to assert influence over the subsidiaries and to foster integration and specialization of their activities. Yet there remain difficult questions which top management must consider with care.

First, timing rationalization with an overall business slump makes the rationalization process seem both more urgent and easier to implement. Brown Boveri's 1972 industrial motors rationalization plans were blasted by a mini capital boom in 1973 whereas SKF's managers attributed their own success in good part to the depressed markets of 1975–1976. Taking advantage of new product introduction may also help cast the rationalization in a more positive light. It is also easier to plan for new machines and productions in a rationalized system than to start by relocating existing activities.

Second, sequencing is important. In a successful rationalization, behaviors and commitments change. Often the new patterns of interaction between subsidiaries induce shifts in power and status, causing great concern to managers. The various coordination issues are raised to bring cooperation between subsidiaries.

How and when to use these issues to gain influence upon subsidiaries most often rests with the decision maker in the product management unit supported by top management. If he or she is too assertive, or a pawn of the coordination committee, the process is ruined.

Significant steps can best be taken when external sources of reward are present. At GTE, for instance, the worldwide product vice president obtained a huge telecommunication order which had to be allocated for capacity reasons; he used his power to allocate production as a means for gaining ascendancy and influence over national subsidiaries. Conversely, steps taken in direct conflict with outside events (as in the Brown Boveri case mentioned above) are likely to fail and jeopardize the whole process.

The sequence of moves to increase the influ-ence of the worldwide product management unit(s) is subject to corporate veto control. Through their power over structure and their allocation of responsibility, top management can set the pace of the process and restrain overassertive managers. Beyond this broad conclusion, no general approach to the sequencing can be developed; sequencing depends on coalitions that can develop between subsidiary managers, on the "feel" for the situation developed by the manager of the product coordination unit, and on the urgency imposed by competitive pressures.

Third, given his/her key role in managing the later parts of the rationalization process, a coordinator must be chosen carefully. There seem to be no general rules. Recognized substantive expertise and experience within the organization are important elements, but not sufficient ones. On the contrary, too much technical emphasis and task orientation would jeopardize the process. The most important element is the ability to provide energy, commitment and drive without using line authority. One means used by several companies is to appoint successful past subsidiary managers as worldwide product coordinators with the idea that they will know what is palatable to their former colleagues and what is not; their previous experience provides them with both an intellectual understanding and an emotional grasp of how to manage a subsidiary or an area. On the other hand, when one of the companies studied appointed *division* managers within its subsidiaries it reached out to recruit managers who had been running worldwide product groups for other MNCs. This company's top management hoped that some degree of reciprocal understanding between newly appointed subsidiary division managers and worldwide coordinators would facilitate a needed rationalization process in some of the activities they controlled. This quickly unlocked a tight situation and revitalized a rationalization that had been stalled for several years.

Wrong timing, sequencing and choice of coordinator(s) seem to be the most frequent cause of unsuccessful rationalization. They deserve much top management attention.

Corporate Management Options to Support the Rationalization

Beyond direct management of rationalization, top management can facilitate its implementation and encourage central coordination in many ways. In particular, it is important to recognize that though national subsidiary managers have considerable autonomy prior to the rationalization, they do not operate in a vacuum: both the corporate and the host country environments contribute to shape the perceptions, premises, and commitments of managers. Therefore an important element of the rationalization process is to modify the organizational context within which subsidiary managers operate.[9] It is important to be aware of the set of administrative procedures that "shape the purposive manager's definition of business problems by directing, delimiting and coloring the focus and perception and determine the priorities which the various demands on him are given."[10]

Corporate management controls an array of variables which structure the context of subsidiary managers and can hinder or facilitate the rationalization process—in particular, the organization's architecture, the systems of measure, evaluation and reward and punishment, the flows of communication to and from subsidiaries, and the career paths of key managers.[11]

COMMUNICATION OF TOP MANAGEMENT PURPOSE

It is important how the intent of rationalization and top management's commitment (or lack of commitment) to its success are signaled to national management groups. A mechanistic view of the social aspects of starting the process should be avoided. To increase the influence of product management without immediately decreasing the influence of national managers requires the development of a social interaction process. Top management's role in bringing product and host country preferences and their sponsors together is most important.

Series of worldwide planning meetings can be scheduled for a few days at a time, and what takes place outside the sessions is often as important as what takes place inside. Systematic patterns of communication between subsidiaries may be developed. Top managers should be personally involved in alleviating the fears of national managers and exploring their reservations. Only top managers and functional staffs constitute a relatively neutral source of arbitration for the conflicts that are bound to develop as rationalization is implemented. Because their actions are visible, top managers can also set precedents which signal the strategy they pursue and set the tone for relationships between host country and product managers.

CHANGES IN MEASUREMENT, EVALUATION, AND REWARD SYSTEMS

Rationalization may not be compatible with tight national profit center accountability. Because decisions which affect the profitability of the subsidiaries are increasingly being influenced by worldwide product management units, maintaining tight profit center accountability leads to frustration and conflict. Thus, during the rationalization process a loosening up of the measurement, evaluation and control systems of national profit centers is needed. Similarly, an incentive system based on national subsidiary results may have to be replaced by one based on overall corporate or worldwide product group results. All companies stress the need for lenient measurement, evaluation and reward systems as a condition for learning and for disassociating personal financial risks from realignments in status and power.

CAREER PATHS AND MANAGEMENT DEVELOPMENT

It is important for top management to assess early in the rationalization process whether the role of subsidiary managers is likely to be diminished. If they have long represented the main level of general management, at some point during the rationalization process shifts in career paths should be considered. Though this is too broad a question to consider here, some of the key issues are worth mentioning. If marketing needs to be differentiated by countries and constitutes a critical task, splitting production and marketing could be considered: marketing would then be left to strong autonomous national companies headed by entrepreneurial managers. On the manufacturing side, only good plant managers are needed nationally. What scope remains for strong national managers? The development of international careers may be difficult, and national managers may resent being deprived of the perquisites of power and responsibility. Good national managing directors do not always make good international staff or product group managers. Also, for personal reasons country managers may loathe the expatriate status and relocations which accompany an international career path.

For all these reasons some attrition is unavoidable among national subsidiary managers and in some cases it may even be sought to facilitate the rationalization process. But the systematic replacement of strong national managers by mere caretakers is not advisable. With the growth of host governments' interventions, workers' participation, and the disillusionment with free trade and free investment, there is a need for the management of an integrated network to remain responsive to national conditions. We have also seen that the extent and benefits of a rationalization can hardly be clearly assessed in advance, and that not all productions, and not all countries can be rationalized without strong penalties. Therefore it is important to have a strong national management group sensitive to the needs of local interests as a balance to worldwide product managers who are likely to overlook national idiosyncracies.

CONCLUSION

Rationalization is not only an economic and technical exercise, but also a complex social and organizational process which aims to develop an integrated multinational business capability. Such a capability is particularly needed in developed countries and mature industries subject to intense price competition. It can bring economic advantages mainly through exploiting economies of scale.

Though an objective diagnosis of economic forces and of the benefits of rationalization is possible, it is likely to be hampered by difficulties of perception, commitment of managers, and power structure shifts. Start-up of a rationalization process requires new commitments from the national subsidiary managers and development of a central body that can draw influence from coordination of export marketing, worldwide market analysis, forecasting and production planning activities, improved export sales, changes in the production process, technology transfer and control over investments and R&D budgets. Full top management support must be provided to the coordinating body and to the rationalization efforts. Early pitfalls in the process include adoption of a firm "blueprint" without subsidiary managers' support, premature constitution of a coordination center, its dependence either on corporate or subsidiary management, attempts to rationalize complex products where the benefits of rationalization are not obvious, and inclusion of too many small or partly owned subsidiaries into the rationalization scheme. Later pitfalls may include poor timing, poor sequencing, lack of top management support and absence of administrative changes. Useful administrative changes include provision of a sense of purpose by top management, changes in the measurement, evaluation and rewards systems, changes in career paths, and staffing of key subsidiary positions.

Yet even carefully planned and well-managed rationalization processes may not be successful. Because rationalization challenges organizational commitments and power relationships and forces their realignment, many internal roadblocks have to be overcome to carry out the process. Some of these roadblocks are predictable in a planning stage, but overcoming them successfully requires constant top management attention at each stage in the process. The rationalization process deserves more research: I have merely tried here to suggest means of facilitating rationalization and some pitfalls to avoid when carrying out the process.

NOTES

1. Cited in Lawrence G. Franko, *The European Multinationals* (Stamford, Conn.: Greylock, 1976).

2. William Abernathy, *The Productivity Dilemma* (forthcoming).

3. See, for instance, John S. McGee, "Economies of Size in Automobile Manufacture," *The Journal of Law and Economics*, pp. 239–273.

4. See Boston Consulting Group. *Perspectives on Experience* (Boston: Boston Consulting Group, 1968).

5. Richard G. Hamermesh, "Responding to Divisional Profit Crises," *Harvard Business Review* (March–April 1977). Stuart Clarke Gilmore, "The Divestment Process," unpublished doctoral dissertation, Harvard Business School, Boston, 1975. Richard Normann, *Management and Statesmanship* (Stockholm: Scandinavian Institutes of Administrative Research, 1976.

6. Yves L. Doz, *Government Power and Multinational Strategic Management* (New York: Praeger 1979).

7. For instance, many prepared food products and strategic products sold to governments or state-owned enterprises.

8. Lawrence G. Franko, *Joint Venture Survival in Multinational Corporations* (New York: Praeger, 1972).

9. Joseph L. Bower, *Managing the Resource Allocation Process* (Boston: Division of Research, Harvard Business School, 1970).

10. Ibid., p. 73.

11. See C. K. Prahalad, "Strategic Choices in Diversified MNCs," *Harvard Business Review* (July–August 1976).

29

POSTINDUSTRIAL MANUFACTURING
Ramchandran Jaikumar

As global competition grows ever fiercer in manufacturing industries, American managers are adopting a new battle cry: "Beat 'em with technology or move—over there." Indeed, since 1975, the boom in information-intensive processing technologies has been explosive. A close look at how U.S. managers are actually using these technologies, however, silences their battle cry in a hurry. Yes, they are buying

Source: Harvard Business Review (November–December 1986), pp. 69–76.

the hardware of flexible automation—but they are using it very poorly. Rather than narrowing the competitive gap with Japan, the technology of automation is widening it further.

With few exceptions, the flexible manufacturing systems installed in the United States show an astonishing lack of flexibility. In many cases, they perform worse than the conventional technology they replace. The technology itself is not to blame; it is management that makes the difference. Compared with Japanese systems, those in U.S. plants produce an order-of-magnitude less variety of parts. Furthermore, they cannot run untended for a whole shift, are not integrated with the rest of their factories, and are less reliable. Even the good ones form, at best, a small oasis in a desert of mediocrity.

Lest this sound unduly harsh, consider the facts summarized in *Exhibit I.* In 1984 I conducted a focused study of 35 flexible manufacturing systems (FMSs) in the United States and 60 in Japan, a sample that represented more than half the installed systems in both countries. The kinds of products they made—large housings, crankcases, and the like—were comparable in size and complexity, and required similar metal-cutting times, numbers of tools, and precision of parts. The U.S. systems had an average of seven machines and the Japanese, six.

Here the similarities end. The average number of parts made by an FMS in the United States was 10; in Japan the average was 93, al-most ten times greater. Seven of the U.S. systems made just 3 parts. The U.S. companies used FMSs the wrong way—for high-volume production of a few parts rather than for high-variety production of many parts at low cost per unit. Thus the annual volume per part in the United States was 1,727; in Japan, only 258. Nor have U.S. installations exploited opportunities to introduce new products. For every new part introduced into a U.S. system, 22 parts were introduced in Japan. In the critical metal-working industries, from which these numbers come, the United States is not using manufacturing technology effectively. Japan is.

I have spent several years examining the experiences of companies that have installed FMSs. (See the insert entitled "Primary Research" for details of the study.) The object has been to observe the most sophisticated form of information-intensive technology in manufacturing. Flexible systems resemble miniature factories in operation. They are natural laboratories in which to study computer-integrated manufacturing, which is rapidly becoming the battleground for manufacturing supremacy around the globe.

The battle is on, and the United States is losing badly. It may even lose the war if it doesn't soon figure out how better to use the new technology of automation for competitive advantage. This does not mean investing in more equipment; in today's manufacturing environment, it is how the equipment is used that is important. Success comes from achieving continuous process improvements through organizational learning and experimentation.

Exhibit I Comparison of FMSs Studied in the United States and Japan

	United States	Japan
System development time years	2.5 to 3	1.25 to 1.75
Number of machines per system	7	6
Types of parts produced per system	10	93
Annual volume per part	1,727	258
Number of parts produced per day	88	120
Number of new parts introduced per year	1	22
Number of systems with untended operations	0	18
Utilization rate* two shifts	52%	84%
Average metal-cutting time per day hours	8.3	20.2

*Ratio of actual metal-cutting time to time available for metal cutting.

TECHNOLOGY LEADERSHIP

The FMS installations surveyed in *Exhibit I* were, as noted, technically alike. They had similar machines and did similar types of work. The difference in results was mainly due to the extent of the installed base of machinery, the work force's technical literacy, and management's competence. In each of these areas, Japan was far ahead of the United States.

In the last five years, Japan has outspent the United States two to one in automation. During that time, 55% of the machine tools introduced in Japan were computer numerically controlled (CNC) machines, key parts of FMSs. In the United States, the figure was only 18%. Of all these machines installed worldwide since 1975, more than 40% are in Japan. What's more, over two-thirds of the CNC machines in Japan went to small and medium-sized companies.

Just counting how much of this technology companies use is not enough. Because software development lies at the heart of this increasingly information-intensive manufacturing process, the technological literacy of a company's workers is critical. In the Japanese companies I studied, more than 40% of the work force was made up of college-educated engineers, and all had been trained in the use of CNC machines. In the U.S. companies studies, only 8% of the workers were engineers, and less than 25% had been trained on CNC machines. Training to upgrade skills was 3 times longer in Japan than in the United States. Compared with U.S. plants, Japanese factories had an average of 2½ times as many CNC machines, 4 times as many engineers, and 4 times as many people trained to use the machines.

Management's Role

A skilled work force and a large installed base of equipment build the foundation for technological leadership. It is the competence of managers, however, that makes such leadership happen. To understand why, we should look more closely at recent experience with FMS technology.

A flexible manufacturing system is a computer-controlled grouping of semi-independent work stations linked by automated material-handling systems. The purpose of an FMS is to manufacture efficiently several kinds of parts at low to medium volumes. All activities in the

system—metal cutting, monitoring tool wear, moving parts from one machine to another, setup, inspection, tool adjustment, material handling, scheduling, and dispatching—are under precise computer control. In operation, an FMS is a miniature automated factory.

The system at one prominent Midwestern heavy-equipment producer consisted of 12 machines that made just 8 different parts for a total volume of 5,000 units a year. Once the FMS went on line, management prevented workers from making process improvements by encouraging them not to make any changes. "If it ain't broke, don't fix it" became the watchword.

The FMS boosted machine uptime and productivity, but it did not come close to realizing its full—and distinctive—strategic promise. The technology was applied in a way that ignored its huge potential for flexibility and for generating organizational learning.

Management treated the FMS as if it were just another set of machines for high-volume, standardized production—which is precisely what it is not. Captive to old-fashioned Taylorism and its principles of scientific management, these executives separated the establishment of procedures from their execution, replaced skilled blue-collar machinists with trained operators, and emphasized machine uptime and productivity. In short, they mastered narrow-purpose production on expensive FMS technology designed for high-powered, flexible usage.

This is no way to run a railroad. Certainly, Frederick W. Taylor's work still applies—but not to this environment. Managing an FMS as if it were the old Ford plant at River Rouge is worse than wrong; it is paralyzing. In this case there was little, if any, attention given to process or program flexibility and almost no support for software improvement. Management failed to utilize the FMS's improved capabilities, from which even greater improvements might have flowed over time.

Not surprisingly, the flexibility achieved by this FMS was much less than that of a stand-alone CNC machining center. And that's the *good* news. The system had four operators per shift, each of whom was responsible for checking gauges, changing hydraulic fluid and parts like drill bits, and making simple diagnoses when something went wrong. These tasks, as specified by management, were very procedural, and no operator had the discretion to change procedures. If anything, the complexity of the FMS forced operators to stick more rigidly to procedure than they did at the stand-alone CNC machining centers.

Goals for Management

How, then, should managers look at FMSs? About what should they ask? For one thing, development time. The systems in the United States take 2½ to 3 years and about 25,000 man-hours to conceive, develop, install, and get running. Japanese systems take 1¼ to 1½ years and 6,000 man-hours. Here, again, the difference is management. U.S. project teams are usually large groups made up of specialists who design systems for a much greater level of flexibility than their companies are prepared to use. This greater complexity means that projects not only take longer but have plenty of bugs when finished. Delays create enormous pressure on software engineers to take shortcuts and seek hard-wired fixes.

At the end of a project, as a rule, the team is disbanded. The engineers assigned to maintain a system, who are usually not its developers, are reluctant to make any changes. They know about all the bugs but are unwilling to tinker with things because "you never know what may happen." The result: inflexibility.

By contrast, the FMS installations in Japan are remarkably flexible. This would not be so troublesome for the United States if the old-fashioned productivity of its systems, for which flexibility gets sacrificed, were better than that of Japanese systems. But it is not. The average utilization rate (metal-cutting time as a percentage of total time) of U.S. flexible manufacturing systems over two shifts was 52%, as opposed to 84% in Japan. Over three shifts, because of reliable untended operations, the figure in Japan was even higher.

Where does so huge a difference come from? In a word, the *reliability* designed into the system. In Japan, system designers strive to create

Exhibit II Comparison of Japanese FMSs with the Systems They Replaced

	FMSs	Conventional Systems
Number of parts produced per system*	182	182
Number of systems with untended operations	18	0
Number of machine tools	133	253
Number of operators three shifts	129	601
Utilization rate two shifts	84%	61%

*To make the comparison useful, I have held the number of parts made by each system constant.
†For three shifts the figure is 92%.

operations that can run untended. Of the 60 FMSs I studied, 18 ran untended during the night shift. Such systems take more time and resources to develop than those that require even a single attendant, because designers have to anticipate all possible contingencies. But the additional costs are well worth it. So demanding a design objective leads in practice to a great deal of advance problem solving and process improvement. The entire project team remains with the system long after installation, continually making changes. Learning occurs throughout—and learning gets translated into ongoing process mastery and productivity enhancement. This learning is what gives rise to, and sustains, competitive advantage.

Most of the systems built in Japan after 1982 have achieved untended operations and system uptime of an astonishing 90% to 99%. Operators on the shop floor make continual programming changes and are responsible for writing new programs for both parts and systems as a whole. They are highly skilled engineers with multifunctional responsibilities. Like the designers, they work best in small teams. Most important, managers see FMS technology for what it is—flexible—and create operating objectives and protocols that capitalize on this special capability. Not bound by outdated mass-

production assumptions, they view the challenge of flexible manufacturing as automating a job shop, not simply making a transfer line flexible. The difference in results is enormous, but the vision that leads to it is in human scale. No magic here—just an intelligent process of thinking through what new technology means for how work should be organized.

FMS ON LINE

To find out more about this "job shop" approach, I examined more closely 22 FMS installations at Hitachi-Seiki, Yamazaki Mazak, Okuma, Murata, Mori-Seiki, Makino, and Fanuc. As *Exhibit II* shows, these systems far outperformed the conventional CNC equipment they replaced.

Both systems produced the same variety of parts. But the FMSs did it with five times fewer workers than the conventional systems. Moreover, it took only half as many flexible machines to produce the same volume of parts as conventional machines. The CNC machines used in both systems were identical; the FMSs, however, also employed robots, special material-handling equipment, automated storage systems, and tool-handling equipment. These support devices added another 30% to hardware costs, but they helped boost average uptime from 61% to 92% and made untended operations possible. These benefits alone more than justified the extra cost; better quality and reduced inventories were a bonus.

Potential FMS users often worry that the systems are difficult to justify strictly in economic terms. Based on the experiences of Japanese companies, these fears are groundless. All 22 systems I studied in Japan met their companies' ROI criterion of a three-year payback.

Even so, the impact of flexible manufacturing on the performance of a company reaches far beyond simple productivity rates and investment calculations. FMSs take on strategic importance when the installed base of flexible systems in a factory reaches a critical mass. Only when separate "islands of automation" in a plant start to link does management realize the possibilities for new kinds of competitive advantage via manufacturing.

Of the six Japanese companies that used flexible automation extensively, three had fully automated fabrication plants. At the time I visited them, they were the only flexible manufacturing factories in the world. Their productivity was stupendous.

Exhibit III compares the performance of one such factory before and after the introduction of total flexible automation, and *Exhibit IV*

Exhibit III Performance of One Factory Before and After Automation

		Before	**After**
	Types of parts produced per month*	543	543
	Number of pieces produced per month*	11,120	11,120
	Floor space required	16,500 m²	6,600 m²
Equipment per system	CNC machine tools	66	38
	General-purpose machine tools	24	5
	Total	90	43
Personnel per system three shifts	Operators	170	36
	Distribution and production control workers	25	3
	Total	195	39
Average processing time per part† days	Machining time	35	3
	Unit assembly	14	7
	Final assembly	42	20
	Total	91	30

*To make the comparison useful, I have held these figures constant.
†This includes time spent in queue.

Exhibit IV Manpower Requirements for Metal-Cutting Operations to Make the same Number of Identical Parts

	Conventional systems United States	Japan	**FMSs** Japan
Engineering	34	18	16
Manufacturing overhead	64	22	5
Fabrication	52	28	6
Assembly	44	32	16
Total number of workers	194	100	43

Note: There is no column here for FMSs in the United States because, at the time of this study, no domestic machine tool producer had an FMS on line.

shows the effect of such performance on cost structure and competition in an industry. Specifically, the exhibit compares the manpower requirements of various manufacturing systems for metal-cutting operations: if it took 100 people in a conventional Japanese factory to make a certain number of machine parts, it would take 194 people in a conventional U.S. factory—but only 43 in a Japanese FMS-equipped factory. If U.S. companies mastered flexible automation as the Japanese have, they would have more than a fourfold increase in labor productivity. This efficiency in labor is part of the reason that smaller companies in Japan have been able to use FMS technology so effectively.

Perhaps even more interesting than such aggregate improvements are their components. The largest manpower reduction in the exhibit is in manufacturing overhead, where an FMS cuts the number of workers from 64 to 5. In engineering, an FMS cuts the number of workers from 34 to 16. One consequence of these reductions (92% in manufacturing overhead, but only 53% in engineering) is to change the composition of the work force: engineers now outnumber production workers three to one. This may not sound like much at first, but it signals a fundamental change in the environment of manufacturing.

Flexible automation shifts the arena of competition from manufacturing to engineering, from running the plant to planning it. In the FMS environment, engineering innovation and engineering productivity hold the keys to success. Engineering now performs the critical line function. Manufacturing has become, by comparison, a staff or support function.

MANAGING ABOVE THE LINE

Picture a "lights out" factory operating untended, with general-purpose CNC machines that make a wide variety of parts and are capable of adapting easily to new demands. If two such factories compete with similar products, competition will focus on price. This is so be-

cause all costs in the development of tools, fixtures, and programs are sunk before the first unit is produced. The only variable costs are those of materials and energy, which usually amount to less than 10% of total costs.

Each factory's profits will erode over time as other companies acquire the same operating capabilities. How, then, would a company stay ahead? One way is by creating new physical assets in the form of better programmed and better managed equipment. Each plant's competitive fate would rest heavily on its ability to create facilities that generate performance advantages—and to do it faster than the competition. When the lion's share of costs are sunk before production starts, the creation and management of intellectual assets becomes the prime task of management.

This is manufacturing's new competitive environment. It may sound like something from the distant future, but the Japanese are doing it now. The crucial variable in this kind of environment is automation—the ability of an FMS to run untended. And Japanese manufacturing companies are becoming increasingly expert in that field.

Exhibit V summarizes my findings from 20 of the 22 Japanese FMSs on the extraordinary degree of automation reflected in different production activities. *Exhibit VI* presents data from these 20 systems on the amount of manual labor time spent on the factory floor to support such levels of automation. Average system losses took 16.6% of total operating time, about a third the figure in U.S. systems. Each 144 hours of metal-cutting time took only 26 hours of manual effort, which included direct labor as well as required activities usually associated with manufacturing overhead. In the United States, manufacturing overhead activities are separated from direct labor and take about ten times longer.

In most plants, 26 hours of manual effort translate into two workers per system for each of two shifts. In all 22 of these FMSs, however, there was a third person on each shift, whose work accounted for part of the 26 hours of man-

Exhibit V Degree of Automation in Production Activities of 20 Japanese FMSs in numbers of systems

	Metal-Cutting operations	Material Handling		Setup		Process Control*	Production Control		Inventory Management	
		Parts	Tools	Parts	Tools		Planning	Dispatching	Parts	Tools
Manual	—	—	—	16	13	—	4	—	—	—
Manual with computer assistance	—	—	—	2	—	—	5	—	—	—
Automated with manual override	2	—	—	—	2	—	10	—	—	15
Untended†	18	20	20	2	5	20	1	20	20	5

*Tool monitoring, inspection, and feedback.
†To qualify as untended, a system had to run without manual assistance for one shift a day and have a 98% utilization rate.

Exhibit VI Production activities in an Average FMS in Japan*

	Metal-Cutting operations	Material Handling		Setup		Process Control*	Production Control		Inventory Management		Total
		Parts	Tools	Parts	Tools		Planning	Dispatching	Parts	Tools	
Average system losses as a percentage of total time	1.6%	5%	—	—	5%	2%	—	3%	—	—	16.6%†
Manual labor time per system hours	2	—	—	11	7	3	2.5	0.5	—	—	26

*An average FMS in Japan has six machines, creating a total of 144 hours of available metal-cutting time per day.
†This figure seems to imply that the system's utilization rate over three shifts would be 83.4%, not 92% as asserted in *Exhibit II*. There is no discrepancy; the figures don't match because problems in some areas, such as material handling, cause system losses that do not result in machine downtime.

ual effort. By dividing the work among three people, the companies that had these systems purposely created extra time for such process-improvement activities as additional test cutting of new parts, observing machine behavior, and examining statistics on performance. In all 22 systems, each of the workers did these nonrequired—but immensely valuable—tasks. The number of people required to do all this in conventional systems making the same parts in the same companies was four times greater.

The distribution of the 26 hours of manual effort is also instructive. More than half were spent loading and unloading pallets. The other major activity, which took 7 hours, was mounting tools and qualifying them on machines. Together, these efforts accounted for 80% of the time spent on manual labor. Workers loaded pallets and mounted tools during the day shift, and the machines ran untended at night. Production planning, a weekly activity, took only one hour of a person's time. Systems making a large variety of parts also had automated methods for production planning. Those with a low variety of parts did it manually.

The FMS installations performed exceptionally well. Delivery performance in each system, tracked during a three-month period, was 100%. The high reliability of individual machines and of the system itself kept the variance in unscheduled downtime to only 2%. The scheduled slack for software testing and process experiments ranged from 4% to 9% of capacity and was more than enough to accommodate any variation in machine reliability. Each system met its production schedule, as long as the schedule observed the constraints of capacity. In addition, only six pieces in a thousand had a quality problem. Of these, three were reworked, usually by the operators themselves. The other three were scrapped. Tool breakage caused most of these quality problems, and the machine operators could make the necessary adjustments.

With such impressive levels of performance, few contingencies demanded management's attention. In fact, executives were largely absent from day-to-day operations. Instead of concerning themselves with internal operations, they focused their attention on how to meet competitive pressures on product performance. In the United States, on the other hand, managers spend so much time on routine problems with quality and production delivery schedules that they have virtually no time left over to plan for long-term process improvement.

As noted before, the prime task of management once the system has been made reliable is not to categorize tasks or regiment workers but to create the fixed assets—the systems and software—needed to make products. This calls for intellectual assets, not just pieces of hardware. Thus the new role of management in manufacturing is to create and nurture the project teams whose intellectual capabilities produce competitive advantage. What gets managed is intellectual capital, not equipment.

The technology of flexible manufacturing has led managers into a drastically altered competitive landscape. This new landscape has a number of important features:

A sharp focus on intellectual assets as the basis for a company's distinctive competence.

A heightened emphasis on the selection of the portfolio of projects a company chooses to manage.

A close attention to the market and to the special competence of process engineers.

A steady adjustment of product mix and price in order to maintain full capacity utilization.

A pointed emphasis on reducing fixed manufacturing costs and the time required to generate new products, processes, and programs.

An intensification of cost-based competition for manufactured products.

I am convinced that the heart of this new manufacturing landscape is the management of manufacturing projects: selecting them, creating teams to work on them, and managing workers' intellectual development. In company after company in Japan, systems engineers with a thorough knowledge of several disciplines have proved the key to the success of flexible manufacturing systems. One rigidly organized Japanese company, recognizing the importance of such versatile teams, now rotates experienced engineers through all manufacturing departments. Another, which already had job rotation, has begun to keep its engineers longer in each area so they can learn more from their FMS experience.

In contrast with the traditional Japanese approach of involving a large number of people in decision making, small teams of highly competent, engineering-oriented people have been most successful with flexible manufacturing. These groups have succeeded because they are given responsibility for both design and operations. They remain on a project until the FMS achieves 90% uptime and untended operations. Perhaps most important, in all the Japanese companies I studied, the teams came entirely from engineering and were given line responsibility for day-to-day operations.

NEW MISSION STATEMENT

The management of FMS technology is taking place in a different manufacturing environment, and thus consists of new imperatives:

Build small, cohesive teams   Very small groups of highly skilled generalists show a remarkable propensity to succeed.

Manage process improvement, not just output   FMS technology fundamentally alters the economics of production by drastically reducing variable labor costs. When these costs are low, little can be gained by reducing them further. The challenge is to develop and manage physical and intellectual assets, not the production of goods. Choosing projects that develop intellectual and physical assets is more important than monitoring the costs of day-to-day operations. Old-fashioned, sweat-of-the-brow manufacturing effort is now less important than system design and team organization.

Broaden the role of engineering management to include manufacturing   The use of small, technologically proficient teams to design, run, and improve FMS operations signals a shift in focus from managing people to managing knowledge, from controlling variable costs to managing fixed costs, and from production planning to project selection. This shift gives engineering the line responsibilities that have long been the province of manufacturing.

Treat manufacturing as a service   In an untended FMS environment, all of the tools and software programs required to make a part have to be created before the first unit is produced. While the same is true of typical parts and assembly operations, the difference in an FMS is that there are no allowances for in-the-line, people-intensive adjustments. As a result, competitive success increasingly depends on management's ability to anticipate and respond quickly to changing market needs. With FMS technology, even a small, specialized operation can accommodate shifts in demand. Manufacturing now responds much like a professional service industry, customizing its offerings to the preferences of special market segments.

Making flexibility and responsiveness the mission of manufacturing flies in the face of Taylor's view of the world, which for 75 years has shaped thinking about manufacturing. FMS technology points inevitably toward a new managerial ethos—an ethos dedicated to the building of knowledge in the flexible service of markets, not merely to the building of things. Scale is no longer the central concern. Size no longer provides barriers to entry. The minimum efficient scale for FMS operations is a cell of roughly six machines and fewer than a half a dozen people. That's the new reality.

Going to FMS-based operations does *not* require lots of money or people. It can be done—at its best, it *is* done—on a small scale. The critical ingredient here is nothing other than the competence of a small group of people. There is no Eastern mystery in this, no secrets known only to the Japanese. We can do it too—if we will.

What, after all, is a manufacturing company? Today, no artist would represent a factory as a huge, austere building with bellowing smokestacks. The behemoth is gone. The efficient factory is now an aggregation of small cells of electronically linked and controlled FMSs. New technology enables these operating cells to be combined in nonlinear ways. No shared base of infrastructure mandates large-scale production integration. The days of Taylor's immense, linear production systems are largely gone.

Unless U.S. managers understand the implications of Japan's mastery of FMS technology, their companies will fall further behind. Flexible manufacturing systems are no longer a theory, a pipe dream. They exist. And the leverage they provide on continuous process improvement is immense. Making automation work means a whole new level of process mastery. A large number of Japanese factories demonstrate its reality every day. They lead the way; we linger behind at our own peril.

30

MANUFACTURING LOGISTICS SYSTEMS FOR A COMPETITIVE GLOBAL STRATEGY

Christopher Gopal

Corporate management in the increasingly competitive manufacturing world has begun to explore concepts of global manufacturing to secure its organization's position in the current marketplace. The key to successful implementation of such concepts is an effective integrated information system. This article explores aspects of that system and the logistics chain, from purchasing through distribution, necessitated by a global policy.

In an increasingly complex and competitive business environment, manufacturing executives are finding that to maintain the status quo is to lose ground and that traditional management techniques must be supplemented with planning that incorporates all market factors. This need has led to the growth of global manufacturing policies.

Both domestic and foreign companies are examining the concepts of global manufacturing more closely than ever. Unlike a multinational manufacturing policy, which emphasizes local production for each market, a global manufacturing policy requires a "world system" perspective. Products or parts can be produced at different locations and shipped wherever a market exists, responsibilities of a particular production location are determined by existing conditions, and centralized planning keeps company operations in line with overall goals. The following complex, sometimes conflicting trends and factors are leading executives to adopt a global manufacturing strategy:

- National markets newly opened or reopened to foreign goods and competition.

- Import restrictions and local content laws in many countries.

Source: Information Strategy: The Executive's Journal (Fall 1986), pp. 19–24.

- Policies in many developing countries that make licensing of foreign firms contingent on their ability to develop export markets.

- Foreign domination of formerly strong domestic markets.

- Foreign firms' use of multinational sourcing and manufacturing to gain cost and quality advantages.

- US firms entering foreign markets, often in competition with strong domestic and multinational firms.

- An increasingly globalized marketplace that supports common products, albeit with local differences and preferences.

The benefits of adopting a global manufacturing policy include improved efficiency through logical planning of manufacturing facilities and centralization of capacity management, improved communication and resource transfer between the domestic product division and international operations, and the development of a strategy that addresses global competition.

Corporate management must proceed carefully when implementing a global manufacturing policy. The cornerstone of a global policy is centralized planning, purchasing, and distribution functions. Such centralization entails the development of a strong logistics network, which is often a difficult task. Logistics strategies are complex even in purely domestic environments, and problems can increase dramatically when strategies are transferred to international operations.

Quality standards must be maintained throughout the logistics network, making effective vendor evaluation and development programs essential for local and international manufacturing operations. A careful assessment of local market requirements and manufacturing capabilities should guide decisions involving the location, configuration, and automation of production facilities. Also, an often-overlooked concern in implementing a global policy is that a manufacturing information system must be designed to support a global strategy.

MANUFACTURING SYSTEMS INTEGRATION

A manufacturing information system to support the centralized planning dictated by a global policy is vital. Exhibit 1 lists elements of a comprehensive traditional manufacturing information system that can be adapted for global manufacturing.

Most packaged systems are designed for a single plant, and their bills of material (BOMs) typically list only component and lead-time requirements. Such BOMs do not provide the comprehensive details of manufacturing supplies, facilities, and materials that global manufacturing requires.

Most manufacturing resource planning

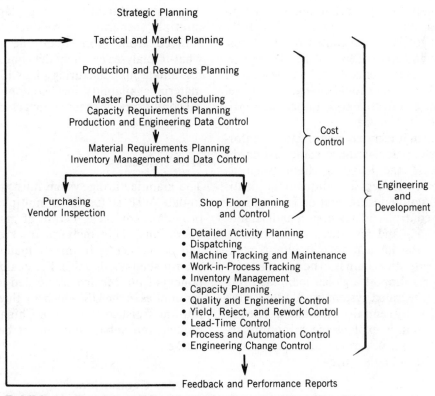

Exhibit 1. Elements of a Traditional Manufacturing Information System

(MRP) systems focus on plant functions, such as obtaining materials on time, manufacturing on time, and maintaining certain levels of raw material, component, work-in-process (WIP), and finished-goods inventories. Global manufacturing requires that such functions be made applicable to multiple suppliers and customers. Traditional systems support data entry to a single host computer through terminals located within the facility; global manufacturing requires rapid data transfer between hosts at separate facilities. Centralized planning demands that accurate and up-to-date inventories be available for all locations to facilitate purchasing and distribution.

The nature of global manufacturing implies the use of different technologies at different manufacturing plants. Therefore, an integrated system must aggregate and present data from different shop floor control modules. Performance measurements and systems also differ from plant to plant, depending on the focus, technology, and goals of each plant. Hence, performance measurements should not be applied across the board but should change as requirements change. Effectiveness, rather than efficiency, must be the goal.

However, an integrated manufacturing information system does require some standardization across the logistics chain, such as standard part numbers for unique item identification, common documentation for engineering change control, and a common understanding of capacity and resource use parameters. Standardization in such areas is vital if planning for the logistics chain is to be centralized.

To properly support a global manufacturing policy, the integrated system must address the needs dictated by centralized planning. The following paragraphs explore the minimum requirements of an integrated information system for global manufacturing.

Multiplant Product Structure.

A system must support multiple sources, plants, and planning parameters (e.g., lead times, yields, and rejection rates) for the same item produced at various locations.

The structure should allocate production responsibilities based on such factors as fixed percentages, capacity limitations, and mandatory practices (e.g., sourcing from a plant in India may require that a certain amount of Indian material be used, in conformance with local content laws). Production can be allocated to several plants if multiplant manufacturing is necessary for a certain component, assembly, or product.

Multitiered Planning.

Production planning and master scheduling should be multitiered to accommodate multiple plants. Traditionally, a product master schedule is based on a single plant's capacity. The system should be able to plan and assess multiple scenarios for products that can be sourced from more than one plant. Such what-if analyses can help the company quickly reevaluate manufacturing plans if labor costs, material availability, local content laws, political conditions, or other factors change at a particular plant.

WIP Tracking.

The manufacturing system must maintain up-to-date WIP status from multiple sources to provide a complete picture of manufacturing operations. This includes tracking products and components, from raw material through the finished-goods stage. For example, if components from Mexico are needed to build subassemblies in the US, which are then assembled into the finished product in China, each component and subassembly must be separately tracked.

Vendor Evaluation.

Vendor evaluation must be part of the global purchasing system. Traditional evaluation criteria, such as delivery performance, price, and reliability, must be augmented by qualitative measures that can be converted to qualified ratings for evaluation purposes. Such measures include stability, technology, capacity, and ability to handle higher technologies and more complex designs. Lists of current and potential vendors should be maintained and updated within the system.

OTHER ISSUES IN GLOBAL SYSTEMS IMPLEMENTATION

Exhibit 2 lists many external factors that affect the implementation of a system for global strategy. Corporate management must carefully assess the ramifications of each factor on the company's proposed system.

Technology Policies and Strategies

An effective global manufacturing system requires a rational plan for establishing appropri-

Exhibit 2.   Nonmanufacturing Issues in System Implementation

Issues	Factors
Technology Policies and Strategies	Level of technologies
	Location of plants
	Technology transfer
	R&D information dissemination
	Market potential
	Supplier potential
	Regulations
	Standards
Centralization versus Decentralization	Information flow
	Reporting
	Performance measurement
	Planning
	Logistics
Education	All aspects of manufacturing
Management Commitment	Espoused
	Actual
	Perceived
Communication	Policies and procedures

ate levels of technology at different production facilities and assigning products, components, or subassemblies to be manufactured at each location. It may be necessary to perform final assembly in a certain country with subassemblies manufactured in another country. Exhibit 3 illustrates a case in which a lower level of technology is necessary for the assembly of the finished product than for the manufacture of the subassemblies. If the finished product is an electronic measuring instrument, for example, integrated circuit manufacturing would require a higher level of technology than final assembly.

In some countries, laws require a certain percentage of local labor and material content, which may justify a lower level of technology. However, a country's potential market growth could outweigh this factor because local production may minimize transportation costs and increase response time to market demands. In such a case, the manufacturing technology may be established at a lower level but should be easily upgraded.

Centralized Management

Corporate planning managers are often unaccustomed to planning a widespread logistics chain and assuming the responsibilities that a global system entails. Local managers in established plants, on the other hand, are accustomed to a higher degree of autonomy in planning, scheduling, and execution than a global system allows. Managers at all levels must be educated on quality awareness, planning and scheduling responsibilities, and job coordination and cooperation.

Since performance measurement techniques must be changed to accommodate each new situation, traditional cost-based measures, such as variance and contribution, are obsolete and may be dangerous. Performance measurements must assess the following factors, which constitute the rationale for adopting a global manufacturing policy:

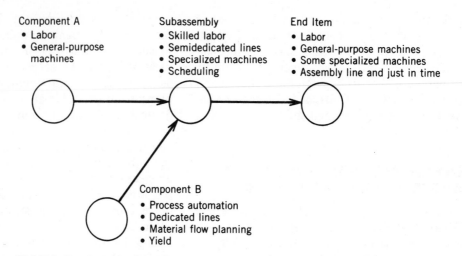

Exhibit 3. Possible Technology Requirements of Different Production Stages

• Delivery performance—The speed and accuracy of delivery to geographically dispersed plants and customers must be carefully measured.

• Quality assurance—The cycle of inspection, rejection, return, and replacement is very costly and time-consuming, and shortages of components attributable to faulty manufacturing can result in stoppages of subsequent processes if safety stock is not maintained. With the increased emphasis on foreign production, quality is a vital concern.

• Cost—A major incentive for manufacturing abroad is lower production cost. Therefore, value-added tracking (i.e., comparing actual cost roll-ups with standards) should be an integral part of the assessment.

Determining and maintaining standards are vital steps in centralized planning. Valid standards are essential for controlling nonmanufacturing activities (e.g., corporate software development) and production activities. Their development should be based on reasonable assumptions and measurements or on well-reasoned hypotheses, if data is unavailable. Standards should be maintained by comparing actual performance with previous standards, and the standards should be updated as new technologies are introduced and efficiency improves.

Commitment, Education, and Communications

The most important non-information system factors that affect the implementation of a glo-bal manufacturing policy are human resource factors. Whether executives can obtain commitment to the change from employees, educate them in the new system, and communicate and synchronize organizational direction may be the ultimate test of their ability to oversee the project.

THE LOGISTICS CHAIN

The requirements for a global manufacturing system will be determined by the configuration of the logistics network. Each logistics function should be analyzed in two ways: as it is currently performed and as it must be adapted to fit the overall plan and direction. A system perspective, or top-down analysis, should be used to avoid the "islands-of-information" syndrome and deter the tendency to directly transfer a local system to an international environment. Based on the overall strategic plan and direction of an organization, a detailed analysis of all aspects of the logistics chain should be made. In this way, long-term and short-term objectives can be translated into policies and procedures for operating the system. Exhibit 4 illustrates the methodology for analyzing and developing the system and the various issues and parameters that must be considered.

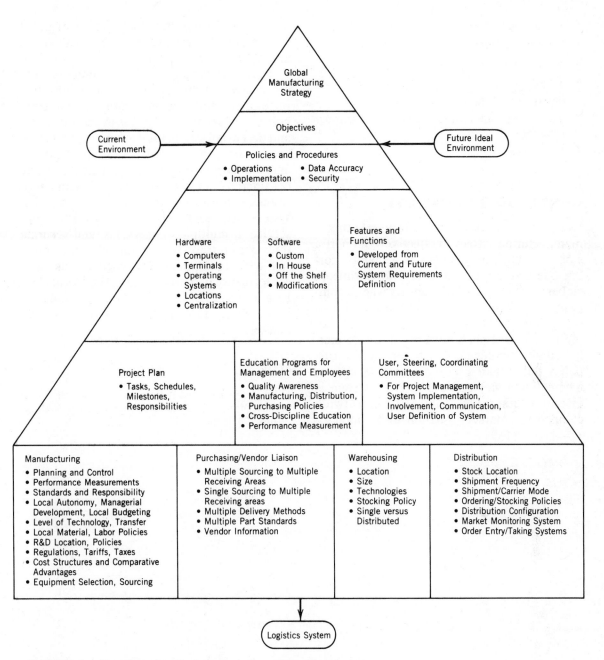

Exhibit 4. Manufacturing System Analysis and Development

The following aspects of the logistics chain should be addressed by an integrated information system for global manufacturing:

- Multiple vendors for similar parts.

- Warehouse planning.

- Accurate lead-time analysis and determination of multiple sources.

- Transportation and lead times.

- Scheduling.
- Delivery performance.
- Variable quality standards.
- Varying scrap, yield, and rejection rates.
- Safety stock requirements.
- Total throughput time (from design through distribution).
- Varying cost structures.

CONCLUDING COMMENTS

Designing, obtaining, and implementing a manufacturing system to effectively support a global manufacturing policy is a major effort but one that can be eminently worthwhile. A global policy may not be necessary when a company uses foreign manufacturing facilities solely to reduce labor and material costs for domestic competition, but when worldwide market conditions dictate a global manufacturing policy rather than a multinational policy, implementing a global manufacturing system is essential to survival. Increasing worldwide competition, market regulation, and market so-phistication are spurring the adoption of global manufacturing strategies by large, multinational manufacturing corporations.

Before a global policy is implemented, a fresh perspective on the capabilities of manufacturing systems and a reexamination of company policy are needed. Such issues as centralization and decentralization, local autonomy and managerial development, education and training, and standard setting and enforcement must be considered, and a companywide investment of resources must be made. Benefits of a global system include better coordination of customer service in multiple markets, fast and accurate information transfer, less difficulty in complying with local laws and regulations, and conformance of both centralized and local planning to overall objectives. The ultimate payoff is the ability to compete effectively in world markets.

NOTES

1. W. H. Davidson and P. Haspeslagh, "Shaping a Global Product Organization," *Harvard Business Review,* 60 (July–August 1982), pp. 125–132.

SECTION 7

R&D AND INNOVATION MANAGEMENT

Multinational and global corporations face important international technology issues. In many industries, new products and processes are necessary for survival. A major reason that many corporations expand abroad is to acquire foreign technology or to exploit technological advantages. Abundant evidence indicates that the market is the most important stimulus for innovation in both consumer and industrial goods. Companies that can gain knowledge and experience with innovations can pass what they have learned to their other operating units.

Through the 1960s, countries developed innovations based on market size and product demand. The United States, as the largest market and highest-income country in the world, held a virtual monopoly on labor-saving innovations. European innovations tended to be material-saving, and Japanese innovations were both material- and space-saving. Obviously, all were responding to demand. The United States, which historically had experienced a shortage of skilled labor, had high labor costs. European firms had high material costs and Japanese firms contended with both high space and high material costs.

In the past two decades this environment has changed. As labor costs increased significantly, Japanese and European companies developed labor-saving innovations. Material costs increased substantially in the United States, providing a stimulus for material-saving innovations. In addition, rising disposable incomes in many countries greatly expanded the number of potential sites for consumer goods innovations.

Scott Paper Company is an example. In 1989, Scott added paper machines in Italy and Spain to those already in France and Belgium. U.S. paper-making technology, superior to European processes, made a cheaper and better product. European sales of Scott products rose from $900 million in 1987 to over $1 billion in 1988. Scott figured that this growth would increase substantially with the additional production sites.[1] Another American company, The

[1]"The U.S. Gets Back in Fighting Shape," *Fortune* (April 24, 1989), pp. 43–48.

Stanley Works, located some of its engineering, design, and manufacturing of certain tools in England because of a burgeoning European Community market.

Growing industrial bases in many countries, coupled with growing similarities in production processes, have increased significantly the number of countries that can provide stimuli for industrial products innovation. For example, West Germany's Siemens plans to acquire American companies to tap technological advances in factory automation, telecommunications, and semiconductors.

It would seem, then, that the more countries in which a firm operates, the more potential opportunities it has to innovate. It would also seem that multinational firms might want to spread their R&D and innovative development across several countries. Widespread operations might both maximize the firm's exposure to innovation opportunities and facilitate commercialization through close market contacts. On the other hand, as country markets become more similar, it can be argued that any market can stimulate R&D and serve as a testing ground and that centralized R&D is far less expensive for the company.

The debate over the optimum organization of R&D activities continues. As we noted, U.S. firms are doing an increasing proportion of their R&D outside the United States. European companies are at least as likely, and perhaps even more likely than U.S. firms, to carry out R&D abroad. Japanese firms continue to locate their R&D facilities in Japan even when they manufacture products for specific foreign markets abroad.

Firms consider political and economic conditions as well as markets when they make their location decisions. Some host governments, particularly in developing countries, view favorably those multinationals that locate their R&D facilities locally. Host government pressure supports decentralization. Multinationals may decide to locate R&D abroad after considering such factors as where they can acquire needed skills, whether they can economically justify the investment, whether foreign countries provide enough incentives, and whether the foreign infrastructure is sufficient.

READING SELECTIONS

The first reading, by Jack Behrman and William Fischer, identifies three alternative primary market orientations shown by transnational corporations: home, host, and world market. The authors studied the overseas R&D activities of 53 U.S. and European multinational corporations and linked their overseas R&D activities to their primary market orientations. They found that the location of R&D activity in the host market orientation firm is likely to be governed by market considerations. But the location of R&D in the world market firm is conditioned primarily by the availability of technical knowledge and talented people.

Arnoud De Meyer and Atsuo Mizushima studied the global R&D efforts of European and Japanese multinationals. They acknowledge that they studied development laboratories rather than research outlets. But, they point out, it is important to think *now* about global competition and the location of R&D facilities. All of the companies studied reported that it was easier to centralize R&D than globalize but there were two major managerial problems that multinationals have to consider.

The first problem is finding the right balance between centralized activities that avoid inefficiencies and duplication, and a level of autonomy that fosters the best deployment of local entrepreneurship and technical expertise. The second problem is optimizing information flows among laboratories and researchers.

The authors conclude that global R&D management will be increasingly important to managers of global operating companies. They provide a number of assertions that could lead to a new model for the management of an international network of laboratories.

The short article by Tadahiro Sekimoto, president of Nippon Electric Corporation (NEC), presents the operating manager's perspective of technological change. In his view, the world is in the midst of a great transformation based on a core technology of information. Computers and communication technology will usher in an information society that will restructure industry. Sekimoto reports that Nippon Electric Corporation has set its sights on R&D as the essential force that propels the company.

Christopher Freeman takes the European perspective of technology and R&D. In the late 1970s, the Organization for Economic Cooperation and Development (OECD) sponsored a survey of R&D specialists in a number of countries. The survey asked whether R&D was becoming more or less important. Respondents were nearly unanimous that R&D was growing and would continue to grow.

Freeman presents five generic technology programs, indicating a need for a taxonomy of technical innovations so that public investment in generic technologies and specific R&D projects can be assessed. His taxonomy distinguishes among four categories of innovation: incremental innovations, radical innovations, changes of "technology system," and change in "technoeconomic paradigm." Freeman argues that the problems of structural change confronting OECD economies are associated with the change from one technoeconomic paradigm to another.

31

TRANSNATIONAL CORPORATIONS: MARKET ORIENTATIONS AND R&D ABROAD

Jack N. Behrman
William A. Fischer

Over the past several decades, the transfer of technology, in its various guises, has become an accepted part of doing business for transnational corporations and has been profitable for many of them. Other things being equal, most transnational corporations would be reluctant to transfer abroad the origins of their technology—their research and development (R&D) activities. Since other things are not equal in reality, however, the transnationals have increasingly found themselves considering where and how they will do their R&D. For many of them this is a relatively new situation, but, given expectations in the developing countries, one which will become more common in the near future.

R&D activities of American firms abroad have increased over the past decade. The 1966 foreign R&D expenditures of American companies were estimated to be $537 million.[1] By 1979:

Expenditures of U.S. firms for research and development performed abroad reached $1.5 billion, increasing 41 percent from 1974 to 1977, compared to a 32 percent increase for industrial research and development performed within the United States.[2]

Yet it was further noted that "the vast majority of U.S. firms do not conduct any research and development abroad. According to the Census Bureau, only an estimated 15 percent of the

Source: *The Columbia Journal of World Business* (Fall 1980), pp. 55–60. Copyright © by the Trustees of Columbia University in the City of New York. Reprinted by permission.

major U.S. industrial performers maintain foreign laboratories. These firms, however, account for nearly one-half of total U.S. company–funded R&D expenditures."[3]

In order to formulate effective policies, officials in developing and developed countries, and in the transnational corporations, need to understand why certain firms choose to pursue R&D abroad while others don't, and what the consequences of such activities are. None of this information is available from the statistics.

Recently, several studies of multinational R&D behavior have chronicled the experiences of transnational firms performing R&D abroad.[4] While these case studies improve our understanding of this phenomenon by supplying more information, they tend to lack a framework enabling them to go beyond mere data collection to a fuller understanding of the dynamics involved in the foreign R&D location decision. On the basis of a substantial amount of interviewing among transnational corporations, we believe that a rather simple taxonomy based upon market orientations can be quite useful in explaining the decision to do R&D abroad.

MARKET ORIENTATIONS

The market orientation of a transnational corporation refers to the market it is primarily interested in serving. There are three possible primary market orientations: home market, host market, and world market. While it is possible for a firm to appear to have several market orientations, they are often mutually exclusive for a given product line.

Home Market Firms

"Home market" firms are primarily concerned with investing abroad for the purpose of serving their domestic market through imports of materials and components. It is unusual for them to have international R&D operations. To the extent that such firms do R&D abroad, it usually is in support of their domestic market objectives. Typical firms of this type are the extractive industries and offshore component assemblers taking advantage of resource availability or low-wage labor in foreign locations to improve their ability to compete domestically. These firms can be expected to have few durable foreign scientific and technical commitments, a highly ethnocentric managerial style, low external orientation on the part of management, and an organizational structure that is largely unaffected by the firm's foreign operations. The products of these firms tend to be highly standardized, often because of their commodity nature, needing no diversified R&D effort.

Host Market Firms

Foreign affiliates of "host market" firms are oriented to the markets of the place where they are located. Included among these firms are industries spanning a range of technical sophistication from chemicals and pharmaceuticals, to foods and tobacco, to services. The products of the firms in this category typically exhibit a high degree of standardization within a market but not necessarily between markets. The management style of these firms can be characterized as polycentric, since a relatively low level of control is exerted by corporate headquarters over a decentralized organizational structure. Their need for R&D abroad is dictated by the diversity of market demands on their products.

World Market Firms

"World market" firms are those whose foreign affiliates are integrated to serve a standardized international market. These firms are typically organized to achieve economies of scale based upon high technology and a high degree of worldwide product standardization, and guided by a geocentric management style and a highly centralized corporate structure. They also have diverse R&D needs reflecting the range of markets they serve and the sources of ideas they must monitor.

THE SAMPLE STUDIED

The utility of these market orientations in explaining foreign R&D behavior among transnational corporations was demonstrated in a study of 35 American and 18 European transnational corporations, undertaken during 1978. The purpose of the study was to determine: what type of R&D is being performed abroad by transnational corporations; how they have come to select their foreign sites; how they manage their foreign R&D activities; what sort of collaborative R&D activities they are engaged in; and the nature of their relationship with host-country governments.[5]

Data collection for the study consisted of structured interviews conducted with top R&D executives in each firm. The average interview lasted approximately two and one-half hours, ranging from one hour in the few firms with little foreign R&D experience to a full day with those with extensive experience. Most of the firms interviewed were chosen because of their foreign R&D experience.

FOREIGN R&D ACTIVITIES OF THE FIRMS STUDIED

Although the firms were selected because of their foreign R&D experiences, the volume of activity discovered was surprising. Among the 31 American transnationals reporting foreign R&D activities, 106 active foreign R&D groups were identified. Furthermore, the European transnationals appeared even more active, with the 18 firms interviewed reporting 100 distinct foreign R&D activities. While most of these foreign activities were smaller in size and more restricted in scope than the R&D activities pursued at home, they were distinctly involved with R&D and were not technical services or quality control.

The firms included in this study were typically large firms (*Fortune* 500 members) whose relatively strong commitment to R&D was evidenced by their membership in the Industrial Research Institute in the U.S. or the European Industrial Research Managers Association. Although they exhibited significant foreign R&D activities, their international manufacturing and marketing operations were far more numerous and dispersed than their R&D activities. Although the firms we shall describe are clearly among the largest in the world in terms of both sales and geographic spread, they are representative of firms pursuing R&D activities in foreign locations, since such activities, by their very nature, are the domain of large multinational organizations.

The large majority of the foreign R&D activities identified among the American transnational corporations belonged to firms with a "host market" orientation (96 out of the 106 foreign R&D activities identified, or 91%). While this reflects, to some extent, the prepon-

derance of "host market" firms in the sample 23 of the 34 American firms (68%) had "host market" orientations it goes beyond a simple proportional relationship. The "host market" companies averaged more than four foreign R&D activities per firm, compared with less than two among the four American "world market" companies, and slightly less than one-half of a foreign R&D activity for each of the seven American "home market" companies (Table 1). All of the European firms, but one, had "host market" orientations. Thus, a comparison of their propensity to pursue R&D abroad cannot be made with their counterparts favoring other market orientations. However, when the European R&D activities are considered along with those of the American firms, the combined 38 "host market" firms account for 184 foreign R&D activities, or 89% of those identified.

Among the American transnational corporations it was possible to discern the nature of the R&D mission assigned to most of the foreign R&D activities. Thirty of the 106 foreign R&D activities (28%) had missions which included new product research, and of these 30 facilities, 25 belonged to "host market" firms and five belonged to "world market" companies (Table 2). Three of the five foreign laboratories of American corporations dedicated to exploratory research belonged to "world market" firms.

Table 1 Foreign R&D Activities of Transnational Corporations

Market Orientation	American Firms	
	Number of Firms	Number of Foreign R&D Activities
Home market	7	3
Host market	23	96
World market	4	7
Not included	1	
	European Firms	
Home market	0	0
Host market	15	88
World market	1	12
Not included	2	

Table 2 Inclusion of New Product: Research Responsibilities in the Missions of Foreign Laboratories (American Firms Only)

Market Orientation	Number of Foreign Laboratories with a New Product Research Mission	Percentage of Foreign Laboratories with a New Product Research Mission
"World market"	5	71%
"Host market"	25	26
"Home market"	0	0

LOCATION OF FOREIGN R&D ACTIVITIES

Over thirty different countries were identified in our interviews as hosting the foreign R&D activities of the firms in the sample. Both American and European firms indicated that their foreign R&D activities were predominantly located in developed countries, such as the U.S., France, the U.K., Japan, Canada, Australia, and Germany, and in advanced developing countries, such as Mexico, Brazil, and India (Table 3).

The "host market" firms appeared most likely to establish R&D activities in developing countries. As it was important to them to get as close to the markets they were serving as possible, they would favorably consider developing country locations when necessary, if the market was an attractive one and if the R&D group could be supported both financially and technically.

THE MOTIVATION TO DO R&D ABROAD

The propensity of various firms to do R&D in the developing countries highlights the topic of motivation to do R&D abroad. "Home market" firms typically have little or no sales in foreign markets. When they do sell to foreign customers, they view it as a direct extension of their domestic business, not requiring any further R&D beyond that which has already been performed for the original, (domestic) market. Because of their extractive operations, and their employment of low-wage workers for assembly operations, "home market" firms tend to have high exposure in the developing world. They have not, however, located much R&D activity in these countries because they typically do not refine raw materials or sell components or finished products in these markets. Accordingly, in those few instances when "home market" companies did consider doing R&D abroad they were most interested in being close to their foreign operations in order to provide technical support.

Firms involved in the international marketing of goods and services designed to satisfy local styles and tastes have a more compelling reason to do R&D abroad. These firms need to

Table 3 Most Popular Sites for Foreign R&D Activities*

American Firms		European Firms	
U.K.	(11)	U.S.	(14)
Australia	(8)	France	(10)
Canada	(8)	Germany	(9)
Japan	(8)	India	(6)
France	(7)	Brazil	(5)
Germany	(6)	U.K.	(5)
Mexico	(6)		
Brazil	(5)		

*Numbers in parentheses refer to the number of corporations reporting an R&D presence in particular country.

be as close to their markets as possible. Illustrative of such motivation is the agricultural chemical firm that needs to test its products in the markets they are intended for and, hence, has facilities in South America to treat South American pest problems, facilities in the Far East to address problems of tropical climates, and facilities in the Philippines to provide market conditions indicative of Japan. Similarly, all of the American pharmaceutical firms interviewed had European formulation laboratories as a result of European preferences for drug administration practices which differ from those in the U.S.

"Host market" firms also tend to endorse the proposition that their foreign affiliates often serve distinctive markets and, as such, are autonomous business entities requiring R&D of their own. Rosemarie Van Rumker's experience with Chemagro Corporation explains just such a philosophy:

Attempts to establish direct *links between research in one country and technology and the market place in another country have largely been unsuccessful. In my experience, the barriers of distance and language can be overcome reasonably well by scientists working within the same discipline, but scientists in one country are not good at answering the specific market needs of another country. . . .*

We believe that the best way to overcome this problem is to have subsidiaries in important markets away from the parent company develop their own complete R&D organizations, to enable them to take full and direct advantage of the opportunities peculiar to their environment, and to be full-fledged practicing members of the scientific and technological community in their country.[6]

While all of the firms interviewed expressed an interest in enhancing their relationship with host country governments, the "host market" firms, with their national market focus, were particularly sensitive to the importance of such

relationships. In a number of cases, this sensitivity resulted in the establishment of foreign R&D activities, some of which have become particularly productive.

The "world market" firms are concerned with the availability abroad of specific types of skills in particular technical areas. This, of course, is in keeping with their propensity to assign new product development responsibility to foreign R&D groups. More than one of the foreign R&D laboratories of the "world market" firms was characterized as having achieved a level of competence in a technical area which far surpassed the capabilities of other research groups in the corporation. Accordingly, "world market" firms typically establish their R&D abroad without regard for the location of their existing international manufacturing and marketing operations. They are much more attracted to the concentration of knowledge and talent than to market size in a foreign country.

A summary of the important criteria for considering or not considering overseas R&D locations by firms in the various market orientation categories is presented in Table 4.

THE CRITICAL MASS OF FOREIGN R&D GROUPS

As Table 4 reveals, one of the principal deterrents to the performance of R&D abroad by transnational firms is their perception that they will be unable to assemble an R&D group large enough and diverse enough to be productive. While the size of an R&D group is a function of many variables, there is substantial agreement within the R&D community that a "critical mass" of R&D professionals must be reached if a laboratory is to be a worthwhile investment. This "critical mass" is the size necessary to ensure rich communications both within the group and between the group and its environment, to allow the degree of scientific and technical interaction among the group's personnel necessary to fulfill its mission, and to acquire whatever instrumentation and organization are

Table 4 Important Criteria for Considering or Not Considering Overseas R&D Locations

	Home Market Firms	Host Market Firms	Worldwide Market Firms
Important criteria for considering an overseas R&D location	1. Proximity to operations	1. Proximity to markets	1. Availability of pockets of skills in particular technical areas
	2. Availability of universities	2. Concept of overseas operations as full-scale business entities	2. Access to foreign scientific and technical communities 3. Availability of adequate infrastructure and universities
Important criteria for not considering overseas R&D locations	1. Products sold in the developing countries are not sophisticated 2. Lack of qualified scientists and engineers 3. Economics of centralized R&D	1. Increasing costs of doing R&D overseas 2. Economics of centralized R&D	1. Economics of centralized R&D 2. Difficulties in assembling R&D teams

necessary for acceptable performance. There is considerable variation in the estimates of "critical mass" for specific situations, but in general, R&D laboratories in industries serving consumer markets (i.e., "host market" firms) require a smaller R&D staff to reach "critical mass" than do laboratories in science based industries. Furthermore, R&D groups in consumer-oriented industries require less sophisticated personnel and less variety in personnel specialization than do R&D groups in science based industries. These observations suggest that "host market" firms are more likely than their counterparts to be in a position to establish R&D in a developing country.

THE ESTABLISHMENT OF R&D ABROAD

There are several ways in which a transnational corporation can establish R&D activities

abroad: it can allow R&D to evolve from technical support activities for marketing or manufacturing; it can directly establish R&D activities abroad with the intention of doing R&D right from the start; it can acquire some other corporation's R&D activities; it can enter into some form of collaborative R&D arrangement with another partner. Just as market orientation appears to affect the location and mission of foreign R&D activities, it influences the means of establishing these activities.

In 71 of the foreign R&D activities of American firms it was possible to ascertain the means of establishment. In approximately one-half of these cases an evolutionary pattern where R&D originated from technical services was evident. Nearly all of these cases were found among "host market" firms and two of the three foreign "home market" laboratories were also in this group. In approximately 28 percent of the cases direct placement was the means of establishment and, while most of these were attributable to "host market" firms, more than 70 percent of the foreign laboratories of "world market" firms were established in this manner. Almost 25 percent of the laboratories were established through acquisition, all of them being by "host market" companies (Table 5).

The data collected on laboratory establishment appears to agree quite well with the findings reported earlier. "Home market" firms are not interested in R&D abroad and so what foreign R&D of theirs does exist is the result of an evolution of capabilities and missions among their technical support activities. Conversely, "world market" firms are interested in pursuing R&D abroad if they can gain access to particular technological skills or communities. Accordingly, they tend to rely more upon direct placement of their foreign R&D activities, as their other foreign commercial operations are not necessarily related to their R&D activities. "Host market" firms need to be close to the markets they serve and they will utilize a variety of methods to get there.

COLLABORATIVE R&D ARRANGEMENTS

At least 28 specific manufacturing joint ventures between parent companies of different nationalities, which required R&D support in some form, were reported in the interviews. All but four of these belonged to "host market" companies. Our interviews indicated quite clearly that the key determinant of *active* R&D participation by a transnational firm in such a venture is the ownership position it commands. Foreign joint ventures will bring forth *new* R&D only when the transnational firm can maintain control over that R&D, namely, when it possesses a majority interest in the joint venture.

HOST-GOVERNMENT RELATIONS

As noted earlier, although all firms professed an interest in maintaining good relationships with host country governments, "host market" firms appeared particularly sensitive to pressure from their hosts. During our interviews, fourteen American and five European firms indicated having received some form of pressure from host country governments hoping to influence their foreign R&D location decisions. Sixteen of these firms had "host market" orientations. Furthermore, 19 foreign R&D laboratories were identified as having their origins in host government pressure, three of these being joint ventures, and in four other cases the pressure resulted in the acquisition of R&D results without a laboratory. The countries most active in attempting to influence transnational corporations were Brazil, France, India, and Japan.

CONCLUSIONS

The data presented in this study argue strongly for the usefulness of a simple taxonomy of

Table 5 Methods of Establishing Foreign R&D Activities*

Market Orientation	Evolution from Technical Service	Direct Placement	Acquisition
"Home market"	2	0	0
"Host market"	33	11	18
"World market"	2	5	0

*The data in this table represent only those instances where the means of establishing the foreign laboratory could be ascertained. All data in this table come from American corporations.

transnational corporations, based upon market orientations. The location and operations of foreign R&D laboratories of transnational corporations can be explained by referring to the market orientations of the firms in question.

The data presented indicated that a considerable amount of R&D is presently being performed abroad by both American and European transnational corporations. While most of this R&D is located in developed countries, there is diversity among the locations selected. This diversity, in part, reflects the varying market orientations of the firms. Market orientation also appears to be an important determinant of the means by which a transnational corporation establishes R&D activities abroad.

The evidence presented suggests that transnational corporations with "host market" orientations are generally most likely to pursue R&D abroad, particularly when developing countries are at issue. They are, however, less likely than their "world market" counterparts to delegate new product research responsibilities to their foreign laboratories, and they also rely heavily upon evolution from technical

services as a means of establishing foreign R&D groups.

NOTES

1. D. Creamer, *Overseas Research and Development by United States Multinationals, 1966–1975* (New York: The Conference Board, 1976), pp. 3–4.
2. "U.S. Industrial R&D Spending Abroad," Industry Studies Group, Division of Science Studies, U.S. National Science Foundation, *Reviews of Data on Science Resources,* NSF 79-304, No. 33 (April 1979), p. 1.
3. Ibid., p. 3.
4. W. T. Hanson, "Multinational R&D in Practice: Eastman Kodak Corporation," *Research Management* (January 1971), pp. 47–50; M. Papo, "How to Establish and Operate a Multinational Lab," *Research Management* (January 1971), pp. 12–19; R. Van Rumker, "Multinational R&D in Practice: Chemagro Corporation," *Research Management* (January 1971), pp. 50–54; R. C. Ronstadt, "International R&D: The Establishment and Evolution of Research and Development Abroad by Seven U.S. Multinationals," *Journal of International Business Studies,* Vol. 9 (1978), pp. 7–24.
5. For a more complete report on this study the reader is advised to see J. N. Behrman and W. A. Fischer, *Overseas R&D Activities of Transnational Companies* (Cambridge, Mass.: Oelgeschlager, Gunn & Hain, 1980).
6. Van Rumker, "Multinational R&D in Practice," p. 52. Emphasis added.

32

▬▬▬▬▬ GLOBAL R&D MANAGEMENT

Arnoud de Meyer
Atsuo Mizushima

Global R&D management, the management of company R&D effort distributed over different countries, a task that concerns multinational firms, has not been widely studied. The authors have therefore carried out in-depth studies of global R&D conducted by 7 European and 15 Japanese companies. Their objective was to identify "best practice" and so construct a framework for future research.

Part of this research was sponsored by Mitsubishi Research Institute (Tokyo).

Source: R&D Management, Vol. 19, no. 2 (April 1989), pp. 135–146.

The authors' conclusions are as follows. Globalisation, that is decentralisation of R&D, has become a necessity for multinationals as a result of the localisation of competition, of product life becoming shorter than development time, and the need to locate laboratories near sources of new technological know-how.

Because foreign acquisitions often lead to the acquisition of laboratories, questions are raised about how best to integrate them with the administrative practices of the "home" organization, whether to reorganize them or to close them down. When it is necessary to set up a new foreign-based laboratory deciding its exact location will require the weighing of factors such as whether the activities are to be market or process oriented, where on the R to D scale the activities will be placed, and how far direction of the laboratory's programmes and work will be decentralised.

Global management also demands special attention to the building of an open communication network among the laboratories, the best form of which has yet to be determined. The main concern in human resources management will be how to select and develop an internationally oriented management corps and how to train R&D professionals to communicate across sites.

If globally dispersed R&D laboratories are to be most effectively used then a new framework for their management needs to be developed. The authors believe that their findings should form a useful starting-point for this task.

INTRODUCTION

Management of research and development activities in laboratories located in different countries (i.e., global R&D management), is not a very widely studied topic. The reason is not that the importance of innovation to internationally operating companies has not been recognised. In fact quite a lot of theory building about the multinational company goes back to Vernon (1966), who proposed with the product cycle theory the fact that the ability to innovate is the *raison d'être* for multinational corporations. The recent literature on global competition stresses even more the importance of innovation for the multinational corporation in its struggle for survival.

Though innovation is thus recognised by many as having much practical importance to international management, the topic of innovations in multinational companies and more particularly the topic of international R&D has received little attention. Past research on multinational corporations has focussed more on strategy or structure, with most attention being paid to the determinants of headquarters-subsidiary relationships as opposed to their consequences (see for an overview Ghoshal and Bartlett, 1986).

Some efforts have been made to investigate certain isolated aspects of distributed R&D. Ronstadt (1977) has carried out an extensive analysis of the international R&D activities of 7 US multinationals. Behrman and Fischer (1980) report on structured interviews at 34 transnational corporations in the US, 16 in Europe and 6 in Japan. Hakanson and Zander (1986) have reported on four in-depth case studies of Swedish companies. Booz, Allen & Hamilton carried out in 1986 a survey of 16 multinationals to identify the most effective approaches for building global competitiveness in technology (Harris, 1987). All of these studies are studies of "best practice." None of them has even attempted to measure the relationship between performance and the practice used. In this paper, we will attempt to summarize the issues and problems in global R&D management, on the basis of these four studies, and our own case-based research. We will also propose a framework for further research.

THE RESEARCH PROJECT

Our own research consists at this stage of seven in-depth case studies of European companies operating multinationally, with research and development activities in more than one country. In each of these case studies, several executives involved in R&D activities were interviewed, and the results of these interviews were complemented with desk research, leading to extensive research cases. Part of the study was carried out in parallel with and sponsored by a Japanese research institute. As a consequence, we had access to data gathered in about 15 Japanese companies which had recently started R&D activities overseas.

The term R&D has to be handled with caution. Most of the laboratories we studied were development laboratories rather than research outlets. Only in a few cases did we have access to data on global research management.

Again, it should be mentioned that we did not attempt at this stage of the research to relate performance of the R&D network to the particular practice of R&D management. Our insights too are "best practice" descriptions which have to be studied with caution.

THE STATE OF THE ART

The Need for International R&D: Why and Where

Why Do Companies Locate R&D Abroad?

The evidence of R&D abroad is scant and based almost solely on US data. The existing statistics indicate that it is still not very common but that it is on the other hand growing. Some data seem to indicate that international R&D is more common for European companies than it is, even today, for US companies. The early internationalisation of European companies during the colonial period, and the fact that Europe consists of a patchwork of a few larger and many fairly small countries, make it all the more understandable why there are quite a few large European companies which have long-standing R&D laboratories in different countries. One should however not

even in Europe overestimate the amount of research carried out abroad. In Sweden for example, the dominant share of R&D (86%) carried out by Swedish multinationals in 1984 was still located in Sweden.

Moreover, the fact that laboratories are located in different countries does not necessarily mean that these Europeans companies have a truly global approach to R&D management. Often, in the past, European companies consisted of a "confederation" of country subsidiaries, which were more or less independently operating, and had developed their own local development capabilities. The sum of these local development activities cannot always be added up to a global approach to R&D.

Though international R&D might not yet be an important activity from a macroeconomic point of view, the strategic management literature indicates that the increasing global competition will require internationally operating companies to rethink the way they have organised their R&D. "While traditionally many multinational corporations could compete successfully by exploiting scale economies or arbitrating imperfections in the world's goods, labour and capital markets, such advantages have tended to erode over time. In many industries, multinational corporations no longer compete primarily with numerous national companies, but with a handful of giants who tend to be comparable in terms of size, international resource access, and worldwide market position. Under these circumstances, the ability to innovate and to exploit those innovations globally in a rapid and efficient manner has become essential for survival, and perhaps the most important sources of a multinational's competitive advantage" (Ghoshal and Bartlett, 1987). From a management point of view the question of how to optimally manage the R&D function becomes all the more urgent.

These authors look at the globalisation in a pro-active way. A more conservative approach was equally prevalent in some of the Japanese companies we studied. The threat of retaliation activities by the US in the US/Japanese trade discussion, and the fear that the European integration after 1992 could lead to the possible creation of "fortress Europe," that is, the closing of the trade borders for outsiders to the big European market, has led many heavily exporting Japanese enterprises to invest in manufacturing facilities overseas. In a technology-intensive world, where the speed of the response to market needs becomes an essential element of the competitive strategy, it is felt that pure marketing and manufacturing activities cannot be sufficient in this process of globalisation. Consequently, this process of globalisation will lead to an increase in the extent to which the company develops peripheral activities around its production facilities, for example, process and product engineering, and ultimately R&D activities.

Another way of looking at what the trigger is for locating R&D abroad has been described earlier by De Meyer (1984). One of the reasons why a firm might consider creating R&D capabilities abroad is that the corporate central research is not able to provide the locally needed technology efficiently and effectively. This problem is in fact a trade-off between the costs associated with the exchange of information—from the parent to the subsidiary and *vice versa,* and associated with markets and/or technology—and the opportunity costs incurred by missed opportunities due to untransferred information on the one hand and the loss of economies of scale and critical mass in R&D on the other. Stated differently, a company will decide to internationalise its R&D activities when the information transaction costs become larger than the costs involved in duplicating the research facilities and organisation. Since information can be market oriented as well as technology oriented, the decision to internationalise R&D can be taken to be closer to the customer as well as to be closer to centres of technical or scientific excellence.

Types of Global R&D Laboratories Ronstadt (1977) describes four types of international

R&D activities. His model is based on the international product lifecycle and it classifies foreign R&D on the basis of their activities:

1. *Transfer technology units* or units established to help certain foreign subsidiaries transfer manufacturing technology from the parent while also providing related technical services for foreign customers.
2. *Indigenous technology units* or units established to develop new and improved products expressly for the foreign market. These products were not the direct result of new technology supplied by the parent organisation.
3. *Global technology units* or units established to develop new products and processes for simultaneous application in major world markets of the company.
4. *Corporate technology units* or units established to generate new technology of a long term or exploratory nature expressly for the parent.

The framework based on these four categories is attractive since it provides a trajectory for the logical evolution of an R&D laboratory overseas. It suggests how to start and develop an international network of laboratories, and it also brings a system of hierarchy to the network of laboratories. But Ronstadt makes the point that the US companies he studied had started their international R&D in all four categories, and that there is no reason why one would have to start with group one. Once started, there seems to be evidence that the vast majority of R&D investments follows the evolutionary pattern from technology transfer unit over indigenous technology unit to global technology unit. This model is of course in agreement with the theory about the international product lifecycle. Globalisation of competition has however brought some doubts about the validity of this model, and we probably have to use Ronstadt's model with necessary caution (De Meyer and Schuette, 1989). The types of laboratories he describes probably still exist, but the evolutionary pattern he sees might have changed.

Behrman and Fischer (1980) found, for example, that more than one-half of the foreign R&D groups of the American transnationals they studied were established through the evolution of skills, capabilities, and missions, from an initial emphasis on technical support to manufacturing and marketing to applied R&D. This is similar to Ronstadt's model. But foreign laboratories with (global or regional) new product responsibilities (including exploratory research) were, however, more likely to be established through direct placement rather than evolution.

Moreover, Ronstadt's model does not provide a useful tool when it comes to the management of laboratories which are "created" through acquisition of foreign companies. In these cases, one can end up with laboratories which are at a totally different stage than the one which the central laboratory is able to manage, and some regression to previous stages is not inconceivable.

The Swedish study (Hakanson and Zander, 1986) summarises the reasons for the increasing shares and volumes of foreign R&D as follows:

- The evolution of technical support functions at foreign subsidiaries to encompass more advanced product development tasks. Entrepreneurial subsidiary managers were able to exploit local market opportunities and attract and retain qualified technical personnel.
- Increasing reliance on acquisitions as a strategy for internal growth.
- International rationalisation of production, that is, the establishment of specialised manufacturing units with groupwide supply responsibility.
- Difficulties in recruiting qualified personnel on the tight Swedish labour market.
- The exploitation of foreign entrepreneurial and technical talent, sometimes in compensation for stagnating R&D at home.
- Advantages of proximity to customers and foreign research establishments.

These reasons include, apart from the market oriented reasons, also explicit supply reasons of availability of personnel (technical or entrepreneurial) or the proximity to the source of technological know-how. They emphasize that more than a few of the foreign R&D laboratories were the byproduct of acquisitions. Ronstadt mentions also that of the 55 R&D investments he studied, 13 were "incidental" because they were simply part of a company which was acquired for other reasons than the technology. The Booz, Allen & Hamilton survey comes to similar conclusions, but adds explicitly the need to meet (or bypass) national regulatory demands.

In our own case studies it became apparent that all the reasons mentioned in the Swedish study have played an important role. In five of the cases, markets were a primary determinant in locating R&D in different countries. But the lack of researchers, for example, in the home countries was definitely a secondary reason. For developments in more advanced technologies such as genetic engineering, too, lack of researchers in the home country and proximity to sources of technology in the US have played a major role. The proximity to sources of technology seems to be a reason which is increasing in importance. An interesting aspect of these types of sources appeared to be that their number is getting higher. Where, for example, for microelectronics it was quite obvious that in the 1960s, Boston and Palo Alto were sufficient to know what was going on, today there seem to be more places where knowledge in this field is created.

Summarising one can say that internationalisation of R&D activities has to do with a range of factors of market development, supply of technology, and is often triggered by acquisitions. Where the international product lifecycle could explain to a large extent internationalisation of R&D in the sixties and seventies, we need today a model which pays more attention than before to the role of supply of technology and global product development. In the concluding section, we will translate some of these findings into research propositions.

Selection of Location The criteria for the selection of the location are of course quite closely related to the reasons for going abroad with R&D. As Behrman and Fischer stress "the most powerful inducements to locate R&D in a particular foreign location appear to be the presence of a profitable affiliate in the foreign country, and a growing and sophisticated market with an adequate scientific and technical structure. The primary obstacles to locating R&D abroad appear to be the firms' perceptions of the economies of centralised R&D and the perceived difficulties of assembling an adequate R&D staff in foreign countries." In no instance was saving money on doing research a primary inducement to decentralise R&D in different countries.

Other reasons that can be found in the literature or which were derived from our own cases are (not in order of importance):

• Proximity to a manufacturing site, to be able to share costly overheads and to have an effective transfer of technology between R&D and manufacturing.

• The availability of adequate local universities, mainly as a stable supply of professionals, and sometimes for the availability of analytical testing or small pilot plant facilities.

• The ability to build up a critical mass of local researchers is most important in those cases where the laboratories carry out global technological research. Although there is considerable variation in the estimates of critical mass, it is clear that it varies with the scientific orientation of an industry and the type of R&D to be performed. Generally consumer oriented industries and process oriented industries require the least critical mass. Estimates vary from 25–30 technical people for paints and chemicals to 100–200 technical people for pharmaceuticals.

• The attractiveness of sources of technical excellence, for example, universities or research institutes, advanced customers or suppliers, and so on.

• Specific environmental conditions, in particular for food, chemical or agricultural research.

• Government requirements to increase the local technological content of the firm's activities. Though it is played down as a reason for the choice of a particular location, one can find that in the case of pharmaceutical development or products having an impact on the environment, local clinical testing is required in order to meet host-country regulations. These firms usually also mention, however, positive reasons such as speeding up the approval procedures if one can collaborate with local regulatory agencies, or the wisdom of using foreign academic researchers who might be on the local boards of health, and so on.

• Excellent communication systems: travel conditions were mentioned, but increasingly the quality of the electronic communications network is envisaged as an asset to a particular location.

• Work permit regulations for expatriates are often mentioned as a minor, though explicit element of the selection decision.

The Management Challenge

We have no record of companies which would indicate that it is easier to do R&D on a global scale than in a geographically centralised approach. Globalisation of R&D is typically accepted more with resignation than with pleasure. Risks of cost escalation, loss of economies of scale, difficulties to reach a critical mass, or risk or unintentional duplication of research are often mentioned as factors which inhibit firms from internationalising their R&D. In one of our own cases, internationalisation was almost described as an unavoidable nightmare, closer to a marketing gimmick than to an effectively contributing R&D outlet.

The two core management problems as we perceive them through the literature and the case studies are:

a. How to find the right balance between (i) a central control of the activities to avoid inefficiencies and unintentional duplication and (ii) a level of autonomy which is high enough to allow for an optimal deployment of local entrepreneurship and technical competence.

b. How to optimise the flows of information between the different laboratories and the individual researchers in those laboratories.

Central Control versus Autonomy: Management Style The Booz, Allen & Hamilton survey puts the management of a network of laboratories into the context of integration. They see primarily two approaches—the "hub" model and the "network" model. In the hub model, the home lab retains leadership in all technologies; centralised decision making is the norm. In the network model, individual laboratories focus on different missions.

To decide how to deploy technological resources, participants in the Booz, Allen & Hamilton survey indicated that they generally analyzed three factors—internal efficiency, market proximity requirements, and external constraints. If the demand for internal efficiency is high, participants favour centralised resources and top-down decision making for several reasons: scale advantages and more effective use of assets reduce costs. Multidisciplinary interaction is optimized. And internal communication is made easier.

When market proximity is critical or when external constraints are of prime consideration, companies tend to adopt the decentralised model.

Behrman and Fischer define four managerial styles influencing R&D activities: (1) absolute centralisation, (2) participative centralisation, (3) supervised freedom and (4) total freedom. They have found only a few examples of the first and the fourth types. The two dominant (and as is suggested implicitly in their description the two most successful) are the second and third types.

What they describe as "participative centralisation firms" tend to exert strong centralised authority over the funding, programmes, and often even over project selection decisions faced by the overseas subsidiaries. There is however some evidence of genuine participa-

tion by the overseas subsidiaries in the management of R&D activities.

"Supervised freedom" firms are characterised by both a number of R&D laboratories abroad and a tendency to place primary responsibility for operational decisions in the hands of foreign R&D management. Coordination appears to be far less formal than attempted by the participatively centralised firms and tends to rely on good personal relationships and lots of travel.

Their framework consists in fact of four discrete points on a continuum ranging from a confederation of non-integrated R&D laboratories to a central R&D laboratory which happens by chance to have its activities in different geographical locations. In our own data, the management style was scattered along this dimension and it became clear that the top R&D manager's attitude towards the desirable position on this dimension permeated his/her whole management approach. The choice of where to position oneself on the scale from absolute freedom to absolute control appears to us to be the central management decision in global R&D management. Coordination and control systems, communication systems, planning, seem all to be a consequence of this particular choice.

If our hypothesis should prove to be correct, the challenging question becomes, of course, what are the criteria which guide the top R&D manager in making this choice? Behrman and Fischer make no comments on the success of either of the forms of organisation they described. They conclude however that the scientific orientation of a firm appears to strongly influence the choice between both. Firms with a strong science-orientation tend to employ participatively centralised management styles. Most of the companies which started their foreign R&D as a direct placement rather than as an evolution from technical services, seemed to favour this participatively centralised management style. Consequently, one can say that the position of the technological work carried out by the laboratory *vis-à-vis* the state of the art is a first factor determining the position on this scale.

In our own case studies, three other factors seem to play a role. One of them is a conglomerate of influences which probably can best be defined as managerial culture, or the company's and the manager's basic attitude towards centralisation. In some of the Swiss/German firms we studied, the whole company seemed to be permeated by a tendency towards centralisation, which was reflected in the R&D management style. The second factor has to do with time. The higher the time pressure, that is, the pressure to shorten the response time to the market's requirements, the higher the tendency seemed to be to go to centralisation. The third factor has to do with the size of the foreign laboratories. The smaller the foreign laboratories, the higher the control exercised over them.

Central Control versus Autonomy: Organisational Structure   Traditionally one finds in the literature on the organisation of decentralised (not necessarily internationally) research laboratories three models, that is,

a.   The functional organisation where the several R&D laboratories report through the R&D function to the CEO, and where central R&D has a strong coordinating function.
b.   The divisionalised organisation where each division has its own divisional R&D reporting through the division manager to the CEO. In these cases a central R&D can have a coordinating and advising role.
c.   The matrix organisation where the subsidiary R&D manager reports both to a divisional and a central R&D manager.

These three approaches can of course easily be translated into an international R&D organisation. Division manager can in such cases be replaced by country manager. In some cases the matrix structure can become a three-dimensional structure in which the local R&D manager has to report to central R&D, the local country manager, and a product or divisional manager.

Hakanson and Zander (1986) propose on the basis of their Swedish study as one of their major conclusions that these traditional practices do not suffice to achieve the required level of international coordination and integration of R&D. They see an evolution to what they call *integrated networks*, characterised by tight and complex controls and high subsidiary involvement in the formulation and implementation of strategies. As a consequence of the strategic allocation of tasks between specialised units, heavy flows of technology, finance, people and materials tie subsidiaries to each other and to the parent. They see as a consequence the requirement for new roles and capacities for headquarters, divisions and subsidiaries. In fact they have developed a somewhat adapted version of the supervised freedom concept of Behrman and Fischer. They summarise their recommendations as follows:

a.   The central task of corporate level R&D staff is to act as a liaison between the R&D organisation and corporate management, that is, monitoring the R&D portfolio of the group to ensure its conformity with overall corporate strategy and to explain technological threats and opportunities in the formulation of corporate strategy.
b.   Divisional R&D staff carries the responsibility for the bulk of the R&D effort and must ensure worldwide coordination of R&D within its product areas. A central task in this context is to allocate R&D responsibilities in a way that both matches the technical capacity of different units and minimises the need for close and costly control.
c.   Line responsibility for foreign R&D units should rest with local subsidiary management with a great amount of discretion as to the allocation of R&D funds. Only in this way will decision processes be flexible enough to permit the rapid exploitation of new business opportunities.

They describe a fairly organic type of organisation which is strongly dependent on an extensive informal communication network, a great deal of lateral contacts, more or less formal co-ordination of committees of peers and a strong common corporate goal which provides the cement which is needed to have all subsidiaries evolving in the same direction.

One should be careful with their conclusions. They are based on a very limited number of cases, and the recommendations have no relation to a direct performance measure. However the concept of the integrated network as opposed to a more traditional structure clearly deserves some reflection.

Comparing our cases with these proposals one can see that none of them are pure forms of the organisational structures which are discussed above. We have found limited matrix structures with strong functional or divisional components, integrated networks, purely functional structures and structures which seem to organically move over the years, following the redistribution of power going on in other functions such as marketing and sales. It is fair to say that none of the cases we studied were pure examples of what management theory would describe. They were in almost every case a mixed form. The value of Hakanson and Zander's framework is probably that they have explicitly recognised the messiness of real organisations, and try to explain how the organisations work in those circumstances.

Communication Flows Communication flows have a twofold role in international research and development. As is stressed by Hakanson and Zander, but also mentioned in countless other publications, communication has an important coordination role. In this sense, it is the variable which can be fine-tuned to influence the position on the managerial style dimension. But beyond this, in R&D communication is at the core of the activities (Allen, 1977). One could argue that management of R&D is to a large extent the management of the information flows between the researchers and between

the research team and the outside sources of information.

Management of global R&D requires a careful monitoring, stimulation or limiting of the flow of information, from corporate headquarters to the subsidiaries, and *vice versa,* but also between the different subsidiaries. To a large extent these communications can be routinised and one can rely on impersonal media, letters, telexes, reports, and so on. Each of our case studies indicated that the companies have developed quite elaborate procedures, ranging from traditional written media, to the sophisticated deployment of worldwide accessible computerised databases.

But in the area of R&D the personal face-to-face communication remains of primordial importance. Indeed personal contacts are critical in several stages of the innovation cycle. Time and again it was stressed during the interviews leading to the case studies that lateral information flows had to be stimulated. Tools which were used by the companies we have studied were:

- a policy to stimulate travel and constant telephone contacts between the subsidiary managers and between the technological specialists;
- regular formal meetings or internal seminars with extensive informal "appendices";
- creation of a company culture which stimulates a very open information exchange;
- organisation of international working groups, project teams, and so on, leading to intense personal interaction between researchers of different countries;
- an active policy of job rotation of scientists and managers between different countries;
- language training.

One would hypothesize that some of the person-to-person communication will be replaced in the near future by real-time communication through electronic networks such as video-conferencing, computer conferences, electronic mail, and so on. Confronted with that hypothesis, most of the interviews accepted this, but most if not all of them indicated that there existed something which we could define as a "half-life time" of confidence in electronic communication.

To be able to collaborate on research projects, the geographically decentralised members of a research team need to trust each other. This trust can only be created through face-to-face encounters. Once separated, the team members can go on working with each other through electronic means, but like radiation, the trust they have in each other will gradually decrease. When this trust drops below a certain level, a new injection of confidence is needed, and this can only be achieved through face-to-face meetings. What the length is of the half-life time of confidence is not at all clear, but most of the companies with extensive experience with electronic communication systems appeared to have experienced this phenomenon.

International Human Resource Management

Managing R&D projects is first and foremost managing R&D professionals. Managing global R&D requires managing R&D professionals with a different cultural and educational background and managing the transfer of R&D "expatriates." The management of intercultural teams does not seem to pose too many problems, when it comes to researchers: the scientific culture seems to dominate local culture. To manage the laboratories two options are conceivable: local managers or expatriates.

Particularly during the start-up phase of an R&D facility, managers and employees are transferred from the parent company to the R&D laboratory. Edstrom and Galbraith (1977) developed a typology of transfers which is helpful in developing a transfer strategy and also for manpower and career planning.

- Transfer for staffing due to lack of local personnel to fill a given position;

- Transfer for management development. Head office employees can be transferred to positions in subsidiaries to learn how to manage in a foreign environment or to learn specific skills which might exist in a particular laboratory.

- Transfer for organizational development.

However, two things have to be kept in mind when transferring parent or third country nationals to a foreign research site:

1. Extensive literature exists on the high failure rate of expatriate managers. The percentages for premature termination of assignments vary between 10%–35% (variation in respect of the managers' parent country and in respect of the host country, e.g. 9 out of 10 expatriates were found to be significantly less successful in Japan than in previous assignments in the US (Zeira and Banai, 1984). The reason most frequently found for this outcome is the inability of the spouse to adjust to the new environment. Predeparture counselling and training can alleviate some of the pressures for the family and prevent severe cases of culture shock.

2. Using expatriate managers to lead a foreign R&D facility blocks the opportunities for promotion of the host country nationals and therefore often results in a decrease in their identification with the organisation. The conviction is intensified with each new rotation of their foreign superiors (Zeira and Harari, 1979). Such a negative promotional situation can, of course, be avoided through actively reinforcing international careers throughout the organization, that is, host country nationals have the opportunity to move beyond the regional level thus pursuing a global career similar to the headquarters' managers and scientists.

When it comes to selecting the manager for an international research laboratory, the common approach is primarily to look for technical competence, which almost always prevents immediate failure on the job. Selectors play safe by placing heavy emphasis on technical qualifications and little on the individual's ability to stimulate, develop and manage researchers.

One of the interviewers summarized that they would always be looking for a technological "star" to manage an international research laboratory.

Parallel to on-the-job individual and organisational development activities, off-the-job activities such as joint training programmes and workshops have to be specifically developed in order to build an international network of scientists and researchers.

In all of our cases, scientists and researchers were included in the routine management training activities of the company. Of course, this gave them the opportunity to meet people from other departments in the organisation. Development activities tailored to the needs of R&D employees were limited to technology updates and in some cases to project management techniques. The opportunity to meet fellow scientists in a non-research related environment in order to build an informal network is thus very limited in light of the fact that managing scientists and researchers is usually viewed by them as very different and demanding.

TOWARDS A NEW FRAMEWORK

The previous sections gave an edited summary of what the literature indicates on management of global R&D. Through our own case studies and access to insights on selected Japanese companies, it became clear, however, that our view on management of global R&D will need a different framework in the near future. We will make an attempt here to summarise some of the elements of such a framework in ten assertions which can be used as hypotheses for further research. There is a big danger in this exercise. While case studies provide ample and verifiable data on the past—and are as such an acceptable methodology to understand frameworks as they were successfully or unsuccessfully applied in the past—they often only provide vague and by definition unverifiable opinions on what is to be expected. Like every forecasting exercise, this one too is full of pitfalls.

A. On the Reasons for Globalisation of R&D

Assertion 1: The accelerated trend towards globalisation of European and Japanese companies has turned what used to be a marginal characteristic of the economy into a key building block of a global competitive posture: international decentralisation of R&D activities has become an essential component of the global firm.

Assertion 2: The sequence suggested by the international lifecycle of sales and marketing, production, technology development and finally research is perhaps still applicable. What has changed is the duration of the period during which one rides down this cycle. Whereas in the 50s and 60s one could have 25 years to go through the cycle, it appears that today it has to be run through in a far shorter period. In earlier periods, one could wait to start up production until sales had grown into a mature position, and one could delay the start of development until production had grown into maturity. The pressure to shorten this time frame leads to a situation where R&D already has to be initiated before one knows the results of production or sales internationalisation. Creation of a laboratory under these circumstances has to happen under higher uncertainties, and with less support of an infrastructure already in place.

Assertion 3: Supply of technology will become an increasingly important reason for globalisation of R&D. Two elements have, however, changed with respect to this reason. Firstly, the production of technological know-how in research institutes or universities is less concentrated in a few centres of excellence than it used to be. Secondly, in some cases the normal diffusion process of scientific knowledge through conferences and publications in refereed journals, appears to be too slow a process. As a consequence, some companies seem to think that the diffusion of technological know-how is faster through their own channels than through the usual channels of scientific community. Thus, they prefer to create a research centre close to the sources of technological know-how and to diffuse it internally, than to wait until this know-how has spread through the international scientific community by means of conferences and publications. One can expect these companies to have a network of more numerous though smaller laboratories.

B. On the Creation of R&D Laboratories Abroad

Assertion 4: Acquisition strategies will lead to an increasing number of laboratories being absorbed. Tools to integrate laboratories after acquisition consist of exchange of researchers, common budgeting and planning, reorganisation or closure of the laboratories. The choice between these different possibilities will be determined by variables such as (a) proximity of the technological activities of the acquired laboratory to the acquiring laboratory; (b) the strategic importance of the acquired laboratory's technological strengths to the acquiring company; (c) the areas of strength of the acquired laboratory on the scale of technological development to fundamental research.

Assertion 5: The technology-driven approach to globalisation of R&D can be based on two different categories of technologies. In some cases we saw the creation of foreign laboratories for technologies related to the existing technological competences of the firm. In other cases, we saw the creation of laboratories specialising in unrelated technologies. One example of this was the creation of an overseas bioengineering venture by a chemicals firm. It will be clear that the degree of risk and the difficulties encountered in the second type of development are expected to be much larger than in the first type.

C. On the Management of an International Network of R&D Laboratories

Assertion 6: Location of global R&D activities will be determined by two categories of factors: (a) what is the orientation of the activities, that is, towards the market (product) or towards the process, and (b) the *type* of activities, that is, where the laboratory is positioned on the scale from technical development to fundamental research. Locations close to production sites, customers, research institutions, sources of researchers or simply close to the world experts in the field, will be determined by those two factors.

Assertion 7: The key management decision in global R&D management is the choice of where one wants to position oneself on the scale of absolute centralisation of the management process to absolute freedom of the management process. This choice determines the type of organisation structure, the patterns of formal and informal communication and the human resource management. This choice is not one which is common to all laboratories of the firm, but will be different from one laboratory to another, depending on the types of activities they perform.

Assertion 8: The choice of centralisation versus freedom is a dynamic choice, that is, it can change over time. It is among other influences determined by the rate of change of the technologies which are developed, the time pressure to deliver results, the managerial culture of the company and the size of the individual laboratories.

Assertion 9: Global R&D management will require new types of organisation structures. The most frequently quoted type of organisation is that of a network of peer laboratories. The precise mechanisms operating in this network are still not well specified.

Assertion 10: The core foci in human resource management in global R&D will be the grooming and selection of the laboratory managers and the training of R&D professionals to increase the exchange of information across sites.

CONCLUSION

Global R&D management will be a major element of the management of globally operating companies. International networks of laboratories are not totally new and the literature provides some details on the management of these laboratories. But on the basis of our own case studies it appears that a new model for the management of such a network of laboratories is needed. We have provided in this paper a number of assertions which could lead to such a new framework.

REFERENCES

Allen, T. J. (1977). *Managing the Flow of Technology.* Cambridge, Mass.: MIT Press.

Behrman, J. N., and W. A. Fischer. (1980). *Overseas Activities of Transnational Companies.* Cambridge, Mass.: Oelgeschlager, Gunn and Hain.

De Meyer. A. (1984, December). Internationalisation of Research and Development. Conference proceedings, EIBA conference. Rotterdam.

De Meyer, A., and H. Schuette. (1989). Trends in the Development of Technology and Their Effects on the Production Structure in the European Community. *INSEAD Working Paper 89/10.*

Edstrom, A., and J. Galbraith. (1977). "Transfer of Managers as a Coordination and Control Strategy in Multinational Firms." *Administrative Science Quarterly.* Vol. 22 (2), pp. 248–263.

Goshal, S., and C. A. Bartlett. (1987, September). Innovation Processes in Multinational Corporations. *Proceedings of the Symposium on Managing Innovation in Large Complex Firms.* INSEAD. Fontainebleau.

Harris, J. M. "The Global Management of R&D Resources," *Outlook.* Vol. 11.

Hakanson, L., and U. Zander. (1986). *Managing International Research and Development.* Stockholm: Mekanforbund.

Ronstadt, R. (1977). *Research and Development Abroad by U.S. Multinationals.* New York: Praeger.

Vernon, R. (1966, May). "International Investment and International Trade in the Product Cycle," *Quarterly Journal of Economics.*

Zeira, Y., and M. Banai. (1984). "Present and Desired Methods of Selecting Expatriate Managers for International Assignments," *Personnel Review.* Vol. 13 (3), pp. 29–35.

Zeira, Y., and E. Harari. (1979). "Host Country Organisations and Expatriate Managers in Europe," *California Management Review.* Vol. 21 (3), pp. 40–50.

33

NEW TECHNOLOGIES AND INDUSTRIAL RESTRUCTURING
Tadahiro Sekimoto

Let me preface my intervention with a number of clarifying remarks. First, though I intend to confine myself to the domestic aspects of technological change, I regard the international perspective as equally important. Second, the focus will be on Japan. Third, my standpoint will be that of industry. It is not my intention to deal with technology from the viewpoint of government policymakers.

THE OUTLOOK FOR TECHNOLOGICAL PROGRESS

Looking back on human affairs from a technological point of view, we see that man has experienced three major transformations. The first was the agricultural revolution, characterised by the transition from a society based on hunting and gathering to one based on cultivation,

Source: "L. D. C. Growth and Development: A Record of Diverse Experience," ed. Organisation for Economic Co-operation and Development, Interdependence and Co-operation in Tomorrow's World. Paris, OECD, 1987.

which made it possible to sustain large populations. In Japan, this change occurred during the Jomon Period (around 2500 BC), by which time the population had reached about ten times its former level.

The second great transformation was the Industrial Revolution. This event began in 18th century England, spreading to other parts of the globe and reaching Japan in the late 19th to early 20th centuries. Its inception was the invention of the steam engine, followed by the internal combustion engine, electric power, steel, chemicals and many other innovative technologies. In parallel to this, the population of the world, and of Japan, grew exponentially.

Today, mankind is faced with its third great transformation, brought about by information technology, biotechnology, new materials technology, energy technologies such as nuclear power, and technologies of space exploration. As in the industrial revolution, there is no single technology which by itself constructs a new social order. There is, however, a core technology here: that of information.

Information technology provides us with an increased intellectual capacity inconceivable in the Industrial Revolution. It will be integrated with other technical areas: with biotechnology to produce bioelectronics; with new materials technology to become, for example, optoelectronics; with nuclear energy technology to become laser-generated nuclear fusion. These technologies will greatly benefit mankind, bringing a shift in emphasis from quantity to quality. The previous two transformations engendered great leaps in population, but the current change will foster qualitative fulfillment for man.

The information technology that will be the cornerstone of the new social order is that integrating computers and communications (C&C). Indeed, computer and communications technologies have already begun to merge, aided by the rapid progress that has been made in digital, semi-conductor and integrated-circuit technology. Thanks to digitalisation, present levels of computing power are 100–200 MIPS (million instructions per second) for general-purpose computers and two GFLOPS (gigaflops, i.e., two billion calculations per second) for supercomputers; communications technology will soon reach a point where 1.6 billion signals per second can be transmitted.

Semi-conductor technology, developed at Bell Laboratories in 1948, has also seen remarkable progress. The amount of memory capacity we can store on a five-millimetre square silicon chip has quadrupled every two years, to the point where currently over 500,000 alphanumeric characters can be stored—a capacity allowing a computer to be put on a single chip. Communications circuitry, too, can be placed on the same chip. This enables the creation of small computers with communications capability, facilitating computerised networks. These developments have made possible distributed information processing systems, one of the common manifestations of C&C. Yet another such manifestation of C&C is the fifth-generation computer, which takes advantage of enormous chip capabilities.

Progress in hardware technology will continue at a rapid pace that will, in fact, accelerate due to such developments as bioelectronics and new materials. Our own research has resulted in numerous breakthroughs, such as new angstrom-level devices that permit molecular control and a biosensor that will pave the way for bioelectronics. Particularly noteworthy is a material that attains fiftyfold performance improvement through trial manufacture in space. This is glass for optical fibres which was made in the Space Shuttle. When this glass was tested, we found that it was transmitting light 10,000 kilometres without the use of repeaters. If space factories which use the advantages of low gravity and vacuum in their manufacturing processes permit the creation of new and high-performance materials which it is not possible to make on earth, hardware technology will take yet another great leap forward. As I said when I joined NEC nearly forty years ago, "those who dominate materials dominate technology." It is vital, therefore, not to underestimate the importance of hardware.

Today, I would add that those who dominate software dominate the world, for software is of inestimable importance in bridging the communications gap between man and machine. At present, extensive training is often required before machines can be operated. In the future, however, artificial intelligence will eventually overcome this problem. For example, artificial "ears" will be able to understand correctly even heavily accented voices, enabling machines to move and operate according to the speaker's wishes. Artificial intelligence will contribute tremendously to the improvement of man-machine interfaces.

TECHNOLOGICAL INNOVATION AND CHANGE IN THE INDUSTRIAL ECONOMY

C&C technology will usher in an information society. This will be a change of immense proportions, altering the very building blocks of civilisation. Years ago we gained insight into this phenomenon from Fritz Machlup and Daniel Bell, and more recently from Alvin Toffler and John Naisbitt. For the sake of convenience, let us analyse here the change in the structure of civilisation à la Toffler. In *The Third Wave,* he listed six structural changes that occur in an industrial society's transformation to an information society.

The first is the change from standardization to post-standardization. Industrial society was characterised by high-volume production of a small variety of items. An information society, however, is capable of small production runs of multiple items which match individual needs. The second is a shift from specialisation to collaboration, with many aspects of society becoming increasingly composite and multi-disciplinary. The third is the shift from synchronisation to flexibility, and liberation from the constraints of time and place. The fourth is the trend away from concentration toward diversification. The fifth is the movement from maximisation to appropriate scale. (From "big is best," we are moving toward "small is beautiful.") Finally, the sixth is the trend away from centralisation toward decentralisation.

These changes will bring shifts in the pattern of industrial activity. For example, post-standardization, as it affects the distribution sector, will bring about diversification in retailing, such as non-store retailing, home shopping and the like. To take another example, that of collaboration, the integration of the distribution of goods and of finance with the information industry is already occurring.

These transformations will trigger a restructuring of industry. The traditional industrial classifications of primary, secondary and tertiary sectors will become increasingly blurred through the emergence of C&C; the hardware of secondary industry will merge with tertiary industry's software. The result is what might be called "2.5 industry." An example of a 2.5 industrial product is an automobile containing microprocessors. This allows the driver to programme various desired driving conditions which the automobile will proceed to execute flawlessly. Computer-aided manufacturing is an example of a 2.5 industry manufacturing process. With no drop in efficiency, different products can be produced simply by making changes in the software—in short, a flexible manufacturing system. This demonstrates the integration of hardware and software taking place in both the processes and the products of manufacturing.

Clearly, there is a need to reassess the validity of the primary, secondary and tertiary classifications. A reclassification of the tertiary industry is currently being considered by the Japan Committee for Economic Development (Keizai Doyukai). The basic idea is to classify industries handling (but not producing) physical commodities as tertiary, and those dealing with "knowledge" and other non–commodity related services as a new quaternary industry sector.

The motive for proposing industrial reclassification is to clarify each nation's stage of industrial development, and contribute to the formulation of national policy and the harmonizing of international economic policies. For instance, a common fallacy in discussing trade friction is to overlook changes in industrial structures; the extent of these changes differs from country to country. If we compare the United States with Japan, for example, there is a large gap between the United States as an "information society" and Japan as a "mature industrial society." It is natural for imbalances to occur in trade consisting primarily of physical goods. Economic relations between the United States and Japan should be evaluated in terms of the current account balance, including services, or of the basic balance. In any event, it is because we must not be bound by old paradigms in a time of qualitative industrial change that I have ventured these proposals.

C&C also alters the nature of work. Many authors have cited the changes taking place in the jobs of skilled workers. The shift from lathes to numerically controlled machinery and robots alters the skill content of jobs, and reduces employment in traditional kinds of work. Even in traditional jobs, dangerous tasks are being eliminated and skills are being upgraded. Moreover, the nature of high-grade technical jobs is undergoing great changes. NEC carried out studies to determine the point at which college-trained engineers felt their skills had become obsolete. The studies revealed that those who joined the firm between twenty and twenty-five years ago had felt that this happened after eleven or twelve years. In contrast, those who joined ten years ago felt the same way after only one or two years. What this indicates is that technical jobs are now undergoing transformation every year or two. Even the engineers themselves are caught up in change.

Creating jobs and providing job security are vital issues for government, the economy and corporate management, issues that in fact demand reconsideration of where we stand. We have reached the limits of industrial society. While the importance of manufacturing will remain, a qualitative change in its nature is taking place. Its former job-creating power is on the decrease. As employment opportunities have grown in industries that have successfully revitalised themselves through information technology, increasing attention is being focussed on the links between the new technologies and jobs.

The current labour market mismatch is primarily one of quality. There is no quick means of dealing with this problem. Comprehensive, steady and determined efforts at the national level are required. At NEC, we are adopting a policy of stepwise improvement. We are improving the content of skilled jobs in general.

We are retraining workers for new jobs, and transferring them to technical jobs. We are also upgrading the content of technical jobs, and moving workers to technical software positions. Because of the great shortage of software technicians, we are actively making use of other employees who show an aptitude for such work. For the task of stepwise job-upgrading, we have established college-level training facilities within the company.

TECHNOLOGICAL INNOVATION AND CORPORATE MANAGEMENT

Periods of transformation are fraught with problems. Management must beware of many pitfalls, some of which are related to adaptation. We must adapt to survive. Yet overadaptation is no guarantee of survival. History shows that a civilisation, as it advances, carries the seeds of its own demise. We must not blindly adhere to management systems that proved successful in the old industrial society, and fail to meet the challenges of the information society. We must devise sensitive means of detection that will continually provide the corporation with feedback on social change, and respond accordingly. That is why NEC has set its sights not only on the continuous creation of new products, new materials and new production processes but also on new markets and new organisations—all part of what Schumpeter defined as innovation.

NEC places particular emphasis on technological development, which it regards as the essential force propelling a company. It is both a support and a source of growth. That is why NEC's ratio of R&D expenditures to revenues is 6 or 7 per cent, whereas the average for the manufacturing sector is only 2 or 3 per cent. Our overall technology-related activities, broadly defined, consume in excess of 10 per cent of revenues. The question arises whether there is not a more accurate method of evaluating the strength of companies that aggressively pursue research and development. The basic elements of a business enterprise are people, goods and money. Yet there is no place in a corporate balance sheet for the human element. If such factors as the intellect, technical capability and know-how of the personnel could be evaluated and recorded on the balance sheet (a sort of "technology premium"), the valuation placed on a company—and indeed, on a nation—would be more accurate.

Of course, as we cross the threshold into the information society, that addition alone is insufficient. In the information society, information would be a fourth management resource. Such issues as the state of a company's information systems and the quality of management attained thereby would be appropriate subjects for listing in the balance sheet, where they could appear under the heading "information premium."

A further area which Japanese corporations need to concentrate on is creativity. The Japanese used to be regarded as skillful imitators. Today, this observation may need to be modified. NEC has long been engaged in creative work, yet because priority was placed on the task of catching up with Western corporations, demonstration of our creativity was accorded relatively low priority. Now we are finally on equal footing with the West, and the time has come for Japan to contribute to the world's store of inventions. Creativity alone, however, will not suffice; sensitivity and the will to overcome obstacles to progress are equally crucial.

The information society will be a challenge to man's intellect and capabilities. I trust that through fora such as the OECD, we will share our experience, our information and our wisdom, devoting ourselves to the creation of a better society. That is crucial for corporate management—and our duty to later generations.

34

THE CHALLENGE OF NEW TECHNOLOGIES
Christopher Freeman

The purpose of this paper is to examine the emergence of new technologies and the contemporary and future problems of technical and structural change associated with their diffusion.[1] The first two sections discuss the widespread view that technical change has accelerated in the last ten years as a result of the emergence of revolutionary new technologies, despite the fact that productivity growth has slowed down. This points to the need for a taxonomy of technical innovations, which is introduced in the third section. In the light of this taxonomy a comparison of some of the major new technologies is made, highlighting the exceptional importance of "information technology" over the next few decades. The characteristics of this new paradigm and the interconnections between technical, social and managerial innovations are discussed in the fourth and fifth sections. The implications for economic growth and for employment are analysed in the sixth and seventh sections. Finally, Section VIII discusses the problems of adaptation of the institutional framework to the opportunities afforded by the new technologies.

Source: "L. D. C. Growth and Development: A Record of Diverse Experience," ed. Organisation for Economic Co-operation and Development, Interdependence and Co-operation in Tomorrow's World. *Paris, OECD, 1987.*

PERCEIVED ACCELERATION OF TECHNICAL CHANGE

It is almost a rarity today to find an article or speech about the contemporary world which does not make some reference to the *accelerating* pace of technical change. Yet this observation, which has become virtually a platitude, is not so obvious or well-founded as those who repeat it often suppose.

Indeed, during the 1970s many economists expressed concern about the *decelerating* pace of technical change and sometimes offered this as one of the principal causes of the slow-down in the growth of productivity from the high rates achieved during the quarter-century after the Second World War. It was often suggested that the levelling off in the growth of R&D expenditures, particularly in the United States and the United Kingdom, was one of the factors underlying the more sluggish behaviour of the economy.

The difference in perception between professional economists and scientists and the widespread public acceptance of the notion of acceleration is in large part due simply to differences in conceptualising the problem. For the economist the rate of technological change is conceptually distinct from the rate of technical change. The latter is usually defined statistically as the "residual" factor explaining that part of measured growth which cannot be attributed to increases in the inputs of labour and capital. Almost any significant slow-down in economic growth therefore implies a deceleration in the rate of technical change so defined. But the underlying rate of technological change may be unaffected, since this refers to changes in the body of knowledge relating to techniques of production.

For scientists or technologists, on the other hand, although they would be hard pressed to measure it, the rate of technical change represents some notion of the outputs of the science-technology system, almost irrespective of how effectively these results are picked up and used

in the economy. It is this notion of technological change as a flow of inventions, innovations and discoveries that is reflected in the popular notion of "acceleration." Not surprisingly, such spectacular achievements of science and technology as the exploration of space, genetic engineering, the development of the microprocessor and of increasingly powerful computing systems, very-large-scale integrated circuits embodying a million components on one chip, and increasingly sophisticated robotic systems lend credibility to the notion of an accelerating pace of technical change.

In addition, it must be taken into account that many industries that previously experienced rather few technical innovations are now experiencing computerisation in one form or another. Even though their productivity may show little or no improvement for a while, the impression is nevertheless created that these banks, offices, insurance companies, retail stores, hotels and other organisations that install computer-based systems are involved in a wave of technical change which was previously imagined to affect only the leading sectors of manufacturing and the defence system.

This points to an extremely important issue which is involved in these differing perceptions. It could indeed be true that the rate of technological change in the sense of outputs of potentially useful discoveries and inventions has been increasing during the 1970s and 1980s, whilst their diffusion and efficient exploitation (technical change) has been much less successful.

When the OECD invited a group of economists, scientists and technologists in the late 1970s to prepare a report on "Science and Technology in the New Economic Context"[4] they investigated this very point. They began their work by asking the question: "Have Science and Technology slowed down?" and instigated a survey of many leading R&D specialists in a number of countries. The result was clear-cut. Scarcely any scientists or technologists believed that the output of science or technology was declining. On the contrary, almost all believed that the science-technology system was offering an expanding and exciting wave of new opportunities to the economy. Moreover, the rate of non-defence R&D expenditure, which had stagnated in the early 1970s, resumed its strong upward growth in the late 1970s (Figure 1). The group therefore concluded that if the rate of technical change, as defined in terms of measured productivity growth, had slowed down, this could not be attributed to weakness in the science-technology system, but must rather be explained in terms of problems in the socio-economic sphere and particularly in terms of structural change and the new investment and training needed to diffuse radically new technologies.

EMERGENCE OF NEW GENERIC TECHNOLOGIES

The OECD Report on "Technical Change and Economic Policy"[5] points to the particular importance of "generic" technologies, which offer scope for innovation and productivity improvement, not just in one particular product or process, but in many. Policies designed to promote such underlying or "enabling" technologies are akin to policies for fundamental scientific research in their power to generate a wide range of new opportunities for technical advance and many externalities, benefitting firms in every sector. The shift in policy from project-type funding to generic technologies marked to some degree the acceptance of the argument advanced by economists such as Nelson and Eads[6], and Henderson[7]: that the commercial stage of development of specific products and processes should be mainly or entirely a matter for private funding, and that public support should be concentrated on the promotion of the underlying "pre-commercial science and technology."

The promotion of generic technologies has indeed become a widespread feature of tech-

nology policy in the OECD area during the 1970s and 1980s and almost every Member country now has programmes designed to give special encouragement and support to some or all of the following technologies:

a. *Information technology.* This has received by far the most attention and is generally defined as a cluster of advanced technologies in the field of

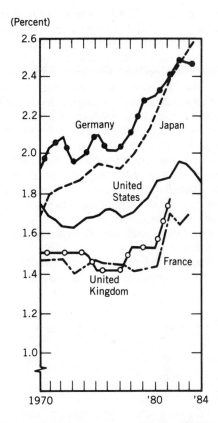

Figure 1 Estimated Ratio of Non-defence R&D Expenditure[1] to GNP

[1]National R & D expenditures excluding government funds for defence.

The US ratio of non-defence R&D-to-GNP continues to be lower than that of Japan and Germany. All three countries showed relatively rapid increases in this ratio from the late 1970s until the end of the decade.

Source: National Science Foundation, International Science and Technology Update (1985).

computing, software, micro-electronics and tele-communications. In the most recent period, during the 1980s, the Japanese announcement of their research programme for the New ("Fifth") Generation of Computers has stimulated a whole series of competitive programmes in other Member countries, with a special emphasis on man-machine interface, expert systems, parallel processing and other features of what will hopefully be a more "intelligent" generation of computers.

b. *Biotechnology.* This too has been a fashionable area for special programmes designed to strengthen both the underlying research capability in a range of relevant disciplines, and the necessary linkages with industrial R&D. However, the scale of commitment is generally at least one order of magnitude less than in the case of information technology, which reflects the far smaller prospects of profitable exploitation in the short and medium-term future. But in the longer term, there is widespread agreement that this technology is likely to offer enormous possibilities for productivity improvements, new products and systems and enhanced quality in a wide range of industries, including in particular agriculture, food, drugs, chemicals, mineral extraction and refining.

c. *Materials technology.* The extremely rapid growth of the micro-electronic industry has itself been a powerful stimulus to many new developments in this field, both in the direct sense of high-purity materials consumed by the industry, and indirectly through the possibilities of improving the quality and economising in the use of materials in many other industries. Whereas in the 1950s and 1960s the OECD area experienced an explosive growth in the production of metals and of bulk synthetic materials, mainly based on petrochemicals, the main trend now is towards the precise tailoring of high-quality composite and other materials to the needs of very specific applications. This requires an underlying capability extending to the whole range of materials technology, both organic and inorganic, and closely related to fundamental research in physics and chemistry.

d. *Energy technology.* After the OPEC crisis of 1973 and 1979, energy technologies were the subject of particularly intensive public support and promotion. In a number of OECD countries nuclear technology had already been an area of very large-scale public investment and continued to benefit from this stimulus. However, "alternative" technologies, such as wind power, solar energy and geothermal energy, as well as energy-conservation technologies, also benefitted. The very considerable success of the latter is demonstrated in Table 1, which shows that energy coefficients in the OECD area have im-

Table 1 Energy and Economic Growth, IEA Member Countries, 1968–1983

	1968	1973	1978	1983	Annual average change (%)		
					1968–73	1973–78	1978–83
Gross domestic product (GDP)[1]	3 177	3 713	4 227	4 595	3.2	2.6	1.7
Total primary energy requirements (TPER)[2]	2 586	3 324	3 592	3 359	4.1	1.6	−1.3
Total final consumption (TFC)[2]	1 929	2 491	2 609	2 398	4.2	0.9	−1.7
TPER/GDP[3]	0.81	0.90	0.85	0.73	2.1	−1.1	−3.0
TFC/GD	0.61	0.67	0.62	0.52	1.9	−1.5	−3.5

[1] In billions of US dollars, 1975 prices and exchange rates.
[2] Million tonnes of oil equivalent, total final consumption equals total primary energy requirements less transformation and distribution losses.
[3] Tonnes of oil equivalent per thousand US dollars.

Sources: Energy Policies and Programmes of IEA Countries, 1983 Review, International Energy Agency, Paris, 1984; *Energy Balances of OECD Countries, 1960–1974,* OECD, Paris, 1970 *Main Economic Indicators,* OECD, Paris, various issues; W. Walker, "Information Technology and the Use of Energy," *Energy Policy,* October 1985.

proved substantially over the past decade. Both in the sphere of materials technology and in the sphere of energy technology it is evident that information technology has had a powerful influence in shifting the focus of technical effort from quantitative expansion to sophisticated conservation techniques and quality control.

e. *Space technology.* As in the case of nuclear technology, programmes related to space technology are very unevenly distributed between countries, with the superpowers accounting for a very high proportion of the total technical effort. Most Member countries of the OECD have some significant commitment to at least some aspects of this technology and recognise in particular its immediate importance for telecommunications and resource survey applications. However, the long-term development of industries actually operating in space is generally regarded as more remote in its economic importance for most if not all the OECD countries.

This listing of five main areas of "generic" technology programmes indicates the growing need for a taxonomy of technical innovations that takes into account the "clustering" of technically and economically interrelated innovations, as well as the traditional distinction between "radical" and "incremental" innovations. Such a taxonomy is particularly important for technology policy in order to provide criteria for assessing the relative importance of public investment both in the generic technologies described and in specific R&D projects.

A TAXONOMY OF INNOVATIONS

Research at the Science Policy Research Unit over the past decade suggests the value of distinguishing between four categories of innovation as follows[8].

Incremental Innovations

These occur more or less continuously in any industry or service activity, although at a varying rate in different industries and over differ-ent time periods. They may often occur not so much as the result of any deliberate research and development activity, but as the outcome of inventions and improvements suggested by engineers and others directly engaged in the production process, or as a result of initiatives and proposals by users. Many empirical studies have confirmed their great importance in improving efficiency in the use of all factors of production.[2] Incremental innovations are particularly important in the follow through period after a radical breakthrough innovation (see below), and frequently associated with the scaling-up of plant and equipment and quality improvements to products and services for a variety of specific applications. Although their combined effect is extremely important in the growth of productivity, no single incremental innovation has dramatic effects, and they may sometimes pass unnoticed and unrecorded.

Radical Innovations

These are discontinuous events and in recent times are usually the result of a deliberate research and development activity in enterprises and/or in university and government laboratories. As Schumpeter insisted, they are unevenly distributed over sectors and over time.[3] Whenever they occur, however, they are important as the potential springboard for the growth of new markets, or in the case of radical process innovations such as the oxygen steel-making process, for big improvements in the cost and quality of existing products. Over a period of decades a radical innovation, such as nylon or the "Pill," may have fairly dramatic effects, but its economic impact remains relatively small and localised, unless a whole cluster of radical innovations are linked together in the rise of entire new industries and services, such as the synthetic materials industry or the semiconductor industry. Strictly speaking, at a sufficiently disaggregative level, radical innovations would constantly require the addition of new rows and columns in an input-output table. But in practical terms, such changes are introduced only in the case of the most important innovations and with long time lags, when their economic impact is already substantial. It generally took about thirty years for statistics of electronic computers and related industries to enter the regular statistical system and even now the process is far from complete.

Changes of "Technology System"

These are far-reaching changes in technology, affecting several branches of the economy, as well as ultimately giving rise to entirely new sectors. All the "generic" technologies listed above have given rise to one, or more "new technology systems." Keirstead[15], in his exposition of a Schumpeterian theory of economic development, introduced the concept of "constellations" of innovations which were technically and economically interrelated. Obvious examples are the clusters of synthetic materials innovations and petrochemical innovations introduced in the 1930s, 1940s and 1950s with the associated developments in machinery for injection moulding and extrusion. Another example is the "cluster" of electrically driven household consumer durables innovations.

Change in "Techno-economic Paradigm" (Technological Revolutions)

These are the "creative gales of destruction" that are at the heart of Schumpeter's long wave theory. They represent those new technology systems which have such pervasive effects on the economy as a whole that they change the "style" of production and management throughout the system. The introduction of electric power or steam power or the electronic computer are examples of such deep-going transformations. A change of this kind carries with it many clusters of radical and incremental innovations, and may eventually embody several new technology systems. Not only does this fourth type of technical change lead to the emergence of a new range of products, services, systems and industries in its own right—it also affects directly or indirectly almost every other branch of the economy. We use the expression "techno-economic" rather than "technological paradigm" because the changes involved go beyond specific product or process technologies and affect the input cost structure and conditions of production and distribution throughout the system. This fourth category would, in our view, correspond to Nelson and Winter's concept of "general natural trajectories" and, once established as a dominant influence on engineers, designers and managers, becomes a "technological regime" for several decades. Schumpeter's long cycles may be regarded as a succession of "techno-economic paradigms."

A new techno-economic paradigm develops initially within the old technological regime, but becomes dominant only after a crisis of structural adjustment involving deep social and institutional changes as well as the replacement of the leading motive branches of the economy. It is essential to bear in mind the long time-scale involved in the diffusion of a new techno-economic paradigm. Some of the early pioneers of computing thought that it would have a revolutionary effect on investment, unemployment and economic growth as early as the 1950s. But it is clear now that an enormous amount of further technical development and training of large numbers of skilled people was necessary before the costs and convenience of computing came down to a level where the new technology could be diffused widely not just in a few leading edge industries but to all branches of manufacturing and services. Biotechnology today is still at the stage of the computing technology of the early 1950s, where costs of development, investment and training limit its applications to a few specialised areas. The "integrated circuit" stage of biotechnology has yet to arrive and the economy-wide effects are still barely perceptible.

THE CHANGING BALANCE OF "HARD" AND "SOFT" TECHNOLOGIES: INFORMATION TECHNOLOGY AS A NEW "TECHNO-ECONOMIC PARADIGM"

From this very brief review of the taxonomy of technical innovations, it is evident that only one of the five "generic" technologies which have been discussed above could qualify today as a change of "techno-economic paradigm": information technology (IT). It is possible, even probable, that third-generation biotechnology will lead to a new technological regime in the first half of the 21st century and space technology in the more distant future, but in terms of present-day economic realities they represent only a tiny proportion of production and trading activities. Table 2 illustrates in a very rough way a number of major factors affecting the diffusion of some of the technologies under consideration.

Clearly, materials technology and energy technology will always have an important place in any industrialised society. But the emphasis in the overall development of industrial technology has shifted in the 1970s away from an extremely energy-intensive and materials-intensive "style" of mass and flow production to a much more flexible, information-intensive style, associated with computerised control and communication systems. We turn now therefore to a somewhat more detailed consideration of the special characteristics of information technology.

Among the important characteristics of the new paradigm are the following:

a. A continuing very high rate of technical change in the IT industries themselves, as well as in a wide range of applications. Underlying this process is the continuing dramatic improvement in large-scale integration of electronic circuits, and the continuing fall in costs which this per-

Table 2 Factors Affecting Diffusion of Four Technologies

Rate of diffusion factors

(5 = most favourable 1 = least favourable)

	Nuclear technology		Space technology		Information technology		Biotechnology	
	Electric power	Other	Civil communi-cation	Other	Electronic industry	Other	Drug industry	Other
Profitability	2	2	2	2	5	2–5	2	1
Competition pressure	2	2	3	2	5	5	4	2
Scale of investment	1	1	2	1	2–5	1–5	2	2
Environmental impact	2	1	4	3	5	4	4	3
Safety	3	2–4	4	2	5	4	4	4
Technical reliability	2	3	4	3	5	4	4	3
Public attitudes	2	2	4	3	5	4	4	3
Change agents								
Government	3	4	4	3	5	5	2	2
Multinational corporations	2	2	3	3	5	5	3	3
Other business	2	2	2	3	5	4	3	3
Military strategy	4	5	1	5	5	5	1	2
Potential range of applications	3	2	3	2	5	5	3	4

mits. As a result of this and parallel developments in opto-electronics and communications technology as well as in computer design and performance, there is a high rate of product obsolescence with rapidly succeeding "generations" of components incorporated into new designs of end-products and systems. The revolutionary developments in integrated circuits have their parallel in communication technology, where fibre optics have made possible similar drastic improvements in costs and performance. The convergence of all these technological advances (Figure 2) means that the capability for communicating, processing and storing information is still improving very rapidly and that it is becoming even cheaper. This has profound consequences for the ability of the new technology in terms of integration and control of productive activities and gives rise to several other characteristics of IT, as follows.

b. Much greater flexibility and speed in model changes and design changes. Whereas mass and

flow production systems of the old paradigm were based on "dedicated" equipment continuously replicating vast numbers of standardized, homogeneous products, the new flexibility conferred by IT permits more rapid changes of tooling and dies, so that small production runs become economic, and the prospects for small and medium-sized firms are changed. Piore[16] has argued that the availability of cheap computers will change the prospects of flexible small-scale craft-based firms so dramatically as to permit them to predominate in the economy generally, as was the case in the 19th century, provided appropriate institutional changes are made. Our own research suggested that marketing, financial and design economies of scale are still very important in these and other industries. Thus the rise of information technology is unlikely to displace the dominant position of large firms. It will, however, lead to a new symbiosis of large firms surrounded by a penumbra of specialised satellite firms, as in the Japanese JIT

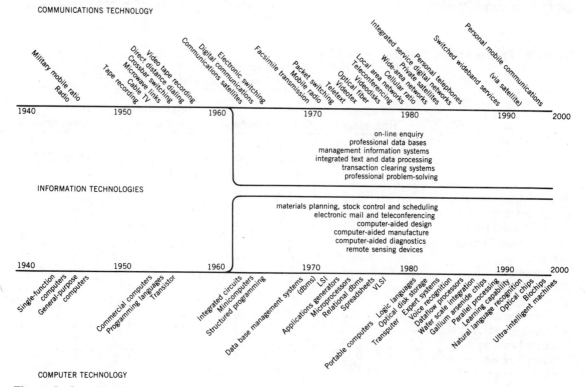

Figure 2 Some Key Events in the Convergence of Information Technology

system or the Benetton subcontracting system, and it will also create many new "niche" types of market throughout the economy.

c. A reduction in electro-mechanical components and in various stages of component transformation as a result of the redesign of products and processes. This leads to substantial materials-saving and energy-saving, as well as a process of structural change involving loss of jobs in some sectors of metals and metal goods and an increase in jobs in some sectors of the electronic components industry, electronic products, and producer services.

d. As a result of the changes outlined above and in particular as a result of the continuing high rate of technical change in the micro-electronics and computer industries themselves, a strong tendency towards a more rapid rate of product and process change and more intense technological competition in other industries also. This in turn strengthens the demand for new skills and services in design, development, software engineering and IT products generally, affecting both in-house skill and employment profiles and the growth of new externally contracted services, information flows and supplies of equipment. The more rapid rate of product and process change is facilitated and stimulated by the diffusion of computer-aided design systems.

e. Speed, reliability and low cost of communicating and storing vast quantities of information relating to sales, inventories and financial transactions generally. Ultimately the whole structure of banking, financial services and distribution are likely to be transformed as a result of the introduction of "electronic funds transfer" based on this capability. Already the information technology revolution has had very far-reaching effects on banks, insurance companies, retail chains and supermarkets, making possible capital and materials saving as well as labour-saving organisational and technical changes.

f. The capability which IT confers to integrate design, manufacture, procurement, sales, administration and technical service in any enterprise. The ultimate tendency is towards computer-integrated manufacturing systems and all-electronic office systems, but these are still some way off and there are many social as well as technical barriers to their full realisation. Neverthe-less, many enterprises are moving in this direction, as exemplified in the rapid take-off of Computer-Aided Design (CAD) systems in many branches of manufacturing and their increasingly close linkages with ordering systems for tooling and parts, as well as with manufacturing schedules. These developments have already had significant effects on the skill profile of industry, affecting drawing offices and design as well as clerical labour and machine shops. In the service industries in manufacturing, the skill profile and the levels of employment in offices are being affected by the introduction of word processors and their integration with new communication systems and information services. Whilst these new developments undoubtedly displace some clerical labour, some draughtsmen and tracers, some middle-management and other employees, they also generate a demand for new skills, which are everywhere in short supply, and for new types of information within firms and from specialist firms in the provision of business and computer services.

g. The capability which IT confers to improve the quality of products, processes, and services. On-line monitoring and control of quantity and quality of output has already led to dramatic improvements in industries as diverse as colour television and passenger cars. It leads to capital-saving, labour-saving, materials-saving and energy-saving improvements in production processes since it reduces the number of rejects and wasted components both for intermediate and final output. This reduces the requirements for inspection and lower management employees, but increases the requirement for skilled systems designers and engineers and the level of responsibility and skills for maintenance and for some types of operative.

h. The capability which IT confers to link up networks of component and material suppliers with assembly-type firms (as in the automobile industry) or with service firms (as in the hotel and catering industries). An equally important function which IT can perform is with respect to the linkages between producers, wholesalers and retailers, as in the clothing industry. In both cases it is the combination and convergence of communications with computer technology (Figure 2) that permits big savings in inventories at all levels in the system, and especially in work-in-progress, and a far more rapid and sensitive response to (even daily) changes in consumer demand.

i. The increased integration of manufacturing and service activities means that it does not make any sense to speak of a "service" economy or a "manufacturing" economy, since both are interdependent. This is evident, for example, in the tendency for suppliers of hardware or components to offer a "service" or at least a subsystem incorporating many service elements. The tendency is clear on a small scale in the mushroom growth of "instant print shops," which are partly in retail distribution and partly in the manufacturing (printing) industry. On a much larger scale it is evident in the supply of design, engineering and other information services, together with entire new plants.

j. Greater international integration of industries, services and markets as a result of much more rapid transmission of information and vastly improved communication flows. This has already had big effects in the communication between offices, production sites and laboratories of large multinational enterprises. Accelerated international transfer of technology and greater mobility of service industries are among the probable consequences of these developments. The financial services industry is already demonstrating the far-reaching consequences of this enhanced mobility, and many countries and regions will ultimately be affected by major changes in the international division of labour.

The listing of these characteristics of the new paradigm is not intended to be exhaustive, but to illustrate some of the main ways in which it is affecting the entire economic system and not just particular products or sectors.

From this discussion it is evident that the new technological regime will differ from that prevailing in the 1950s and 1960s in many important respects. "Intangible" investment in information systems is becoming the critical resource in all areas of the economy rather than dedicated fixed investment in plant and machinery. The computerised control and communication system is now the nerve-centre and the "memory" not just of sophisticated weapon systems such as aircraft, ships and missiles, but now increasingly of almost every large firm and government department.

The design, development and continued improvement of such information systems is now the concern not just of the suppliers, locked as they are in an intense technological competition for this enormous world market, but also increasingly of specialised groups of software suppliers within each of the user organisations. As Tim Brady and Peter Senker[17] have emphasized, the maintenance of software systems is now a critical function in their continued successful operation and improvement and accounts for an increasingly high proportion of total system cost (Figure 3).

This shift from "hard" to "soft" technologies has very great consequences for the structure of industry and management, since it involves not only all the changes already listed above, but also a completely new role for those industries previously regarded as "passive" recipients of technology from the manufacturing sector. Hitherto the surveys of R&D in all the OECD countries have shown the major service industries essentially as non-performers of R&D, which was heavily concentrated in the manufacturing sector and public utilities such as energy, transport and communications. With the emergence of strong systems software groups in banks, insurance companies, distribution, travel agents and professional services, this picture will change dramatically.[4] The changes are so far-reaching that they affect the management style of all firms and all types of central and local government organisations.

MERGING OF SOCIAL, MANAGERIAL AND TECHNICAL INNOVATIONS

Schumpeter insisted on the interdependence of organisational and technical innovations, and

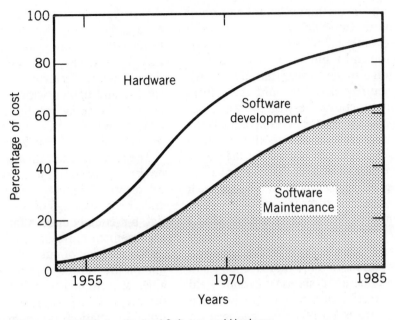

Figure 3   The Relative Costs of Software and Hardware
Source: Steve Olson, "Pathways of Choice," *Mosaic* (July–August 1983), p. 6.

nowhere is this more apparent than in the case of information technology. Most of the economic and technical advantages which it makes possible depend upon changes in management organisation and behaviour. Many of them depend upon more far-reaching structural change and social innovations on a larger scale. This section looks briefly at some of the implications of IT at the level of the enterprise, whilst the following sections consider the economic and social implications at the level of the national and international economy.

One of the major advantages of information technology, as already indicated above, is the capability which it confers to integrate design, production and marketing far more effectively than earlier management systems of control and communication. This means, for example, that with the introduction of CAD, it is possible to link the design stage with the planning of the production process, and the ordering of tools, components and materials needed for the

newly designed or redesigned products. At the same time inventory control at all stages—materials, work-in-progress and finished products—can be greatly improved, both as a result of better internal communication and control and as a result of information networks involving suppliers, and with marketing and distributors.

These changes can lead to a much closer integration of product and process innovation, since the product and process can be designed virtually simultaneously. On the other hand it can lead to a much more sensitive and rapid response to signals from the market, since production schedules can be adjusted very quickly to changes in demand for a particular style, colour, size, type or other specification of products.[5] However, it is not always easy for established large corporations to change their management style and structure in order to adapt to these new possibilities of "flexibility" and "systemation." In his assessment of the major transformation in the management system at General Motors, Gooding[19] describes it as a "Cultural Revolution," which involved not just the acquisition and assimilation of several software firms but also the reorganisation of design and manufacturing activities and the relocation of many functions. Very often, the initial response of management is to resist or delay the type of "cultural revolution" upon which GM has embarked and to opt instead for the piecemeal introduction of isolated "islands" of automation in the office, factory or warehouse, such as the stand-alone word processor or the individual Computer Numerical Control (CNC) machine tool. Whilst such small-scale experimentation and "learning by doing" is usually a necessary precursor to more radical changes in office and production systems, it cannot yield more than a fraction of the benefits which can be won by more far-reaching changes in organisation. The MIT project on the world car industry has shown that the main impact of the intense competition from Japanese automobile firms has not been so much on the large-scale use of robotics, important as this undoubtedly is, as in the whole system of management organisation, the relationship with suppliers and the training of workers.

There is an interesting parallel here with the early stages of the introduction of electric power at the turn of the century. As Warren Devine[20] points out, the growth in the share of electric power, from 5 per cent of the mechanical drive for US industry in 1900 to 53 per cent in 1920, was possible only after the acceptance of a major change in factory organisation—from the old system, based on one large steam engine driving a number of shafts through a complex system of belts and pulleys, to a system based initially on electric group drive and later on unit drive, that is, one electric motor for each machine.[6]

Unit drive gave far greater flexibility in factory layout since machines were no longer placed in line with shafts, making possible big capital savings in floor space. Unit drive meant

that trolleys and overhead cranes could be used on a large scale, unobstructed by shafts and belts. Portable power tools increased even further the flexibility and adaptability of production systems. Factories could be made much cleaner and lighter, which was very important both for working conditions and for product quality and process efficiency. Production capacity could be expanded much more easily.

The attainment of the full benefits of electric power depended not just upon a cluster of radical technical innovations made in the 1870s and 1880s, although of course these were essential, but equally upon a far-reaching change in management philosophy and plant layout, and on the redesign of much production equipment and on the training and retraining of many engineers, technicians and skilled workers. This interdependence of technical and organisational innovations is even more apparent in the case of information technology.

In numerous cases of adoption of IT, the dominance of older equipment and administrative systems has led to a very slow realisation of potential productivity gains and even to declines in productivity, where management has been unable to cope with the teething problems, or where the necessary adaptation of the technology to the specific requirements of the sector has not been undertaken. The new growth opportunities arising from technical change are therefore heavily dependent upon an associated process of organisational and social change, as well as upon further technical innovations and considerable investment in new equipment and software. Some observers believe that this organisational change is now an even bigger problem than the new investment.

A good example of the way in which organisational innovations can generate very substantial productivity gains is the Italian clothing firm, Benetton. This is one of the fastest-growing firms in the world in what has hitherto been regarded as a "traditional" industry with a rather slow rate of technical change. Established only in 1965, the firm opened its first retail shop outside Italy in 1970 in France[21]. It now has over 1000 retail shops outside Italy, including 400 in France and (most recently) about 100 in the United States and a rapidly growing number in Japan. Exports have risen from 5 per cent of total sales in 1976 to over 50 per cent since 1983, whilst total sales increased more than tenfold over the past decade.

This extraordinarily rapid rate of growth and competitive success was based on a whole series of organisational and technical innovations. The organisational and labour costs are lower than typical competitors (Table 3) whilst the retailers and Benetton both get a higher profit margin. Sales per employee here are much higher than those of comparable European competitors. An advanced information system now enables sales and market data from the retail outlets and from Benetton sales agents in various countries to feed into the warehousing and manufacturing system. This in turn makes possible big economies in inventories, whilst at

the same time ensuring a very rapid response to world-wide customer demand, that is, the customers can actually get the colour and size they want.

This example illustrates both the interdependence of organisational and technical innovations and the potential for the rejuvenation of traditional industries that is afforded by information technology. The extent to which these opportunities can be realised more widely throughout the economy is discussed in the next three sections.

NEW GROWTH OPPORTUNITIES ARISING FROM REJUVENATION OF TRADITIONAL INDUSTRIES AND EMERGENCE OF NEW PRODUCTS, PROCESSES AND SERVICES

In assessing the growing impact of the new techno-economic paradigm, it is necessary to

Table 3 An Analysis of Costs and Profits for a Typical Benetton Shop and Comparisons with Competitors

	Typical Benetton shop	Shop of European competition	American specialised chain store
Annual sales in $	150 000	150 000	400 000
Selling space (in sq. ft.)	400	1 200	2 000
Storage space		300	150
Initial margins, as % of sales prices	44%	50%	52%
Median price for unit in $	30	40	55
Employee hours per week	90	200	230
Selling hours per week	45	45	76
Average store inventory at cost in $	30 000	50 000	95 000
Expense categories as % of sales:			
Cost of goods sold	61%	55%	56%
Labour	14%	29%	22%
Rent	5%	7%	5%
Other	8%	6%	8%
Profit (net)	12%	3%	9%

Source: Harvard Business School, ISTUD, 1984.

take into account all that has been said about the problems of structural adjustment, before a "good match" is achieved between the new paradigm and the institutional framework. This process is very uneven between different countries and different industrial sectors. In this section we discuss the extremely uneven diffusion of the new technological paradigm from a few leading sectors to the economy as a whole.

The TEMPO project at SPRU attempted to analyse the long-term changes in labour and capital productivity in the principal sectors of the British economy (the forty industries distinguished in the Cambridge growth model) from 1948 to 1984. The account which follows is based on the five volumes analysing the main sectors and the forthcoming full summary[22]. In our view, although there are important national variations, the broad picture which is described below is characteristic of all the major OECD industrial economies.

When we analyse changes in labour productivity and in capital productivity over the past twenty years at a sufficiently disaggregated level, we find the following picture:

a. The sectors with the highest rates of growth in labour productivity are the electronic industries, and especially the computer industry and the electronic component industry (Figure 4). These are the industries which make the greatest use of their own technology for design, production, stock control, marketing and management (Figure 5). They are also the only industrial sectors which show a substantial rise in capital productivity. They are the sectors which demonstrated the advantages of the new technologies for everyone else and may be described as the "carrier" and "motive" branches of the new paradigm, which will play in the 1980s and 1990s a role analogous to that of the automobile, oil and consumer durable industries in the previous half-century.

b. In those sectors that have been heavily penetrated already by micro-electronics, both in their product and process technology, there is also evidence of a considerable rise in labour productivity and even some advance in capital productivity in the most recent period. This applies, for example, to the scientific instruments industry, to the telecommunications industry, and to the watch industry. These sectors have now become virtually a part of the electronics industry.

c. In sectors where micro-electronics has been used on an increasing scale over the past ten years but older technologies still predominate in product and process technology, there is a very uneven picture. Some firms have achieved very high productivity increases and have clearly demonstrated the possibilities of rejuvenation through a combination of process innovation and redesign of products. In other firms there is stagnation or even declining productivity. This is the case, for example, in the printing industry, in the machine-building industries and in the clothing industry. This uneven picture is completely consistent with Salter's[25] vision of the spread of new technologies within established industries through new capital investment. In many cases information technology is introduced in a piecemeal fashion in one department or for one activity and not as part of an integrated system. As we have already noted, there may even be a temporary fall in productivity because of the lack of the necessary skills in design, in software, in production engineering, in maintenance, and in management generally. Problems of institutional and organisational adaptation are extremely important, and flexibility in this social response varies greatly between countries, as well as between enterprises. Among OECD countries, Japan and Sweden appear to have been particularly successful in making progress in the area of "mechatronics."

d. Sectors producing standardized homogeneous commodities on a flow production basis in rather large plants have made considerable use of information technology in their process control systems and in various management applications. They were indeed among the earliest users of computers for these purposes. This applies especially to the petrochemical and steel industries. IT has helped them to achieve considerable improvements in their use of energy and materials, but capital productivity usually shows decline. To understand this phenomenon it is essential to recognise that these industries are amongst those most heavily affected by the shift

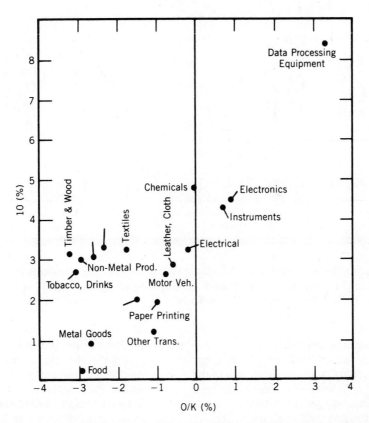

Figure 4 Post-War Growth in Labour (Q/L) and Capital Productivity (Q/K) in the UK Manufacturing Sectors (1948–1984, by SIC Sector)

Q: net output; L: employees; K: official CSO capital stock estimates. All figures are average annual growth rates. Level of disaggregation is the highest one available in terms of capital stock estimates, except for Electronics, which has been estimated on the basis of Soete and Dosi[23]. All sectors have been normalised to their 1980 Standard Industrial Classification definition [24].
Source: Soete (1986).

from an energy-intensive and materials-intensive mass production technological paradigm to an information-intensive paradigm. At the height of the consumer durables and vehicles consumption boom of the 1950s and 1960s, they were achieving strong labour productivity gains based on big plant economies of scale. With the change in technological paradigm, the slowdown of the world economy, and the rise in energy prices in the 1970s, they often faced problems of surplus capacity and high costs based on below-capacity production levels.

However, a combination of rationalisation and closure of the "tail" of low productivity surplus capacity with process innovation in the more advanced plants enables even these industries to resume their productivity advance as well as to improve the quality of their products and inventory control.

e. Some service sectors have been considerably affected by information technology, such as banking and insurance. In these sectors, although the diffusion of new technology is uneven, both by firm and by country, there is evidence of signifi-

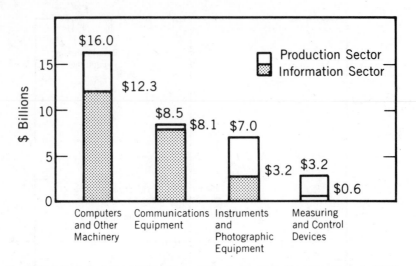

Figure 5   Who Uuses High-Tech Equipment? (Allocation of Private Domestic Final Shipments in 1982)
Source: Morgan Stanley Economics estimates based on input-output industry distribution tables provided by the Interindustry Service of Data Resources, Inc., United States.

cant gains in labour productivity. This phenomenon is rather important because hitherto it has often been observed that the service sector of the economy was not capable of achieving the type of labour productivity gains achieved in manufacturing. Information technology now offers the potential (and already in some cases the reality) of achieving such gains outside manufacturing. However, the progress of technology depends heavily on institutional and structural changes, and especially upon the growth of a capability for software design and maintenance within the service industries.

f. In most service sectors, information technology still has diffused only to a small extent, and these areas are still characterised by very low labour productivity gains, or none at all. The stagnation in labour productivity in these sectors may be attributed to the lack of information technology, but it certainly cannot be attributed to the impact of information technology. These account for by far the larger part of the tertiary sector.

g. Finally, there is a group of service industries that are completely based on information technology and are among the fastest-growing in the world economy. They include especially the software industry and related computerised information services and data banks. These already employ hundreds of thousands of people in the OECD countries, but their impact so far has been mainly in the area of producer services, supplying software, information, design and consultancy services to a broad range of firms in every branch of the economy, as these firms attempt to adopt and modify information technology for their own particular needs. In the future, it can be expected that new consumer information services will also experience (even more) rapid growth, as the infrastructural investment in telecommunications and experience in the provision of such services and products makes them cheaper and more attractive to households. At present the standard of provision is still rather poor and the design of services leaves much to be desired.[7]

The diffusion of new information services is still at a primitive level of provision so far as domestic users are concerned. The day of the "intelligent" refrigerator, the "intelligent" washing-machine and computer-controlled domestic energy systems has not yet dawned. This can be expected to change radically over the next twenty years, providing a major new source of growth of consumer demand and substantial further employment growth in the service and manufacturing industries responding to this demand. However, the introduction of new services, such as "tele-banking" and "tele-shopping," depends also on institutional innovations and on the capacity of various service industries to make radical innovations themselves. These problems are discussed further in the next section, but we first discuss the implications of this process for the growth of employment in new industries and the loss of employment in other sectors of the economy.

IMPLICATIONS FOR EMPLOYMENT, EDUCATION AND TRAINING

One of the main problems in the inconclusive debate on micro-electronics and employment in the 1970s and the many studies which were carried out in the OECD countries over the past ten years was an inadequate conceptualisation of information technology. In our survey of this research for IBM[27] we pointed out that there were at least four different ways of looking at information technology and its employment effects.

The first approach regards the debate about the new technology as essentially a continuation of the "automation" debate of the 1950s and uses expressions such as "factory automation" or "office automation" as though they were virtually synonymous with information technology. The emphasis in this approach is almost entirely on process innovation. Not surprisingly it usually leads to pessimistic estimates of labour displacement.

The second approach regards the IT "industries" as major new branches of the economy capable of imparting an upward impetus to employment in their own right. Thus, for example, it is pointed out that as a result of its extraordinary growth in the 1960s and 1970s, the computer industry in the United States now employs more people than the automobile industry. The "IT sector" in this approach comprises both manufacturing and service industries, whose growth may be analysed in the same way as that of vehicles, electrical machinery or garages and motor repair services, once the necessary re-classification of industrial output and employment statistics has been satisfactorily performed. A typical example is shown in Table 4 from the Office of Technology Assessment (OTA)'s recent report on Information Technology R&D (1985). The emphasis in this approach is on the IT industries as providers of new products and new services. But this approach also underestimates the expansionary effects on employment, since it is confined to the leading edge sectors. The great majority of new jobs in any sustained expansion must come in other industries and services.

The third approach, pioneered by social scientists such as Daniel Bell and Fritz Machlup[28], puts the emphasis on information activities wheresoever they are performed. Bell[29] introduced the notion of the "post-industrial society" and sociologists and economists taking this route tend to stress the growth of information-related occupations in every industry and service as a long-term trend characteristic of the twentieth century, leading to what is often described as the "Information Society." This approach is not necessarily concerned mainly or exclusively with electronic or computer technology, although these have received increasing emphasis in recent times.

The fourth approach, which we ourselves adopt, comprises elements of all three of those which have been described and defines "information technology" both as a new range of products and services and as a technology which is capable of revolutionising the processes of production and delivery of all other industries and services. The scope for such a new technology itself is new, having emerged in the last couple of decades as a result of the convergence of a number of interrelated radical advances in the field of micro-electronics, fibre optics, software engineering, communications

Table 4 Employment Levels in the US Information Technology Industries
Employees (in thousands)

	1972	1982	Percentage change 1972–1982
Manufacturing[1]			
Computers	145	351	+142
Office equipment	34	51	+50
Radio and television receiving sets	87	63	−28
Telephone and telegraph equipment	134	146	+9
Radio and television communications equipment	319	454	+42
Electronic components	336	528	+57
Totals, manufacturing	1 055	1 593	
Services			
Telephone and telegraph	949	1 131	+11
Computing[2]	149	360	+141
Radio and television broadcast[3]	68	81	+19
Cable television[4]	40	52	+30
Totals, services	1 206	1 624	

[1] Estimates provided by the US Department of Commerce, Bureau of Industrial Economics.
[2] Figures are for 1974 and 1983. *Source:* US Industrial Outlook, 1984.
[3] Figures are for 1979 and 1983. *Source:* Federal Communications Commission in telephone interview with the staff of the Office of Technology Assessment (US Congress), May 1984.
[4] Figures are for 1981 and 1982. Ibid. (FCC).

Source: US Congress, Office of Technology Assessment, "Information Technology R&D," Washington, D.C., 1985.

and computer technology. An approach to information activities that ignores the specific features of the new technologies is in danger of overlooking many of the economic and social consequences of these technologies, including their employment effects.

Our approach puts the emphasis on the new technology and not just on the information. For this reason we described the change as a new techno-economic paradigm. We argue that only this fourth approach can yield satisfactory results from the standpoint of the overall economic and employment effects of IT, since the first approach (automation) has an implicit bias towards job displacement, and the second (IT industries) towards job creation, but in a narrow sphere. The third approach is more a theory of occupational trends than of employment. But the new information technologies affect industrial structure, as well as occupational structure. Moreover, they have other specific features which cannot be ignored in considering the problems of structural change and adjustment which have arisen in all the OECD Member countries.

If we adopt this fourth approach, then the employment effects of new technology depend upon the process of structural adjustment and are amenable to policies which influence this process. Here, economists differ in the emphasis which they place on various aspects of structural adjustment, and these differences relate to basic issues in economic theory. Nevertheless, almost all economists would agree that problems of structural adjustment to the rise of new industries and technologies (and the decline of some old ones) are an important part of the agenda for overcoming unemployment problems. Disagreement stems from the difficulty of assessing the relative significance of factor-price mechanisms on the one hand and overcoming institutional and structural rigidities on the other. The analysis here emphasizes that these inflexibilities are exceptionally important in relation to the far-reaching changes that are involved in the adoption of information technology.

Over the past fifteen years the rate of unemployment has been higher both at the peak and at the trough of capacity utilisation in each successive business cycle, as is shown by OKUN curve analysis.[30] That the problem is not simply one of aggregate demand (although this may be important in some countries) is also suggested by consideration of the evidence on skill shortages. Even in countries with very high levels of general unemployment, such as the United Kingdom and the Netherlands, there have been persistent and acute shortages of high-level skills in software design, computer science, systems analysis and related areas. These shortages have persisted throughout the 1970s and 1980s despite efforts to increase the supply, which are handicapped by shortages of teachers of these subjects throughout the system.

The importance of these shortages cannot be assessed by a simple comparison of aggregate numbers of unemployed with numbers of vacancies. Seen in terms of the paradigm change which has been described above, these shortages represent the critical bottle-neck in the "cultural revolution" needed in so many firms and so many industries. Without these skilled people it is simply not possible to embark on the design and redesign of products and processes to utilise information technology. Moreover, without an adequate supply of skilled people, investment in new capital equipment may actually lead to a fall in both capital and labour productivity, because of an inability to maintain the equipment, use it to full capacity and integrate it with other parts of the system.

A survey of more than twenty research projects in all the major OECD Member countries showed great differences in methodology and in conclusions about the employment effects of information technology. But there was one point of absolutely universal agreement: the critical importance of education, training and retraining of the labour force[27]. Even in those countries—Japan and Sweden are examples—which are well-known for the scale and thoroughness of their training and retraining programmes, there were also persistent shortages of certain key skill categories. On the one hand this indicates the world-wide universal nature of the technological paradigm change which we are considering; on the other it indicates that these skills are needed, not just in one or two science-intensive industries, or in defence electronics, but everywhere, both for the rejuvenation of old industries and the growth of new ones.

An aggregative approach to unemployment and vacancies disguises the true problem in another way. It is not just a question of new high-level skills, crucial though these are. It is also a question of the transformation of the skill profile of the labour force at all levels. The craftsmen who operate and maintain new types of capital goods have often been trained mainly or only with electro-mechanical rather than electronic equipment. The substitution process which takes place everywhere is of course highly desirable, but it is likely to be very inefficient unless accompanied by extensive retraining. Above all, Japanese experience brings out the value of continuous training and retraining of all levels of the work-force to gain the full advantages of new technology. The organisational innovations which, as we have seen, are an essential accompaniment of technical innovation, are likely to be effective only if implemented in conjunction with such retraining programmes. Adaptability to such changes also requires a high level of general education and of computer literacy throughout the population.

Whilst the need for major programmes of education, training and retraining is world-wide, the ways in which these changes are introduced is necessarily country-specific, because of the institutional variety in Member countries. For example, the Japanese pattern is based on extensive provision of general education and higher education for a very high proportion of school-leavers. This is followed by intensive and prolonged training organised by firms that devote great resources to these programmes and believe that the investment is justified by the returns in terms of quality of output, productivity, company morale, industrial relations and adaptability to technical change. On the other hand, in Sweden (and in other countries with greater mobility of labour between firms), public provision of training and retraining plays a much bigger role.

The case of education and training is one instance, albeit a very important one, of the general problem of adaptation of the institutional and social framework to the new techno-economic paradigm. We now turn to consider these wider issues at the national and international level.

ADAPTATION OF COUNTRIES' SOCIAL, LEGAL AND INSTITUTIONAL FRAMEWORK

This paper has argued that the problems of structural change now confronting all the OECD economies are associated with the transition from one techno-economic paradigm to another.

Economists studying technical innovation have used a variety of expressions to describe this type of far-reaching radical change involving a new perception of the whole way in which business is organised.[8]

Whilst there are similarities in all these concepts, the approach of Carlotta Perez[34] is the most systematic and has some important distinguishing features in relation to the structural

crises of adaptation, with which we are concerned. The development of a new "techno-economic paradigm" involves a new "best practice" set of rules and customs for designers, engineers, entrepreneurs and managers, which differ in many important respects from the previously prevailing paradigm. Such technological revolutions give rise to a whole series of rapidly changing production functions for both old and new products. Whilst the exact savings in either labour or capital cannot be precisely foreseen, the general economic and technical advantages to be derived from the application of the new technology in product and process design become increasingly apparent and new "rules of thumb" are gradually established. Such changes in paradigm make possible a "quantum leap" in potential productivity, which however is at first only realised in a few leading sectors. It takes decades for the productivity gains to be realised throughout the economy as a result of a process of learning, adaptation, incremental innovation and institutional change.

Perez places great emphasis on changes in the institutional and social framework and has suggested that boom periods of expansion occur when there is a "good match" between a new techno-economic "paradigm" or "style" and the socio-institutional climate. Depressions represent periods of mismatch between the emerging new paradigms and the institutional framework. The widespread generalisation of the new paradigms, not only in the "leading" branches but also in many other branches of the economy, is possible only after a period of change and adaptation of many social institutions to the potential of the new technology. Whereas technological change is often very rapid, there is usually a great deal of inertia in social institutions, buttressed by the social and political power of established interest groups as well as by the slow response times of many individuals and groups.[9]

In the present period of structural change, a new information-intensive techno-economic paradigm has emerged, based on the extraordinarily low costs of storing, processing and communicating information. Because this technology permits far more precise control of all production processes in real time, and of stocks and distribution, it offers great potential for cost-savings not just in labour but also in capital, energy and materials. This is linked to a potential for providing a wide range of new products and services and higher quality of existing goods and services. But its diffusion is hindered and its productivity potential is not realised because of institutions and management styles which are still geared to the old paradigm. The structural crisis of the 1980s is in this perspective a prolonged period of social adaptation to this new paradigm.

The mismatch between the skills that are needed for the efficient exploitation of the new technologies and the available skill profile of the labour force is the most obvious manifestation of the general problem of institutional and structural adaptation confronting the OECD economies. But it is no less important to consider the problem of the transformation of the capital stock.

In considering capital stock and capacity utilisation it is essential to consider disaggregated data, as well as aggregate national trends. As in the parallel case of unemployment and vacancies, aggregate statistics can disguise the real process of structural change by suggesting considerable surplus capacity throughout the economy, when in fact this is concentrated in industries and in types of equipment which are not technologically and economically viable. This "surplus" capacity may exist side by side with shortages of capacity in the newer industries and technologies. It is for this reason that the whole issue of "capital mismatch" unemployment should be taken seriously, and with it the related issue of capital productivity.

Whilst of course the trend of labour productivity and the way in which it is affected by new technology is central, it cannot be isolated from the trend in capital productivity and capital-saving technical change. Micro-level studies indicate that IT can have important effects on capital productivity in relation to stocks of materials, work-in-progress and finished products. New types of "intelligent" capital goods may show rising capital productivity whereas older types of capital equipment generally have shown a falling trend in the OECD countries over the past decade or so. This aspect of the problem is important in considering the possible effects of IT as a stimulus to a broad-based wave of new investment, offering prospects of rising profitability and expansion in the OECD economies.

The change in the profile of capital stock also involves major changes in policies and institutions. Many investment incentive schemes in the past, both at the regional and national level, have been based on a priority for large capital-intensive plants. The Japanese "Technopolis" project[37] indicates the change in direction that regional policy and investment incentives will have to take in the future. It puts the main emphasis in regional policy on restructuring through information technology and the associated research, education and communications infrastructure. Japanese policies seem to be moving further now in the direction of emphasizing software and service provision, rather than physical investment in new plant.

New investment in the telecommunication infrastructure has an exceptional importance in this context, comparable to the railway and road networks in previous waves of technical change. Many of the new producer and consumer services that will provide a major expansionary impetus to the world economy over the next few decades (Figure 6) depend upon this investment.

It is rather unlikely that the necessary changes in the telecommunications industry can take place within monopolistic structures, whether public or private. Especially in the field of local networks, the development of autonomous growth poles would seem to be essential for widespread diffusion of new services.

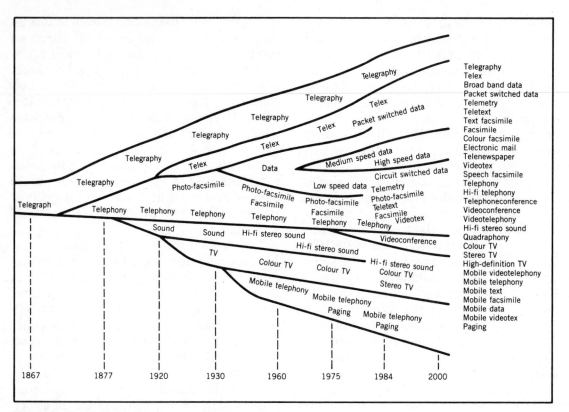

Figure 6 The Evolution of Diverse Telecommunications Services
Source: Electronic Times, May 2, 1985, article by C. Partridge.

There are still plenty of demand niches that need to be identified, where the long painstaking process of user feedback effects has yet to be set in motion. In view of the generic nature of the technology it would be surprising if one single firm would be able to cope with the enormous diversity of user demand and requirements.

The emergence of entirely new services, such as tele-shopping and tele-banking, will depend very heavily on the telecommunications network and on more far-reaching legislative and institutional changes. The same holds for any trend towards the "electronic cottage"—the shift in the creation of employment away from the town, factory and office to the domestic household and rural networks.

The diffusion of IT is still in its infancy and the future course of development is in part a process of social experiment and innovation. Obviously, the OECD countries have much to learn from each other in such a period. There is a growing search for new social and political solutions in such areas as flexible working time, shorter working hours, re-education and re-training systems, regional policies based on creating favourable conditions for information technology (rather than tax incentives to capital-intensive mass production industries), new financial systems, new ways of regulating telecommunications, possible decentralisation of management and government, higher quality of social services and access to data banks at all levels. But so far, changes have seemed partial and relatively minor. If the Keynesian revolution and the profound transformation of social institutions in the Second World War and its aftermath were required to unleash the post-war boom, then social innovations on a much more significant scale are likely to be needed now. This applies especially to the international dimension of world economic development which, however, lies beyond the scope of this paper.

NOTES

1. Much earlier work at the OECD has discussed problems of the measurement of scientific and technical activities[1], and analytical reports[2] have demonstrated the relevance of R&D to economic performance, particularly in relation to policies for basic research and education[3].

2. For example, Hollander's study[9] of productivity gains in Du Pont rayon plants or Townsend's study[10] of the Anderton shearer-loader in the British coal-mining industry. SPRU research on technical change in the UK economy since the war confirmed the importance of these incremental changes in every sector, but especially in industries such as chemicals[11] or textiles[12] following the introduction of new materials, such as synthetic fibres, and the exploitation of novel process technology during the scaling-up and rapid market expansion period in the 1950s and 1960s.

3. SPRU research did not, however, support the view of Mensch[13] that their appearance is concentrated particularly in periods of deep recessions[14].

4. The present "Frascati"[1] statistics do not capture these new developments since software applications are largely excluded from both R&D measures and patent statistics. New statistics and methods of measurement will certainly be needed, and the OECD is already involved in this work.

5. Carlotta Perez[18] has identified these dominant characteristics of information technology as "systemation" and "flexibility."

6. Under the old system all the shafts and countershafts rotated continuously and a breakdown could affect the entire factory. As Warren Devine[20] points out, *"Replacing a steam engine with one or more electric motors, leaving the power distribution system unchanged, appears to have been the usual juxtaposition of the new technology upon the framework of an old one . . . Shaft and belt power distribution systems were in place and manufacturers were familiar with their problems. Turning line shafts with motors was an improvement that required modifying only the front end of the system . . . As long as the electric motors were simply used in place of steam engines to turn long line shafts the*

shortcomings of mechanical power distribution systems remained."

It was not until after 1900 that manufacturers generally began to realise that the indirect benefits of using unit electric drive were far greater than the direct energy-saving benefits.

7. Again, there is an instructive analogy here with the diffusion of electric power in households. For a considerable time, it was not usually cheaper to use electricity for lighting, cooking, and many household appliances, and as Adrian Forty[26] pointed out, *"On the whole, as electricity supply engineers frequently complained, the standard of design was not high. In some cases, such as certain domestic clothes washing machines, the appliances were manual models to which an electric motor had been attached. Some electric cookers had been made by installing electric elements in the cast-iron carcase of gas cookers, while those that were purpose-built often looked very much like gas cookers. Even where, as in the case of electric fires, the product was not a direct substitute for a manual or gas appliance, there was rarely much about the designs to indicate their specifically electrical nature, and the level of efficiency was generally unspectacular. The extravagant claims that were sometimes made for the luxury of the all-electric home were hardly justified by the appliances themselves, which could not in any case be put to more than occasional use because of the high price of electricity."*

8. Nelson and Winter[31] have used the expression "generalised natural trajectories" to describe the phenomenon. Keirstead[15] spoke of "constellations" of innovations, interrelated technically and economically. Dosi[32] has used the expression change of "technological paradigm" and made comparisons with the analogous approach of Kuhn[33] to "scientific revolutions" and paradigm changes in basic science. In these terms "incremental innovation" along established technological trajectories may be compared with Kuhn's "normal science."

9. Institutional rigidities in such periods of structural change have also been brought out strongly by other studies such as those of Olsen[35] and the Kiel Institute[36].

REFERENCES

1. OECD, *The Measurement of Scientific and Technical Activities: Frascati Manual*, Paris, 1963 and revised editions, 1970 and 1981.
2. For example, OECD, *Gaps in Technology*, Paris, 1968, General Report and reports on six industrial sectors. OECD, *Science, Growth and Society* (Brooks Report), 1971.
3. For example, OECD, *Conditions for Success in Technological Innovation* (K. Pavitt, ed.), Paris, 1975. *Government and Allocation of Resources to Science*, 1966.

4. OECD, *Technical Change and Economic Policy: Science and Technology in the New Economic Context,* Paris, 1980.

5. Ibid.

6. Eads, G., and R. R. Nelson. "Government Support of Advanced Civilian Technology," *Public Policy,* Vol. 19, no. 3, pp. 415–427.

7. Henderson, P. "Two British Errors: Their Probable Size and Some Possible Lessons," *Oxford Economic Papers,* Vol. 29 (1977).

8. The following section is based largely on C. Freeman, and C. Perez, "The Diffusion of Technical Innovations and Changes of Techno-economic Paradigm," paper for DAST Conference, University of Venice, March 1986.

9. Hollander, S. *The Sources of Increased Efficiency; A Study of Du Pont Rayon Plants.* Cambridge, Mass.: MIT Press, 1965.

10. Townsend, J. F. *Innovations in Coal-Mining Machinery—the Anderton Shearer-Loader and the Role of the NCB and Supply Industries in Its Development,* SPRU Occasional Paper No. 3, University of Sussex, 1976.

11. Clark, J. (ed.), *Technological Trends and Employment,* Vol. 1, Aldershot: Gower Press, 1984.

12. Soete, L. L. G. (ed.), *Technological Trends and Employment,* Vol. 3, Aldershot: Gower Press, 1985.

13. Mensch, G., *Das technologische Patt,* Umschau, Frankfurt, 1975, and English translation, *Stalemate in Technology,* Bollinger, New York, 1979.

14. Freeman, C., J. A. Clark, and L. L. G. Soete, *Unemployment and Technical Innovation: A Study of Long Waves in Economic Development.* London: Frances Pinter, 1982.

15. Keirstead, B. S. *The Theory of Economic Change.* Toronto: Macmillan, 1948.

16. Piore, M., and C. Sabel. *The Second Industrial Divide.* New York: Basic Books, 1984.

17. Brady, T., and P. Senker. *Economic Incentives and Training: Changing Skill Requirements in Computer Maintenance,* Manpower Services Commission, Bradford, 1986.

18. Perez, C., "Micro-electronics, Long Waves and World Structural Change: New Perspectives for Developing Countries," *World Development,* Vol. 13, no. 3 (1985) pp. 441–463.

19. Gooding, K. "The Cultural Revolution at GM," *Financial Times,* November 13, 1984.

20. Devine, W. "From Shafts to Wires: Historical Perspective on Electrification," *Journal of Economic History,* Vol. XLIII(2), pp. 347–372.

21. Belussi, F. "The Diffusion of Innovations in Traditional Sectors: The Case of Benetton," SPRU, University of Sussex, mimeo, 1986.

22. Freeman, C., and L. L. G. Soete. *Technical Change and Full Employment,* Oxford: Blackwell, 1986, and Clark, J. A., K. Guy, L. L. G. Soete, C. Freeman, and A. A. D. Smith (eds.), *Technological Trends and Employment,* 5 Vols. Aldershot: Gower, 1984, 1985, 1986.

23. Soete, L. L. G., and G. Dosi, *Technology and Employment in the Electronics Industry.* London: Frances Pinter, 1983.

24. Soete, L. L. G., and C. Freeman, "Innovation Diffusion and Employment Policies," Paper for Venice Conference on Innovation Diffusion, DAST, March 1986.

25. Salter, W. *Productivity and Technical Change.* Cambridge: Cambridge University Press, 1960.

26. Forty, A. *Objects of Desire: Design and Society 1850–1980.* London: Thames and Hudson, 1981, p. 187.

27. Freeman, C., and L. L. G. Soete, *Information Technology and Employment: An Assessment,* IBM (Europe), 1985. The following section draws on this report.

SECTION 8

CORPORATE CULTURE AND HUMAN RESOURCE MANAGEMENT

Many multinational corporations are becoming global rather than multidomestic in their strategy and structure. We might expect these companies to shed the narrow cultural perspective of headquarters and become culturally homogeneous world companies. Global managers would adopt a global managerial culture that would encompass all subsidiaries. These managers would feel equally at home in their companies' Japanese, French, Indonesian, or U.S. operations and would adopt culture-free human resource policies.

In fact, one's own national culture is an astonishingly powerful factor in multinational and even global management. No matter how large a company becomes or in how many environments it operates, cultural factors will have a profound impact. Culture can be defined as "that complex whole which includes knowledge, belief, art, morals, law, customs and any capabilities and habits acquired by man [and woman] as a member of society."[1] Some components of culture are attitudes, religion, education, norms, social organization, language, and community organization. Geert Hofstede calls culture "a selective programming of the mind."[2]

People in a particular culture think, feel, and react in patterned ways and have a collective personality. Multinational managers must understand the elements of their home-country cultures and those of their host-country subsidiary managers. They need to operate in local environments while still retaining their headquarter's culture and perspective. Japanese multinational managers, for example, are adept at learning host-country customs and norms while keeping their own their language, habits, and managerial practices intact. Americans tend to act and feel like Americans, regardless of where they work.

[1]Edward B. Tylor, "Primitive Culture," in Vern Terpstra, *The Cultural Environment of International Business* (Cincinnati, Ohio: South-Western, 1978), p. xii.
[2]Geert Hofstede, *Culture's Consequences* (Beverly Hills, Calif.: Sage Publications, 1980), p. 13.

The enculturation process, or the way in which communities pass rules of behavior from generation to generation, begin in infancy. Verbal and nonverbal communication transmits cultural elements so subtly that people are not aware they are being patterned. There are an almost endless number of cultural "rules" that we observe without thinking about them. Most of us converse at a culturally defined distance. When we move either closer or farther away, we feel uncomfortable.

The concept of being "on time" is also culturally determined. Americans keep appointments at the agreed-upon hour. Others may arrive an hour later than the agreed-upon time, but still be "on time." The most critical and the most trivial aspects of management are influenced by cultural traditions and patterns.

Firms also have cultures that guide managerial behavior. Some companies foster cooperative behavior while others thrive on internal competition. Firms may have explicit norms of dress, behavior, and relationships. Some managers are expected to show up at meeting after meeting while others communicate through computerized mail. Some companies expect managers to take an interest in employees' personal lives; others care only about the employees' work. New employees on every level are taught prevailing corporate norms, values, and rules. Their own national cultures interrelate and interact with the corporate culture. This is an ongoing process of conflict, cooperation, and accommodation.

Headquarters' strategy determines how and to what extent home-country and host-country managers and cultures interact. The nature of products, differences in customer preference, employee relations, legal requirements, and financial arrangements all play a part. Headquarters' national and corporate culture profoundly affects the management of one subsidiary firm but may have little relevance to another.

Managers of multinational firms should seek to maximize the positive interaction of national and corporate cultural elements. Managerial skills, attitudes, and commitments should fit the firm's global strategy. But, even when managers try to treat the firm as a single unit with overall planning, objective setting, and goal implementation, they cannot ignore culture. In practice, most MNCs combine home- and host-country national cultures with corporate culture. Each company's headquarters and subsidiaries interact in unique combinations consistent with an overarching uniform strategy for the MNC as a whole.

For many years, scholars adopted Perlmutter's model of staffing policy: ethnocentric, polycentric, and geocentric.[3] The ethnocentrically oriented firm tends to think of its nationals as superior to managers in host countries. It assumes that what works at home will work abroad. This viewpoint leads headquarters to overlook the importance of local conditions and to make assumptions based on faulty data. Standards, procedures, and cultural biases

[3]Howard V. Perlmutter, "The Tortuous Evolution of the Multinational Corporation," *Columbia Journal of World Business,* 1969, pp. 9–18.

appropriate in the home country are often not transferable to subsidiaries in different cultures.

Host-country, or polycentric, orientation carries its own set of problems for the MNC. When host-country managers are given virtual autonomy, they may run their subsidiaries almost independently of headquarters. It becomes difficult, if not impossible, for top management to implement a global strategy. Although communication and cultural interactions may be easier within the subsidiary, interactions between headquarters and operating units will be impaired.

Geocentric orientation means the firm has a worldwide outlook. Ideally, top management treats the firm as a single unit with overall planning, objective setting, and goal implementation. Managers are selected without regard to nationality and cultural attitudes. Their skills and their commitment to the firm's global strategy are the basis for selection.

Perlmutter observed that none of these models exists in pure form and that most MNCs work out their own hybrid combination of home and host policies. More recent work in cross-cultural management demonstrates the continued importance of culture in every aspect of the firm's operations. They explore the complex mechanisms that companies use to manage cultural diversity. MNCs no longer ignore national and corporate culture; rather, they use them to foster the most effective use of their resources.

READING SELECTIONS

The four articles in this section examine the impact of culture on management and human resource allocation. The first article, by Nancy Adler, Robert Doktor, and S. Gordon Redding, deals with the differences in national cultures. It reviews comparative and cross-cultural management and particularly the differences in East-West cultural relations.

The authors note that scholarship used to focus on the Atlantic Basin but now has shifted, both conceptually and geographically, to the Pacific. The article examines the major debates in cross-cultural management and addresses central questions such as: Does organizational behavior vary across cultures? How much of the difference can be attributed to culture? Is the variance of organizational behavior worldwide increasing, decreasing, or remaining stable? How can organizations best manage outside their own cultures? How can organizations best manage cultural diversity? The authors point out that researchers may misinterpret East-West managerial comparisons because of their own ethnocentric perspective. It is critical, they stress, that managers present their own view of the world in such a way that it can be understood and appreciated by others.

The second article looks inside the firm and the interaction between national and corporate culture. Susan Schneider points out the complex interactions that exist between subsidiaries embedded in local national cultures and the national and corporate culture of the MNC parent. She reviews the general components of culture, noting that multiple definitions tend to be confusing and lead to different assumptions about the nature of human relationships. These differences have implications for human resource policies that are developed at headquarters and imposed upon subsidiaries. Schneider describes how national culture affects human resource choices in planning and staffing, appraisal and compensation, and selection and socialization. She poses, and attempts to answer, two very important questions: To what extent can corporate culture override national culture differences to create a global company? and Is it even desirable to override national differences?

In "Organizing for Worldwide Effectiveness: The Transnational Solution," Christopher Bartlett and Sumantra Ghoshal find that globalizing and localizing forces work simultaneously in multinational corporations. They note first that for historical reasons, very few companies are organized in such a way that they can respond to both localizing and globalizing forces. The authors note generally that the external environment shapes company tasks but MNCs' ability to perform is constrained by their corporate culture or "administrative heritage."

American and European companies tend to be "decentralized federations" of subsidiaries. Japanese companies concentrate operations at home and are less successful at building responsive worldwide operating units. They examine the strategies of two giant electronics firms: Matsushita and Philips. Matsushita Electric Company controls its global strategy from the center in Japan but has implemented flexible and responsive management worldwide. Philips, the Dutch-based electronics giant, builds effective national operations worldwide. The authors also note that a few MNCs are in the process of developing organizational capabilities to respond to both localizing and globalizing forces. These companies have developed the ability to manage across national borders, retaining flexibility while still achieving global integration. L. M. Ericsson, the Swedish telecommunications company, is an example of such a company. Ericsson is successful because it has a clearly defined and tightly controlled set of operating systems, it uses personnel effectively, and it resolves differences through subsidiary boards and other interunit decision forums. Bartlett and Ghoshal conclude that companies must think globally and act locally for long-term success.

Peter Lorange, in the final article, addresses human resource management in joint ventures. When managers from different national and corporate cultures are brought together in a new enterprise, they often have different strategies, values, and experiences. The author presents a conceptual framework for these ventures based on the relative degree of strategic importance of the venture to each partner and the desired degree of control by each partner over resources.

Lorange examines six crucial issues for joint ventures in multinational settings. These are (1) where managers should be assigned, (2) which partner controls a particular manager, (3) how managers trade off time spent in operating or strategic tasks, (4) how biases in human resource performance are avoided, (5) issues of loyalty to the joint venture or parent, and (6) individual manager career planning issues. He concludes that the joint venture will have to establish its own strong human resource function to motivate people in appropriate ways and to develop skills in managers who will eventually be used in the parent company and in other joint ventures.

35

FROM THE ATLANTIC TO THE PACIFIC CENTURY: CROSS-CULTURAL MANAGEMENT REVIEWED

Nancy J. Adler and Robert Doktor
in collaboration with S. Gordon Redding

This article reviews the areas of comparative and cross-cultural management and discusses the impact of cultural diversity on international organizational behavior. With the growing shift of business from the Atlantic to the Pacific Basin East-West cultural differences are becoming increasingly significant. Research in developmental psychology, sociology, and anthropology shows that there are major differences among the cognitive processes of people from different cultures. In the era of the global corporation, cultural diversity has to be recognized, understood, and appropriately used in organizations. It is suggested that cross-cultural management would greatly benefit from comparative studies considering the impact of the cognitive aspects of culture on managerial practice.

Japanese and American management is 95 percent the same, and differs in all important respects.
T. Fujisawa, cofounder of Honda Motor Corporation

International commerce is vital to national prosperity. According to Robert Frederick, chairman of the National Foreign Trade Council, 80% of United States industry now faces international competition. The growing interdependence of national economies has created a demand for managers sophisticated in international business and skilled in working with people from other cultures. Even as the decade began, a major study of United States industrial competitiveness concluded that where a global

Source: Journal of Management, Vol. 12, no. 2 (1986), pp. 295–318. Copyright 1986 by the Southern Management Association 0149-2063 86 52.00.

market exists, firms operating on a worldwide basis may have advantages over those that restrict themselves to a domestic market, even one as large as that of the United States. Just to remain competitive, the world of business is asking international questions and demanding global answers.

The field of comparative management developed to increase our understanding of worldwide business. A relatively recent phenomenon, it has paralleled the internationalization of the firm and the rise of the multinational corporation (MNC) following World War II. Only a decade ago, Evans (1976) anticipated the potential of this new field:

Thus far, the field of organization theory has failed to come to grips with the cultural component of the environments in which organizations are embedded. This is not at all surprising because there are formidable conceptual and methodological obstacles to overcome. The fact that MNCs operate in a multitude of cultural and societal settings not only poses a challenge to executives but also provides an opportunity for organizational researchers to use this worldwide organizational phenomenon as a vehicle for research. (p. 241)

Today, the move from the multinational to the global corporation marks yet another fundamental change in perspective. Corporate structures will no longer be primarily multidomestic, but rather truly global in their strategy, structure, markets, and resource bases.

For years, scholars have called for research that would explain and analyze the relationship between management and culture (e.g., Roberts, 1970; Sorge, 1983; Weinshall, 1977). Others have argued that the growing body of organization theory literature (research conducted within one country, usually the United States) should be integrated with the comparative management literature (research conducted in more than one country) (Joynt, 1985). Cross-cultural management research has attempted to do just that: inform people working in organizations whose employees or clients span more than one culture. Cross-cultural management studies the behavior of people interacting within and between organizations around the world. It describes and compares organizational behavior across cultures, and, perhaps most important for managers, seeks to understand and improve the effectiveness of people interacting with colleagues from different cultures. Cross-cultural management thus expands domestic management knowledge and practice to encompass international, global, and multicultural spheres.

This article documents the development of the comparative and cross-cultural management fields through a discussion of the major issues each has addressed. That development has focused primarily on Western research traditions and paradigms. Paralleling the shift of business from the Atlantic to the Pacific Basin, we move from the field's conceptually Occidental history to an Oriental perspective. This shift, both geographical and conceptual, foreshadows the move from the Atlantic to the Pacific century.

CROSS-CULTURAL MANAGEMENT: SOME MAJOR DEBATES

The fields of comparative and cross-cultural management address five central questions.[1] First, does organizational behavior vary across cultures? Second, how much of the observed difference can be attributed to cultural determinants? Third, is the variance in organizational behavior worldwide increasing, decreasing, or remaining the same? Fourth, how can organizations best manage within cultures other than their own? Fifth, how can organizations best manage cultural diversity, including using diversity as an organizational resource? This includes a macro-level question: the implications for government and economic policy of one form of organization being found to be more efficient than others in a given environment. Although more research has been done on the first three questions, scholars in the field have considered all five. We review each separately.

Cross-Cultural Variance

Does organizational behavior vary across cultures? Or, perhaps more important, do the relationships between organizational factors (e.g., work climate, leadership style, decision-making processes, degree of formalization) and organizational outcomes (e.g., performance, satisfaction, commitment of organizational members) vary from one nation to the next? Crozier (1964) contended that the research community has often ignored cultural differences altogether:

Intuitively . . . people have always assumed that bureaucratic structures and patterns of action differ in different countries. . . . Men of action know it and never fail to take it into account, but contemporary social scientists . . . have not been concerned with such comparisons. (p. 210)

Single-Culture Studies Single-culture studies have attempted to document aspects of organizational behavior in many countries, but they are not designed to identify similarities and differences. Almost half (47.2%) of all recent cross-cultural management articles report on single-culture studies (Adler, 1983b). Examples include such articles as "Politics, Bureaucracy, and Worker Participation: The Swedish Case" (Albrecht, 1980). "Cultural and Situational Determinants of Job Satisfaction Amongst Management in South Africa" (Blunt, 1973), "Early Chinese Management Thought" (Chang, 1976), and "Managerial Attitudes of Greeks: The Roles of Culture and Industrialization" (Cummings & Schmidt, 1972).

Comparative Studies Comparative studies have focused on whether there is a difference among organizations operating in two or more cultures. About a third (34.2%) of all cross-cultural management articles report findings from comparative research (Adler, 1983b). Examples of comparative research include such articles as "Worker Participation Contrasts in Three Countries" (Foy & Gadon, 1976), "The Impact of Culture Upon Managerial Attitudes, Beliefs and Behavior in England and France" (Graves, 1972), and "Social Performance Goals in the Peruvian and the Yugoslav Worker Participation System" (Hoover, Troub, Whitehead, & Flores, 1978). Although some studies find more similarities and others more differences, it is clear that neither the behavior of people in organizations nor the relationships between behavior and organizational outcomes are identical worldwide.

Nation Versus Culture In both single-culture and comparative studies, nation and culture have been used as if they were synonymous, with national boundaries separating one cultural group from another. Rarely have more specific definitions of culture been used, nor has domestic cultural heterogeneity been considered. In essence, the majority of these studies should be labeled cross-national rather than cross-cultural.

Cultural Determination

Given that differences exist, can they be explained by cultural determinants? In other words, can organizational characteristics which influence or determine human behavior in work situations be explained by cultural factors? Are the relationships between organizational behavior and organizational outcomes, whether similar or different across countries, contingent upon cultural variables? As a number of authors have indicated, the question is not merely whether organizations differ across cultures but whether the differences are caused by cultural factors.

Culture Culture and cultural influences are concepts which neither anthropology nor management has defined consistently. Tylor (1877) defined culture as "that complex whole which includes knowledge, belief, art, law, morals, customs and any capabilities and habits acquired by a man as a member of society" (p. 1). Linton (1945) described culture as "the configuration of learned behavior and the results of behavior whose component elements are shared and transmitted by members of a particular society" (p. 32). Barnouw (1963) wrote that "a culture is a way of life of a group of people, the configuration of all of the more or less stereotyped patterns of learned behavior, which are handed down from one generation to the next through the means of language and imitation" (p. 4). Kroeber and Kluckhohn (1952), in cataloging more than a hundred definitions of culture, gave one of the more comprehensive and generally accepted:

Culture consists of patterns, explicit and implicit of and for behavior acquired and transmitted by symbols, constituting the distinctive achievement of human groups, including their embodiment in artifacts; the essential core of culture consists of traditional (i.e., historically derived and selected) ideas and especially their attached values; culture systems may, on the one hand, be considered as products of action, on the other as conditioning elements of further action. (p. 181)

Culture is, therefore, (a) something that is shared by all or almost all members of some social group, (b) something that the older members of the group try to pass on to the younger members, and (c) something (as in the case of morals, laws, or customs) that shapes behavior or structures one's perception of the world (Carrol, 1982, p. 19).

In Hofstede's (1980) more recent work, culture is defined as

the collective programming of the mind which distinguishes the members of one human group from another. . . . the interactive aggregate of common characteristics that influence a human group's response to its environment. (p. 25)

. . . Culture is not a characteristic of the individual: it encompasses a number of people who were conditioned by the same education and life experience. When we speak of the culture of a group, a tribe, a geographical region, a national minority, or a nation, culture refers to the collective mental programming that these people have in common: the programming that is different from that of other group, tribes, regions, minorities, or nations. (p. 48)

Such a definition implies a clear and important distinction between (a) the shared ideas which shape and influence social action and (b) the action itself as played out in the social system. Culture appears to be increasingly agreed upon by theorists as being the former (Child, 1981, p. 324; Keesing, 1974; Kroeber & Parsons, 1958, pp. 582–583; Parsons, 1973, p. 36), although this convenient analytical distinction does not show how ideas and action are con- nected in real life. Theorists concerned primarily with such a sociological question agree that even though cultural patterns are observable in the realm of social action, culture itself exists at another level of analysis.

The idea of culture as mind-state raises the problem of reductionism and an explanatory cul-de-sac, whereas using social patterns for explanation removes the understanding of their determinants. A recent review of the sociological literature on culture (Wuthnow, Hunter, Bergesen, & Kurzweil, 1984) stresses the embryonic nature of the discipline. Even so, fruitful progress may be marked, and more predicted, with culture being accepted as an observable aspect of human behavior, manifest in social interaction and tangible objects like organizations, but resting on symbolic frameworks, mental programs, and conceptual distinctions in people's minds (Hicks & Redding, 1983; Redding, 1982).

These collective mental programs may be termed *cognitive maps*. Because cognitive maps vary across cultures, their effects upon managerial action can also vary and at times even become severely dysfunctional. Although the number of analytic dimensions needed to describe and classify cultural similarities and differences is unknown, recognizing the existence of each culture's unique set of cognitive maps and their potential impact upon managerial action, however measured, is extremely important.

Culture's Influence. However defined, culture influences people's values, attitudes, and behaviors, which in turn collectively define their culture. Culture influences organizations through societal structures such as laws and political systems and also through the values, attitudes, behavior, goals, and preferences of participants (clients, employees, and especially managers). The circular nature of culture has made it difficult, if not impossible, to separate cultural causation from determination by other societal factors. Is the influence of the educational system a cultural influence? The influence of the legal system? The influence of the political system? The answers have depended on various researchers' definitions of culture. From our perspective, culture is certainly not identical to other primary societal structures, but it strongly influences their form and function. Specific educational, political, legal, and economic systems exist in a given society partly because of their cultural heritage.

From the viewpoint of organizational culture, the question becomes: Do organizational culture and structure determine people's behavior in organizations, or does national or ethnic cultural conditioning limit the organization's influence? Does the culture that enters the organization through employees limit the influence of management-created organizational culture and structure (Adler & Jelinek, 1986)? Apparently, yes.

However, it may be that our Western cognitive conditioning leads us to separate culture from other societal influences and the organization from its environment. Westerners tend to see categories, distinctions, and separateness, whereas people conditioned by Eastern cultures are more likely to see continuity and connectedness (Maruyama, 1980, 1982, 1984).

In 1982, Solange-Perret conducted a particularly important study attempting to distinguish between national and cultural impacts on management.[2] She used Kluckhohn and Strodbeck's (1961) five dimensions to identify the underlying cultural variance between American and French managers working in United States- and French-based subsidiaries of a major American corporation. The five dimensions used were relationship to self, others, external environment, activity, and time. Using observation and interview techniques, she documented fundamental differences in managerial styles and control systems between the two subsidiaries. Her data revealed parallels between the variance in fundamental cultural orientations and the actual work behavior and attitudes of the two groups. Solange-Perret is currently replicating the study.

Convergence Versus Divergence

Is the diversity of behavior in organizations across cultures increasing, decreasing, or remaining the same? Trying to resolve what is commonly labeled the *convergence/divergence dichotomy,* scholars ask whether organizations worldwide are becoming more similar (convergence) or are maintaining their culturally based dissimilarity (divergence).

Convergence Adherents of the convergence (or universalist) perspective argue that organizational characteristics across nations are mostly free of the particularities of specific cultures (e.g., Cole, 1973; Form, 1979; Hickson, Hinnings, McMillan, & Schwitter, 1974; Kerr, Dunlop, Harbison, & Myers, 1952; Negandhi, 1979, 1985). This position suggests that as an outcome of "common industrial logic"—most notably of technological origin—institutional frameworks, organizational patterns and structures, and management practices across countries are converging.

For example, Child (1981) and Child and Tayeb (1983) concluded that organizational variance today depends much more on contingencies other than culture than it has previously:

Contingencies of technological development, market and geographical diversification, large-scale production and close interdependence with other organizations . . . impose a logic of rational administration which it becomes functionally imperative to follow in order to achieve levels of performance sufficient to ensure the survival of the organization. . . . It is argued that this logic is in all societies, irrespective of culture, economic or political systems, steadily pervading the design and management of organizations which are subject to high performance requirements either because of competitive pressure or because of ex-

ternal demands for their effectiveness. Cultural differences are therefore of diminishing importance. (Child & Tayeb, 1983, p. 27)

In full agreement, Levitt (1983) declared that

a powerful force drives the world toward a converging commonality, and that force is technology. It has proletarianized communication, transport, and travel. It has made isolated places and impoverished peoples eager for modernity's allurements. . . . The result is a new commercial reality—the emergence of global markets for standardized consumer products on a previously unimagined scale of magnitude. Corporations geared to this new reality benefit from enormous economies of scale in production, distribution, marketing, and management. By translating these benefits into reduced world prices, they can decimate competitors that still live in the disabling grip of old assumptions about how the world works.

Gone are accustomed differences in national or regional preference. (p. 92).

He added that "different cultural preferences, national tastes and standards, and business institutions are vestiges of the past" (p. 96). Similarly, based on their comparative analysis of organizations, Hickson, McMillan, Azumi, and Horvath (1979) concluded that although organizations worldwide are far from identical, the key relationships among organizational variables remain constant across cultures.

Divergence By contrast, other scholars argue that organizations are culture-bound, rather than culturally free, and are remaining so (e.g., Hofstede, 1980; Laurent, 1983; Lincoln, Hanada, & Olson, 1981; Meyer & Rowan, 1977). These scholars conclude that the principle of *equifinality* applies to organizations functioning in different cultures (Negandhi, 1973) and that many equally effective ways to manage exist. The most effective depend, among other contingencies, on the culture(s) involved.

For example, Bass and Eldridge (1973) found distinct differences in managerial objectives among the 12 countries they studied. England (1975), although finding differences, found more similarities than expected in managerial values across the United States, Japan, Korea, India, and Australia. Heller and Wilpert (1979) identified several important country-specific differences in their eight-country comparative study (including the United States, the United Kingdom, Germany, Sweden, the Netherlands, France, Spain, and Israel) of managerial attitudes and decision-making behavior. Similarly, Laurent (1983) documented fundamental differences in managers' assumptions and conceptualizations among nine Western European countries and the United States.

Whereas the above studies found countries using distinctly different managerial styles, other studies have identified clusters of similar countries. This difference has much to do with the particular variables and sets of countries studied. For example, Haire, Ghiselli, and Porter (1966), in studying the managerial attitudes of 3,641 managers in 14 countries, clustered the countries into five groups: Nordic European (Denmark, Germany, Norway, Sweden), Latin European (Belgium, France, Italy, Spain), Anglo-American (England and the United States), developing countries (Argentina, Chile, India), and Japan. Of all the attitudinal differences they observed, 25% of the variance was associated with national differences, leading them to infer that although "cultural influence is present and substantial, it is not overwhelming" (p. 9).

Hofstede (1980), in a landmark study of 160,000 employees working in 40 countries for a major American multinational, identified four dimensions on which styles of work differ: power distance, uncertainty avoidance, individualism/collectivism, and masculinity/femininity.

Convergence or divergence? The studies are inconclusive. Perhaps, instead of asking whether there are similarities or differences, we should be asking when there are similarities and when differences. And if differences exist, when are there consistent patterns of cultural clustering as opposed to individual expressions of distinct cultures?

Accordingly, this third-level question should perhaps be: When do organizations converge and when do they maintain their cultural specificity? In surveying the cross-cultural management literature, Child (1981) observed that reputable scholars using equally reputable methodologies were forming opposite conclusions— some finding convergence, some divergence. Analyzing the studies, he discovered that the majority of those focusing on macro-level variables were finding few differences across cultures, whereas those examining micro-level variables were observing many significant differences. Similarly, Aiken and Bacharach (1979) have suggested that cultural effects are more manifest in the "various patterns in organizational members" (p. 216) than in such areas as structure, procedures, and rules. Perhaps, as suggested by the Fujisawa quotation that opens this article, our organizations are becoming more similar in terms of structure and technology, whereas people's behavior within those organizations continues to manifest culturally based dissimilarities.

Although culture may continue to affect the formal institutional level, the increasing prevalence of common technology tends to reduce its impact. Because culture is in part defined at the level of cognitive maps, we should probably expect to observe the most profound differences at the informal rather than the formal organizational level.

Beyond Comparison: Intercultural Interaction

Management, as a profession, is not an academic discipline. For managers, understanding cultural similarities and differences and their causes, although interesting and necessary, is not sufficient. International managers need to know how to act when working in foreign cul-

tures. Interaction, not merely comparison, is the essence of most managerial action. What happens when people from different cultures work together? In what ways do people modify their within-culture styles when working with people from other cultures? What are the most effective ways to approach foreign colleagues and clients? International managers' jobs involve a high level of cross-cultural interaction, which has been largely overlooked by management researchers. Fewer than one fifth (18.6%) of all cross-cultural management research articles have focused on interaction (Adler, 1983b).

Interaction The cross-cultural communication and psychology literature suggests that people behave differently with members of their own culture than they do with members of foreign cultures. Research in nonbusiness contexts has demonstrated that when people from various cultures interact, the differences among them become salient (Bouchner & Ohsako, 1977; Bouchner & Perks, 1971). Moreover, when people confront actual differences in interpersonal situations, they tend to exaggerate those differences (Sherif & Hovland, 1961; Vassiliou, Triandis, Vassiliou, & McGuire, 1980). In addition, perceived similarity, not difference, predicts satisfaction with work relationships (Bass, Burger, Doktor, & Barrett, 1979; Polakos & Wexley, 1983; Wexley, Alexander, Greenwalt, & Couch, 1980).

In international exchanges, "the greater the cultural differences, the greater is the likelihood that barriers to communication will arise and that misunderstandings will occur" (Mishler, 1965, p. 555). Peterson and Shimada (1978) have even questioned whether "managers from significantly different cultures such as Japan and the United States can ever completely understand each other" (p. 803). Moreover, research suggests that the relationships among managers may deteriorate when differences become very apparent (Stening, 1979).

Current studies comparing intracultural and intercultural negotiating behavior document that Japanese and American business people modify their within-culture styles when negotiating internationally (Graham, 1985). Likewise, English and French-Canadian business people alter their intracultural negotiating behavior when bargaining across cultures (Adler & Graham, 1986). An interesting study of such areas of subtle tension, this time in an entirely Asian geographical context (although in a largely Western intellectual one), is reported by Everett, Krishnan, and Stening (1984). They studied the stereotypes of one another held by groups of Southeast Asian and Japanese managers in subsidiaries of Japanese companies and concluded that there were "serious limitations to the exportability of the Japanese style of management" (p. 149). This recent research shows that we cannot assume that managers behave identically in within-culture and cross-cultural situations.

Synergy from Cultural Diversity

Managers must learn to use cultural diversity as an advantage, rather than as a disadvantage, to the organization. Although a sizable body of literature describes the impacts of diversity on small-group processes, decision making, and creative problem solving, few researchers have focused on intercultural interaction within work settings. Even fewer have asked proactive, action-research questions investigating the creation of organizational benefits from cultural diversity.

Because culture tends to be invisible and, when visible, is usually seen as causing problems for the organization, the phrasing of this fifth question is particularly important. Only infrequently do people view cultural diversity as benefiting the organization. For example, international executives attending management seminars at the European Management Institute (INSEAD) in France were asked to list the advantages and disadvantages of cultural diversity to their organizations. Although every executive could list several disadvantages, only 30% of them could list even one advantage.[3] Similarly, in a Canadian study, only 1 of 60 organizational development consultants surveyed mentioned an advantage to the organization from cultural diversity, whereas all 60 mentioned disadvantages (Adler, 1983c). Likewise, all of the 52 corporate and academic experts attending the 1981 McGill International Symposium on Cross-Cultural Management could identify several problems but few benefits of diversity (Adler, 1983a).

Sufficient research on cultural synergy in organizational settings has yet to be conducted, but Maruyama (1973, 1980, 1982, 1984) has given us one of the best paradigms both for thinking about the potential benefits of diversity and for understanding our historical blindness to its possibilities for organization and management. Maruyama proposes four meta-types of causality: nonreciprocal causal models, independent event models, homeostatic causal-loop models, and morphogenetic causal-loop models. The four correspond respectively to the organizational approaches of international, multidomestic, multinational, and global firms. Each is discussed briefly in terms of its conceptualization of cultural homogeneity and heterogeneity.

In nonreciprocal causal models, causality is linear and unidirectional (A→B→C→D→E). Homogeneity is considered natural, desirable, and good, and heterogeneity an abnormality or error. Cultural diversity is viewed as the source of all conflict, inconvenience, and inefficiency. The parts are subordinated to the whole. Under this assumption of nonreciprocal causality, homogeneity is viewed as basic and natural, and change is seen as evolving through a competitive survival of the fittest model. The organizational analogy is the international firm, in which the headquarters' culture is assumed to apply universally and management believes that there is one best way to manage. The culture of top management dominates all parts of the organization. This approach is in accordance with the insistence on a strong organizational culture for international as well as domestic firms.

In independent event models, events are seen as random. Therefore, the question of causality lacks explanatory power. Management views the organization as an aggregate of individuals who think and act independently. Thus, cultural conditioning is either ignored or treated as an irrelevant myth. The organizational analogy is the multidomestic firm, an organization with highly independent operations in many countries. Multidomestic firms recognize cultural differences, and, unlike international firms, reject attempts to have everyone working the same way. Multidomestic firms regard each national unit as independent and fairly autonomous, with random rather than planned interaction among the parts. Management makes no attempt to create mutually beneficial combinations among domestic operations. When necessary, consensus is expected to cancel out differences and allow for concerted action. Multidomestic firms recognize cultural diversity, although harboring no illusion that they can control it or benefit from it.

In homeostatic causal-loop models, causal relations form stable loops. Organizational structures (patterns of heterogeneity) are maintained in equilibrium by causal loops. The organizational analogy is the multinational firm. Diversity (or geographic differentiation) is basic, indispensable, and desirable, whereas homogeneity is the source of competition and conflict. Cultural interaction and heterogeneity are considered beneficial. Change and evolution can come only from external forces causing the organization to adapt to new, stable patterns of equilibrium.

In morphogenetic causal-loop models, causal relations form loops, but heterogeneity goes beyond homeostasis and generates new patterns of mutually beneficial relations among the interacting elements, thus raising the level of sophistication of the whole system. Unlike homeostatic models, in which external forces cause change, morphogenetic models can internally generate their own evolution: They constantly create new, improved, mutually beneficial systems of interaction. The organizational analogy is the global firm, which considers heterogeneity essential and indispensable. The global firm constantly seeks and generates new patterns through international interaction, which is developmental, evolutionary, and, as is necessary for evolution, degenerative.

In moving from international, multidomestic, and multinational firms to the era of the global corporation, our approach to recognizing, understanding, modeling, and using cultural diversity is changing. Research is required on organizational uses of morphogenetic causal-loop models to create synergy from cultural diversity. It is no longer valuable to ask if cultural diversity is salient. The global organization needs to develop ways to create and manage evolving systems of cultural synergy.

FROM THE ATLANTIC TO THE PACIFIC CENTURY

As the world enters the Pacific century, the differing impacts of Occidental and Oriental culture on managerial interaction have become highly significant. Yet, most management scholars to date have focused on the Atlantic rim rather than on the Pacific rim. Existing research on Asian managers is based on Western theoretical models that fail to account for differences between Occidental and Oriental cultures and mind-sets. (We note here that although the term "American" refers to all peoples of North and South America, we use it as a shorthand and writing convenience to refer to the citizens of the United States of America.)

Questioning the universal applicability of theories developed and tested in the West, Azumi (1974) suggested that "if the perspective of social science as developed in the West is inadequate, that must be demonstrated by the creation of a new and better social science instead of developing separate social sciences for different societies" (p. 527). Such a new social science, including the science of management, would account for cultural diversity rather than assume a mono-cultural perspective. More important, it would recognize differences between Oriental and Occidental mind-sets and their implications for international managerial action. In other words, it would form a solid theoretical base for comparative studies that would examine cultures and their cognitive maps and predict their impact on organizational behavior.

Single-Culture Management Studies

Espousing an admittedly simplistic mechanical model, observation alone reveals differences in the behavioral characteristics of managers from various Asian countries. Single-culture studies on Japanese, South Korean, and Chinese management practices have documented these differences.

Studies have shown that Japanese managers and workers have a sense of identity with their work groups (Befu, 1983b; Cole, 1979; Doi, 1962; Gibney, 1982; Kumagai, 1981; Tung, 1984), an ethic of cooperativeness (Befu, 1983a; Kawai, 1981; Ouchi & Jaeger, 1978), a high dependence on the larger entity (Abegglen, 1984; Cole, 1979; Conner, 1976; Doi, 1973; Minami, 1980), a strong sensitivity to status (Cole, 1979; Dore, 1978; Hofstede, 1980; Pascale, 1978), and an active respect for the interests of individuals and for each individual as a person (Deutsch, 1984; De Vos, 1973; Graham & Sano, 1984; Moran, 1985).

South Korean managers have been observed to exhibit the Confucian virtues of familism, filial piety, and loyalty and obedience to authorities, including their leaders (Chung, 1978; Nam, 1971). They desire to contribute to the national well-being (Chung, 1978; England & Lee, 1971), tend to hold strong personal opinions (Nam, 1971), and are uninclined to adopt systems of shared management, or power

equalization within the organization (England & Lee, 1971; Harbron, 1979).

Ethnic Chinese managers, whether from the People's Republic of China (PRC) or from Taiwan, Hong Kong, or Singapore, have been shown to honor a tight set of business rules, many of them unwritten (Benedict, 1946; Chui, 1977; Tung, 1981a). They possess what Redding (1977) has referred to as a "siege mentality," characterized by excessive anxiety, especially concerning material security (Chui, 1977). They see money as a security surrogate, emphasize hard work, thrift, and competitiveness (Chui, 1977; Lemming, 1977; Nevis, 1983; Silin, 1976), and believe in Confucian familism (Redding & Wong, 1986; Sterba, 1978; Tung, 1981b; Yang, 1973).

Comparative Management Studies

Of the few comparative studies of organizations, the majority focus on comparisons between Japan and the West. The Japanese view of conflict between the whole and its parts and conflict among parts is different from that of the West (Kawai, 1981; Kumon, 1984; Minami, 1980; Suzuki, 1976; Yamauchi, 1974). The Japanese also tend to see more complementarity and interconnectedness in opposites than do Westerners, who tend to see only conflict between opposites (Mendenhall & Oddou, 1987).

Keys and Miller (1984) suggested three "underlying factors at the heart of the Japanese system that foster the development of the various management theories and models" (p. 349): a long-range planning horizon, commitment to lifetime employment, and collective responsibility. Noting that these factors were rooted in Japanese culture, they hypothesized a causal relationship between cognitive maps (implicit cultural views of the world) and specific management practices. Similarly, Doktor (1983a), comparing differences in behavior and time-use patterns between Japanese and American chief executive officers (CEOs), identified cognitive maps as a primary explanatory variable. He found that Japanese CEOs tended to be more deliberate, more planning oriented, and less frenetic in their behavior than their American counterparts.

Although few comparative management studies focus on Asian countries other than Japan, those that do are important because they pay attention to cognitive factors. For example, in comparing American managers with those in the PRC, Nevis (1983) noted the strong relationship between mind-sets and productivity. The Cultural Revolution brought about two major attitudes or mind-sets which affected productivity in the PRC. First, great caution about standing out in any way became the norm. Second, in order to reward loyalty to the work unit and to the nation, the idea of equal sharing became prevalent. It was better to have everyone share equally what little there was than to give extra rewards to those who stood out as highly productive workers. Thus, poor performance and good performance were rewarded equally.

Investigators studying organizations in Hong Kong (Lau, 1977; Redding, 1980; Redding & Hicks, 1983) and Taiwan (Silin, 1976) have reported that although work itself is highly individualized and competitive, official positions are only loosely designated. Apparently, ethnic Chinese people's subjective environment has enough authority to make explicit demarcation of official positions and roles less necessary than in the West. Consistent with these findings, Hofstede (1980) found that managers in Hong Kong prefer low levels of uncertainty avoidance.

Schollhammer's (1969) survey of approaches to comparative management showed researchers' tendency to concentrate on socioeconomic variables or managerial attitudes but not on cognition. Robert's (1970) survey of cross-cultural management research indicated the relevance of studies on meaning, communication, and perception, but failed to refer to any single study on cognition per se. Likewise, Weinshall's (1977) edited collection of works on the linkages between culture and management, for all its strengths, contained not a single study of cognition.

Within Asia, most research has been done on Japan. Dunphy and Stening (1984) compiled a comprehensive annotated bibliography of over 400 Japanese research articles on organizational behavior and management, published in English. Of the Japanese studies, very few (4%) are comparative studies which consider the impact of the cognitive aspects of culture on managerial practice.

Notable among those scholars who consider cognition is Kumon (1984), who as cited by Mendenhall & Oddou (1987), has summarized the differences between the cognitive processing of information by Japanese and Westerners, observing that

the nature of Japanese reasoning is "analytical" whereas that of Westerners can be characterized as "comprehensive." Thus the cognitive process of Japanese, in most cases, goes from the whole to its parts. For them to understand something is to divide it into parts. . . . [T]he cognitive process of Westerners tends to proceed from individual elements to a larger whole. . . . [W]hen individual objects which were first taken separately are put together forming one whole, Westerners say they comprehend it. Comprehension is just the opposite of division. (pp. 8–9)

Sociological Studies

As indicated earlier, sociological literature, unlike most management literature, generally supports both the importance of the subjective environment's influence on organizational behavior and the need for organizational analysis at the individual level, both within cultures and across cultures. Silverman (1970), in arguing that the unique role of sociologists is to understand the subjective logic of social situations, stressed the importance of this understanding to comparative management research. He identified five issues that foreshadowed comparative management's current methodological dilemma: (a) the nature of the predominant meaning structure and its associated system in different organizations, and the extent to which they rely on varying degrees of coercion or consent, (b) the characteristic pattern of involvement of the actors' differing attachment to rules and to definitions of their situation, (c) the typical strategies used by the actors to attain their ends, (d) the relative ability of different actors to impose their definition of the situation upon others, and (e) the origin and pattern of change of meaning structures in different organizations.

All these issues emphasize individuals' definitions of the situations they are in, an emphasis reflected in the emergence of such approaches as ethnomethodology (Cicourel, 1972; Garfinkel, 1967) and the action frame of reference (Harre & Sekord, 1972; Silverman, 1970). Bougon, Weick, and Binkhorst (1977) gave more specific attention to cognition as a factor in organizational analysis and presented an empirically based picture of organizational participants' "cause maps." They concluded that

social settings are defined and must be analyzed in terms of the participant's epistemology: organization problems are mind-environment problems. . . . Cause maps will help us find that by a non-logical, but highly intelligent mental process, organization participants perform translation from the world of experience to the world of mind. (p. 23)

Supporting the concept of mind-environment problems and focusing attention on the informal side of organizational behavior, Lammers and Hickson (1979), in their review of the comparative organization theory literature, concluded that "there are grounds to suspect that specific traditions, value patterns, ideo-

logies, and norms (originating, for example, in cognitive maps) are bound to differentiate as much or even more than structural factors, between societies" (p. 275).

That there are major differences between the cognitive processes of Orientals and Occidentals often comes as a surprise to both sides. Each side is inherently unable to step outside its own world view to see the possibility of alternatives. Yet, the Western literatures of psychology, philosophy, and anthropology that describe and analyze Oriental peoples consistently refer to such cognitive differences.

Developmental Psychology Studies

Research concerned with the development of cognitive styles has demonstrated a relationship between elements of socioeconomic status and the propensity for cognitive differentiation or what is often termed *field articulation* (Witkin, Dyke, Faterson, Goodenough, & Karp, 1962). As a cognitive style dimension, individuals have been shown to vary from low field articulation (being intuitive, holistic, socially dependent, other directed, and motivationally diffuse) to high field articulation (being analytical, systematic, emotionally self-controlled, perceptually discriminating, socially independent and self-reliant, and motivationally focused). Poverty of the socioeconomic environment has been shown to be related to a focus on security and biological needs, immediate gratification, and obedience to well-tried methods of coping with daily needs. These conditions are inimical to the development of field articulation. Therefore, cultures in areas of high national economic development and modernization are more likely to demonstrate the cognitive characteristics of high field articulation (Gruenfeld & MacEachron, 1975). Triandis (1973) has expanded this view by suggesting that the level of economic development both affects and is dependent on the ability of members to respond and adjust to increasing environmental complexity. Gruenfeld and MacEachron (1975) have demonstrated that the degree of field articulation among managers and technicians correlates with their respective countries' economic development indices. Thus, cognitive aspects of culture appear to be somewhat developmentally related to national economic conditions, and finding major differences in cognitive functioning among regions of the world with significantly different economic histories, traditions, and levels of development ought not to be surprising.

Causes of Misinterpreting Data Across Cultures

To understand our cultural myopia, we may consider Needham's (1978) explanation of how the idea of causation developed via one route in the West, beginning with the ancient Greeks and culminating in Newtonian physics, while taking a totally different route in China:

We are driven to the conclusion that there are two ways of advancing from primitive truth. One was the way taken by some of the Greeks: to refine the ideas of causation in such a way that one ended up with a mechanical explanation of the universe, just as Democritus did with his atoms. The other way is to systematise the universe of things and events into a structural pattern which conditioned all the mutual influences of its different parts. In the Greek world view, if a particle of matter occupied a particular place at a particular time, it was because another particle had pushed it there. In the other view, the particle's behavior was governed by the fact that it was taking its place in a "field of force" alongside other particles that are similarly responsive: causation here is not "responsive" but "environmental." (p. 166)

Another aspect of cause-and-effect relations is what might be called the building blocks of explanation. When thinking about a problem, Westerners normally use abstract concepts such as "productivity," "morale," and "leadership style." By contrast, the Oriental mind tends to use more concrete ideas such as, "How can we improve product quality and thus increase export sales?" (Redding, 1980). Nakamura (1964) identified the following contrasting characteristics as typical of Oriental thinking: (a) an emphasis on perception of the concrete, on the particular rather than the universal, and a lack of development of abstract thought; (b) a central focus on practicality; and (c) a concern for reconciliation, harmony, and balance.

Some Westerners tend to denigrate Orientals' style of thinking as nonspecific and therefore primitive, but Needham (1978) has defended its richness and strength. He has noted that many Western scholars embrace "total system" and "contingency" concepts in most branches of science, including management, but that they rarely associate these approaches with Oriental cognitive processes. Nonetheless, these frameworks reflect an approach that is fundamental to the Oriental perspective. The striking validity of Oriental thinking for dealing with complexity was elegantly argued by Capra (1975) in the context of post-Heisenberg physics.

Maruyama (1985), in relating cognitive issues to comparative management, has expanded upon similar points:

The principles, styles and methods of management are affected by mind patterns, which may vary from individual to individual and from culture to culture. As the cultural heterogeneity increases, managers become aware of some new phenomena:

1. *That management principles and methods must be adapted both to the cultural heterogeneity within the office and to the local culture;*
2. *That there are significant individual differences within each culture;*
3. *That some managers and workers from the local culture may look excellent if judged by the criteria of the superior from a foreign culture, but they*

may be cultural deviants who reject their own culture, and whose credibility may be very high among foreigners but very low among their compatriots;

4. *That those who appreciate both local and foreign cultures are a valuable asset.*

... It is posited here that in any larger culture there are all types of individual mind patterns, but that cultural differences exist in the distribution of various individual types as well as in the social dynamics of the interaction among different types: some types are officially accepted or encouraged while others are relegated to the social periphery, ignored, instititionally suppressed, individually repressed, latent or nonverbalized. (p. 126)

In considering Maruyama's implications, we note that the foundation of all managerial interaction, especially in the less-prescribed domain of the informal organization, is ultimately the unique set of cognitive maps in the manager's head. These maps are the basic components of culture and may become organizationally dysfunctional when differences among interacting cultures become more salient. As the world moves out of the Atlantic century into the Pacific century, cultural differences are likely to become far more significant. Some of the East-West cognitive differences outlined here must therefore be considered in future comparative management research.

Clearly, methodologies relying on data collected without attention to cognitive dimensions will lack reliability in the Pacific century. Earlier attempts to deal with these methodological issues (Adler, 1984; England & Harpaz, 1983; Sekaran, 1983) have addressed the fundamental question of measurement validity. For example, a questionnaire designed for cross-cultural equivalence may be used to compare managers' values or attitudes across various European and North American cultures. The questionnaire itself, however, may contain an implicit Western paradigm of causality. Simple translation, reverse translation, and other procedures for maintaining equivalence of literal meaning do nothing to address Orientals' alternative paradigm of causality. For example, rating a leadership dimension in order to measure an organization's climate presupposes a causal link between individual initiative and results, a link not accepted in Japanese mind-sets. This lack of causal equivalence plagues almost all methodologies using interpretive data rather than strictly observed behavior. In East-West managerial comparisons, data interpreted and filtered either by the subject or by the researcher are always suspect because of the potential impact of differing cognitive maps of causality.

Precautions must also be taken in interpreting and drawing implications from analyzed data in Oriental/Occidental comparisons. For example, one major theme within the popular literature comparing the decision making of American and Japanese managers has been that the Japanese are more "holistic," the Americans more "segmented" (Ouchi, 1981). But "segmented" may not be a bipolar opposite of "holistic." The Japanese may be segmented and holistic simultaneously. This very combination of cognitive patterns may be a significant dynamic in Japanese managerial success.

Another recurring theme in the literature on Japanese management, especially on the decision-making process, is the importance of the group. However, a crucial difference between Japanese and Western conceptions of the group is often overlooked. In the United States, people frequently associate the concept of group with affiliation. In Japan, however, affiliation is not the main subliminal perception. Grouping implies a sense of interrelatedness among all natural elements—including, in this case, group members. Interrelatedness is coupled with a blurring of physical barriers, including those among individual human bodies. It is interrelatedness—with everything being a part of everything else—that results in strong social cohesion, not, as frequently hypothesized by Westerners, a powerful need for affiliation among organizational members. For example, Ouchi and Jaeger (1978) argued that their Type Z organization would be appropriate where it could fulfill a need for stability and affiliation, as in the segment of American society adversely affected by urbanization and a geographically mobile work force. Apparently, these authors inferred that the strong dynamic of "groupism" in Japan means the same as a greater sense of American-style affiliation needs.

Ouchi and Jaeger's (1978) causation map may be an accurate description of Japanese dynamics. It may be that Japanese workers are cognitively more similar to American workers than different from them. Perhaps Japanese sociocultural values are similar to American values, and differences in managerial practice account for higher Japanese productivity: On the other hand, it may be that decision-making behavior in Japan and the United States differs quite markedly, and, moreover, that one culture's behavior is inappropriate for use in another culture.

Furthermore, differences in cognitive modeling behavior among cultures suggest that researchers and managers belonging to one culture may misinterpret the meaning of another culture's decision-making behavior. Therefore, even in cases where one culture's decision-making techniques seem to be appropriate for another, misapplication may occur due to erroneous analysis of the underlying way of seeing the world implicit in each culture, as illustrated by the example of equating Japanese groupism with a need for affiliation.

IMPLICATIONS FOR THE PRACTICE OF MANAGEMENT

A key element in the process of management anywhere in the world is being able to anticipate future actions of colleagues and competitors. Much of the research reviewed and analyzed in this article addresses this issue through the metaphor of cognitive style. Often, when we have trouble understanding and predicting the future behavior of our colleagues, peers, or competitors, we attribute these difficulties to language problems or to idiosyncrasies in their behavior. But these prediction and understanding problems may arise from lack of appreciation of the thought processes manifested by foreigners in our managerial environment. Part of our inability to understand or predict the future behavior of our peers, colleagues, and competitors may be caused by our inability to understand how they are modeling the world and what kind of causal dimensions they use to see the world. The question, "Shall we do business with these people or not?" is really the question, "Do we understand how they are thinking about the world?" (Williamson, 1986). Finally, our ability to present our view of the world so that it can be understood and appreciated within the cognitive paradigms held by significant foreign colleagues determines, in large measure, our own acceptance by and relevance in an increasingly multicultural managerial environment.

IMPLICATIONS FOR FUTURE RESEARCH

The forces of technological rationality drive organizations toward common work flows, operating procedures, and structures. On the level of interpersonal interaction, particularly in the informal organization, national culture mediated through cognitive maps results in a variety of behaviors among members. Therefore, understanding the demands of rational technology is insufficient for understanding organizational behavior across cultures; we must also understand the realities constructed by the respective participants. Progress in cross-cultural management research depends as much upon our understanding of the relationship between culture and cognition as it does upon our understanding of any other set of variables in the complex world of management research in the Pacific century.

NOTES

1.   The first three questions are based on the conceptualization of Peter J. D. Dreath (1985).

2.   Dissertation research conducted under the guidance of Professor Joseph deStefano, Faculty of Business Administration, University of Western Ontario, Canada.

3.   Data collected by Professors Andre Laurent (INSEAD) and Nancy J. Adler (McGill University) during the "Managerial Skills for International Business" executive seminars at INSEAD (France), 1981–1983. Unpublished research, summarized in N. J. Adler, *International Dimensions of Organizational Behavior* (Boston: Kent Publishing, 1986), Chap. 4, pp. 76–98.

REFERENCES

Abegglen, J. C. (1984). *The strategy of Japanese business.* Cambridge, Mass.: Ballinger.

Adler, N. J. (1983a). Cross-cultural management: Issues to be faced. *International Studies of Management and Organization,* 13(1–2), 7–45.

Adler, N. J. (1983b). Cross-cultural management research: The ostriche and the trend. *Academy of Management Review,* 8(2), 226–232.

Adler, N. J. (1983c). Organizational development in a multicultural environment. *Journal of Applied Behavioral Science,* 19(3), 350–365.

Adler, N. J. (1984). Understanding the ways of understanding: Cross-cultural management reviewed. In R. N. Farmer (Ed.), *Advances in international comparative management:* Vol. I, pp. 31–67. Greenwich, Conn.: JAI Press.

Adler, N. J., and Graham, J. L. (1986). Cross-cultural interaction: The international comparison fallacy. Working paper, McGill University, Faculty of Management, Montreal.

Adler, N. J., and Jelinek, M. S. (1986): Is "organization culture" culture bound? *Human Resource Management,* 25(1), 73–90.

Aiken, M., and Bacharach, S. B. (1979). Culture and organizational structure and process: A comparative study of local government administrative bureaucracies in the Walloon and Flemish regions of Belgium. In C. J. Lammers and D. J. Hickson (Eds.), *Organizations alike and unlike,* pp. 215–250. London: Routledge & Kegan Paul.

Albrecht, S. L. (1980). Politics, bureaucracy, and worker participation: The Swedish case. *Journal of Applied Behavioral Science,* 16(3), 229–317.

Azumi, K. (1974). Japanese society: A sociological review. In A. D. Tiedemann (Ed.), *An introduction to Japanese civilization,* pp. 515–535. New York: Columbia University Press.

Barnouw, V. (1963). *Culture and personality.* Homewood, Ill.: The Dorsey Press.

Bass, B. M., Burger, P. C., Doktor, R., and Barrett, G. V. (1979). *Assessment of managers.* New York: The Free Press.

Bass, B., and Eldridge, L. (1973). Accelerated managers' objectives in twelve countries. *Industrial Relations,* 12, 158–171.

Befu, H. (1983a). Giri and Ninjo. In *Kodansha Encyclopedia of Japan,* Vol. 3, p. 34. Tokyo: Kodansha.

Befu, H. (1983b). Groups. In *Kodansha Encyclopedia of Japan,* Vol. 3, p. 63. Tokyo: Kodansha.

Befu, H. (1983c). On. In *Kodansha Encyclopedia of Japan,* Vol. 6, p. 105. Tokyo: Kodansha.

Benedict, R. (1946). *The chrysanthemum and the sword.* New York: Houghton Mifflin.

Blunt, P. (1973). Cultural and situational determinants of job satisfaction amongst management in South Africa. *Journal of Management Studies,* 10(2), 133–140.

Bouchner, S., and Ohsako, T. (1977). Ethnic role salience in racially homogeneous and heterogeneous societies. *Journal of Cross-Cultural Psychology,* 8, 455–492.

Bouchner, S., and Perks, R. W. (1971). National role evocation as a function of cross-cultural interaction. *Journal of Cross-Cultural Psychology,* 2, 157–164.

Bougon, M., Weick, K., and Binkhorst, D. (1977). Cognition in organizations: An analysis of the Utrecht Jazz Orchestra. *Administrative Science Quarterly,* 22(4), 1977.

Capra, F. (1975). *The Tao of physics.* New York: Bantam.

Carrol, M. P. (1982). Culture. In J. Freeman (Ed.), *Introduction to sociology: A Canadian focus,* pp. 19–40. Scarborough, Ontario: Prentice Hall.

Chang, Y. N. (1976). Early Chinese management thought. *California Management Review.* 19(2), 71–76.

Child, J. (1981). Culture, contingency and capitalism in the cross-national study of organizations. In L. L. Cummings and B. M. Staw (Eds.), *Research in organizational behavior,* Vol. 3, pp. 303–356. Greenwich, Conn.: JAI Press.

Child, J., and Tayeb, M. (1982–1983). Theoretical perspectives in cross-national organizational research. *International Studies of Management and Organization,* 7(3–4).

Chui, V. C. L. (1977). Managerial beliefs of Hong Kong managers. Unpublished master's thesis. University of Hong Kong.

Chung, K. H. (1978, October). *A comparative study of managerial characteristics of domestic, international, and governmental institutions in Korea.* Paper presented at the Midwest Conference in Asian Affairs, Minneapolis, Minn.

Cicourrel, A. V. (1972). *Cognitive sociology: Language and meaning in social interaction.* London: Penguin.

Cole, R. E. (1973). Functional alternatives and economic development: An empirical example of permanent employment in Japan. *American Sociological Review,* 38, 424–438.

Cole, R. E. (1979). *Work, mobility, and participation: A*

comparative study of American and Japanese industry. Berkeley: University of California Press.

Conner, J. W. (1976). Joge kankei: A key concept for an understanding of Japanese-American achievement. Psychiatry, 39, 266–279.

Crozier, M. (1964). The bureaucratic phenomenon. Chicago: University of Chicago Press.

Cummings, L. L., and Schmidt, S. M. (1972). Managerial attitudes of Greeks: The roles of culture and industrialization. Administrative Science Quarterly, 17(2), 265–272.

Deutsch, M. F. (1984). Doing business with the Japanese. New York: New American Library.

DeVos, G. A. (1973). Socialization for achievement: Essays on the cultural psychology of the Japanese. Berkeley: University of California Press.

Doi, T. (1973). The anatomy of dependence. Tokyo: Kodansha.

Doi, T. (1962). Amae: A key concept for understanding Japanese personality structure. In R. J. Smith and R. K. Beardsley (Eds.), Japanese culture, pp. 253–287. Chicago: Adline.

Doktor, R. (1983a). Culture and the management of time: A comparison of Japanese and American top management practice. Asia Pacific Journal of Management, 1(1), 65–71.

Doktor, R. (1983b). Some tentative comments on Japanese and American decision making. Decision Science, 14(4), 607–612.

Dore, R. P. (1978). Shinohata: Portrait of a Japanese village. New York: Pantheon Books.

Dunphy, D. C., and Stening, B. W. (1984). Japanese organization behavior and management. Hong Kong: Asian Research Service.

England, G. W. (1975). The manager and his values: An international perspective from the USA, Japan, Korea, India and Australia. Cambridge, Mass.: Ballinger.

England, G. W., and Harpaz, I. (1983). Some methodological and analytic considerations in cross-national comparative research. Journal of International Business Studies, 14(2), 49–59.

England, G. W., and Lee, R. (1971). Organizational goals and expected behavior among American, Japanese, and Korean managers: A comparative study. Academy of Management Journal, 14(4), 425–438.

Evans, W. M. (1980). Organization Theory. New York: John Wiley.

Everett, J. E., Krishnan, A. R., and Stening, B. W. (1984). Through a glass darkly: Southeast Asian managers' mutual perceptions of Japanese and local counterparts. Singapore: Eastern Universities Press.

Form, W. (1979). Comparative industrial sociology and the convergence hypothesis. Annual Review of Sociology, 5, 1–25.

Foy, N., and Gadon, H. (1976). Worker participation contrasts in three countries. Harvard Business Review, 54(3), 71–84.

Garfinkel, H. (1967). Studies in ethnomethodology. Englewood Cliffs, N.J.: Prentice-Hall.

Gibney, F. (1982). Miracle by design: The real reasons behind Japan's economic miracle. New York: Times Books.

Graham, J. L. (1985). Cross-cultural marketing negotiations: A laboratory experiment. Marketing Science, 4(2), 130–146.

Graham, J. L., and Sano, Y. (1984). Smart bargaining: Doing business with the Japanese. Cambridge, Mass.: Ballinger.

Graves, D. (1972). The impact of culture upon managerial attitudes, beliefs and behavior in England and France. Journal of Management Studies, 10, 40–56.

Gruenfeld, L. W., and MacEachron, A. E. (1975). A cross-national study of cognitive style among managers and technicians. International Journal of Psychology, 10(1), 27–55.

Haire, M., Ghiselli, E. G., and Porter, L. W. (1966). Managerial thinking: An international study. New York: John Wiley.

Harbron, J. (1979). Korea's Executives Are Not Quite "The New Japanese." The Business Quarterly, 44(3), 16–19.

Harre, R., and Sekord, P. F. (1972). The explanation of social behaviour. Oxford: Blackwell.

Heller, R. A., and Wilpert, B. (1979). Managerial decision making: An international comparison. In G. W. England, A. R. Negandhi, and B. Wilpert (Eds.), Functioning organizations in cross-cultural perspective. Kent, Ohio: Kent State University Press.

Hicks, G. L., and Redding, S. G. (1983). The story of the East Asian economic miracle. Part 2: The culture connection. Euro-Asia Business Review, 2(2), 18–22.

Hickson, D. J., Hinnings, C. R., McMillan, C. J. M., and Schwitter, J. P. (1974). The culture-free context of organization structure: A tri-national comparison. Sociology, 8, 59–80.

Hickson, D. J., McMillan, C. J., Azumi, K., and Horvath, D. (1979). Grounds for comparative organization theory: Quicksands or hard core? In C. J. Lammers and D. J. Hickson (Eds.), Organizations alike and unlike, pp. 25–41. London: Routledge & Kegan Paul.

Hofstede, G. (1980). Culture's consequences: International differences in work-related values. Beverly Hills, Calif.: Sage Publications.

Hoover, J. D., Troub, R. M., Whitehead, C. J., and Flores, L. G. (1978). Social performance goals in the Peruvian and the Yugoslav worker participation systems. In J. Susbauer (Ed.), Academy of Management Proceedings '78, pp. 241–246. San Francisco.

Joynt, P. (1985). Cross-cultural management: The cultural context of micro and macro organizational variables. In P. Joynt and M. Warner, Managing in different cultures, pp. 57–68. Oslo: Universitetsforlaget.

Kawai, H. (1981). *Crisis of the Japanese "hollow structure" [Nihonteki chuku kozo no kiki]*. Tokyo: Chuo Koron.

Keesing, R. M. (1974). Theories of culture. *Annual Review of Anthropology,* 3, 73–97.

Kerr, C. J., Dunlop, T., Harbison, F., and Myers, C. A. (1952). *Industrialism and industrial man.* Cambridge, Mass.: Harvard University Press.

Keys, J. B., and Miller, T. R. (1984). The Japanese management theory jungle. *Academy of Management Review,* 9, 342–353.

Kluckhohn, C., and Strodbeck, F. L. (1961). *Variations in values orientations.* Evanston. Ill.: Row, Peterson.

Kroeber, A. L., and Kluckhohn, C. (1952). *Culture: A critical review of concepts and definitions.* Cambridge, Mass: Harvard University Press.

Kroeber, A. L., and Parsons, T. (1958). The concepts of culture and of social systems. *American Sociological Review,* 23, 582–583.

Kumagai, H. (1981). A dissection of intimacy: A study of bipolar posturing in Japanese social interaction—*amaeru* and *amayakasu,* indulgence and deference. *Culture, Medicine and Psychiatry,* 5, 249–272.

Kumon, S. (1984). Some principles governing the thought and behavior of Japanists (contextuals). *Journal of Japanese Studies,* 8, 5–28.

Lammers, C. J., and Hickson, D. J. (1979). Towards a comparative sociology of organizations. In C. J. Lammers and D. J. Hickson (Eds.), *Organizations alike and unlike,* pp. 3–20. London: Routledge & Kegan Paul.

Lau, S. (1977). Managerial style of traditional Chinese firms. Unpublished master's thesis, University of Hong Kong.

Laurent, A. (1983). The cultural diversity of Western management conceptions. *International Studies of Management and Organization,* 8(1–2). 75–96.

Lemming, F. (1977). *Street studies in Hong Kong.* Hong Kong: Oxford University Press.

Levitt, T. (1983). The globalization of markets. *Harvard Business Review,* 83(3), 92–102.

Lincoln, J. R., Hanada, M., and Olson, J. (1981). Cultural orientations and individual reactions to organizations: A study of employees of Japanese-owned firms. *Administrative Science Quarterly,* 26, 93–115.

Linton, R. (1945). *The cultural background of personality.* New York: Appleton-Century.

Maruyama, M. (1973). Paradigmatology and its application to cross-disciplinary, cross-professional and cross-cultural communication. *Dialectica,* 29(3–4), 135–196.

Maruyama, M. (1980). Mindscapes and science theories. *Current Anthropology,* 21(5), 389–600.

Maruyama, M. (1982). New mindscapes for future business policy and management. *Technology Forecasting and Social Change,* 21, 53–76.

Maruyama, M. (1984). Alternative concepts of management: Insights from Asia and Africa. *Asia Pacific Journal of Management,* 1(1), 100–111.

Mendenhall, M., and Oddou, G. (1987). The cognitive, psychological and social contexts of Japanese management, *Journal of Management,* forthcoming.

Meyer, J. W., and Rowan, B. (1977). Institutionalized organizations: Formal structures as myth and ceremony. *American Journal of Sociology,* 83, 340–363.

Minami, H. (1980). *Encyclopedia on human relations of the Japanese* [Nihonjin no Ningen Kankei Jiten]. Tokyo: Kodansha.

Mishler. A. L. (1965). Personal contact in international exchanges. In H. C. Kelman (Ed.), *International behavior: A social-psychological analysis,* pp. 555–561. New York: Holt, Rinehart and Winston.

Moran, R. T. (1985). *Getting your yen's worth: How to negotiate with Japan, Inc.* Houston, Tex.: Gulf Publishing.

Nakamura, H. (1964). *Ways of thinking of Eastern peoples.* Honolulu. East-West Center Press.

Nam, W. S. (1971). *The traditional pattern of Korean industrial management.* ILCORK Working Paper No. 14. University of Hawaii, Social Science Research Institute.

Needham, J. (1978). *The shorter science and civilization in China.* Cambridge: Cambridge University Press.

Negandhi, A. R. (1973). *Management and economic development: The case of Taiwan.* The Hague: Martinus Nijhoff.

Negandhi, A. R. (1979). Convergence in organizational practices: An empirical study of industrial enterprise in developing countries. In C. J. Lammers and D. J. Hickson, *Organizations alike and unlike,* pp. 323–345. London: Routledge & Kegan Paul.

Negandhi, A. R. (1985). Management in the Third World. In P. Joynt and M. Warner, *Managing in different cultures,* pp. 69–97. Oslo: Universitetsforlaget.

Nevis, E. C. (1983). Cultural assumptions and productivity: The United States and China. *Sloan Management Review,* 24(3), 17–28.

Ouchi, W. G., and Jaeger. A. M. (1978). Theory Z organization: Stability in the midst of mobility. *Academy of Management Review,* 3(2), 305–314.

Ouchi, W. G. (1981). *Theory Z: How American business can meet the Japanese challenge.* Reading, Mass.: Addison-Wesley.

Parsons, T. (1973). Culture and social system revisited. In L. Schneider and C. M. Benjean (Eds.), *The idea of culture in the social sciences.* Cambridge: Cambridge University Press.

Pascale, R. T. (1978). Zen and the art of management. *Harvard Business Review,* 56(2), 153–162.

Peterson, R. B., and Shimada, J. Y. (1978). Sources of management problems in Japanese-American joint ventures. *Academy of Management Review,* 3, 796–805.

Polakos, E. D., and Wexley, K. N. (1983). The relationship

among perceptual similarity, sex and performance ratings in manager-subordinate dyads. *Academy of Management Journal, 26,* 129–139.

Redding, S. G. (1977). Some perceptions of psychological needs among managers in South-East Asia. In Y. H. Poortinga (Ed.), *Basic problems in cross-cultural psychology,* pp. 338–344. Amsterdam: Swets and Zeitlinger.

Redding, S. G. (1980). Cognition as an aspect of culture and its relation to management processes: An exploratory view of the Chinese case. *Journal of Management Studies,* 17(2), 127–148.

Redding, S. G. (1982). Thoughts on causation and research models in comparative management for Asia. *Proceedings of the Academy of International Business Conference on Asia Pacific Dimensions of International Business,* pp. 1–38. University of Hawaii.

Redding, S. G., and Hicks, G. L. (1983). *Culture, causation and Chinese management.* Unpublished manuscript, University of Hong Kong, Mongkwok Ping Management Data Bank.

Redding, S. G., and Wong, G. (1986). The psychology of Chinese organizational behavior. In M. H. Bond (Ed.), *The psychology of Chinese people.* Hong Kong: Oxford University Press.

Roberts, K. H. (1970). On looking at an elephant: An evaluation of cross-cultural research related to organizations. *Psychological Bulletin.* 74(5), 327–350.

Schollhammer, H. (1969). The comparative management theory jungle. *Academy of Management Journal,* 12(1), 81–97.

Sekaran, U. (1983). Methodological and theoretical issues and advancements in cross-cultural research. *Journal of International Business Studies,* 14(2), 61–73.

Sherif, M., and Hovland, C. I. (1961). *Social judgment: Assimilation and contrast effects in communication and attitude change.* New Haven, Conn.: Yale University Press.

Silin, R. H. (1976). *Leadership and values: The organization of large scale Taiwanese enterprises.* Cambridge, Mass.: Harvard University Press.

Silverman, D. (1970). The theory of organizations. London: Heinemann.

Solange-Perret, M. (1982). *Impact of cultural differences on budget.* Unpublished doctoral dissertation, University of Western Ontario, London, Ontario, Canada.

Sorge, A. (1983). Cultured organizations. *International Studies of Management and Organization,* 12, 106–138.

Stening, B. W. (1979). Problems in cross-cultural contact: A literature review. *International Journal of Intercultural Relations,* 3, 269–313.

Sterba, R. L. A. (1978). Clandestine management in the Imperial Chinese bureaucracy. *Academy of Management Review,* 3(1), 69–78.

Suzuki, H. (1976). *The transcendents and the climate* [Choetsusha to fudo]. Tokyo: Taimedo.

Triandis, H. C. (1973). Subjective culture and economic development. *International Journal of Psychology,* 8, 163–182.

Tung, R. L. (1981a). Management practices in China. *China International Business,* 64–105.

Tung, R. L. (1981b), Patterns of motivation in Chinese industrial enterprises. *Academy of Management Review,* 481–489.

Tung, R. L. (1984). Business negotiations with the Japanese. Lexington, Mass.: Lexington Books.

Tylor, E. B. (1877). *Primitive culture: Researchers into the development of mythology, philosophy, religion, language, art and custom,* Vol. 1. New York: Henry Holt.

Vassiliou, V., Triandis, H. C., Vassiliou, G., and McGuire, H. (1980). Interpersonal contact and stereotyping. In H. C. Triandis (Ed.), *The analysis of subjective culture,* pp. 89–115. New York: John Wiley.

Weinshall, T. D. (1977). *Culture and management.* London: Penguin.

Wexley, K. N., Alexander, R. A., Greenwalt, J. P., and Couch, M. A. (1980). Attitudinal congruence and similarity as related to interpersonal evaluations in manager-subordinate dyads. *Academy of Management Journal,* 23, 320–330.

Williamson, O. E. (1986). *The economic institutions of capitalism.* New York: The Free Press.

Witkin, H. A., Dyke, R. B., Faterson, H. F. Goodenough, D. R., and Karp. S. A. (1962). *Psychological differentiation.* New York: John Wiley.

Wuthnow, R., Hunter, J. D., Bergesen, A., and Kurzweil, E. (1984). *Cultural analysis: The work of Peter L. Berger, Mary Douglas, Michel Faucault, and Jurgen Habermas.* London: Routlege & Kegan Paul.

Yamauchi, T. (1974). *Logos and lemma* [Rogosu to remma]. Tokyo: Iwanami Shoten.

Yang, H. L. (1973). *The practice of nepotism: A study of sixty Chinese commercial firms in Singapore.* Unpublished manuscript, University of Singapore.

36

NATIONAL VS. CORPORATE CULTURE: IMPLICATIONS FOR HUMAN RESOURCE MANAGEMENT

Susan C. Schneider

Corporate culture has been described as the "glue" that holds organizations together by providing cohesiveness and coherence among the parts. Multinational companies are increasingly interested in promoting corporate culture to improve control, coordination, and integration of their subsidiaries. Yet these subsidiaries are embedded in local national cultures wherein the underlying basic assumptions about people and the world may differ from that of the national and corporate culture of the multinational. These differences may hinder the acceptance and implementation of human resource practices, such as career planning, appraisal and compensation systems, and selection and socialization. This article discusses the assumptions about people and about the world underlying these HRM practices as they may differ from those of the national culture of the subsidiary. Finally, issues concerning the use of corporate culture as a mechanism for globalization will be raised.

Corporate culture has received a great deal of attention in the last five years. Popular books such as *In Search of Excellence* (Peters and Waterman, 1982) and *Corporate Cultures* (Deal and Kennedy, 1982), have sold millions of copies to eager executives in many countries. Although the academic community has taken a more cautious approach, they too are interested (Schein, 1985; Smircich, 1983; see also *ASQ,* September, 1983). While the popular press has implied that excellent companies have strong corporate cultures, the link between strong culture and performance can be challenged. Different environments require different strategies; the corporate culture needs to fit that strategy (Schwartz and Davis, 1981). In the case of the MNC, there is the need to ad-

The author would like to thank Paul Evans, Andre Laurent, Randall Schuler and the anonymous reviewers for their helpful suggestions.

Source: Human Resource Management, Summer 1988, Vol. 27, no. 2, pp. 231–246. © 1988 by John Wiley & Sons, Inc. CCC 0090-4848/88/020231-16$04.00

dress the fit of corporate culture with the different national cultures of their subsidiaries to assure strategy implementation, particularly HRM strategy.

Corporate culture has been discussed as a means of control for headquarters over their subsidiaries (see special issue of *JIBS,* 1984; in particular, Baliga and Jaeger; Doz and Prahalad). In this view, corporate culture serves as a behavioral control, instilling norms and values that result in following "the way things are done around here." The methods by which this is accomplished are: recruiting "like-minded" individuals, that is, those that share the values of the company; socialization through training and personal interaction; and developing strong organizational commitment through various other HR policies such as life time employment, stock option plans, recreational and housing facilities, and expatriate rotation. These methods are frequently used by Japanese firms but also the so-called excellent companies such as IBM, Hewlett-Packard, Digital Equipment known for their strong corporate cultures (Pascale, 1984).

Corporate culture is in part managed through the HRM practices (Evans, 1986). Some of these practices, however, may not be appropriate given the beliefs, values, and norms of the local environment, that is, the national culture wherein the subsidiary is embedded. Problems arise in transferring corporate culture through these practices in an effort to achieve globalization. More attention needs to be paid to the possible clash of assumptions underlying national and corporate cultures (Laurent, 1986; Adler and Jelinek, 1986).

The purpose of this article is to explore the potential clash of the corporate culture of a multinational organization and the national culture of the local subsidiary, paying particular attention to human resource practices. First, the construct of culture will be reviewed. Then the assumptions underlying human resource management practices will be discussed, questioning their fit within different national cultures. Specific attention will be paid to the implications for human resource management practices such as career planning, performance appraisal and reward systems, selection and socialization, and expatriate assignments. Case examples are used to illustrate the problem. Finally, the article will raise an issue often expressed by multinational companies—what does it mean to be a truly international company? What does "global" really look like? It will also question the use of corporate culture as a homogenizing force and as a mechanism of control.

CULTURE

The construct of culture has caused much confusion. While there are multiple definitions, they tend to be vague and overly general. This confusion is added to by the multiple disciplines interested in this topic, which while increasing richness, does not necessarily increase clarity. Anthropologists, sociologists, psychologists, and others bring with them their specific paradigms and research methodologies. This creates difficulties in reaching consensus on construct definitions as well as their measurement or operationalization.

The model developed by Schein (1985) helps to organize the pieces of the culture puzzle. According to this model, culture is represented at three levels: (1) behaviors and artifacts; (2) beliefs and values; and (3) underlying assumptions. These levels are arranged according to their visibility such that behavior and artifacts are the easiest to observe, while the underlying assumptions need to be inferred. To understand what the behaviors or beliefs actually mean to the participants, the underlying assumptions have to be surfaced. This is most difficult as assumptions are considered to be taken for granted and out of awareness.

This model can be applied to both corporate and national cultures. Laurent (1986) argues, however, that corporate culture may modify the first two levels but will have little impact on the underlying assumptions that are embedded in the national culture. This raises the issue as to whether the behaviors, values, and beliefs prescribed by corporate culture are merely complied with or truly incorporated (Sathe, 1983). This is particularly relevant to concerns regarding motivation, commitment, and the possibility of employees sharing a common "worldview," that is, the very reasons for promoting a strong corporate culture. Although it can be argued that changes in behavior may result in changes in underlying assumptions over time, the unconscious nature of these assumptions makes this unlikely (Schein, 1985).

The underlying assumptions prescribe ways of perceiving, thinking, and evaluating the world, self, and others. These assumptions include views of the relationship with nature and of human relationships (Schein, 1985; Kluckholn and Strodtbeck, 1961; Wallin, 1972; Hall, 1960; Hofstede, 1980; Laurent, 1983). The relationship with nature reflects several dimensions: (1) control over the environment; (2) activity vs. passivity or doing vs. being; (3) attitudes towards uncertainty; (4) notions of time; (5) attitudes towards change; and (6) what determines "truth." Views about the nature of human relationships include: (1) task vs. social orientation; (2) the importance of hierarchy, (3) the importance of individual vs. group. For example, some cultures, often Western, view man as the master of nature, which can be harnessed and exploited to suit man's needs; time, change, and uncertainty can be actively managed. "Truth" is determined by facts and measurement. Other cultures, often Eastern, view man as subservient to or in harmony with nature. Time, change, and uncertainty are accepted as given. "Truth" is determined by spiritual and philosophical principles. This attitude is often referred to as "fatalistic" or "adaptive."

Assumptions regarding the nature of human relationships are also different. The importance of social concerns over task, of the hierarchy, and of the individual vs. the group are clearly different not only between the East and West, but also within Western cultures. In Eastern cultures, for example, importance is placed on social vs. task concerns, on the hierarchy, and on the group or collective (Hofstede, 1980). By contrast, in Western cultures, the focus is more on task, on the individual and the hierarchy is considered to be of less importance. However, research by Hofstede (1980) and Laurent (1983) demonstrate that along these dimensions there is variance between the U.S. and Europe as well as within Europe.

HUMAN RESOURCE PRACTICES IN MNCs

The differences described above have implications for human resource policies that are developed at headquarters and that reflect not only the corporate culture but the national culture of the MNC. Problems may arise when these policies are to be implemented abroad. According to Schuler (1987), MNCs can choose

from a menu of human resource practices that concern: planning and staffing, appraising and compensating, and selection and socialization. Within this menu there are several options which need to be in line with the overall corporate strategy and culture. They also need to take into account the differences in the national cultures of the subsidiaries where they are to be implemented. This section will describe how national culture may affect these choices. In many cases, the description and examples of both corporate and national culture are exaggerated and/or oversimplified. As this is done for purposes of demonstration, it must be remembered that there remains variance within as well as between national and corporate cultures.

Planning and Staffing

Planning can be considered along several dimensions such as formal/informal, and short term/long term. Career management systems represent formal, long term human resource planning. These systems may be inappropriate in cultures where man's control over nature or the future is considered minimal if not sacrilege, for example, as in the Islamic belief, "Inshallah" (if God wills). Derr (1987) found that national culture was a key determinant of the type of career management systems found within Europe.

Some career management systems assume that people can be evaluated, that their abilities, skills, and traits (i.e., their *net worth* to the company) can be quantified, measured, and fed into a computer. As one British HR manager said, "A lot of that material is highly sensitive; You just don't put it into a computer." On the other hand, Derr (1987) found that the French used highly complex and sophisticated computerized systems. This may reflect a humanistic vs. engineering approach (social vs. task orientation).

Secondly, it may assume that evaluation reflects past performance and predicts future performance, which means that evaluation is based on DOING rather than BEING (active vs. passive). In other words, evaluation is based on *what* you achieve and *what* you know (achievement), and *not* on *who* you are (a person of character and integrity) and *who* you know (ascription). In the U.S., concrete results are the criteria for selection and promotion (Derr, 1987). An American general manager of the U.K. region complained that people around there got promoted because of the schools they went to and their family background, not on what they accomplished. This is also common in France, where ties with the "grandes écoles" and the "grands corps" are important for career advancement.

Third, it may assume that data banks can be created of "skills" that can then be matched to "jobs," that jobs can be clearly defined and that specific skills exist to fit them. One Dutch HR manager said that the major problems of long term planning in high technology industries is that the nature of the job in three to five years is unpredictable. IBM says it hires for careers, not jobs; Olivetti says "potential," not "skills" is most important. These differences may reflect underlying assumptions regarding uncertainty and the relationship between the individual and the group (here, organization), for example, careers vs. jobs. For example, in Japan job descriptions are left vague and flexible to fit uncertainty and to strengthen the bond between the individual and the company. In the U.S. and France, job descriptions tend to be more specific, which may reduce uncertainty but which permits more job mobility between organizations.

Also, the nature of the skills acquired is a function of the national educational system. In many European countries, particularly France, mathematics and science diplomas have status and engineering is the preferred program of further study. This system encourages highly technical, narrowly focused specialists which may make functional mobility more difficult. In the U.S. and the U.K., psychology and human rela-

tions is valued and more generalists are welcomed. Derr (1987) found that in identifying high potentials, the French valued technical and engineering expertise whereas the British preferred "the classical generalist" with a "broad humanistic perspective." Knife and fork tests, assessment of table manners and conversation skills, as well as personal appearance were considered to be important criteria for selection in the U.K.

Many career management systems also assume geographic mobility of the work force. Geographic mobility may reflect assumptions regarding the task vs. social orientation, and the group vs. the individual. Europeans are considered more internationally oriented than Americans, as they tend to stay longer in each country and move to another country assignment rather than return home (Tung, 1987). Yet, one Belgian general manager stated that the biggest problem in developing leadership was getting people to move; "Belgians would rather commute 2 hours a day to Brussels than to leave their roots. How can you get them to go abroad?" In a survey done in one MNC, the British were most likely to be willing to relocate, while the Spanish were less so, perhaps reflecting economic considerations in Britain and importance of family in Spain. Derr (1987) found 70% of Swedish sample reporting it difficult to relocate geographically due to wives' careers. This is similar to Hofstede's (1980) findings that Sweden has the least differentiation between male and female roles, increasing the likelihood that women would have careers.

Finally, these systems may assume that people want to be promoted. While self-actualization needs are supposedly the same in all countries (Haire et al., 1966), it is not clear that self-actualization means promotion. Nor is it certain that Maslow's hierarchy of needs is universal, as McClelland (1961) found different levels of need for achievement in different societies. In collective societies, wherein the emphasis is on the group over the individual, need for affiliation may be much more important

(Hofstede, 1980). In Sweden, egalitarianism as well as the desire to keep a low profile to avoid "royal Swedish envy" (i.e., others coveting your position) may make promotion less desirable. Also, promotion may mean more time must be devoted to work, which means less time for family and leisure, or quality of life. If promotion includes a raise, this may not be desirable due to the Swedish tax structure.

Overall, the notion of career management systems in which people are evaluated in terms of skills, abilities, and traits that will be tested, scored, and computerized may appear impersonal, cold, and objective. These systems may be seen as treating human beings as things, instrumental towards achieving company goals, with no concern for their welfare or for their "soul." Employees should be like family and friends, you don't evaluate them, they are to be unconditionally loved. Even seeing them as "human resources" may be considered questionable.

Appraisal and Compensation

Performance appraisal and compensation systems are also examples of cultural artifacts that are built upon underlying assumptions. As mentioned before, performance appraisal implies that "performance," i.e., what is "done" or "achieved," is important and that it can be "appraised," that is, measured objectively. What is appraised is thus behavior and not traits. In Japanese firms, however, there is more concern with judging a person's integrity, morality, loyalty, and cooperative spirit than on getting high sales volume. Furthermore, for the Japanese, the notion of "objective" truth is usually neither important nor useful; "objectivity" refers to the foreigners' point of view while "subjectivity" refers to the host's viewpoint (Maruyama, 1984).

Giving direct feedback does not take into account "saving face" so crucial to many Eastern cultures where confronting an employee with "failure" in an open, direct manner would be considered to be "very tactless." The intervention of a third party may be necessary. Appraisal also assumes that the feedback given will be used to correct or improve upon past performance. This requires that individuals receiving the feedback are willing to evaluate themselves instead of blaming others or external conditions for their performance (or lack thereof). This assumes a view of man as having control over the environment and able to change the course of events. It also assumes that what will happen in the future is of importance, that the present provides opportunity, and/or that the past can be used as a guide for future behavior.

Appraisal and compensation systems are often considered to be linked in Western management thinking, as in the case of management by objectives (MBO). Here it is espoused that people should be rewarded based on their performance, what they do or achieve, or for their abilities and skills and not on their traits or personal characteristics. Management by objective (MBO) assumes the following.

1. goals can be set (man has control over the environment);
2. with 3, 6, 12, or 18 month objectives (time can be managed);
3. their attainment can be measured (reality is objective);
4. the boss and the subordinate can engage in a two-way dialogue to agree on what is to be done, when, and how (hierarchy is minimized);
5. the subordinate assumes responsibility to meet the agreed upon goals (control and activity); and
6. the reward is set contingent upon this evaluation (doing vs. being).

Problems with the transfer of MBO to other cultures have been discussed before (Hofstede, 1980; Laurent, 1983; Trepo, 1973). In Germany, MBO was favorably received because of preference for decentralization, less emphasis on the hierarchy (allowing two-way dialogue), and formalization (clear goals, time frames, measurement and contingent rewards). In

France, however, this technique was less successfully transferred (Trepo, 1973). Due to the ambivalent views towards authority, MBO was viewed suspiciously as an exercise of arbitrary power and a manipulative ploy of management. Given that power is concentrated in the hands of the boss (importance of hierarchy), subordinates would be held responsible without having the power to accomplish goals. Within this perspective, the notion of the boss and subordinate participating in reaching a decision together is quite foreign. Also, although the French have a preference for formalization, for example, bureaucratic systems, things tend to get accomplished outside the system rather than through it—"systeme D" or management by circumvention (Trepo, 1973). Other European managers complain that use of MBO is particularly American as it encourages a short term focus and, as it is tied to rewards, encourages setting lower, more easily attainable goals than necessarily desirable ones.

Tying performance to rewards is also suspect. It would be difficult for most Western managers to consider implementing a system at home whereby the amount that family members are given to eat is related to their contribution to the family income. Yet in the workplace the notion of pay for performance seems quite logical. In African societies, which tend to be more collective, the principles applied to family members apply to employees as well; nepotism is a natural outcome of this logic. One multinational, in an effort to improve the productivity of the work force by providing nutritious lunches, met with resistance and the demand that the cost of the meal be paid directly to the workers so that they could feed their families. The attitude was one of "how can we eat while our families go hungry?"

Preferences for compensation systems and bonuses are clearly linked to cultural attitudes. In one MNC's Danish subsidiary, a proposal for incentives for salespeople was turned down because it favored specific groups, that is, ran counter to their egalitarian spirit. Furthermore,

it was felt that everyone should get the same amount of bonus, not 5% of salary; in fact, there should be no differences in pay. In Africa, savings are managed or bonuses conferred by the group in a "tontine" system wherein everyone gives part of their weekly salary to one group member. Although each member would get the same if they saved themselves, it is preferred that the group perform this function.

The relative importance of status, money, or vacation time varies across countries and affects the motivating potential of these systems. One compensation and benefits manager explained that for the Germans, the big Mercedes wasn't enough; a chauffeur was also needed (status concerns). In Sweden, monetary rewards were less motivating than providing vacation villages (quality of life vs. task orientation). Also, there were different expectations regarding pensions, in part a function of the government and inflation. In Southern European countries the pension expected was 40% of salary, while in the Nordic countries up to 85%, which may reflect different roles of government in society as embedded in the "civic culture" (Almond and Verba, 1963).

Selection and Socialization

One of the major concerns of many multinational companies is the training and development of their human resources. This includes concern for the level of skills at the operating levels, the development of indigenous managerial capability, and the identification and nurturing of "high potentials," that is, those who will play major future leadership roles. At every level, this requires not only acquiring specific skills, for example, technical, interpersonal, or conceptual (Katz, 1974), but also acquiring the "way things are done around here"—the behaviors, values, and beliefs and underlying assumptions of that company, that is, the corporate culture.

Selection is one of the major tools for developing and promoting corporate culture (Schein,

1985). Candidates are carefully screened to "fit in" to the existing corporate culture, assessed for their behavioral styles, beliefs, and values. IBM, for example, may be less concerned with hiring the "typical Italian" than hiring an Italian who fits within the IBM way of doing things. For example, IBM attempts to avoid power accumulation of managers by moving them every two years (it's said that IBM stands for "I've Been Moved"), which may not suit the Italian culture wherein organizations are seen as more "political" than "instrumental" (Laurent, 1983).

One HR manager from Olivetti said that those Italians who want more autonomy go to Olivetti instead of IBM. He described the culture of Olivetti as being informal and non-structured, and as having more freedom, fewer constraints, and low discipline. Recruitment is based on personality and not "too good grades" (taken to reflect not being in touch with the environment). This encouraged hiring of strong personalities, that is, impatient, more risk-taking and innovative people, making confrontation more likely and managing more difficult.

Socialization is another powerful mechanism of promoting corporate culture. In-house company programs and intense interaction during off-site training can create an "esprit de corps," a shared experience, an interpersonal or informal network, a company language or jargon, as well as develop technical competencies. These training events often include songs, picnics, and sporting events that provide feelings of togetherness. These rites of integration may also be accompanied by initiation rites wherein personal culture is stripped, company uniforms are donned (t-shirts), and humiliation tactics employed, for example, "pie-in-the-face" and "tie-clipping" (Trice and Beyer, 1984). This is supposed to strengthen the identification with the company (reinforce the group vs. the individual).

Other examples are to be found in Japanese management development "Hell Camps"

wherein "ribbons of shame" must be worn and instruction must be taken from "young females" (*International Management,* January 1985). IBM management training programs often involve demanding, tension-filled, strictly prescribed presentations to "probing" senior managers (Pascale, 1984). These "boot camp" tactics are designed to create professional armies of corporate soldiers. These military metaphors may not be well accepted, particularly in Europe or other politically sensitive regions.

Artifacts of corporate culture campaigns (stickers, posters, cards, and pins) remind members of the visions, values, and corporate goals, for example, "Smile" campaigns at SAS, Phillips "1 Billion" goal buttons, and G.M. corporate culture cards carried by managers in their breast pockets. Many Europeans view this "hoopla" cynically. It is seen as terribly "American" in its naïveté, enthusiasm, and childishness. It is also seen as controlling and as an intrusion into the private or personal realm of the individual. Statements of company principles on the walls are often referred to sceptically. One HR manager thought that it was "pretty pathetic to have to refer to them." Others feel that it is very American in its exaggeration and lack of subtlety.

Expatriate transfers are also used for socialization and development of an international "cadre" (Edstrom and Galbraith, 1977). The rotation of expatriates from headquarters through subsidiaries and the shipping of local nationals from the subsidiaries to headquarters occur for different reasons, such as staffing, management development, and organization development. These reasons tend to reflect different orientations of headquarters towards their subsidiaries: ethnocentric, polycentric, and geocentric (Ondrack, 1985; Edstrom and Galbraith, 1977; Heenan and Perlmutter, 1979; Evans, 1986).

Differences between American, European, and Japanese firms have been found in the use of transfers for purposes of socialization or as a system of control. U.S. firms rely more on local managers using more formal, impersonal numbers controls, while the European firms rely on the use of the international cadre of managers using more informal, personal control (La Palombara and Blank, 1977; Ondrack, 1985). The Japanese rely heavily on frequent visits of home and host country managers between headquarters and subsidiaries, using both socialization and formalization (Ghoshal and Bartlett, 1987).

Some external conditions affect the use of expatriates, such as local regulations requiring indigenous management and increasingly limited mobility due to the rise of dual career and family constraints. Also, willingness to make work vs. family tradeoffs differ between countries, the Europeans less likely to do so than the Americans (Schmidt and Posner, 1983). It is also reported that the young Japanese managers are less willing to make the same sacrifices to work than their parents were. Therefore, there may be convergence in these trends but for different reasons, for example, task vs. social orientation or individual vs. group orientation.

This section discussed the assumptions underlying various HRM practices and explored their possible clash with the assumptions of the national cultures of subsidiaries. This clash can cause problems in implementing HRM practices designed at headquarters. The differences in underlying assumptions, however, may provide only the excuse. The extent to which these practices are seen as flowing in one direction, down from headquarters to subsidiaries, may influence the extent to which these practices are adopted and to what extent the behavior, beliefs, and values of the corporate culture are incorporated or even complied with. Ethnocentric vs. geocentric attitudes determine whether there is hope for going global and whether "truly international" is really possible. The next section will discuss some important con-

cerns regarding the use of corporate culture in realizing this global vision.

GOING GLOBAL

Many American multinationals are moving from having international divisions to embracing a "global" or "worldwide" perspective, that is, stage II to stage III development (Scott, 1973). Even European multinationals having longer histories of international business due to smaller domestic markets, a colonial heritage and greater proximity of "foreign" countries, are asking, "How can we become more international?"

What does international or global really look like? Do they mean the same thing? Some companies point to the reduced number of expatriates in local subsidiaries, the use of third country nationals, and multinational composition of their top management team as evidence of their "internationalization" (Berenbeim, 1982). Many are clamoring for "corporate culture" to provide the coordination and coherence sought. In one American MNC, the European regional headquarters president saw himself vis-à-vis the national affiliates as "a shepherd that needs to let the flock wander and eat grass but get them all going in one direction—to the barn. You don't want to end up alone in the barn at the end of the day." Is corporate culture necessary for global integration? Will socialization work as a control strategy? Several issues are raised that need careful consideration: need for differentiation vs. integration; autonomy vs. control; and national vs. corporate boundaries.

Differentiation versus Integration

To what extent can corporate culture override national culture differences to create a global company? Is that desirable or even possible? This raises the issue of the extent to which global vs. local HRM practices are needed to integrate a global company. In the case of global practices, care must be taken so that "geocentric" looks different from "ethnocentric" while remaining sensitive to needs for differentiation. In the case of local, it means determining what needs to be done differently in the context of requirements for integration.

Marketing and HRM have traditionally been functions left decentralized in multinational-subsidiary relationships. Yet, global marketing has been proclaimed the wave of the future (Levitt, 1983) despite obvious local market and customer differences. Global HRM runs along similar logic with similar risks. Is HRM necessarily culture-bound? Does competitive advantage derive from global HRM? Homogenized HRM may weaken competitive advantage by trying to ignore or minimize cultural differences instead of trying to utilize them (Adler, 1986).

Contingency arguments abound. Doz and Prahalad (1984) argue that the simultaneous need for global integration and local responsiveness must be managed. Evans (1986) argues for the product/market logic to determine the socio-cultural strategy for adaptation. Ghoshal and Nohria (1987) argue that the level of environmental complexity and the level of local resources should determine the levels of centralization, formalization, or socialization used for control in headquarters-subsidiary relationships. These prescriptions are all quite rational but may overlook important resistances arising from the following issues regarding autonomy and boundaries.

Control versus Autonomy

Visions of going global with corporate culture as a strategy for control may have some unforeseen consequences. While Schein (1968) has likened socialization to brainwashing, Pascale (1984) says the maligned "organization man" of the 1960s is now "in." At what point will the push to conform be met with an equal if not stronger push to preserve uniqueness? Dostoyevsky (1960) said that man would even behave self destructively to reaffirm his autonomy. What reactance may be provoked by socialization efforts? Those managers selected out or who "drop out" may be valuable not only by providing their expertise but also by providing an alternative perspective. Certain cultures, both national and corporate, that value conformity over individuality may be better able to use corporate culture as a mechanism for control but may lose the advantage of individual initiative.

Hofstede's (1980) research demonstrates that even within a large multinational, famous for its strong culture and socialization efforts, national culture continues to play a major role in differentiating work values. Laurent (1983) has demonstrated that there is greater evidence for national differences regarding beliefs about organizations in samples of single MNCs than in multicompany samples. These findings may point to a paradox that national culture may play a stronger role in the face of a strong corporate culture. The pressures to conform may create the need to reassert autonomy and identity, creating a cultural mosaic rather than a melting pot.

The convergence/divergence argument (Webber, 1969) states that economic development, technology, and education would make possible globalization whereas differential levels of available resources and national cultures would work against this. A simple comparison of U.S. and Japanese management practices demonstrates that the level of economic development, industrialization, or education is not going to bring about convergence. According to Fujisawa, Founder of Honda, "Japanese and U.S. management is 95% alike and differs in all important aspects."

Equal and opposing forces for unification and fragmentation coexist (Fayerweather, 1975) as seen within and between countries.

The ongoing case of trade policies between Canada and the U.S. (Holsti, 1980) and the hopes for the future of the EEC trade agreements in 1992 rest precariously on this tension. Issues of asymmetry and interdependence between multinationals and host country governments (Gladwin, 1982) and between multinational headquarters and their subsidiaries (Ghoshal and Nohria, 1987) make globalization efforts precarious. Therefore, attempts by headquarters to control subsidiaries through more "subtle" methods, such as corporate culture, should take into account the dependency concerns and autonomy needs of the subsidiary and anticipate their resistance.

For example, efforts to educate Western managers to "understand" Japan met with local resistance (Pucik, personal communication) as ignorance may provide the autonomy zone desired by the local managers. Socialization as a power equalizer as argued by Ghoshal and Nohria (1987) is suspect and will be rejected for precisely this reason. As one general manager of a national subsidiary said regarding the European regional headquarters of a U.S. based MNC, "As long as we give them the numbers they leave us alone." And U.S. headquarters? "They don't have the foggiest idea about what's going on really. They get the numbers. They get 100 million dollars a year in profit and that's probably about as much as they want to know about." Perhaps formal reporting preserves autonomy and will thus be preferred regardless of the logic of globalization.

Boundaries: National versus Corporate

In the 1960s, multinationals threatened to take over the world; host country governments' sovereignty was at risk (Vernon, 1971, 1977). However, through the transfer of technology and managerial capacity, the power became more symmetrical, even tipping the scale in the other direction as seen at one point in the rash of nationalizations that occurred in the 1970s (Kobrin, 1982). While the balance has subsequently restabilized, larger forces, such as the rise of religious fundamentalism in some areas, threaten this stability.

National boundaries are again threatened. Economic victory in lieu of military victory seems to have created "occupation douce." This is reflected in the anxieties of Americans as they see their country becoming owned by "foreigners" and the Japanese invasion of Wall Street. Mitterand, President of France, said recently that in the future the French might become the museum keepers, relying on tips from Japanese tourists.

The vision of developing an international cadre of executives through frequent and multiple transfers designed to encourage the loss of identification with their country of origin and its transfer to the corporation (Edstrom and Galbraith, 1977) is frightening. In these global "clans," corporate identification may come to override community and even family identification (Ouchi and Jaeger, 1978). These citizens of the world, men and women without countries, only companies, become corporate mercenaries. One story has it that a French IBM executive arriving at JFK airport in New York while searching for his entry visa pulled out his IBM identification card. The customs official, seeing it said, "Oh, it's O.K., you're IBM, you can go ahead." Business schools train these corporate soldiers, dispatching them to multinationals to control the world through finance and management consulting. Perhaps now is the time for academics and practitioners to sit back and reflect about the implications.

REFERENCES

Adler, N. J. *International dimensions of organizational behavior.* Belmont, Calif.: Kent, 1986.

Adler, N. J., and Jelinek, M. Is "Organizational Culture" culture bound? *Human Resource Management,* 1986, 25 (1), 73–90.

Administrative Science Quarterly, 1983, 28 (3).

Almond, G. A., and Verba, S. *The civic culture: Political attitudes and democracy in five nations.* Princeton, N.J.: Princeton University Press, 1963.

Baliga, B. R., and Jaeger, A. M. Multinational corporations: Control systems and delegation issues. *Journal of International Business Studies,* 1984, 15 (2), 25–40.

Berenbeim, R. *Managing the international company: Building a global perspective.* New York: The Conference Board, Report no. 814, 1982.

Deal, T., and Kennedy, A. *Corporate cultures: The rites and rituals of corporate life.* Reading, Mass.: Addison-Wesley, 1982.

Derr, C. Managing high potentials in Europe. *European Management Journal,* 1987, 5 (2), 72–80.

Dostoyevsky. *Notes from the underground.* New York: Dell, 1960.

Doz, Y., and Prahalad, C. Patterns of strategic control within multinational corporations. *Journal of International Business Studies,* 1984, 15 (2), 55–72.

Edstrom, A., and Galbraith J. Transfer of managers as a co-ordination and control strategy in multinational organizations. *Administrative Science Quarterly,* 1977, 22, 248–263.

Evans, P. The context of strategic human resource management policy in complex firms. *Management Forum,* 1986, 6, 105–117.

Fayerweather, J. A conceptual scheme of the interaction of the multinational firm and nationalism. *Journal of Business Administration,* 1975, 7, 67–89.

Ghoshal, S., and Bartlett A. Organizing for innovations: Case of the multinational corporation. WP INSEAD No. 87/04, 1987.

Ghoshal, S., and Nohria, N. Multinational corporations as differentiated networks. WP INSEAD No. 87/13, 1987.

Gladwin, T. Environmental interdependence and organizational design: The case of the multinational corporation. WP NYU No. 82-13, 1982.

Haire, M., Ghiselli, E., and Porter, L. *Managerial thinking—An international study.* New York: John Wiley, 1966.

Hall, E. T. The silent language of overseas business. *Harvard Business Review,* 1960, 38 (3), 87–95.

Heenan, D. A., and Perlmutter, H. V. *Multinational organization development: A social architectural perspective.* Philippines: Addison-Wesley, 1979.

Hofstede, G. *Culture's consequences.* Beverly Hills, Calif.: Sage Publications, 1980.

Holsti, J. Change in the international system: Integration and fragmentation. In R. Holsti, R. Siverson, and A. George (Eds.), *Change in the International System.* Boulder, Colo.: Westview, 1980, 23–53.

Journal of International Business Studies, Fall 1984.

Katz, R. Skills of an effective administrator. *Harvard Business Review,* 1974, 90–102.

Kluckholn, F., and Strodtbeck, F. *Variations in value orientations.* Evanston, Ill.: Row, Peterson, 1961.

Kobrin, S. *Managing political risk assessments: Strategic response to environmental change.* Berkeley: University of California Press, 1982.

La Palombara, J., and Blank, S. *Multinational corporations in comparative perspective.* New York: The Conference Board, Report No. 725, 1977.

Laurent, A. The cross-cultural puzzle of international human resource management. *Human Resource Management,* 1986, 25 (1), 91–102.

Laurent, A. The cultural diversity of western conceptions of management. *International Studies of Management and Organizations,* 1983, 13 (1–2), 75–96.

Levitt, T. The globalization of markets. *Harvard Business Review,* 1983 (May–June), 92–102.

McClelland, D. *The achieving society.* New York: D. Van Nostrand, 1961.

Maruyama, M. Alternative concepts of management: Insights from Asia and Africa. *Asia Pacific Journal of Management,* 1984, 100–110.

Ondrack, D. International transfers of managers in North American and European MNE's. *Journal of International Business Studies,* 1985, XVI (3), 1–19.

Ouchi, W. G., and Jaeger, A. M. Type Z organization: Stability in the midst of mobility. *Academy of Management Review,* 1978, 3 (2), 305–314.

Pascale, R. The paradox of "Corporate Culture": Reconciling ourselves to socialization. *California Management Review,* 1984, 27 (2), 26–41.

Peters, T., and Waterman, R. *In search of excellence.* New York: Harper & Row, 1982.

Sathe, V. Implications of corporate culture: A manager's guide to action. *Organizational Dynamics,* 1983 (Autumn), 5–23.

Schein, E. H. Organizational socialization and the profession of management. *Industrial Management Review,* 1968, 9, 1–15.

Schein, E. H. *Organizational culture and leadership.* San Francisco: Jossey-Bass, 1985.

Schmidt, W., and Posner, B. *Management values in perspective.* New York: AMA, 1983.

Scott, B. The industrial state: Old myths and new realities. *Harvard Business Review,* 1973 (March–April), 133–148.

Schuler, R. Human resource management practice choices. In R. Schuler and S. Youngblood (Eds.), *Reading in Personnel and Human Resource Management,* 3rd ed. St. Paul, Minn.: West, 1987.

Schwartz, H., and Davis, S. Matching corporate culture and business strategy. *Organizational Dynamics,* 1981 (Summer), 30–48.

Smircich, L. Studying organizations as cultures. In G. Morgan (Ed.), *Beyond Method: Strategies for Social Research.* Beverley Hills, Calif.: Sage Publications, 1983.

Trepo, G. Management style à la Francaise. *European Business*, 1973 (Autumn), 71–79.

Trice, H. M., and Beyer, J. M. Studying organizational culture through rites and ceremonials. *Academy of Management Review*, 1984, 9 (4), 653–669.

Tung, R. Expatriate assignments: Enhancing success and minimizing failure. *Academy of Management Executive*, 1987, 1 (2), 117–126.

Vernon, R. *Sovereignty at bay.* New York: Basic Books, 1971.

Vernon, R. *Storm over the multinationals.* Cambridge, Mass.: Harvard University Press, 1977.

Wallin, T. The international executive baggage: Cultural values of the American frontier. *MSU Business Topics*, 1972 (Spring), 49–58.

Webber, R. Convergence or divergence? *Columbia Journal of Business,* 1969, 4 (3).

37

ORGANIZING FOR WORLDWIDE EFFECTIVENESS: THE TRANSNATIONAL SOLUTION

Christopher A. Bartlett
Sumantra Ghoshal

The enormous success of Japanese companies that burst into the international competitive arena in the 1960s and 1970s has triggered a barrage of analysis and advice in the Western business press. Most of this analysis highlighted the convergence of consumer preferences worldwide, the impact of changing technologies and scale economies on international industry structures, and the emergence of increasingly sophisticated competitive strategies that have led to a rapid process of globalization in a large number of worldwide businesses.[1]

As Western companies have searched for the source of the newcomers' incredible ability to sell everything from automobiles to zippers, one conclusion has gained increasing credibility: companies that are unable to gain firm strategic control of their worldwide operations and manage them in a globally coordinated manner will not succeed in the emerging international economy. There are few senior managers in the

West who are unaffected by the implications of this message.

The concerns of top managers in Japan, however, have been quite different and have focused on the forces of localization that have also been gathering strength in the recent past. Like their Western counterparts, they have been sensitized not only by their own experiences, but also by stories in the Japanese business press, which have been focused on the growing barriers to trade and, most recently, the impact of a strengthening yen in offsetting the efficiencies of global-scale Japanese plants. These managers are much more sensitive to the flip side of globalization—the growing demand of host governments for local investments, the building resistance of consumers to standardized homogenized global products, and the changing economics of emerging flexible manufacturing technologies that are making smaller-scale production and more tailored products feasible.

In the course of a study of some of the world's leading Japanese, European, and American multinationals, we found that these globalizing and localizing forces are working simultane-

Source: California Management Review (Fall 1988), pp. 54–74.

ously to transform many industries.[2] But for historical reasons, few companies have built the organizational capabilities to respond equally to both of these forces.

Many of the European- and American-based companies had well-established networks of fairly independent and self-sufficient national subsidiaries—"decentralized federations" we call them. Those with such organizations had little difficulty in responding to the increased demands from their host governments or adapting to shifts in consumer preferences worldwide, and their strategic posture was often literally multinational—multiple national positions, each highly sensitive to its local market. The problem with this strategy and the organizational structure that supported it was that it was difficult to coordinate and control these worldwide operations in order to respond to the global forces.

Most of the Japanese companies we studied had the opposite problem. Their operations tended to be concentrated in the home country—we term them "centralized hubs"—and this gave them the ability to capture the opportunities presented by the global forces. Indeed, the strategic posture of these companies was literally global—the world was considered as an integrated whole. Such an approach made these companies less successful in building worldwide operating units that were sensitive and responsive to the countervailing forces of localization.[3]

THE CONSTRAINT OF A COMPANY'S HERITAGE

As the international operating environment became more complex over the past decade or so, the great temptation for companies was to try to imitate the organizational characteristics and strategic postures of their competitors. For example, in the United States, multinational managers are being advised to "rein in far-flung autonomous subsidiaries, produce standard-ized global products, and pull decision-making power back to the home office," with the reminder that "this is a formula that, not coincidentally, many Japanese companies have used for years."[4]

But the appropriate response to the developing international demands cannot be captured in a formula—and certainly not one that is imitative of companies in totally different situations. The problem is that while a company's tasks are shaped by its external environment, its ability to perform those tasks is constrained by what we term its "administrative heritage"—the company's existing configuration of assets, its traditional distribution of responsibility, and its historical norms, values, and management style.[5] This internal organizational capability is something that cannot be changed overnight or by decree, and one of the important lessons for management is to shift its attention from a search for the ideal organization structure to a quest for ways in which to build and leverage the company's existing capabilities to make them more responsive to the ever-changing external demands.

That is not to deny that there are lessons to be learned from other companies—indeed our research indicates quite the opposite. However, the important lesson is that either blind imitation simply to eliminate obvious differences or wholesale adoption of another company's organizational approach or strategic posture is likely to end in failure. In the first part of this article, we distill some of the important transferable lessons that *can* be learned from companies that manage global coordination effectively and from those that have been most successful in developing and managing a responsive and flexible localized approach. Although the lessons are drawn from a broader study, we will emphasize the importance of a company's administrative heritage by comparing and contrasting the approaches of two leading consumer electronics companies and suggesting ways in which they can learn from each other.

But while such lessons are helpful, they do not provide the full solution. Today's operating environment in many worldwide businesses demands more than efficient central management and flexible local operations—it requires companies to link their diverse organizational perspectives and resources in a way that would allow them to leverage their capabilities for achieving global coordination and national flexibility simultaneously. In response to this need, a few companies have evolved beyond the simpler multinational or global approach to international business and developed what we term a *transnational* capability—an ability to manage across boundaries.[6] In the final part of the article, we will describe some of the characteristics of such an organization, and will suggest some steps that can be taken to build these capabilities.

MAKING CENTRAL MANAGEMENT FLEXIBLE: LESSONS FROM MATSUSHITA

For companies that expanded internationally by establishing fairly independent and self-sufficient subsidiary companies around the world, the task of imposing some kind of global direction or achieving some measure of coordination of activity is often a Herculean challenge. The problem that has confronted successive generations of top management at Philips is typical. The Dutch-based electronics giant has built a justifiable reputation as one of the world's most innovative companies, yet has continually been frustrated in its attempt to deliver its brilliant inventions to the world's markets. The recent failure of its VCR system is a classic example.

Despite the fact that it was generally acknowledged to be technologically superior to the competitive VHS and Beta formats, the Philips V2000 system failed because the company was unable to commercialize it. Within the company there is no shortage of theories to

explain the failure: some suggest that those who developed the product and its competitive strategy were too distant from the market; others feel the barriers between research, development, manufacturing, and marketing led to delays and cost overruns; and another group points to the fact that worldwide subsidiaries were uninvolved in the project and therefore uncommitted to its success. All these explanations reflect organizational difficulties and have some element of truth.

On the other hand, Matsushita Electric Company, Philips' archrival in consumer electronics, has built the global leadership position of its well-known Panasonic and National brands on its ability to control its global strategy from the center in Japan—yet it has been able to implement it in a flexible and responsive manner throughout its worldwide operations. As we tried to identify the organizational mechanisms that were key to Matsushita's ability to provide strong central direction and control without becoming inflexible or isolated, three factors stood out as the most important explanations of its outstanding success:

- gaining the input of subsidiaries into its management processes;
- ensuring that development efforts were linked to market needs; and
- managing responsibility transfers from development to manufacturing to marketing.

By examining how these core mechanisms work in Matsushita, managers in other companies may see ways in which they can gain more global coordination without compromising local market sensitivity.

Gaining Subsidiary Input: Multiple Linkages

The two most important problems facing a centrally managed multinational company are that those developing the new product or strategy may not understand market needs or that those required to implement the new direction are not committed to it. Matsushita managers are very conscious of these problems and spend much time building multiple linkages between headquarters and overseas subsidiaries to minimize their impacts. These linkages are designed not only to give headquarters managers a better understanding of country level needs and opportunities, but also to give subsidiary managers greater access to and involvement in headquarters decision-making processes.

Matsushita recognizes the importance of market sensing as a stimulus to innovation and does not want its centrally driven management process to reduce its environmental sensitivity. Rather than trying to limit the number of linkages between headquarters and subsidiaries or to focus them through a single point (as many companies do for the sake of efficiency), Matsushita tries to preserve the different perspectives, priorities, and even prejudices of its diverse groups worldwide and tries to ensure that they have linkages to those in the headquarters who can represent and defend their views.

The organizational systems and processes that connect different parts of the Matsushita organization in Japan with the video department of MESA, the U.S. subsidiary of the company, illustrate these multifaceted interlinkages. The vice president in charge of this department has his career roots in Matsushita Electric Trading Company (METC), the organization with overall responsibility for Matsushita's overseas business. Although formally posted to the United States, he continues to be a member of the senior management committee of METC and spends about a third of his time in Japan. This allows him to be a full member of METC's top management team that approves the overall strategy for the U.S. market. In his role as the VP of MESA, he ensures that the local operation effectively implements the agreed video strategy.

At the next level, the general manager of MESA's video department is a company veteran who had worked for 14 years in the video product division of Matsushita Electric, the central production and domestic marketing company in Japan. He maintains strong connections with the parent company's product division and is its link to the local American market. Two levels below him, the assistant product manager in the video department (one of the more junior-level expatriates in the American organization) links the local organization to the central VCR factory in Japan. Having spent five years in the factory, he acts as the local representative of the factory and handles all day-to-day communication with factory personnel.

None of these linkages is accidental. They are deliberately created and maintained and they reflect the company's open acknowledgement that the parent company is not one homogeneous entity, but a collectivity of different constituencies and interests, each of which is legitimate and necessary. Together, these multiple linkages enhance the subsidiary's ability to influence key headquarters decisions relating to its market, particularly decisions about product specifications and design. The multiple links not only allow local management to reflect its local market needs, they also give headquarters managers the ability to coordinate and control implementation of their strategies and plans.

Linking Direction to Needs: Market Mechanisms

Matsushita's efforts to ensure that its products and strategies are linked to market needs does not stop at the input stage. The company has created an integrative process that ensures that the top managers and central staff groups are not sheltered from the pressures, constraints, and demands felt by managers on the front line of the operations. One of the key elements in achieving this difficult organizational task is the company's willingness to employ "market mechanisms" for directing and regulating the activities located at the center. Because the system is unique, we will describe some of its major characteristics.

Research projects undertaken by the Central Research Laboratories (CRL) of Matsushita fall into two broad groups. The first group consists of "company total projects" which involve developing technologies important for Matsushita's long-term strategic position and that may be applicable across many different product divisions. Such projects are decided jointly by the research laboratories, the product divisions, and top management of the company and are funded directly by the corporate board. The second group of CRL research projects consists of relatively smaller projects which are relevant to the activities of particular product divisions. The budget for such research activities, approximately half of the company's total research budget, is allocated not to the research laboratories but to the product divisions. This creates an interesting situation in which technology-driven and market-led ideas can compete for attention.

Each year, the product divisions suggest research projects that they would like to sponsor and which would incorporate their knowledge of worldwide market needs developed through their routine multiple linkages to subsidiaries. At the same time, the various research laboratories hold annual internal exhibitions and meetings and also write proposals to highlight research projects that they would like to undertake. The engineering and development groups of the product divisions mediate the subsequent contracting and negotiation process through which the expertise and interests of the laboratories and the needs of the product divisions are finally matched. Specific projects are sponsored by the divisions and are allocated to the laboratories or research groups of their choice, along with requisite funds and other resources.

The system creates intense competition for projects (and the budgets that go with them) among the research groups, and it is this mechanism that forces researchers to keep a close market orientation. At the same time, the product divisions are conscious that it is their money that is being spent on product development and they become less inclined to make unreasonable or uneconomical demands on R&D.[7]

The market mechanism also works to determine annual product styling and features. Each year the company holds what it calls merchandising meetings, which are, in effect, large internal trade shows. Senior marketing managers from Matsushita's sales companies worldwide visit their supplying divisions and see on display the proposed product lines for the new model year. Relying on their understanding of their individual markets, these managers pick and choose among proposed models, order specific modifications for their local markets, or simply refuse to take products they feel are unsuitable. Individual products or even entire lines might have to be redesigned as a result of input from the hundreds of managers at the merchandising meeting.

Managing Responsibility Transfer: Personnel Flows

Within a national subsidiary, the task of transferring responsibility from research to manufacturing and finally marketing is facilitated by the smaller size and closer proximity of the units responsible for each stage of activity. This is not so where large central units usually take the lead role, and Matsushita has built some creative means for managing these transitions. The systems rely heavily on the transfer of people, as is illustrated by the company's management of new product development.

First, careers of research engineers are structured so as to ensure that most of them spend about five to eight years in the central research laboratories engaged in pure research, then they spend another five years in the product divisions in applied product and process development, and finally they spend the rest of their working lives in a direct operational function, usually production, wherein they take up line management positions. More important, each engineer usually makes the transition from one department to the next along with the transfer of the major project on which he has been working.

The research project that began Matsushita's development of its enormously successful VCR product was launched in the late 1950s under the leadership of Dr. Hiroshi Sugaya, a young physicist in the company's Central Research Laboratory. As the product evolved into its development stage, the core members of Dr. Sugaya's team were kept together as they transferred from CRL to the product development and applications laboratory located in the product division. After a long and difficult development process, the product was finally ready for commercial production in 1977, and many of the team moved with the project out into the Okanyama plant.[8]

In other companies we surveyed, it was not uncommon for research engineers to move to development, but not with their projects, thereby depriving the companies of one of the most important and immediate benefits of such moves. We also saw no other examples of engineers routinely taking the next step of actually moving to the production function. This last step, however, is perhaps the most critical in integrating research and production both in terms of building a network that connects managers across these two functions, and also for transferring a set of common values that facilitates implementation of central innovations.

Another mechanism that integrates production and research in Matsushita works in the opposite direction. Wherever possible, the company tries to identify the manager who will head the production task for a new product under development and makes him a full-time member of the research team from the initial stage of the development process. This system not only injects direct production expertise into the development team, but also facilitates

transfer of the innovation once the design is completed. Matsushita also uses this mechanism as a way of transferring product expertise from headquarters to its worldwide sales subsidiaries. Although this is a common practice among many multinationals, in Matsushita it has additional significance because of the importance of internationalizing management as well as its products.

As with the multiple linkages and the internal market mechanisms, this organizational practice was a simple, yet powerful tool that seemed to be central to Matsushita's ability to make its centrally driven management processes flexible, sensitive, and responsive to the worldwide opportunities and needs. More important, these three organizational mechanisms are simple enough to be adopted, probably in some modified form, by other companies. They meet the needs of those trying to build an organization process that allows management at the center more influence and control over worldwide operations, without compromising the motivation or operating effectiveness of the national units.

MAKING LOCAL MANAGEMENT EFFECTIVE: LESSONS FROM PHILIPS

If Matsushita is the champion of efficient centrally coordinated management, its Netherlands-based competitor, Philips, is the master of building effective national operations worldwide. And as surely as Philips' managers envy their Japanese rival's ability to develop products and strategies in Osaka that appear to be implemented effortlessly around the globe, their counterparts in Matsushita are extremely jealous of Philips' national organizations that are not only sensitive and responsive to their local environments, but are also highly innovative and entrepreneurial.

For example, the company's first color TV set was built and sold not in Europe, where the parent company is located, but in Canada, where the market had closely followed the U.S. lead in introducing color transmission; Philips' first stereo color TV set was developed by the Australian subsidiary; teletext TV sets were created by its British subsidiary; "smart cards" by its French subsidiary; a programmed word processing typewriter by North American Philips—the list of local innovations and entrepreneurial initiatives in the company is endless.

While Matsushita has had no difficulty in establishing effective sales organizations and assembly operations around the world, top management has often been frustrated that its overseas subsidiaries do not exhibit more initiative and entrepreneurial spark. Despite pleas to its overseas management to become more self-sufficient and less dependent on headquarters for direction, the company has found that the decentralization of assets that accompanies its "localization" program has not always triggered the kind of independence and initiative that had been hoped for.

Out of the many factors that drive Philips' international organization, we were able to identify three that not only appear central to the development and maintenance of its effective local management system, but also may be adaptable to other organizations that are trying to promote national innovativeness and responsiveness within a globally integrated organization:

- Philips' use of a cadre of entrepreneurial expatriates;
- an organization that forces tight functional integration within a subsidiary; and
- a dispersion of responsibilities along with the decentralized assets.

A Cadre of Entrepreneurial Expatriates

Expatriate positions, particularly in the larger subsidiaries, have been very attractive for Philips' managers for several reasons. With only 7% or 8% of its total sales coming from Holland, many different national subsidiaries of the company have contributed much larger shares of total revenues than the parent company. As a result, foreign operations have enjoyed relatively high organizational status compared to most companies of similar size with headquarters in the United States, Japan, or even the larger countries in Europe. Further, because of the importance of its foreign operations, Philips' formal management development system has always required considerable international experience as a prerequisite for top corporate positions. Finally, Eindhoven, the small rural town in which corporate headquarters is located, is far from the sophisticated and cosmopolitan world centers that host many of its foreign subsidiaries. After living in London, New York, Sydney, or Paris, many managers find it hard to return to Eindhoven.

Collectively, all these factors have led to the best and the brightest of Philips' managers spending much of their careers in different national operations. This cadre of entrepreneurial expatriate managers has been an important agent in developing capabilities of local units, yet keeping them linked to the parent company's overall objectives. Further, unlike Matsushita where an expatriate manager typically spends a tour of duty of three to six years in a particular national subsidiary and then returns to the headquarters, expatriate managers in Philips spend a large part of their careers abroad continuously working for two to three years each in a number of different subsidiaries.

This difference in the career systems results in very different attitudes. In Philips, the expatriate managers follow each other into assignments and build close relations among themselves. They tend to identify strongly with the national organization's point of view, and this shared identity makes them part of a distinct subculture within the company. In companies like Matsushita, on the other hand, there is very little interaction among the expatriate managers in the different subsidiaries, and most tend to see themselves as part of the parent company temporarily on assignment in a foreign country.

One result of these differences is that expatriate managers in Matsushita are far more likely to take a custodial approach which resists any local changes to standard products and policies. In contrast, expatriate managers in Philips, despite being just as socialized into the overall corporate culture of the company, are much more willing to be advocates of local views and to defend against the imposition of inappropriate corporate ideas on national organizations. This willingness to "rock the boat" and openness to experimentation and change is the fuel that ignites local initiative and entrepreneurship.[9]

Further, by creating this kind of environment in the national organization, Philips has had little difficulty in attracting very capable local management. In contrast to the experience in many Japanese companies where local managers have felt excluded from a decision-making process that centers around headquarters management and the local expatriates only, local managers in Philips feel their ideas are listened to and defended in headquarters.[10] This too, creates a supportive environment for local innovation and creativity.

Integration of Technical and Marketing Functions within Each Subsidiary

Historically, the top management in all Philips' national subsidiaries consisted not of an individual CEO but a committee made up of the heads of the technical, commercial, and finance functions. This system of three-headed management had a long history in Philips, stemming from the functional backgrounds of the founding Philips brothers, one an engineer and the other a salesman. Although this management philosophy has recently been modified to a system which emphasizes individual authority and accountability, the long tradition of shared responsibilities and joint decision

making has left a legacy of many different mechanisms for functional integration at multiple levels. These integrative mechanisms within each subsidiary in Philips enhance the efficiency and effectiveness of local decision making and action in the same way that various means of cross-functional integration within Matsushita's corporate headquarters facilitates its central management processes.

In most subsidiaries, integration mechanisms exist at three organizational levels. First, for each product, there is an article team that consists of relatively junior managers belonging to the commercial and technical functions. This team evolves product policies and prepares annual sales plans and budgets. At times, subarticle teams may be formed to supervise day-to-day working and to carry out special projects, such as preparing capital investment plans, should major new investments be felt necessary for effectively manufacturing and marketing a new product.

A second tier of cross-functional coordination takes place at the product group level, through the group management team, which again consists of both technical and commercial representatives. This team meets monthly to review results, suggest corrective actions, and resolve any interfunctional differences. Keeping control and conflict resolution at this low level facilitates sensitive and rapid responses to initiatives and ideas generated at the local level.

The highest level coordination forum within the subsidiary is the senior management committee (SMC) consisting of the top commercial, technical, and financial managers in the subsidiary. Acting essentially as a local board, the SMC provides an overall unity of effort among the different functional groups within the local unit, and assures that the national unit retains primary responsibility for its own strategies and priorities. Again, the effect is to provide local management with a forum in which actions can be decided and issues resolved without escalation for approval or arbitration.

Decentralized Authority and Dispersed Responsibility

While Matsushita's localization program was triggered by political pressures to increase local value added in various host countries, the company had also hoped that the decentralization of assets would help its overseas units achieve a greater measure of local responsiveness, self-sufficiency, and initiative. To management's frustration, such changes were slow in coming.

Philips, on the other hand, had created such national organizations seemingly without effort. The difference lay in the degree to which responsibility and authority were dispersed along with the assets. Expanding internationally in the earliest decades of the century, Philips managers were confronted by transport and communications barriers that forced them to delegate substantial local autonomy to its decentralized operating units. The need for local units to develop a sense of self-sufficiency was reinforced by the protectionist pressures of the 1930s that made cross-shipments of products or components practically impossible. During World War II, even R&D capability was dispersed to prevent it from falling into enemy hands, and the departure of many corporate managers from Holland reduced the parent company's control over its national operations abroad.

In the postwar boom, while corporate managers focused on rebuilding the war-ravaged home operations, managers in foreign units were able to capitalize on their well-developed autonomy. Most applied their local resources and capabilities to build highly successful national businesses, sensitive and responsive to the local needs and opportunities. In doing so, they achieved a degree of local entrepreneurship and self-sufficiency rare among companies of Philips' size and complexity.

Although it would be impossible for another company to replicate the historical events that resulted in this valuable organizational capability, the main characteristics of their develop-ment are clear. First, it must be feasible for offshore units to develop local capabilities and initiative, and this requires the decentralization of appropriate managerial and technological resources along with the reconfiguration of physical assets.

While this is necessary, it is not sufficient, however, as Matsushita and many other companies have begun to recognize. Local initiatives and entrepreneurial action must not only be feasible, they must also be desirable for local managers. This requires the legitimate delegation of responsibilities and authority that not only gives them control over the decentralized resources, but rewards them for using them to develop creative and innovative solutions to their problems.[11] Only when the decentralization of assets is accompanied by a dispersion of responsibilities can local management develop into a legitimate corporate contributor rather than simple implementers of central direction.

BUILDING TRANSNATIONAL CAPABILITIES: LESSONS FROM L. M. ERICSSON

In multinational corporations, the location of an opportunity (or threat) is often different from where the company's appropriate response resources are situated. This is so because environmental opportunities and threats are footloose, shifting from location to location, while organizational resources, contrary to the assumptions of many economists, are not easily transferable even within the same company. Further, the location of a company's strategic resources—plants and research centers are good examples—is related not only to actual organizational needs and intentions, but also to the idiosyncracies of the firm's administrative history. The result is a situation of environment-resource mismatches: the organization has excessive resources in environments that are relatively noncritical, and very limited or even no resources in critical markets that offer the greatest opportunities and challenges.

Such environment-resource mismatches are pervasive in MNCs. For many historical reasons, Ericsson has significant technological and managerial capabilities in Australia and Italy, even though these markets are relatively unimportant in the global telecommunications business. At the same time, the company has almost no presence in the United States, which not only represents almost 40% of world telecommunications demand but is also the source of much of the new technology: Procter & Gamble is strong in the United States and Europe, but not in Japan where important consumer product innovations have occurred recently and where a major global competitor is emerging. Matsushita has appropriate technological and managerial resources in Japan and the U.S., but not in Europe, a huge market and home of archrival Philips.

Rectifying these imbalances in the configuration of their organization resources is taking these companies a long time and, since the relative importance of different environments will continue to change, the problem will never be fully overcome. The need, therefore, is not simply to make adjustments to the geographic configuration or resources, but also to create organizational systems that allow the spare capacity and slack resources in strong operating units to be redirected to environments in which they are weak.

Simply creating effective central and local management does not solve this mismatch problem, and to succeed in today's demanding international environment, companies must develop their organizational capabilities beyond the stages described in the first part of this article. The limitation of companies with even the most well-developed local and central capabilities is that the location of resources also tends to determine the locus of control over those resources. Whether organizationally mandated or not, local management develops strong influence on how resources available locally are to be used. Further, organizational commitments are usually hierarchical, with local needs taking precedence over global needs. Consequently, at the core of resolving the problem of environment-resource mismatches is the major organizational challenge of loosening the bonds between ownership and control of resources within the company.

Among the companies we studied, there were several that were in the process of developing such organizational capabilities. They had surpassed the classic capabilities of the *multinational* company that operates as decentralized federation of units able to sense and respond to diverse international needs and opportunities, and they had evolved beyond the abilities of the *global* company with its facility for managing operations on a tightly controlled worldwide basis through its centralized hub structure. They had developed what we termed *transnational* capabilities—the ability to manage across national boundaries, retaining local flexibility while achieving global integration. More than anything else this involved the ability to link local operations to each other and to the center in a flexible way, and in so doing, to leverage those local and central capabilities.

Ericsson, the Swedish telecommunications company, was among those that had become most effective in managing the required linkages and processes, and we were able to identify three organizational characteristics that seemed most helpful in facilitating its developing transnational management capabilities:

- an interdependence of resources and responsibilities among organizational units;
- a set of strong cross-unit integrating devices; and
- a strong corporate identification and a well-developed worldwide management perspective.

Interdependence of Resources and Responsibilities

Perhaps the most important requirement of the transnational organization is a need for the organizational configuration to be based on a principle of reciprocal dependence among units. Such an interdependence of resources and responsibilities breaks down the hierarchy between local and global interests by making the sharing of resources, ideas and opportunities a self-enforcing norm. To illustrate how such a basic characteristic of organizational configuration can influence a company's management of capabilities, let us contrast the way in which ITT, NEC, and Ericsson developed the electronic digital switch that would be the core product for each company's telecommunications business in the 1980s and beyond.

From its beginnings in 1920 as a Puerto Rican telephone company, ITT built its worldwide operation on an objective described in the 1924 annual report as being "to develop truly national systems operated by the nationals of each company." For half a century ITT's national "systems houses" as they were called within the company, committed themselves to integrating into their local environments and becoming attuned to national interests and market needs. All but the smallest systems houses were established as fully integrated, self-sufficient units with responsibility for developing, manufacturing, marketing, installing, and servicing their own products.

With the emergence of the new digital electronic technology in the 1970s, however, this highly successful strategic posture was threatened by the huge cost of developing a digital switch. Since no single systems house would be able to muster the required technological and financial resources on its own or recoup the investment from its local market, the obvious solution was for ITT to make the System 12 digital switch project a corporate responsibility. However, given their decade of operating independence, the powerful country unit managers were unwilling to yield the task of developing the new switch to the corporate R&D group—and indeed, little expertise had been gathered at the center to undertake such a task.

By exercising their considerable influence, the European systems houses were able to capture the strategic initiative on System 12, but then began disagreeing about who should take what role in this vital project. Many of the large systems houses simply refused to rely on others for the development of critical parts of the system; others rejected standards that did not fit with their view of local needs. As a result, duplication of effort and divergence of specifications began to emerge, and the cost of developing the switch ballooned to over $1 billion.

The biggest problems appeared when the company decided to enter the battle for a share of the deregulated U.S. market. Asserting its independence, the U.S. business launched a major new R&D effort, despite appeals from the chief technological officer that they risked developing what he skeptically termed "System 13." After further years of effort and additional hundreds of millions of dollars in costs, ITT acknowledged in 1986 it was withdrawing from the U.S. central switching market. The largest and most successful international telecommunications company in the world was blocked from its home country by the inability to transfer and apply its leading edge technology in a timely fashion. It was a failure that eventually led to ITT's sale of its European operations and its gradual withdrawal from direct involvement in telecommunications worldwide.

If effective global innovation was blocked by the extreme independence of the organizational units in ITT, it was impeded in NEC by the strong dependence of national subsidiaries on the parent company. The first person in NEC to detect the trend toward digital switching was the Japanese manager in charge of the company's small U.S. operation. However, his role was one of selling corporate products and developing a beachhead for the company in the U.S. market. Because of this role, he had a hard time convincing technical managers in Japan of a supposed trend to digitalization that they saw nowhere else in the world.

When the U.S. managers finally were able to elicit sufficient support, the new NEAC 61 digital switch was developed almost entirely by headquarters personnel. Even in deciding which features to design into the new product, the central engineering group tended to discount the requests of the North American sales company and rely on data gathered in their own staff's field trips to U.S. customers. Although the NEAC 61 was regarded as having good hardware, customers felt its software was unadapted to U.S. needs. Sales did not meet expectations.

Both ITT and NEC recognized the limitations of their independent and dependent organizations systems and worked hard to adapt them. But the process of building organizational interdependence is a slow and difficult one that must be constantly monitored and adjusted. In our sample of companies, Ericsson seemed to be the most consistent and experienced practitioner of creating and managing a delicate balance of interunit interdependency. The way in which it did so suggests the value of a constant readjustment of responsibilities and relationships as a way of adapting to changing strategic needs while maintaining a dynamic system of mutual dependence.

Like ITT, Ericsson had built, during the 1920s and 1930s, a substantial worldwide network of operations sensitive and responsive to local national environments; but like NEC, it had a strong home market base and a parent company with technological, manufacturing, and marketing capability to support those companies. Keeping the balance between and among those units has required constant adjustment of organizational responsibilities and relationships.

In the late 1930s, management became concerned that the growing independence of its offshore companies was causing divergence in technology, duplication of effort, and inefficiency in the sourcing patterns. To remedy the problem they pulled sales and distribution control to headquarters and began consolidating responsibilities under product divisions. While worldwide control improved, the divisions eventually began to show signs of isolation and short-term focus. Thus, in the early 1950s the

corporate staff functions were given more of a leadership role. It was in this period that the central R&D group developed a crossbar switch that became an industry leader. As the product design and manufacturing technology for this product became well-understood and fully documented, however, Ericsson management was able to respond to the increasing demands of host governments to transfer more manufacturing capacity and technological know-how abroad. Once again, the role of the offshore subsidiaries increased.

This half a century of constant ebb and flow in the roles and responsibilities of various geographic, product, and functional groups allowed Ericsson to build an organization in which all these diverse perspectives were seen as legitimate and the multiple capabilities were kept viable. This multidimensional organization gave the company the ability to quickly sense and respond to the coming of electronic switching in the 1970s. Once it had prevented the emergence of strong dependent or independent relationships, product development efforts and manufacturing responsibilities could be pulled back to Sweden, without great difficulty. Where national capabilities, expertise, or experience could be useful in the corporate effort, the appropriate local personnel were seconded to headquarters. Having established overall strategic and operational control of the digital switching strategy, however, corporate management at Ericsson was then willing to delegate substantial design, development, and manufacturing responsibilities to its international subsidiaries, resulting in a reinforcement of the interdependence of worldwide operations.

Sourcing of products and components from specialized plants have long provided a base of interdependence, but recently that has been extended to product development and marketing. For example, Italy is the company's center for global development of transmission system development, Finland has the leading role for mobile telephones, and Australia develops the company's rural switch. Further, headquarters has given some of these units responsibility for handling certain export markets (e.g., Italy's responsibility for developing markets in Africa). Increasingly, the company is moving even advanced core system software development offshore to subsidiary companies with access to more software engineers than it has in Stockholm.[12]

By changing responsibilities, shifting assets, and modifying relationships in response to evolving environmental demands and strategic priorities, Ericsson has maintained a dynamic interdependence among its operating units that has allowed it to develop entrepreneurial and innovative subsidiary companies that work within a corporate framework defined by knowledgeable and creative headquarters product and functional groups. This kind of interdependence is the basis of a transnational company—one that can think globally and act locally.

Interunit Integrating Devices

Although the interdependence of resources and responsibilities provides a structural framework for the extensive use of interunit cooperation, there is a need for effective organizational integrating mechanisms to link operations in a way that taps the full potential of the interdependent configuration.

Compared to some companies in our study where relationships among national companies were competitive and where headquarter-subsidiary interactions were often of an adversarial nature, the organizational climate in Ericsson appeared more cooperative and collaborative. The establishment and maintenance of such attitudes was important since it allowed the company's diverse units to work together in a way that maximized the potential of their interdependent operations. We identified

three important pillars to Ericsson's success in interunit integration:

- a clearly defined and tightly controlled set of operating systems;
- a people-linking process employing such devices as temporary assignments and joint teams; and
- interunit decision forums, particularly subsidiary boards, where views could be exchanged and differences resolved.

Ericsson management feels strongly that its most effective integrating device is strong central control over key elements of its strategic operation. Unlike ITT, Ericsson has not had strong or sophisticated administrative systems (it introduced strategic plans only in 1983), but its operating systems have long been structured to provide strong worldwide coordination. Knowing that local modifications would be necessary, the company designed its digital switch as a modular system with very clear specifications. National units could custom-tailor elements of the design to meet local needs without compromising the integrity of the total system design. Similarly, Ericsson's global computer-aided design and manufacturing system allowed the parent company to delegate responsibility for component production and even design without fear of losing the ability to control and coordinate the entire manufacturing system.

Rather than causing a centralization of decision making, management argues that these strong yet flexible operating systems allow them to delegate much more freely, knowing that local decisions will not be inconsistent or detrimental to the overall interests. Rather than managing the decisions centrally, they point out they are managing the parameters of decisions that can be made by local units, thereby retaining the flexibility and entrepreneurship of those units.

But in addition to strong systems, interunit cooperation requires good interpersonal relations, and Ericsson has developed these with a long-standing policy of transferring large numbers of people back and forth between headquarters and subsidiaries. It differs from the more common transfer patterns in both direction and intensity, as a comparison with NEC's transfer process will demonstrate. Where NEC may transfer a new technology through a few key managers, Ericsson will send a team of 50 or 100 engineers and managers from one unit to another for a year or two; while NEC's flow is primarily from headquarters to subsidiary, Ericsson's is a balanced two-way flow with people coming to the parent not only to learn, but also to bring their expertise, and while NEC's transfers are predominantly Japanese, Ericsson's multidirectional process involves all nationalities.[13]

Australian technicians seconded to Stockholm in the mid-1970s to bring their experience with digital switching into the corporate development effort established enduring relationships that helped in the subsequent joint development of a rural switch in Australia a decade later. Confidences built when a 40-man Italian team spent 18 months in Sweden in the early 1970s to learn about electronic switching, provided the basis for the subsequent decentralization of AXE software development and the delegation of responsibility for developing the corporate transmission systems to the Italian company.

But any organization in which there are shared tasks and joint responsibilities will require additional decision-making and conflict-resolving forums. In Ericsson, often divergent objectives and interests of the parent company and the local subsidiary are exchanged in the national company's board meetings. Unlike many companies whose local boards are pro forma bodies whose activities are designed solely to satisfy national legal requirements, Ericsson uses its local boards as legitimate forums for communicating objectives, resolving differences and making decisions. At least one, and often several senior corporate managers are members of each board, and subsidiary board meetings become an important means for coordinating activities and channelling local ideas and innovations across national lines.

National Competence, Worldwide Perspective

If there is one clear lesson from ITT's experience, it is that a company cannot manage globally if its managers identify primarily with local parochial interests and objectives. But as NEC has learned, when management has no ability to defend national perspectives and respond to local opportunities, penetration of world markets is equally difficult. One of the important organizational characteristics Ericsson has been able to develop over the years has been a management attitude that is simultaneously locally sensitive and globally conscious.

At the Stockholm headquarters, managers emphasize the importance of developing strong country operations, not only to capture sales that require responsiveness to national needs, but also to tap into the resources that are available through worldwide operation. Coming from a small home country where it already hires over a third of the graduating electrical and electronics engineers, Ericsson is very conscious of the need to develop skills and capture ideas wherever they operate in the world. But, at the same time, local managers see themselves as part of the worldwide Ericsson group rather than as independent autonomous units. Constant transfers and working on joint teams over the years has helped broaden many managers' perspectives from local to global, but giving local units systemwide mandates for products has confirmed their identity with the company's global operations. It is this ability for headquarters and subsidiary managers to view the issues from each other's perspective that distinguishes the company that can think globally yet act locally.

CONCLUSION: ORGANIZATIONAL CAPABILITY IS KEY

There are few companies that have not recognized the nature of the main strategic tasks facing them in today's complex international business environment. Philips' managers have understood for years that they need to build global scale, rationalize their diverse product lines, and establish a more integrated worldwide strategy. And while their counterparts at Matsushita have recently made localization a company watchword, this is just the culmination of years of effort to build more self-sufficient and responsive national subsidiaries which the company recognizes it will need to remain globally competitive. If changes have been slow in coming to both companies, it is not for the lack of strategic clarity about the need for change but for want of the organizational ability to implement the desired change.

In the course of our study, we found that managers engaged in a great deal of cross-company comparison of organizational capabilities. And the managerial grass inevitable looked greener on the other side of the corporate fence. Philips' managers envied their Japanese competitors' ability to develop global products, manufacture them centrally, and have them launched into markets worldwide on a time cycle that would be virtually impossible in their own organization. On the other hand, as Matsushita's managers face growing pressure from host governments worldwide, and as they feel the vulnerabilities of their central sourcing plants in an era of the strong yen, they view Philips' worldwide network of self-sufficient, well-connected, and innovative national organizations as an asset they would dearly love to have. But the apparently small step from admiration to emulation of another company's strategic capabilities usually turns out to be a long and dangerous voyage.

What we suggest is that managers ignore battle cries calling for "standardization, rationalization, and centralization" or any other such simplistic quick-fix formulas. What is needed is a more gradual approach that, rather than undermining a company's administrative heritage, both protects and builds on it. Having built flexible central and local management capabilities, the next challenge is to link them in an organization that allows the company to do what it must to survive in today's international environment—think globally and act locally. For most worldwide companies it is the development of this transnational organizational capability that is key to long-term success.

NOTES

1. See, for example. Theodore Levitt. "The Globalization of Markets," *Harvard Business Review* (May–June 1983), pp. 92–102; Michael Porter, "Changing Patterns of International Competition," *California Management Review,* 28(2) (Winter 1986), pp. 9–40; and Gary Hamel and C. K. Prahalad, "Do You Really Have a Global Strategy," *Harvard Business Review* (July–August 1985), pp. 139–148.

2. The research on which this article is based consisted of a three-year-long in-depth study of nine leading American, Japanese, and European multinational companies in three diverse industries. We interviewed over 235 managers in the headquarters and a number of different national subsidiaries of these companies to uncover how these companies with their diverse national backgrounds and international histories were adapting their organizational structures and management processes to cope with the new strategic demands of their operating environments. The companies studied were Philips, Matsushita, and General Electric in the consumer electronics industry; Ericsson, NEC, and ITT in the telecommunications switching industry; and Unilever, Kao, and Procter & Gamble in the branded packaged products business. The complete findings of this study will be reported in our forthcoming book *Managing Across Borders: The Transnational Solution* to be published by the Harvard Business School Press.

3. For a more detailed explication of the decentralized federation and centralized hub forms of multinational organizations, see Christopher A. Bartlett, "Building and Managing the Transnational: The New Organizational Challenge," in Michael E. Porter, ed., *Competition in Global Industries* (Boston: Harvard Business School Press, 1986).

4. "Rebuilding Corporate Empires—A New Global Formula," *Newsweek,* April 14, 1986, p. 40.

5. The concept of administrative heritage is explained more fully in Christopher Bartlett (op. cit.) and also in Christopher Bartlett and Sumantra Ghoshal, "Managing

Across Borders: New Strategic Requirements," *Sloan Management Review* (Summer 1987), pp. 7–17.

6. The organization we describe as the transnational has a long but discontinuous history in the international management literature. The concept of such an organizational form was manifest in Howard Perlmutter's celebrated paper, "The Torturous Evolution of the Multinational Corporation," *Columbia Journal of World Business* (January–February 1969), pp. 9–18. Similarly, C. K. Prahalad and Yves Doz's idea of a multifocal organization is described in *The Multinational Mission: Balancing Local Demands and Global Vision* (New York: The Free Press, 1987); Gunnar Hedlund's definition of the heterarchy in "The Hypermodern MNC—A Heterarchy?" *Human Resource Management* (Spring 1986), pp. 9–35; and Roderick White and Thomas Poyneter's description of the horizontal organization in "Organizing for Worldwide Advantage," presented at the seminar on Management of the MNC at the European Institute for Advanced Studies in Management, Brussels, on June 9–10, 1987, are conceptually similar to what we describe as the transnational organization, though the models differ significantly in their details.

7. Westney and Sakakibara have observed a similar system of internal quasi-markets governing the interface between R&D and operating units in a number of Japanese computer companies. See Eleanor Westney and K. Sakakibara, "The Role of Japan-Based R&D in Global Technology Strategy," *Technology in Society,* No. 7, (1985).

8. See Richard Rosenbloom and Michael Cusumano, "Technological Pioneering and Competitive Advantage: Birth of the VCR Industry," *California Management Review,* 29/4 (Summer 1987), pp. 51–76, for a full description of this interesting development process.

9. See John Van Mannen and Edgar H. Schein, "Toward a Theory of Organizational Socialization," in Barry Staw, ed., *Research in Organizational Behavior* (Greenwich, Conn.: JAI Press, 1979) for a rich and theory-grounded discussion on how such differences in socialization processes and career systems can influence managers' attitudes toward change and innovation.

10. See Christopher Bartlett and Hideki Yoshihara, "New Challenges for Japanese Multinationals: Is Organizational Adaptation Their Achilles' Heel?" *Human Resource Management,* 27/4 (Spring 1988), pp. 1–25, for a fuller discussion of some of the personnel management implications of managing local nationals in a classic centralized hub Japanese organization.

11. The need for both feasibility and desirability for facilitating innovativeness of organizations has been suggested by Lawrence Mohr, "Determinants of Innovation in Organizations," *American Political Science Review,* 63 (1969).

12. For a detailed discussion of how managers make such choices and how new responsibilities and relationships are developed, see Christopher Bartlett and Sumantra Ghoshal, "Tap Your Subsidiaries for Global Reach," *Harvard Business Review* (November–December 1986), pp. 87–94.

13. The effectiveness of personnel transfers as an integrative mechanism in multinational companies has been highlighted by many authors, most notably by E. Edstrom and J. R. Galbraith, "Transfer of Managers as a Coordination and Control Strategy in Multinational Organizations," *Administrative Science Quarterly* (June 1977).

38

HUMAN RESOURCE MANAGEMENT IN MULTINATIONAL COOPERATIVE VENTURES
Peter Lorange

INTRODUCTION

Human resource management has increasingly been recognized as a critical dimension of strategic management (Tichy, 1983; Beer et al.,

Source: Human Resources Management (Spring 1986), Vol. 25, no. 1, pp. 133–148. © 1986 by John Wiley & Sons, Inc.

1984; Fombrun et al., 1984; Chakravarthy, 1985). Above all, it is becoming clearer that the human resource is a strategic resource that should be managed in a more explicit, proactive manner. Even though it cannot be allocated and generated in a way entirely analogous to the financial resources of a corporation, it is still an integral part of strategic management. A strategic resource is defined as a resource that can be shifted from one business strategy application to another (Lorange, 1980), not only financial funds or technological know-how, but also human resources. Without the growth of human resources as a strategic resource within a corporation, it will be difficult to secure the long-term strategic future of the corporation, even though financial resources might be adequate.

We are currently witnessing an increase of cooperative ventures as vehicles for implementing strategy, particularly in multinational contexts where joint ventures, licensing agreements, project cooperation, and other methods of cooperation are becoming commonplace. The reasons for the growth of cooperative ventures are manifold: they may make scarce strategic resources last longer by utilizing complementary resources from several partners; they may allow faster market penetration; they may be a political necessity, and so on (Lorange, 1986a). The human resource function is particularly critical to successful implementation of such cooperative ventures. Several strategic human resource issues surrounding these cooperative ventures are not well understood; therefore, the purpose of the present article is to raise and discuss a number of them.

First, a conceptual scheme for classifying cooperative ventures proposed elsewhere (Lorange, 1986b), will be delineated briefly in the next section. Six human resource management issues as they related to the four types of cooperative modes identified in the conceptual scheme will then be considered. Finally, the conclusion will entail a synthesis of the strategic human resource management function within each of the four cooperative venture archetypes.

The present paper is preliminary and the arguments are normative. The research is part of a broader effort to study strategic management of cooperative multinational ventures based on clinical experience in a number of cooperative ventures.

CONCEPTUAL FRAMEWORK FOR COOPERATIVE VENTURES

It can be argued that the choice of a cooperative venture should satisfy several requirements of each participating partner. The cooperative venture must create a value-added chain by bringing together synergistic factors for a combined output greater than the sum of the outputs of each participating partner. The combined output must result in a competitive product or service, in comparison with alternative sources of supply.

The cooperative venture must also be useful for the pursuance of each partner's own individual strategy. The venture may still, of course, be of a different strategic importance to the various partners. For some partners, the cooperative venture may be an integral factor in the implementation of its overall strategy. For other partners, however, it may play a relatively minimal strategic role in this sense. Of course, this does not imply that the cooperative venture would be of little value; the dividend streams from the joint venture might still be tangible.

A partner in a joint venture may wish to keep a certain degree of discretionary control over its unique resources. Some strategic resources, such as unique technological skills or relevant marketing know-how, may not as readily be made available to the other partners as other, more common know-hows. The protection of exclusive know-hows may be particularly necessary in cases in which the joint venture is pertinent to the implementation of a parent's strategy.

Exhibit 1 portrays a two-dimensional conceptual framework for cooperative ventures, based on the relative degree of strategic importance of the venture to each partner, and the relative degree of retained discretionary control over its own resources desired by each partner. The overall rationale for the framework of this exhibit suggests an interplay among the two types of dimensions that are postulated to be

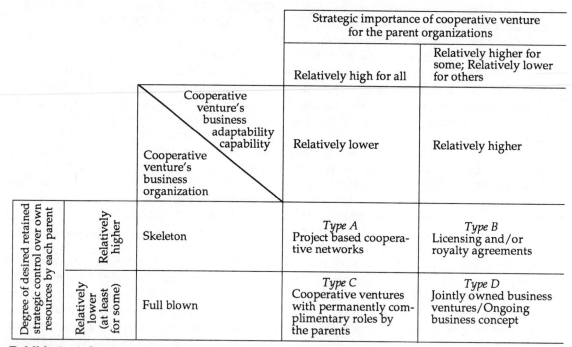

			Strategic importance of cooperative venture for the parent organizations	
			Relatively high for all	Relatively higher for some; Relatively lower for others
		Cooperative venture's business adaptability capability — *Cooperative venture's business organization*	Relatively lower	Relatively higher
Degree of desired retained strategic control over own resources by each parent	Relatively higher	Skeleton	*Type A* Project based cooperative networks	*Type B* Licensing and/or royalty agreements
	Relatively lower (at least for some)	Full blown	*Type C* Cooperative ventures with permanently complimentary roles by the parents	*Type D* Jointly owned business ventures/Ongoing business concept

Exhibit 1   A Conceptual Framework for Cooperative Ventures

important determinants of the cooperative venture's strategic context: the importance of the joint venture to the parent organizations and the degree of desired control over strategic resources retained by the parents.

Exhibit 1 also suggests several organizational forms that may be appropriate for the cooperative venture. At one extreme, the cooperative venture may be a full-blown business organization in its own right, in many ways analogous to an independent business organization. This organizational design would be implemented under circumstances in which one or more of the parent organizations have become comfortable with relinquishing exceedingly tight strategic controls over their critical resources. On the other hand, if one or more of the parents feel that they must maintain tight control over critical strategic resources, the organizational form of the cooperative venture might be more skeletal or temporary, with a number of organiza-

tional functions carried out by the partners on behalf of the cooperative venture.

The conceptual scheme also offers implications for a cooperative venture organization's capacity to be adaptable to new environmental opportunities. One might expect that a full-blown organization would be able to adapt relatively easily to new business opportunities, as would a freestanding business organization. There will typically be considerable adaptive constraints due to a lack of immediately available strategic resources within a less full-blown organization, on the other hand, due to agreements among the parents on behalf of the cooperative venture.

Exhibit 1 illustrates four types of cooperative ventures which may result from this conceptual framework. Somewhat arbitrarily they can be labeled *cooperative ventures with permanently complementary roles by the parents* (such as franchising), *licensing and/or royalty agree-*

ments, project-based cooperative networks, and jointly owned ventures based on ongoing business concepts.

In the following sections, human resource management functions as they apply to the four types of cooperative ventures will be considered. We shall claim that critical human resource management issues must be addressed differently for each of the four archetypes. It will become apparent that a unidimensional approach to human resource management, without recognizing the uniqueness of each type of cooperative venture, may result in suboptimal human resource management.

SIX CRITICAL HUMAN RESOURCE MANAGEMENT ISSUES

Based on preliminary clinical studies, six issues appear to be among the particularly crucial ones for human resource management within cooperative ventures in multinational settings. In the following paragraphs, the manner in which each of these issues can be approached in the context of the four cooperative venture archetypes will be discussed. The six issues are as follows:

- assignment of managers to cooperative ventures: who should be assigned where?
- the human resource transferability issue: who controls a particular manager?
- the trade-off in time-spending between operating and strategic tasks among various managers involved in the cooperative venture.
- judgment calls regarding the performance of the human resource in the established cooperative venture: how to avoid biases.
- human resource loyalty issues: the cooperative venture versus the parent.
- individual managers' career planning issues: how can they achieve career progression through cooperative venture assignments?

Assignment of Human Resources to Cooperative Ventures

A difficult issue in the assignment of managers to a cooperative venture is the identification of the best persons for each job. A cooperative venture must be created in such a way that it possesses relevant complementarities and synergies, so as to allow the cooperative venture to generate a satisfactory output through a meaningful value-added process. Managers will usually be assigned by the partners, and often they will have worked for one of them beforehand. Various partners' perceptions of the types of human skills and talents needed may differ. Some partners may have unrealistic biases regarding the quality of the managerial capabilities being assigned, and some may not wish to assign their best people because they want to keep them in their own organizations. The assigned managers may be competent as individuals but unable to work together in a cooperative organizational context due to cultural differences, communication problems, and so on. These are only a few of the issues that may impact upon the staffing of a cooperative venture.

In a project-based cooperative network, there will not be one common organization in the classical sense to be staffed jointly, but separately staffed organizational "modules" to be provided by each of the partners under their largely individual jurisdictions. Appropriate staffing is still important because there must be compatability between managers from the different organizations. Managers being allocated to this project-based organization must be able to understand one another and develop a meaningful communication pattern. The representatives from each parent organization must, above all, be able to communicate the key concepts of their package to be contributed to the project. Equally important, each member must be able to understand the unique features of the other members' packages so as to "translate" it to integrated, project-based opportunities. As such, the creation of compatible organizational entities is of major importance to this kind of project-based network.

As to the assignment of managers to cooperative ventures based on licensing and/or royalty agreements, there will also be two separate complementary organizational entities which must interact. The licensor must assign staff capable of providing sufficient training and organizational assistance for adequate transfer of know-how. Sufficiently competent managers must also be assigned to the venture from the licensee, to promote the transfer of know-how. Due to the relative difference in the strategic importance of the cooperative venture for the parents, it is a danger that one of the partners might be tempted to assign "second stringers," thereby creating another potential source of friction.

For cooperative networks with permanently complementary roles by the parents in which a new, temporary organization must be created, assigning human resources to the project should be accomplished according to at least the following three criteria. First, assigned human resources must reflect the necessary specialized skills that each partner has agreed to contribute to the joint venture. These skills must be of adequate quality; thus, second or third stringers should normally not be assigned to the project. Second, the managers assigned must be sufficiently compatible in style to communicate and work together in effecting the cooperative venture. This requires team-work and cooperation across functions, not isolation within each specialized camp. Third, the assigned managers must have the ability to provide adequate feedback to their respective parent organizations, giving continuous ad-hoc support for unforeseen backup activities within a reasonable amount of time.

The assignment of critical management resources to jointly owned, ongoing business ventures also requires that management commitments be made for longer periods of time.

Usually, the joint venture organization will also attract human resources within time from sources other than the parent organization. The assigned managerial resources must have relevant capabilities and must be of adequate quality. The overall blend of these human resources must have a cultural dimension to allow the development of an effective ongoing concern. The difference in importance of the cooperative venture to each of the partners makes it possible that a partner assigns relatively weak management resources to the venture.

In summary, the assignment of relevant management resources to various cooperative ventures is critical, but in different ways. For instance, for cooperative networks with permanently cooperative roles by the parents, the development of a workable common culture will be the challenge. On the other hand, with less formalized cooperative venture organizations, such as for project-based cooperative networks and licensing, the critical management assignment issue is to employ people who can communicate and interact with one another effectively in such settings. In the more formal, full-blown, jointly owned, ongoing venture, the parents' role in the assignment of human resources may become less of an issue over time, because the jointly owned organization may have to gradually bring in necessary human resources on its own, as in an independent business.

Transferability of Human Resources

By definition, a resource is strategic only if it can be freely transferred from one application to another, that is, divested from an established, hopefully successful strategy, to an emerging strategy to be built for the future. Financial resources have traditionally been those most frequently considered for strategic reallocation (Henderson, 1979). However, the same principle applies to other strategic resources, such as unique technological know-how and human resources. But human resources can, of course, not be considered a "commodity" to be allocated in a mechanistic way; in this respect, they are different from financial resources. An adequate ethical and human rights foundation must be established for human resources to be strategically transferable from one work application to another. In the present context this implies that parents must be able to transfer human resources to and/or from the cooperative venture, and they might also be transferred within the cooperative venture from old to new job applications. In the latter case, the human resource has direct strategic value to the cooperative venture organization itself. The transferred human resource has strategic value to the parent organization due to its discretionary "power" to transfer it back. It must thus be ascertained whether the cooperative venture and/or a particular parent has discretionary decision-making powers in managerial reassignments, and within which strategic context these decisions are made. This is applicable to all of the four archetypal settings. An issue to be dealt with in a later section concerns the degree of influence decision-makers actually have over a given manager so that reassignment considerations do not lead to discontent or resignation.

The partners in a project-based cooperative network will typically maintain their own organizational capabilities within the cooperative franchising network. In such an organization, the human resource transfer issues may center on how each partner provides human resources "on loan" to the project, such as that of technical specialists being temporarily assigned to a project. The transfer of human resources tends to be temporary and is controlled by the parents. The parent in question also controls which type of assignment the manager in question will go to after the project-based venture is completed. Of course, the human resources which do not have sufficient alternative applications may be dismissed after the project is terminated. It often seems to be the case, in fact, that too many human resources are let go when a particular strategic project is over, thereby creating a "stop-go" human resource management approach which might deprive parent organizations of important strategic human assets. It should be noted that a parent organization will keep its own benefits in mind when consenting to reassign some of its key people on loan. Therefore, it may at times be difficult for the parent to justify such an arrangement, even though the competitive network as a whole might clearly benefit. Any overall half-heartedness or paranoia regarding this type of human resource assignment may, in the long run, hamper the successful development of a project-based cooperative network approach.

A similar situation might typically exist for a licensing type of cooperative arrangement. A licensor may transfer human resources temporarily to a licensee for training and technical assistance, provided that he has sufficient human resources available and that he can retrieve this resource.

As to the transfer of key human resources in a cooperative network with permanently complementary roles by the parents, the parent organizations will in principle be obligated to make available the relevant managerial resources. Each partner must, however, also have available sufficient additional human resources to cover their own independent needs. Given the nature of this type of cooperative venture, each parent organization should put particular emphasis on developing the capability to "take back" human resources, as these human skills may have significant strategic value in future organizational contexts. Some transfer of human resources among partners may at times also be necessary. For instance, a franchisor may provide human resources "on loan" to a franchisee, such as technical specialists being temporarily assigned to a franchisee. A franchisee may also "loan" human resources to a franchisor, say, to strengthen the franchisor's market understanding and ensure that the franchising package remains relevant and adapted to market realities.

In jointly owned, ongoing business ventures, the issue is whether or not a parent organization is willing to transfer critical human resources to the new business venture. These strategic human resources would normally be assigned to the joint venture for a long period of time, perhaps for the entire remaining working career of the managers in question. The parents may thus have to transfer strategic human resources on a net basis during the initial phase and will not necessarily get them returned. Human resource management decisions will gradually be handled by the joint venture organization. Within the joint venture, human resources will have to be regenerated and developed and reallocated to new jobs therein, as in an independent business organization. Given the opportunity, however, the parent organizations should attempt to "welcome back" relevant human resources from the joint venture, and not automatically release them so that they might "accidentally" end up with competing organizations.

Managers' Time-Spending Patterns: On Operating vs. Strategic Task Trade-Offs?

Regarding the implementation of the strategies of a cooperative venture, it is worthwhile to keep in mind that this requires expenditure of efforts at the present time in order to develop a position with future prospective payoffs. This typically might result in an immediate lessening of operating results due to the diversion of resources for strategic use. In settings with full-blown cooperative venture organizations, these may execute independent judgment regarding how much resources to spend on the implementation of business strategies on their own. In this case, the cooperative organization has to carry out a set of operating duties simultaneously with its development of new strategies; as such, sufficient human resources will have to be earmarked for strategic development as well as for operating tasks. In the less fully developed skeleton organization, these strategic tasks will mainly be carried out by the partners on behalf

of the cooperative venture. It is therefore key in the latter type of setting that the parent organizations are willing to spend resources in a coordinated fashion to facilitate this strategic development.

Thus, it must be ascertained *where* in a cooperative network do the human resources reside which have the responsibilities, capabilities, and capacity to carry out the development of further strategic moves. In other words, how does the cooperative network, on its own or together with the parent partners, meet the challenge of tackling *both* operating *and* strategic tasks on a parallel, ongoing basis? This leads to different considerations regarding the role of human resources in these trade-offs between operating and strategic challenges in each of the four archetypes.

In a project-based cooperative network organization, a common understanding and a clear division of labor between the managers of the participating organizations must be apparent, with respect to time allotted to strategic tasks such as further development of the technical base for the project cooperation and additional marketing efforts. The premise behind this is that future projects might result as a consequence of such coordinated strategy developments—if no future potential cooperation is contemplated then the issues discussed in this section will be largely irrelevant. Usually, these activities will involve specific hands-on cooperation between the various participant organizations, sometimes in the form of task forces. The managers assigned to such committees must have the time, energy, and motivation to actively contribute to such strategic development work, using some of the time normally spent in their own organizations for strategy development or on operating tasks.

In a licensing cooperative organization, strategic development tends to take place independently within the licensor and the licensee organizations. Thus, each organization must provide the relevant human resource capacity for strategic self-renewal. Here, too, some of this will involve joint cooperation, as in project-based cooperative ventures.

Relatively few free standing strategic development tasks will be typically carried out within the cooperative venture with permanently complementary roles by the parents, because it is created to take advantage of a strategic opportunity based on a pooling of the partner organizations' strategic capabilities. Thus, to some extent there will be independent adaptation and strategic self-renewal by each parent, to ensure that they set aside sufficient human resources to maintain unique capabilities. This splitting up of the responsibilities to adapt by strategic developments carried out by the partners alone may not be enough, however. Common strategic adaptive efforts may have to be carried out by the cooperative venture itself. In a franchising organization, for instance, a common understanding and a clear division of labor between the managers of the franchisor and franchisee organizations must be had as to time allotted to common strategic tasks, such as further development of the franchising package and additional marketing adaptability moves.

The joint, ongoing business cooperative venture organization faces a situation that is in many ways parallel to any independent business organization, in that it must be able to draw sufficient human resources from the operating mode to further develop its own strategy. If the joint venture is too thinly staffed, strategic development will suffer, and an eventual lack of self-renewal and decreasing strategic focus will result. The challenge, similar to that of any type of business organization, is to allot sufficient organizational energy and time for the pursuit of business self-renewal and further strategic development. This must always be done in parallel with the other operating tasks. Parent organizations must not exercise so much near-term pressure for operating results that the cooperative venture is left with insufficient resources for its staffing for strategic self-renewal.

Human Resource Competency Issues: Avoidance of Judgment Biases

Human resources assigned to cooperative ventures must be able to satisfy the skill requirements of the value-added chain in carrying out the functional activities for which each partner is responsible. The importance of choosing appropriate persons for assignment for specific tasks has been emphasized previously in Section A. In this section, human competency and skill assessment issues within the various types of cooperative ventures once in operation will be discussed. Thus, the challenge is how to judge managers in terms of how well they are able to carry out their assignments, once the assignments of executives have been made.

In project-based cooperative ventures, the bulk of the judgments regarding managerial competencies in carrying out their jobs will have to largely be executed by each partner on his own. The partners must be able to exercise human resource competency and performance judgments to develop a relevant way to execute their team roles. Although the partners will have to make human resource performance and competency judgments largely on their own, in some instances it may not be uncommon that the partners also make joint human resource judgments regarding team effectiveness and contributions towards making the cooperative project work, based on their experience regarding desirable human characteristics in this respect.

In licensing cooperative ventures, each partner will also have to make human resource performance judgments and considerations largely on their own, as in project-based cooperative networks. In addition, the licensor and the licensee must jointly assess the issue of the cooperative licensing ventures' ability to be trained, that is, executives' performance and their abilities to give and absorb information as part of a fairly standardized learning and communication process.

Judgments in human resource performance and competency issues are also critical in cooperative networks with permanently complementary roles by the parents. The partners must cooperate in assessing their performance of one another's functional specialists. Given that each partner may feel that he will be solely responsible for making the human performance judgments that fall within his given sphere of competence, this may lead to biases, such as looking too favorably upon the performance of managers from one's own organization. This may result in the inadvertent buildup of second string functional specialists who cannot perform as effectively within the cooperative network as is desirable. For this reason, human resource performance and competency judgment issues should be dealt with by all of the partners in cooperation. In these situations, it may be appropriate to use joint performance review committees to make judgments and give feedback that is as free as possible from individual partner culture biases.

Judgments in human resource performance and competency must also be kept strictly in mind in the going concern cooperative venture. Several joint ventures have failed because they have been inappropriately staffed, due in part to lack of cooperation between myopic, biased parent organizations. In some instances, a partner may, for instance, have intended to get rid of some managers by unloading them on the cooperative venture. Whatever the case, it is imperative that the jointly owned cooperative venture establishes a thorough human resource performance review, so that ameliorating actions can be taken with regard to less than adequate performance within the jointly owned organizational setting.

Management Loyalty Issues: To the Cooperative Venture or to the Parent?

A manager may at times find himself in conflict between loyalty to his parent organization vs. loyalty to the cooperative venture organiza-

tion to which he is presently assigned. These loyalty conflicts may be difficult and the management of them must be considered an integral part of the human resource management of cooperative ventures. The nature of these divided loyalty issues in the context of each of the four archetypes will now be described.

Divided loyalty issues are usually minimal in project-based cooperative networks, because the partner's employees will, of course, naturally tend to be loyal to their respective organizations. There may be "raiding" of good managers within such cooperative networks, however. A partner may easily notice outstanding human talents, given the typically close cooperation within such transparent arrangements. Thus, some managers may transfer between various partners. This may cause stress in the cooperative mode of the network, and the partners usually do well not to overdo such raiding of one another's talents.

For licensing types of cooperative arrangements, loyalty division similarly does not tend to be a major issue. Technical advisors "on loan" from the licensor will usually remain loyal to the licensor. If a technical advisor remains in an assigned advisory capacity for too long, however, loyalty may diminish. Therefore, to avoid "defections," it may make sense to rotate key technical advisors on a regular, scheduled basis.

Loyalty issues may become problematic in joint cooperative projects with permanently complementary roles by the parents. Each employee is ordinarily "on loan" from the parent organization and usually expects to return to the parent after some time. At the same time they must be "loyal" to their temporary assignment if it is to succeed. This may involve having to take positions which may go against the original parent organization's wishes. Professional integrity and judgment are key in implementing such assignments. Problem areas that may create such conflicts may most typically come up regarding transfer pricing and other pricing issues. In this context, the employees must be loyal to the project organization, as a practice of professional management conduct. The parent organization must have enough maturity and cultural tolerance to understand that this type of conflict is inevitable. They must not "punish" former employees who have been involved in such divided loyalty conflicts. A mature approach on the part of the parents is necessary to prevent the development of a feeling of paranoia among key employees.

Assigned executives tend to be loyal to the cooperative venture organization in the going concern cooperative context. Most employees can expect to stay with the cooperative venture for a long period of time in this instance. They may rarely return to their old parent organization at all; in fact, if a conflict arises, they would be expected to side with the cooperative venture. In global settings, there can be a problem when a national from a parent moves to a cooperative venture in another country. Despite this reassignment, he may often be perceived as still being associated with the parent organization. The loyalty issue can then become difficult and stressful for the executives involved. A similar situation can arise when national loyalty conflicts with loyalty to the cooperative venture's business which pursues global strategies that may be at odds with strict national interests.

Individual Managers' Career and Benefits Planning

Individual executives must be motivated to perform their assigned strategic tasks within the cooperative venture. To achieve this, one must above all create the appearance of future career relevance and a sense of job security. Assignment to a joint venture may make one's future career appear uncertain. An employee may wonder what types of jobs will be waiting, if any, after the joint venture assignment is over, and if others who remain in the parent organization will be assigned to the interesting new jobs on a "fast track" basis, while he is "forgot-

ten" in the joint venture assignment. Steps must be taken to ameliorate employees' feelings of "being forgotten" by the parent while assigned to the cooperative venture. A fast-track, up-and-coming executive may feel that the joint venture assignment is a side-track, that he is "out of sight and out of mind," and that this assignment will actually impair the further development of his career. Parent organizations must offer career planning to inform up-and-coming talents of potential assignments that might be available after the joint venture. However, there must be a certain degree of formality in the career-planning system to make it credible. A clear-cut career planning approach can counter the ambiguity and riskiness associated with a cooperative venture assignment.

Joint venture assignments may require relocation, which can impact on quality of living in general. This is often expensive, may be potentially disturbing for the family, may require a change of housing, and so on. Individual managers' economic and emotional discomforts must be minimized in this respect. In a cooperative venture setting, the split decision-making roles among the parents must take this issue into consideration. An executive must be able to maintain the employee benefits he would have accrued in the parent organization. Thus, the individual manager should not feel he is losing salary, retirement benefits, bonus eligibility, fringe benefits, and so on; he should be able to draw on these benefits after he temporarily leaves for the joint venture. How these career planning and benefits issues apply to each of the four archetypes will be considered next.

Within the project-based type of cooperative venture, the individual executive's career outlook and incentives will have to be closely aligned with the administrative procedures of each parent organization. The temporary nature of the project-based organization may present a problem for the individual who desires to grow, unless his parent organization provides a sensitivity to offering stimulating opportunities for further individual growth by giving the executive the opportunity to transfer to a meaningful new job within the partner's organizations or to another project-based venture assignment. The compartmentalization of jobs into free-standing temporary organization assignments should not engender a lack of willingness to implement career planning within the overall system. This overall view must override the somewhat narrower temporary organizational focus.

For a licensing type of cooperative venture, the licensee must motivate its employees to support the implementation of the license agreement. This can be facilitated by implementing a career development plan within the licensee organizations. The licensor must similarly ensure that it motivates the advisors working with the licensees to approach these jobs without fearing that they are being exploited or side-tracked. This group of executives must not feel that they are "out in the cold" and have reached an organizational dead end. Systematic job rotation schemes must be utilized for these advisors.

In the cooperative ventures with permanently complementary roles by the parents, the executive must, above all, have a strong feeling of job security. These strategic projects often involve temporary assignments, which might engender uncertainty and anxiety in the employees, as to what type of jobs they will go to next. Many of them will have to find entirely new jobs outside the present cooperative organizational network. The temporary nature of these assignments must not cause so much anxiety and perceived loss of job security that the employees become dysfunctional. Career planning seems essential here so that the employee knows what he is coming back to.

The career planning of the employees in the jointly owned business organization should be tied in with the joint venture organization itself. Here too, an employee should be given the opportunity to return to the parent organization if he so wishes, to avoid the fear of stagnating within the joint venture organization or of

being deprived of promotional opportunities elsewhere in one of the parents. However, he must decide quickly whether he wants to stake out his career in the parent or the joint venture. It is important to be explicit regarding preference and expectation for the broader or narrower career tracks.

CONCLUDING COMMENTS

In conclusion, the human resource management function will at times differ quite dramatically in cooperative venture contexts compared to that of the better-known, wholly owned corporate settings. Further, the human resource function may differ dramatically among different types of cooperative ventures, such as between the four types of cooperative ventures which have been identified.

In a project-based type of cooperative venture, the human resource management function will largely be carried out by each partner in a "compartmentalized" manner and largely on behalf of their own organizational entities. However, the strategic human resource management functions must be coordinated to some degree, particularly in the attempt to develop a relatively homogenous type of value system in approaching central dimensions of the cooperative project business, such as when it comes to attitude towards quality, competitiveness in securing follow-on projects, and so on. Also, the establishment of a common communication style can be a major determinant to success. This can be enhanced by allowing for consultation among the parents regarding such issues as dealing with biases in human resource assessments, allowing for broader career opportunities, and so on.

A similar type of quite separate human resource management arrangements among the partners will have to be made in licensing-type cooperative agreement settings. However, the human resource management groups of the licensor and licensee must find ways to cooperate to a certain extent, above all, in the assignment of advisors to the licensee.

The human resource function will probably also to some extent be dealt with independently by each parent in the cooperative venture with permanently complementary roles by the parents. In this setting there must, however, be solid coordination between the various human resource management functions of the parents, so that a common organizational approach can be established, which is functioning with the necessary compatibility among members' styles. A separate parallel human resource management function may have to be established within the cooperative venture itself, complementing the parents' human resource management capabilities.

Finally, regarding the jointly owned ongoing cooperative venture business, a strong, full-fledged human resource management function will have to be established within the joint venture itself. This function will have to find ways to work closely with that of each parent, however, particularly during the first years. The human resource function within the joint venture must gradually encourage the development of new human resource capabilities which can enhance the strategic progress of the joint venture.

Overall, the human resource management function within all types of cooperative ventures will have to attempt to undertake two types of tasks. First, it will attempt to assign and motivate people in appropriate ways, so that the value creation within the cooperative venture will proceed as well as possible. To create such an arrangement requires particular attention to job skills, compatability of styles, communication compatability, and so on. Second, human resources will have to be managed strategically. This means that human resources will not only have to be allocated with a view towards the needs of the cooperative venture activity, but also with a view towards potential repatriation to a parent, to be used later in other contexts for other strategic purposes. As such, the cooperative venture must be seen as a vehicle to produce not only financial rewards, but also managerial capabilities, which can be used later in other strategic settings.

REFERENCES

Beer, Michael, Spector, Bert, Lawrence, Paul R., Mills, D. Quinn, and Walton, Richard E. *Managing Human Assets.* New York: The Free Press, 1984.

Chakravarthy, Balaji S. "Human Resource Management and Strategic Change: Challenges in Two Deregulated Industries," *Wharton School Working Paper,* Philadelphia, 1985.

Fombrun, Charles, Tichy, Noel M. and Devanna, Mary Anne. *Strategic Human Resource Management.* New York: John Wiley, 1984.

Henderson, Bruce C. *Henderson on Corporate Strategy.* Cambridge, Mass.: Abt Books, 1979.

Lorange, Peter. *Corporate Planning: An Executive Viewpoint.* Englewood Cliffs, N.J.: Prentice-Hall, 1980.

Lorange, Peter. "Cooperative Strategies: Planning and Control Considerations," to appear in Hood, Neil, and Walne, Jan-Erik, *Strategies in Global Competition.* Chichester: Wiley, 1986a.

Lorange, Peter. "Cooperative Ventures in Multinational Settings: A Framework," to appear in Johanson, Jan, and Hallen, Lars, *International Markets as Networks.* Sweden: Uppsala, 1986b.

Tichy, Noel M. *Managing Strategic Change.* New York: John Wiley, 1983.

INDEX